Montreal Canadiens'
Toe Blake.

Pittsburgh Steelers'
Chuck Noll.

Green Bay Packers'
Vince Lombardi.

Ron Smith

# The Sporting News
## CHRONICLE
### — OF —
## 20TH CENTURY
## SPORT

MALLARD PRESS

Notre Dame's Knute Rockne.

Los Angeles Lakers' Pat Riley.

Cleveland Browns' Paul Brown.

Brooklyn Dodgers'
Walter Alston.

Oklahoma's
Bud Wilkinson.

Boston Celtics'
Red Auerbach.

MALLARD PRESS
An imprint of BDD Promotional Book Company, Inc.
666 Fifth Avenue
New York, N.Y. 10103

Mallard Press and its accompanying design and logo are
registered trademarks of BDD Promotional Book Company,
Inc. Registered in the U.S. Patent and Trademark Office.

Copyright © 1992 The Sporting News Publishing Company

Design © 1992 Reed International Books Limited

First published in the United States of America
in 1992 by The Mallard Press by arrangement with Octopus
Illustrated Publishing, a part of Reed International Books,
Michelin House, 81 Fulham Road, London SW3 6RB, England

All rights reserved

For copyright reasons this edition may not be sold
outside the United States of America

ISBN 0-792-45720-X

Printed and bound in Hong Kong

Photographic Acknowledgements
The photographs in this book were obtained from
The Sporting News and the Bettmann Archive.

# Contents

UCLA's
John Wooden.

New York Yankees'
Joe McCarthy.

# introduction

by John D. Rawlings, Editor of *The Sporting News*

*Why is it that nothing defines the North American psyche more accurately than its relentless obsession with sports? When society thrives, its citizens win the game. When society falters, its citizens suffer the defeat. It has been that way for more than a hundred years, and it is likely to continue that way for 200 more.*

The rules of sports are clear, well defined and universally accepted. Rules governing other parts of our existence are not always so precise and often change minute to minute. On the playing field, it is an easy-to-understand case of "us" versus "them". Off the field, players become muddled and their goals unfocused. Athletic contests provide an orderly package summed up with an unequivocal winner and loser. They fill our need for a life so tidy.

While the reasons behind this attraction are open to debate, the passions and emotions triggered by sports are undeniable. As historian and educator Jacques Barzun said, "Whoever wants to know the heart and mind of America had better love baseball." And *The Sporting News*, which has been charting the course of the National Pastime and other competitive contests longer than any other medium, provides a perfect barometer to assess the state of

Ty Cobb.                    Jack Dempsey.                    Babe Ruth.

that "heart and mind" in a chronicle of Century sports.

When Alfred Spink recognized a voracious sports appetite and hunger for a national perspective, he acted decisively, launching *The Sporting News* in 1886—17 years before the Boston Red Sox upset the Pittsburgh Pirates in the first World Series, 32 years before the Toronto Arenas captured a Stanley Cup for the newly formed NHL, 47 years before the Chicago Bears beat the New York Giants in the first championship game, 61 years before the Philadelphia Warriors beat Chicago in the first NBA Super Bowl.

Decade by decade, each infused with its own colorful personalities and indelible memories, *TSN* was there to provide insight and information. And as the various sports matured and grew, so did *The Sporting News*. The format of this book reflects that growth, simple and easy to follow in the early years expansive and more complicated as the century unwinds.

The names, the faces, the personalities they're all on these pages, from the Ty Cobbs, Babe Ruths and Jack Dempseys of the early years to the Joe Montanas, Magic Johnsons and Wayne Gretzkys of the 1980s and '90s. The great athletes and their moments of success and failure race across pages like Jesse Owens streaking for Olympic gold.

*The Sporting News* is happy to bring these vibrant characters and dramatic moments back to life. But remember, this is not a sports encyclopedia – it is an exciting trip down memory lane. Take your time, enjoy the journey, browse through several wonderful generations of sports nostalgia while bracing for the future. And take note, because the moments of today will be what your grandchildren will admire in their reflections of tomorrow.

*Wayne Gretzky.*          *Magic Johnson .*          *Joe Montana.*

# THE 1900s

*Like an infant trying to balance his quivering legs before taking that first step toward adulthood, the North American sports scene teetered on the edge of respectability as the Twentieth Century dawned.*

Baseball had poured a solid foundation in the United States and ice hockey was deeply rooted in the various provinces of Canada, but most other sports featured amateur athletes with little or no hope of a professional future. Football, basketball, golf, tennis: all were searching for their identities.

*Boxer Jack Johnson.*

*Washington pitcher Walter Johnson.*

Baseball already had its identity. But it also had a reputation — as a rowdy, spikes-high, pugilistic sport played by unsavory characters who espoused hooliganism and violence. Such conditions repulsed much of the gentility that otherwise might have been attracted to the emerging National Pastime. If the game was to prosper, a strong hand would be needed.

That strong hand arrived in the person of Byron Bancroft (Ban) Johnson, a former sportswriter who founded the American League in 1901, forced rival National League officials to merge under a National Agreement two years later and then helped rule the sport fastidiously for the next 24 years. By the end of 1903, the two leagues were being governed by a common authority and existed as two eight-team alignments that would endure for the next 50 years.

While baseball was looking for discipline, hockey was

# ROLL OF HONOR

## GOLF

### US OPEN

| Year | Winner | Year | Winner |
|------|--------|------|--------|
| 1900 | Harry Vardon | 1905 | Willie Anderson |
| 1901 | Willie Anderson | 1906 | Alex Smith |
| 1902 | Laurie Auchterlonie | 1907 | Alex Ross |
| 1903 | Willie Anderson | 1908 | Fred McLeod |
| 1904 | Willie Anderson | 1909 | George Sargent |

## TENNIS

### US OPEN

| Year | Men's Winner | Women's Winner |
|------|--------------|----------------|
| 1900 | Malcolm D. Whitman | Myrtle McAteer |
| 1901 | William A. Larned | Elisabeth Moore |
| 1902 | William A. Larned | Marion Jones |
| 1903 | Laurie Doherty | Elisabeth Moore |
| 1904 | Holcombe Ward | May Sutton |
| 1905 | Beals Wright | Elisabeth Moore |
| 1906 | William J. Clothier | Helen Homans |
| 1907 | William A. Larned | Evelyn Sears |
| 1908 | William A. Larned | Maud Barger-Wallach |
| 1909 | William A. Larned | Hazel Hotchkiss |

Challenge round system (defending champion automatically qualifies for following year's final) used until 1911.

## HORSE RACING

### KENTUCKY DERBY

| Year | Winner | Jockey |
|------|--------|--------|
| 1900 | Lieut. Gibson | Jimmy Boland |
| 1901 | His Eminence | Jimmy Winkfield |
| 1902 | Alan-a-Dale | Jimmy Winkfield |
| 1903 | Judge Himes | Hal Brooker |
| 1904 | Elwood | Frankie Prior |
| 1905 | Agile | Jack Martin |
| 1906 | Sir Huon | Roscoe Troxler |
| 1907 | Pink Star | Andy Minder |
| 1908 | Stone Street | Arthur Pickens |
| 1909 | Wintergreen | Vincent Powers |

### PREAKNESS STAKES

| Year | Winner | Jockey |
|------|--------|--------|
| 1900 | Hindus | H. Spencer |
| 1901 | The Parader | F. Landry |
| 1902 | Old England | L. Jackson |
| 1903 | Flocarline | W. Gannon |
| 1904 | Bryn Mawr | E. Hildebrand |
| 1905 | Cairngorm | W. Davis |
| 1906 | Whimsical | Walter Miller |
| 1907 | Don Enrique | G. Mountain |
| 1908 | Royal Tourist | Eddie Dugan |
| 1909 | Effendi | Willie Doyle |

### BELMONT STAKES

| Year | Winner | Jockey |
|------|--------|--------|
| 1900 | Ildrim | Nash Turner |
| 1901 | Commando | H. Spencer |
| 1902 | Masterman | John Bullmann |
| 1903 | Africander | John Bullmann |
| 1904 | Delhi | George Odom |
| 1905 | Tanya | E. Hildebrand |
| 1906 | Burgomaster | Lucien Lyne |
| 1907 | Peter Pan | G. Mountain |
| 1908 | Colin | Joe Notter |
| 1909 | Joe Madden | Eddie Dugan |

## BASEBALL

### WORLD SERIES

| Year | Winner | Pennant Winner (series score) |
|------|--------|-------------------------------|
| 1903 | Boston Red Sox | (Pittsburgh Pirates, 5-3) |
| 1904 | No series | |
| 1905 | New York Giants | (Philadelphia Athletics, 4-1) |
| 1906 | Chicago White Sox | (Chicago Cubs, 4-2) |
| 1907 | Chicago Cubs | (Detroit Tigers, 4-0-1) |
| 1908 | Chicago Cubs | (Detroit Tigers, 4-1) |
| 1909 | Pittsburgh Pirates | (Detroit Tigers, 4-3) |

searching for direction. Already entrenched as Canada's national sport, amateur teams were competing for the prestigious Stanley Cup on a challenge basis in seven-on-seven games played with unsophisticated equipment and uneven rules. Rough play, frequent feuding among teams and disrespect for officials were the order of the day and by the end of the decade, the Stanley Cup had officially been passed into sole possession of newly created professional leagues.

One of the decade's significant developments was a 1906 meeting in New York that resulted in the formation of an organization that later would become the National Collegiate Athletic Association. With more than 60 colleges embracing the idea of a national rules committee to legislate the brutal game of college football, the sport took a major step along its evolutionary trail.

The bottom line is that early-century sports mirrored the growing pains being felt by the chiefly agrarian societies they were attempting to entertain. Those societies were unorganized, lacked sophistication in their regard for athleticism and were unyielding to the winds of change. The common man found it difficult to embrace what he considered the sports of the elite — tennis, golf and horse racing primarily—and showed little regard for their showcase events. He preferred raw physical power and endurance, such as boxing, which unwittingly produced one of the century's biggest steps forward. In 1908, Jack Johnson defeated Tommy Burns in a heavyweight bout, thus becoming the first black champion to be crowned in any major sport.

*New York Giants pitcher Christy Mathewson.*

# 1900

## JANUARY - DECEMBER

# U.S. wins Davis cup

An American team of Malcolm D. Whitman, Dwight F. Davis and Holcombe Ward made short work of a challenging team from the British Isles, winning a 3-0 decision and the rights to the first Davis Cup trophy.

The format for the series played at the Longwood Cricket Club near Boston called for two singles matches on August 8, a doubles match on August 9 and two more singles matches the following day. But, with the United States holding an insurmountable 3-0 lead, heavy rains forced the cancellation of the final-day activity.

The British team, which arrived late and played without practice, quickly fell victim to the Americans' quickness and net-rushing tactics.

Davis, donor of the prize cup, opened play with a 4-6, 6-2, 6-4, 6-4 victory over Ernest Black

*Dwight F. Davis and the prize cup he donated for international tennis competition, 24 years later.*

and Whitman, the U.S. singles champion, quickly disposed of Arthur Gore, 6-1, 6-3, 6-2. Davis and Ward made certain of victory on the second day when they defeated Black and Roger Barrett, 6-4, 6-4, 6-4, in doubles play.

# Americans in Paris steal Olympic show

The tally is complete and the French athletes have been declared "official" winners of the second modern Olympic Games, held in Paris. But don't be fooled by France's inflated medal count of 102. The Americans stole the show.

The 55-member U.S. contingent, made up primarily of college and club athletes with no official organization, walked away with 53 medals. And they only competed in the track and field segment which they completely dominated, and might have swept had not French officials insisted on running numerous finals on a Sunday. Many U.S. athletes refused to compete on that July 15 Sabbath.

Overall, the 1900 Games failed to meet expectations. Held in conjunction with the World's Fair being staged in Paris, the Olympics were really nothing more than a sideshow. The events were spread out over five months, facilities and organization were poor and attendance was bad.

The big U.S. winner was Alvin Kraenzlein, who captured the 60-meter sprint, the 110- and 200-meter hurdles and the long jump.

# Jeffries retains title

James J. Jeffries, making his third title defense since winning the heavyweight crown from Bob Fitzsimmons last year, knocked out former champ James J. Corbett in the 23rd round of a May 11 bout on Coney Island.

It was a battle of contrasting styles as Jeffries, fighting with bulldog determination and brute strength, tried to catch up with the smaller, quicker Corbett. The crowd of 7,000 at the arena of the Seaside Athletic Club cheered Corbett's every move but sensed that it was only a matter of time. Gentleman Jim simply did not have the punching power and his strategy of tiring Jeffries did not work.

Playing to the crowd throughout the fight, Corbett stayed away from Jeffries' power for 22 rounds before inexplicably choosing to mix it up with the champ in round 23. Jeffries backed him into a corner and dropped him with a powerful right to the jaw. Corbett had to be carried back to his corner and revived, but amazingly showed little sign of wear and tear.

*Gentleman Jim Corbett, another notch in Jim Jeffries' heavyweight championship belt.*

# 1901

# New A.L. is a threat to established N.L.

Byron Bancroft (Ban) Johnson, the former Cincinnati sportswriter and now entrepreneur, has got his new "major league" off the ground and it is beginning to look like a serious threat to the established National League.

The American League began play, April 24, with franchises located in Philadelphia, Boston, Chicago, Washington, Detroit, Cleveland, Baltimore and Mil-

*Byron (Bancroft) Johnson, the brains behind the American League.*

waukee. It opened with such marquee performers as Cy Young, Nap Lajoie, John McGraw, Jimmy Collins, Joe McGinnity, Chick Stahl, Buck Freeman and Wilbert Robinson who Johnson and his cohorts have lured from the rosters of N.L. teams, hoping to establish the new league as a credible entity. Their task has been made easier by the $2,400 yearly salary ceiling that National League officials have stubbornly refused to raise.

Johnson's audacity in placing three of his teams in direct competition with N.L. clubs (Philadelphia, Chicago and Boston) and the willingness of the outlaw circuit to conduct wholesale player raids concerns many of the established owners. Others believe the new league will soon collapse and their prodigal players will return.

From this vantage point, it appears Johnson is extremely well organized and has the financial backing to carry this campaign to a conclusion. But only time will tell.

# Chisox 1st A.L. champs

Pittsburgh Pirates, 7½-game winners over the Philadelphia Phillies in the National League, and the Chicago White Sox, four-game victors over the Boston Pilgrims in the new American League, are the baseball champions of 1901.

Of particular interest on the A.L. ledger is the list of individual winners, which looks like a Who's Who of former National League stars.

The Philadelphia Athletics' Nap Lajoie, who played last season for the cross-town Phillies in the N.L., stole the show offensively, winning the A.L. Triple Crown with a .422 batting average, 14 home runs and 125 runs batted in. Chicago player-manager Clark Griffith enjoyed the best winning percentage among pitchers with his 24-7 record (.774) and Boston's Cy Young led the league with 33 victories and a 1.62 earned-run average.

St. Louis Cardinals outfielder Jesse Burkett led the N.L. with a .382 average, Cincinnati's Sam Crawford topped the home run charts with 16 and Honus Wagner led the league with 126 RBIs. Two Pirate hurlers, Jack Chesbro (21-10) and Jesse Tannehill (2.18), led in winning percentage and ERA, respectively.

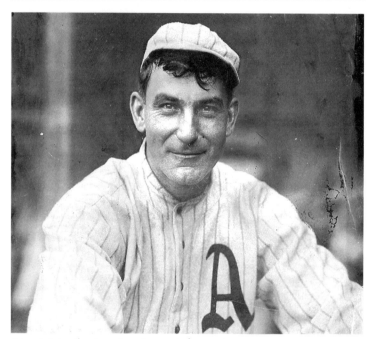

*Nap Lajoie, the American League's first major superstar.*

# Canadian wins race

Jim Caffrey of St. Patrick's Athletic Association in Hamilton, Ontario, knocked more than 10 minutes off his own record, April 19, and ran to an impressive victory in the fifth annual Boston Marathon.

Caffrey completed the 24-mile, 1,230-yard course in 2:29.23, easily beating the 2:39.44 he recorded while winning the race last year. Another Canadian, William Davis of Hamilton, also came in under Caffrey's 1900 time, finishing second in 2:34.45. The first American finisher was S.A. Mellors of Yonkers, N.Y. Mellors finished the race 15 minutes behind Caffrey in 2:44.34.

The course runs from Ashland, Mass., to the Boston Athletic Association in Boston. Thirty-seven runners started the race on a warm, cloudy afternoon and traversed roads that were a little dusty, but otherwise in good condition.

# 1902

The 1902 Michigan Wolverines, first Rose Bowl champions.

## U.S. team foils a British invasion

Buoyed by its unexpected success in the 1900 Davis Cup competition in Boston, the United States braced for another British invasion. The August 6, 7 and 8 matches were scheduled for the Crescent Athletic Club at Bay Ridge in Brooklyn and the Americans did not disappoint.

Malcolm D. Whitman and William A. Larned, the crack U.S. singles players, both were up two sets over their English opponents on the first day of play when the rains came. When play resumed the next morning, however, Whitman went on to a 6-1, 6-1, 1-6, 6-0 victory over Joshua Pim, but Larned fell to Reggie Doherty, 2-6, 3-6, 6-3, 6-4, 6-4.

There were no interruptions in the afternoon and both Americans recorded straight-sets victories, Whitman beating Reggie Doherty and Larned stopping Pim. Reggie and Laurie Doherty beat Holcombe Ward and Dwight F. Davis, 3-6, 10-8, 6-3, 6-4 in doubles, but an American victory already had been sealed.

## Coming up Roses

Michigan's "point-a-minute" Wolverines have taught West Coast promoters a valuable lesson—Western football is no match for the style of football being played in the East and Midwest. Coach Fielding Yost's Wolverines, getting five touchdowns from senior Neil Snow, pounded Stanford, 49-0, before 7,000 fans in the inaugural Rose Bowl on January 1.

Officials at Tournament Park in Pasadena, Calif., stunned by the lopsided score, have not announced whether this New Year's Day football game will become an annual event. But Stanford players and coaches can take consolation in the fact that this Michigan team has steamrolled every opponent on its schedule.

The Wolverines ended their season with an 11-0 record, having outscored their opponents, 550-0. No team, in fact, managed to penetrate the Wolverine 35-yard line, four opponents never crossed mid-field and three teams were held to three or less first downs.

## A.L. enjoys success

The powerful Pittsburgh Pirates romped to a 27½-game victory in the National League while the Philadelphia Athletics captured the American League pennant. But the real story of 1902 was the growing power of Ban Johnson and his success in managing to establish the A.L. as a legitimate major league.

Perhaps the most shocking figures are those registered at the turnstiles. By season's end, the A.L. had outdrawn its rival, 2,228,000 to 1,684,000, and had produced a decisive edge in each of the four cities where the leagues competed for fan support. Some of this can be attributed to continued player raids. Some can be attributed to Johnson's superior leadership.

When, for instance, the Athletics' Nap Lajoie was ordered by the Pennsylvania Supreme Court to rejoin his original team, the Phillies, Johnson transferred Lajoie's contract to Cleveland. Lajoie could not return to Pennsylvania for games against the Athletics, but Johnson had secured his services for the A.L.

Johnson did suffer one major setback at midseason when John McGraw bolted Baltimore with several key players to manage the N.L.'s New York Giants. But he retaliated, December 9, announcing that the A.L. had purchased grounds to build a stadium in New York. That salvo brought quick inquiries from N.L. officials about Johnson's terms for peace.

---

### ★ SPORTS WATCH ★

**JUL:** San Francisco fight fans watched heavyweight champion James J. Jeffries retain his title with an eighth-round knockout of Bob Fitzsimmons.

**SEP:** The Chicago Cubs' infield took on a poetic look when shortstop Joe Tinker, second baseman Johnny Evers and first baseman Frank Chance appeared in a game together for the first time.

**OCT:** New Yorker Genevieve Hecker won her second straight U.S. Amateur golf title with a 4 and 3 victory over Louisa Wells at Brookline, Mass.

---

Football fans watch Michigan and Stanford in the first Rose Bowl game at Tournament Park in Pasadena, Calif.

# 1903

## JANUARY-DECEMBER

# Powerful Pirates fall to upstart Red Sox

Considering the intense hostility that has existed between the established National League and the fledgling American League, it came as a surprise when Pittsburgh Owner Barney Dreyfuss, his Pirates closing in on an N.L. pennant, and Boston Owner Henry Killilea, his Red Sox leading the A.L., agreed to stage a best-of-nine postseason playoff series for the "world championship of baseball."

But even more surprising was the manner in which the upstart Red Sox dispatched the Pirates, five games to three, behind the strong pitching of Bill Dinneen and 36-year-old Cy Young. That pair combined to pitch 69 of the 71 innings the Red Sox hurlers totaled in the first fall classic, more than offsetting the

heroic work of Pittsburgh righthander Deacon Phillippe, who pitched five complete games and 44 innings.

Phillippe and right fielder Jimmy Sebring got the heavily favored Pirates off to a good start. With the Deacon throwing a six-hitter and Sebring hitting the first home run in "World Series" history while driving in four runs, the Pirates prevailed, 7-3. Dinneen fired a three-hit shutout to even the Series for the Red Sox in Game 2, but Phillippe prevailed in both the third and fourth games, beating Boston, 4-2 and 5-4. The first World Series was following form.

Young and Dinneen, however, changed that. Young pitched complete-game victo-

ries in Games 5 and 7 and Dinneen matched that effort in Games 6 and 8. Dinneen's final-game 3-0 victory was his second shutout of the Series and the Red Sox's fourth straight win, wiping out Pittsburgh's 3-1 advantage.

Although the Red Sox took great delight in their stunning victory, the most important thing was that the two leagues had finally buried the hatchet—at least temporarily. And with the Red Sox striking a big blow for A.L. equality and baseball fans enjoying the postseason proceedings, many officials are now promoting the "World Series" as an annual showcase event.

*Talented Cy Young was a major factor in Boston's upset victory over National League powerhouse Pittsburgh in baseball's first World Series.*

*New baseball allies Garry Herrmann (left), owner of the National League's Cincinnati Reds, and Ban Johnson, American League president.*

# Johnson dictates terms of treaty

When the rival American and National Leagues opened peace talks in January, it quickly became apparent just how powerful Ban Johnson has grown. The A.L. president controlled the talks and managed to come away with virtually everything he wanted.

N.L. officials sought a merger between the two circuits, but Johnson, backed by his A.L. owners, said no. Johnson's demands included: recognition

of the A.L. as a major league, respect for the reserve clause in the contracts of the players his league had signed, permission to keep practically all of the pirated players and the right to place a team in New York.

Despite the protests of New York Giants officials John T. Brush and John McGraw to the last point, the National Leaguers acceded. In return, Johnson promised not to put a team in Pittsburgh.

A National Agreement was signed that would allow the leagues to coexist peacefully and a three-man national commission was formed to rule on all disputes. The board members are Garry Herrmann, owner of the Cincinnati Reds, Johnson and the president of the National League.

# 1904

## Boston Brushed aside

It comes as no surprise that New York Giants Owner John T. Brush and Manager John McGraw have flatly rejected the challenge of the Boston Red Sox to a second "World Series".

The Red Sox's surprise victory over the Pirates last year could have something to do with the rejection. But more likely it is a result of Brush's intense dislike for Ban Johnson and the bad blood between Johnson and McGraw, stemming back to 1902 when McGraw, then manager of the A.L.'s Baltimore team, left in midseason for a job with the Giants. Johnson did not help matters last year when he placed the Highlanders in New York, ignoring the Giants' territorial rights.

"Why should we play the upstarts?" asked McGraw. "When we won the National League pennant, we became champions of the only real major league."

Brush asserted there was no reason why "the dignity of the pennant of the National League should be 'cheapened' by playing a series with the best club of a minor league."

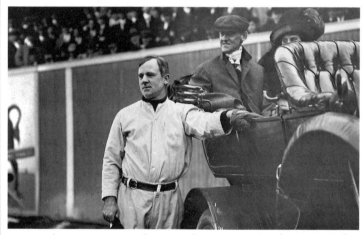

*New York Giants Owner John T. Brush (in carriage) and Manager John McGraw scoffed at the idea of playing Boston in a second World Series.*

### ★ SPORTS WATCH ★

**APR:** Brooklyn defeated Boston, 9-1, in its first Sunday home game, getting around New York's Blue Law by not charging admission but stipulating that fans had to buy scorecards to get into the park.

**JUL:** The New York Giants had their 18-game winning streak snapped by the Philadelphia Phillies, but they took comfort in their N.L.-leading 53-18 record.

**AUG:** May Sutton, a talented 16-year-old from California, defeated Elisabeth Holmes Moore, 6-1, 6-2, to become the youngest U.S. singles champion ever.

## St. Louis Olympics

The third modern Olympic Games staged in St. Louis, Mo., was simply a showcase for American athletics: the United States captured a whopping 238 medals, including golds in 21 of the 22 track and field events. The Games lacked an international flavor and resulted in poor attendance.

Without competitors from such high-profile countries as Great Britain and France, the Games became a hot battle for status between many of the U.S. athletic clubs and colleges. That wasn't all bad because the competition was high quality.

Four athletes finished as triple winners. Archie Hahn won golds in the 60-, 100- and 200-meter sprints; H.L. Hillman swept the 400-meter run and the 200- and 400-meter hurdles; J.D. Lightbody won the 800- and 1,500-meter runs as well as the 2,500-meter steeplechase, and Ray Ewry took the standing high jump, standing broad jump and hop, step and jump.

## Year of the Iron Men

It was the year of the Iron Men in major league baseball and the numbers produced by three New York pitchers—Joe McGinnity and Christy Mathewson of the Giants and Jack Chesbro of the Highlanders—border on the unbelievable.

McGinnity led National League pitchers with 51 games, 408 innings pitched, 35 victories, nine shutouts and an .814 winning percentage. Teammate Mathewson chipped in with 48 games, 368 innings, 33 victories and four shutouts. The duo accounted for 64 percent of the Giants' 106 league-leading wins.

But even McGinnity was outdone by Chesbro, who led the American League with 55 games, an incredible 454 innings and 41 victories. Chesbro pitched six shutouts and completed 48 of his 51 starts. His season, however, ended on a negative note when he uncorked a ninth-inning wild pitch on the final day of the season, allowing Boston to score the winning run and clinch the pennant over his Highlanders.

*New York Giants Iron Man Joe McGinnity.*

# 1905

## Jeffries retires as unbeaten champion

James J. Jeffries, the undefeated king of boxing's heavyweight division since 1899, announced his retirement from the ring on May 13, and handpicked the two contenders to fight for his vacated crown. Jeffries, who had never even been knocked down in the ring, cited lack of opposition as the reason for his decision, pointing out that he already had beaten most of the leading contenders twice.

The 6-foot-2, 220-pound battering ram selected Marvin Hart and Jack Root to fight for his vacated crown. He also agreed to referee the July 3 bout and then officiated as Hart scored a 12th-round knockout in Reno, Nev.

Jeffries, who had won the title in 1899 when he knocked out Bob Fitzsimmons and then defended it seven times, headed for his alfalfa ranch in California after the Hart-Root match. He announced to the press that he plans to live out his retirement there.

## ★ SPORTS WATCH ★

**JUL:** For the first time in Wimbledon history, an overseas player, 17-year-old May Sutton of the United States, captured the singles championship with a 6-3, 6-4 win over Dorothea K. Douglass.

**AUG:** An 18-year-old Detroit rookie named Ty Cobb made his big-league debut with a double off New York Highlanders ace Jack Chesbro.

**OCT:** A Pacific Coast League baseball game between the Oakland Oaks and Portland Beavers was attended by one fan.

## New Brush strokes

After listening to media criticism and public indignation over his refusal to play the A.L.'s Boston Red Sox in a postseason series last year, New York Giants Owner John T. Brush did an abrupt about-face and embraced the idea of an annual "World Series" with open arms.

Brush, in fact, drew up the guidelines under which the recent 1905 event was contested. Besides outlining a revenue formula, the John T. Brush Rules call for—among other things—a best-of-seven format.

Those new guidelines were in effect when Brush's Giants dispatched the A.L.'s Philadelphia Athletics in an incredible five-game all-shutout spectacular. The incomparable Christy Mathewson, allowing only 14 hits over a six-day span, held Philadelphia scoreless three times while teammate Joe McGinnity and the Athletics'

## Michigan streak ends

Time finally ran out on the University of Michigan's 56-game unbeaten streak.

Sporting an incredible five-year record of 55-0-1 (the Wolverines had fought to a 6-6 tie with Minnesota in 1903) and having outscored opponents 495-0 in running up 12 straight victories this season, Coach Fielding Yost took his Michigan team to face the University of Chicago in a December 2 season-ending matchup that would decide the Western Conference championship. With 27,000 screaming Chicago fans supporting the Maroons' hopes for a major upset, a fierce defensive battle ensued.

The only breakthrough occurred in the first half, when Chicago's Walter Eckersall drove a low punt between Michigan's Al Barlow and Denny Clark near the goal line. Clark attempted to carry the ball from the end zone but was tackled by the Maroons' Maurice Catline for a Chicago safety. It turned out to be the game's only score.

Chicago had snatched away the conference championship and the Wolverines were left to ponder an unmatched five-year string of success during which they had outscored opponents, 2,821-42.

*University of Michigan Coach Fielding Yost.*

*Christy Mathewson zeroed in on the Philadelphia A's in the New York Giants' World Series victory.*

Chief Bender pitched the other two shutouts.

Mathewson won the opener, 3-0, the third game, 9-0, and the clincher, 2-0. McGinnity lost Game 2 to Bender, 3-0, but recorded a 1-0 victory in Game 4. Red Ames, who worked one inning, was the only other Giant pitcher to see action.

# Hitless Wonders win Battle of Chicago

The Chicago White Sox, the Hitless Wonders of the American League, pulled off a major upset, defeating the cross-town Cubs in a six-game World Series.

Most Chicagoans and other baseball fans had considered the powerful Cubs, winners of 116 games during the regular season, prohibitive favorites to defeat the scrappy White Sox, who captured the A.L. pennant despite a team batting average of only .228.

Surprisingly, the Sox batted even worse in the Series (.198), making their success story even more improbable. But the White Sox's pitchers, primarily starters Nick Altrock, Frank Owen, Big Ed Walsh and Doc White, didn't require much offensive help. They held the Cubs to a .196 composite aver-

*White Sox lefthander Doc White.*

age and 18 runs, seven of which were scored in the Cubs' Game 2 victory.

As a result of this upset, any lingering doubts about the American League's ability to compete with National League teams have been laid to rest.

*Chicago White Sox ace Ed Walsh helped deflate the Cubs with a shutout and two World Series victories.*

# A football facelift

In what is being hailed as a major breakthrough, a newly appointed committee has redefined the nature of college football with a series of far-reaching rules changes designed to open up the game and remove the brutality that resulted in 18 deaths and 149 injuries last year.

The most significant changes are the legalization of the forward pass and the creation of a neutral zone—the length of the ball—between the two rush lines. The hope is that these rules will eliminate mass-formation football and the brutality it promotes.

That brutality has resulted in public outrage and a call from President Theodore Roosevelt for drastic reform. With that in mind, the Chancellor of New York University, Henry M. McCracken, invited representatives of the nation's colleges to assemble in New York and that meeting resulted in the formation of the National Intercollegiate Football Conference.

From the meeting came the rules committee that met January 12. Other changes include the reduction of game time from 70 to 60 minutes, increase of the distance to be gained in three downs from five to 10 yards and the addition of a second umpire to officiate with the referee and linesman.

# The Silver Seven

The Stanley Cup reign of Ottawa's famed Silver Seven came to an end, March 17, but not before they displayed some of the swashbuckling style that marked their three-year stay atop the hockey world.

Facing a two-game total-goals series with the Montreal Wanderers that would decide the Eastern Canadian Hockey Association championship as well as possession of the Cup, the Silver Seven were embarrassed, March 14, when they were thrashed, 9-1, in the opener. With their chances for retaining the Cup now slim and none, the Seven hoped to at least regain some lost respect.

Playing before a large home crowd and delivering the kind of hard and fierce body checks that had earned them a national reputation, the Silver Seven did more than that in Game 2. They built a 3-1 halftime lead and then, on the strength of Harry Smith's six goals, increased their second-half margin to 9-1.

But the Wanderers answered with two Lester Patrick goals that resulted in a 9-3 final. The Wanderers had prevailed, 12-10, ending a three-year, eight-series Stanley Cup reign in which the Silver Seven had outscored opponents 151-74, while losing only three of the 20 games played.

# 1907

## Tom Longboat earns Boston Marathon win

Tom Longboat, a strong-lunged Canadian Indian, clipped more than five minutes off the existing Boston Marathon record on April 19. Longboat's time of 2:24.20 bettered the mark set in 1901 by fellow Canadian Jim Caffrey.

Longboat settled in behind the leaders for the first five miles before moving into the lead. He was 50 yards ahead of Tom Petch of Toronto at 15 miles and increased his margin to a quarter of a mile at the 18-mile marker.

Longboat really turned it on over the latter stages of the race and left the field in his wake. He finished 3½ minutes ahead of American Robert Fowler, who also was under Caffrey's previous record time.

More than 100 runners were in the starting field for the 11th annual Boston spectacular.

### ★ SPORTS WATCH ★

**APR:** New York Giants catcher Roger Bresnahan, wearing wooden shinguards, showed off his new innovation during a game against Philadelphia.

**AUG:** The big-league debut of Washington fireballer Walter Johnson resulted in a 3-2 loss to the Detroit Tigers.

**DEC:** Phog Allen, successor to Dr. James Naismith as Kansas University basketball coach, watched his Jayhawks roll over Ottawa, 66-22, in their home opener at Lawrence, Kan.

## Football committee changes more rules

The American Intercollegiate Football Rules Committee followed up on its revolutionary 1906 recodification efforts with more changes that will affect how college football is played in the future. The committee agreed on many rules alterations in its January 26 and 27 meeting at the Murray Hill Hotel in New York, but three major changes were put into effect.

The big one concerned the forward pass, which was legalized at last year's session. No longer will teams unsuccessfully attempting a pass be penalized by losing possession of the ball. Now teams will be given a 15-yard penalty for a bad pass, hopefully encouraging them to take more chances at critical times.

The rules committee also increased the length of halves from 30 to 35 minutes and added a field umpire to back up the referee. All of the changes will be in effect for the 1907 season and all could have a significant impact.

## Cubs make amends

After their embarrassing loss to the cross-town White Sox last year, the powerful Chicago Cubs were anxious to make amends. First they took out their frustration on the rest of the National League, winning 107 regular-season games and finishing 17 lengths ahead of second-place Pittsburgh. Then they set their sights on the American League-champion Detroit Tigers.

*Chicago Cubs righthander Ed Reulbach.*

After the teams played to a 3-3 first-game tie that was called after 12 innings because of darkness, the Cubs showcased their outstanding pitching staff. Jack Pfiester, Ed Reulbach, Orval Overall and Mordecai Brown each took their turn, stopping Detroit by scores of 3-1, 5-1, 6-1 and 2-0.

The Tigers concluded the Series with a .209 average and six runs. Cubs pitchers finished with a sparkling 0.75 earned-run average and third baseman Harry Steinfeldt batted .471 while leading an offensive charge that included 18 stolen bases. Ty Cobb, the 20-year-old Detroit outfielder who had just won his first A.L. batting title with a .350 mark, was held to four hits and a .200 average.

Things might have been different if the Tigers hadn't let victory slip through their fingers in Game 1. Leading 3-2 with two out and two Cubs on base in the ninth inning, Tigers starter Bill Donovan struck out pinch-hitter Del Howard. The third strike, however, got away from catcher Charlie Schmidt and Steinfeldt scored the tying run.

*Harry Steinfeldt wielded a big bat in the Cubs' World Series triumph over Detroit.*

# 1908

## The London Olympics

Despite some bickering and petty disputes, the London Olympic Games were a remarkable success. Flawlessly organized, the Games were truly international in flavor because London officials broadened the base of competitors and avoided the regional atmosphere of their host predecessors.

The United States continued to dominate the showcase track and field competitions, but new faces from new countries began to make their marks. One of the most exciting victories was recorded by South African sprinter Reggie Walker, one of the most dramatic by American marathoner Johnny Hayes. The unheralded Walker shocked an excellent field with his 10.8-second victory in the 100-meter dash. Hayes won the marathon when an Italian named Dorando collapsed only yards away from victory.

Of special note were the performances of Americans Mel Sheppard, a winner in the 800- and 1,500-meter events, Ray Ewry, who brought his career Olympic medal count up to eight with victories in the standing high jump and standing broad jump, and the record-setting run (15 seconds flat) of Forrest Smithson over the 110-meter hurdles.

As usual, the host country, with many more athletes competing, captured medal honors. Great Britain won 145.

## Giants lose pennant on blunder by Merkle

Fate has played a cruel trick on the New York Giants and first baseman Fred Merkle, turning the latter's September 23 baserunning mistake into a "boneheaded" play that will long live in baseball infamy.

The play occurred with two out in the bottom of the ninth inning of a 1-1 game against Chicago at New York's Polo Grounds. The Giants, locked in a torrid pennant race with the rival Cubs, had Merkle stationed at first base and Moose McCormick running at third when Al Bridwell delivered a single to center, apparently insuring an important Giants' victory. As McCormick headed home, Merkle made a dash straight for the center-field clubhouse, thus avoiding the rush of jubilant spectators pouring onto the field.

Cubs second baseman Johnny Evers, noticing that Merkle had failed to touch second, thus setting up a forceout, called for the ball and frantically appealed to umpire Hank O'Day. "Out," said the arbiter. But with the mayhem reigning on the field and most players already retired to their respective clubhouses, O'Day had no recourse but to send the confusing matter to the league directors for a ruling. In the hours that followed, the Giants continued to claim victory while the Cubs insisted the game was a tie.

League officials eventually agreed with the Cubs, adding

★ SPORTS WATCH ★

**AUG:** Heavyweight champion Tommy Burns knocked out Bill Squires for the third time in 13 months in the 13th round of a bout at Sydney, Australia.

**OCT:** The Chicago Cubs, N.L. pennant winners by virtue of New York Giant Fred Merkle's baserunning blunder, made short work of Detroit in a five-game World Series.

**NOV:** Harvard ended Yale's 42-game college football unbeaten streak when it defeated the Elis, 4-0, in the final game of the season at New Haven, Conn.

*Fred Merkle's "boner" cost the New York Giants a pennant.*

that the game would have to be replayed in the unlikely event that the two teams would be deadlocked atop the National League standings at the end of their 154-game schedules. But that's exactly what happened. When all was said and done, both teams sported 98-55-1 records and a one-game, winner-take-all confrontation was scheduled for the Polo Grounds.

But not even a delirious crowd of Giants fans, filling the stadium and watching from the bluffs surrounding the park, or the strong right arm of Christy Mathewson could stop the inevitable. With Joe Tinker providing the offense and Mordecai Brown the pitching, Chicago rolled to a 4-2 victory.

Merkle's "boner" had cost the Giants a pennant.

*Olympic jumping jack Ray Ewry.*

# 1909

## Phillies, Pirates open impressive new parks

*An overflow crowd, dressed to kill, turned out to watch the first game at Philadelphia's new Shibe Park.*

Philadelphia's Shibe Park opened, April 12, as baseball's first steel-and-concrete stadium and Pittsburgh's Forbes Field followed suit two months later. Both have played to rave reviews.

Shibe Park, the creation of Athletics Owner Ben Shibe, welcomed 30,162 fans on opening day and thousands more had to be turned away. After ceremonies dedicating the new structure, players and fans were introduced to a symmetrical configuration that measured 360 feet down the lines and 420 feet to center. With Eddie Plank pitching a six-hitter, the A's christened their new home with an 8-1 victory over Boston.

The Pirates dedicated their $2 million park on June 30, four months after Owner Barney Dreyfuss had broken ground. An overflowing crowd of 30,338 watched the Pirates drop a 3-2 decision to the Chicago Cubs. Forbes Field has irregular dimensions of 360 feet to left, 376 to right and 462 to straightaway center.

## Pirates edge Tigers

The Detroit Tigers, five-game World Series losers in each of the last two seasons to the powerful Chicago Cubs, tried, tried again in the 1909 fall classic. But the happy prospect of not having to face the Cubs was tempered by the knowledge that the Chicagoans had won 104 games in the regular season—and finished 6½ games behind Pittsburgh in the National League pennant race.

The powerful Pirates, who had won 110 times, showed the Tigers why when the Series opened in Pittsburgh and Babe Adams pitched a six-hit, 4-1 victory. But Detroit fired right back with a 7-2 triumph of its own. This victory-swapping pattern was to continue throughout the Series.

The Pirates recorded 8-6 and 8-4 victories in the third and fifth games, the Tigers answered with 5-0 and 5-4 wins (both victories by George Mullin) in Games 4 and 6.

Game 7 was no contest. With Adams recording his third victory and Honus Wagner and Dots Miller driving in two runs apiece, the Bucs rolled, 8-0, and won their first championship. The Tigers had lost for the third year in a row.

A Series sidelight was the matchup of Wagner, who had just won his seventh N.L batting title, and Ty Cobb, the Tiger youngster who had just won the A.L. Triple Crown. Wagner batted .333 and drove in seven runs; Cobb batted only .231 with six RBIs.

*A pair of aces: Pittsburgh's Honus Wagner (left) and Detroit's Ty Cobb discuss hitting before Game 1 of the World Series.*

## Lafayette wins with last gasp touchdown

Frank Irmschler, a substitute halfback, blocked a field-goal attempt with six seconds remaining and ran 92 yards with the loose ball to give Lafayette a 6-0 victory, October 23, over previously undefeated Princeton in one of the wildest finishes ever witnessed on a football field.

Princeton was on the Leopards' 10-yard line with time running out and victory within its grasp.

But as Logan Cunningham received the ball and put his foot into the dropkick that could have preserved Princeton's unbeaten (5-0) record, Irmschler came firing between guard and tackle, blocked the kick and ran for the winning touchdown after the ball conveniently bounced into his arms.

A few minutes earlier, another Cunningham field-goal try had bounced off the goal post and three times in the second half Princeton had advanced within the Lafayette 25, only to stall. The win lifted Lafayette's record to 4-0.

# boxing

## Jack Johnson and the "Great White Hopes"

*The story of the first black heavyweight champion of the world*

That Jack Johnson possessed a stylish, deadly boxing proficiency that made him superior to anyone in the world was bad enough. That he approached his profession with mocking defiance and a self-confidence that bordered on arrogance was added insult.

But the most annoying thing about Johnson was that he was *black*, and he was heavyweight champion of the world, the symbolic physical king of the universe. In an era when blacks still were walking a fine line between slavery and freedom, Johnson was punching holes in the accepted theories of white supremacy. He was a threat to the social order, a menace that had to be disposed of. He was a white society's worst nightmare.

Born in the humble seaport surroundings of Galveston, Tex., Jack Arthur Johnson would never have passed for anybody's hero. He left school after fifth grade and bounced from job to job, blindly searching for his life's calling. He found it when he became janitor for a local gymnasium.

The sweat, the sounds and smells of the gym, the demands of hard work and discipline all were addictive to his senses. He began training with weights,

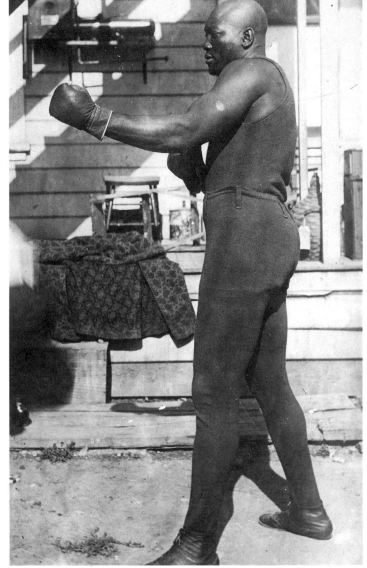

*World champion Jack Johnson.*

*Johnson stands over Jeffries, the fallen Great White Hope.*

punching bags and jumping ropes while dedicating himself to the science of boxing— everything he could pick up from the daily activity.

Whether sparring, fighting against circus ringers or volunteering for informal bouts in strange alleyways, Johnson would do anything to refine his skills. He quickly developed a reputation as a great defensive fighter and master of the feint.

Johnson soon conquered Galveston, then drifted through Chicago, New York and Boston before finally turning professional in 1897.

From that point until he became champion in 1908, Johnson would fight an astounding 77 matches, losing only three times. But most of those fights were against fellow blacks. The white heavyweight champions, in keeping with the mores of the society they entertained, refused to fight "inferior" black men.

Heavyweight champ John L. Sullivan challenged all contenders in 1892, with one exception. "I will not fight a Negro," he said. Future champs Jim Corbett, Bob Fitzsimmons and James J. Jeffries followed Sullivan's lead.

But when Jeffries retired undefeated in 1905 for lack of competition, the door opened a little. Tommy Burns eventually claimed Jeffries' abdicated crown and fought a series of also-rans for two years. Johnson literally pursued the champion from New York to London, to Paris, back to London and then to Sydney, Australia, trying to corner him into a match. Burns, thinking he would win easily, finally agreed, on two conditions: He, as champ, would get $35,000 to Johnson's $5,000, and the match would be refereed by Burns' manager.

## "Jim Jeffries must emerge from his alfalfa farm and remove the golden smile from Jack Johnson's face. Jeff, it's up to you."

**JACK LONDON**
*writing in the* New York Herald

Burns spent the week before the December 26, 1908, match hurling racial digs at Johnson. That was a big mistake. When Sydney police finally jumped into the ring during the 14th round to break up the fight, Johnson was wearing his patented smile and Burns was a bloody mess. Johnson could have knocked him out, but chose to inflict what he considered well-deserved punishment.

*Johnson is introduced before his 1910 fight with Jim Jeffries.*

"I figured that Burns had something coming to him," Johnson said. "I certainly wished to give him his $35,000 worth."

Jack Johnson was the heavyweight champion of the world and white America was appalled. Blacks were supposed to be second-class citizens, not symbols of physical manhood. The call went out for a "Great White Hope" to dethrone this pretender and there was only one logical choice.

"Jim Jeffries must emerge from his alfalfa farm and remove the golden smile from Jack Johnson's face. Jeff, it's up to you," wrote Jack London in his Burns-Johnson fight story for the *New York Herald*.

Jeffries, overweight and out of shape, at first refused the plea. But pressure mounted daily and fans everywhere begged the former champion to come out of retirement. He

eventually gave in to the outcry.

The "Fight of the Century" was scheduled for July 4, 1910, in Reno, Nev. Jeffries trained hard and assured his national following, "I realize full well just what depends on me and I am not going to disappoint the public." For Johnson, it was a double opportunity to silence critics who had labeled him an undeserving champion and to wreak more havoc on the white community.

He did just that. With the crowd chanting "Jeff, it's up to you," Johnson danced and floated around the ring, pounding the 35-year-old former champion into oblivion. The "Great White Hope" never stood a chance and was knocked down three times in the 15th round, the final time for good.

"I could never have whipped Jack Johnson at my best," Jeffries later told reporters. "I couldn't have reached him in a thousand years."

News of Johnson's victory touched off race riots in many cities around the country and rekindled the cry for a new "Great White Hope." But there was none on the horizon and desperate Americans would have to survive Jack Johnson for five more years. Johnson did not make it easy.

The champion enjoyed his life in the fast lane as much as his ability to distress white supremacists. That he preferred the company of white women was particularly disturbing—and, for Johnson,

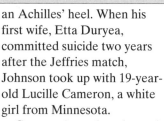

an Achilles' heel. When his first wife, Etta Duryea, committed suicide two years after the Jeffries match, Johnson took up with 19-year-old Lucille Cameron, a white girl from Minnesota.

Cameron's mother charged Johnson with abduction of her daughter across a state border for immoral purposes, a federal crime under the 1910 Mann Act. But Cameron, who later married Johnson, would not substantiate the charge. Johnson was not so fortunate when Belle Schreiber, a white prostitute with whom he once had lived and traveled, accused him of violating the same law.

A trial was held in 1913, the jury brought in a guilty verdict (a one-year sentence) and Johnson skipped bail and fled to France. A fugitive in his own country, he boxed occasionally and traveled around Europe giving boxing exhibitions and theatrical performances. It wasn't until April 5, 1915, that Johnson fought his next big match—and met his Waterloo.

Jess Willard, a 6-foot-6, 250-pound giant from Kansas, was not a great boxer, but he did have endurance and punching power. The hope was that Willard could wear down Johnson in this scheduled 45-round match in the heat of Havana, Cuba, and eventually put him away. It worked.

The 37-year-old Johnson outclassed the 28-year-old challenger for 20 rounds, but could not put him down. Suddenly the champ ran out of gas. Willard finally hit paydirt with a powerful left-right combination in the 26th round and Johnson's reign of terror over White America was over.

Johnson returned to the United States in 1920 and served his sentence at the federal prison in Leavenworth, Kan., before fading into obscurity. Ironically, he died in a car accident in Raleigh, N.C., in 1946, the year before Jackie Robinson broke the color barrier in baseball.

*Challenger Stanley Ketchel takes the count in a 1909 bout.*

*North Americans were on the move as the decade opened and the agrarianism of the early 1900s was giving way to a new urban industrial society — wealthier, more mobile and interested in expanding its sports and entertainment horizons.*

S uch interest can be illustrated by two developments: The inaugural Indianapolis 500, run in 1911, drew 80,000 curious spectators and a 1914 national championship amateur baseball game played in Cleveland attracted more than 100,000. Not surprisingly, enterprising sportsmen were ready, willing and able to satisfy such a widespread entertainment hunger.

When Shibe Park in Philadelphia and Forbes Field in Pittsburgh opened their gates for the

Track and football star Jim Thorpe.

Boxer Jack Dempsey.

Chicago White Sox outfielder Shoeless Joe Jackson.

first time in 1909, they sparked an explosion of baseball stadia, most of them large steel and concrete facilities that would help fuel the popularity of the game. By 1916, seven more teams had opened new ballparks and baseball fans were flocking to games in ever-increasing numbers.

College football officials took heed and, seeing an opportunity to generate athletic funds, began building massive structures and presenting their games on Saturday afternoons. When Yale erected a 67,000-seat facility in 1913, the stage was set for a stadia mania that would grip the sport in the following decade.

Team sports, with their ability

to tap into regional pride and enthusiasm, continued to generate the most interest, but new heroes, capable of giving their sports a temporary spotlight, were beginning to surface.

Through the first half of the decade, the nation would literally sit on the edge of its seat as boxing promoters sent a series of "Great White Hopes" against black heavyweight champion Jack Johnson. When 6-foot-7 giant Jess Willard finally satisfied the white establishment by knocking out Johnson in 1915, the sport was quickly moving toward its first million-dollar purse and one of its most popular champions—Jack Dempsey, who unseated Willard in 1919.

While tennis was still awaiting the arrival of big Bill Tilden in 1920, golf fans already were enjoying the superstar play of Walter Hagen and horse racing enthusiasts were toasting the 1919 success of Sir Barton, the sport's first winner of the coveted Triple Crown, and record-setting colt Man o'War.

This is not to say that everything was proceeding smoothly. World War I threw a shroud over the nation, called away athletes for service and drastically reduced the schedules of many sports. Baseball was forced to deal with a rival major league and the hint of a scandal that would rock the sport in 1920. And hockey was fighting an identity crisis that would eventually culminate with the formation of the National Hockey League in 1917.

But not even the ominous shadow of a world war could hide the sports prosperity that lay just around the corner. And when athletes, coaches and fans returned from their war-time duties, the time was right for a new order of commitment. The first "Golden Age of Sports" was just around the corner.

# ROLL OF HONOR

## AUTO RACING

### INDIANAPOLIS 500

| Year | Winner | Speed |
|------|--------|-------|
| 1911 | Ray Harroun | 74.602 mph |
| 1912 | Joe Dawson | 78.719 mph |
| 1913 | Jules Goux | 75.933 mph |
| 1914 | Rene Thomas | 82.474 mph |
| 1915 | Ralph DePalma | 89.840 mph |
| 1916 | Dario Resta | 84.001 mph |
| 1917 | Not held | |
| 1918 | Not held | |
| 1919 | Howard Wilcox | 88.050 mph |

## GOLF

| Year | US OPEN Winner | PGA |
|------|----------------|-----|
| 1910 | Alex Smith | |
| 1911 | John McDermott | |
| 1912 | John McDermott | |
| 1913 | Francis Ouimet | |
| 1914 | Walter Hagen | |
| 1915 | Jerry Travers | |
| 1916 | Chick Evans | Jim Barnes |
| 1917 | Not held | Not held |
| 1918 | Not held | Not held |
| 1919 | Walter Hagen | Jim Barnes |

## HORSE RACING

### KENTUCKY DERBY

| Year | Winner | Jockey |
|------|--------|--------|
| 1910 | Donau | Fred Herbert |
| 1911 | Meridian | George Archibald |
| 1912 | Worth | Carroll Shilling |
| 1913 | Donerail | Roscoe Goose |
| 1914 | Old Rosebud | John McCabe |
| 1915 | Regret | Joe Notter |
| 1916 | George Smith | Johnny Loftus |
| 1917 | Omar Khayyam | Charles Borel |
| 1918 | Exterminator | William Knapp |
| 1919 | Sir Barton | Johnny Loftus |

### PREAKNESS STAKES

| Year | Winner | Jockey |
|------|--------|--------|
| 1910 | Layminister | R. Estep |
| 1911 | Watervale | Eddie Dugan |
| 1912 | Colonel Holloway | C. Turner |
| 1913 | Buskin | James Butwell |
| 1914 | Holiday | A. Schuttinger |
| 1915 | Rhine Maiden | Douglas Hoffman |
| 1916 | Damrosch | Linus McAtee |
| 1917 | Kalitan | E. Haynes |
| 1918* | War Cloud | Johnny Loftus |
| 1918* | Jack Hare Jr. | Charles Peak |
| 1919 | Sir Barton | Johnny Loftus |

### BELMONT STAKES

| Year | Winner | Jockey |
|------|--------|--------|
| 1910 | Sweep | James Butwell |
| 1911 | Not held | |
| 1912 | Not held | |
| 1913 | Prince Eugene | Roscoe Troxler |
| 1914 | Luke McLuke | Merritt Buxton |
| 1915 | The Finn | George Byrne |
| 1916 | Friar Rock | E. Haynes |
| 1917 | Hourless | James Butwell |
| 1918 | Johren | Frank Robinson |
| 1919 | Sir Barton | Johnny Loftus |

*In 1918 the Preakness Stakes was run in two divisions: War Cloud winning in the Eastern Division and Jack Hare Jr. in the Western Division.

## BASEBALL

### WORLD SERIES

| Year | Winner | Pennant Winner (series score) |
|------|--------|-------------------------------|
| 1910 | Philadelphia Athletics | (Chicago Cubs, 4-1) |
| 1911 | Philadelphia Athletics | (New York Giants, 4-2) |
| 1912 | Boston Red Sox | (New York Giants, 4-3-1) |
| 1913 | Philadelphia Athletics | (New York Giants, 4-1) |
| 1914 | Boston Braves | (Philadelphia Athletics, 4-0) |
| 1915 | Boston Red Sox | (Philadelphia Phillies, 4-1) |
| 1916 | Boston Red Sox | (Brooklyn Dodgers, 4-1) |
| 1917 | Chicago White Sox | (New York Giants, 4-2) |
| 1918 | Boston Red Sox | (Chicago Cubs, 4-2) |
| 1919 | Cincinnati Reds | (Chicago White Sox, 5-3) |

## HOCKEY

### STANLEY CUP

| Year | Champion | Finalist (series score) |
|------|----------|-------------------------|
| 1917-18 | Toronto Arenas | (Vancouver Millionaires, 3-2) |
| 1918-19 | No champion—series canceled after five games because of flu epidemic | |
| 1919-20 | Ottawa Senators | (Seattle Metropolitans, 3-2) |

## TENNIS

### US OPEN

| Year | Men's Winner | Women's Winner |
|------|--------------|----------------|
| 1910 | William A. Larned | Hazel Hotchkiss |
| 1911 | William A. Larned | Hazel Hotchkiss |
| 1912 | Maurice McLoughlin | Mary K. Browne |
| 1913 | Maurice McLoughlin | Mary K. Browne |
| 1914 | Richard Williams | Mary K. Browne |
| 1915 | Bill Johnston | Molla Bjurstedt |
| 1916 | Richard Williams | Molla Bjurstedt |
| 1917 | Lindley Murray | Molla Bjurstedt |
| 1918 | Lindley Murray | Molla Bjurstedt |
| 1919 | Bill Johnston | Hazel Hotchkiss-Wightman |

# 1910

## JANUARY - DECEMBER

## Coombs, Bender pitch Athletics past Cubs

Philadelphia Manager Connie Mack was short of pitchers as he prepared to face the powerful Chicago Cubs in the World Series. So he simply told ailing starter Eddie Plank to take it easy and turned matters over to his two aces, 31-game winner Jack Coombs and 23-game winner Chief Bender.

That strategy proved too much for Chicago.

Coombs and Bender combined to pitch every inning of the Athletics' five-game Series victory and they received plenty of offense from the likes of Eddie Collins, Frank Baker and Danny Murphy. The young A's, 102-game winners in capturing the American League pennant, averaged seven runs per game in the Series and held the Cubs, 104-game winners in earning

*A's righthander Jack Coombs, a three-game World Series winner.*

their fourth National League pennant in five years, to an average of three.

Coombs won three Series games, although Bender produced a better earned-run average (1.93 to 3.33) while splitting his two decisions.

## Elis upset Princeton, silence the critics

Yale, criticized all week after its November 5 21-0 loss to lowly Brown, took out its frustration on unbeaten Princeton, November 12, and defeated the Tigers, 5-3, before 25,000 fans at Princeton.

Fred Daly's Elis outfought the Tigers in one of the school's most valiant efforts in years. Yale entered the game 5-2-1 while Princeton carried a 7-0 mark into its season-ending contest.

Keying all day on star running back Tal Pendleton, the

Elis made Princeton work for every inch of ground. The Tigers did strike first, using a Pendleton field goal to forge a 3-0 halftime lead, but the rest of the game belonged to Yale.

The Elis finally broke through in the third quarter when Springer Brooks recovered a fumble at the Tiger 25 and quarterback Arthur Howe pulled a major surprise by throwing a touchdown pass to John Kilpatrick. That score, the first allowed by Princeton this season, proved to be costly.

### ★ SPORTS WATCH ★

**JAN:** The newly organized Montreal Canadiens played their first game as members of the National Hockey Association at Montreal's Jubilee Rink.

**APR:** A baseball first: U.S. President William Howard Taft threw out a ceremonial first pitch for Washington's opening day game against Chicago.

**JUL:** New Comiskey Park, the biggest stadium in baseball, opened with the hometown White Sox losing a 2-0 decision to the St. Louis Browns.

## Johnson declares Cobb top batsman

American League President Ban Johnson has officially declared Detroit's Ty Cobb winner of the A.L. batting championship over Cleveland's Nap Lajoie. But Johnson's October 16 ruling will not end the controversy over the manner in which the issue was decided.

Cobb entered the final day of the season with a .383 average and a comfortable lead over Lajoie. So the Tigers' star

decided to sit out. However, strange things were happening in St. Louis, where the Indians were playing a doubleheader against the Browns.

In his first at-bat, Lajoie tripled to left. He then bunted successfully seven straight times, finishing 8-for-8 and lifting his average to .384. Browns' rookie third baseman Red Corriden had been ordered to play deep by St. Louis Manager Jack O'Connor, ostensibly to protect the youngster from getting nailed by one of Lajoie's patented line drives. But many observers suspected the Browns of trying to help Lajoie win out over the unpopular Cobb.

Johnson was furious. He immediately met with the principals, banished O'Connor

*Cleveland's Nap Lajoie and Detroit's Ty Cobb pose in a Chalmers automobile, the kind given annually to the league batting champion. The final averages of the two American League stars were so close in 1910 that Chalmers awarded both a new car.*

from baseball and ordered a check of Cobb's official average. He announced one week after the season that a discrep-

ancy had been found and Cobb's final mark, authenticated by the A.L., was .385— one point above Lajoie.

# 1911

## 4 Thorpe field goals too much for Harvard

Jim Thorpe kicked four field goals, including the game-winner from 48 yards out in the fourth quarter, as Carlisle Industrial School pulled off an 18-15 shocker over Harvard, November 11, before 25,000 disappointed spectators at Harvard Stadium in Cambridge, Mass.

Thorpe, one of the most talented all-round athletes this country has ever produced, started the game with his right leg wrapped from knee to ankle and limping noticeably. But that didn't stop him from throwing his body around on defense or handling most of Carlisle's ball-carrying chores.

Harvard, coming off a tough 8-6 loss to Princeton last week, fought to a 9-6 halftime lead and appeared to be in control. But Coach Glenn (Pop) Warner's Indians scored the next 12 points and held on for dear life after Harvard's Robert Storer picked up a blocked punt and raced into the end zone for a fourth-quarter touchdown.

*Jim Thorpe, considered by many the world's greatest all-round athlete, was at his best on the football field while playing for Carlisle Industrial School.*

Carlisle, which improved its record to 4-0, scored its only touchdown in the third period on Possum Powell's short plunge. Thorpe's running helped Carlisle get into position for the score.

## American wins Open

John McDermott, a 21-year-old former caddie, outdueled Mike Brady and George Simpson in an 18-hole playoff, June 26, to become the first American-born winner of the U.S. Open golf championship.

McDermott, forced to play the final 18 holes of his Saturday round in heavy rain, covered the 6,636-yard Chicago Golf Club course in 79 strokes, leaving him tied with Brady and Simpson at 307 after 72 holes. When the threesome teed off for the playoff round on Monday, they had to contend with extreme heat, heavy wind and wet greens.

McDermott, born in Atlantic City, N.J., came home with an 80, two strokes ahead of Brady and five ahead of Simpson. The victory was especially satisfying for McDermott, who had lost in a 1910 playoff to Alex Smith.

Pleasing also was the fact that no other American-born golfer had ever won this tournament, which had been dominated through its 16-year history by Britons.

---

### ★ SPORTS WATCH ★

**AUG:** William A. Larned defeated Maurice McLoughlin in straight sets to win his fifth straight U.S. singles championship at Newport Casino two months after Hazel Hotchkiss rolled to her third consecutive U.S. singles championship at Philadelphia.

**OCT:** The hitting heroics of Frank (Home Run) Baker carried the Philadelphia Athletics to a six-game triumph over the New York Giants and their second straight World Series win.

---

## Harroun takes first Indianapolis 500 race

Ray Harroun, driving a six-cylinder Marmon Wasp, took the lead on the 190th mile and then held off all challengers to win the inaugural Indianapolis 500 at the Indianapolis Motor Speedway.

Harroun, who posted a winning time of 6 hours, 41 minutes, 8 seconds while averaging 74.602 miles per hour, collected the $10,000 first-place money plus another $5,000 in special prizes. More than 80,000 fans turned out for the accident-filled Memorial Day spectacular that was not lacking for excitement.

The most serious accident occurred during the race's 30th mile when a car driven by Arthur Greiner lost a tire and spun into the rail, throwing both Greiner and S.P. Dickson, his riding mechanic, from the vehicle. Dickson was killed immediately while Greiner suffered only a fractured arm.

Harroun finished the race about 30 seconds ahead of Ralph Mulford's Lozier while David Bruce-Brown's Fiat trailed by another half minute.

*Cars line up and gentlemen prepare to start their engines for the first Indianapolis 500-mile race.*

## Giants lose on World Series misplay

A 10th-inning error by New York center fielder Fred Snodgrass opened the door and the Boston Red Sox stepped through with a pair of runs for a 3-2 victory over the Giants in the decisive eighth game of the World Series, October 16, at Boston's Fenway Park.

The New Yorkers took a 2-1 lead in the 10th inning with Christy Mathewson on the mound, and literally gave this one away. The Giants' 10th-inning horror story started when Snodgrass, camped under Clyde Engle's innocent-looking fly ball, inexplicably let it drop.

With Engle on second base after the misplay, Harry Hooper was robbed of a hit when Snodgrass partially redeemed himself by making a great running catch. But Engle tagged and advanced to third on the play and Steve Yerkes drew a walk. Disaster struck again when Tris Speaker lifted a foul pop between home plate and first base.

Catcher Chief Meyers and first baseman Fred Merkle, whose single had given the Giants the lead in the top of the inning, converged on the ball. But neither took control and it dropped untouched between them. Given a new life, Speaker singled home Engle with the tying run.

With Yerkes now stationed at third and Speaker on first, Duffy Lewis was walked intentionally. Third baseman Larry Gardner's deep fly ball scored the Series-winning run.

The Series had been evenly played, with Boston pitcher Smokey Joe Wood, a 34-game winner during the season, earning three victories. Wood, in fact, was the Game 8 winner after relieving starter Hugh Bedient. Giants pitcher Rube Marquard, a 26-game winner during the regular campaign, was a two-time Series winner.

The eighth game was necessary because darkness ended Game 2 after 11 innings with the teams tied 6-6.

*Fred Snodgrass dropped a fly ball and the New York Giants dropped a World Series heartbreaker to Boston.*

**★ SPORTS WATCH ★**

**MAR:** Playing three 20-minute periods and six players to a side for the first time in Stanley Cup competition, the Quebec Bulldogs of the National Hockey Association defeated Moncton, two games to none.

**APR:** Two new concrete baseball stadiums were opened: Redland Field (later Crosley Field) in Cincinnati and Fenway Park in Boston.

**JUL:** American Indian Jim Thorpe earned worldwide acclaim with his victories in the pentathlon and decathlon at the Stockholm Olympic Games.

**OCT:** The National League produced its first Triple Crown winner of the century: Chicago's Heinie Zimmerman batted .372 with 14 homers and 103 RBIs.

## Frustrated DePalma comes up 1 lap short

Ralph DePalma was cruising around the 2.5-mile rectangular track at the Indianapolis Motor Speedway with nothing but fate standing between him and the $20,000 first-place money in the second Memorial Day 500-mile extravaganza.

But fate can be cruel, and it certainly was on this day.

DePalma, driving a ghost-grey German Mercedes, held a 10-mile lead over second-place runner Joe Dawson with 15 miles (six laps) to go. But suddenly his engine began stammering, courtesy of a broken connecting rod that had torn a hole in his crankcase. What to do: Pull into the pits and probably get back on the track in time to insure a top five finish?

Or take a risk and go for broke?

DePalma chose the latter course and his Mercedes chugged around the track, losing both oil and speed at an alarming pace. Barely hitting 20 miles per hour as the home-stretch of the 199th lap appeared, the car, starved for oil, finally clanked and died.

DePalma and his riding mechanic did the only thing they could think of. They got out and pushed. As they finally reached the pit area, exhausted, Dawson's blue National roared by, completing its 197th lap. The race was over for DePalma and Dawson, a 23-year-old from Indianapolis, sped to victory and the $20,000 first-prize reward.

*Driver Ralph DePalma (gripping wheel) and mechanic Rupert Jeffkins push DePalma's broken-down 2,500-pound Mercedes toward the pits, trailed by an Indianapolis 500 official. DePalma was leading when the car stopped, a little more than one lap from the finish line.*

# 1913

## U.S. recovers Cup

After 11 years of disappointment, the United States finally has recovered the Davis Cup.

That long-overdue accomplishment was achieved on July 28, when an American team composed of Maurice McLoughlin, Norris Williams and Harold Hackett squeaked out a 3-2 victory over the British team of Cecil Parke, Charles Dixon and Roger Barrett on Wimbledon's famed Centre Court.

The outlook was not bright when McLoughlin, the top American player, lost to Parke in the opening match, an 8-10, 7-5, 6-4, 1-6, 7-5 thriller. But Williams fought back with an equally exciting 8-6, 3-6, 6-2, 1-6, 7-5 victory over Dixon and then McLoughlin and Hackett outlasted Dixon and Barrett in a five-set doubles match.

McLoughlin insured the U.S. victory with an 8-6, 6-3, 6-2 second-day win over Dixon. Parke's five-set victory over Williams only made the final score respectable.

The 1913 challenge round was the deepest ever with a record seven teams joining the competition. The Americans had to beat Australasia, Germany and Canada to reach the final round.

## Irish, Dorais pass test

In the first notable intersectional game in Notre Dame history, Fighting Irish quarterback Gus Dorais unveiled an offensive strategy that is sure to influence the way college football is played in the years to come. Dorais put on an aerial display that produced 13 completions in 17 attempts for 243 yards and a stunning 35-13 win over Army in a November 1 game at West Point, N.Y.

Although passing was legalized in 1906, most teams have thrown only as a last-ditch attempt to move the ball when their ground games are stymied. When the forward pass is used, it is mostly on a spot basis in which the quarterback throws into a predetermined area.

But the passing strategy designed by Coach Jesse Harper and executed superbly by Dorais could change that thinking. The quarterback hit

*Gus Dorais, a passing pioneer during his days as Notre Dame quarterback, went on to coach for the University of Detroit and the Detroit Lions of the National Football League.*

his targets in full stride and proved how devastating a balanced run/pass offense can be.

One of Dorais' completions, a 25-yarder in the first quarter, was caught for a touchdown by end Knute Rockne.

---

### ★ SPORTS WATCH ★

**MAR:** Joseph Malone scored nine goals in the opener and the NHA's Quebec Bulldogs went on to sweep the Sydney Millionaires in a two-game set for the Stanley Cup.

**APR:** Brooklyn unveiled new Ebbets Field with a 3-2 exhibition game victory over the Yankees and Dodger outfielder Casey Stengel christened the park with its first home run.

**AUG:** Maurice McLoughlin used his cannon serve to dispose of Richard Norris Williams in four sets and win his second straight U.S. singles championship.

**SEP:** Jerry Travers won his fourth U.S. Amateur golf title and second straight with a 5 and 4 victory over John G. Anderson at Garden City, N.Y.

---

*Francis Ouimet, the first amateur to win the U.S. Open, is flanked by Harry Vardon (left) and Ted Ray, the two Englishmen he defeated in a playoff.*

## Amateur wins Open

Francis Ouimet, a 20-year-old employee of a sporting goods company, stunned the golf community, September 30, when he defeated British stars Harry Vardon and Ted Ray in a playoff for the U.S. Open championship. Ouimet shot an 18-hole playoff round of 72 at The Country Club in Brookline, Mass., to become the second American-born player and the first amateur ever to win this 19-year-old event.

Ouimet's victory, considered a real breakthrough for both American and amateur golf, follows on the heels of John McDermott's triumphs in the 1911 and '12 Opens after more than a decade and a half of foreign rule. Vardon, who won the U.S. Open in 1900, shot a playoff round 77 while Ray was one stroke further back at 78.

Ouimet, Vardon and Ray were tied at 304 after the final regulation round.

# 1914

## Federal League opens for business

With the signing of shortstop Joe Tinker to manage the Chicago Whales and pitcher Mordecai Brown to manage in St. Louis, the new Federal League has stressed its intentions to exist as a third major league.

The new circuit's president, James A. Gilmore of Chicago, has put together top-flight ownership groups for franchises that will play out of Chicago, St. Louis, Brooklyn, Baltimore, Kansas City, Pittsburgh, Buffalo and Indianapolis in the upcoming campaign. And Gilmore has suggested that the

*Joe Tinker, manager of the Federal League's Chicago Whales.*

owners will do what is necessary to make the league work, including the pirating of players from the well-established American and National leagues.

War has been declared and it looks like serious business.

## Colorful Hagen wins Open championship

Walter Hagen, a brash, talented young shotmaker with a bright future on the American golf tour, ignored the sweltering August heat and fired a record-tying four-round total of 290 to capture the 20th U.S. Open championship at the Midlothian Country Club near Chicago.

The 21-year-old Hagen, decked out in white flannel trousers and a multi-colored silk shirt with a red bandana knotted around his neck, became just the third American-born golfer to win the event and he did it in style, matching the record four-round total of George Sargent in 1909. The colorful Rochester, N.Y., native set a fast early pace with a record-shattering first-round 68 and then followed that with rounds of 74, 75 and 73.

Hagen, who had carried a one-stroke lead into Saturday morning's round, did suffer through some anxious moments as Chicagoan Chick Evans made a belated rush that fell one stroke short of forcing a playoff.

## Miracle Braves roll to Series sweep

The 1914 Boston Braves will henceforth be known as the Miracle Braves—a nickname that was twice earned.

The Braves, managed by George Stallings, rested at the bottom of the National League standings in mid-July and many fans were praying for a merciful end to their suffering. But the Braves suddenly caught fire, moving up to second place by mid-August and storming into first place on September 8. By season's end, the Braves had run off an amazing 68 victories in their last 87 games and owned a 10½-game edge over the second-place New York Giants and the team's first-ever N.L.

pennant. Miracle No. 1 was complete.

But now came the difficult task of facing off against the powerful Philadelphia Athletics in the World Series. The A's, winners of three of the last four classics, were managed by Connie Mack and featured such hitters as Eddie Collins, Home Run Baker and Stuffy McInnis plus a pitching staff that boasted seven hurlers with 10 or more wins.

But that didn't seem to make much difference to the Braves, who fed the A's a steady diet of pitching (Dick Rudolph, Bill James and Lefty Tyler) and hitting (Hank Gowdy batted .545,

*Four of Boston's 1914 miracle workers were (left to right) Hank Gowdy, Dick Rudolph, Lefty Tyler and Joe Connolly.*

Johnny Evers .438) and rolled to an unlikely sweep by scores of 7-1, 1-0, 5-4 and 3-1.

Miracle No. 2 was complete.

And the team that had finished 52 games behind the pennant-winning Giants two years ago now reigned as king of the hill.

# 1915

## Federal League out of business

The outlaw Federal League no longer exists, but that's not to say it won't continue to have a far-reaching impact on baseball.

New Cubs Owner Charles Weeghman (right) with Manager Fred Mitchell (left) and pitcher Grover Cleveland Alexander.

In the wake of player raids and intra-city battling for the sports dollar, American League and National League owners broke down and negotiated a peace settlement with the newcomers.

As one of the conditions of the agreement, Charles Weeghman, owner of the Federal League's Chicago Whales franchise, was allowed to buy the Chicago Cubs. Likewise, Phil Ball, owner of the outlaw St. Louis franchise, was given permission to purchase the Browns. Federal League players will be placed in a pool and major league teams will be allowed to buy back those who had originally jumped from their clubs.

Only the outlaw Baltimore club refused to accept terms of the surrender. The Feds sued major league baseball under the Sherman Antitrust Act and actually won a lower-court decision before the major leagues won an appeal to the United States District Court of Illinois.

Indianapolis and Chicago were the pennant winners in the Federal League's two years of existence.

## Tennis at Forest Hills

Bill Johnston defeated Maurice McLoughlin, the California Comet, to win the 1915 U.S. singles championships, 1-6, 6-0, 7-5, 10-8. But of more importance is the fact that the tournament was played for the first time at the West Side Tennis Club in Forest Hills, N.Y.

That ended a string of 34 consecutive years that the men's singles and doubles events were held at Newport Casino in Newport, R.I. The marriage of the tennis championships and the

Newport facility dates back to 1881.

The move to Forest Hills was made because tennis is enjoying an upsurge in popularity and the West Side Tennis Club provides a bigger facility with better access. Located just outside of New York City, Forest Hills figures to draw a lot more fans.

Officials at Newport have created the Newport Invitation tournament, a men's singles and doubles program, to fill the void that has been created.

One of Ty Cobb's many talents was his daring, take-no-prisoners baserunning style.

## Ty Cobb continues his record assault

He may not be the best liked player in baseball, but there's no denying Ty Cobb knows how to play the game. The Detroit star provided two more records this season that major league players will be shooting at for years to come.

Cobb hit .369, leading American League batters for a record ninth year in a row. Included in that stretch are two .400 seasons (.420 in 1911 and .410 in 1912) and his Triple Crown campaign of 1909—a .377 average, nine

home runs and 115 runs batted in.

He also stole a record 96 bases this season, a mark that is likely to hold up for many years. At age 32, Cobb already is closing in on the magic 3,000-hit mark and by the time his career ends, he conceivably could hold career records in every important offensive category.

Like him or not, Cobb has made sure that he will not be forgotten for many years to come—if ever.

# 1916

# Georgia Tech rambles to 222-0 football rout

The president of Cumberland College, a small-school football force at the turn of the century but no longer competitive, wanted to get some national exposure. Why not play a game against a major college power?

Bad idea. Georgia Tech Coach John Heisman agreed to play the Lebanon, Tenn., school, October 7, but only if the challenger deposited a $3,000 check as forfeit money in case it did not field a team. Cumberland did round up 15 players for the trip to Atlanta, but did not even bother to practice. What followed was, to put it kindly, a blowout.

Tech had 32 possessions in the game and scored touchdowns on all of them. The Ramblin' Wreck didn't need to attempt a pass. Tech scored on 19 of its 29 rushes, netting 501 yards on the ground. Tech also scored on six interception returns, five of nine punt runbacks and one of five kickoff returns. Everett (Strup) Strupper scored 49 points, making eight touchdowns and kicking one extra point. He rushed eight times for 165 yards and six touchdowns and he scored on both of his punt returns.

The score was 63-0 after one quarter, 126-0 at halftime, 180-0 after three quarters and 222-0 at the end of the game.

*Coaching genius and trophy namesake John Heisman.*

### ★ SPORTS WATCH ★

**MAR:** The Montreal Canadiens won their first Stanley Cup, defeating the Portland Rosebuds of the PCHA in a five-game series.

**APR:** The Chicago Cubs dedicated new Wrigley Field with a 7-6 victory over the Cincinnati Reds.

**JUN:** Amateur golfer Chick Evans pulled off a shocking double, winning both the U.S. Open and the U.S. Amateur in the same year.

# Zuppke's Illinois shocks "Perfect" Minnesota

Minnesota, the so-called "perfect team that nobody could beat," met its Waterloo, November 4, during a Western Conference game in Minneapolis. Twice-beaten Illinois brought the Gophers back to earth with a 14-9 victory that sent shockwaves through the football world.

Minnesota had outscored its opponents, 236-14, in rolling up a 4-0 record and the Illini did not figure to offer much resistance. The question around Gopher country was not whether Illinois could win, but whether it could score.

The Illini provided that answer right away. Getting the ball on their first possession at the Minnesota 45 following a punt, Coach Bob Zuppke's troops marched straight downfield on a 25-yard pass from quarterback Bart Macomber to Dutch Sternaman and

*Bob Zuppke, architect of Illinois' major upset over Minnesota.*

Macomber's short touchdown run. On Minnesota's next possession, Illinois' Ren Kraft picked off Arnold Wyman's pass and ran the interception back 55 yards for another touchdown.

The shocked Gophers, shut out in the first half, rallied for a touchdown and safety in the third quarter to cut the lead to 14-9. Illinois, however, buckled down defensively and held on for the upset.

# Barnes fights back to capture inaugural PGA title

Jim Barnes, a tall Englishman with nerves of steel, continued his successful run on the United States golf tour, October 14, when he calmly sank a four-foot putt on the 36th hole of his match-play round with Scotsman Jock Hutchison for a 1-up victory in the inaugural PGA

Championship at the Siwanoy Country Club in New York.

Barnes, who was trailing his inexperienced opponent 4-down after eight holes of the morning round, earned the $500 first prize, a diamond-studded gold medal and the Rodman Wanamaker Trophy for his victory. But Hutchison, who now lives in Pittsburgh, made the talented shotmaker work for everything he got.

Barnes fought back to trail Hutchison by one hole after the morning round and then shot 73 over the final 18 holes. Hutchison, who shot 77-76 for his two Saturday rounds, missed a four-foot putt on the 18th green that could have forced a playoff.

# 1917

## Giants self-destruct again in World Series

The New York Giants, in keeping with a growing tradition of costly misplays, were at it again, October 15, when a fourth-inning gaffe helped the Chicago White Sox to a 4-2 victory and a six-game triumph in the World Series.

With 33,969 mortified fans looking on at New York's Polo Grounds, the Giants rekindled painful memories of the 1908 baserunning mistake by Fred Merkle that cost them a pennant and Fred Snodgrass' muff of an easy fly ball that contributed to their defeat in the 1912 World Series.

Trailing the White Sox three games to two and locked with the American Leaguers in a 0-0 fourth-inning Game 6 battle, the Giants suddenly came unraveled. First third baseman Heinie Zimmerman fielded Eddie Collins' routine grounder and made a bad throw that resulted in a two-base error.

Then right fielder Dave Robertson dropped Joe Jackson's fly ball.

Things quickly got worse. With Collins on third and Jackson on first, Happy Felsch grounded back to pitcher Rube Benton, who saw Collins break and threw to Zimmerman. The third baseman tried to run down Collins, who bounded past catcher Bill Rariden midway between third and home. Unfortunately for the Giants, nobody had bothered to cover the plate and it became a futile chase—the slow-footed Zimmerman trying to catch the fleet-footed Collins. The run scored and so did two more when Chick Gandil followed with a single.

With Red Faber on the mound in search of his third Series victory, the White Sox were home free. The Giants were left with egg on their faces —again.

*Chicago Cubs lefty Jim (Hippo) Vaughn, who ran out of luck after nine no-hit innings.*

## Chicago Cubs fans witness a double no-hitter

The 3,500 fans who braved bitterly cold and windswept conditions to attend a May 2 game at Chicago's Weeghman Park were rewarded with one of the great pitching matchups of all time. Cincinnati's Fred Toney and Chicago's Jim (Hippo) Vaughn spelled double trouble on this day.

Toney was outstanding as he began mowing down Cubs hitters without incident. When nine innings were complete, only Cy Williams had reached base against the righthander— both times on walks. But Vaughn, a fireballing left-hander, was equally effective. Only three Reds reached base in nine innings, two on walks and one on an infield error.

Never before had baseball produced a double no-hitter. But, unfortunately, one of these efforts would go to waste.

The breakthrough came in the top of the 10th inning when Cincinnati shortstop Larry Kopf produced the game's first hit—a clean single to right— off Vaughn and came around to score on two errors and a swinging bunt.

Toney returned to the mound and retired the Cubs in order. He had a 10-inning no-hitter and Vaughn had a severe case of frustration.

---

### ★ SPORTS WATCH ★

**OCT:** The University of California ended Washington's 63-game college football unbeaten streak with a resounding 27-0 victory at Berkeley, Calif.

**DEC:** Rice University ended the Texas Longhorns' 44-game basketball winning streak with a 24-18 triumph in Austin, Tex.

---

*New York Giants third baseman Heinie Zimmerman chases Chicago's Eddie Collins across the plate as catcher Bill Rariden, out of position, looks on in Game 6 of the World Series.*

## Seattle wins Cup

The Seattle Metropolitans of the Pacific Coast Hockey Association became the first American team ever to win a Stanley Cup when they defeated the Montreal Canadiens in a four-game series.

The Canadiens, representing the National Hockey Association, won the series opener, 8-4, but the rest of the playoff belonged to the Metropolitans. Seattle scored 6-1, 4-1 and 9-1 victories, leaving no doubt where the Cup belonged.

The first and third games were played under PCHA rules (seven players to a side, forward passing allowed in the center zone and no substitutes allowed for penalized players), the second and fourth contests under NHA rules (six players, no forward passing anywhere and no substitutes for penalized players).

# 1918

**JANUARY - DECEMBER**

## Red Sox's pitching too much for Cubs

Carl Mays and Babe Ruth won two games apiece and four Boston pitchers combined for a 1.70 earned-run average as the Red Sox defeated the Chicago Cubs in a six-game World Series.

The fall classic was actually the late summer classic as baseball followed up its shortened schedule with an early September Series to accommodate wartime restrictions. And the Red Sox, winners in their four previous Series appearances, wasted little time setting the tone for the way it would be played.

Ruth shut out the Cubs in the opener, 1-0, as Stuffy McInnis drove in the only run. Chicago's Lefty Tyler won a 3-1 decision in Game 2 and Mays stopped the Cubs 2-1 in Game 3.

When all was said and done, neither team had scored more than three runs in a game and the Cubs had outhit the Red Sox, .210 to .186. Ruth led Boston with two runs batted in and nobody hit a home run.

*Babe Ruth was a young, slim and versatile player in 1918 when he helped pitch and bat the Boston Red Sox to a six-game World Series victory over the Chicago Cubs in a shortened war-time season.*

## Navy strategy fails

In one of the more bizarre conclusions ever witnessed in college football, Great Lakes Naval Training Station defeated Navy 7-6 in a November 23 game at Annapolis.

With a Rose Bowl bid riding on the outcome, unbeaten Navy led 6-0 and was threatening again with less than five minutes to play. Facing a second-and-goal from the Great Lakes 8-yard line, Navy's Bill Ingram drove through left tackle and was met by defensive tackle Con Ecklund, who stripped the ball free. It bounced into the end zone where defensive back Harry Eileson scooped it up and began a long run upfield.

Eileson broke through the Navy line and had nothing but daylight between him and the tying touchdown. Then, from out of nowhere, came a flying body that hit him and dragged him to the turf at the Navy 30. Who was that guy?

That guy was William Saunders, a Navy reserve who jumped off the bench to stop a touchdown. Eileson was helped to his feet by a teammate and escorted to the end zone.

"Touchdown," said the referee, and Great Lakes kicked the conversion to complete the upset.

### ★ SPORTS WATCH ★

**MAR:** Montreal's Joe Malone captured scoring honors in the NHL's first season, collecting 44 goals in 20 games.

**MAY:** Exterminator, with William Knapp in saddle, ran to the roses at Churchill Downs and captured the Kentucky Derby with a time of 2:10$^{4}/_{5}$.

**MAY:** Sunday baseball became legal in Washington D.C. when officials determined that the city's large war-time population needed recreational outlets.

## NHL ends 1st season

The newly formed National Hockey League ended its inaugural season, March 30, when the Toronto Arenas defeated Pacific Coast Hockey Association champion Vancouver in a five-game playoff for the Stanley Cup.

The Arenas were one of five teams awarded franchises in November 1917 and one of three that actually played and finished the league's first-season schedule. The Montreal Canadiens and Ottawa Senators also played full 22-game slates while the Montreal Wanderers disbanded after six games because of a January 2 fire that burned down their Westmount Arena. Quebec was awarded rights to a franchise but failed to produce a team to take it up.

The schedule was split, Montreal winning the opening segment with a 10-4 record and Toronto winning the second with a 5-3 mark. The Arenas and Canadiens played a two-game, total-goals series to determine the NHL's representative in the Stanley Cup playoff, Toronto winning, 10-7.

The Arenas won the three games played under NHL rules (six players to a side, no forward passing anywhere and substitutes allowed for penalized players), while Vancouver took those played under PCHA rules (seven players to a side, forward passing allowed in the center zone and no substitutes for penalized players).

# 1919

**JANUARY · DECEMBER**

## Dempsey pounds out easy win over Willard

Jack Dempsey, a 24-year-old former saloon fighter, captured the world heavyweight boxing title July 4, in Toledo, Ohio, when he pounded defending champion Jess Willard in three rounds.

Dempsey, giving away 50 pounds to his 6-foot-7 opponent, quickly earned the favor of the 45,000 spectators who braved a 110-degree temperature to watch the young challenger knock Willard down six times in the opening round. With the champion offering little resistance, Dempsey pounded away. The end came 30 seconds after the finish of the third round, when Willard's seconds threw in the towel.

As the unmarked Dempsey celebrated, Willard's face was a mass of blood. There was a bad cut under a right eye that was completely closed, his mouth

*Jack Dempsey (right) made short work of big Jess Willard and won the heavyweight championship.*

was bleeding profusely and six teeth were missing.

Willard reportedly walked away with $100,000 from gate receipts, while Dempsey picked up $27,500.

## Sir Barton's trifecta

Sir Barton, a 3-year-old chestnut colt, captured the $10,000 Belmont Stakes, thus becoming the first Triple Crown winner in horse racing history.

Sir Barton, owned by J.K.L. Ross and ridden by Johnny Loftus, set an American record for $1\frac{3}{8}$ miles by covering the Belmont Track course in $2:17\frac{2}{5}$. He finished five lengths in front of Sweep On and another eight lengths ahead of Natural

Bridge, both W.R. Coe entries.

Loftus held Sir Barton back in the early going, preferring to let Sweep On set the pace. But he let the son of Star Shoot burst into the lead on the far turn and then let out the reins as he headed for home.

Sir Barton is the first colt ever to capture the big three—the Kentucky Derby, Preakness and Belmont—in the same year.

*Johnny Loftus aboard Triple Crown winner Sir Barton.*

**★ SPORTS WATCH ★**

**JUN:** Walter Hagen won his second U.S. Open golf title, shooting a playoff round 77 to defeat Mike Brady by a stroke at the Brae Burn Country Club in West Newton, Mass.

**SEP:** Bill Johnston overpowered young Bill Tilden and recorded a straight-set victory in the singles finals of the U.S. tennis championships at Forest Hills.

**SEP:** Detroit outfielder Ty Cobb batted .384 to win his record 12th—and last—American League batting title.

## Flu ends Cup series

They didn't win, but the Montreal Canadiens upheld the honor of the two-year-old National Hockey League in their recent Stanley Cup series with Pacific Coast Hockey Association champion Seattle. The Canadiens, fighting a serious flu epidemic, fought valiantly before being forced to withdraw when five members of their team became too ill to take the ice in Game 6.

With the playoff series deadlocked at two games apiece (there was one tie), PCHA President Frank A. Patrick was in position to call for a forfeit.

But he very sportingly declined.

Seattle had rolled to 7-0 and 7-2 victories in the first and third games, with Montreal winning 4-2 in Game 2 and the fourth game ending in a 0-0 tie, despite two overtime periods. The Canadiens won the fifth game, 4-3, March 29 when the stricken Jack McDonald heroically jumped onto the ice in overtime and scored the winner.

But with five players running temperatures up to 105 degrees on the day of Game 6 and two, McDonald and Joe Hall, in critical condition, the Canadiens threw in the towel.

# THE 1920s

As the curtain rose on "The Roaring Twenties," baseball was engulfed by a dark cloud that threatened the deepest fibers of its existence. With the game's reputation on the gallows, a Cook County, Ill., grand jury returned indictments against eight members of the Chicago White Sox for conspiring to fix the 1919 World Series.

Such news was not accepted graciously by baseball fans, many of whom still were reeling from the social fallout of war. Baseball needed a savior—and it needed him fast.

What it got was two for the price of one. Enter Kenesaw Mountain Landis, the crusty, iron-fisted federal judge who became the sport's first commissioner in November 1920, and Babe Ruth, the colorful New York Yankee outfielder who ushered in a new era of baseball prosperity with his uncanny ability to hit prodigious home runs to the outer reaches of man's imagination.

Landis' role was simply defined—use his newly created dictatorial powers to bring integrity back to the game. The Judge performed that job admirably for 24 years, starting with his 1921 lifetime ban against the eight Black Sox.

With the stench of scandal thus removed, Ruth began dominating the game, overshadowing such contemporary greats as John McGraw, Ty Cobb and teammate Lou Gehrig. And with an adoring public roaring its approval, he began belting home runs in record numbers:

Illinois' Galloping Ghost, Red Grange.

## ROLL OF HONOR

### AUTO RACING

**INDIANAPOLIS 500**

| Year | Winner | Speed |
|------|--------|-------|
| 1920 | Gaston Chevrolet | 88.618 mph |
| 1921 | Tommy Milton | 89.621 mph |
| 1922 | Jimmy Murphy | 94.484 mph |
| 1923 | Tommy Milton | 90.954 mph |
| 1924 | L.L. Corum & Joe Boyer | 98.234 mph |
| 1925 | Peter DePaolo | 101.127 mph |
| 1926 | Frank Lockhart | 95.904 mph |
| 1927 | George Souders | 97.545 mph |
| 1928 | Louis Meyer | 99.482 mph |
| 1929 | Ray Keech | 97.585 mph |

### GOLF

| US OPEN | | PGA CHAMPIONSHIP | |
|---------|--------|---------|--------|
| Year | Winner | Year | Winner |
| 1920 | Edward Ray | 1920 | Jack Hutchison |
| 1921 | Jim Barnes | 1921 | Walter Hagen |
| 1922 | Gene Sarazen | 1922 | Gene Sarazen |
| 1923 | Bobby Jones | 1923 | Gene Sarazen |
| 1924 | Cyril Walker | 1924 | Walter Hagen |
| 1925 | Willie MacFarlane | 1925 | Walter Hagen |
| 1926 | Bobby Jones | 1926 | Walter Hagen |
| 1927 | Tommy Armour | 1927 | Walter Hagen |
| 1928 | Johnny Farrell | 1928 | Leo Diegel |
| 1929 | Bobby Jones | 1929 | Leo Diegel |

54 in 1920, 59 in 1921 and 60 in 1927 for what many considered the greatest team in baseball history.

In the wake of Ruth's long-ball exploits, other teams began looking for muscular hitters who could create instant offense with one swing of the bat. And with fans clamoring for more offensive excitement, officials began changing rules that previously had favored pitchers.

But other seeds of change took longer to germinate. When the first radio broadcast of a game took place in 1921, the idea was chastised unmercifully by the journalistic community. And when Branch Rickey set up the first farm system for the St. Louis Cardinals, McGraw called it a "stupid idea." Baseball was king, but other sports were beginning to take root.

The framework for the National Football League was built in 1920, college football, now playing to large crowds in massive new stadia, continued to develop more sophisticated passing attacks and the National Hockey League, growing in prestige north of the border, expanded to the United States.

Other sports were being lifted into prominence by Ruthian-like performers. Bill Tilden and Helen Wills dominated tennis courts around the world while Gene Sarazen, Walter Hagen and Bobby Jones captured the imaginations of golf fans. Jack Dempsey and Gene Tunney ruled the boxing world, which prospered through its alliance with radio.

Ironically, this "Golden Age" closed with Ruth trying to become the first six-figure athlete in team-sports history. As he haggled with the Yankees in 1929, the country was plunging into the Great Depression.

*Boxer Gene Tunney.*

## HORSE RACING

### KENTUCKY DERBY

| Year | Winner | Jockey |
|------|--------|--------|
| 1920 | Paul Jones | Ted Rice |
| 1921 | Behave Yourself | Charles Thompson |
| 1922 | Morvich | Albert Johnson |
| 1923 | Zev | Earl Sande |
| 1924 | Black Gold | John Mooney |
| 1925 | Flying Ebony | Earl Sande |
| 1926 | Bubbling Over | Albert Johnson |
| 1927 | Whiskery | Linus McAtee |
| 1928 | Reigh Count | Chick Lang |
| 1929 | Clyde Van Dusen | Linus McAtee |

### PREAKNESS STAKES

| Year | Winner | Jockey |
|------|--------|--------|
| 1920 | Man o'War | Clarence Kummer |
| 1921 | Broomspun | F. Coltiletti |
| 1922 | Pillory | L. Morris |
| 1923 | Vigil | B. Marinelli |
| 1924 | Nellie Morse | John Merimee |
| 1925 | Coventry | Clarence Kummer |
| 1926 | Display | John Maiben |
| 1927 | Bostonian | Whitey Abel |
| 1928 | Victorian | Sonny Workman |
| 1929 | Dr. Freeland | Louis Schaefer |

### BELMONT STAKES

| Year | Winner | Jockey |
|------|--------|--------|
| 1920 | Man o'War | Clarence Kummer |
| 1921 | Grey Lag | Earl Sande |
| 1922 | Pillory | C.H. Miller |
| 1923 | Zev | Earl Sande |
| 1924 | Mad Play | Earl Sande |
| 1925 | American Flag | Albert Johnson |
| 1926 | Crusader | Albert Johnson |
| 1927 | Chance Shot | Earl Sande |
| 1928 | Vito | Clarence Kummer |
| 1929 | Blue Larkspur | Mack Garner |

## BASEBALL

### WORLD SERIES

| Year | Winner | Pennant Winner (series score) |
|------|--------|-------------------------------|
| 1920 | Cleveland Indians | (Brooklyn Dodgers, 5-2) |
| 1921 | New York Giants | (New York Yankees, 5-3) |
| 1922 | New York Giants | (New York Yankees, 4-0-1) |
| 1923 | New York Yankees | (New York Giants, 4-2) |
| 1924 | Washington Senators | (New York Giants, 4-3) |
| 1925 | Pittsburgh Pirates | (Washington Senators, 4-3) |
| 1926 | St. Louis Cardinals | (New York Yankees, 4-3) |
| 1927 | New York Yankees | (Pittsburgh Pirates, 4-0) |
| 1928 | New York Yankees | (St. Louis Cardinals, 4-0) |
| 1929 | Philadelphia Athletics | (Chicago Cubs, 4-1) |

*New York Yankee slugger Lou Gehrig.*

## HOCKEY

### STANLEY CUP

| Year | Champion | Finalist (series score) |
|------|----------|-------------------------|
| 1920-21 | Ottawa Senators | (Vancouver Millionaires, 3-2) |
| 1921-22 | Toronto St. Pats | (Vancouver Millionaires, 3-2) |
| 1922-23* | Ottawa Senators | (Vancouver Maroons, 3-1) (Edmonton Eskimos, 2-0) |
| 1923-24* | Montreal Canadiens | (Vancouver Millionaires, 2-0) (Calgary Tigers, 2-0) |
| 1924-25 | Victoria Cougars | (Montreal Canadiens, 3-1) |
| 1925-26 | Montreal Maroons | (Victoria Cougars, 3-1) |
| 1926-27 | Ottawa Senators | (Boston Bruins, 2-0, with two ties) |
| 1927-28 | New York Rangers | (Montreal Maroons, 3-2) |
| 1928-29 | Boston Bruins | (New York Rangers, 2-0) |
| 1929-30 | Montreal Canadiens | (Boston Bruins, 2-0) |

*Because of an agreement between the NHL and the two western leagues (WCHL and PCHA), the NHL winner had to play the champions of each league during the Stanley Cup Finals.

## TENNIS

### US OPEN

| Year | Men's Winner | Women's Winner |
|------|--------------|----------------|
| 1920 | Bill Tilden | Molla Bjurstedt-Mallory |
| 1921 | Bill Tilden | Molla Bjurstedt-Mallory |
| 1922 | Bill Tilden | Molla Bjurstedt-Mallory |
| 1923 | Bill Tilden | Helen Wills |
| 1924 | Bill Tilden | Helen Wills |
| 1925 | Bill Tilden | Helen Wills |
| 1926 | Rene Lacoste | Molla Bjurstedt-Mallory |
| 1927 | Rene Lacoste | Helen Wills |
| 1928 | Henri Cochet | Helen Wills |
| 1929 | Bill Tilden | Helen Wills |

# 1920

Cleveland second baseman Bill Wambsganss tags out Otto Miller to complete an unprecedented World Series triple play against Brooklyn in Game 5.

## An Indian uprising

Nobody can blame the Cleveland Indians for feeling emotionally drained following their incredible season of tragedy and triumph.

Working their way toward their first-ever American League pennant, the Cleveland roller-coaster took a big dip, August 16, when shortstop Ray Chapman, leading off the fifth inning of a game against the New York Yankees, was struck on the head by a pitch from Carl Mays. Chapman was rushed to New York's St. Lawrence Hospital, where he died of massive head injuries at age 29—the first major league player ever to die as the result of injuries in a game.

The Indians, however, persevered through the dark weeks that followed and topped the A.L. standings. That earned them the right to square off against National League champion Brooklyn in a World Series that will long be remembered for its remarkable firsts.

They all occurred in Game 5, starting in the opening inning when Cleveland's Elmer Smith connected for the first grand slam in Series history. Three innings later, the Indians' Jim Bagby, a 31-game winner during the season, connected for the first-ever Series homer by a pitcher.

But the crowning achievement occurred in the fifth when second baseman Bill Wambsganss caught a line drive and pulled off a rare unassisted triple play. The Dodgers, obviously rattled by this unlikely series of events, went on to lose the game, 8-1, and the Series, five games to two.

## Man o' War shows record Belmont form

Most race enthusiasts who showed up for the June 12 running of the Belmont Stakes expected to see a Man o' War victory. But Samuel D. Riddle's marvelous 3-year-old colt gave them much more than that.

In a wire-to-wire exhibition of incredible speed, Man o' War, with Clarence Kummer aboard, shocked a crowd of 25,000 at Belmont Park by covering the $1\frac{3}{8}$-mile distance in a world-record time of $2:14\frac{1}{5}$, $2\frac{3}{5}$ seconds faster than the distance had ever been run.

The American record at $1\frac{3}{8}$ miles had been set last year when Sir Barton, the first Triple Crown winner in horse racing history, ran in $2:17\frac{2}{5}$. And Man o' War was not even challenged. Only one other colt was entered in the Belmont and G.W. Loft's Donnacona finished a

The great Man o' War with Clarence Kummer in saddle.

sixteenth of a mile behind the winner.

Many are calling Man o'War the greatest racer of all time. Others admit that the son of Fair Play is surely the best colt ever produced in the United States. Man o' War was not entered in the Kentucky Derby but ran away from a good Preakness Stakes field in May.

### ★ SPORTS WATCH ★

**JAN:** Quebec's Joe Malone scored an NHL-record seven goals in a game against the Toronto St. Patricks.

**MAY:** Boston's Joe Oeschger and Brooklyn's Leon Cadore both pitched 26 innings in the longest game in major league history. The contest ended in a 1-1 tie.

**SEP:** The United States walked away with 95 medals to capture team honors in the Olympic Games at Antwerp, Belgium.

## Yankees pay $125,000 for Ruth's contract

The New York Yankees, in need of offensive punch in their outfield, purchased the contract of Boston pitcher-outfielder Babe Ruth on January 3. The Yankees paid an incredible $125,000 for the 26-year-old, who set a major league record with 29 home runs last year.

Boston Owner Harry Frazee said he sold Ruth's contract because he thought it an injustice to keep him with the Red Sox, who are becoming a one-man team. But it is more likely that he parted with his star player because of Ruth's demand for a big contract increase and because of his own financial difficulties.

Yankee co-Owner Colonel Jacob Ruppert says Ruth will become an everyday player, taking over in right field.

# 1921

## Giants beat Yankees in New York battle

The first one-city World Series was played in Chicago in 1906. But New York's Yankees and Giants took that one step further this year, playing a fall classic in one stadium — the Polo Grounds. Both teams had something to prove.

The Giants had played in four World Series since 1905, losing all of them. The Yankees had never won an American League pennant and were looking to showcase a powerful lineup that featured Babe Ruth and young Bob Meusel. Babe Ruth had just completed his second Yankee season with a major league-record 59 home runs, 171 RBIs

and a .378 batting average.

With the opening game being broadcast by sportswriter Grantland Rice on radio, the Yanks rode the pitching of Carl Mays to a 3-0 victory. Waite Hoyt, who did not allow an earned run in 27 Series innings, topped Mays the next day when he fired a two-hit, 3-0 shutout.

But the Giants won the next two games and, after falling to Hoyt again in Game 5, swept the next three to close out the best-of-nine Series. The injured Ruth, who had hit his first Series homer in Game 4, sat out the Giants' Series-closing 2-1 and 1-0 victories.

*Centre College quarterback Bo McMillin breaks past Harvard defenders for his game-winning touchdown scamper.*

## Centre College stuns undefeated Harvard

Little Centre College figured to be a sacrificial lamb when it traveled to play powerful, unbeaten Harvard, October 29. But the

Praying Colonels of Danville, Ky., had other ideas. Giving a valiant defensive effort, Centre pulled off a 6-0 victory.

**AUG:** Harold Arlin performed the first radio broadcast of a major league game over station KDKA in Pittsburgh. The Pirates beat the Phillies, 8-5.

**SEP:** Walter Hagen became the first American-born golfer to win the PGA Championship, defeating Jim Barnes, 3 and 2, at Inwood Country Club on Long Island, N.Y.

**SEP:** American Bill Tilden swept the Wimbledon and U.S. singles titles for the second year in a row.

## Relentless Dempsey batters Frenchman

It was billed as "the battle of the century," but Jack Dempsey put that notion to rest in the fourth round, July 2, when he retained the world heavyweight boxing championship by knocking out Frenchman Georges Carpentier before 90,000 fans in Jersey City, N.J.

After relentlessly stalking his smaller opponent through three rounds and more than a minute of the fourth, Dempsey landed a short left to the face and a powerful right to the ear that knocked Carpentier to the canvas for the count of nine. The Frenchman jumped back up but was greeted by a left to the face and rights to the ribs and jaw. He went down for the count.

Carpentier's fate actually was sealed in the second round when he caught Dempsey on the jaw with a punch that broke his thumb and sprained his wrist. Without a healthy right hand, Carpentier was finished.

The fight produced a number

*Jack Dempsey was in prime condition when he stepped in the ring to face Frenchman Georges Carpentier.*

of firsts. It was the first to feature a legitimate European contender, the first broadcast on radio and the first with a million-dollar purse. The crowd was the largest in boxing history.

The loss not only ruined Harvard's hopes for a perfect season, but it snapped a 25-game unbeaten streak that dated back to 1916.

The Harvard players were not surprised by Centre's toughness. The teams had met in 1920 and played to a 14-14 halftime standoff before Harvard took charge for a 31-14 victory. But its hopes of wearing down the

Colonels on this occasion after a 0-0 first half proved groundless.

Centre broke through in the third quarter after a punt and penalty put the ball on the Harvard 32. On the next play, quarterback Bo McMillin broke through right tackle, cut left to the sideline and outran all defenders for the game's only score.

# baseball

## The "Black Sox" scandal

*The gambling scam of the century that besmirched the good name of America's national pastime*

White Sox pitchers Lefty Williams (left) and Eddie Cicotte (second from left): primary figures in the World Series fix.

"Regardless of the verdict of juries, no player who throws a game, no player who entertains proposals or promises to throw a game, no player who sits in conference with a bunch of crooked players and gamblers where the ways and means of throwing games are discussed and does not promptly tell the club about it, will ever play professional baseball."

With these historic words, Judge Kenesaw Mountain Landis, the recently ordained first commissioner of baseball, exercised his dictatorial powers and officially closed the books on the most sordid chapter of the sport's long history. Eight members of the Chicago White Sox, almost two years after

Shoeless Joe Jackson.

conspiring with gamblers to fix the 1919 World Series, had been banished for life.

Landis' August 3, 1921, ruling must have come as a shock to pitchers Eddie Cicotte and Lefty Williams, first baseman Chick Gandil, shortstop Swede Risberg, third baseman Buck Weaver, outfielders Joe Jackson and Happy Felsch and utility infielder Fred McMullin. Only the day before, they had been pronounced not guilty of criminal charges by a Chicago jury. The prosecution's case had been destroyed by the mysterious disappearance of all paperwork concerning the fix, including signed confessions of Cicotte, Jackson and Williams, from the Cook County district attorney's office.

Jury or no jury, by this time the baseball community was resigned to the fact that the eight players had indeed conspired to throw the 1919 Series. There had been suspicions of foul play in 1919 when the Cincinnati Reds, heavy underdogs to the powerful Chicago White Sox, posted a stirring five games to three upset that raised questions about the performances of several key Chicago players.

The first clue of conspiracy

actually had surfaced before the fall classic even opened. The White Sox had been established as heavy favorites in gambling circles and the early money supported the odds. But suddenly, as the teams prepared to open play on October 1, the odds shifted drastically. Some high rollers were pumping in serious money on Cincinnati and the odds now were about even.

The details of how the eight White Sox went about their dark duties are somewhat sketchy. But there is no denying that their Series play left plenty of room for suspicion. Game 1 opened with Cicotte hitting Reds leadoff man Morrie Rath with a pitch, supposedly the signal to bettors that the fix was on. Cicotte, a 29-game winner during the regular season, was battered by the Reds while Cincinnati starter Dutch Ruether pitched a six-hitter for a 9-1 victory.

Game 2 was equally puzzling

as Williams, a 23-game winner during the regular campaign, dropped a 4-2 decision to the Reds' Slim Sallee. The loss was puzzling because the Sox outhit the Reds, 10-4, but Williams, who would go on to lose all three of his Series starts with a distressing 6.61 earned-run average, uncharacteristically walked six batters.

White Sox fans relaxed when the Series moved to Chicago for Game 3 and rookie Dickie Kerr responded with a three-hit shutout. But the Reds continued their surprising play by recording 2-0 and 5-0 victories in Games 4 and 5. Cicotte started in the fourth game and contributed to his downfall with two fifth-inning errors that resulted in the game's only runs.

Ordinarily, four wins would mean victory in a World Series, but baseball officials had decided to make this classic a best-of-nine affair to take advantage of intense postwar interest. Their bad timing prolonged the travesty.

The White Sox suddenly came to life in Games 6 and 7, Kerr pitching his team to a 5-4, 10-inning verdict and Cicotte winning a 4-1 decision. But Williams took the mound for Game 8 and the Reds struck.

Scoring four runs in the first inning, Cincinnati knocked Williams out of the game and rolled to a 10-5 Series-clinching victory.

For the record, Jackson batted a Series-leading .375 but admitted letting up in key situations. Weaver contributed a .324 mark and Gandil supplied winning hits in the third and sixth games. But Gandil hit only .233, Felsch and Risberg batted .192 and McMullin got one hit in two pinch-hitting appearances.

## "Say it ain't so, Joe!" the youngster pleaded with his hero. "Yes, I'm afraid it is," Jackson reportedly replied.

While most of the nation accepted the outcome as a simple case of David knocking off Goliath, those closer to the game suspected otherwise. Rumors of a fix before the Series, the strange shift in betting odds and the suspicious performances of several top players led to serious concern. And embarrassment for White Sox Owner Charles A. Comiskey, who launched an exhaustive, behind-the-scenes investigation to get at the truth.

Comiskey wasn't alone. American League President Ban Johnson initiated an investigation of his own and, as the 1920 season was drawing to a close with the White Sox,

Chicago's 1919 infield featured (left to right) third baseman Buck Weaver, shortstop Swede Risberg, second baseman Eddie Collins and first baseman Chick Gandil. All but Collins were banned from baseball.

Cleveland and New York locked in a torrid pennant race, a bombshell was dropped on the baseball world. Cicotte, Jackson and Williams had confessed their roles in the Series fix and implicated the other five conspirators. On September 28, with Chicago one game behind Cleveland with three games left to play, a Cook County grand jury returned indictments and all eight were suspended. The player-depleted Sox lost two of their last three games and the Indians captured the pennant.

Perhaps the most poignant picture of the Black Sox disgrace was painted by a reporter who described the scene as Shoeless Joe Jackson left the grand jury room after confessing his part in the conspiracy. Jackson, a career .356 hitter and one of the most idolized players in the game, felt a tug at his arm and looked down into the eyes of a young boy. "Say it ain't so, Joe!" the youngster pleaded with his hero. "Yes, I'm afraid it is," Jackson reportedly replied.

The most-asked question after all was said and done was why. Why would eight players on one of the best teams ever assembled risk their careers on such a sordid venture? The answer most likely was greed— and resentment of Comiskey for the notoriously low salaries he paid his players. Comiskey allegedly even held Cicotte out of several late-season starts to keep him from winning his 30th game, which would have earned the spitballer a bonus.

Ironically, however, some reports say that Cicotte ($10,000) is the only player who actually received a payoff from the gamblers. Other reports claim that several other players received $5,000 apiece. And several of the players, most notably Buck Weaver, continued to maintain their innocence, if not in prior knowledge of the fix, at least in carrying it through.

Weaver, in fact, continued to petition for reinstatement every year right up to his death in 1958. Jackson supporters, pointing out that Shoeless Joe was uneducated and incapable of understanding the complicity with which he was involved, have continued working to get his name cleared so voters can consider him for inclusion in baseball's Hall of Fame. All pleas have been denied.

What cannot be denied is that the quick, ruthless and decisive action of Landis brought integrity back to the sport as its reputation stood on the gallows, waiting for the trap door to drop. Thanks to baseball's new supreme ruler, it never did.

Judge Kenesaw Mountain Landis, supreme ruler of baseball.

# 1922

## Princeton rallies to beat Chicago

Princeton's "team of destiny," sometimes down but never out, pulled off one of football's more incredible comebacks, October 28, and escaped with a 21-18 victory over Amos Alonzo Stagg's powerful Chicago team.

The improbable victory, a result of two fourth-quarter touchdowns, left a packed house at Chicago's Stagg Field sitting in stunned silence. Princeton was making its first intersectional trip to the Midwest.

Unbeaten Chicago, much bigger than the scrappy Tigers, dominated the first three quarters and built an 18-7 lead. But destiny began smiling on the Tigers as the fourth quarter opened.

With Chicago expecting to receive a punt, a bad center snap bounced right into the arms of Princeton's Howard Gray, who sprinted 42 yards for a touchdown. Moments later, the Tigers marched easily to the Chicago 3, from where Burly Crum punched the ball into the end zone. Suddenly Princeton led, 21-18.

But Chicago took the ensuing kickoff and quickly passed its way downfield. The Maroon punched to Princeton's 1-yard line and there the ball sat on fourth down with one second left to play.

John Thomas got the call and hit the middle of Princeton's line. No hole. The little Tigers held and Princeton had its fifth victory without a loss.

*The always colorful and flamboyant Walter Hagen.*

## Hagen triumphs in British golf tourney

Walter Hagen, battling against the elements and two determined Englishmen, earned a hard-fought one-stroke victory, June 23, in the British Open golf championship at Royal St. George's Golf Club in Sandwich, England.

Hagen, who finished with a four-round total of 300, edged out British stars Jim Barnes and George Duncan in becoming the first American-born golfer ever to win this prestigious event. American Jock Hutchison captured the title last year,

## Canton Bulldogs capture 1st "NFL" title

The Canton Bulldogs are the first champions of the National Football League.

It should be clarified, however, that the National Football League is merely the new name for the American Professional Football Association, the league formed two years ago to bring some order to the pro football chaos. And the Bulldogs, indeed the first champions of the NFL, are really the league's third champions, following in the footsteps of the Akron Pros (1920) and the Chicago Staleys (1921). Just to add to the confusion, the "Staleys" of Chicago Owner and Coach George Halas are now going to be called the "Bears."

The Bulldogs, under the guidance of player-coach Guy Chamberlin, recorded a 10-0-2 record in their just-completed championship season.

*George Halas, the Chicago Staleys' founder, coach and two-way end.*

but he was born in Scotland.

Hutchison held a one-stroke lead over J.H. Taylor after a third round that was played in morning rain. Hutchison ignored the storm and came home with a 73 while Hagen struggled to a 79, Barnes to a 77 and Duncan to a disastrous 81. Hagen and Barnes were two

back entering the afternoon competition, Duncan six behind.

But Hutchison faltered on the fourth hole, taking a 7, and Barnes took a 6 on the par-3 third hole. Hagen, meanwhile, was carving out a steady round of 72 that would carry him to victory.

# 1923

## American tennis has new queen of the courts

Helen Wills, a 17-year-old Californian, continued her rise up the tennis ladder, August 18, when she needed only 33 minutes to beat defending champion Molla Mallory, 6-2, 6-1, in the singles finals of the U.S. championships.

Playing before 6,000 fans at the West Side Tennis Club's new stadium at Forest Hills, the youngster delivered one of the event's most decisive beatings. Mallory was the country's top woman player and had won the title in seven of the last eight years. Her 1922 victory had come at the expense of Wills.

Wills had christened the new horseshoe-shaped stadium a week earlier when she defeated Kathleen McKane, England's top female player, 6-2, 7-5, in the first match of the inaugural Wightman Cup series. The U.S.

Helen Wills, the new American queen of the tennis courts.

team of top women players swept past their English counterparts in that event.

The new stadium, which cost $150,000 to build and seats 13,000, is the second concrete facility in the world devoted strictly to tennis. The other is at Wimbledon.

---

### ★ SPORTS WATCH ★

**SEP:** Heavyweight boxing champion Jack Dempsey successfully defended his crown with a second-round knockout of Luis Firpo at New York's Polo Grounds.

**SEP:** Two good-looking New York rookies, Bill Terry of the Giants and Lou Gehrig of the Yankees, made their big-league debuts.

**DEC:** The Canton Bulldogs ran away with their second straight NFL championship, recording an impressive 11-0-1 record in league play.

---

## Yankees win first World Series title

It seemed only fitting that the 1923 World Series should open at beautiful new Yankee Stadium and end less than a mile away at the ancient Polo Grounds. The Yankees were on the rise, the Giants were desperately trying to hold on to their place in the hearts of fickle New York fans.

When it was over on October 16, the Yanks owned their first-ever championship and had avenged the Series losses to the Giants in 1921 and '22. The Yankees, who rolled to a 16-game margin in winning their third straight American League pennant, spotted the Giants a two games to one advantage and then streaked to a six-game victory behind the pitching of Herb Pennock, Bob Shawkey and Joe Bush and the three-home run barrage of Babe Ruth.

It was Ruth, fittingly, who had christened new Yankee Stadium when it opened its gates for the first time on April 18. Playing before a baseball-record opening day crowd of 74,200, the Bambino rose to the occasion with a three-run homer in the Yanks' 4-1 victory over Boston.

## Talented Jones wins dramatic U.S. Open

Bobby Jones, conquering his explosive temper and shaking off a six-year jinx that had kept him from winning a major golf title, downed Robert A. Cruickshank, 76-78, in an 18-hole playoff, July 15, to capture the U.S. Open championship at Long Island's Inwood Country Club.

The talented 21-year-old Atlantan had to call on his incredible shotmaking ability on the 18th hole. Jones and Cruickshank finished the 17th tied at 72 and both got into trouble off the tee, Cruickshank topping his drive into a patch of rough to the left of the fairway and Jones pushing his into the right rough.

Cruickshank could only play onto the fairway, but Jones blasted a 1-iron 190 yards, leaving it six feet from the pin. Cruickshank, obviously rattled

The near-perfect swing of U.S. Open winner Bobby Jones.

by the turn of events, hit his next shot into a trap and settled for a final-hole bogey.

Jones, only the fourth amateur ever to win the Open, had let a two-shot lead slip away when he double bogeyed the final hole of regulation. But he didn't make that mistake in the Monday playoff and was mobbed by an appreciative gallery that carried him off the green.

# 1924

**JANUARY - DECEMBER**

## The Four Horsemen and the "Galloping Ghost"

October 18, 1924. That date should stand tall in the annals of college football.

"Outlined against a blue-grey October sky, the Four Horsemen rode again. In dramatic lore, they are known as Famine, Pestilence, Destruction and Death. These are only aliases. Their real names are Stuhldreher, Miller, Crowley and Layden. . . ."

So read the poetic words of sportswriter Grantland Rice, who was moved to such lofty praise after watching Notre Dame's talented backfield lead the Fighting Irish to a 13-7 victory over a powerful Cadet team. Right halfback Don Miller rushed 19 times for 148 yards and left halfback Jim Crowley ran for 102 yards and a touchdown. Fullback Elmer Layden added 60 yards and a touchdown and quarterback Harry Stuhldreher flawlessly directed the Irish offense.

The victory helped propel Notre Dame to a 10-0 record and the 1924 national championship.

But the Four Horsemen had to share their big day with another talented performer. As the University of Illinois prepared to dedicate its new Memorial Stadium with a game against unbeaten Michigan, junior Red Grange was preparing to gallop into football immortality.

The Illini's Galloping Ghost returned the opening kickoff 95 yards for a touchdown and then reeled off scoring runs of 67, 56 and 44 yards as the Illini streaked to a 27-0 first-quarter lead. Grange added a 13-yard touchdown run in the third quarter and threw a 20-yard TD pass in the fourth. By the game's end, Illinois owned a 39-14 victory with Grange accounting for 402 yards.

*The Four Horsemen of Notre Dame.*

## NHL buys American

The great National Hockey League experiment began, December 1, when the newly formed Boston Bruins opened their inaugural season as members of what previously had always been a Canadians-only fraternity.

And the Bruins opened in style, defeating the Montreal Maroons, 2-1, on Carson Cooper's two third-period goals at Boston Arena. The 7-year-old NHL, looking to expand its horizons to the fertile sports markets of the United States, opens its 1924-25 season as a six-team league, with the expansion to Boston and the formation of the Maroons franchise. The NHL had competed primarily as a four-team league up to now.

## Senators win Series on bad-hop grounder

Fate has not been kind to baseball's Washington Senators over the years, but it made up for it in the October 10, Game 7 conclusion to the World Series at the Griffith Stadium, in Washington DC.

The 31,667 spectators included U.S. President Calvin Coolidge, who watched rookie Manager Bucky Harris deliver a two-run game-tying single in the eighth inning and veteran Walter Johnson shut the door on the New York Giants for four innings.

With one out in the 12th, Muddy Ruel lifted a pop foul behind the plate. But New York catcher Hank Gowdy tripped over his own mask and failed to make the catch. Reprieved, Ruel doubled and then held second when Johnson reached on an error by shortstop Travis Jackson.

*U.S. President Calvin Coolidge and Washington Manager Bucky Harris before Game 7.*

The Giants' fortunes hit rock bottom when the next batter, Earl McNeely, drove a routine grounder toward third baseman Fred Lindstrom. Bracing to start an inning-ending double play, Lindstrom watched the ball strike something hard and bound high over his head. Ruel scored and Washington had its first championship.

# 1925

## JANUARY-DECEMBER

## Michigan's title hopes sink in sea of mud

Michigan Coach Fielding Yost watched helplessly, November 7, as his Wolverines' national championship hopes floundered in a sea of mud at Chicago's Soldier Field.

Northwestern won the game 3-2, but a five-day rainstorm that pelted the Chicago area and continued through the game was the real culprit. This powerful Michigan team had not allowed a point through five games and had outscored opponents, 180-0.

But the Wolverines spent the afternoon against Northwestern slipping, sliding, fumbling and punting. By game's end, they had gained only 35 total yards without recording a first down. And an 18-yard Tiny Lewis field goal, after quarterback Benny Friedman's first-quarter fumble, gave Northwestern all the points it needed. The Wildcats later gave Michigan an intentional safety.

Yost's disappointment was compounded in the weeks that followed when Michigan blew away Ohio State, 10-0, and Minnesota, 35-0. Despite outscoring their opponents 227-3 over an entire season, the Wolverines lost a game and Dartmouth was proclaimed national champion.

## Tilden wins sixth straight U.S. title

Big Bill Tilden, reaffirming his claim as the world's best tennis player, captured his sixth consecutive United States championship, September 19, with a 4-6, 11-9, 6-3, 4-6, 6-3 victory over Bill Johnston.

The 14,000 fans who packed the center-court arena at the West Side Tennis Club at Forest Hills, N.Y., were treated to one of the most exciting finals in the history of the event. That surprised many observers, who expected Tilden to crush Johnston as he had done in both the 1923 and '24 finals. Johnston was in rare form and took the defending champ to the brink of defeat in the 2-hour, 10-minute marathon.

Johnston played almost flawlessly to win the opening set and then reached set point three times in the second, only to see Tilden perform one of his

*Big Bill Tilden, master of the tennis universe.*

patented comebacks. Tilden fell behind in both the third and fifth sets before recovering in his usual dramatic fashion.

The victory marked the fifth time Tilden, a two-time Wimbledon champion, had defeated Johnston in the finals of this event after losing to him in 1919.

## DePaolo tops 100 mph in Indianapolis win

Peter DePaolo, driving a Duesenberg Special, averaged a record 101.127 miles per hour and held off the challenge of Dave Lewis' innovative front-drive Junior 8 Special to win the 15th running of the Indianapolis 500 at the Motor Speedway.

DePaolo became the first driver to crack the 100-mph barrier over the course of an entire race, but Lewis averaged 100.82 mph and third-place finisher Phil Shafer, also driving a Duesenberg Special, finished at 100.18.

More than 145,000 fans were treated to an exciting race. DePaolo held the lead at the 250-mile mark but had to give way to a relief driver so doctors could treat his bloody and blistered hands. While he was out, Lewis went ahead and led until the 400-mile mark when, exhausted and needing a break, he also gave way to relief.

DePaolo, now bandaged and back at the wheel, regained the lead and held off a late blitz to win by less than a minute.

*Indianapolis 500 winner Peter DePaolo with his winning Duesenberg team.*

# 1926

## JANUARY - DECEMBER

## Alabama rallies late to win Rose Bowl

Halfback Johnny Mack Brown caught two long touchdown passes during a 20-point Alabama third-quarter blitz and the Crimson Tide hung on to defeat Washington, 20-19, in a Rose Bowl battle of unbeatens. The victory was Alabama's 10th straight while the loss dropped the Huskies to 10-1-1.

Washington appeared to have this game under control.

★ SPORTS WATCH ★

**MAY:** Washington's Big Train, Walter Johnson, became only the second pitcher in big-league history to win 400 games when he beat the St. Louis Browns, 7-4.

**JUL:** Bobby Jones became the first golfer ever to win the British and U.S. Opens in the same year.

**SEP:** Gene Tunney became heavyweight champion of the world when he recorded a unanimous 10-round decision over Jack Dempsey in Philadelphia.

With their star halfback George Wilson setting up one score with an interception and then passing 20 yards to Johnny Cole for a second, the Huskies had built up a big lead of 12-0 by halftime. But Wilson was injured just before the intermission and remained on the bench as the third period opened. Alabama was not slow to take advantage of its opportunity.

In seven minutes, quarterback Pooley Hubert carried on every play of a 41-yard scoring drive and then connected on 63 and 33-yard bombs to Brown, devastating scores which gave the Tide a 20-12 lead.

Washington Coach Enoch Bagshaw had seen enough. Wilson returned and fired a 27-yard touchdown pass to George Guttormsen. But the damage had been done.

Alabama halfback Johnny Mack Brown evades Washington tacklers and heads for the end zone with one of his two touchdown catches in the Crimson Tide's 20-19 Rose Bowl victory.

## NHL expands to 10

The National Hockey League will play the 1926-27 season as a 10-team circuit and its teams will compete for the Stanley Cup in a complicated playoff format involving the top three teams from two divisions.

With the addition of three more franchises in the United States, the NHL has aligned five teams in both the International Division and the American Division. With the creation of a second New York franchise, one in Chicago and another in Detroit, there are now more American teams than Canadian. Boston joined the league in 1924 and Pittsburgh and the New York Americans were added last year.

The three new clubs will be stocked with players who competed last season in the Western Canadian Hockey League. When the WCHL announced it was ceasing operations, the NHL bought the entire league with the intention of allocating players according to need.

The folding of the WCHL also brings the Stanley Cup under the sole province of the NHL. Under a new playoff formula, the second and third-place teams in each division will meet in a two-game postseason series that will be decided by total goals. The winners will meet the first-place teams under the same format and the winners from each division then will compete in a five-game Stanley Cup series.

## U.S. wins another Davis Cup

The United States Davis Cup team, sparked by the first-day singles play of Bill Tilden and Bill Johnston, scored a 4-1 victory over its French challenger and captured its seventh consecutive Davis Cup.

Johnston got the Americans off to a good start, September 9, at the Germantown Cricket Club in Philadelphia when he defeated Rene Lacoste, 6-0, 6-4, 0-6, 6-0, and Tilden, winner of six straight U.S. singles titles, needed only 53 minutes to dispatch Jean Borotra, 8-6, 6-4, 8-6. The U.S. doubles team of

US Davis Cup star Bill Tilden.

Dick Williams and Vincent Richards clinched the American victory September 10 with a 6-4, 6-4, 6-2 win over Henri Cochet and Jacques Brugnon.

The one success for France was the final-day victory for Lacoste over Tilden, snapping Big Bill's Davis Cup winning streak at 13.

# 1927

## JANUARY-DECEMBER

★ S P O R T S  W A T C H ★

**JAN:** The Harlem Globetrotters, organized by Abe Saperstein, played their first game at Hinckley, Ill.

**JUL:** Ty Cobb, now performing for the Philadelphia Athletics, collected his 4,000th career hit, a double off Detroit's Sam Gibson.

**SEP:** Walter Hagen beat Joe Turnesa to capture his record fourth consecutive PGA Championship at Cedar Crest Country Club in Dallas.

**DEC:** The New York Giants earned their first-ever NFL championship by compiling an 11-1-1 league record.

*Heavyweight champion Gene Tunney struggles to his feet after being knocked down in the seventh round of his controversial long-count fight with Jack Dempsey.*

# The long-count fight

Gene Tunney retained his world heavyweight boxing title, September 22, with a unanimous 10-round decision over Jack Dempsey before 150,000 fans at Chicago's Soldier Field. But the controversial outcome will be debated for many years.

That's because in the seventh round, Dempsey knocked the champion to the canvas and seemingly stood on the brink of regaining the title he had lost to Tunney a year earlier. But as Tunney sat helplessly near the ropes, Dempsey hovered over him, ignoring the attempts of referee Dave Barry to motion him to a neutral corner. In accordance with the Illinois State Athletic Commission boxing rules, the count was held up. Dempsey finally realized his mistake and hustled to the opposite corner as the count began. But Tunney, now regaining his senses, arose at the count of nine and managed to fend off Dempsey's charge for the rest of the round.

"Intentionally or otherwise, I was robbed of the championship," Dempsey charged after the fight. "In the seventh round Tunney was down for a count of fourteen or fifteen . . . and the inefficiency of the referee or the timekeeper, or both, deprived me of the fight."

When the fight concluded three rounds later, Tunney was a clear-cut winner. The former Marine, making his first title defense since his unanimous 1926 title-winning decision over Dempsey in Philadelphia, outboxed his opponent and held a decisive edge in every round except the third and seventh.

The largest ringside crowd in boxing history was joined by an estimated audience of 50 million fans listening to NBC's radio description of the fight.

# The Yankee machine

A two-out, ninth-inning wild pitch by Pittsburgh's John Miljus allowed Earle Combs to score from third base with the winning run, October 8, as the New York Yankees wrapped up their storybook season with a 4-3 victory over the Pirates and a four-game World Series sweep.

A delirious Yankee Stadium crowd of 57,909 exploded when Combs crossed the plate to break the 3-3 tie and give the Yankees their second World Series championship. The game featured a home run and three runs batted in by Babe Ruth.

This Yankee team, which won the other three Series games by scores of 5-4, 6-2 and 8-1, likely will be remembered as one of the greatest ever assembled. The New Yorkers rolled to an American League-record 110 victories during the regular season.

Ruth, with his major league-record 60 home runs, was the headliner of the Yankees' offensive machine, but Manager Miller Huggins had plenty of weapons. Ruth and Lou Gehrig combined for 107 home runs and the Yankees' "Murderer's Row" of Ruth, Gehrig, Bob Meusel and Tony Lazzeri combined for 544 RBIs. Ruth batted .356, Gehrig .373, Meusel .337 and Combs .356.

Want pitching? Try these

*New York Yankee Manager Miller Huggins, flanked by sluggers Babe Ruth (left) and Lou Gehrig (right).*

numbers: Waite Hoyt tied for the A.L. lead with 22 wins and finished second in earned-run average (2.63), Wilcy Moore won 19 games and led the league with a 2.28 ERA, Herb Pennock won 19 games and Urban Shocker won 18.

# The legend of the Bambino

*The story of the sporting colossus who dominated baseball in the "Roaring Twenties"*

Nothing in the childhood of George Herman Ruth suggested that he was destined for fame and glory. An unruly Baltimore street kid who was constantly testing the boundaries of his parents' control, the 7-year-old youngster was turned over to the Xaverian Brothers of St. Mary's Industrial School for Boys.

It was at St. Mary's that Ruth received a heavy dose of discipline, guidance and the first of several nicknames—Babe. He also began showcasing the talents that one day would carry him to the peak of baseball immortality.

Pitch, hit, field—the young Ruth could do it all. As a 19-year-old at St. Mary's in 1914, Ruth caught the attention of the International League's Baltimore Orioles, who signed the youngster and then sold his contract to the American League's Boston Red Sox. From 1915 through 1919, the 6-foot-2, 195-pound lefthander with the moon-shaped face, contagious smile and blazing fastball would compile an 87-45 record and win three World Series games.

Yes, the Red Sox had quite a pitching prodigy on their hands. But there was something else about this self-confident, almost arrogant, kid. He could hit, and he could do it with a force and power never before witnessed on the baseball field. In 1918, while splitting his time between the mound and the outfield, Ruth tied for the league lead with 11 home runs in 95 games. He hit a major league-record 29 in 1919—and some of them soared majestically into the outer reaches of everybody's imagination.

He was, undeniably, the stuff of which legends are made—but not just because of the incredible abilities he was unveiling almost daily to a hero-hungry public. He also had personality, flair and a sense for the theater.

"He was magical," said Harry Hooper, Boston's right fielder when Ruth broke into baseball. "A real showman. And it just poured out of him naturally. You either have that in you or you don't. And the fans knew it right away. The minute we'd all come out on the field to warm up, you'd hear them yelling, 'Babe, Babe.' And he'd laugh and wave and lift up his cap. They loved him and he loved them. It was real, right from the beginning."

But this love affair was doomed, thanks to Red Sox Owner Harry Frazee. Having produced another in a line of Broadway musical flops, Frazee accepted New York Yankee Owner Jacob Ruppert's offer of $125,000 for Ruth. On January 3, 1920, Frazee sold out and the city of Boston began paying the price.

New York and Babe Ruth were the perfect union. Ruth required a large stage that could choreograph his show.

*With Manager Miller Huggins.*

New York needed a first-class act worthy of its reputation. Baseball needed both as it faced the consequences of the Black Sox scandal, a World Series "fix" that would rock its very foundation.

Playing full-time in right field for the Yankees, the Bambino caught national attention by hitting 54 home runs in his first New York campaign. He followed that with a 59-homer blitz in 1921.

"He is the most destructive force ever known in baseball," said Yankee Manager Miller Huggins.

But there was another side to Ruth that Huggins did not find so appealing. Babe played hard by sunlight and even harder after sunset, when he gave full rein to his gargantuan appetite for food, drink and frolic. Curfews were for adolescents; pleasures of the world were designed for weakness of his flesh.

"If you have a young son who is in the first stages of discovery, a youngster whose days are filled with riotous

*Young Babe Ruth (second row left) and his St. Mary's school team.*

romping, pleasure and glory. . . then you have a small edition of Babe Ruth," said former pitcher and Ruth teammate Waite Hoyt. "The guy just never grew up . . . His love was baseball—the fans his friends and the world his playground."

As Babe's numbers grew, so did his disregard for authority. His .378 batting average, 59 homers and 171 RBIs in 1921 seemed to create in his mind a position of power that made him responsible to no one. Trouble followed.

From 1922 through '25, Ruth tested his power on baseball Commissioner Kenesaw Mountain Landis, Huggins and Ruppert, losing lots of money in fines and playing time to suspensions. He also lost more than six weeks in 1925 to an intestinal abscess, the so-called "bellyache heard 'round the world."

Through it all, Ruth continued to hit home runs—35 in 1922, 41 in '23, 46 in '24 and 47 in '26—but it wasn't until 1927 that the Babe, and his Yankee teammates, really exploded.

Featuring a murderous lineup that boasted four .300 hitters and four 100-RBI men, the Yankees won 110 times and captured their fifth pennant of the decade by a whopping 19 games. It was, arguably, the greatest team ever assembled and its marquee player was Babe Ruth—the 60-home run man.

The magical No. 60 came on the last day of the regular campaign—the Yanks' 154th game—against Washington pitcher Tom Zachary. It was a record, everybody predicted, that would stand the test of time. And stand it did for 34 years, until 1961, when another Yankee, Roger Maris, belted 61 homers—in 162 games.

Ruth's flair for the dramatic was always on exhibit, but never moreso than in 1932, when he faced off against Chicago pitcher Charlie Root in Game 3 of the World Series.

*The Sultan of Swat.*

*Ruth (right), Gehrig (left) and football legend Knute Rockne.*

The Yankees had won the first two games and this one was deadlocked at 4-4. As he stepped to the plate, Ruth could hear taunts from the Chicago dugout. There were hard feelings and emotions were running high.

Ruth, who had homered in his first at-bat against Root, watched four pitches (two balls and two strikes) and listened as the intensity in Wrigley Field grew to fever pitch. Then, suddenly, he gestured toward center field, as if that's where he intended to deposit Root's next pitch. Was that the message? Or was Ruth merely pointing to Root? Or

addressing the Cubs' bench with an exaggerated sweeping motion?

Whatever the case, Ruth drove Root's next offering over the center-field wall. The Yankees went on to win, 7-5, and then swept the Series from the Cubs. For 70 years the question has endured—did he call his shot?

"What do you think of the nerve of that big monkey calling his shot and getting away with it?" asked teammate Lou Gehrig, obviously a believer.

"If he had, I would have decked him with the next pitch," countered Root.

Ruth never volunteered an answer, preferring to let the arguments rage and the legend grow. It continued to do so long after he ended his career with the Yankees in 1934, long after he ended his major league career with the Boston Braves in 1935 and long after his 1948 death following a bout with cancer.

Among the many impressive marks left by Ruth were 714 career homers, a record that would stand for almost four decades, a slugging percentage of .690 that is likely never to be broken and a career .342 batting average. Among his

many notable firsts were the 1923 homer that christened new Yankee Stadium, a.k.a. the House That Ruth Built, the first All-Star Game homer in 1933 and the first three-homer Series games (1926 and '28).

But more importantly, Ruth left a larger-than-life legacy that transcends numbers and accomplishments. He arrived at a time when baseball needed a savior, a diversion from the fallout of world war and scandal, and he performed that role with exceptional flair.

"Babe was no ordinary man," Hoyt said. "He was not alone the idol of the fans, he was a superman to the ballplayers. Ruth possessed a magnetism that was positively infectious. When he entered a clubhouse or a room, when he appeared on a field, it was as if he was the whole parade. There seemed to be flags waving, bands playing constantly."

He was, indeed, master of his baseball universe.

*A 1947 Yankee Stadium farewell.*

# 1928

## JANUARY - DECEMBER

## Rangers roll to 1st Cup victory

Frank Boucher blasted home a dramatic shorthanded goal, April 14, to give the 2-year-old New York Rangers a 2-1 victory over the Montreal Maroons and their first Stanley Cup.

The goal broke a tense Game 5 struggle in an exciting series that had Montreal Forum fans on the edge of their seats. All the games were played in Montreal because Madison Square Garden had been committed to a circus.

Game 2 was one of the most memorable contests in hockey history. With the game scoreless early in the second period, Rangers goalie Lorne Chabot was rushed to the hospital after getting hit by a shot just above the eye.

With no other goaltenders on his roster, New York Coach Lester Patrick shocked everybody by donning Chabot's bloody, sweat-soaked gear and leading the Rangers back onto the ice. His determined players, knowing that their 44-year-old, white-haired boss was a former defenseman, tightened their game and made it through the second period scoreless.

Both teams broke through for one goal in the third period and the game went into overtime. At 7:05 of the extra period, Boucher threaded his way between the Maroon defenders and beat goalie Clinton Benedict.

Patrick, who had made 18 saves, was carried aloft to the dressing room on the shoulders of his players.

*Years after his memorable performance in goal for the New York Rangers, Lester Patrick put on the pads and posed for photographers.*

## Leo Diegel wins PGA

Little Leo Diegel officially ended Walter Hagen's four-year reign as PGA champion, October 5, when he recorded an easy 6 and 5 victory over Chicagoan Al Espinosa and claimed the 1928 tournament title at Five Farms Club in Baltimore. But Diegel actually had sealed Hagen's fate two days earlier when he knocked off the five-time champion with a 2 and 1 quarterfinal victory.

Nobody can deny that Diegel's title was well earned. First he ended Hagen's 22-match PGA win streak when he sank a three-foot birdie putt on the 17th hole. Then he handed Gene Sarazen the worst drubbing of his outstanding career, closing him out on the 28th green for a 9 and 8 victory. After that, the final match-play round

*Leo Diegel watches his drive during action in the PGA Championship.*

was merely a formality.

Diegel, a winner in the Canadian Open a week ago, finished Espinosa on the 31st green and claimed the title Hagen had held since 1924.

## Amsterdam Olympics

The United States "officially" captured team honors in the showcase track and field events at the Amsterdam Olympic Games, but most Americans would call the squad's performance disappointing.

Of the 12 running events staged, Americans won only three times—and two of their victories were relay events. Ray Barbuti's victory in the 400-meter final and the record-setting triumphs of the 400-meter and 1,600-meter relay teams were small consolation after failures in the sprints, hurdles and distance events. Only the

Americans' performance in the field events saved the day.

The star of the track and field competition was a 19-year-old Canadian named Percy Williams, who came out of nowhere to capture golds in the 100-meter and 200-meter sprints. An American highlight was swimmer Johnny Weismuller, who set an Olympic record in the 100-meter freestyle.

More than 4,000 athletes representing 43 nations competed in the summer portion of the Games, which included women in the track and field segment for the first time.

### ★ SPORTS WATCH ★

**JUL:** World heavyweight boxing champion Gene Tunney announced that he will retire from the ring.

**SEP:** Glenna Collett fired a record 76 on the morning round and then went on to defeat Virginia Van Wie, 13 and 12, to win her third U.S. Women's Amateur title at Hot Springs, Va.

**SEP:** Ty Cobb got the final hit of his illustrious career—No. 4,191—as a pinch-hitter off Washington's Bump Hadley.

# 1929

## The wrong-way run

California defensive lineman Roy Riegels' dream play turned into a nightmare, January 2, and cost the Golden Bears a Rose Bowl victory over undefeated Georgia Tech.

With the Yellow Jackets controlling the ball at their own end of the field during the second quarter of a 0-0 game, Riegels picked up a fumble at the Tech 35-yard line and took off for the end zone.

"I was running toward the sidelines when I picked up the ball," he said after the game. "I started to turn toward my left, toward Tech's goal. Somebody shoved me and I bounded off into a tackler. In pivoting to get away from him, I completely lost my bearings."

Disoriented, Riegels raced toward his own goal before teammate Benny Lom caught up and turned him around at the Golden Bears' 1-yard line. He was tackled at the 3 and the Bears, trying to kick out of trouble, then had their punt blocked out of the end zone. Tech was awarded a safety and Stumpy

*This photo sequence shows the wrong-way run of California's Roy Riegels after recovering a Georgia Tech fumble in the Rose Bowl. In the last picture, Riegels is stopped by a teammate before he enters his own end zone.*

Thompson later ran 15 yards for a touchdown to help the Yellow Jackets to an 8-7 victory and a 10-0 season-ending record.

## A's Game 4 explosion rocks Cubs

The Philadelphia A's World Series-deciding fifth-game victory over the Chicago Cubs was merely a formality. The fall classic actually had been decided two days earlier, in the seventh inning of Game 4.

After dropping the first two games at home, the Cubs had rebounded for a 3-1 triumph in Game 3 at Philadelphia's Shibe Park. They appeared on the verge of squaring things at two games apiece when they carried an 8-0 lead into the seventh inning of Game 4. Nobody was prepared for what happened.

Al Simmons' leadoff home run looked like too little too late. But Jimmie Foxx, Bing Miller, Jimmie Dykes and Joe Boley all followed with singles and before the dust could clear, the Athletics had plated 10 runs. The key homer was a Mule Haas drive that the Cubs' Hack Wilson lost in the sun, allowing a three-run inside-the-park.

Just like that the A's were back in control. They won Game 4, 10-8, and Howard

*Rival World Series managers Connie Mack (left) of the Athletics and Joe McCarthy of the Cubs.*

Ehmke and Rube Walberg pitched the Series-clinching 3-2 victory.

## Albie destroys Army

Expectations were not high for the 80,000 fans who flocked to the Yale Bowl, October 26, to see their Elis take on mighty Army. The Cadets were 4-0 and once-beaten Yale appeared to be overmatched.

And that indeed seemed to be the case as Army raced to a 13-0 lead. But Yale Coach Mal Stevens had a trick up his sleeve —5-foot-6, 140-pound sophomore quarterback Albie Booth.

Booth, too elusive for the huge Army linemen, carried the ball on almost every play of a second-quarter drive that ended with his short TD plunge. He then rattled off a 35-yard third-quarter run and added the kick that gave Yale its first lead, 14-13.

Then, taking an Army punt at his own 35, Booth embarked on a dramatic 65-yard journey through Cadet tacklers for Yale's clinching touchdown. After kicking his third extra point, he was carried from the field by delirious teammates.

Final score: Albie Booth 21, Army 13.

*With strong determination and impressive resiliency, North American sports were marching toward prosperity and great riches as "The Roaring Twenties" came to an end. Nothing, it seemed — not in-house bickering, not ineptitude, not a world war, not scandal — could stem the tide of growth and progress.*

Chicago football star Bronko Nagurski.

**B**ut those who harbored such notions were brought to their knees in 1929 when the stock market crashed and the continent plunged into deep depression. Growth and progress would take a backseat for the next 10 years as the sports world struggled to keep its head above water.

That it succeeded in doing so is a tribute to the patience, dedication and creativity of those who called the shots for their respective sports. With the national income cut in half from 1929 to '32, profit ledgers suffered. Baseball's gate receipts fell more than $6 million in four years, and college football attendance dropped drastically. Other sports were delivered similar economic blows.

There was little anyone could do except tighten the belt, make prudent economic decisions and wait for the worst to pass. After the Depression hit rock bottom in the early '30s, baseball owners looked for creative ways to bring fans back to their parks.

The sport's first All-Star Game was played in 1933 before a full house at Chicago's Comiskey Park, Sunday baseball finally received unanimous support and in 1935 innovative

Cincinnati General Manager Larry MacPhail brought night baseball to the major leagues.

Baseball's Depression-era losses were not confined to the pocketbook. Babe Ruth announced his retirement in 1935 and four years later, New York ironman Lou Gehrig, stricken with amyotrophic lateral sclerosis, bid a tear-jerking farewell to a packed house at Yankee Stadium. But two shiny new stars arrived to take their place—colorful righthander Dizzy Dean, unofficial leader of St. Louis' Gas House Gang, and Yankee Clipper Joe DiMaggio, one of the best center fielders

The Cardinals' Dean boys, Paul (left) and Dizzy.

ever to play the game.

While most sports were buckling down under economic strain, horse racing was enjoying a growth boom. That's because state governments, looking for a new tax base to generate money, began legalizing pari-mutuel betting. It didn't hurt that three outstanding colts captured Triple

Crowns in the decade.

A number of other outstanding performances took place, including the first-ever Grand Slams in golf (Bobby Jones in 1930) and tennis (Don Budge in 1938).

Joe Louis arrived on the boxing scene in 1937 and began knocking out heavyweight opponents with regularity.

Other notable developments: The National Football League introduced its championship game in 1933; the Orange, Sugar and Cotton Bowls were introduced to college football fans and the Associated Press began selecting the sport's national champions; college basketball took its first steps toward major status by unveiling the National Invitation Tournament in 1938 and the NCAA Tournament a year later, and the role of women in sports became more pronounced—particularly in golf, tennis and the suddenly booming Olympic movement.

# ROLL OF HONOR

## AUTO RACING

### INDIANAPOLIS 500

| Year | Winner | Speed |
| --- | --- | --- |
| 1930 | Billy Arnold | 100.448 mph |
| 1931 | Louis Schneider | 96.629 mph |
| 1932 | Fred Frame | 104.144 mph |
| 1933 | Louis Meyer | 104.162 mph |
| 1934 | William Cummings | 104.863 mph |
| 1935 | Kelly Petillo | 106.240 mph |
| 1936 | Louis Meyer | 109.069 mph |
| 1937 | Wilbur Shaw | 113.580 mph |
| 1938 | Floyd Roberts | 117.200 mph |
| 1939 | Wilbur Shaw | 115.035 mph |

## GOLF

### MASTERS

| Year | Winner | Year | Winner |
| --- | --- | --- | --- |
| 1934 | Horton Smith | 1937 | Byron Nelson |
| 1935 | Gene Sarazen | 1938 | Henry Picard |
| 1936 | Horton Smith | 1939 | Ralph Guldahl |

### US OPEN / PGA CHAMPIONSHIP

| Year | Winner | Year | Winner |
| --- | --- | --- | --- |
| 1930 | Bobby Jones | 1930 | Tommy Armour |
| 1931 | Billy Burke | 1931 | Tom Creavy |
| 1932 | Gene Sarazen | 1932 | Olin Dutra |
| 1933 | John Goodman | 1933 | Gene Sarazen |
| 1934 | Olin Dutra | 1934 | Paul Runyan |
| 1935 | Sam Parks Jr. | 1935 | Johnny Revolta |
| 1936 | Tony Manero | 1936 | Denny Shute |
| 1937 | Ralph Guldahl | 1937 | Denny Shute |
| 1938 | Ralph Guldahl | 1938 | Paul Runyan |
| 1939 | Byron Nelson | 1939 | Henry Picard |

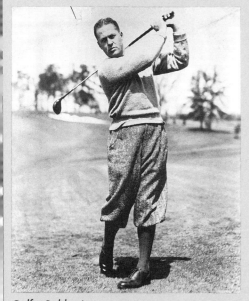

*Golfer Bobby Jones.*

## HORSE RACING

### KENTUCKY DERBY

| Year | Winner | Jockey |
| --- | --- | --- |
| 1930 | Gallant Fox | Earl Sande |
| 1931 | Twenty Grand | Charles Kurtsinger |
| 1932 | Burgoo King | Eugene James |
| 1933 | Brokers Tip | Don Meade |
| 1934 | Cavalcade | Mack Garner |
| 1935 | Omaha | Willie Saunders |
| 1936 | Bold Venture | Ira Hanford |
| 1937 | War Admiral | Charles Kurtsinger |
| 1938 | Lawrin | Eddie Arcaro |
| 1939 | Johnstown | James Stout |

### PREAKNESS STAKES

| Year | Winner | Jockey |
| --- | --- | --- |
| 1930 | Gallant Fox | Earl Sande |
| 1931 | Mate | George Ellis |
| 1932 | Burgoo King | Eugene James |
| 1933 | Head Play | Charles Kurtsinger |
| 1934 | High Quest | Robert Jones |
| 1935 | Omaha | Willie Saunders |
| 1936 | Bold Venture | George Woolf |
| 1937 | War Admiral | Charles Kurtsinger |
| 1938 | Dauber | Maurice Peters |
| 1939 | Challedon | George Seabo |

### BELMONT STAKES

| Year | Winner | Jockey |
| --- | --- | --- |
| 1930 | Gallant Fox | Earl Sande |
| 1931 | Twenty Grand | Charles Kurtsinger |
| 1932 | Faireno | Tom Malley |
| 1933 | Hurryoff | Mack Garner |
| 1934 | Peace Chance | W.D. Wright |
| 1935 | Omaha | Willie Saunders |
| 1936 | Granville | James Stout |
| 1937 | War Admiral | Charles Kurtsinger |
| 1938 | Pasteurized | James Stout |
| 1939 | Johnstown | James Stout |

## BASEBALL

### WORLD SERIES

| Year | Winner | Pennant Winner (series score) |
| --- | --- | --- |
| 1930 | Philadelphia Athletics | (St. Louis Cardinals, 4-2) |
| 1931 | St. Louis Cardinals | (Philadelphia Athletics, 4-3) |
| 1932 | New York Yankees | (Chicago Cubs, 4-0) |
| 1933 | New York Giants | (Washington Senators, 4-1) |
| 1934 | St. Louis Cardinals | (Detroit Tigers, 4-3) |
| 1935 | Detroit Tigers | (Chicago Cubs, 4-2) |
| 1936 | New York Yankees | (New York Giants, 4-2) |
| 1937 | New York Yankees | (New York Giants, 4-1) |
| 1938 | New York Yankees | (Chicago Cubs, 4-0) |
| 1939 | New York Yankees | (Cincinnati Reds, 4-0) |

## BASKETBALL

### NCAA TOURNAMENT FINAL

| Year | Winner | Finalist (score) |
| --- | --- | --- |
| 1939 | Oregon | (Ohio State, 46-33) |

## FOOTBALL

### NFL CHAMPIONSHIP

| Year | Winner | Finalist (score) |
| --- | --- | --- |
| 1933 | Chicago Bears | (New York Giants, 23-21) |
| 1934 | New York Giants | (Chicago Bears, 30-13) |
| 1935 | Detroit Lions | (New York Giants, 26-7) |
| 1936 | Green Bay Packers | (Boston Redskins, 21-6) |
| 1937 | Washington Redskins | (Chicago Bears, 28-21) |
| 1938 | New York Giants | (Green Bay Packers, 23-17) |
| 1939 | Green Bay Packers | (New York Giants, 27-0) |

## HOCKEY

### STANLEY CUP

| Year | Champion | Finalist (series score) |
| --- | --- | --- |
| 1930-31 | Montreal Canadiens | (Chicago Black Hawks, 3-2) |
| 1931-32 | Toronto Maple Leafs | (New York Rangers, 3-0) |
| 1932-33 | New York Rangers | (Toronto Maple Leafs, 3-1) |
| 1933-34 | Chicago Black Hawks | (Detroit Red Wings, 3-1) |
| 1934-35 | Montreal Maroons | (Toronto Maple Leafs, 3-0) |
| 1935-36 | Detroit Red Wings | (Toronto Maple Leafs, 3-1) |
| 1936-37 | Detroit Red Wings | (New York Rangers, 3-2) |
| 1937-38 | Chicago Black Hawks | (Toronto Maple Leafs, 3-1) |
| 1938-39 | Boston Bruins | (Toronto Maple Leafs, 4-1) |
| 1939-40 | New York Rangers | (Toronto Maple Leafs, 4-2) |

## TENNIS

### US OPEN

| Year | Men's Winner | Women's Winner |
| --- | --- | --- |
| 1930 | John Doeg | Betty Nuthall |
| 1931 | Ellsworth Vines | Helen Wills-Moody |
| 1932 | Ellsworth Vines | Helen Jacobs |
| 1933 | Fred Perry | Helen Jacobs |
| 1934 | Fred Perry | Helen Jacobs |
| 1935 | Wilmer Allison | Helen Jacobs |
| 1936 | Fred Perry | Alice Marble |
| 1937 | Don Budge | Anita Lizane |
| 1938 | Don Budge | Alice Marble |
| 1939 | Bobby Riggs | Alice Marble |

# 1930

## Life is just grand for golf champ Jones

Bobby Jones, one of the greatest craftsmen ever to swing a golf club, etched his name into the sport's history books, September 27, when he defeated Gene Homans, 8 and 7, in the final of the U.S. Amateur championship, thus becoming the first man ever to win four major titles in the same year.

Jones, in fact, accomplished his seemingly impossible feat in a five-month span, winning the British Open and Amateur and the U.S. Open and Amateur. He also became the first American to win the U.S. Amateur five times.

More than 18,000 fans at Merion Cricket Club in Ardmore, Pa., cheered the 27-year-old on every shot. The match turned out to be more of an exhibition than a contest, a glor-

*Grand slammer Bobby Jones (right) with his trophies (left to right): British Amateur, British Open, Walker Cup, U.S. Open and U.S. Amateur.*

ious salute and victory parade for the greatest golfer in the world.

Jones easily closed out his opponent on the 29th hole with a par putt and then had to fight off the advances of a delirious

crowd, with the help of a Marine escort, to get back to the clubhouse. When that difficult journey was complete, Jones officially accepted the mantle as the first Grand Slam winner in sports history.

## Schmeling cries foul, defeats Sharkey

German Max Schmeling, incapacitated by a low blow from Jack Sharkey, captured the world heavyweight boxing championship in a confusing, controversial decision, June 12, before 80,000 fans at New York's Yankee Stadium. Schmeling becomes the first European ever to hold the crown and the first fighter ever to be awarded the title on a foul.

Sharkey appeared to be in control as the fourth round neared an end. But Schmeling made a charge and Sharkey fired a left hook that landed well below the belt. Schmeling crumpled to the canvas, writhing in pain.

Referee Jim Crowley hesitated before checking with judge Harold Barnes, who told him the blow clearly was a foul. Still he hesitated and the bell rang to end the round. Schmel-

*Max Schmeling writhes in pain, courtesy of a low blow from Jack Sharkey.*

ing's handlers had to carry their fighter to the corner, petitioning all the while for Crowley to make the call. Crowley looked at the German sitting helplessly in his corner, checked again with Barnes and finally ruled Sharkey a loser by disqualification. When the confusion and pandemonium of the moment had subsided, Sharkey stood stunned in his corner.

The fight, worth $175,000 for each boxer, was for the crown vacated by Gene Tunney, who retired as champion on July 31, 1928.

## Gallant Fox captures Belmont, Triple Crown

The June 7 Belmont Stakes duel between Harry Payne Whitney's Whichone and William Woodward's Gallant Fox was everything it was supposed to be. But the wrong horse won, at least in the eyes of many of the 40,000 racing fans who braved a drizzling rain to make Whichone the hot 3-5 favorite.

Gallant Fox, underestimated because of his victories over weak fields in the Kentucky Derby and Preakness Stakes, held off Whichone's late challenge and pulled away to a four-length victory while setting a

Belmont track record over 1½ miles. The winning time of 2:31⅗ established Gallant Fox as the second Triple Crown winner in horse racing history, following in the footsteps of Sir Barton, the 1919 winner of the Kentucky Derby, Preakness and Belmont.

Gallant Fox, with Earl Sande in the saddle, led from start to finish, although Whichone, ridden by Sonny Workman, did pull even briefly on the homestretch. Whichone had defeated Gallant Fox in the horses' only prior meeting.

### ★ SPORTS WATCH ★

**JUL:** After an eight-year absence from Wimbledon's winner's circle, Bill Tilden earned his third—and last—major title.

**SEP:** Chicago Cubs slugger Hack Wilson finished the season with an N.L.-record 56 home runs and a major league-record 190 RBIs.

**DEC:** Adolph Rupp, new basketball coach at the University of Kentucky, watched his Wildcats open their season with a 67-19 home victory over Georgetown.

# 1931

*Former Notre Dame Coach Knute Rockne watching his Fighting Irish during practice drills.*

## Rockne dies in plane crash

A nation went into mourning, March 31, when it was disclosed that Notre Dame football Coach Knute Rockne was one of eight passengers killed in a plane crash near Bazaar, Kan.

The 43-year-old Rockne, a former Notre Dame player (1910-14) and the school's coach since 1918, was aboard a 10-passenger Trans-Continental and Western Airways flight from Kansas City to Los Angeles, where he was going to make a football film and tend to personal business. The plane inexplicably lost its engines above the clouds over southeastern Kansas and went plummeting into a pasture in the Flint Hills cattle country.

Called by many the greatest coach in the history of the game, Rockne produced a 105-12-5 record in 13 years. Among his best Irish teams were the 1920 squad that featured George Gipp, the 1924 group that included the Four Horsemen and the 1929 and '30 undefeated national championship squads.

A strong proponent of the great American work ethic, Knute Rockne is credited with developing the backfield shift, refining forward passing strategy and promoting a new concept in line play.

## Canadiens win 2nd straight Stanley Cup title

Superb goaltending by George Hainsworth and goals by John Gagnon and Howie Morenz lifted Montreal to a 2-0 Game 5 victory over Chicago, April 14, giving the Canadiens their second straight Stanley Cup title.

So ended one of the most exciting and dramatic postseason exhibitions ever staged by the National Hockey League. The Flying Frenchmen had to work for everything they got in their five-game semifinal series against Boston and their championship matchup against Chicago. Seven of the 10 games were decided by one goal and five of the contests were decided in overtimes that required more than 120 minutes of extra play.

The Canadiens opened the final series with a 2-1 victory at Chicago, but the Black Hawks took the lead when John Gottselig and Marvin Wentworth scored overtime goals at 24:50 and 53:50 of Games 2 and 3, respectively.

With their backs planted squarely against the wall, the Canadiens rallied from a two-goal deficit in Game 4 to achieve a 4-2 victory and they went on to complete their comeback in the finale.

## Southern California rally stuns defending champion Notre Dame

Southern California, the last team to beat Notre Dame (the final game of the 1928 season), performed the feat again, November 21, in a dramatic cliffhanger at South Bend. The Trojans spotted the Fighting Irish a 14-0 lead after three quarters and then rallied for a 16-14 victory before 50,731 stunned fans.

The game, decided in the final minute by Johnny Baker's 33-yard field goal, marks the rise of Southern Cal as a contender for the national championship—an honor held by Notre Dame in 1929 and '30 under the coaching direction of the late Knute Rockne. The loss was the first for the Irish in 26 games (25-0-1).

Notre Dame appeared to have this game well in hand. But the Trojans engineered two long drives that ended with Gus Shaver touchdown runs, and only a blocked extra-point attempt kept the Irish clinging to a one-point lead.

Southern Cal, however, got the ball back with four minutes remaining and Shaver quickly completed two long passes that put the Trojans in position for Baker's last-second heroics.

# 1932

## Chicago goes indoors, wins NFL playoff

The Chicago Bears defeated the Portsmouth Spartans, 9-0, December 18, in the first title-deciding postseason game in National Football League history.

When the Bears and Spartans tied for the NFL's regular-season title, a playoff game was scheduled for Chicago's Wrigley Field. But snow and extreme cold negated that idea and in desperation opportunistic officials decided to move the game *inside*. That's right, *inside* Chicago Stadium.

Dirt already covered the arena floor, courtesy of a circus that had just finished its dates. But other adjustments were needed to prepare for this unusual game.

The tight quarters permitted only an 80-yard-long field with the goal posts being moved from the end lines to the goal lines. Because of the walls edging the playing surface, it was decided that the ball would be moved laterally toward midfield

*Indoor football in tight quarters at converted Chicago Stadium.*

any time a play ended too close to the sideline.

The game drew 11,198 fans, who were rewarded with an exciting contest, decided on a fourth-quarter touchdown pass from Bronko Nagurski to Red Grange.

## Los Angeles Olympics

The recently concluded Los Angeles Olympic Games are being hailed as the best-organized, smoothest-running and most-successful international competition ever staged. That is high praise considering that many skeptics, noting the economic depression gripping the world, had predicted failure.

But great weather, record crowds and outstanding performances from athletes representing 37 countries dictated otherwise. When the international athletes, coaches and officials arrived, they found a state-of-the-art complex with an Olympic Village constructed to house all male competitors. The women athletes stayed in a Los Angeles hotel.

When the competition began, the United States, with more than three times as many athletes as any other nation, won 104 medals. The top American track and field competitors were Eddie Tolan, who captured the 100- and 200-meter

*Multi-talented Babe Didrikson (right) soars over a hurdle en route to a victory during competition in the Summer Olympic Games at Los Angeles.*

sprints, and 18-year-old Mildred (Babe) Didrikson, a double winner in the 80-meter hurdles and the javelin.

In addition to the facilities, athletes were impressed by the Games' innovative equipment —automatic timers and photo-finish cameras that helped put an end to the arguments and bickering that had marred other Olympic Games.

## Sarazen wins Open, doubles his pleasure

Gene Sarazen, playing his last 28 holes in 100 strokes, captured his second U.S. Open golf championship, June 25, with a four-round total of 286 and a three-stroke victory over Phil Perkins and Bobby Cruick-shank at Long Island, N.Y. With the victory, Sarazen becomes only the second golfer to win both the British Open and U.S. Open in the same year.

A gallery of 10,000 watched Sarazen swing around the 6,815-yard Fresh Meadows Country Club course in a U.S. Open-record 66 strokes after a morning round of 70. Sarazen's blitz actually began on the ninth hole of the morning round when he carded a birdie 2 and he then proceeded to play the back nine and the front nine of the afternoon round in 64 strokes.

Sarazen, who had won his first British Open title two weeks earlier at Sandwich, England, had not won the U.S. Open since 1922. Only Bobby Jones had won the U.S. and British championships in the same year.

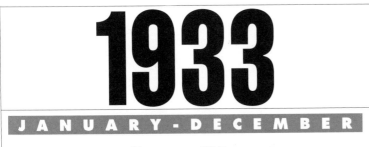

# 1933

## Bears claw Giants

It was supposed to be offense versus defense on December 17, when the New York Giants squared off against the Chicago Bears at Chicago's Wrigley Field in the National Football League's first scheduled championship game—a matchup of division winners in the realigned NFL.

Prior to this year, the championship of the single-division NFL had been decided in regular-season play. The lone exception was 1932, when the Bears and Portsmouth finished the season tied for first and met in a playoff to decide the title.

But this championship game carried an official NFL stamp and the Bears, coached by George Halas, proved they were not just another pretty defense. In a game filled with a surprising number of forward passes and laterals, the Bears beat the offensive-minded Giants at their own game and snuck away with a 23-21 victory.

*The Bears' Bill Hewitt (no helmet) laterals to Billy Karr on the winning touchdown play in the 1933 NFL title game.*

Chicago, winner of the Western Division with a 10-2-1 record, scored the winning points against the Eastern Division champs (11-3) with less than a minute to play. Bronko Nagurski took a handoff and passed 13 yards downfield to end Bill Hewitt. Hewitt grabbed the pass and lateraled to end Billy Karr, who ran 19 yards for the touchdown.

The Giants had scored 244 points during the regular campaign, 111 more than the Bears.

## Foxx, Klein capture Triple Crowns

For the first time, baseball produced two Triple Crown winners in the same season—and they both played for Philadelphia teams.

Jimmie Foxx enjoyed a monstrous season for the Athletics, with a .356 average, 48 home runs and 163 runs batted in. Not to be outdone by his cross-city rival, the Phillies' Chuck Klein averaged .368 with 28 homers and 120 RBIs.

Foxx was rewarded for his efforts with the A.L. Most Valuable Player award, but Klein was beaten out in the N.L. voting. That honor went instead to New York lefthander Carl Hubbell, who led the league with 23 victories, 10 shutouts and a 1.66 earned-run average.

Klein was shut out again on November 21, when the financially struggling Phillies, who lost 92 games and finished 31 lengths behind the first-place Giants, sold his contract to the Chicago Cubs for $125,000 and three young players.

*Incomparable Yankee slugger Babe Ruth crosses the plate after hitting the first home run in All-Star Game history.*

## Chicago fans embrace All-Star exhibition

Based on the reaction of Chicago's baseball fans to the All-Star exhibition played, July 6, at Comiskey Park, the sport's executives are considering making the game an annual event.

Most of the credit has to go to Arch Ward, the *Chicago Tribune* sportswriter who conceived the idea in conjunction with Chicago's Century of Progress Exposition. But not even he could have predicted the excitement such a game would generate.

With 47,595 fans looking on and cheering every pitch, the stars of the American League outshined their National League counterparts in a 4-2 victory. The fans were rewarded with home runs by New York Yankee slugger Babe Ruth and St. Louis Cardinals player-manager Frankie Frisch and strong pitching from the likes of Yankee Lefty Gomez and New York Giant Carl Hubbell.

But mostly it was a fun day that piqued the interest of fans who seemed to relish the idea of watching the game's brightest stars all gathered together on the same field.

### ★ SPORTS WATCH ★

**APR:** Toronto recorded a 1-0 semifinal playoff victory over Boston in the longest NHL game (164 minutes and 24 seconds) ever played.

**OCT:** Boston Redskins' back Cliff Battles became the NFL's first 200-yard single-game rusher when he carried 16 times for 215 yards against the New York Giants.

**NOV:** Two new entries in the NFL: Bert Bell's Philadelphia Eagles and Arthur J. Rooney's Pittsburgh Steelers.

# 1934

## Giants' "Sneak" attack

The New York Giants' slim hopes of defeating the talent-laden, unbeaten Chicago Bears in the December 9 National Football League championship game were further diminished when Coach Steve Owen checked the playing conditions at New York's Polo Grounds. The weather was frigid, a razor-edged wind cut across the field and the surface was hard, slick and icy.

He did not react when Ray Flaherty, an All-Pro Giants end, told him that his college team had once fared better under similar conditions by using basketball shoes rather than cleats. But with the Bears holding a 10-3 halftime lead, Owen mentioned Flaherty's comment to trainer Gus Mauch, who quickly sped off to find a telephone.

Bears led 13-3 after three quarters, when Mauch and club-house attendant Abe Cohen arrived with armloads of sneakers. The players quickly dove into the pile and the turnaround was incredible.

No longer slipping and sliding, halfback Ken Strong reeled off touchdown runs of 42 and 11 yards and the Giants stunned the Bears by scoring 27 points in the final 10 minutes. Final score: Giants 30, Bears 13.

## Hubbell steals show

The American League wiped out an early 4-0 deficit on July 10, to record a 9-7 victory over the National League in baseball's second All-Star Game. But the highlight of this "offensive" battle was the pitching performance turned in by New York Giants' lefthander Carl Hubbell.

Starting the game and pitching before his home fans at New York's Polo Grounds, Hubbell allowed a leadoff single to Detroit's Charlie Gehringer and then walked Washington's Heinie Manush. But he quickly settled down and used his devastating screwball to strike out Yankees Babe Ruth and Lou Gehrig and Philadelphia slugger Jimmie Foxx.

Hubbell continued his magic in the second, striking out Chicago's Al Simmons and Washington's Joe Cronin. After Yankee catcher Bill Dickey ended Hubbell's strikeout streak at five with a single, Hubbell fanned opposing pitcher Lefty Gomez.

Hubbell went on to complete his scoreless three-inning stint with six strikeouts and could have been the winning pitcher. But N.L. relievers Lon Warneke, Van Lingle Mungo and Dizzy Dean couldn't hold a 4-0 lead and the A.L. stormed back to win.

*Soon-to-be pitching hero Carl Hubbell (left) of the New York Giants greets American League starter Lefty Gomez of the Yankees before the All-Star Game.*

## Smith captures Masters inaugural

The inaugural Masters golf tournament, an invitation-only event hosted by Bobby Jones on a beautiful Augusta, Ga., course he helped to design, came to a dramatic conclusion, March 25, when Horton Smith sank a four-foot par putt on the 18th green for a one-stroke victory over Craig Wood.

That putt, set up by a gritty 10-footer for a birdie at 17, earned Smith first-prize money of $1,500 and the title Master of Masters.

With Wood sitting in the Augusta National clubhouse after posting a four-round total of 285, Smith approached the 17th green needing a birdie on one of the last two holes to claim victory. He played a chip shot

*Horton Smith en route to victory in the inaugural Masters golf tournament.*

10 feet from the pin and then calmly rolled it in to take the lead.

Jones, who gave up retirement long enough to compete in his own event, never was a factor. He shot a 76 in the opening round and then followed with rounds of 74, 72 and 72 for 294, 10 strokes behind Smith.

# 1935

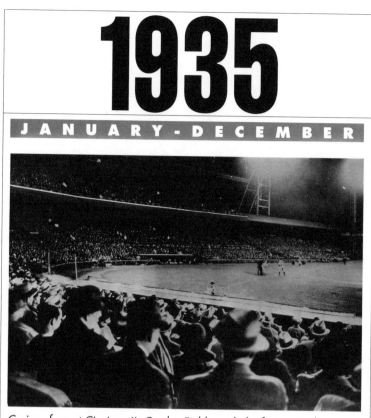

*Curious fans at Cincinnati's Crosley Field watch the first major league game played under lights.*

## Reds see the light

Cincinnati General Manager Larry MacPhail has had to do a lot of talking and convincing, but tradition-minded major league baseball executives finally are beginning to see the light—literally.

Armed with the knowledge that artificial lights and night baseball already had spelled profits for, and in some cases the salvation of, numerous minor league clubs during the height of the Depression in the early 1930s, MacPhail lobbied long and hard to convince big-league owners that such an experiment was a worthy pursuit at the major league level. With a general belief that night baseball was simply a novelty that would pass with time, they finally acceded to MacPhail and granted the Reds permission to play no more than seven night games this year—and only with permission from their opponents.

The breakthrough event occurred on May 24, and Mac-Phail did not lack for ceremony.

In the White House, President Franklin D. Roosevelt pressed a button that transformed Crosley Field into a glittering wonderland and new National League President Ford Frick watched from the stands as the Reds defeated the Philadelphia Phillies, 2-1.

A turnout of 20,422 to watch the game helped mark the event as a rousing success.

## Wills-Moody rallies to win 7th Wimbledon

Helen Wills-Moody, on the comeback trail after a two-year layoff, captured her record-tying seventh Wimbledon singles title, July 6, with a heart-stopping 6-3, 3-6, 7-5 victory over old rival Helen Jacobs.

Wills-Moody, who only began playing competitively again about a month ago, thrilled 19,000 Centre Court fans with a stirring comeback after Jacobs reached match point with a 5-2 third-set lead. Suddenly attacking the net with ferocity, Wills-Moody showed glimpses of her old form in running off five straight games to secure the victory.

The seven Wimbledon titles

*Helen Wills-Moody: A successful comeback.*

match the record set by Dorothea Lambert Chambers in the first two decades of this century. Jacobs now has lost four times in the Wimbledon finals, three times to Wills-Moody.

### ★ SPORTS WATCH ★

**JAN:** Bucknell overpowered Miami and Tulane slipped past Temple in the inaugural Orange and Sugar Bowls, played in Miami and New Orleans, respectively.

**JUN:** Belair Stud's Omaha, ridden by Willie Saunders, became horse racing's third Triple Crown winner by sweeping the Kentucky Derby, Preakness Stakes and Belmont Stakes.

**SEP:** Glenna Collett-Vare won her record sixth U.S. Women's Amateur golf title with a 3 and 2 victory over 17-year-old Patty Berg.

## Pilney sparks big Irish comeback

After three quarters had been contested in the November 2 battle of the unbeatens at Columbus, O., Notre Dame's prospects for a perfect season looked dim. Ohio State held a 13-0 lead and was dominating play.

Until, that is, Irish quarterback Andy Pilney decided to take matters into his own hands. First Pilney returned a punt to the Buckeye 13-yard line, threw a 12-yard pass to Frankie Gaul

and handed off to fullback Steve Miller for a touchdown. Then he engineered an 80-yard drive that concluded with a 15-yard TD pass to Mike Layden. But two extra point failures left Ohio State clinging to a one-point lead.

Notre Dame's onside kick failed, but the Buckeyes generously fumbled, Notre Dame's Hank Pojman recovering at the Irish 49. With 55 seconds remaining, Pilney couldn't find

any open receivers so he scrambled 32 yards to the Buckeyes' 19. Pilney, unfortunately, was hurt on the play and had to be carried from the field.

But his replacement, Bill Shakespeare, came in and wrote the perfect ending—a touchdown pass to Wayne Millner with 32 seconds remaining. The Irish had their ninth straight victory and the Buckeyes had to deal with 81,000 disgruntled fans.

# 1936

## Red Wings overcome Maroons in NHL marathon

It started off as a nondescript series-opening playoff game between Detroit and the Montreal Maroons, two teams with Stanley Cup aspirations. But it ended as one of the most bitterly fought, dramatic and endurance-testing contests ever played.

With 9,500 fans looking on at the Montreal Forum, the Red Wings and Maroons did battle in a close-to-the-vest, hard-checking game that ended in a scoreless tie through regulation. The teams played a fourth period. . .a fifth. . .a sixth. . .a seventh. . .nothing. The eighth session also concluded with no scoring, although a quick flurry near the end had the fans on the edge of their seats.

Having passed the previous NHL record for longest game (a

*Detroit's Modere Bruneteau, unlikely hero of the NHL's longest game.*

1933 playoff contest between Boston and Toronto) earlier in the sixth extra period, the Red Wings finally broke through at the 16:30 mark. Hector Kilrea, leading a two-man break on Montreal goalie Lorne Chabot, fed a nice pass to rookie Modere Bruneteau, who faked the sliding Chabot and scored.

The game, which did not end until 2:20 a.m., featured great efforts by goalies Lorne Chabot and Norman Smith. Smith, starting his first playoff game, made 90 saves.

---

★ **SPORTS WATCH** ★

**FEB:** Ty Cobb, Babe Ruth, Christy Mathewson, Honus Wagner and Walter Johnson were announced as the first electees to the new Baseball Hall of Fame.

**FEB:** Great Britain pulled off a stunning upset, beating Canada, 2-1, to win the hockey segment of the Winter Olympic Games at Garmisch-Partenkirchen, Germany.

**DEC:** Stanford's Hank Luisetti introduced his one-handed set shot to an amazed New York audience at Madison Square Garden and the Cardinal snapped Long Island's 43-game win streak with a 45-31 victory.

---

*Grimy-faced Indianapolis 500 winner Louis Meyer poses with wife June next the the Packard pace car, which was part of his winning package.*

## Meyer wins 3rd Indy

Californian Louis Meyer roared to his record-setting third victory in the Indianapolis 500 on May 30, thrilling the 166,000 spectators with the fastest time recorded in the 25-year-old event.

Covering the 500 miles in 4 hours, 35 minutes and 3.39 seconds, Meyer averaged 109.069 miles per hour around the 2½-mile Indianapolis Motor Speedway track in his four-cylinder Ring-Free Special. Meyer, a winner in 1928 and '33, collected $35,000 in first-place money and lap prizes.

Of the original 32 starters, 15 finished the race. Meyer made only two quick stops and took over the lead just before halfway. He controlled the second half of the event.

Meyer finished three miles ahead of fellow Californian Ted Horn.

---

## Double honor for Jay

With the death of John W. Heisman, athletic director of the Downtown Athletic Club of New York City, the name of the statuette that will be awarded annually to the outstanding college football player in the United States has been changed to the Heisman Memorial Trophy.

The first such award, last year, was won by the University of Chicago's Jay Berwanger. Called the Downtown Athletic Club Trophy, it was intended for the best college player east of the Mississippi River.

Berwanger recorded another notable first on February 8, when he was selected by the National Football League's Philadelphia Eagles as the No. 1 choice in the circuit's first-ever draft of college players.

---

## Gophers win AP honor

The Minnesota Gophers have won the first college football national championship awarded by the Associated Press. The 7-1 Gophers outdistanced No. 2 Louisiana State and No. 3 Pittsburgh in voting by the nation's sportswriters and broadcasters.

Minnesota also was ranked No. 1 in the first-ever poll released by AP on October 19. But it was upset by Northwestern and briefly relinquished the top ranking. The Wildcats, trounced by Notre Dame, 26-6, three weeks later, finished seventh in the final poll.

# 1937

**JANUARY-DECEMBER**

## Thousands mourn hockey great Morenz

More than 10,000 friends, former teammates and admirers showed up at the Montreal Forum, March 11, to pay tribute to Howie Morenz, the Canadiens' hockey great who died three days before of a heart attack at age 34. Thousands more lined the streets to see the hearse wend its way to the cemetery.

It was a tremendous outpouring of emotion for the man most people consider the greatest player of all time. The little center, who spent most of his 14-year National Hockey League career with Montreal, scored 270 goals and 467 points. But numbers do not tell the whole story.

Morenz was the top gate attraction in a league that badly needed stars and the familiar sight of No. 7 speeding down the center of the ice on one of his patented rushes was worth the price of admission. Morenz led the NHL in scoring two times and was a three-time recipient of the Hart Trophy.

On January 28, Morenz suffered a leg fracture during a game against Chicago. He still was in the hospital recovering when he suffered the fatal heart attack.

*The great Howie Morenz in 1936 as a member of the Chicago Black Hawks.*

## Joe Louis captures heavyweight crown

Joe Louis, the Brown Bomber from Detroit, recorded an impressive eighth-round knockout of champion James J. Braddock, June 22, and captured the heavyweight title before 60,000 screaming fans at Chicago's Comiskey Park.

Louis survived a first-round knockdown and then punished the reigning champ the rest of the way before putting him away with a thundering right to the jaw one minute and 10 seconds into the eighth round. Braddock, battered, bruised and bleeding, crumpled in the center of the ring and made no attempt to get to his feet. He eventually had to be carried to his dressing room.

The 23-year-old Louis entered the scheduled 15-round bout as a heavy favorite over the 31-year-old Braddock, who was making his first defense of the title he won from Max Baer two years ago. The New Yorker stunned Louis in the opening round when he sent him to the canvas, but the rest of the fight belonged to the challenger.

## Baugh passes test

The Redskins concluded their first season in Washington with a bang, beating the Chicago Bears, 28-21, in the December 12 National Football League championship game. The fuse was lit by the strong right arm of a rookie quarterback out of Texas Christian University.

"I think that Sammy Baugh is going to change football with his arm," said Chicago's Bronko Nagurski.

Firing the ball 35 times against the Bears, Slingin' Sammy completed 17 passes for 335 yards and three touchdowns. The 15,870 fans at Chicago's Wrigley Field watched incredulously as Baugh connected with Wayne Millner for a 78-yard fourth-quarter touchdown that tied the game

*Washington's Slingin' Sammy Baugh cuts loose with a pass over Bears defenders during the Redskins' 28-21 NFL Championship victory at Chicago's Wrigley Field.*

21-21 and then, with time running out, threw a 35-yard TD strike to Ed Justice. The winning score came after Washington's Don Irwin faked a punt and ran three yards for a key first down.

The Redskins, playing out of Boston, had lost last year's title game to the Green Bay Packers. But they moved to Washington and won the NFL's Eastern Division title with an 8-3 record. The championship game victory was simply icing on the cake.

---

**★ SPORTS WATCH ★**

**JAN:** Texas Christian defeated Marquette, 16-6, in the inaugural New Year's Day Cotton Bowl classic at Dallas.

**MAR:** Basketball rule changes: The center jump after each score was eliminated and teams now have 10 seconds to advance the ball over the center-court line.

**JUN:** Samuel Riddle's War Admiral, with Charles Kurtsinger aboard, won horse racing's Triple Crown with a 2:28⅗ track-record victory in the Belmont Stakes.

# track and field

## The Jesse Owens Olympics

*America's black athletes expose
the myth of the Nazis' "master race"*

Technically, aesthetically and competitively, the Olympic Games staged in 1936 Berlin approached perfection. The state-of-the-art equipment, facilities, housing compounds and organization that made this Olympiad the greatest international spectacle ever choreographed were products of a $30 million investment to showcase the "new Germany."

Record attendance, record receipts and record performances far exceeded even the most ambitious of projections and the Games, despite the heavy atmosphere of political unrest that pervaded all of Europe at this time, succeeded in promoting a general spirit of good fellowship among the participants.

But historical perspective paints a different picture of the Berlin Olympics. That can be attributed in great part to the American press, which chose to focus much of its attention on political issues above competition. That led to exaggeration in many cases and promoted larger-than-life myths that have endured, and even grown, with the passage of years. Give a great big assist to the journalistic community

for turning the 1936 Games into the Jesse Owens and Adolf Hitler show.

Hitler and his Nazi party had taken control of Germany in 1932, shortly after the 1936 Games had been awarded to Berlin. Seeing an opportunity to create a favorable impression of his country while planning a course that would soon engulf the world in war, he spared no expense. Hitler's theories on Aryan superiority had been well publicized, but he assuaged the fears of international Olympic officials with his promise to keep politics and discrimination away from the sports arena. Hitler, however, did not stay away. And that proved to be a problem.

Der Führer probably could have avoided a lot of embarrassment by doing his homework. Americans had been dominating Olympic track and field events for years, and black athletes had recently moved to the forefront of this competition. Hitler was about to watch his Aryan philosophies take a well-publicized beating, and Owens would play a major role.

When the first day of competition began before 110,000 enthusiastic fans at

*Jesse Owens, sprinting to a 200-meter Olympic victory, 1936.*

Reich Stadion, so did the controversy. Hitler, seated in the official box, and the massive crowd were thrown into an excited frenzy when a German athlete, Hans Woellke, shattered the Olympic record on his second toss in the shot put, winning not only the first gold medal of the Games but also the first track and field gold in German history. A second German, Gerhard Stoeck, took third in the event and Hitler summoned both for public congratulations.

When three Finns swept the 10,000-meter run finals, they, too, were publicly acclaimed. And a one-two finish by two German girls in the javelin earned another greeting from Der Führer, who already had stayed well beyond his allotted time. Only one more final would be decided on this day and competition in the high jump was just ending when Hitler abruptly departed. The winner of that event: Cornelius Johnson, an American black. Second place: Dave Albritton, another American black.

Whether Hitler intentionally snubbed Johnson is a matter of debate, but the American press jumped on the story. Only it became Owens, not Johnson, who was snubbed. The fuse had been lit.

## "When we were over there I saw Hitler every day. I wasn't concerned with Hitler or the political aspects surrounding the Games. We weren't as well informed then about world affairs as youngsters are today."

**JESSE OWENS**

Owens, the son of an Alabama sharecropper who had risen to fame as a record-setting sprinter and long jumper for Ohio State University, had run his 100-meter semifinal heat on that first day, setting a world record (10.2 seconds) that was later disallowed because of a

*The record-setting 4 x 100-meter relay team (left to right): Owens, Ralph Metcalfe, Foy Draper and Frank Wykoff.*

following wind. But he was just getting started. Dominating the scene like no athlete before him, Owens would go on to win four gold medals, set several Olympic and world records and win over the German fans who were so ready to chastise him a few days before.

Owens held off a late challenge by fellow American Ralph Metcalfe to win the 100 meters, he set an Olympic and world record for 200 meters around a turn, he long jumped over 26 feet for the first time in Olympic history and he ran the opening leg on America's world-record-setting 4 x 100-meter relay team. He was, simply stated, marvelous.

Whether Hitler thought so will never be known. He watched most of the competition in stone-faced silence. After his early excitement over German success had worn off, he realized full well that his Aryan superiority principals did not apply to the cinder track. Owens became a political football back home, with daily newspaper reports telling readers that Hitler had snubbed America's newest hero after each one of his victories. The truth of the matter, however, is that Hitler had not publicly honored any athlete after the first-day competition, having been warned by International Olympic Committee President Henri de Baillet Latour to cease and desist. Whether Hitler ever could have brought himself to shake the hand of a black athlete is unknown. But the "snub" story, created and enhanced by newspapers and black organizations, is an exaggeration that caught even Owens off guard.

"As far as I'm concerned, no," Owens said years later when asked if he really was snubbed by Hitler. "There are a lot of myths about the incident and I'm glad there are because people will remember Hitler and in that way they will remember me.

"We must remember that the Olympic Games are run strictly by the International Olympic Committee. Nobody, but nobody, rains on their parade at that time. Heads of government don't have any part in the Games except for a few functions during the opening and closing ceremonies".

When the 23-event track and field program ended, 16 Olympic records had been broken and another had been equaled. Five world records had been shattered. American athletes had earned 12 gold medals, one more than all the other nations combined. Black athletes had successfully led the charge and won the admiration of the sports-crazy German crowds.

Record books will tell you that German athletes went on to lead all nations with 89 medals (the U.S. earned 56) in the Berlin Olympics. That, of course, was a source of great national pride for Hitler and the host nation. But there is no denying that Germany's thunder had been stolen by a quiet, unassuming athlete from Alabama, a youngster who would reign as a world hero and American legend for years.

The 1936 Games belonged to Jesse Owens and would become known simply as the Jesse Owens Olympics.

*Owens soars to victory in the long jump final.*

*Owens (right) welcomed home.*

# 1938

**JANUARY-DECEMBER**

*Cincinnati lefty Johnny Vander Meer works on his second straight no-hitter during the first-ever night game at Brooklyn's Ebbets Field.*

## Johnny on the spot

Top billing for the night of June 15 went to Ebbets Field in Brooklyn, where the Dodgers were about to play host to Cincinnati in the first park other than Crosley Field to be illuminated by lights. But a young left-handed pitcher stole the show.

Four days earlier, Johnny Vander Meer had fired his first career no-hitter against Boston, defeating the Braves, 3-0. Now, working under the bright lights of Ebbets Field, Vander Meer rose to the occasion and duplicated that feat, throwing his second consecutive no-hitter in a 6-0 victory over the Dodgers.

It marked the first time in baseball history that a pitcher had thrown consecutive no-hitters. And it marked only the eighth time that a pitcher had achieved two career no-hitters.

Vander Meer almost faltered in the ninth inning against the Dodgers when he walked the bases loaded with one out. But he got a force out at the plate and a fly out to end the game.

## Don Budge is grand

Don Budge, the red-headed giant from Oakland, Calif., has completed the most amazing one-season success story in tennis history. Budge's 6-3, 6-8, 6-2, 6-1 victory over Gene Mako in the September 24 final of the United States championships at the West Side Tennis Club in Forest Hills, gives him a record-setting four major titles in the same year.

The 23-year-old Budge completed his Grand Slam with the ease that most observers had predicted. Mako, Budge's regular doubles partner, did manage to win one set (the only one Budge dropped in the tournament), but the two-time U.S. champion dominated.

The victory gives Budge same-season titles in the Wimbledon, French, Australian and U.S. championships, not to mention doubles and mixed doubles titles at both Wimbledon and Forest Hills. He also was a key figure in the United States' defense of its Davis Cup title against Australia.

Budge was not the only record-setting champion at Forest Hills. Fellow Californian Alice Marble captured her second U.S. title, dispatching Australian Nancye Wynne, 6-0, 6-3, in a record 22 minutes.

*Don Budge returns a shot during competition in the U.S. singles championships, the final step of his Grand Slam journey.*

---

**★ SPORTS WATCH ★**

**JUN:** Heavyweight champion Joe Louis, avenging the only loss of his career, knocked out Max Schmeling in the first round of a fight at Yankee Stadium.

**SEP:** Patty Berg won her first U.S. Women's Amateur golf title with a 6 and 5 victory over Estelle Lawson Page at the Westmoreland Country Club in Wilmette, Ill.

**NOV:** Seabiscuit, ridden by Georgie Woolf, set a Pimlico track record and pulled off a stunning upset with a three-length victory over 1937 Triple Crown winner War Admiral.

---

## Temple rips Colorado in NIT inaugural

The tall, talented Temple Owls put on a show of strength for 14,497 fans at New York's Madison Square Garden, March 16, overpowering Colorado, 60-36, and capturing the inaugural National Invitation Tournament championship.

The victory, which gives the 23-2 Owls a mythical national title, was never in doubt as Temple ran out to a 10-1 lead, increased the margin to 15 at halftime and cruised through a second half that featured a lot of playing time for Coach Jimmy Usilton's second unit.

Don Shields captured individual scoring honors for Temple with 16 points, although Howie Black and Ed Boyle were right behind him with 14 apiece. Mike Bloom and Don Henderson, Temple's 6-foot-6 middle men, swatted away any Buffalo shots from close range. Jack Harvey (11) and Whizzer White (10) combined for 21 of Colorado's 36 points.

Temple reached the finals with victories over Bradley (53-40) and Oklahoma A&M (56-44). Colorado, which ended its season 15-6, scored a one-point semifinal victory over New York University.

# 1939

## Riggs wins easily; Marble survives

Bobby Riggs, a brash 21-year-old shotmaker from Los Angeles, made quick work of 19-year-old Welby Van Horn, September 18, to add the United States singles championship to the Wimbledon title he captured earlier in the year.

Riggs' 6-4, 6-2, 6-4 victory before 10,000 fans at the West Side Tennis Club in Forest Hills, N.Y., set the stage for Alice Marble's dramatic 6-0, 8-10, 6-4 victory over Helen Jacobs in the women's final. Marble, like Riggs, is the reigning Wimbledon champion.

Riggs, who narrowly lost to Don McNeill in the French championship final, employed his full arsenal of shots against Van Horn and kept the youngster off balance, forcing numerous mistakes.

Alice Marble fell behind the four-time U.S. title holder, 3-1, in the third set before storming back for the victory.

*Wimbledon and U.S. singles champion Alice Marble.*

## Oregon captures NCAA tourney

The University of Oregon has won the new NCAA-approved college basketball tournament, put together by the nation's basketball coaches. The Ducks defeated Texas and Oklahoma in the preliminary rounds and then dispatched Ohio State, 46-33, in the March 27 title game at Evanston, Ill.

The tournament's format featured eight teams playing preliminary-round games at different regional sites. The scope of the field was limited because six top teams were competing in the National Invitation Tournament, a basketball playoff that began a year ago and spawned the idea for the NCAA showcase.

Howard Hobson's Oregon team wrapped up the championship with a big second half that allowed it to pull away from the slower Buckeyes. John Dick led the Ducks with 15 points and Bobby Anet added 10.

### ★ SPORTS WATCH ★

**JAN:** The NFL played its first Pro Bowl game with the champion New York Giants beating a team of all-stars, 13-10, at Wrigley Field in Los Angeles.

**JUN:** A star-studded cast of former greats gathered at Cooperstown, N.Y., for the dedication of the Baseball Hall of Fame's museum and took part in a six-inning game at Doubleday Field.

**AUG:** The first major league game ever televised was aired by New York station W2XBS from Brooklyn's Ebbets Field. The Reds beat the Dodgers, 5-2.

*A touching moment during "Lou Gehrig Day" ceremonies at Yankee Stadium.*

## Lou Gehrig's tribute

*Babe Ruth (right) and Lou Gehrig.*

In a dramatic tribute, 61,808 roaring New York fans bid an emotional farewell to Lou Gehrig between games of a July 4 doubleheader at Yankee Stadium.

The two games between the Yankees and Washington Senators were merely background for the festivities honoring Gehrig, the great Iron Horse who two months ago was tragically forced by ill health to retire after playing in a record 2,130 consecutive games. Gehrig's outstanding career was cut short when he was diagnosed as having a form of infantile paralysis.

Joining in the ceremony were members of the 1927 Yankees, the record-setting championship team of which Gehrig was a vital cog. Babe Ruth, Bob Meusel, Tony Lazzeri and other former stars were escorted onto the field by the Seventh Regiment Band. The current Yankees joined the activities along with the Senators and various other officials. A human rectangle was formed around home plate and Gehrig, obviously weak and fraught with emotion, emerged from the dugout to a thunderous ovation.

Tributes were delivered, gifts were presented and finally Gehrig moved to the microphone, choked back his emotion and began speaking in a slow, even manner.

"What young man wouldn't give anything to mingle with such men for a single day as I have for all these years?" he told the crowd. "You've been reading about my bad break for weeks now. But today I think I'm the luckiest man on the face of the earth."

# THE 1940s

*From the golden heights of prosperity in the 1920s to the depths of desolation in the '30s—the fall was swift, merciless and sobering. It was a hard lesson that was not lost on the North American sports community: Proceed, but do so with caution.*

*Minneapolis Lakers star George Mikan.*

That course proved wise as the new decade opened with a bang. Evidence was mounting that Americans were shedding the austerity of the Depression and were embracing their sports diversions in greater numbers than ever before. Good health appeared to be returning to the economy and many predicted a sports boom unprecedented in scope and intensity.

But sports booms and other non-essential forward progress would have to wait. On December 7, 1941, Japanese planes unleashed their fury on Pearl Harbor. The United States was back at war.

This time, however, it was different. Whereas a majority of events were either cancelled or schedules reduced during World War I, Americans refused to let that happen as World War II became a part of their daily lives. Sports were a necessary diversion, even though many of the country's best athletes were fighting a different kind of battle.

Baseball players like Hank Greenberg and Ted Williams heeded Uncle Sam's call, as did many players from all the sports. There were cancellations of some major individual events and several unstable pro football franchises went under, but for the most part college and

*Montreal Canadiens star Maurice (Rocket) Richard.*

## ROLL OF HONOR

### AUTO RACING

#### INDIANAPOLIS 500

| Year | Winner | Speed |
|---|---|---|
| 1940 | Wilbur Shaw | 114.277 mph |
| 1941 | Floyd Davis & Mauri Rose | 115.117 mph |
| 1942 | Not held | |
| 1943 | Not held | |
| 1944 | Not held | |
| 1945 | Not held | |
| 1946 | George Robson | 114.820 mph |
| 1947 | Mauri Rose | 116.338 mph |
| 1948 | Mauri Rose | 119.814 mph |
| 1949 | Bill Holland | 121.327 mph |

### GOLF

| MASTERS | | US OPEN | |
|---|---|---|---|
| Year | Winner | Year | Winner |
| 1940 | Jimmy Demaret | 1940 | Lawson Little |
| 1941 | Craig Wood | 1941 | Craig Wood |
| 1942 | Byron Nelson | 1942 | Not held |
| 1943 | Not held | 1943 | Not held |
| 1944 | Not held | 1944 | Not held |
| 1945 | Not held | 1945 | Not held |
| 1946 | Herman Keiser | 1946 | Lloyd Mangrum |
| 1947 | Jimmy Demaret | 1947 | Lew Worsham |
| 1948 | Claude Harmon | 1948 | Ben Hogan |
| 1949 | Sam Snead | 1949 | Cary Middlecoff |

| PGA CHAMPIONSHIP | | US WOMEN'S OPEN | |
|---|---|---|---|
| Year | Winner | Year | Winner |
| 1940 | Byron Nelson | 1946 | Patty Berg |
| 1941 | Vic Ghezzi | 1947 | Betty Jameson |
| 1942 | Sam Snead | 1948 | Babe Zaharias |
| 1943 | Not held | 1949 | Louise Suggs |
| 1944 | Bob Hamilton | | |
| 1945 | Byron Nelson | | |
| 1946 | Ben Hogan | | |
| 1947 | Jim Ferrier | | |
| 1948 | Ben Hogan | | |
| 1949 | Sam Snead | | |

## HORSE RACING

### KENTUCKY DERBY

| Year | Winner | Jockey |
|------|--------|--------|
| 1940 | Gallahadion | Carroll Bierman |
| 1941 | Whirlaway | Eddie Arcaro |
| 1942 | Shut Out | Wayne Wright |
| 1943 | Count Fleet | Johnny Longden |
| 1944 | Pensive | Conn McCreary |
| 1945 | Hoop Jr. | Eddie Arcaro |
| 1946 | Assault | Warren Mehrtens |
| 1947 | Jet Pilot | Eric Guerin |
| 1948 | Citation | Eddie Arcaro |
| 1949 | Ponder | Steve Brooks |

### PREAKNESS STAKES

| Year | Winner | Jockey |
|------|--------|--------|
| 1940 | Bimelech | F.A. Smith |
| 1941 | Whirlaway | Eddie Arcaro |
| 1942 | Alsab | Basil James |
| 1943 | Count Fleet | Johnny Longden |
| 1944 | Pensive | Conn McCreary |
| 1945 | Polynesian | W.D. Wright |
| 1946 | Assault | Warren Mehrtens |
| 1947 | Faultless | Doug Dodson |
| 1948 | Citation | Eddie Arcar |
| 1949 | Capot | Ted Atkinson |

### BELMONT STAKES

| Year | Winner | Jockey |
|------|--------|--------|
| 1940 | Bimelech | Fred Smith |
| 1941 | Whirlaway | Eddie Arcaro |
| 1942 | Shut Out | Eddie Arcaro |
| 1943 | Count Fleet | Johnny Longden |
| 1944 | Bounding Home | G.L. Smith |
| 1945 | Pavot | Eddie Arcaro |
| 1946 | Assault | Warren Mehrtens |
| 1947 | Phalanx | R. Donoso |
| 1948 | Citation | Eddie Arcaro |
| 1949 | Capot | Ted Atkinson |

## BASEBALL

### WORLD SERIES

| Year | Winner | Pennant Winner (series score) |
|------|--------|-------------------------------|
| 1940 | Cincinnati Reds | (Detroit Tigers, 4-3) |
| 1941 | New York Yankees | (Brooklyn Dodgers, 4-1) |
| 1942 | St. Louis Cardinals | (New York Yankees, 4-1) |
| 1943 | New York Yankees | (St. Louis Cardinals, 4-1) |
| 1944 | St. Louis Cardinals | (St. Louis Browns, 4-2) |
| 1945 | Detroit Tigers | (Chicago Cubs, 4-3) |
| 1946 | St. Louis Cardinals | (Boston Red Sox, 4-3) |
| 1947 | New York Yankees | (Brooklyn Dodgers, 4-3) |
| 1948 | Cleveland Indians | (Boston Braves, 4-2) |
| 1949 | New York Yankees | (Brooklyn Dodgers, 4-1) |

## BASKETBALL

### NBA CHAMPIONSHIP

| Year | Winner | Finalist (series score) |
|------|--------|-------------------------|
| 1946-47 | Philadelphia Warriors | (Chicago Stags, 4-1) |
| 1947-48 | Baltimore Bullets | (Philadelphia Warriors, 4-2) |
| 1948-49 | Minneapolis Lakers | (Washington Capitols, 4-2) |
| 1949-50 | Minneapolis Lakers | (Syracuse Nationals, 4-2) |

### NCAA TOURNAMENT FINAL

| Year | Winner | Finalist (score) |
|------|--------|------------------|
| 1940 | Indiana | (Kansas, 60-42) |
| 1941 | Wisconsin | (Washington State, 39-34) |
| 1942 | Stanford | (Dartmouth, 53-38) |
| 1943 | Wyoming | (Georgetown, 46-34) |
| 1944 | Utah | (Dartmouth, 42-40 OT) |
| 1945 | Oklahoma A&M | (New York University, 49-45) |
| 1946 | Oklahoma A&M | (North Carolina, 43-40) |
| 1947 | Holy Cross | (Oklahoma, 58-47) |
| 1948 | Kentucky | (Baylor, 58-42) |
| 1949 | Kentucky | (Oklahoma A&M, 46-36) |

## FOOTBALL

### NFL CHAMPIONSHIP

| Year | Winner | Finalist (score) |
|------|--------|------------------|
| 1940 | Chicago Bears | (Washington Redskins, 73-0) |
| 1941 | Chicago Bears | (New York Giants, 37-9) |
| 1942 | Washington Redskins | (Chicago Bears, 14-6) |
| 1943 | Chicago Bears | (Washington Redskins, 41-21) |
| 1944 | Green Bay Packers | (New York Giants, 14-7) |
| 1945 | Cleveland Rams | (Washington Redskins, 15-14) |
| 1946 | Chicago Bears | (New York Giants, 24-14) |
| 1947 | Chicago Cardinals | (Philadelphia Eagles, 28-21) |
| 1948 | Philadelphia Eagles | (Chicago Cardinals, 7-0) |
| 1949 | Philadelphia Eagles | (Los Angeles Rams, 14-0) |

## HOCKEY

### STANLEY CUP

| Year | Champion | Finalist (series score) |
|------|----------|-------------------------|
| 1940-41 | Boston Bruins | (Detroit Red Wings, 4-0) |
| 1941-42 | Toronto Maple Leafs | (Detroit Red Wings, 4-3) |
| 1942-43 | Detroit Red Wings | (Boston Bruins, 4-0) |
| 1943-44 | Montreal Canadiens | (Chicago Black Hawks, 4-0) |
| 1944-45 | Toronto Maple Leafs | (Detroit Red Wings, 4-3) |
| 1945-46 | Montreal Canadiens | (Boston Bruins, 4-1) |
| 1946-47 | Toronto Maple Leafs | (Montreal Canadiens, 4-2) |
| 1947-48 | Toronto Maple Leafs | (Detroit Red Wings, 4-0) |
| 1948-49 | Toronto Maple Leafs | (Detroit Red Wings, 4-0) |
| 1949-50 | Detroit Red Wings | (New York Rangers, 4-3) |

## TENNIS

### US OPEN

| Year | Men's Winner | Women's Winner |
|------|--------------|----------------|
| 1940 | Don McNeill | Alice Marble |
| 1941 | Bobby Riggs | Sarah Palfrey-Cooke |
| 1942 | Ted Schroeder | Pauline Betz |
| 1943 | Joseph Hunt | Pauline Betz |
| 1944 | Frank Parker | Pauline Betz |
| 1945 | Frank Parker | Sarah Palfrey-Cooke |
| 1946 | Jack Kramer | Pauline Betz |
| 1947 | Jack Kramer | Louise Brough |
| 1948 | Pancho Gonzales | Margaret Osborne-du Pont |
| 1949 | Pancho Gonzales | Margaret Osborne-du Pont |

professional team sports tightened their belts and managed to muddle through.

As it turned out, the world crisis merely stimulated interest and whetted the sports appetite. When the fighting ceased, it quickly became evident that new seeds of growth were taking root—a growth that would exceed even the wildest of expectations.

Improved air service would trigger a wild rush of expansion. NBC, CBS and ABC soon would become the most important initials in athletics as television looked to expand its own horizons. Organized labor soon

would be looking to unionize the sports community. And blacks who had fought alongside whites for freedom against Germany and Japan soon would be fighting for justice in their own country—a fight that drew national attention with Jackie Robinson's 1947 arrival in major league baseball.

Some other notable developments: The National Basketball Association formed and played its first season in 1946-47; the big men—Bob Kurland and George Mikan—arrived in college basketball; pro football triggered expansion to the West Coast and fought survival wars

against two rival leagues; Notre Dame and Army combined for six college football national titles, the New York Yankees and St. Louis Cardinals combined for seven World Series championships, Toronto captured five Stanley Cups and horse racing produced four Triple Crown winners, the last the sport would see for 25 years.

Top individual honors went to Army backs Doc Blanchard and Glenn Davis, Mr. Inside and Mr. Outside of college football, baseball's ever-popular Joe DiMaggio, boxing's unbeatable Joe Louis and Ben Hogan, golf's rising superstar.

*Golfer Byron Nelson.*

# 1940

*Oil-smeared but happy Wilbur Shaw encircled by well-wishers in Victory Lane after winning the Indianapolis 500.*

## Shaw survives a rainy Indianapolis 500 finish

Wilbur Shaw, negotiating the final 125 miles in a driving rain under a yellow caution flag, captured his record-tying third Indianapolis 500 and became the first driver ever to win consecutive races.

Shaw, who won the Memorial Day spectacular in 1937, finished second in 1938 and triumphed again last year, averaged 114.277 miles per hour in his maroon Boyle Maserati, considerably less than the speed Indianapolis Motor Speedway officials had predicted. But that's because the drivers were locked in position at 80 mph over the final quarter—the stage where most races are won or lost.

Shaw took the lead at the 250-mile mark and then, with dark clouds lurking overhead, hurried through his second pit stop. He managed to get back onto the track with the lead and that proved fortunate. Twenty-five miles later, lightning flashed, rain pelted the backstretch and the yellow lights flickered on.

There was no letup in the rain and Shaw literally cruised to victory. Pole-sitter Rex Mays finished second in his Bowes Seal Fast Special.

### ★ SPORTS WATCH ★

**FEB:** In the first televised basketball games, Pittsburgh beat Fordham and New York University beat Georgetown at Madison Square Garden in New York.

**APR:** Cleveland fireballer Bob Feller became only the second pitcher to throw an opening day no-hitter, beating Chicago 1-0 at Comiskey Park.

**OCT:** Cincinnati's 2-1 Game 7 victory over Detroit gave the Reds their first World Series victory since 1919, the year of the infamous Black Sox scandal.

## Cornell gives up its "fifth-down" victory

Cornell sported an 18-game unbeaten streak when it traveled to Hanover, N.H., for a mid-November game against 3-4 Dartmouth. Coach Earl Blaik's Big Green was not expected to offer much of a test.

An outstanding defensive battle ensued and neither team could break through in the first three quarters. When Dartmouth's Bob Krieger finally kicked a field goal with just over four minutes remaining, it appeared the Big Green had a major upset in the bag. But this game was far from settled.

Cornell took Dartmouth's kickoff and promptly moved to the Big Green 6-yard line. Cornell ran three plays to the 1, referee Red Friesell moved the ball back five yards on a substitution penalty and Scholl then threw an incomplete pass.

Dartmouth's ball, right? Wrong. Friesell, having lost count of the plays, allowed Cornell to line up for a fifth down and Scholl passed to Bill Murphy, who dove into the end zone for a touchdown.

But that wasn't the end of the story. Cornell Coach Carl Snavely reviewed films the next day and admitted to Cornell Athletic Director James Lynah and President Ezra Day that the fifth down had indeed occurred. Day sent a telegram to Dartmouth Athletic Director William T. McCarter and Blaik relinquishing claim to the victory. The Dartmouth officials accepted and sent back a telegram of appreciation for Cornell's fine sportsmanship.

Simple as that.

## Chicago Bears get sweet revenge

*Chicago quarterback Sid Luckman and Coach George Halas seem to be enjoying the final moments of the Bears' 73-0 NFL title-game victory over Washington.*

The Washington Redskins, and Owner George Preston Marshall in particular, have nobody but themselves to blame for the football massacre that took place, December 8, at Washington's Griffith Park.

Having lost to the Redskins, 7-3, three weeks earlier in a hard-fought regular-season game was bad enough, but the Chicago Bears were stung by the words of Marshall and several players. "The Bears are crybabies," Marshall said. "When the going gets tough, the Bears quit."

That was all Chicago Coach George Halas needed to stir his team into a frenzy for the National Football League championship game. Just 55 seconds into the contest, halfback Bill Osmanski took a handoff and raced 68 yards for a touchdown. The massacre was underway.

When the dust finally cleared, the Bears owned a 73-0 victory, having outgained the beleaguered Redskins, 382 yards to 22. Halas later admitted that he would have let his Bears score 100 points if possible.

## Indian pitchers end DiMaggio's streak

The Cleveland Indians failed to slow New York's pennant express on July 17, in Cleveland, but they did record a different kind of victory. The Yankees won the game, 4-3, but the Indians stopped Joe DiMaggio's 56-game hitting streak.

The streak, which started on May 15 when DiMaggio singled off Chicago's Edgar Smith, was on the line when he came to the plate to face Jim Bagby Jr. in the eighth inning after grounding out twice to third baseman Ken Keltner (off Al Smith) and walking in his previous plate appearances.

Bagby induced DiMaggio to ground the ball to shortstop Lou Boudreau, who started a double

*Yankee Clipper Joe DiMaggio (left) and Boston's Ted Williams.*

play, ending DiMaggio's streak.

During the course of the streak, the longest in major league history, DiMaggio collected 91 hits in 223 at-bats for a .408 average, 15 home runs and 55 runs batted in.

---

### ★ SPORTS WATCH ★

**JUN:** Eddie Arcaro rode Whirlaway to victory in the Belmont Stakes, helping the 3-year-old colt become horse racing's fifth Triple Crown winner.

**JUL:** Lefty Grove earned his 300th career victory by pitching the Boston Red Sox to a 10-6 win over Cleveland.

**OCT:** Dodger catcher Mickey Owens' passed ball opened the Game 4 floodgates and the Yankees went on to dispatch Brooklyn in a five-game World Series.

---

*Upset-minded Billy Conn takes a left to the face from heavyweight champion Joe Louis.*

## Louis survives scare, knocks out Conn

Joe Louis, struggling in his heavyweight title fight against a former world light heavyweight champion, crashed home a series of savage blows in the 13th round and knocked out Billy Conn in a June 18 bout at New York's Polo Grounds.

The Brown Bomber, making his 18th defense of the title he won four years ago, stunned Conn with a right to the jaw. When the challenger tottered back, his knees buckling, Louis leaped in for the kill. Conn went down and was counted out with two seconds remaining in the round.

Conn, a Pittsburgh product, used his superior speed and quickness to keep Louis off balance through 12 rounds. With 54,487 excited fans cheering him on, Conn connected regularly with his punches and managed to stay away from Louis' lethal right hand. The rounds were rated even through 12 and anticipation of an incredible upset was building with every passing minute.

But that was not to be. Conn, after defying critics and odds-makers for 12 rounds, elected to trade blows with Louis in the 13th and paid the price. Louis shattered his dream, leaving Conn only with the consolation of having extended boxing's greatest champion to the limit in one of the sport's most exciting title fights.

---

## Williams tops .400, enjoys memorable campaign

The 1941 season will be memorable for Boston slugger Ted Williams, if not for the pitchers who are paid to get him out.

First Williams etched his name into All-Star Game history, July 8, when he slammed a two-out, three-run, ninth-inning home run off Chicago Cubs pitcher Claude Passeau in a game played at Detroit's Briggs Stadium. The shot gave the American League a 7-5 victory over the National League.

Then Williams rejected an offer to let him sit out Boston's season-ending doubleheader to protect his .400 (actually .39955) average.

"I don't care to be known as a .400 hitter with a lousy average of .39955," Williams said. "If I'm going to be a .400 hitter, I want to have more than my toenails on the line."

Williams proceeded to collect six hits in eight at-bats in the doubleheader off Philadelphia Athletics pitchers. His final average: .406. Williams is the first player to hit .400 since Bill Terry batted .401 for the New York Giants in 1930. Detroit's Harry Heilmann was the last American Leaguer to do it, batting .403 in 1923.

## The Bronx Bombers

*Joe DiMaggio fosters Babe Ruth's legacy at Yankee Stadium*

The foundation for success having been poured and his skills having eroded, Babe Ruth passed into retirement in 1935. He had ruled as king of baseball in "The Roaring Twenties" while pioneering the long-ball era and ushering in a decade of prosperity for the New York Yankees.

The Bambino was instrumental in six New York pennants and three World Series victories in the 1920s under Manager Miller Huggins and another pennant and Series triumph in 1932 under Joe McCarthy. But then there was silence for three years. Not to worry, the Yanks were just reloading.

*Joltin' Joe DiMaggio.*

Ammunition arrived in 1936 in the form of Joe DiMaggio, a shy, soft-spoken youngster of Italian extraction who had been setting the Pacific Coast League on its ear for three seasons. DiMaggio had compiled a 61-game hitting streak for the San Francisco Seals in 1933 and had batted .398 in 1935. The press overpowered him with great expectations. New York fans envisioned a Ruthian-like hero.

But during the rookie's first camp in St. Petersburg, Fla., he injured his ankle and then suffered a badly burned foot during treatment under a diathermy lamp. He didn't make his major league debut until May 3, a rainy Sunday afternoon at Yankee Stadium.

But what a debut it was. DiMaggio broke into the major leagues with two singles and a triple as the Yankees pounded the St. Louis Browns, 14-5. So much for first-game jitters. DiMaggio went on to hit .323, the first of 13 .300-plus Yankee campaigns, with 29 home runs and 125 runs batted in.

With first baseman Lou Gehrig, a holdover from the great Yankee teams of the 1920s, batting .354 with an American League-leading 49 homers and 152 RBIs in his second-to-last big season, the Yankees romped to a record

*DiMaggio (right) and veteran Lou Gehrig at spring training in 1937.*

19½-game bulge over Detroit. In the first Subway Series since 1923 and the Yankees' first fall classic without Ruth, the Bronx Bombers defeated the New York Giants in six games. The first dynastic block was in place.

From 1936 through '43 under McCarthy's quiet but firm leadership, the Yankees would compile a .652 winning percentage (799-427) while collecting seven pennants and six World Series titles. They averaged 99.9 victories in that span and never won a pennant by fewer than nine games.

"When he (McCarthy) was with the Yankees, he never became too friendly with any

*One of DiMaggio's home runs.*

of his players, but he made them realize he was interested in all of them," DiMaggio said. "And he was particularly careful to see that the players didn't have too good a time.

"If we'd win an important game, McCarthy would frown on any kind of celebration. He wanted the players to think about the next day and you'd find yourself doing it after awhile. There wasn't any choice. With McCarthy around, there never was any chance to become impressed with your own importance."

Teamwork and pride were qualities nurtured by McCarthy and handed down from veterans to rookies. Gehrig passed them on to youngsters like DiMaggio, Tommy Henrich and Joe Gordon. They passed them on to Charlie Keller, Yogi Berra, Phil Rizzuto, Billy Martin, Mickey Mantle and other future Yankees. Winning became a Yankee expectation, a habit that fed on itself.

## "You're a Yankee, and Yankees always hustle."

### JOE DIMAGGIO

The Yankees used 1936 as a springboard to a record four consecutive World Series victories. A lineup that included Gehrig, DiMaggio, second baseman Tony Lazzeri, shortstop Frank Crosetti, third baseman Red Rolfe, catcher Bill Dickey and outfielders George Selkirk and Jake Powell fronted a pitching staff that featured Red Ruffing, Lefty Gomez and Monte Pearson. Outfielders Henrich and Keller arrived in 1937 and '39, respectively. Gordon replaced Lazzeri in 1938.

Gehrig enjoyed his last big season in 1937, batting .351 with 37 homers and 159 RBIs. DiMaggio enjoyed his first monster campaign, hitting .346 with a league-leading 46 homers and 167 RBIs. Gehrig would drop off to .295 in 1938 and fall victim in '39 to amyotrophic lateral sclerosis, a crippling, incurable disease that

*DiMaggio and new Manager Casey Stengel in 1949.*

would force him out of the Yankee lineup after 2,130 consecutive games and take his life two years later.

Without Gehrig, the mantle of leadership fell on DiMaggio's shoulders and he wore it well through his retirement in 1951. He captured Most Valuable Player awards in 1939, '41 and '47, he compiled an amazing 56-game hitting streak in '41 and he played in 10 World Series.

"There's something about DiMag that commands respect and indicates leadership," said former teammate Joe Page, an outstanding relief pitcher for the Yankees from 1944-50. "As long as I can remember, when the Yankees took the field, they all waited for Joe to make the first break. Nothing was said about this ritual, but everybody held back and waited for Joe to lead us out."

Whereas Ruth led by bombast and force of personality, DiMaggio led by example and grace. He was poetry in motion, whether grazing the center-field pasture at Yankee Stadium, running the bases or swinging a bat.

"Don't think for a moment he didn't show emotion," Page said. "I remember a game in Detroit one day when I was on third base. Snuffy Stirnweiss tripled between the outfielders and I jogged home, turning to watch the fielders chase the ball. After I crossed home plate, DiMaggio grabbed me and chewed me out for not running. 'You're a Yankee,' he said, 'and Yankees always hustle.'"

With such stars as DiMaggio, Henrich, Ruffing and shortstop Phil Rizzuto lost to the service during World War II, the Yankee reign was interrupted in 1944, '45 and '46. McCarthy left in '46 and Bucky Harris managed the Yankees to another Series title in '47, but it wasn't until Casey Stengel's arrival two years later that order was restored.

Under Casey's sometimes comic exterior lied a strategic mind and a no-nonsense demeanor. He had a great knack for getting the most out of his players while providing humorous relief.

He won over suspicious fans and sportswriters by directing the Yankees to a record five consecutive World Series titles from 1949 through '53 and his teams captured five more pennants and two more Series in the next seven campaigns. During Stengel's tenure, another baton was passed. DiMaggio turned over his center-field duties to the rookie Mantle.

After Ralph Houk's Yankees won four pennants and two more Series from 1961 to '64, the dynasty came to a screeching halt. The franchise that had won 22 pennants and 16 World Series in 29 years, would not appear in another World Series until 1976.

The Yankee era of total domination was over, but what a ride it was.

*Yankee outfield 1940: DiMaggio, Charlie Keller and Tommy Henrich.*

# 1942

## Rose Bowl moves east

Don Durdan ran 15 yards for one touchdown and passed 32 yards for another, January 1, as Oregon State upset previously unbeaten Duke, 20-16, in the 1942 Rose Bowl game—at Durham, N.C.

With the recent bombing of Pearl Harbor and the involvement of the United States in World War II, military conditions forbade the gathering of large crowds on the West Coast. It seemed the New Year's Day spectacular would have to be canceled, but Duke Coach and Athletic Director Wallace Wade came to the rescue when he offered his school's stadium as a replacement for the normal Pasadena, Calif., site.

His offer was accepted and the Rose Bowl moved east. Wade's 9-0, No. 2-ranked Blue Devils went south.

Durdan's run opened the scoring in the first quarter and his 32-yard third-quarter strike to George Zellick gave the 7-2 Beavers a 14-7 lead. After Duke tied again, Oregon State took the lead for good when Gene Gray caught a 32-yard bomb from Bob Dethman. The Blue Devils did drop Durdan in the end zone for a fourth-quarter safety, but they never really threatened again.

### ★ SPORTS WATCH ★

**JAN:** Alabama managed only one first down but used seven interceptions and five fumble recoveries to produce a 29-21 Cotton Bowl win over Texas A&M.

**SEP:** Ted Williams, Boston's Splendid Splinter, carved out Triple Crown numbers: a .356 average, 36 homers and 137 RBIs.

**DEC:** Green Bay's Don Hutson became the first NFL player to top the single-season 1,000-yard barrier in receptions, catching 74 passes for 1,211 yards and 17 TDs.

## Maple Leafs pull off incredible comeback

The Toronto Maple Leafs, on the verge of elimination six days earlier, completed the most dramatic comeback in National Hockey League history, April 18, when they defeated the Detroit Red Wings, 3-1, and captured their first Stanley Cup title in 10 years.

Two third-period goals by Dave Schriner and another by center Pete Langelle wiped out a 1-0 Detroit lead and helped the Maple Leafs become the first team ever to win a playoff series after losing the first three games. A Toronto record crowd of 16,218 at Maple Leaf Gardens went wild when the final buzzer signaled a Cup victory that had appeared so hopeless a few days before.

## Torrid Nelson masters Hogan

*Sweet-swinging Byron Nelson disposed of fellow Texan Ben Hogan in an 18-hole Masters playoff.*

It was a playoff matchup made in heaven, and fellow Texans Byron Nelson and Ben Hogan didn't let anybody down. Nelson, playing like a well-oiled machine after an opening-hole double bogey, fired a playoff-round 69, April 13, and held on for a one-stroke victory in the ninth Masters golf tournament at Augusta National.

The 30-year-old Nelson, who had watched Hogan birdie the 18th hole on Sunday to force the playoff, got off to a bad start Monday when he hit a tree with his drive and carded a six on the par-4 first hole. But, trailing by three strokes after five holes, Nelson turned the match around with one of the most incredible stretches of golf ever witnessed. He birdied 6, 11, 12 and 13 and rolled in an eagle putt on 8.

Hogan, who had played par golf over the same eight holes, had lost six strokes—and suddenly trailed by three. Aided by Nelson's final-hole bogey, Hogan managed to pull within one, but he never really was in contention over the back nine.

*Toronto goaltender Turk Broda (1) fends off Red Wings right winger Joe Carveth during action in Game 6 of the Stanley Cup final series at Detroit, which the Leafs won 3-0.*

After dropping the first three games to the Red Wings, the Leafs entered the third period of Game 4 in Detroit trailing, 3-2, and less than 20 minutes away from elimination.

But captain Syl Apps scored the tying goal in that game and then set up the winner a few minutes later. That was the spark needed. The Leafs held on for a 4-3 victory, captured the fifth game, 9-3, and shut out the Red Wings in Game 6, 3-0.

# 1943

## Luckman burns 'Skins

It was billed as the battle of the quarterbacks, Chicago's Sid Luckman versus Washington's Slingin' Sammy Baugh. But that confrontation never really materialized as the Bears pounded the Redskins, 41-21, in the National Football League's championship game before 34,320 spectators at Chicago's Wrigley Field.

Luckman held up his part by completing 15 of 27 passes for 276 yards and a title-game record five touchdowns, but Baugh suffered a concussion on Washington's first offensive play and spent the opening half on the bench. He came back to throw two second-half TD passes, but the game was already out of hand.

Fans had been hoping the quarterbacks would deliver the kind of record-setting performances they had witnessed during regular-season games of November 14.

Luckman battered the New

*Chicago's Sid Luckman won his much-anticipated duel with Washington's Sammy Baugh, leading the Bears to an NFL championship game victory.*

York Giants that day by passing for 453 yards and seven touchdowns, both NFL records, in a 56-7 victory at New York's Polo Grounds. Baugh fired four touchdowns and intercepted four Frank Sinkwich passes in Washington's 42-20 win over Detroit at Washington.

*Jake LaMotta (left) en route to an upset over Sugar Ray Robinson.*

## Sugar Ray Robinson finally meets match

Jake LaMotta, a tough, rock-hard New York street kid, pulled off a stunning upset, February 5, when he won a unanimous 10-round decision over Sugar Ray Robinson in a welterweight fight before 18,930 fans at Olympia Stadium in Detroit.

The loss was the first for Robinson in 130 bouts. Regarded as "the best fighter pound for pound that boxing has ever produced," Sugar Ray had won 89 straight amateur bouts and 40 more since turning professional in 1940. Thirty-two of his pro victories had been by knockouts.

But Robinson met his match on this night. Dancing and jabbing in the early rounds, Robinson appeared to be in control. But LaMotta, who had lost to Robinson four months earlier, stalked his opponent relentlessly and worked non-stop on his body. Patience paid off and late in the eighth round, LaMotta connected with a right to the body and a left to the head that drove Robinson through the ropes onto the ring apron.

Only the bell saved Sugar Ray, but LaMotta continued his assault in the ninth and tenth rounds. That was enough to insure his 41st career victory against five losses.

## Triple Crown

Count Fleet stormed to a 30-length victory in the 75th running of the Belmont Stakes, June 5, becoming the sixth Triple Crown winner in the history of American horse racing.

But the son of Reigh Count, owned by Mrs. John D. Hertz and ridden by Johnny Longden, accomplished something that no other horse had been able to do. In winning all six starts in 1943, the colt also became the first ever to win all five spring specials—the Wood Memorial, the Kentucky Derby, Preakness Stakes, Withers Mile and Belmont.

Count Fleet led from wire to wire in outdistancing Fairy Manhurst, son of former great Man o' War, and Deseronto. A 1-20 favorite going into the race, Count Fleet improved his career record to 16 victories in 21 starts and kept intact his streak of never having finished out of the money.

---

**★ SPORTS WATCH ★**

**FEB:** Frank Calder, president of the NHL since its formation in 1917, died and was replaced by Mervyn (Red) Dutton.

**MAR:** Wyoming claimed the championship of the NCAA Tournament by dispatching Georgetown, 46-34, in the final at New York.

**OCT:** World Series losers to St. Louis in 1942, the Yankees turned the tables on the Cardinals in an easy five-game victory. The Yankees have appeared in seven of the last eight fall Classics, winning six.

---

# 1944

## Baseball does part for war effort

With the 1942 decree of President Franklin Delano Roosevelt that all American sports should continue to be played during World War II, baseball officials dug in and prepared for hard times. They did not have to wait long.

The major problem, of course, has been the massive talent drain. More than 50 percent of major league players have been called into service and replacements are difficult to find. When last season opened, the St. Louis Cardinals had lost 260 farm hands and had reduced their farm system from 22 teams to six. Only nine minor leagues were operating and baseball was advertising on the pages of *The Sporting News* for players.

Some teams were destroyed by their service losses, others prospered when the quality of play dropped, like the St. Louis Browns, long a symbol of American League ineptitude. The Browns won their first pennant in 43 years this season and captured two of the first three games of the World Series before falling to the Cardinals in six.

Other cost-cutting measures have helped the major leagues cope. Travel restrictions have been adopted and spring training sites have been moved north. But despite the difficult times, baseball has still managed to play a considerable part in the war effort.

*Many top professional athletes such as Detroit slugger Hank Greenberg heeded the call to war-time duty.*

Most obvious has been the numerous benefit games that have raised millions of dollars for relief.

## St. John's repeats

The Redmen of St. John's, striving to become the first back-to-back winners in the seven-year history of the National Invitation Tournament, rolled to a surprising 47-39 victory over DePaul in the March 26 NIT finals before 18,374 partisan fans at New York's Madison Square Garden.

Keeping pace with the heavily favored Blue Demons and bottling up Mikan in the middle, St. John's finished the first half with a slender 26-24 lead. But disaster struck DePaul six minutes after the break when Mikan picked up his fourth foul and went to the bench. St. John's, leading 35-31 at that point, quickly increased the margin to 10 and DePaul never really threatened again.

Mikan led all scorers with 13 points. Ray Wertis scored 12 for St. John's.

### ★ SPORTS WATCH ★

**JUN:** Joe Nuxhall became the youngest player in major league history (15 years, 10 months) when he pitched ²/₃ of an inning in Cincinnati's 18-0 loss to the St. Louis Cardinals.

**NOV:** Kenesaw Mountain Landis, who as baseball's first commissioner had ruled over the game since 1920, died of a heart attack in Chicago at age 78.

**DEC:** The Green Bay Packers captured their third championship game victory and their sixth NFL title with a 14-7 triumph over the New York Giants.

## Cadets sink Navy in battle for No. 1

No. 1 Army versus No. 2 Navy. It was billed as the battle of the titans and a capacity crowd of 66,639 turned out at Baltimore's Municipal Stadium for the December 2 game that would decide a national championship while generating millions of dollars for the country's war bond effort.

By the end of the day, Army was unanimously being hailed as the quickest, deepest and most talented service squad ever assembled. The Cadets' 23-7 mastery of the Midshipmen left no doubters.

"This is the best team I ever coached," said Army Coach

*Army Coach Red Blaik with Mr. Inside Doc Blanchard (left) and Mr. Outside Glenn Davis (right).*

Red Blaik after watching backs Dale Hall, Doc Blanchard and Glenn Davis run over, around and through one of the best defensive lines in college football. "These boys were great out there this afternoon. That's just what I expected."

Hall scored Army's first touchdown on a 24-yard second-quarter run, Blanchard scored on a 10-yard run early in the fourth quarter and Davis iced the cake with a scintillating 50-yard burst around right end. The touchdown was Davis' NCAA-record 20th of the season and he also finished the campaign with a record 11.5-yard rushing average.

# 1945

*Freezing Washington Redskins try to stay warm on the sideline during the NFL championship game against the Rams at Cleveland.*

## Rams Owner Reeves eyes westward move

Cleveland Rams Owner Dan Reeves and Washington Redskins boss George Preston Marshall have agreed to a rematch of their December 16 National Football League championship game, won by the Rams, 15-14, at Cleveland's Municipal Stadium. The teams will play again next year at the Los Angeles Coliseum in a preseason game that will benefit *Los Angeles Times* Charities.

This decision has an obvious ulterior motive. Reeves has been trying to relocate his financially pinched Rams to the West Coast and apparently believes the charity game will open the doors to the Coliseum as a home field. The Coliseum has existed as an amateur stronghold since the 1932 Olympic Games were held there.

Reeves covets the idea of becoming the first professional franchise to locate on the West Coast and he has stepped up his campaign since learning that the new All-America Football Conference, which will begin operations next season, plans to locate two teams there (Los Angeles and San Francisco.).

If Reeves' petition to the other NFL owners draws approval next month, he will bring a championship-caliber team to a fertile Los Angeles sports market. Leading the charge will be quarterback Bob Waterfield, the rookie who fired two touchdown passes in the Rams' title-game victory over Washington.

## Byron Nelson enjoys record campaign

It is unlikely that any professional golfer will ever enjoy the kind of year that Byron Nelson just put together. He recorded 18 victories, 11 of them in succession, and record money winnings of $63,336.

That Nelson's success coincides with World War II and the absence of many players from the tour (a blood disorder prevents Nelson from serving) should not diminish from his accomplishments. In 30 tournaments he averaged 68.33 strokes and he had 17 straight rounds under 70 with no four-round totals over par. He was, simply, magnificent.

That success follows a 1944 campaign in which he won eight tournaments and led the tour with money winnings of $37,968. He has won two Masters, one U.S. Open and two PGA Championships in his career, the second PGA this year. None of the other major tournaments were held this year because of the war.

## Mikan sparks DePaul victory

*Talented big man George Mikan carried DePaul to victory in the National Invitation Tournament.*

Talented DePaul center George Mikan completed a record blitz with a 34-point effort against Bowling Green on March 26, lifting the Blue Demons to a 71-54 victory and the championship of the eighth annual National Invitation Tournament.

With 18,166 fans looking on at New York's Madison Square Garden, the 6-foot-10 Mikan overcame a slow start and dominated play under the basket. Bowling Green jumped out to an 11-0 lead, but the Blue Demons kept their poise and took control midway through the first half.

With Mikan doing most of the offensive damage, they forged a 30-22 halftime lead and then controlled the tempo the rest of the way. The confrontation between Mikan and 6-foot-11 Bowling Green center Don Otten turned into a mismatch after five minutes of play.

Mikan, the tournament's most outstanding player, finished his three-game blitz of West Virginia, Rhode Island and Bowling Green with 120 points—a 40-point average. The highlight was his Garden-record 53-point explosion in the semifinal round against Rhode Island.

### ★ SPORTS WATCH ★

**APR:** One-armed outfielder Pete Gray made his major league debut for the St. Louis Browns, singling once in four at-bats.

**APR:** Baseball owners elected Kentucky Senator Albert (Happy) Chandler to succeed Kenesaw Mountain Landis as baseball commissioner.

**NOV:** Cleveland receiver Jim Benton caught 10 passes for an NFL-record 303 yards and one touchdown in the Rams' 28-21 victory over Detroit.

# 1946

## Aggies repeat NCAA victory

Oklahoma A&M, riding the tall shoulders of 7-foot center Bob Kurland, held off a determined North Carolina second-half rally and captured its second straight NCAA Tournament championship, on March 26, at Madison Square Garden.

The Aggies' 43-40 victory, much like their 49-45 win over New York University in last year's final, was made possible by the inside work of Kurland. He scored 23 points against North Carolina and held Tar Heels center Horace McKinney to five points, forcing him to foul out midway through the second half.

After lifting its lead to 13, Oklahoma A&M had to hold off the late assault of forward

*Aggie Bob Kurland, 7-foot, was the big gun in Oklahoma A&M's two straight NCAA Tournament victories.*

John Dillon, who scored 16 points. But Dillon's efforts were too little too late.

Coach Henry Iba's Aggies, 31-2 this season and 58-6 over the last two, posted easy wins over Baylor and California en route to becoming the first to win consecutive NCAA titles.

## ★ SPORTS WATCH ★

**JAN:** Texas quarterback Bobby Layne ran for four touchdowns, passed for two others and kicked four extra points in the Longhorns' 40-27 Cotton Bowl victory over Missouri.

**AUG:** Ben Hogan captured his first major golf title with a 6 and 4 victory over Ed Oliver in the PGA Championship at Portland Golf Club.

**SEP:** Patty Berg defeated Betty Jameson, 5 and 4, at Spokane, Wash., in the inaugural Women's Open Championship, an event run by the new Women's Professional Golf Association.

**DEC:** The Cleveland Browns compiled a 12-2 record to capture league honors as the eight-team All-America Football Conference completed its first season.

## Williams puts on show

Boston slugger Ted Williams, playing before his home fans at Fenway Park, collected four hits, including a pair of homers, and drove in five runs as the American League belted the Nationals, 12-0, in the July 9 All-Star Game.

After a one-year cancellation of the midsummer classic because of World War II, most of baseball's big names were back in uniform and ready for action. Unfortunately for the National Leaguers, most of the action occurred when the A.L. players were batting.

Cleveland's Bob Feller, Detroit's Hal Newhouser and St. Louis' Jack Kramer held the N.L. to three hits and Yankee Charlie Keller and Williams provided home runs.

But the highlight of the game was an eighth-inning matchup of Williams against Pittsburgh pitcher Rip Sewell, the man known for his slow, high-arcing "ephus pitch." With the score at 9-0 and two runners on base, 34,906 fans wondered what would happen if. . .

They didn't have to wonder long. Sewell wound up like he was going to throw a fastball and delivered his "ephus." Williams swung mightily and just tipped the ball. Everybody broke up laughing. Sewell threw another "ephus" for a ball and a third, which Williams belted for his second homer of the game.

*A. L. boppers (left to right) Mickey Vernon, Ted Williams, Johnny Hopp and Dixie Walker.*

## Assault wins Crown

Assault, convincing everybody once and for all that he belongs in horse racing's select company, captured the June 2 Belmont Stakes to become the sport's seventh Triple Crown winner.

Despite victories in the Kentucky Derby and Preakness Stakes, Assault went off in the Belmont as a 7-5 second favorite behind Lord Boswell. But the chocolate-colored King Ranch 3-year-old upset the odds with a powerful stretch run that produced a three-length victory over Natchez. Lord Boswell was never in the race and finished fifth in the six-horse field.

Assault, with Warren Mehrtens in saddle, covered the 1$\frac{1}{2}$-mile test in 2:30$\frac{4}{5}$ and joined a Triple Crown roster that includes Sir Barton, Gallant Fox, Omaha, War Admiral, Whirlaway and Count Fleet. He won $77,400 for owner Robert J. Kleberg and raised his career earnings to $316,270.

# Slaughter runs wild, Cardinals win Series

Enos (Country) Slaughter's mad dash around the bases produced the winning run and Harry Brecheen's clutch pitching sealed the verdict as the St. Louis Cardinals defeated the Boston Red Sox, 4-3, in a dramatic Game 7 conclusion to the World Series.

After Boston had tied the game in the top of the eighth on Dom DiMaggio's two-run double, the hustling Slaughter led off the bottom of the inning with a single off Bob Klinger. But he could not advance as the Boston pitcher retired Whitey Kurowski and Del Rice. Now it was up to Harry Walker.

The Cardinal left fielder delivered, lining a shot toward the left-center-field gap. Boston center fielder Leon Culberson made an outstanding play, cutting the ball off and firing it back to the infield—quickly enough to hold Slaughter at third.

Wrong. Slaughter never slowed down as he rounded the

*St. Louis' Enos Slaughter slides across the plate with the World Series' winning run against Boston after his "Mad Dash" around the bases.*

bag and headed home. Shortstop Johnny Pesky took the relay and hesitated, obviously surprised at Slaughter's bold move. His hurried throw was up the third-base line and the Cardinals had a 4-3 lead.

Brecheen, already a two-time Series winner as a starter, had relieved Murry Dickson in the eighth. He added to the excitement in the ninth when he allowed the first two Red Sox, Rudy York and Bobby Doerr, to reach base with singles. But with 36,143 fans on the edge of their seats, he induced Pinky

Higgins to hit into a forceout, retired Roy Partee on a foul pop and completed the Cardinals' sixth World Series victory by getting Tom McBride to ground into another force.

The victory capped a memorable season in which the Cardinals tied for first place with Brooklyn and captured their fourth flag in five years by beating the Dodgers two straight in a best-of-three pennant playoff, the first in baseball history.

Howie Pollet pitched the Redbirds to a 4-2 victory in the playoff opener at St. Louis and

Dickson and Brecheen combined for an 8-4 win at Brooklyn. Boston and St. Louis alternated victories through the first six games of the World Series.

# Irish nip Army — in poll

The final Associated Press college football poll has determined what a well-publicized midseason clash failed to decide —Notre Dame is No. 1, Army is No. 2.

That determination was made by the nation's sportswriters and broadcasters, who most likely were influenced by Army's struggle against Navy in the season finale. Army, which had held the top spot all season before slipping at the end, finished with a 9-0-1 record. The Irish were 8-0-1.

The only blemish on both teams' ledgers came from their midseason clash, on November

9, at Yankee Stadium. The No. 2 Irish entered the game 5-0, Army came in at 7-0. Notre Dame had outscored its opponents, 177-18. Army owned a 208-55 edge over its opposition.

Everybody braced for an offensive explosion. But Notre Dame blanketed Army star running backs Doc Blanchard and Glenn Davis and the Cadets returned the favor by shutting down Irish quarterback Johnny Lujack. Final score: Army 0, Notre Dame 0.

The national championship would have to be decided by voters rather than the teams involved.

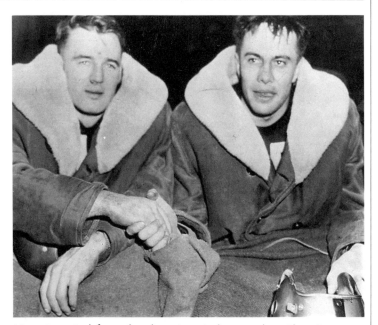

*Notre Dame's defense shut down Army's dynamic duo: Glenn Davis (left) and Doc Blanchard.*

# 1947

## 2 Giants suspended in gambling probe

New York Giants quarterback Frank Filchock and fullback Merle Hapes have been suspended indefinitely by National Football League Commissioner Bert Bell for their impropriety in failing to report a bribe offer before the Giants' December 15, 1946, championship game against the Chicago Bears.

New York fans were stunned on the morning of the title game when the Giants reported that Filchock and Hapes had been offered $2,500 to ensure that they lost the game by more than the 10 points by which Chicago was favored. The players also were offered winnings from a $1,000 bet that was to be placed against the Giants and lucrative off-season employment.

Hapes admitted receiving the offer and was not allowed to play. Filchock, however, denied that he had been approached and Bell, lacking evidence, allowed him to compete. Filchock played well, throwing two touchdown passes despite suf-

*New York Giants quarterback Frank Filchock (40), the subject of a gambling scandal hours earlier, is tackled by Chicago's Bulldog Turner (66) during action in the NFL championship game.*

fering a first-quarter broken nose. But the Bears had too much offense and rolled to a 24-14 victory.

At the subsequent trial of gambler Alvin Paris, Filchock admitted that he, too, had been approached and had lied because he wanted one more chance to play in a championship game. He now will pay the price.

*One of the few Rose Bowl highlights for UCLA was the record 103-yard kickoff return by Al Hoisch (7).*

## Illinois whips UCLA

Pacific Coast Conference members may be wondering about the wisdom of their agreement to meet a Big Nine Conference representative annually in the Rose Bowl. In the first meeting under that contract on January 1, Illinois rolled into Pasadena, Calif., and embarrassed No. 4-ranked and previously undefeated UCLA, 45-14.

Illinois, ranked fifth by the Associated Press despite two losses, unveiled its fleet and elusive corps of running backs for the 90,000 spectators and com-

pletely dominated the bigger and slower Bruins. The Fighting Illini took control with a 19-point second-quarter surge and put the game out of reach with a 20-point explosion in the fourth quarter. The biggest damage was done by Buddy Young and Julie Rykovich, each of whom rushed for 103 yards.

The one bright spot for UCLA was a Rose Bowl-record 103-yard kickoff return for a touchdown by Al Hoisch in the second quarter.

## Utes win in NIT; Crusaders triumph in NCAA

In the most dramatic two-night stand in college basketball history, Madison Square Garden hosted the March 24 and 25 coronation of two champions—Utah in the National Invitation Tournament and Holy Cross in the NCAA Tournament.

The Utes pulled off a stunning upset on March 24, defeating powerful Kentucky, 49-45, in the NIT final. With 18,467 fans looking on, Utah slowed the Wildcats' offense to a crawl and prevented them from garnering their second straight NIT victory. Tourney most valuable player Vern Gardner and Arnie Ferrin each scored 15 points and triggered a defensive effort that led to Kentucky's third loss in 37 games.

With 18,445 fans in attendance the next night, Holy Cross stopped Oklahoma, 58-47. The Sooners led by three points at halftime and trailed by only three with less than three minutes remaining before the Crusaders pulled away.

Holy Cross, which finished 27-3, was keyed by George Kaftan, who scored 18 points and won outstanding player honors. Oklahoma's Gerald Tucker led all scorers with 22 points.

**JAN:** Former catcher Josh Gibson, one of the foremost sluggers in Negro League baseball history, died of a brain tumor at age 35.

**MAR:** A good-looking youngster named Gordie Howe finished his first NHL season in Detroit with seven goals and 15 assists in 58 games.

**MAR:** The Cleveland Indians and New York Giants have announced plans to set up the first spring training camps in Arizona, while the Brooklyn Dodgers will move from their Florida headquarters to Havana, Cuba.

**APR:** The Chicago American Gears, featuring the inside presence of George Mikan, won the National Basketball League championship with a three games to one victory over the Rochester Royals.

**APR:** In the first all-Canada Stanley Cup final in 12 years, the Toronto Maple Leafs scored a six-game victory over Montreal.

**JUN:** California won the first NCAA Division I College World Series, beating Yale, 8-7, in the tournament's championship game in Kalamazoo, Mich.

**JUN:** Cincinnati's Ewell Blackwell, who no-hit the Boston Braves on June 18, lost his bid for second straight no-hitter four days later when Brooklyn's Eddie Stanky singled with one out in the ninth inning.

# Fulks leads Warriors

Joe Fulks scored 34 points and Howie Dallmar provided the game-winning basket with a minute left to play, April 22, giving the Philadelphia Warriors an 83-80 win over the Chicago Stags and a four games to one victory in the first championship series of the Basketball Association of America.

The Warriors had finished the league's inaugural season in second place, 14 games behind the Washington Capitols, in the Eastern Division while Chicago won Western honors. But the Stags beat Washington in the first round of the playoffs and Philadelphia advanced with wins over St. Louis and New York.

The new circuit, with Maurice Podoloff as its commissioner, opened play with 11 teams based in Boston, Toronto, Providence, New York, Philadelphia, Washington, Pittsburgh, Cleveland, Detroit, Chicago and St. Louis. Competing against the more established National Basketball League, the BAA set up in a two-division structure with 60-game schedules and a six-team playoff format.

Fulks was the premier performer, compiling a league-best 23.2-point average that included a 41-point January 14 explosion against Toronto.

## " SPORTS TALK "

*"My pitching secret? It's simple. Nobody likes to hit a man who wears glasses."*
**DIZZY TROUT**
Detroit Tigers righthander

# Baseball honors Ruth

April 27 was "Babe Ruth Day" throughout the baseball world and players, managers, officials and fans everywhere took time out to honor the game's most cherished superstar. But nowhere was the tribute more poignant than at Yankee Stadium, where 58,339 fans gathered to say a fond, loving farewell before a scheduled game between the Yankees and Washington Senators.

After receiving awards and gifts from the many officials and dignitaries in attendance, Ruth enjoyed a thunderous greeting as he stepped to the microphone. He looked thin and weak from a series of operations to combat throat cancer and his voice was raspy and subdued. But he still flashed the same Ruthian smile and he spoke straight from the heart. His closing words, piped in to ballparks around the major leagues, were both simple and elegant.

*Babe Ruth, his voice hoarse from cancer, speaks to a full house at Yankee Stadium on a day in his honor.*

"The only real game in the world, I think, is baseball," he said. "There's been so many lovely things said about me, I'm just glad I had the opportunity to thank everybody."

With that, the 53-year-old Ruth flashed his patented smile, waved to the crowd and walked into the Yankee dugout.

# Durocher suspended

Baseball Commissioner A.B. (Happy) Chandler shocked the city of Brooklyn, April 9, when he announced the suspension of Dodgers Manager Leo Durocher for the 1947 season—less than a week before opening day. Chandler's action, the most drastic ever taken against a major league manager, reprimands Durocher for conduct "detrimental to baseball."

Chandler had opened an investigation when Durocher charged former Brooklyn boss Larry MacPhail, now president of the New York Yankees, with having alleged gamblers in his box during a Yankee-Dodger spring training game at Havana, Cuba. An irate MacPhail filed defamation charges against both Durocher and Dodger President Branch Rickey with the commissioner's office.

Chandler listened to testimony from numerous players and officials before announcing Durocher's punishment and clearing both Rickey and MacPhail. Durocher, who has a checkered history of on and off-field indiscretions, will be replaced on an interim basis by coach Clyde Sukeforth.

*Always argumentative Brooklyn Manager Leo Durocher will have to sit out the 1947 season under suspension.*

# baseball

## The breaking of the color barrier in baseball

*Jackie Robinson paves the way for the participation of blacks in team sports*

Robinson signs as Dodger boss Branch Rickey looks on.

"The Brooklyn Dodgers today purchased the contract of Jackie Robinson from the Montreal Royals."

This understated, one-sentence press release was handed out to writers at Ebbets Field on April 10, 1947. Without fanfare, without so much as a drum roll or a wink of his eye, Dodger boss Branch Rickey tore down a 60-year-old sociological barrier and forever changed the national pastime. The transaction and the manner in which it was publicized were typical enough, but the message left out one important detail: Jackie Robinson was *black*.

The announcement did not catch anybody by surprise. Rickey had signed Robinson and four more blacks in 1945 to play for the Dodgers' International League team at Montreal. Rickey's intentions, clear enough already, were strengthened when the 27-year-old batted a league-leading .349, stole 40 bases and led second basemen in fielding while helping the 1946 Royals capture the Junior League

Jackie Robinson in 1946.

World Series. When Robinson batted .625 in seven 1947 exhibition games against Brooklyn, baseball stood on the brink of a breakthrough.

There were immediate outcries of indignation when Robinson was called up, not all of them spoken with southern accents. There were chastisements, character assassinations and threats of boycott from officials, players and fans around the major

leagues. Some Dodger players took a wait-and-see attitude while other reactions ranged from stand-offishness to outright hostility. Before Robinson arrived in Brooklyn, southern players on the Dodgers circulated a petition demanding that he not be promoted to the majors. The move dried up when shortstop Pee Wee Reese, a southerner, the team captain and later Robinson's close friend, refused to sign and Rickey agreed to trade any unhappy players.

Robinson's April 15 debut at Ebbets Field, marking the first appearance of a black in major league baseball since the 1880s, was unspectacular. Batting second and playing first base, a new position, the rookie was fed a steady diet of curveballs from Boston's Johnny Sain and went 0 for 3.

Robinson got his first big-league hit, a bunt single, in his second game, hit his first home run in his third contest and

stole his first base in the fifth game. The steal led to the only run in a battle against Philadelphia and provided sweet revenge for a torrent of verbal abuse Robinson had endured from Phillies Manager Ben Chapman, the most belligerent bench jockey in the National League.

Acceptance in the Dodger clubhouse came grudgingly, but it did come. First several of Robinson's teammates began saying "hello" to him. Soon he was being invited to participate in clubhouse card games on road trips. By the end of a rookie season in which the speedy Robinson batted .297, hit 12 home runs, stole a league-high 29 bases, captured Rookie of the Year honors and helped the Dodgers win the N.L. pennant, he was being hailed by teammates as one of the team's key performers.

"No other ballplayer on this club, with the possible exception of Bruce Edwards, has done more to put the

*Robinson, a daring baserunner, raises the dirt as he steals home against the Cubs in 1948.*

*Robinson became a hero and cult figure for the black community.*

Dodgers up in the race than Robinson has," said outfielder Dixie Walker, a southerner and an outspoken adversary at the beginning of the season. "He is everything that Branch Rickey said he was when he came up from Montreal."

All was not smooth sailing that first season, either inside the Dodger clubhouse or on the field. "It isn't too tough on me," Robinson wrote to his high school baseball coach during the season. "I have played with white boys all my life. But they haven't played with a Negro before, and it sure is rough on some of them."

Abuse from rival fans and players started early and continued throughout the season. Robinson, as programmed by Rickey, simply took it and turned the other cheek, striking back in the only way he could—with base hits and his daring, combative play. The first time Brooklyn traveled to St. Louis, the Cardinals threatened a boycott that was cut short by N.L. President Ford Frick's warning that those who take part "will be suspended and I don't care if it wrecks the National League for five years."

Robinson later was spiked (maliciously he believed) by Cardinals Enos Slaughter and Joe Garagiola. After the Slaughter incident in August, a group of Brooklyn players came to Robinson and said, "If they give you the works, give it back to them—and the team

will be behind you 100 percent." That was the day Robinson won his first major battle.

Jackie Robinson, a 6-foot, 195-pound Californian, was not the first black to carve his niche in the white sports world, but it was his pioneering in the national game that really opened the door for racial integration. The National Football League's Los Angeles Rams signed Kenny Washington and Woody Strode and the All-America Football Conference's Cleveland Browns signed Marion Motley and Bill Willis in 1946, beating the Dodgers to the punch and ending more than a decade of football segregation.

Individual performers, such as boxing great Joe Louis and 1936 Olympic hero Jesse Owens, had risen to the top of their professions, but the integration of team sports was a much touchier issue. Cleveland's Larry Doby and the St. Louis Browns' Hank Thompson and Willard Brown followed Robinson into the major leagues in 1947, as did another Dodger—pitcher Don Bankhead.

To pave the way for his "sociological experiment" and make it work, Rickey painstakingly laid the groundwork. First he needed the right man, both athletically and character-wise.

Rickey and his scouts settled on Robinson, a 26-year-old shortstop with the Kansas City Monarchs. The youngster, a

former four-sport star at UCLA and an Army lieutenant during World War II, did not smoke, drink or swear and he was intelligent and patient to a fault. He understood the plight and handicaps of his race and was willing to address the issues with resolve—and silence.

Rickey formed committees of top black citizens in every N.L. city and drafted a formal "how to handle the job" itinerary for Robinson. The list of do's and don'ts was long, but basically he was told to wear "an armor of humility," to turn the other cheek, never strike back or argue on the field and avoid adulation with the same fervor that he avoided retaliation. That was not easy because he played in every ballpark before throngs of black fans who were there to see their hero. Robinson always left by a secret exit and he was not allowed to accept social invitations.

"I had to fight hard against loneliness, abuse and the knowledge that any mistake I made would be magnified because I was the only black man out there," Robinson wrote in his 1972 autobiography. "Many people resented my impatience and honesty, but I never cared about acceptance as much as I cared about respect."

Robinson's breakthrough was especially difficult because

he had to do it twice—first for Montreal in 1946, then for Brooklyn. But by 1948 he was established as an integral part of the Dodger team (now playing his natural position of second base) and in 1949 he batted an N.L-leading .342, drove in 124 runs and earned the league's MVP citation. In 1955, he helped Brooklyn win the city's first and only World Series.

Robinson, a career .311 hitter and six-time All-Star who retired after the 1956 season, died of a heart attack in 1972, a decade after his election to the baseball Hall of Fame and 13 years after the Boston Red Sox became the last major league team to integrate.

*A natural second baseman, Robinson played first in his rookie season.*

# 1947

## JULY-DECEMBER

## Babe's streak hits 17

Babe Didrikson Zaharias scored an easy 9 and 8 victory over Dot Kielty in the Broadmoor women's golf final in Colorado Springs, July 19, running her incredible streak of tournament victories to 17 straight.

Zaharias, who recently became the first American ever to win the British Ladies Championship when she defeated Jacqueline Gordon, 5 and 4, at the Gullane Number One course in Scotland, finished the morning round 5-up on Kielty and continued to pull away in the afternoon. Earlier in the tournament, the incomparable

*Babe Didrikson Zaharias—17 and still counting.*

Babe fired a course-record 68.

Zaharias, the 1946 U.S. Women's Amateur winner, has not lost a tournament since June of last year.

## Kramer stops Parker

Frank Parker won the hearts of the 14,000 fans at the West Side Tennis Club at Forest Hills, September 14. But Jack Kramer won his second straight U.S. singles championship and acclaim as the top player in the world.

Kramer, who already owned the Wimbledon singles and U.S. doubles (with Ted Schroeder) titles, figured to be a heavy favorite over the 31-year-old Parker, who had played a grueling three-hour semifinal match the previous day against John Bromwich. But Parker changed that thinking with an inventive slow-down strategy that helped him build a shocking two-set advantage.

Kramer seemed baffled by the drop shots, lobs, floaters and other off-speed deliveries Parker threw at him in the early going. But he finally adjusted and took control with his vaunted power game. When all was said and done, Kramer owned a 4-6, 2-6, 6-1, 6-0, 6-3

victory and Parker owned the respect of the fans, who gave him a long, thunderous ovation.

In the women's final, Louise Brough defeated Wimbledon champion Margaret Osborne, 8-6, 4-6, 6-1, and captured her first major championship.

*Jack Kramer, winner of two straight U.S. singles championships.*

## Worsham edges Snead

Lew Worsham sank a 2½-foot putt on the 18th green during a June 14 playoff round with Sam Snead to win the U.S. Open golf title at St. Louis Country Club. Snead, a colorful Virginian and reigning British Open champion, had missed a putt of similar length moments earlier, setting Worsham up for the kill.

The loss was especially bitter for Snead, who had dropped a dramatic 15-foot birdie putt on the same hole in Sunday's final round to force a tie at 282. The golfers remained tied through 17 holes on Monday and both faced short putts for par. But when Snead stepped up to his ball, Worsham called for a measurement. Snead was ruled away and, his concentration broken momentarily, missed the putt badly. Worsham didn't and captured the $2,500 first prize.

Of special significance to this tournament was a single camera stationed behind the 18th green that fed station KSD-TV and 600 television sets in St. Louis. A harbinger, perhaps, of things to come?

# Big-play Cardinals overcome Eagles for title

The resourceful Chicago Cardinals used one big play in each quarter to fashion a 28-21 victory over the Philadelphia Eagles in the December 28 National Football League championship game held at Chicago's Comiskey Park.

The Cardinals did not move the ball as steadily as the Eagles, but they did move with flair. Elmer Angsman twice galloped for 70-yard runs (in the second and fourth quarters) while Charley Trippi scored on a 44-yard first-quarter run and a 75-yard third-quarter punt return.

Those four long-gainers more than offset the excellent passing of Philadelphia quarterback Tommy Thompson, who completed 27 of 44 passes for 297 yards and a touchdown. Thompson surpassed the championship-game records for attempts and completions set by Sammy Baugh in 1937.

The title-game appearance was the first for both teams since two-conference scheduling began in 1933. The Eagles qualified by beating Pittsburgh in a playoff after the teams tied for the Eastern Conference title with 8-4 marks.

# Yankees survive Dodger heroics

*Cookie Lavagetto is escorted from the field by police and a Dodger teammate after breaking up Floyd Bevens' no-hit attempt in the ninth inning of Game 4 and giving Brooklyn a come-from-behind World Series victory over the Yankees.*

*Dodger left fielder Al Gionfriddo makes his game-saving catch in Game 6 of the World Series against Joe DiMaggio and the Yankees.*

History will show that the New York Yankees prevailed in a hotly contested seven-game World Series against Brooklyn. But it was the Dodgers who cornered the Series market on heroics.

Trailing 2-1 in games and 2-1 with two out in the ninth inning of Game 4, the Dodgers gained new life when pinch-hitter Cookie Lavagetto hit a two-run double off the right-field wall at Ebbets Field. Lavagetto's blow ruined Floyd Bevens' bid for the first no-hitter in World Series history and provided Brooklyn with an unlikely 3-2 victory.

The Dodgers were at it again in Game 6, trailing three games to two but holding a precarious 8-5 lead in the bottom of the sixth with two Yankees on base and Joe DiMaggio at the plate. The Yankee Clipper slammed a Joe Hatten pitch toward the left-field bullpen and it appeared the game would be tied. But Dodger left fielder Al Gionfriddo, inserted moments earlier for defensive purposes, raced to the fence and made an improbable, twisting catch, robbing DiMaggio of a home run and preserving an 8-6 victory.

There was no stopping the Yankee express, however. The Bronx Bombers used the outstanding relief pitching of Joe Page to win 5-2 in Game 7 and claim their 11th World Series championship.

# Columbia ends long Army streak

David slayed Goliath again, October 25, but this time the battle took place at Baker Field in New York. Columbia 21, Army 20. The Lions' unlikely comeback victory (they trailed 20-7 at halftime) ended Army's 32-game unbeaten streak and gave the Cadets an early exit from the race for a national championship.

Much of Army's misfortune could be traced to Columbia's Bill Swiacki, whose eight receptions included a 28-yard fourth-quarter touchdown and a 36-yarder setting up Columbia's winning TD on the Army 3-yard line. When Lou Kusserow ran over for the score and Ventan Yablonski kicked the extra point, Army trailed for the first time since October 12, 1946.

That loss took the steam out of an Army team that was trying to adjust to life without its vaunted backfield of Glenn Davis, Doc Blanchard and Arnold Tucker. And it opened the door for Notre Dame and Michigan to wage a valiant battle for the Associated Press' No. 1 ranking.

The Irish finally won that honor, compiling a 9-0 record and finishing atop the AP poll for the second straight year. Michigan also finished 9-0 but had to settle for second.

# 1948

## Kentucky, Bills win

New York basketball fans who watched the finals of the NIT and NCAA Tournament on March 17 and 23 at Madison Square Garden were convinced of one thing—St. Louis University and Kentucky are the best teams in the country.

The Billikens, champions of the Missouri Valley Conference, rolled to a 65-52 victory over New York University behind the 24-point effort of Ed Macauley in the NIT and Kentucky had an even easier time with Baylor in the NCAA, cruising to a 58-42 victory and lifting its final record to 36-3.

St. Louis Coach Ed Hickey played his third-stringers for the last five minutes of the Bills' game against NYU and Kentucky Coach Adolph Rupp removed his Fabulous Five—center Alex Groza, forwards Wallace (Wah Wah) Jones and Cliff Barker and guards Ralph Beard and Ken Rollins—midway through the fourth quarter.

Macauley was named outstanding player in the NIT while Groza earned that honor in the NCAA Tournament.

---

*Ed Macauley was the big gun in St. Louis' run to the NIT championship at Madison Square Garden.*

## Blake's ankle injury breaks up "Punch Line"

The successful career of Montreal left winger Hector (Toe) Blake came to a crashing halt, January 11, when the veteran suffered a double fracture of his ankle while being checked into the boards by New York Ranger Bill Juzda. Canadiens fans also will mourn the passing of Montreal's deadly "Punch Line," which featured Blake, center Elmer Lach and Maurice (Rocket) Richard.

Blake won the Art Ross Trophy as the National Hockey League's leading scorer and the Hart Trophy as the NHL's most valuable player to his team after the 1938-39 season. He teamed with Lach starting in 1940 and Richard during the 1942-43 season, at which time the famed "Punch Line" was born.

Lach captured two scoring titles and won the Hart in 1944-45. Richard became the first player to score 50 goals in a season in 1944-45 and won the Hart in 1946-47. All three were regular NHL All-Stars.

*Montreal's famed Punch Line featured (left to right) Maurice (Rocket) Richard, Elmer Lach and Hector (Toe) Blake.*

## A near-perfect ending

It was a battle of unbeatens when fourth-ranked Penn State (9-0) and third-ranked Southern Methodist University (9-0-1) squared off in the New Year's Day Cotton Bowl classic in Dallas. And 60 minutes of football merely confirmed what everybody already suspected—this was a perfect matchup.

It didn't appear that way at first, however, as SMU star Doak Walker threw a first-quarter touchdown pass to Paul Page and then ran three yards himself for a second-quarter TD. With halftime approaching, the Mustangs held a comfortable 13-0 advantage.

But the Nittany Lions struck 18 seconds before intermission when Elwood Petchel fired a 37-yard scoring strike to Larry Cooney. Petchel connected again, this time on a four-yarder to Wally Triplett late in the third period, and the game was tied—both teams having missed a key extra point.

It was all defense the rest of the way and the 47,000 fans in attendance had to settle for a 13-13 non-verdict—and two undefeated teams.

# Citation wins Crown

Calumet Farm's Citation ran away with the June 12 Belmont Stakes and became the seventh horse in racing history to win the Kentucky Derby, Preakness Stakes and Belmont in the same year. The victory also enabled Eddie Arcaro to become the first jockey ever to ride two Triple Crown winners.

The rest of the field was overmatched as Citation began pulling away on the backstretch and continued to increase his lead right up to the finish line. Even without being pushed, Citation tied the track record (2:28⅕) and roared to a six-length victory—his 18th in 20 career races.

"He's the greatest horse I've ever seen," said Arcaro, who now has ridden four Belmont victors, including Whirlaway, Calumet Farm's other Triple Crown winner, in 1941. "Maybe I shouldn't have let him win by so much, but I couldn't take any chances for that kind of money."

The victory was worth $77,700 to Calumet Farm. Second place went to Better Self with Vulcan's Forge third.

*Triple Crowners Citation and jockey Eddie Arcaro enjoy life in the winner's circle after their victory in the Kentucky Derby.*

# Toronto sweeps aside Red Wings

Harry Watson and Ted Kennedy scored two goals apiece and the Toronto Maple Leafs overpowered the Detroit Red Wings, 7-2, April 14, for a convincing four-game sweep of their Stanley Cup final series.

The Leafs, who beat Montreal in a six-game Cup final last year, were never really threatened in posting 5-3, 4-2, 2-0 and 7-2 victories over the outgunned Red Wings. Watson, a 21-goal scorer during the regular season, connected five times in the series against Detroit.

*Toronto captain Syl Apps and Coach Hap Day admire the Stanley Cup after the Maple Leafs' four-game sweep of Detroit.*

Also getting in on the fun in Game 4 was veteran center Syl Apps, who scored a goal in his final National Hockey League game. Toronto's final two victories were recorded on Detroit ice.

# Hogan wins 1st Open

Ben Hogan carved up the Riviera Country Club course in Los Angeles with a 72-hole record 276 and finally broke through for his first U.S. Open golf championship on June 12. Jimmy Demaret at 278 and Jim Turnesa at 280 also finished under the previous Open record of 281.

But this tournament belonged to the 135-pound Hogan, who fired a 68 and 69 over the lengthy layout during his Saturday rounds and became the first golfer to win the Open and the PGA Championship in the same year since Gene Sarazen accomplished the feat in 1922. The 7,020-yard Riviera is the longest course ever used in the Open and it suited Hogan's game just fine.

Demaret matched Hogan's 68-69 finish, but could never pull closer than the final two strokes. Hogan made the final-round turn in 33 and slipped only once coming home—a bogey on the 15th.

The victory was worth $2,000 to Hogan.

# 1948

## The London Olympics

The taste of war was still bitter in the mouths of the British when London was invaded in July and August by a different kind of force—some 6,000 athletes from 59 countries to compete in the summer Olympic Games. The British proved to be excellent hosts under difficult circumstances and the Games went off smoothly, even though rain plagued several of the track and field events.

The big winner was the United States, which ran off with 84 medals and far outdistanced its closest competitor. The American men were especially efficient in the swimming program, where they swept everything, and track and field, where they won 11 of the 24 events. The men's basketball team, featuring 7-foot Bob Kurland and five starters from the University of Kentucky, won

Olympic decathlon champion Bob Mathias clearing the bar on the pole vault.

easily, defeating France, 65-21, in the final.

The American highlights of the track and field competition were Harrison Dillard's major

upset victory in the 100-meter dash and the decathlon victory by 17-year-old wonder boy Bob Mathias, who compiled 7,139 points.

## Yankee slugger Ruth dies of cancer

A saddened nation paused, August 16, to digest the passing of one of its greatest heroes. Yankee slugger Babe Ruth, king of the baseball world during his home run-hitting heyday in the 1920s and early '30s, died after a long battle with throat cancer at New York's Memorial Hospital.

Ruth, who set an incredible 54 major league records and 10 additional American League marks during his 22-year big-

Crowds line the streets of New York City as the casket bearing the body of Babe Ruth arrives at St. Patrick's Cathedral for funeral services.

league career, had been waging an intense battle against the cancer for two years. He died in his sleep at 8 p.m. with his family at his bedside, including wife Claire and his two adopted

daughters—Mrs. Daniel Sullivan and Mrs. Richard Flanders.

Notes and statements of condolence began pouring in immediately, from statesmen like President Harry Truman and

former President Herbert Hoover to baseball officials and former friends and teammates.

Ruth's two most famous records were the 60 home runs he hit in 1927 and his career total of 714 homers. Both of those marks should stand for a long time.

## NBA is growing by leaps and bounds

With one big strategic swoop, Basketball Association of America Commissioner Maurice Podoloff increased his league's chances for survival while cutting the heart out of the rival National Basketball League.

No sooner had the Baltimore Bullets captured the BAA's second championship on April 21

than Podoloff began working on getting the NBL's four best teams to jump leagues. He had the largest cities and best arenas they needed. They had the star-quality players Podoloff needed.

When the Minneapolis Lakers, Rochester Royals, Fort Wayne Pistons and Indianapolis Kautskys agreed to jump

during the summer, the BAA became a strong 12-team circuit with such new players as George Mikan, Jim Pollard, Bob Davies and Arnie Risen.

As if losing its four best teams wasn't enough, two other NBL franchises, Toledo and Flint, folded and Commissioner Piggy Lambert resigned because of ill health.

**JUL:** Chicago White Sox outfielder Pat Seerey became the fifth major league player to hit four home runs in one game, his fourth providing the winning run in an 11-inning 12-11 victory over the Philadelphia A's.

**SEP:** Some numbers to digest: Bob Crues hit 69 home runs, drove in 254 runs and batted .404 for Amarillo of the West Texas-New Mexico League.

**SEP:** Pancho Gonzales, a 20-year-old Californian, defeated South African Eric Sturgess, 6-2, 6-3, 14-12, in the U.S. singles final at Forest Hills.

**NOV:** Chicago played host to the second annual NHL All-Star Game and defending-champion Toronto lost for the second year in a row, falling 3-1 to a select team of stars.

**NOV:** An NHL-record 10 major penalties were called when the Toronto Maple Leafs brawled their way to a 2-0 victory over the Canadiens at Montreal.

**DEC:** Cleveland capped its perfect 15-0 season with a 49-7 victory over the Buffalo Bills in the All-America Football Conference championship game at Cleveland's Municipal Stadium.

# Indians go on warpath

First the Cleveland Indians dashed hopes for an all-Boston World Series by beating the Red Sox in a one-game American League pennant playoff. Then they cruised past the National League's Braves in a six-game World Series that ended, October 11, with a 4-3 victory.

Player-manager Lou Boudreau took matters into his own hands against the Red Sox in the October 4 playoff, belting two home runs and a pair of singles in the Indians' 8-3 victory at Fenway Park. Then he turned to his talented pitching staff for the World Series.

Even with ace Bob Feller losing two games (he dropped a 1-0 decision to Johnny Sain in the opener and got battered around in an 11-5 loss in Game 5), the Indians controlled the Braves' offense. Bob Lemon won twice and allowed only three earned runs, rookie lefthander Gene Bearden threw a Game 3 shutout and Steve Gromek outdueled Sain, 2-1, in Game 4.

The Series appearance was Cleveland's first since 1920.

*Manager Lou Boudreau waves to the crowd (left) as he is driven through the streets of Cleveland along with his wife and team Owner Bill Veeck after the Indians' World Series triumph over the Boston Braves.*

# Eagles get revenge, soar to NFL title

It was a rematch of the 1947 National Football League championship game between the Chicago Cardinals and Philadelphia Eagles—with a twist. The city of Philadelphia was pelted by a blizzard on the morning of December 19, and the Shibe Park field turned into a white mass of ice and snow.

With 36,309 brave fans looking on, it became apparent early that ball control and patience would be the order of the day. Vision was limited to a few yards, hands were numb, fingers were frostbitten and feet were frozen.

Eagles quarterback Tommy Thompson went for broke early and connected with Jack Ferrante on a 65-yard touchdown pass. But the play was called back on an offside penalty and Thompson played it close to the vest the rest of the way.

His patience paid dividends in the third quarter when Eagles lineman Bucko Kilroy recovered a fumble at the Chicago 17. Three plays later, Steve Van Buren, the NFL's leading rusher for the second straight year, pounded over from the 5 and the Eagles had the only score they would need.

And Philadelphia had its first-ever NFL championship—and sweet revenge.

*Patience paid off for the Philadelphia Eagles and quarterback Tommy Thompson.*

# Michigan finishes No.1

The Michigan Wolverines turned the tables on Notre Dame and walked away with a national championship, courtesy of the Associated Press' final college football poll.

Both the Fighting Irish and Wolverines finished the season undefeated, as they had in 1947 when Notre Dame was given the final top ranking. But the Irish struggled in their home opener against Purdue, winning 28-27, and had to rally in the last half minute of the game to tie Southern California in their season finale.

The Wolverines, however, won all nine of their games by at least a touchdown and polished off Purdue, 40-0. Capping this success story was the selection of Michigan's Bennie Oosterbaan as Coach of the Year by the American Football Coaches Association. Oosterbaan becomes the second straight Michigan coach to win the award. Fritz Crisler was honored last year.

# 1949

## Champ Louis retires

Joe Louis, boxing's Brown Bomber, submitted a letter of resignation to National Boxing Association Commissioner Abe J. Greene, March 1, relinquishing the heavyweight title he had held since June 22, 1937. Louis' championship reign, which covered 11 years, 8 months and included 25 successful defenses, was the division's longest.

The Alabama-born Louis, who now plans to promote the sport, said in his letter, "I am certain you know how sorry I must be to let the championship go this way. I have held it for a long time and I won it in the ring. I expected to lose it the same way I won it. This is the way champions should be made.

"However, things have developed so that I think I ought to stick to the decision to retire that I made some time ago."

Louis also submitted a follow-up letter requesting permission to stage a title fight between Ezzard Charles and Jersey Joe Walcott, the division's top contenders. Greene gave him a go-ahead for June.

## Kentucky wins again

Alex Groza scored 25 points and a stingy Kentucky defense held Oklahoma A&M scoreless for an 8½-minute stretch of the second half as the Wildcats rolled to a 46-36 victory, March 26, and claimed their second consecutive NCAA Tournament title.

The victory in Seattle climaxed an outstanding 32-2 season in which Adolph Rupp's Wildcats methodically staked their claim as the No. 1 college team in the nation. The Associated Press, introducing its nationwide basketball poll, agreed and crowned Kentucky as undisputed national champion.

If there was any doubt going into the NCAA final, it was quickly removed by Kentucky's domination of the second-ranked Aggies (23-5). Coach Henry Iba's defensive standout, 6-foot-7 Bob Harris, was no match for the quicker Groza and fouled out early in the second half.

*Kentucky Coach Adolph Rupp and star player Alex Groza, the principals behind the Wildcats' two straight NCAA Tournament victories.*

## Hogan's future cloudy after car accident

Doctors who performed a two-hour abdominal operation on golf great Ben Hogan, tying off the principal blood vessels in his legs, now question whether the two-time PGA champion and 1948 U.S. Open winner will ever walk again. The operation was performed after complications arose while Hogan was recovering from a February 2 automobile accident.

Hogan, who had opened the 1949 season with victories in the Crosby and Long Beach Open tournaments, was driving home to Fort Worth, Tex., after losing a playoff to Jimmy Demaret in the Phoenix Open. Ben and wife Valerie were driving near the small town of Van Horn when their Cadillac collided with a Greyhound bus that was attempting to pass a truck. Hogan threw himself across Valerie, trying to shield her from the impact, and thus saved his own life. The force of the blow drove the steering column through the driver's seat.

Hogan suffered a fractured pelvis, broken collar bone, broken rib, broken ankle and damage to his left knee. The abdominal operation was required when blood clots began to form and his condition became serious.

*Golfer Ben Hogan relaxes in the sunshine outside a Dallas hospital, two months after his near-fatal car accident.*

# Masters champ Snead adds PGA triumph

Slammin' Sammy Snead, playing before a strongly partisan crowd in his home state of Virginia, defeated Johnny Palmer of North Carolina, 3 and 2, in the May 31 final of the PGA Championship at the Hermitage Country Club in Richmond. The victory makes Snead the first golfer ever to win the PGA and Masters in the same year.

Snead and Palmer were tied after the 18-hole morning round, but the 37-year-old veteran took control quickly in the afternoon when he birdied the fourth, sixth and seventh holes. Snead added a birdie 2 at the 13th and closed out his 30-year-old opponent on the 34th green.

The victory, Snead's third of the year, was worth $3,500 and increased his tour-leading winnings for the year to $12,610. Snead, who recorded a three-stroke victory in the Masters in April, has now won four major titles—two PGA Championships, one British Open and one Masters.

*Double major winner Slammin' Sammy Snead.*

# Charles defeats Walcott for title

Ezzard Charles scored a unanimous 15-round decision over Jersey Joe Walcott on June 22, before 25,932 fight fans at Chicago's Comiskey Park, staking partial claim to the heavyweight title vacated by Joe Louis in March.

The 28-year-old Charles is now heavyweight champion according to the National Boxing Association. But the New York State Athletic Commission preferred a series of elimination bouts.

Neither fighter seemed willing to take control, preferring to stay back and play it cautiously. Part of the reason was that Charles hurt his left hand in the fourth round and Walcott injured his right hand in the third. As a result, there were no knockdowns or serious cuts and the fight was lacking in drama and excitement.

# Underdog Toronto clips Detroit's Wings

Never mind that the Toronto Maple Leafs had struggled to a 22-25-13 regular-season record and a disappointing fourth-place finish. Never mind that the Detroit Red Wings were National Hockey League champions after a 34-19-7 campaign. This was playoff hockey, and the two-time defending champion Leafs were on a roll.

After disposing of Boston in a five-game preliminary series, Toronto faced off against Detroit and began rolling threes, as in 3-2, 3-1, 3-1, 3-1 victories that produced their second straight Cup final sweep of the Red Wings. Walter Broda was outstanding throughout the series in goal and the offensive highlight was Sid Smith's Game 2 hat trick.

Toronto's victory marked the first time an NHL team had ever won three straight titles and the first time a fourth-place club had ever won the Stanley Cup. Clarence (Happy) Day also claimed a record as the first coach to win three consecutive championships.

## ★ SPORTS WATCH ★

**JAN:** Fourth-ranked California watched its perfect season go up in smoke as No. 7-ranked Northwestern pulled off a 20-14 Rose Bowl shocker.

**FEB:** Joe DiMaggio became baseball's first six-figure man when he signed a $100,000 contract with the New York Yankees.

**FEB:** Willie Pep, world featherweight champion from 1942 to '48, regained his lost crown with a unanimous 15-round decision over Sandy Saddler at New York's Madison Square Garden.

**APR:** Prior to the season opener at Yankee Stadium, team officials unveiled a center-field monument to Babe Ruth and plaques honoring Lou Gehrig and Miller Huggins.

**JUN:** NHL officials, attending their annual meeting in Montreal, agreed to increase the 1949-50 schedule from 60 to 70 games.

**JUN:** Capot, a second-place finisher in the Kentucky Derby, went on to win the Preakness and Belmont Stakes, falling just short of becoming horse racing's ninth Triple Crown winner.

# A.L. wins "Star" war

The DiMaggio brothers, Boston's Dom and the Yankees' Joe, combined for four hits and four RBIs to lead the American League to a sloppy 11-7 victory over the National League in the June 12 All-Star Game at Brooklyn's Ebbets Field.

But the real story of this contest was the appearance of black players for the first time in the midsummer classic. Three Brooklyn Dodgers, Jackie Robinson, Roy Campanella and Don Newcombe, played for the Nationals while Cleveland's Larry Doby competed for the A.L. squad. Robinson, who broke the color barrier two years ago in the same park, was the only black to get a hit (a first-inning double). Newcombe pitched 2²/₃ innings, allowing two runs.

Five N.L. errors, two of which led to four unearned runs in the first inning, contributed greatly

*All-Star principals (left to right) Jackie Robinson of the Brooklyn Dodgers, Sid Gordon of the New York Giants and Joe DiMaggio of the New York Yankees.*

to the A.L.'s victory. So, too, did the one-hit pitching of Yankee Vic Raschi, who set down the N.L. over the last three innings to protect the 11-7 lead. St. Louis' Stan Musial and Pittsburgh's Ralph Kiner hit home runs in a losing cause.

# New NBA begins play

When the Anderson Packers swept past the Oshkosh All-Stars to win the 1948-49 National Basketball League championship, the down-but-not-out circuit began making plans for a new season. The NBL pulled off a life-saving coup by getting four graduating starters (Alex Groza, Ralph Beard, Wah Wah Jones and Cliff Barker) from the glamorous University of Kentucky

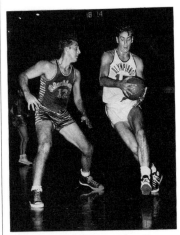

*Former Kentucky star Alex Groza (right) was the point producer for the Indianapolis Olympians, who joined the new NBA under a merger arrangement.*

team to turn professional as the heart of the new Indianapolis Olympians franchise. Kentucky won two straight NCAA Tournament titles and its four stars were members of the 1948 U.S. Olympic squad.

It was a master stroke and the Basketball Association of America immediately pressed for a merger. What emerged, August 3, was the new National Basketball Association, a bulky 17-team league that stretched from Boston to Denver. Ten teams were retained from the BAA, six NBL teams were accepted and Indianapolis was the one new entry.

Commissioner Maurice Podoloff has set up a three-division format and, because of travel restrictions, has instituted an unbalanced schedule. Eastern and Central Division teams will play 68 games with Western Division clubs slated for 62. Inter-divisional matchups will be kept to a minimum.

Confusing, yes, but the bottom line is that the new NBA is unchallenged as the major professional circuit.

# Gonzales rallies to win second U.S. title

Pancho Gonzales overcame first-set adversity and a two-set deficit to pull off a dramatic 16-18, 2-6, 6-1, 6-2, 6-4 victory over Ted Schroeder and win his second straight U.S. singles championship before 13,000 excited center-court spectators at Forest Hills.

Gonzales and Schroeder, the reigning Wimbledon singles champion, battled for one hour and 13 minutes in the marathon opening set, the longest ever played in a championship final. The 21-year-old Gonzales served 17 aces in the set and had five chances to put his fellow Californian away. But Schroeder would not go down and eventually pulled off a first-set victory.

The disappointment of that loss carried over and Gonzales bowed meekly in the second set before regaining his composure. But once refreshed, he began dominating with his rocket serves, blazing passing shots and confident volleys. The

tiring Schroeder proved to be no match for the youngster and could not stop the onslaught.

The women's singles title, considerably less dramatic, was captured for the second year in a row by Margaret Osborne-du Pont, who won in straight sets over Doris Hart. Du Pont scored a 6-4, 6-1 victory.

# Eagles overcome Rams, rule NFL again

The Philadelphia Eagles, unwilling to let little things like snow or rainstorms get them down, defeated the Los Angeles Rams on December 18, to claim their second straight National Football League championship in the first title game ever played on the West Coast.

The Eagles, who had defeated the Chicago Cardinals in a 1948 blizzard for their first title, performed their magic this time in the pouring rain. The 27,980 Los Angeles fans who braved the elements to watch their Rams' normally prolific passing attack instead witnessed a stingy Philadelphia defensive effort and the Eagles' opportunistic offense.

The only scoring occurred in the second quarter on a Tommy Thompson-to-Pete Pihos 31-yard pass and in the third period when defensive end Leo Skladany blocked a Los Angeles punt and returned it two yards for a touchdown.

Running back Steve Van Buren took care of the clock, snuffing out the Rams' chances by grinding out title-game records of 196 yards on 31 carries.

# NFL adds three AAFC teams

The end of the 4-year-old All-America Football Conference was announced, December 9, two days before the Cleveland Browns defeated the San Francisco 49ers, 21-7, in the league's final championship game. When the final gun saluted Cleveland's fourth straight title-game victory, the Browns, 49ers and Baltimore Colts officially became members of the National Football League.

The addition of those three clubs brings the NFL's membership to 13 teams. Coach Paul Brown's Cleveland club, which compiled a 47-4-3 four-year record behind such stars as Otto Graham, Mac Speedie, Marion Motley, Dante Lavelli, Dub Jones and Lou Groza, will join five NFL regulars in the six-team American Conference. The 49ers, with an overall record of 38-14-2 in the AAFC, will join the Colts and five NFL regulars in the seven-team National Conference.

The players from now-defunct AAFC teams will be placed into a pool and allocated around the league according to necessity. One important rule change accompanies the merger —all teams now will operate with free substitution.

*Quarterback Otto Graham, shown running the ball during a late 1940s All-America Football Conference game against the New York Yankees, was the foundation of the Cleveland Browns' dynasty.*

# Irish win national title

The decade closed with Notre Dame capturing its third national college football championship in four years.

Notre Dame's only real scare came in its final game against unranked Southern Methodist. Notre Dame owned a 13-0 halftime lead, but the Mustangs roared back behind halfback Kyle Rote and tied the game at 20-20 in the fourth quarter. Notre Dame responded with a 57-yard game-winning drive for a 27-20 victory.

There were plenty of challengers for the top spot in the final Associated Press poll. Bud Wilkinson's Oklahoma team finished No. 2 with a 10-0 record, California matched that mark and was ranked No. 3 and 9-0 Army ranked fourth.

One of the more interesting stories was turned in by College of the Pacific, which finished 11-0 and No. 10. With 5-foot-8 quarterback Eddie LeBaron directing traffic, Pacific outscored its opponent, 575-66.

*Notre Dame Coach Frank Leahy, undefeated since his return from service in World War II.*

# THE 1950s

*The fuse had been lit and a technological explosion was about to open the door to revolutionary change, a blast that would redefine the boundaries and values of a continent in transition.*

St. Louis slugger Stan Musial.

More durable and efficient automobiles would carry a more mobile society to the suburbs, improved air travel would help trigger a population shift to the west and more sophisticated methods of communication would link the two coasts.

The *most sophisticated* of those methods was television. The impact of the little tube already was being felt by North American sports as the new decade dawned and those with foresight were beginning to grasp the tremendous power this innovation someday would wield. But first, some lessons would have to be learned.

Television equipment and techniques were crude and limiting and single-camera telecasting dictated that programmers gravitate to the tight, easy-to-follow action of arena sports such as boxing and wrestling. But that didn't stop them from experimenting with the more active games, a courtship that would blossom into full commitment and marriage in the 1960s.

That marriage would mean money—lots of money. And with that prospect just around the corner, sports officials from both the professional and amateur ranks began jockeying for position. That new infatuation with television quickly exposed some distasteful realities.

With the exodus to the suburbs and the growth of major

Montreal Canadiens' star Jean Beliveau.

## ROLL OF HONOR

### AUTO RACING

#### INDIANAPOLIS 500

| Year | Winner | Speed |
|------|--------|-------|
| 1950 | Johnnie Parsons | 124.002 mph |
| 1951 | Lee Wallard | 126.244 mph |
| 1952 | Troy Ruttman | 128.922 mph |
| 1953 | Bill Vukovich | 128.740 mph |
| 1954 | Bill Vukovich | 130.840 mph |
| 1955 | Bob Sweikert | 128.209 mph |
| 1956 | Pat Flaherty | 128.490 mph |
| 1957 | Sam Hanks | 135.601 mph |
| 1958 | Jim Bryan | 133.791 mph |
| 1959 | Rodger Ward | 135.857 mph |

### GOLF

| MASTERS | | US OPEN | |
|------|--------|------|--------|
| Year | Winner | Year | Winner |
| 1950 | Jimmy Demaret | 1950 | Ben Hogan |
| 1951 | Ben Hogan | 1951 | Ben Hogan |
| 1952 | Sam Snead | 1952 | Julius Boros |
| 1953 | Ben Hogan | 1953 | Ben Hogan |
| 1954 | Sam Snead | 1954 | Ed Furgol |
| 1955 | Cary Middlecoff | 1955 | Jack Fleck |
| 1956 | Jack Burke Jr. | 1956 | Cary Middlecoff |
| 1957 | Doug Ford | 1957 | Dick Mayer |
| 1958 | Arnold Palmer | 1958 | Tommy Bolt |
| 1959 | Art Wall Jr. | 1959 | Billy Casper |

| PGA CHAMPIONSHIP | | US WOMEN'S OPEN | |
|------|--------|------|--------|
| Year | Winner | Year | Winner |
| 1950 | Chandler Harper | 1950 | Babe Zaharias |
| 1951 | Sam Snead | 1951 | Betsy Rawls |
| 1952 | Jim Turnesa | 1952 | Louise Suggs |
| 1953 | Walter Burkemo | 1953 | Betsy Rawls |
| 1954 | Chick Harbert | 1954 | Babe Zaharias |
| 1955 | Doug Ford | 1955 | Fay Crocker |
| 1956 | Jack Burke Jr. | 1956 | Kathy Cornelius |
| 1957 | Lionel Hebert | 1957 | Betsy Rawls |
| 1958 | Dow Finsterwald | 1958 | Mickey Wright |
| 1959 | Bob Rosburg | 1959 | Mickey Wright |

metropolises, sports officials began looking to the previously ignored but more fertile markets. *Fertile* as in *big*. The result was a rash of franchise shifts and talk of expansion—in search of that all-important bottom line.

The official linking of sports to big business was made in 1957, when the New York Giants and Brooklyn Dodgers, two of the most glamorous and beloved franchises in baseball, jolted their adoring fans with the announcements they were moving to the West Coast. Those moves followed on the heels of the Boston Braves moving to Milwaukee, the St. Louis Browns moving to Baltimore and the Philadelphia Athletics moving to Kansas City. Before Milwaukee, baseball had not seen a franchise shift in 50 years.

The decade was not without its lively moments and major developments. The 24-second clock speeded up pro basketball and made it a more attractive experience, the new American Football League arrived in 1959 to challenge the NFL and the Soviet Union sent its first Olympic team to the 1952 Games at Helsinki.

It also was a decade of domination. The Yankees captured six World Series in baseball, the Cleveland Browns won seven division titles and three NFL championships, the Montreal Canadiens won five Stanley Cups, the Minneapolis Lakers captured four NBA titles, and two powerful college teams, football's Oklahoma Sooners and basketball's San Francisco Dons, compiled record winning streaks of 47 and 60 games, respectively.

The most dramatic moment, however, was provided by baseball's Bobby Thomson, who won the 1951 National League pennant for the New York Giants with his "Shot Heard 'Round the World."

*Boxer Rocky Marciano.*

## HORSE RACING

### KENTUCKY DERBY

| Year | Winner | Jockey |
|------|--------|--------|
| 1950 | Middleground | William Boland |
| 1951 | Count Turf | Conn McCreary |
| 1952 | Hill Gail | Eddie Arcaro |
| 1953 | Dark Star | Hank Moreno |
| 1954 | Determine | Raymond York |
| 1955 | Swaps | Bill Shoemaker |
| 1956 | Needles | David Erb |
| 1957 | Iron Liege | Bill Hartack |
| 1958 | Tim Tam | Ismael Valenzuela |
| 1959 | Tomy Lee | Bill Shoemaker |

### PREAKNESS STAKES

| Year | Winner | Jockey |
|------|--------|--------|
| 1950 | Hill Prince | Eddie Arcaro |
| 1951 | Bold | Eddie Arcaro |
| 1952 | Blue Man | Conn McCreary |
| 1953 | Native Dancer | Eric Guerin |
| 1954 | Hasty Road | Johnny Adams |
| 1955 | Nashua | Eddie Arcaro |
| 1956 | Fabius | Bill Hartack |
| 1957 | Bold Ruler | Eddie Arcaro |
| 1958 | Tim Tam | Ismael Valenzuela |
| 1959 | Royal Orbit | William Harmatz |

### BELMONT STAKES

| Year | Winner | Jockey |
|------|--------|--------|
| 1950 | Middleground | William Boland |
| 1951 | Counterpoint | David Gorman |
| 1952 | One Count | Eddie Arcaro |
| 1953 | Native Dancer | Eric Guerin |
| 1954 | High Gun | Eric Guerin |
| 1955 | Nashua | Eddie Arcaro |
| 1956 | Needles | David Erb |
| 1957 | Gallant Man | Bill Shoemaker |
| 1958 | Cavan | Pete Anderson |
| 1959 | Sword Dancer | Bill Shoemaker |

## BASEBALL

### WORLD SERIES

| Year | Winner | Pennant Winner (series score) |
|------|--------|-------------------------------|
| 1950 | New York Yankees | (Philadelphia Phillies, 4-0) |
| 1951 | New York Yankees | (New York Giants, 4-2) |
| 1952 | New York Yankees | (Brooklyn Dodgers, 4-3) |
| 1953 | New York Yankees | (Brooklyn Dodgers, 4-2) |
| 1954 | New York Giants | (Cleveland Indians, 4-0) |
| 1955 | Brooklyn Dodgers | (New York Yankees, 4-3) |
| 1956 | New York Yankees | (Brooklyn Dodgers, 4-3) |
| 1957 | Milwaukee Braves | (New York Yankees, 4-3) |
| 1958 | New York Yankees | (Milwaukee Braves, 4-3) |
| 1959 | Los Angeles Dodgers | (Chicago White Sox, 4-2) |

## BASKETBALL

### NBA CHAMPIONSHIP

| Year | Winner | Finalist (series score) |
|------|--------|-------------------------|
| 1950-51 | Rochester Royals | (New York Knicks, 4-3) |
| 1951-52 | Minneapolis Lakers | (New York Knicks, 4-3) |
| 1952-53 | Minneapolis Lakers | (New York Knicks, 4-1) |
| 1953-54 | Minneapolis Lakers | (Syracuse Nationals, 4-3) |
| 1954-55 | Syracuse Nationals | (Fort Wayne Pistons, 4-3) |
| 1955-56 | Philadelphia Warriors | (Fort Wayne Pistons, 4-1) |
| 1956-57 | Boston Celtics | (St. Louis Hawks, 4-3) |
| 1957-58 | St. Louis Hawks | (Boston Celtics, 4-2) |
| 1958-59 | Boston Celtics | (Minneapolis Lakers, 4-0) |
| 1959-60 | Boston Celtics | (St. Louis Hawks, 4-3) |

### NCAA TOURNAMENT FINAL

| Year | Winner | Finalist (score) |
|------|--------|------------------|
| 1950 | CCNY | (Bradley, 71-68) |
| 1951 | Kentucky | (Kansas State, 68-58) |
| 1952 | Kansas | (St. John's, 80-63) |
| 1953 | Indiana | (Kansas, 69-68) |
| 1954 | La Salle | (Bradley, 92-76) |
| 1955 | San Francisco | (La Salle, 77-63) |
| 1956 | San Francisco | (Iowa, 83-71) |
| 1957 | North Carolina | (Kansas, 54-53, 3 OT) |
| 1958 | Kentucky | (Seattle, 84-72) |
| 1959 | California | (West Virginia, 71-70) |

## FOOTBALL

### NFL CHAMPIONSHIP

| Year | Winner | Finalist (score) |
|------|--------|------------------|
| 1950 | Cleveland Browns | (Los Angeles Rams, 30-28) |
| 1951 | Los Angeles Rams | (Cleveland Browns, 24-17) |
| 1952 | Detroit Lions | (Cleveland Browns, 17-7) |
| 1953 | Detroit Lions | (Cleveland Browns, 17-16) |
| 1954 | Cleveland Browns | (Detroit Lions, 56-10) |
| 1955 | Cleveland Browns | (Los Angeles Rams, 38-14) |
| 1956 | New York Giants | (Chicago Bears, 47-7) |
| 1957 | Detroit Lions | (Cleveland Browns, 59-14) |
| 1958 | Baltimore Colts | (New York Giants, 23-17 OT) |
| 1959 | Baltimore Colts | (New York Giants, 31-16) |

## HOCKEY

### STANLEY CUP

| Year | Champion | Finalist (series score) |
|------|----------|-------------------------|
| 1950-51 | Toronto Maple Leafs | (Montreal Canadiens, 4-1) |
| 1951-52 | Detroit Red Wings | (Montreal Canadiens, 4-0) |
| 1952-53 | Montreal Canadiens | (Boston Bruins, 4-1) |
| 1953-54 | Detroit Red Wings | (Montreal Canadiens, 4-3) |
| 1954-55 | Detroit Red Wings | (Montreal Canadiens, 4-3) |
| 1955-56 | Montreal Canadiens | (Detroit Red Wings, 4-1) |
| 1956-57 | Montreal Canadiens | (Boston Bruins, 4-1) |
| 1957-58 | Montreal Canadiens | (Boston Bruins, 4-2) |
| 1958-59 | Montreal Canadiens | (Toronto Maple Leafs, 4-1) |
| 1959-60 | Montreal Canadiens | (Toronto Maple Leafs, 4-0) |

## TENNIS

### US OPEN

| Year | Men's Winner | Women's Winner |
|------|--------------|----------------|
| 1950 | Arthur Larsen | Margaret Osborne-du Pont |
| 1951 | Frank Sedgman | Maureen Connolly |
| 1952 | Frank Sedgman | Maureen Connolly |
| 1953 | Tony Trabert | Maureen Connolly |
| 1954 | Vic Seixas | Doris Hart |
| 1955 | Tony Trabert | Doris Hart |
| 1956 | Ken Rosewall | Shirley Fry |
| 1957 | Mal Anderson | Althea Gibson |
| 1958 | Ashley Cooper | Althea Gibson |
| 1959 | Neale Fraser | Maria Bueno |

# 1950

## CCNY doubles pleasure

City College of New York, unranked and almost bypassed for postseason play, defeated No. 1-ranked Bradley for the second time in 10 days and pulled off an incredible double victory by winning both the National Invitation Tournament and NCAA Tournament in the same season.

The Beavers' 71-68 victory over Bradley in the NCAA final

### "SPORTS TALK"

*"I don't think they have been lucky and I don't think they've just been hot. They simply found themselves. And if they stay hale and hearty, I think we can beat anybody and that includes Bradley again."*

**NAT HOLMAN**
City College of New York Coach

at New York's Madison Square Garden culminated an improbable string of upsets that included victories over defending champion San Francisco, No. 3-ranked Kentucky, Duquesne and Bradley in the NIT and No. 2 Ohio State, No. 5 North Carolina State and Bradley again in the NCAA.

CCNY earned their NIT bid by sweeping the so-called "subway series" among metropolitan New York schools. They qualified for the NCAA because they advanced farther in the NIT than any other New York team. Once in, there was no stopping Nat Holman's charges.

Featuring a lineup of 6-foot-4 senior Irwin Dambrot and sophomores Floyd Layne, Al Roth, Ed Warner and Ed Roman, CCNY swept through the NIT field and surprised Bradley with a 69-61 victory. Things got a little tighter in the

*CCNY's Norm Mager (33) and Floyd Layne (3) battle North Carolina State's Sam Razino during semifinal action in the NCAA Final Four.*

NCAA with the Beavers recording a one-point decision over Ohio State and a five-point victory over N.C. State.

But they were cruising with a 58-47 lead midway through the second half of the title game against Bradley when disaster almost struck. The Beavers wilted when the Braves began pressing man-to-man and sud-

denly their lead was one, 69-68. Bradley had a chance to take the lead in the closing seconds, but Dambrot stole the ball from Gene Melchiorre and fed Norm Mager downcourt for the clinching basket.

The seven tournament victories lifted CCNY's final record to 24-5 while Bradley ended its season at 32-5.

## Williams gets rich; Feller takes pay cut

Boston slugger Ted Williams, the American League's Most Valuable Player last season, became baseball's highest-paid player, February 7, when he signed a contract for $125,000. But Cleveland ace righthander Bob Feller headed the other direction on January 18, taking a $20,000 pay cut—at his own suggestion.

Williams, who won the A.L. Triple Crown in both 1942 and '47 by leading the league in batting average, home runs and runs batted in, just missed doing it again last season when he hit

.343 with 43 homers and 159 RBIs. He led in home runs and tied with teammate Vern Stephens for the RBI lead, but Detroit's George Kell edged Williams by .0002 for the batting title.

Feller, a five-time 20-game winner and the author of two no-hitters, was not satisfied with what he considered a lackluster 1949 season (a 15-14 record and 3.75 earned-run average) and told Cleveland officials that he deserved to take a cut in his $65,000 salary. The Indians complied.

*Cleveland's ace righthander Bob Feller.*

# Lakers win NBA title

George Mikan, dominating the middle with his usual force, scored 40 points, April 23, and Jim Pollard added 16 to lead Minneapolis to a 110-95 victory over Syracuse and a six-game win in the first championship series of the new National Basketball Association.

Mikan, who led the 17-team circuit with a 27.4-point average during the regular campaign, was constantly being worked over by the Syracuse big men during the title series but still managed to muscle his way to the basket. The play was intense throughout and the final game was marred by three fights.

The series concluded the NBA's first season following the NBL-BAA merger. Syracuse won the Eastern Division with a 51-13 record, Minneapolis and the Rochester Royals tied for the Central Division title at 51-17 and the Indianapolis Olympians, made up mostly of former University of Kentucky stars, won the Western Division with a 39-25 mark. Alex Groza of the Olympians finished second to Mikan with a 23.4-point average.

*Minneapolis Coach John Kundla gets a victory ride from big George Mikan as Slater Martin (left) and Jim Pollard (right) lend a hand after the Lakers' six-game victory over Syracuse in the first NBA championship series.*

# Red Wings win Cup

Pete Babando fired home a backhander 8:31 into the second overtime period, April 23, and Detroit escaped with a four games to three victory over the New York Rangers in the Stanley Cup finals.

The 4-3 home-ice final-game victory came only after the Red Wings had overcome an early 2-0 Rangers lead for the second straight night. The Rangers, fourth-place finishers during the regular season, had upset Montreal in five games and were within one game of winning the Cup by virtue of their inspired play in the first five games of the final series.

But the regular-season champs would not wilt and fought back for a 5-4 victory, April 22, and a 3-3 tie after regulation in Game 7. After a scoreless first overtime, Babando scored his second goal of the game off a faceoff just to the left of New York goalie Claude Rayner.

Detroit, winning its first Stanley Cup since 1943, played the series without high-scoring Gordie Howe, who was injured in a preliminary-round game.

# A stirring comeback

*Ben Hogan defied all odds and came back from a near-fatal automobile accident to win the U.S. Open.*

Ben Hogan, displaying the talent and determination that had made him the most feared golfer on the PGA tour prior to his February 1949 near-fatal car accident, shot a playoff-round 69 to defeat Lloyd Mangrum and George Fazio to win the U.S. Open at the Merion Golf Club in Ardmore, Pa.

Hogan's heartening and inspirational comeback was aided by a two-stroke penalty assessed against Mangrum on the 16th green during the playoff. Mangrum lifted his ball to blow away a bug, clearly a rule violation. But Hogan, leading by one stroke at the time, removed any doubt on the par three 17th when he rolled in a 50-foot birdie putt and clinched his four-stroke victory.

Hogan's biggest test had come on Saturday when he walked a double round for the first time since his January return to golf. The 36-hole tour did indeed prove a serious test for his aching legs and the Texan staggered over the six closing holes, blowing a three-stroke lead and tying Mangrum and Fazio at 287.

But he was in top form during the Sunday playoff and never faltered en route to earning the $4,000 first prize, winning his second U.S. Open title and reestablishing his position as the No. 1 golfer in the world.

# 1950

## JULY - DECEMBER

*National League All-Star Game heroes Ralph Kiner (left) and Red Schoendienst (right) with Manager Burt Shotton.*

## Late homer lifts N.L.

St. Louis Cardinals second baseman Red Schoendienst had watched the first 10 innings of the July 11 All-Star Game from the National League bench at Chicago's Comiskey Park. He did not take the field until the 11th when he replaced Brooklyn's Jackie Robinson defensively, and he did not step to the plate until the 14th, when he led off against Detroit lefthander Ted Gray.

But Schoendienst was not about to let an opportunity like this slip away. He promptly deposited a Gray pitch into the left-field seats and the N.L. had a 4-3 victory, snapping a four-game American League winning streak.

The Nationals had tied the score in the ninth when Pittsburgh slugger Ralph Kiner homered off Detroit's Art Houtteman. New York Giants curveballer Larry Jansen and Cincinnati's Ewell Blackwell were outstanding over the last eight innings for the N.L., while the Americans got a good effort from Yankee Allie Reynolds.

The victory reduced the A.L. lead in this series to 12-5.

## Du Pont wins again

It seems only right that Margaret Osborne-du Pont and Louise Brough are doubles partners, particularly when you consider how their careers have mirrored each other over the last four years.

It started in 1947 when du Pont won the women's singles title at Wimbledon and Brough captured the U.S. singles championship at Forest Hills. But over the next three years they traded roles, du Pont reigning at Forest Hills and Brough sweeping away all comers at Wimbledon.

Du Pont's latest victory occurred, September 5, at the West Side Tennis Club when she defeated Doris Hart, 6-3, 6-3. Another irony is that Hart, who had beaten du Pont twice and Brough three times in other tournaments this year, was the loser in four of the eight Wimbledon and U.S. finals won by this duo.

## Charles rocks Louis

*Heavyweight champion Ezzard Charles, after pounding Joe Louis in the former champ's comeback.*

Joe Louis, attempting to become the first boxer ever to win the heavyweight championship twice, paid a stiff price. The Brown Bomber, desperately needing money to pay his taxes, came out of retirement in the hopes of regaining the crown he had relinquished almost 17 months ago. His spirit was willing, but his flesh was weak.

Ezzard Charles pummeled the 36-year-old former champ into submission, battering his way to a unanimous 15-round decision on September 27, at New York's Yankee Stadium. Louis, far below the form that allowed him to hold the championship from 1937 to '49, was little more than a punching bag and his bloody, swollen face reflected that sad fact.

The only thing Charles did not do was put Louis down, although he came close in the 14th round. The loss was the second in Louis' career (he was knocked out by Max Schmeling in 1936) and the victory strengthened Charles' claim on the undisputed heavyweight championship.

# Sisler bombs Brooklyn

Center fielder Richie Ashburn threw out the potential winning run at the plate in the bottom of the ninth inning and Dick Sisler hit a dramatic three-run homer in the 10th to give the Philadelphia Phillies a 4-1 victory over Brooklyn and their first National League pennant in 35 years.

The October 1 game at Brooklyn's Ebbets Field was the culmination of an outstanding pennant race that had the Whiz Kids leading the Dodgers by one game with one to play. The Phillies' Robin Roberts, making his third start in five days, and Brooklyn's Don Newcombe both were looking for their 20th victories and an over-

capacity crowd of 35,073 was on hand to witness the proceedings. Nobody was disappointed.

The game was tied 1-1 through 8½ innings when the Dodgers put their first two men on base in the ninth. Duke Snider promptly singled to center, but Ashburn's clutch throw gunned down runner Cal Abrams trying to score from second. Roberts escaped further trouble and Newcombe faltered in the 10th.

The Phillies' bubble burst, however, when the New York Yankees swept them in the World Series, winning their second straight classic and 13th overall.

*Philadelphia's Dick Sisler gets a big welcome at home plate after hitting a three-run, pennant-winning home run against the Brooklyn Dodgers.*

*Cleveland Coach Paul Brown (wearing white scarf) leads a victory celebration after the Browns had won the NFL championship in their first try after moving over from the All-America Football Conference.*

# A streaky season

Call it the year of the streaks.

First Notre Dame, national champion in three of the last four years, had its 38-game unbeaten streak snapped, October 7, by Purdue, 28-14. Then Army's 28-game unbeaten streak was ended by an unimpressed Navy team, 14-2. Notre Dame, 37-0-2 since September 28, 1946, went on to lose three more times and finished at 4-4-1, dropping out of the Associated Press Top 20 for the first time in 10 years.

On the other side of the pic-

ture, Oklahoma powered its way to a 10-0 season and claimed its first national championship. The Sooners, ranked No. 1 by both the AP and the new United Press International college football polls, ended the regular season with an unbeaten string of 31. Fifth-ranked California ran its regular-season unbeaten mark to 30, although the Golden Bears have fallen in each of the last two Rose Bowls.

Army finished No. 2 despite its loss to Navy and Texas captured third-place honors.

# Browns rule as champs of NFL

Paul Brown could not be blamed if he wanted to gloat. Just a little bit, perhaps. Maybe a sly smile for all those critics who said his Cleveland Browns would be a second-rate team in the tougher National Football League.

Well, the Browns now are NFL champions—in their first

season of playing with the big boys following the demise of the All-America Football Conference, the rival league Cleveland ruled for its four-year lifespan (47-4-3, four championships).

They showed everybody by tying for the American Conference crown with a 10-2 record and then beating the co-champion New York Giants, 8-3, in a playoff.

But their biggest victory occurred, December 24, at Cleveland, where the Browns defeated the Los Angeles Rams, 30-28, in a dramatic NFL championship game that featured a passing duel between Cleveland's Otto Graham (22 completions in 33 attempts for 298 yards and four touchdowns) and the Rams' Bob Waterfield (18 of 32 for 312 yards and one TD). The game was decided when Lou Groza drilled a 16-yard field goal with 28 seconds to play.

The Browns had, indeed, showed everybody.

# 1951

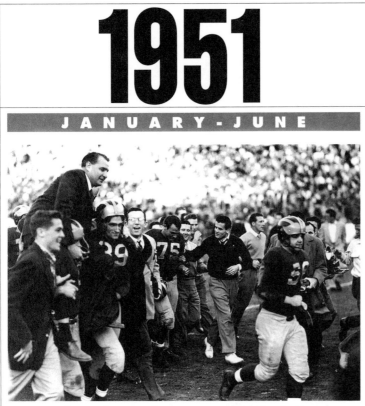

*Ecstatic Michigan players and rooters carry Coach Bennie Oosterbaan off the field after the Wolverines' victory over California in the Rose Bowl.*

## Cal's Rose Bowl jinx

It's becoming something of a tradition. California goes undefeated during the regular season then loses to a Big Ten team in the Rose Bowl. It doesn't matter which Big Ten team. Any one will do.

On this New Year's Day, the 9-0-1 and fifth-ranked Golden Bears dropped a 14-6 decision to Michigan. Last year the 10-0 and third-ranked Bears fell to Ohio State, 17-14. In the 1949 Rose Bowl, the 10-0 and fourth-ranked Bears lost to Northwestern, 20-14.

The Michigan loss was es-pecially disheartening because it looked like California might finally break the pattern. They entered the fourth quarter with a 6-0 lead, having completely outplayed the Wolverines while scoring on a 39-yard pass from Jim Marinos to Bob Cummings.

But Chuck Ortmann passed Michigan into position for Don Dufek, a 113-yard rusher during the game, to score on a short plunge with less than six minutes left to play. And then Michigan padded its one-point lead when Dufek ran seven yards for a touchdown.

## Inspired Kentucky upsets No. 1 Sooners

Bud Wilkinson's Oklahoma Sooners, having already won the 1950 national championship with a 10-0 record while stretching their unbeaten streak to 31 games, had nothing to gain and everything to lose. Paul (Bear) Bryant's No. 7-ranked Kentucky Wildcats (10-1) were playing for pride, fired up by the opportunity to knock off college football's No. 1-ranked team.

Everything was ripe for an upset and the Wildcats did not disappoint, handing the Sooners a 13-7 loss before 82,000 fans in the New Year's Day Sugar Bowl at New Orleans. Ken-

## A basketball scandal

College basketball was rocked to its very foundation on February 18, when three key players for City College of New York, an unprecedented double winner of last year's NCAA Tournament and National Invitation Tournament, were arrested for "fixing" games. But the admitted links of Ed Roman, Al Roth and Ed Warner to professional gamblers, it turned out, were just the tip of the iceberg.

First New York District Attorney Frank Hogan's investigation uncovered that players from three other New York schools, Long Island University, Manhattan College and New York University, also had been involved in bribery. Then the scandal spread to other parts of the country, eventually smearing 35 athletes from seven institutions for their parts in fixing 86 games in 22 different cities. It was originally believed that most of the gambling activity was centered at New York's Madison Square Garden.

The most spectacular disclosures were that Kentucky and Bradley, two powerhouses during the period in question, also were involved. Former Kentucky stars Alex Groza and Ralph Beard admitted their part in shaving points during regular-season, NCAA Tournament and NIT games, ending their professional careers with the Indianapolis Olympians of the National Basketball Association in disgrace.

*Paul (Bear) Bryant, coach of the opportunistic Kentucky Wildcats.*

tucky scored early on a 25-yard pass from quarterback Babe Parilli to Wilbur Jamerson and struck again in the third quarter on Jamerson's one-yard run.

Oklahoma, meanwhile, lost five fumbles and encountered an inspired Kentucky defense. The Sooners scored in the final six minutes when Billy Vessels took a pitchout and lobbed a 17-yard pass to Merrill Green.

# Rochester Royals hold off upstart Knicks

With the stench of scandal settling uncomfortably over New York and college basketball, fans needed something to fill the void. To say that the New York Knicks' timing was impeccable is something of an understatement.

The young Knicks, third-place finishers in the Eastern Division of the new streamlined (10-team) NBA, caught New York's attention when they upset Boston and Syracuse in the opening playoff rounds. But they really generated publicity when they dragged Rochester through a seven-game championship series before falling to the Royals, 79-75, in the April 21 final at Rochester.

The veteran Royals, featuring Arnie Risen and Bob Davies, looked dominant as they won the first three games of the title matchup. But the Knicks, rallying behind Max Zaslofsky, Harry Gallatin, Connie Simmons and Dick McGuire, forced a seventh game that was not decided until Davies sank two free throws in the final seconds.

The title was the first for Rochester and ended the two-year reign of George Mikan and the Minneapolis Lakers.

Two Bob Davies free throws in the final seconds of Game 7 gave the Rochester Royals an NBA championship series victory over the New York Knicks.

# Ben Hogan brings a monster to knees

Ben Hogan "brought the monster to its knees," June 16, with a spectacular final-round 67 that gave him a two-stroke victory over Clayton Heafner and his second straight U.S. Open golf championship.

The "monster" was the tough Oakland Hills course in Birmingham, Mich., that humbled competitors, including Hogan, through much of the four-round event. The little Texan, who dramatically came back from his 1949 car accident to win the Open last year, played the Oakland Hills layout in 76-73-71-67 for a winning total of 287. He trailed Jimmy Demaret by two strokes after the third round and needed to come back with a big effort yesterday afternoon.

"Under the circumstances, it was the greatest round I have played," said Hogan, who earlier in the year won his first Masters title. "My friends said last night that I might win with a pair of 69s. It seemed too much on this course. It is the hardest course I have ever played."

Ben Hogan (right), winner of the Masters, looks on as Bobby Jones congratulates low amateur Charlie Coe (left). Hogan later added his second straight U.S. Open to his growing list of major titles.

# The overtime series

When Toronto's Sid Smith slid the puck past Montreal goaltender Gerry McNeil at 5:51 of overtime in Game 1 of the Stanley Cup series, two patterns were established. Toronto would prevail and every game of the Maple Leafs' five-game victory would end in an extra session.

Game 2 went to Montreal when the great Maurice (Rocket) Richard beat Toronto goalie Turk Broda to a loose puck in front of the net and scored after 2:55 of overtime. Then Ted Kennedy, Harry Watson and Bill Barilko scored overtime goals in successive games to give Toronto its fourth Cup in five years.

The Leafs' April 21 clincher was the most dramatic game of the series. Toronto, behind 2-1, pulled its goalie and Tod Sloan scored from a scramble with 32 seconds remaining. Barilko then scored at 2:53 of overtime.

# 1951

## A little bit of fun

It was the greatest promotional stunt in baseball history and only Bill Veeck, new owner of the St. Louis Browns, could have pulled it off.

With Frank Saucier the scheduled leadoff hitter for the Browns in the second game of an August 19 doubleheader against Detroit at Sportsman's Park, Manager Zack Taylor made a switch. With miniature bat in hand, out walked Eddie Gaedel, a 26-year-old midget wearing uniform number $1/8$, to pinch-hit.

Taylor was questioned by home plate umpire Ed Hurley, but the manager produced an official, signed contract and the game restarted. Gaedel, all 3-foot-7 of him, squatted into his stance and watched as Tiger pitcher Bob Cain walked him on four pitches. Jim Delsing was sent in as a pinch-runner.

Gaedel was released the next day when American League President Will Harridge, saying the use of a midget was not in the best interests of baseball, negated the contract. But Veeck already had his victory over baseball's establishment.

"Ball," says umpire Ed Hurley as Bob Swift catches the high pitch to St. Louis midget Eddie Gaedel.

## Sugar Ray avenges loss to British champ

Sugar Ray Robinson put on quite a show for 61,370 fans, September 12, as he regained the middleweight championship he lost to Randy Turpin by scoring a technical knockout of the British champion in the 10th round at New York's Polo Grounds.

The 31-year-old Robinson, who was battered by the 23-year-old Turpin in their first meeting on July 10 in London, looked more like his old self as he worked over his opponent with a series of jabs and quick combinations. Ahead on points in the 10th, he connected with a right to Turpin's jaw that floored the champion for the count of nine.

Turpin struggled to his feet and Robinson went after him with a vicious attack that left him dazed and bleeding. The

Sugar Ray Robinson looks back at a fallen Randy Turpin in the 10th round of their title fight.

referee intervened with eight seconds remaining in the round.

The fight established middleweight records for both attendance and receipts. Robinson will collect 30 percent of the net receipts.

## 554 yards: Rams QB goes on a record binge

Norm Van Brocklin, replacing injured quarterback Bob Waterfield, bombed the New York Yanks for a National Football League-record 554 yards and five touchdowns as the Los Angeles Rams rolled to a 54-14 victory before 30,315 delighted fans at the Los Angeles Coliseum.

The NFL season opener was a showcase for the former Oregon quarterback. He connected on touchdown passes of one, 46, 47 and 26 yards to Elroy (Crazy Legs) Hirsch, 67 yards to Vitamin Smith and scored another himself on a one-yard run. Van Brocklin, whose 554 yards surpassed the previous record of 468 by Chicago's Johnny Lujack, just missed a sixth TD pass when Tommy Kalmanir was stopped inches short of the goal line.

The Rams set NFL records with 34 first downs and 735 total yards.

# Thomson's home run wins N.L. pennant

"The Giants win the pennant! . . .The Giants win the pennant, and they're going crazy!"

So went the dramatic call of radio announcer Russ Hodges, October 3, as the New York Giants' Bobby Thomson circled the bases after hitting "The Shot Heard 'Round the World." Pandemonium reigned at the Polo Grounds. Giants' players celebrated. Excited fans stormed the field.

Numbed by the events, the Brooklyn Dodgers hurried toward their center-field clubhouse, dodging onrushing fans, realizing that, for the second year in a row, their National League pennant hopes had been dashed by a last-game, final-inning three-run homer.

Only this one was an especially bitter pill to swallow. The Dodgers had controlled this pennant race from the outset and appeared uncatchable when they extended their August 11 lead to a whopping 13½ games over the second-place Giants. But New York then went 37-7, including a 13-1 stretch run that forced a first-place tie and a three-game playoff for only the second in N.L. history.

The Giants gained the upper hand in the playoff, October 1, when they beat the Dodgers, 3-1, on the strength of Thomson's two-run homer at Ebbets Field, but the Dodgers squared the series with a 10-0 victory at the Polo Grounds, Clem Labine allowing six hits.

Things looked bleak for the Giants as 20-game winner Don Newcombe, carried a 4-1 lead into the ninth inning of Game 3. But Alvin Dark and Don Mueller singled and, after Monte Irvin had fouled out,

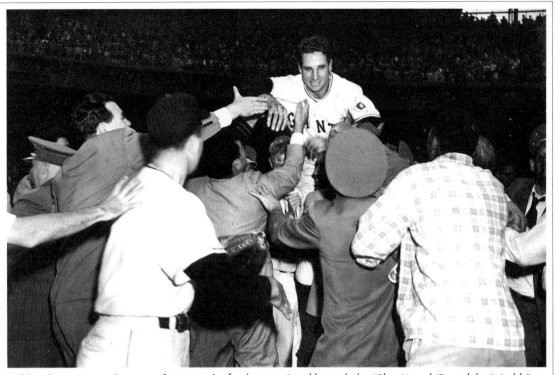

Bobby Thomson was the toast of New York after beating Brooklyn with the "Shot Heard 'Round the World."

Whitey Lockman slapped a run-scoring double down the left-field line. Dodger Manager Chuck Dressen, his team now leading 4-2, called in Ralph Branca from the bullpen to pitch to Thomson.

On Branca's third pitch, Thomson stroked a line drive toward left field. Dodger left fielder Andy Pafko watched the ball disappear. Giants win, 5-4. Pandemonium!

That the Giants went on to lose a six-game World Series to the New York Yankees—the Yanks' third straight Series triumph—is inconsequential. They had staged the most dramatic pennant-winning comeback in history and Thomson's home run would live forever as one of baseball's most unforgettable moments.

# Browns finally lose in NFL title contest

The Cleveland Browns had successfully proven themselves as the class of the National Football League in 1950. Now it was up to other NFL teams to do the proving.

It didn't happen during the regular season as the Browns rolled to an 11-1 record and their second straight American Conference crown. And it didn't seem likely that the youthful Los Angeles Rams, 8-4 winners of the National Conference, could upset them in the December 23 championship game.

But with 57,522 home fans looking on, the Rams put a defensive blanket on All-Pro quarterback Otto Graham and All-Pro fullback Marion Motley and battled to a 17-17 fourth-quarter tie with the explosive Browns. Midway through that

The strong arm of Los Angeles Rams quarterback Norm Van Brocklin brought an end to Cleveland's title-game winning streak.

final period, it was Rams quarterback Norm Van Brocklin who suddenly turned the tables to become explosive himself.

Having set up the Cleveland defense for a running play, Van Brocklin unloaded a bomb that Tom Fears grabbed between two defenders before racing away for a 73-yard touchdown. The Rams had a 24-17 victory and the Browns tasted defeat for the first time in a football championship game.

# 1952

## JANUARY · JUNE

## Lovellette scores 33, Jayhawks win NCAA

It was like running into a brick wall, and that analogy was not lost on St. John's University players.

"He is the greatest center we ever played against," said Redmen captain Jack McMahon. "He's too big," added center Bob Zawoluk.

"He" referred to Kansas 6-foot-9 center Clyde Lovellette, who had just put on a basketball exhibition during the March 26 NCAA Tournament final at Seattle. Lovellette scored 33 points against the Redmen, lifting Kansas to an 80-63 victory and giving Coach Phog Allen the crown jewel of his distinguished coaching career—a national championship.

St. John's vainly tried to neutralize Lovellette with a full-court press, but the Jayhawks still got the ball to him and he scored often on a series of short hook shots and tip-ins. Kansas led 41-27 at the half and never really was threatened en route to its 26th win against two losses.

Lovellette set tournament records with 69 rebounds and 141 points, including 44 against St. Louis in the Western Regional final.

*Kansas University's NCAA Tournament victory was the crown jewel in Phog Allen's long and distinguished coaching career.*

### ★ SPORTS WATCH ★

**MAR:** Three goals in 21 seconds: Chicago's Bill Mosienko set an NHL record.

**MAR:** Detroit goaltender Terry Sawchuk won his first Vezina Trophy after recording 12 shutouts and a sterling 1.90 goals-against average.

**MAR:** Philadelphia's Paul Arizin averaged 25.4 points per game, breaking the three-year hold of Minneapolis' George Mikan on the NBA scoring title.

**JUN:** Boston Braves' lefthander Warren Spahn tied the major league single-game record of 18 strikeouts, but lost a 15-inning thriller to Chicago, 3-1.

**JUN:** The St. Louis Cardinals scored 14 runs in the last three innings and wiped out an 11-0 deficit in a 14-12 victory over the New York Giants.

## Right on the Button

It was showtime in Oslo, Norway, and five-time world figure skating champion Dick Button did not disappoint. Having unveiled a daring new double axel in winning the free-skating portion of the competition as a brash 18-year-old during the 1948 Games in St. Moritz, Switzerland, the Harvard senior had prepared another surprise for 1952—a triple loop.

In a breathtaking performance that further established his superiority in men's figure skating, Button flawlessly executed three complete revolutions and landed smoothly to complete the rest of his program. All nine judges awarded him first place.

Button was one of four gold-medal winning performers for the United States—the best American showing ever in the Winter Games. Leading the way was skier Andrea Mead

*Dick Button, two-time Olympic gold medal-winning figure skater, dazzled at St. Moritz with a smooth triple loop.*

Lawrence, a 19-year-old Vermont housewife who earned golds in the regular and giant slalom, and Ken Henry, a winner in the 500-meter speed skating sprint. The U.S. total of 11 medals was second only to Norway's 16.

## Maryland stuns Vols

For the second straight year, college football's crowned national champion saw its bid for a perfect season go down the drain in a New Year's Day Sugar Bowl upset.

Tennessee, 10-0 and No. 1 in both the final Associated Press and United Press International polls, met undefeated and third-ranked Maryland. The Terrapins prevailed, 28-13.

Maryland stunned the Vols and 82,000 fans at Tulane Stadium with a three-touchdown blitz during a seven-minute stretch of the first half. Ed Fullerton scored on a two-yard run in the first quarter, Bob Shemonski scored on a short pass from Fullerton in the second period and quarterback Jack Scarbath plunged one yard for another score.

Fullerton iced the game in the third quarter when he intercepted a Hank Lauricella pass and returned it 46 yards for a touchdown. Maryland Coach Jim Tatum then turned matters over to big fullback Ed Modzelewski, who proceeded to outrush the entire Volunteer team, 153-81.

*Outstanding women's golf champion Patty Berg.*

# Berg's 64 sets new women's record

Patty Berg, president and co-founder of the Ladies Professional Golf Association and one of the greats of the game, fired a women's world record 64, April 26, over the 6,339-yard Richmond (Va.) Country Club course during the opening round of the Richmond Open.

The incredible round, which beat by two strokes the former women's record shared by Babe Zaharias and Opal Hill, included 10 birdies, two bogeys and a front-nine 30 that required only 11 putts. Berg, who has won more than 90 tournaments in her illustrious career, sank birdie putts of 25 feet on the sixth hole, 15 feet on the ninth, 31 feet on the 16th and 12 feet on the 18th. She was using a new putter.

"It was the greatest round of golf I have ever played," Berg said. "I wouldn't sell this putter for $100."

Berg's 64 gave her a seven-stroke lead. Her playing partner, Marlene Bauer, tied the previous women's course record of 71, but was lost in the shuffle.

# Montreal Rockets past Boston

Maurice Richard lived up to his nickname, April 8, when he rocketed the length of the ice and scored a spectacular goal that broke a 1-1 tie and lifted the Montreal Canadiens past Boston in Game 7 of a semifinal Stanley Cup series at the Montreal Forum. The 3-1 victory (Montreal's Billy Reay added an empty-net goal) finished off a see-saw battle.

Richard, who had been knocked out during a second-period collision and had not played through 16 minutes of the finale, finally got the call from Coach Dick Irvin and immediately became a factor. Richard took a pass from Emile Bouchard in his own end, stick-handled past Boston's Real Chevrefils, shot down the ice, around a startled Bill Quackenbush and fired a low shot past Bruins goaltender Jim Henry for his record 47th career playoff goal at 16:19. The 14,598 Forum fans went wild, littering

*A bloody-faced Rocket Richard is congratulated by Boston goalie Jim Henry after scoring the goal that broke the Bruins' back in a tough Stanley Cup semifinal series.*

the ice with programs, money, overshoes, hats and anything else they could find to throw.

But their happiness was short-lived. Detroit allowed Montreal only two goals and swept the Stanley Cup final series in four straight games.

# Lakers survive Knicks scare

New York again extended its heavily favored opponent to seven games in the National Basketball Association championship series, and again the Knicks fell short.

The Minneapolis Lakers, looking for their third title in four years, simply had too much size. And too much George Mikan. With the 6-foot-10 center scoring 22 points and dominating the boards along with fellow big men Jim Pollard and Vern Mikkelsen, the Lakers rolled to an 82-65 Game 7 triumph at Minneapolis, ending a see-saw victory-swapping battle.

Mikan might have been the moving force, but it was Pollard who came off the bench in the fourth quarter to provide the winning spark. After sitting out the previous two games with a back injury, Pollard scored 10 final-quarter points to ignite the winning surge.

Minneapolis' victory culminated the NBA's most stable season. The same 10 teams that finished the 1950-51 campaign started and finished in 1951-52.

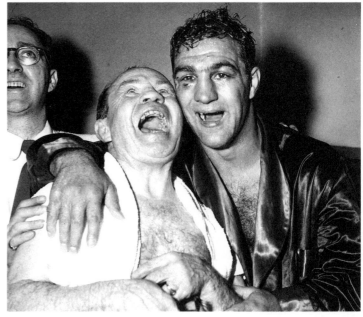

*Celebration time for heavyweight champion Rocky Marciano (right) and trainer Charlie Goldman.*

# Powerful Marciano rocks Walcott in 13th

There is nothing pretty about Rocky Marciano. He is awkward, crude in style and apparently oblivious to punishment as he stalks an opponent awaiting the opportunity to deliver a knockout blow. But Marciano's approach is effective and he now reigns as the new heavyweight champion of the world.

The 28-year-old Brockton, Mass., bomber recorded his 43rd consecutive victory and 38th knockout, September 23, when he delivered a powerful right to the jaw of champion Jersey Joe Walcott in the 13th round of a title bout at Philadelphia's Municipal Stadium. Walcott sagged backward into the ropes and slid head-first to the canvas. Pandemonium broke out as many of the 40,379 fans rushed the ring to congratulate the new champion.

Marciano's bid to become boxing's first white heavyweight champion since James J. Braddock was defeated by Joe Louis in 1937 was in serious jeopardy entering the round. The 38-year-old Walcott had controlled the fight and was ahead on all cards. He had even knocked Marciano down in the first round and the new champ was bruised and bleeding.

But in the end, youth won out and Marciano was able to seize his moment, just as Gene Tunney had against Jack Dempsey 26 years ago in the same arena.

# Connolly, Sedgman roll to U.S. title victories

The 13,000 spectators who crowded into the West Side Tennis Club at Forest Hills, to watch the September 7 men's and women's singles finals got to go home early. First they watched 24-year-old Australian Frank Sedgman destroy 38-year-old Gardnar Mulloy, 6-1, 6-2, 6-3, in a 47-minute match. Then they watched 17-year-old Californian Maureen Connolly whip off a 6-3, 7-5 win over Doris Hart. The U.S. singles champion-ships are the second straight for both Sedgman and Connolly, following their first Wimbledon singles victories earlier in the year. Sedgman, who lost only 40 games in the entire tournament, becomes only the third foreigner to win the U.S. title two consecutive years. Mulloy was the oldest player to reach the finals since William Larned in 1911.

> ## " SPORTS TALK "
>
> *"I didn't think yesterday I could do it. But I did and now I'm finished. This will be my last decathlon."*
>
> **BOB MATHIAS**

# American Olympians outduel Soviets at Helsinki

*Olympic decathlon champion Bob Mathias throwing the discus.*

The United States won the medal count at the Summer Olympic Games in Helsinki, Finland, but the real story was the presence, for the first time in Olympic history, of a powerful team from the Soviet Union. The Games became almost a dual meet between the Russians and Americans, with the U.S. surging at the end for a 75-68 medal-count victory. Included among the American medals were 41 golds, 18 more than the Russians could manage.

Politics aside, one of the biggest stories was the world-record performance of Bob Mathias in the decathlon. The Tulare, Calif., native, a winner at age 17 in the 1948 decathlon at the Games in London, amassed 7,887 points to win the event by the largest margin in Olympic history.

Overall, the U.S. won 14 of the 24 men's track and field events while the Soviet women pulled a similar sweep. The Americans also made excellent showings in swimming, diving and boxing and they beat the Russians twice on the basketball court, winning 86-58 in a preliminary game and 36-25 in the final. The American basketball team featured 7-foot Bob Kurland, formerly of Oklahoma A&M, and 6-foot-9 Clyde Lovellette, the former Kansas star.

# Martin to the rescue

The ever-raucous fans of Brooklyn, packed into the friendly bleachers of cozy Ebbets Field, were more vocal and euphoric than ever. The Dodgers had a three games to two World Series lead over the big bad New York Yankees and there was justifiable anticipation that Brooklyn soon would have its first championship flag to fly with all those National League pennants.

But euphoria turned to discomfort when home runs by Yogi Berra and Mickey Mantle offset two homers by Brooklyn's Duke Snider and the Yankees rallied for a Series-tying 3-2 victory. The discomfort heightened the next day when Mantle homered again and the Yanks carried a 4-2 lead into the bottom of the seventh.

The Dodgers, however, fought back, loading the bases against Vic Raschi with one out. Yankee Manager Casey Stengel called Bob Kuzava from the bullpen and the lefthander induced Snider to pop out. Jackie Robinson followed with another popup near the mound.

But as Kuzava stood transfixed and the runners circled the bases at full speed, first baseman Joe Collins searched fran-

*Brooklyn's Jackie Robinson watches as Yankee second baseman Billy Martin streaks in to catch a pop fly and rescue the New Yorkers in Game 7 of the World Series.*

tically for a ball he could not find. Recognizing the dilemma, second baseman Billy Martin sprinted in and made a miraculous knee-high catch.

Kuzava set down the Dodgers the rest of the way and the Yankees had their record-matching fourth consecutive Series victory. The Dodgers were denied a championship for the sixth time in as many tries.

## Youngsters Beliveau, Geoffrion put on show

A delighted crowd of 14,641 Canadiens fans got a glimpse of the future on December 18, when youngsters Jean Beliveau and Bernie Geoffrion combined to score all six goals in a 6-2 victory over the New York Rangers at the Montreal Forum.

But the night really belonged to Beliveau, the 6-foot-1, 190-pound center who was on loan from the Quebec Aces of the Quebec Senior League. Beliveau, the much publicized amateur who was called up by the

Canadiens for a three-game trial, scored the game's first goal midway through the first period off a goal-mouth pass from Maurice Richard and then added two more goals within a two-minute span of the second period to break a 2-2 tie.

Geoffrion scored late in the first period and twice more in the third to help second-place Montreal overcome the last-place Rangers. Beliveau is expected to sign a professional contract with Montreal before the 1953-54 season.

*A happy group of Detroit Lions surround Coach Buddy Parker (wearing hat) and celebrate their 17-7 NFL title game win over Cleveland.*

# Lions hand Cleveland 2nd title-game loss

Cleveland won its third straight American Conference title since joining the National Football League in 1950 and appeared in its third consecutive NFL title game. But for the second time in a row, the Browns went down to defeat in the season ender, this time to the Detroit Lions before 50,934 fans at Cleveland's Municipal Stadium.

Detroit's 17-7 December 28 conquest was the result of clutch defensive play and just enough offense from quarterback Bobby Layne and halfback Doak Walker.

The Lions' defense allowed Cleveland 384 offensive yards but buckled down whenever the Browns made a deep penetration. Layne scored on a two-yard run and Walker sprinted 67 yards for another touchdown. Pat Harder's 36-yard fourth-quarter field goal sealed the victory after Cleveland's Chick Jagade had run seven yards for the Browns' only touchdown in the third period.

Detroit had reached the championship game by virtue of its 31-21 victory over the Los Angeles Rams in a National Conference playoff.

# 1953

## Hoosiers win NCAA

Bob Leonard sank a free throw with 27 seconds remaining and Kansas failed to convert a last-second shot, giving Branch McCracken's Indiana Hoosiers an exciting 69-68 win over the Jayhawks in the March 18 finals of the NCAA Tournament at Kansas City.

Dean Kelley tied the game for Kansas at 68-68 with just over a minute remaining and then fouled Leonard as the Hoosiers played for the last shot. Leonard missed the first free throw but connected on the second, setting the stage for Kansas reserve Jerry Alberts to miss an off-balance buzzer-beater.

The teams were evenly matched through a 41-41 first half. The Hoosiers owned a tenuous 68-65 lead when Charles Kraak was called for a charge and reacted angrily, drawing a technical. A free throw and Kelley's basket tied the game.

*Indiana Coach Branch McCracken with his starting five (left to right): Charles Kraak, Bob Leonard, Don Schlundt, Dick Farley and Burke Scott.*

Don Schlundt played well to lead Indiana with 30 points while B.H. Born kept Kansas close with an excellent 26-point effort. Indiana finished at 23-3, all of its losses coming on last-second shots, and Kansas finished at 19-6.

## Braves flee Boston

The Braves, charter members of the National League and fixtures in Boston for 77 years, will open the 1953 season in a new home—County Stadium in Milwaukee. The franchise shift is the first in major league baseball since 1903, when Baltimore of the fledgling American League moved to New York.

The shift is a result of sagging attendance and lost revenue in recent years. The Braves drew only 281,000 fans last season and Owner Lou Perini reported a loss of $700,000. Perini, who claims that Boston has become a one-team city since the arrival of television, petitioned N.L. owners to okay the move and received unanimous approval on March 18.

The short-notice move creates minor problems in scheduling and travel arrangements, but the biggest obstacle was getting permission from the Milwaukee Brewers of the American Association. The Brewers, who have played in Milwaukee for more than half a century, accepted a cash payment for their territorial rights and agreed to move to Toledo.

The Braves will play their first home game in County Stadium, a new $5 million facility, on April 14.

*Baseball Commissioner Ford Frick (left) and National League President Warren Giles (right) were on hand for Wisconsin Gov. Walter Kohler's curtain-raising pitch for Milwaukee baseball.*

## Cousy's record 50 points

Bob Cousy, the ball-handling wizard of Boston, scored a playoff record 50 points, March 21, against the Syracuse Nationals, giving the Celtics a 111-105 four-overtime victory at Boston Garden. The win allowed Boston to advance to the second round of the National Basketball Association playoffs for the first time.

Cousy's scoring record was not a thing of beauty, but then neither was the game. The former Holy Cross star managed only 10 field goals while hitting 30 of 32 free throw attempts. There were 107 fouls called in the game and no other player scored more than five field goals in the 68 minutes of action. Each team made 27 field goals; each team attempted 65 free throws.

Cousy hit a long set shot to tie the game with five seconds remaining in the third overtime and then hit five free throws and two field goals in the fourth overtime to secure the victory. Cousy's 50 points bettered George Mikan's mark of 47.

# Amazing Ben Hogan wins 3 majors in one year

Ben Hogan's golf comeback in 1950 was heart-warming. His 1951 U.S. Open triumph was dramatic and sensational. But his 1953 overall performance—winning three majors within a three-month span—was downright scary.

How good is this guy? Good enough to win the Masters in April while knocking five strokes off the tournament record. Good enough to win his fourth U.S. Open in June, this time by a whopping six strokes while leading after every round. Good enough in July to record a four-stroke victory in his first British Open.

The latter was the crowning jewel and it did not come as easily as the final score would indicate. Hogan braved wind, rain and cold to play Scotland's ancient Carnoustie course in a final-round 68, and he struggled to the clubhouse exhausted, chilled and feverish. The grueling 36-hole final day took such a toll that Hogan announced immediately afterward that he was taking the rest of the year off and would come back next spring to defend his Masters title.

That means he will skip the upcoming PGA Championship and his chance at a one-season grand slam.

# Williams to return

The Boston Red Sox received good news in June when it was learned that slugging outfielder Ted Williams is being ordered back to the United States to get treatment for an ear and nose ailment. That's good news because Williams is alive and well after flying 38 missions as a Marine Corps captain in Korea.

Most of those missions went off routinely, but Williams did receive a major scare on February 19, when his F-9 Panther jet was hit by small-arms fire. He perilously flew his burning plane back over enemy lines and somehow crash-landed it on an allied airfield.

There have been rumors that Williams, who has been overseas for 5 1/2 months, will be released from his military commitment soon after his return, but nobody knows when he will be free to rejoin the Red Sox. The four-time American League batting champion and two-time Most Valuable Player also lost three years to military service as a flight instructor during World War II.

The 35-year-old Williams is one of several major leaguers involved in the Korean conflict.

*Ted Williams was fighting a different kind of war in 1953.*

Among the other notables are New York Giants center fielder Willie Mays and Brooklyn pitcher Don Newcombe.

## ★ SPORTS WATCH ★

**JAN:** Southern California snapped the Big Ten Conference's Rose Bowl winning streak at six, beating Wisconsin, 7-0, in the New Year's Day classic.

**JAN:** Alabama exploded for a postseason-record 61 points in a 61-6 Orange Bowl triumph over Syracuse.

**MAR:** Detroit star Gordie Howe finished the season with 49 goals, one short of Maurice (Rocket) Richard's record of 50.

**APR:** The Minneapolis Lakers won their fourth NBA championship in five years, knocking off the New York Knicks in five games.

**APR:** The Montreal Canadiens won their first Stanley Cup in seven years, beating Boston in a fast five-game final.

**MAY:** St. Louis Browns pitcher Bobo Holloman became just the third pitcher to throw a no-hitter in his first big-league start, stopping the Philadelphia Athletics, 6-0.

*Young Yankee slugger Mickey Mantle admires the display put together in honor of his 565-foot home run.*

# Young Mantle blasts a 565-foot rocket

In an amazing show of raw power, 21-year-old New York Yankee slugger Mickey Mantle blasted an incredible home run that cleared the 50-foot outer wall of Washington's Griffith Stadium and came to rest in the back yard of a house, 565 feet away from home plate. It was possibly the longest ball ever hit.

Batting righthanded against Senators lefty Chuck Stobbs with two out and Yogi Berra on first base in the fifth inning of an April 17 game, Mantle sent a shot toward left-center field.

The ball cleared the bleacher fence, 391 feet from the plate, glanced off a football scoreboard that sits atop the 50-foot outer fence and bounded out of sight.

The ball traveled 460 feet in the air and there's no telling how much farther it might have gone had it cleared the scoreboard. It marked the first time a ball had ever been hit completely out of Griffith Stadium on the fly to left field. The Yankees went on to defeat the Senators, 7-3.

# 1953

## Two pro franchises relocate in Baltimore

Baltimore has been twice blessed. First Carroll Rosenbloom purchased what was left of the defunct Dallas Texans and planted a new and better Colts franchise in the city. Then a syndicate headed by Clarence Miles bought the struggling St. Louis Browns on September 29, and received quick approval from American League baseball owners to move the team to Baltimore.

The Colts and "Orioles," as the Browns will be known, will join the Bullets of the National Basketball Association as major league franchises in Baltimore. The Colts will play their first National Football League season this year while the Orioles are scheduled to begin A.L. play in 1954.

Owner Bill Veeck's petition to move the Browns to Baltimore earlier in the year was rejected because the other A.L. owners wanted him out of the league. Veeck sold his interests to the Baltimore syndicate for $2,475,000.

The new Colts flopped last season as the Texans and finished the year as a road team under league direction. Rosenbloom hopes the new Colts will have more success than their predecessors, the former All-America Football Conference team that folded one season after merging into the NFL in 1950.

## Connolly completes sweep of majors

Maureen Connolly, the perky 18-year-old blonde from California, defeated Doris Hart, 6-2, 6-4, to win her third straight U.S. singles championship and complete the first grand slam in women's tennis.

Connolly's September 7 victory before 12,000 fans at Forest Hills, was the last leg of her worldwide blitz that included grass-court victories in the French, Australian and Wimbledon championships. Her feat of sweeping all four majors in one year matches the 1938 effort of Don Budge in the men's division.

Connolly needed only 43 minutes to dispose of Hart, the hard-luck veteran who has lost to Connolly in each of the last two U.S. championships as well as in the French and Wimble-

*Maureen (Little Mo) Connolly and hardware after completing the first women's Grand Slam in the U.S. singles championship at Forest Hills.*

don finals this year. Hart used every trick to slow up her young adversary, but Connolly's speed and ground strokes were too much. The final was like the rest of the tournament: Connolly did not lose a set.

Neither did Tony Trabert of Cincinnati, who recorded a 6-3, 6-2, 6-3 victory over Vic Seixas in the men's singles final.

## Amazing eagle lifts Worsham to victory

Lew Worsham was not optimistic. He trailed Chandler Harper in the August 9 final round of the World Championship of Golf and was getting ready to hit his 140-yard approach to the 18th green at Tam o' Shanter in Chicago. He needed to get down in two to force a playoff for the record $25,000 first prize.

Adding to Worsham's discomfort were the fans who, fighting for a vantage point, formed a horseshoe-shaped path to the green and a final-

*Lew Worsham (left) accepts the $25,000 check he earned with his incredible final-hole eagle in the World Championship of Golf tournament in Chicago.*

round national television audience—a first for golf.

Worsham studied his shot, selected a wedge and quickly made his swing. Everybody watched incredulously as the ball hit on the front of the long green, bounced three times and curled into the hole for an eagle. The tournament was over and Harper's apparently winning 279 total was only second best. So was his $10,000 check.

Instantaneously, Worsham had risen from No. 20 to No. 1 on the PGA money-winning list and golf had been transformed into a camera-friendly sport.

"It was the luckiest shot I ever had in my life," Worsham said after completing his final-round 68.

# Detroit wins 2nd straight NFL title

It was an error-filled and sloppy game by National Football League standards, but the Detroit Lions' 17-16 championship game victory over Cleveland, December 27, had all the ingredients needed to please a gathering of 54,577 fans at Detroit's Briggs Stadium.

Especially pleasing was the knowledge that the Lions' second straight NFL title had come on a 33-yard touchdown pass from Bobby Layne to Jim Doran with just over two minutes remaining. That play wiped out a 16-10 Cleveland advantage forged out by two fourth-quarter field goals kicked by Lou Groza.

Detroit's first touchdown, a one-yard run by Doak Walker, was set up in the opening quarter by Cleveland quarterback Otto Graham's fumble. It was just the beginning of a miserable day for Graham, who inexplicably managed to complete only two passes on 15 attempts for a paltry 40 yards. Two were intercepted, including a desperation bomb after Detroit had scored its winning touchdown.

*Opportunistic Detroit Lions' quarterback Bobby Layne.*

# Irish lose national title, coach

A 14-14 November 21 tie with Iowa kept Notre Dame from winning another national championship, but an exciting victory over Georgia Tech earlier in the season proved more costly in the long run.

The No. 1 Irish played host to Georgia Tech, October 24, in a battle of unbeatens. Tech, in fact, had not lost in 31 games dating back to November 11, 1950. But Johnny Lattner and company proved more than the Yellow Jackets could handle and Notre Dame rolled to a 27-14 victory.

But not without paying a price. With the Irish leading 7-0 at halftime, Coach Frank Leahy suddenly collapsed in the locker room. He was rushed to the hospital where his problem was diagnosed as an intestinal spasm.

The Irish chalked up three more wins before tying Iowa. Undefeated Maryland was declared No. 1 by both the Associated Press and United Press International polls, with Notre Dame second. It would have been the fifth national championship for Leahy, who announced, under doctor's orders, his retirement after the season. He leaves the game with an outstanding career record of 107-13-9.

*New York Yankee World Series heroes (left to right) Billy Martin, Ed Lopat and Mickey Mantle.*

# Frustrated Dodgers fall to Yankees again

The Brooklyn Dodgers were on a roll. They had won 105 regular-season games, coasting to the National League pennant by a comfortable 13 lengths over second-place Milwaukee, and were feeling pretty good about their chances in the World Series. They were loaded with offense, pitching and defense and if they were ever going to beat the hated New York Yankees, this was the year.

Sorry, Bums. For the seventh time in the team's history, and the fifth time against the Yankees, the Dodgers went down to World Series defeat. Never had this proud franchise won a fall classic and here were the Yankees, winners of 16 World Series, picking up their record fifth straight.

Billy Martin, who had made the shoe-top catch in the 1952 Series that saved the day for the Yankees, killed the Dodgers with his bat this time, collecting 12 hits, including the last one in the bottom of the ninth inning of Game 6 to secure a 4-3 victory.

The Yankees were victorious in the first two games and the last two, falling victim to Carl Erskine's 14-strikeout effort in Game 3 and Duke Snider's four-RBI rampage in Game 4.

## ★ SPORTS WATCH ★

**JUL:** Betsy Rawls defeated Jackie Pung in an 18-hole playoff at Rochester (N.Y.) Country Club to win her second U.S. Women's Open golf title in three years.

**SEP:** Rookie watch: Chicago Cubs shortstop Ernie Banks connected for his first major league home run against St. Louis and pitcher Gerry Staley.

**OCT:** Center Jean Beliveau signed a professional contract to play with the NHL's Montreal Canadiens.

**NOV:** The United States Supreme Court decided that baseball is not subject to antitrust laws because it is a sport, not a business.

# 1954

## "Too full of Alabama"

Rice halfback Dicky Moegle turned in one of the great all-time performances in postseason play, January 1, when he ran for 265 yards and three touchdowns in Rice's 28-6 victory over Alabama before 75,504 fans in the Cotton Bowl. But Alabama fullback Tommy Lewis stole his thunder.

Moegle's 79-yard touchdown burst early in the second quarter had given Rice a 7-6 lead and the Owls regained possession on their own 5-yard line. Moegle took a handoff, blasted through the Crimson Tide defense and apparently was on his way to a 95-yard TD run when Lewis jumped off the Alabama bench and threw him to the ground at the Tide 40.

Referee Cliff Shaw awarded Moegle his touchdown and the speedster added a 34-yard TD scamper later in Rice's lopsided victory. But after the game, all attention was focused on Lewis.

"I guess I'm too full of Alabama," said the youngster who had scored Alabama's only touchdown, a one-yard plunge

*Rice halfback Dicky Moegle goes down, courtesy of an illegal touchdown-saving tackle by Tommy Lewis (lying on back), who jumped off the Alabama sideline.*

in the first quarter. "I didn't know what I was doing.... I kept telling myself I didn't do it. I didn't do it. But I knew I did."

The victory lifted Rice's record to 9-2. Alabama fell to 6-3-3.

## Furman's top gun scores 100 points

Frank Selvy, Furman's human scoring machine, set a single-game basketball record, February 13, when he pumped in an amazing 100 points against little Newberry College during a high-scoring massacre in Greenville, S.C.

Selvy, who broke the previous record of 73 points set by Temple's Bill Mikvy in 1951, connected on 41 of 66 field-goal attempts and 18 free throws in Furman's 149-95 victory. That 149-point outburst also was a record, but it came against a school with a male enrollment of 269.

Selvy finished his season with a 41.7-point scoring average, having hit the 50 barrier eight times. Both his average and his single-season total of 1,209 points are NCAA records that are not likely to be approached for some time.

## No. 1 Maryland loses

*Oklahoma's Larry Grigg speeds around Maryland defenders en route to the only touchdown in the Sooners' Orange Bowl upset of the top-ranked Terrapins.*

Larry Grigg ran 26 yards for a second-quarter touchdown and Oklahoma's tenacious defense took care of the rest as the Sooners defeated No. 1-ranked Maryland, 7-0, before a record crowd of 68,718 in Miami's Orange Bowl. It marked the third time in four years that the No. 1 team of both the Associated Press and United Press International had lost in a New Year's Day bowl game.

The Big Seven champions, 8-1-1 entering the game, established their defensive dominance early when they stopped the 10-0 Terrapins on a fourth-down plunge inches from their goal line. Maryland, playing without injured quarterback Bernie Faloney, also missed two first-half field-goal attempts.

In addition to his touchdown run, Grigg recovered a fumble and intercepted a pass as the Sooners handed the Terrapins their first shutout in 50 games. When the clock ran out, the Oklahoma players hoisted Coach Bud Wilkinson onto their shoulders and gave him a victory ride from the field.

### "SPORTS TALK"

*"I've seen a lot of drama in athletics, but Gordie Howe has given me the greatest thrills of all."*

**JACK ADAMS**
Detroit Red Wings Coach

*"I never was in danger of being knocked out and I thought I won."*

**EZZARD CHARLES**
after his June heavyweight championship fight with champion Rocky Marciano

# Vukovich wins second consecutive Indy 500

Bill Vukovich, auto racing's Mad Russian, drove his Fuel Injection Engineering Special to a record-tying second straight victory in the 500-mile Memorial Day spectacular at the Indianapolis Motor Speedway. Vukovich, who matched the doubles posted by Wilbur Shaw and Mauri Rose, averaged a record 130.840 mph in recording his 70-second triumph.

Vukovich defied stiff odds in coming from a seventh-row start in this rugged endurance test. He had difficulty qualifying his winning 1953 roadster and did not make the field until the final day. His chances of fighting through the 33-car field seemed remote.

But with 200,000 fans watching on a cool, gusty and overcast day, Vukovich drove brilliantly. He reached third place at the 150-mile mark and finally took the lead for good with 125 miles to go. He never looked back, crossing the finish line with a comfortable margin over second-place Jimmy Bryan in a Dean Van Lines Special.

Vukovich collected $74,934 in first-place money.

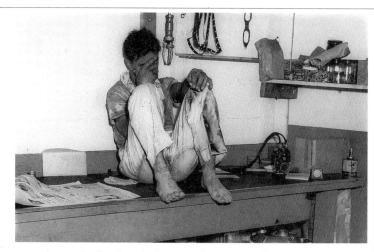

*An exhausted Bill Vukovich slumps in the garage after winning his second straight Indianapolis 500.*

# Musial: 5 home runs in a doubleheader

Six-time National League batting champion Stan (The Man) Musial muscled his way into the record books, May 2, with a five-home run doubleheader barrage against the New York Giants at St. Louis' Busch Stadium. Despite Musial's heroics, the Cardinals could manage only a split, winning the first game 10-6 and losing the nightcap 9-7.

Musial connected three times in the opener, twice off left-hander Johnny Antonelli and once off righthander Jim Hearn. The three-time Most Valuable Player hit a pair of second-game homers against knuckleballer Hoyt Wilhelm.

Musial's five homes brought in nine runs, three coming on his eighth-inning opening-game blast that broke a 6-6 tie. He also had a single in his 6-for-8 two-game performance. The previous record for home runs by one player in a doubleheader was four.

*St. Louis slugger Stan Musial between games of his five-homer doubleheader.*

# Red Wings win Stanley Cup again

Tony Leswick's drive from the blue line bounced off defenseman Doug Harvey's glove, over the shoulder of Montreal goaltender Gerry McNeil and into the net for a spectacular overtime goal that handed the Detroit Red Wings their third Stanley Cup in five years.

The goal, which came at 4:29 of overtime in the April 16 game at Detroit, ended a rugged series that the Wings once had led three games to one. The Canadiens, however, fought back, winning the fifth game, 1-0, on Ken Mosdell's goal at 5:45 of overtime and the sixth game, 4-1. But Montreal's luck ran out in Game 7 and the Red Wings, regular-season National Hockey League champions for the sixth straight year, regained the Stanley Cup.

Detroit dominated three of the first four games. In Game 2 the Canadiens exploded for three goals (two by Rocket Richard and one by Dickie Moore) in a 56-second span of the opening period and hung on for a 3-1 victory.

McNeil was playing in only his third game since coming back from an injury. Jacques Plante played in Montreal's four-game semifinal sweep of Boston and in the first four games against the Red Wings.

# 1954

## Palmer wins Amateur

Arnold Palmer, a 24-year-old blaster from Latrobe, Pa., defeated 43-year-old Robert Sweeny, 1-up, August 28, to win the U.S. Amateur golf championship at the Country Club of Detroit.

The 36-hole battle was decided on the final green. Palmer trailed Sweeny by two holes after the morning round and only took the lead at the 32nd hole. Palmer birdied 33 to go 2-up, but Sweeny cut the margin back to one at the 35th hole to keep the match alive.

Sweeny hit his drive into the right rough and was forced to play two shots to the green. Palmer hit a perfect drive and put his second shot 40 feet from the pin. When the youngster rolled his putt to within three inches of the cup, Sweeny conceded and Palmer had his first U.S. Amateur win in five tries.

Palmer shot a 70 over the final 18 holes to Sweeny's 74.

*Babe Didrikson-Zaharias, back on the tour after a cancer operation last spring, shows off her record third U.S. Women's Open golf trophy.*

## Babe beats the odds

Babe Didrikson Zaharias punctuated her comeback from a cancer operation with an overpowering 12-stroke victory, July 3, in the U.S. Women's Open golf championship at Salem Country Club in Peabody, Mass. The three-time Open champion, who has won four tournaments since undergoing the operation last spring, ended with a 72-hole total of 291.

Zaharias, visibly tired as she neared the end of her 36-hole final-day test, showed her emotions as she accepted the $2,000 first-place check.

"When I was in the hospital, I prayed that I could play again," she said. "Now I'm happy because I can tell people not to be afraid of cancer."

Zaharias, who was named "the greatest woman athlete of

*Roger Bannister hits the finish line just ahead of Australian John Landy to win "The Mile of the Century" in 3:58.8.*

## Bannister nips Landy

It was billed as "The Mile of the Century". Before 35,000 fans at the British Empire Games in Vancouver, B.C., and a transcontinental television audience estimated at 40 million, Roger Bannister and John Landy staged the greatest show in the history of track and field.

Bannister had become the first man ever to break the 4-minute mile on May 6 when he posted a 3:59.4. That remained the recognized world record, even though Landy recorded an unofficial 3:58 on June 21. Their meeting in the Empire Games was much anticipated and the National Broadcasting Company of the United States combined its efforts with the Canadian Broadcasting Company to make this the most widely viewed sports event in television history.

When the race started, Landy set a torrid pace and Bannister followed. The Australian led all the way until Bannister suddenly made his move with 100 yards to go. The Englishman drove past him, hit the tape and collapsed into the arms of some waiting friends. Bannister's time: 3:58.8. Landy's time, 3:59.6. Both were under the once sacred 4-minute barrier.

"I looked back on the inside," Landy said. "Just then he went by me on the outside. I shifted into high gear but couldn't catch him."

the half century" by an Associated Press poll in 1949, recorded rounds of 72-71-73-75 in her inspirational victory.

# Giants stun Indians

A magnificent catch by center fielder Willie Mays and the timely hitting of Dusty Rhodes were decisive as the New York Giants pulled off a shockingly easy four-game sweep of the powerful Cleveland Indians in the World Series.

The Indians, winners of an American League-record 111 games during the regular season, looked like sure winners in Game 1 when, with two runners on base and the score tied 2-2 in the eighth inning, Vic Wertz belted a deep drive to the outer reaches of New York's Polo Grounds. Mays pursued the ball and, facing the wall, made an incredible over-the-shoulder catch 460 feet from home plate. The Giants won the game in the 10th inning when Rhodes pinch-hit a three-run homer off Cleveland starter Bob Lemon.

The Giants won again the next day when Rhodes pinch-hit a two-run single and added a solo homer in a 3-1 victory. And they followed that with a 6-2 win at Cleveland, Rhodes getting another two-run pinch-hit single. New York wrapped up the Series, October 2, with a 7-4 triumph.

Rhodes finished with four hits in six at-bats and seven runs batted in.

*Willie Mays making "The Catch."*

*World Series Giants Willie Mays (left) and Dusty Rhodes.*

# A's relocate to K.C.

Arnold Johnson, the 47-year-old Chicago industrialist who recently bought the Athletics from the Mack family, received a double dose of good news on November 8. Both the sale and the transfer of the team to Kansas City were approved by American League owners.

The news ended weeks of haggling and speculation concerning the future of the down-trodden A's franchise, which was a charter member of the A.L. under the direction of Connie Mack. The Athletics, winners of nine pennants and five World Series in their proud history, had fallen on hard times recently and were losing the battle of Philadelphia to the National League's Phillies.

There had been some A.L. opposition to Johnson because of his close association with New York Yankees co-Owner Dan Topping and his ownership of Yankee Stadium, which Johnson has agreed to sell.

The A's will open next season in Kansas City's Municipal Stadium, which will be expanded from 17,000 seats to 36,000. The stadium has been the home of the Kansas City Blues, a Yankee farm team that Topping plans to relocate. The franchise transfer is the third in major league baseball in 20 months.

# Eskimos pull Grey Cup shocker

Jackie Parker, a former Mississippi State University football star, scooped up a wild lateral pass with three minutes remaining and ran 85 yards for the touchdown that gave Edmonton a 26-25 victory over Montreal in the Canadian Football League championship game. The Eskimos' November 27 victory at Toronto's Varsity Stadium ranks as one of the great upsets in the 45-year history of the Grey Cup classic.

Montreal, considered by many the most powerful football team ever developed in Canada, took an 18-14 halftime lead and the Alouettes increased their margin in the fourth quarter.

But former Maryland quarterback Bernie Faloney directed the Eskimos on a 103-yard drive in the final period and then Parker interrupted a Montreal drive by picking up Chuck Hunsinger's wild pitch.

Edmonton's victory means the Cup will go to Western Canada for the first time since 1948, when Calgary defeated Ottawa.

# 1955

## Shocker: Little Mo gives up tennis

Maureen Connolly, the 20-year-old queen of women's tennis, pulled a shocker on February 22, when she announced her retirement. The three-time Wimbledon and U.S. singles champion was injured in a horse riding accident last July and has not been satisfied with the progress of her rehabilitation.

Connolly, a winner of all nine major tournaments she entered and the first woman ever to win all four majors in one year (1953), was riding when her horse was frightened by a passing cement truck and shied, pinning her against the vehicle. Her fibula was broken and the tendons and muscles in her calf were deeply gashed.

Little Mo said that her leg has not responded well to surgery and exercise, spoiling her plan to return to action this year. She also said a factor in her decision was her plan to marry Norman Brinker, a 23-year-old former member of the United States equestrian team, in June.

*Maureen Connolly, the first grand slam performer in women's tennis.*

## Russell, Jones get job done for Dons

With high-flying center Bill Russell swatting away everything near the basket and guard K.C. Jones doing a masterful defensive job on high-scoring Tom Gola of La Salle, No. 1-ranked San Francisco scored a surprisingly easy 77-63 victory in the March 19 final of the NCAA Tournament at Kansas City.

The 28-1 Dons, who had escaped a 57-56 scare from Oregon State in the Western Regional finals at Corvallis, Ore., did not break a serious sweat in posting a 62-50 semifinal victory over Colorado and then broke open their game against La Salle with a first-half burst.

Jones, giving away five inches

*University of San Francisco playmaker and defensive wizard K.C. Jones (right).*

to the taller Gola, used his superior quickness and athleticism to hold the La Salle star to 16 points while posting 24 himself. Russell was his usual intimidating self, blocking numerous shots, grabbing 25 rebounds and scoring 23 points, 18 of them coming in San Francisco's first half blitz.

Third-ranked La Salle finished with a 26-5 record.

## Campbell suspends Richard; Montreal fans riot

National Hockey League President Clarence Campbell suspended volatile Montreal winger Rocket Richard for the remainder of the 1954-55 season on March 16.

The decision came in the wake of a wild melee in the waning moments of a March 13 game between the Canadiens and Bruins at Boston. After being cut on the head during a clash with Boston's Hal Laycoe, Richard went berserk and attacked the Bruin three different times with his stick. Linesman Cliff Thompson, trying to restrain Richard, also was punched twice by the NHL's all-time leading goal scorer.

After listening to evidence at the March 16 hearing, Campbell acted to curb Richard's long pattern of outrageous behavior. But he paid the price for his decision the next night when, while attending a game against Detroit at the Montreal Forum, he became the target of irate Canadiens fans in an ugly scene that eventually turned into a full-scale riot.

Campbell had to be hustled to safety and the game was called after one period with Detroit leading, 4-1. Rioters poured out of the Forum and began vandalizing and looting nearby stores — a demonstration that carried on for several hours before police could bring the situation under control.

And what did Richard's suspension mean to the Canadiens in the long run? Detroit beat Montreal in a tough seven-game Stanley Cup final that ended April 14. With Richard on the ice, the Canadiens might well have turned around that result.

# Vukovich dies at Indy

Bill Vukovich, the foremost auto racing driver in the country, died in a fiery five-car crash during the Memorial Day Indianapolis 500 at the Indianapolis Motor Speedway. Vukovich, who had won the last two Indy 500s, was 36 years old.

Leading after 140 miles in his bid for a record-breaking third consecutive victory, Vukovich approached a four-car tangle on the backstretch and veered to pass. But an axle snapped on Roger Ward's car and suddenly there was a mass of wreckage flying everywhere. Vukovich's Hopkins Special, going an estimated 150 miles per hour, hit a car, did a flip in midair, crashed on its nose, bounced high, hit again and landed upside down. As flames engulfed the car and the pinned Vukovich, patrol workers rushed to his aid. They were too late. None of the other drivers involved in the accident were seriously injured.

Most of the 175,000 fans lost their zest for the remainder of the race, which Bill Sweikert went on to win in his John Zink Special, averaging 128.209 mph. They had just witnessed the worst tragedy at the track since 1939, when defending champion Floyd Roberts died in a crash.

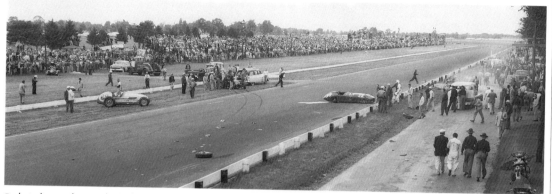

*Debris litters the track and Speedway workers try to free two-time Indianapolis 500 winner Bill Vukovich from the wreckage of the accident that took his life.*

---

# Offensive Chisox drop 29-6 bomb on Athletics

The Chicago White Sox belted seven home runs out of Kansas City's Municipal Stadium and tied a modern major league run-scoring record in a 29-6 bombing of the Athletics on April 23.

The massacre began in the first inning when Bob Nieman hit a three-run homer off Kansas City's Bobby Shantz and continued in the second when Chicago scored seven times off Shantz and reliever

*Chicago's Bob Nieman: Two homers, seven RBIs.*

Leroy Wheat. When all was said and done, the White Sox had matched the 1950 record of the Boston Red Sox while collecting 29 hits, one short of the modern record set by the 1953 New York Yankees.

Nieman and Sherm Lollar both homered twice and Walt Dropo, Minnie Minoso and pitcher Jack Harshman also connected. Nieman drove in seven runs, Lollar and Minoso five apiece. Lollar and Chico Carrasquel both collected five hits.

---

# New rules aid NBA

When Syracuse edged Fort Wayne, 92-91, to complete its seven-game National Basketball Association championship series victory, April 10, on its home court, fans were treated to an exciting finish devoid of the tactical fouling that had plagued the league since its inception. Give credit to two revolutionary 1954-55 rule changes that could redirect the NBA's future course.

The new 24-second clock that requires teams to shoot within that specified time or lose possession of the ball has received rave reviews. So, too, has the bonus free-throw rule that gives an extra charity toss for each foul committed in a quarter beyond the specified limit of six. These amendments mean a faster, cleaner game is being played and fan enthusiasm has reached a new high.

While team scoring skyrocketed from an average of 79.5 in 1953-54 to 93.1 this season, the number of fouls have decreased proportionately. The run-and-gun Boston Celtics averaged 101.4 points per game over their 72-game schedule and the scores should continue to increase as the teams refine their game plans and master the nuances of the new rules.

# football

## The team from the "Humpty-Dumpty" league

*The upstarts from the AAFC beat the best of the NFL and dominate pro football for a decade*

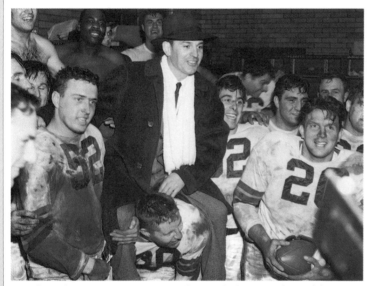

Coach Paul Brown at center stage of annual Championship celebrations.

Brown and QB Otto Graham.

Bert Bell, the National Football League's commissioner and chief trumpet blower, couldn't stop smiling late in 1949 when the NFL completed merger negotiations with the 4-year-old All-America Football Conference and agreed to admit the circuit's top three teams. Bell's league now was stronger than it had ever been before and he was especially enjoying the idea of choreographing the NFL's "game of the half century."

The upstart Cleveland Browns, dominating champions of the AAFC four years running, versus the powerful Philadelphia Eagles, champs of the "real league" the last two years. It was put-up or shut-up time for the Browns; it was Philadelphia's chance to teach the newcomers some football humility.

The Browns, coached by Paul Brown and featuring such stars as Otto Graham, Marion Motley, Lou Groza, Mac Speedie, Dante Lavelli and Dub Jones, would have to defend their honor in

Philadelphia, on a 1950 fall night before the rest of the league would begin regular-season play. The Eagles, coached by Greasy Neale and represented by such talents as Steve Van Buren, Pete Pihos, Alex Wojciechowicz and Chuck Bednarik, had already defeated the College All-Stars at Chicago's Soldier Field.

What this football war boiled down to was Philadelphia's outstanding "Eagle Defense," a 5-4 alignment that had outside linebackers chucking the ends, trying to control Cleveland's high-powered T-formation offense, directed by Graham. It was not even close.

"We'd had five years to think about this great day," Brown said after his team had destroyed the Eagles, 35-10, before a stunned crowd of 71,237. "All kinds of nasty things were said about our league.

"We were physically and emotionally ready for that test. The Cleveland team on this day was the best I ever saw on a given day—anywhere, in any kind of competition."

"Jeez, they got a lotta guns," moaned Neale after watching Graham complete 21 of 38 passes for 346 yards and 246-pound fullback Motley bowl over Eagle defenders. The victory launched Cleveland on the road to a final 10-2 regular season (including another victory over the Eagles), an 8-3 victory over the New York Giants in an American Conference title showdown and an exciting 30-28 championship game triumph over the Los Angeles Rams.

The team from the

"Humpty-Dumpty league" ruled the NFL in its first season and there was no denying what the AAFC had discovered four years earlier: this was one of the greatest professional teams ever assembled.

That was a tribute to Brown, The Great Innovator who recruited and molded players into his own image using advanced football concepts. Brown, a former high school coach in Massillon, O., and college coach at Ohio State, where his team won the 1942 national championship, was at Great Lakes Naval Station when he accepted the challenge to build a professional team from scratch. He formed the nucleus of his first squad with players he had coached, coached against or scouted in high school, college and the service. Two of his recruits, Motley and Bill Willis, were the first blacks to play professional football since 1933 and the only ones to compete in the AAFC in 1946.

Whereas most coaches

*Aptly-named Cleveland wide receiver Mac Speedie.*

*Rifle-armed Otto Graham.*

viewed football as a six-months-on, six-months-off proposition, Brown turned it into a year-round science. He and his assistants became the first to break down game films, the first to take offensive stars and turn them into defensive players, the first to use intelligence tests as a guide to potential, the first to call plays from the sideline with a rotating guard system and the first to develop precision timing pass patterns.

But his greatest skill was in selecting talent, as evidenced by the presence of six future Hall of Famers. Graham ran

the offense and dominated the AAFC with his passing, Groza played offensive tackle and handled place-kicking duties, Motley ran over undersized defenders, Willis was an incredibly quick defender, Lavelli was a lightning-fast receiver and Frank Gatski was a steady center. There were other stars like halfbacks Dub Jones and Edgar Jones, Speedie and receiver-punter Horace Gillom.

What they added up to were four years of misery for outmanned AAFC opponents and similar headaches for deeper, but still outgunned, NFL teams. The Browns dominated the AAFC with a four-year 47-4-3 record, including the first perfect campaign (15-0 in 1948) ever compiled by a professional team. Much of the Browns' success could be traced to the leadership of Graham and a receiving corps featuring Lavelli, Speedie and Gillom.

"Anybody can complete passes when you've got ends like those fellows getting under them," Graham said. "They're three of the fastest ends in the business. They'd make any quarterback look good."

The Browns were so good in the late 1940s that they

unwittingly contributed to the collapse of the AAFC. They dominated to the point that fans from other cities gave up hope and even their own fans bègan to stay away. Cleveland crowds slipped from the 70,000 range in 1946 to below 30,000 in 1949.

After the merger and their first NFL championship, the Browns rolled to their second straight American Conference title, winning their last 11 games after losing the opener to San Francisco. But this time the pass-happy Rams denied Cleveland its sixth straight championship, beating the Browns, 24-17, in the title game.

It was more of the same in 1952 and '53 as Cleveland cruised to conference titles but lost in the championship game to Detroit, 17-7 and 17-16. In

*Edgar Jones (90) blocks for bruising fullback Marion Motley.*

the 1953 loss to the Lions, Graham completed only two of 15 passes for 20 yards and complained later, "This is the worst I've felt in my life."

This sudden crack in the Browns' armor was the result of players like Speedie and tackle John Kissell jumping to Canada and others, like Motley and Willis, retiring. But the defections were not enough to derail Cleveland's express for two more seasons—Graham's final two as quarterback.

After a 1-2 start in 1954, the Browns won eight games in a row, captured another conference title and squared

off against Detroit again in the championship game. But this time the Lions saw a different side of Graham, who threw for three touchdowns and ran for three more in a 56-10 victory.

## "Anybody can complete passes when you've got ends like those fellows getting under them."

**OTTO GRAHAM**
*Cleveland Browns quarterback*

Graham had intended to retire, but Brown coaxed him into playing one more season. Graham responded by leading the league in passing, directing the Browns to the NFL's best record (9-2-1) and closing out

his career with another big championship game: two touchdown passes and two TD runs in a 38-14 pasting of the Rams.

Graham took a legacy into retirement that most likely will never be matched by any quarterback in professional football: 10 seasons, 10 trips to the title game, seven championships. The Browns, in fact, would make it back to the championship game only three times in the next 33 years.

"That's 10 straight years," marveled Brown after 1955. "It was a goal I aimed at, but I didn't think it could be done."

# Musial's late homer lifts N.L. to victory

St. Louis slugger Stan Musial brought a sudden end to the second-longest All-Star Game in baseball history, July 12, when he hit a leadoff home run in the bottom of the 12th inning to give the National League a come-from-behind 6-5 victory over the American League at Milwaukee's County Stadium.

Musial's blast off Boston's Frank Sullivan capped a determined N.L. rally from an early 5-0 deficit. The Americans scored four runs in the first inning, three coming on Yankee Mickey Mantle's homer, and added a solo tally in the sixth. But the N.L. fought back with two runs in the seventh and three more in the eighth to set up Musial's record-breaking fourth All-Star home run.

Milwaukee's Gene Conley delighted his home fans by striking out the side in the top of the 12th and earning the victory after relieving Joe Nuxhall, the Cincinnati lefty who had pitched 3⅓ innings of two-hit relief.

The game was played on the same day that funeral services were held in Chicago for Arch Ward, the former *Chicago Tribune* sports editor who founded the midsummer classic in 1933.

*Eddie Arcaro rides Nashua (right) to a 6½-length victory in the $100,000 match race against Bill Shoemaker and Swaps.*

# Nashua beats Swaps

Belair Stud's Nashua, ridden masterfully by Eddie Arcaro, powered his way to 6½-length victory over Swaps, August 31, in the much-ballyhooed $100,000 winner-take-all match race at Washington Park in Chicago. Nashua's resounding victory gave owner William Woodward Jr. sweet revenge for his colt's only defeat of the year — a 1½-length loss to Swaps in the Kentucky Derby.

The race, broadcast nationally on both television and radio, was a match made in heaven. Once-beaten Nashua, the Preakness and Belmont winner, versus unbeaten Swaps, victor in the Derby. East (Nashua) versus West (Swaps). Arcaro versus Bill Shoemaker.

Swaps went off as the 3-10 favorite, but Arcaro bolted his horse out of the gate and never looked back. Shoemaker tried to keep Swaps in the race, but Nashua really poured it on when he reached the home turn. He romped to victory in 2:04½ over the 1¼-mile course.

The victory was the ninth in 10 starts for Nashua. Swaps, not nominated for either the Preakness or Belmont, has won eight times in nine outings.

*N.L. pitching stars Gene Conley (left) and Joe Nuxhall (center) examine the bat that Stan Musial (right) used to hit his All-Star Game-ending home run.*

# Trabert wins 3 legs of tennis grand slam

Tony Trabert made short work of Australian champion Ken Rosewall, September 11, recording a 9-7, 6-3, 6-3 victory and capturing the U.S. singles championship at the West Side Tennis Club in Forest Hills. The victory was Trabert's second at Forest Hills and his third in major events this year.

The big Cincinnati native exacted a measure of revenge for the American Davis Cup team's recent humiliation against the Australians. Rose-wall and Lewis Hoad, key figures in the Aussies' 5-0 Cup victory, both were struck down in straight sets by Trabert, Hoad in the semifinals.

Trabert, who earlier won the Wimbledon, French and National Clay Courts titles, has enjoyed the finest year since Don Budge recorded the first-ever grand slam in 1938.

In the women's final, Doris Hart earned her second straight U.S. title with a 6-4, 6-2 victory over Patricia Ward of England.

**AUG:** Arnold Palmer recorded his first professional golf victory, winning by four strokes over Jack Burke Jr. in the Canadian Open.

**SEP:** The youngest batting champion in major league history: Detroit's Al Kaline topped A.L. hitters with a .340 average.

**SEP:** New York Giants center fielder Willie Mays belted a National League-leading 51 home runs.

**OCT:** Joe O'Brien drove trotter Scott Frost to harness racing's first Triple Crown—wins in the Yonkers Trot, Hambletonian and Kentucky Futurity for 3-year-olds.

**NOV:** The Green Bay Packers grabbed Alabama quarterback Bart Starr in the 1956 NFL draft—in the 17th round.

**DEC:** Oklahoma captured its second national championship of the decade and stretched its winning streak to 29, three short of the major college record.

# Sugar Ray completes his amazing comeback

The incomparable Sugar Ray Robinson defied the odds, December 9, and claimed the world middleweight boxing crown for an unprecedented third time when he knocked out Carl (Bobo) Olson in the second round of a fight in Chicago.

The 35-year-old Robinson, flashing the form that had carried him to 136 professional victories against only four defeats during a career that began in 1940, was in control from the opening bell and pummeled the champ at will. Olson finally hit the canvas when Robinson connected with a solid right to the jaw nine seconds before the end of the second round.

Despite two previous losses to Robinson, the 27-year-old Olson entered the fight as a clear favorite because of Sugar Ray's long layoff. Robinson won the middleweight crown for the first time in 1951, quickly lost it to England's Randy Turpin, won it back the same year and then relinquished it in December 1952 to try his hand at show business.

He returned to boxing earlier this year and completed his surprisingly successful comeback with the victory over Olson.

# Graham's swan song

Otto Graham completed his outstanding career on December 26, with a brilliant farewell performance, running for two touchdowns, throwing for two more and directing the Cleveland Browns to a 38-14 National Football League title game victory over the Los Angeles Rams at the Los Angeles Coliseum.

When the game was over, the massive crowd of 85,693, most of them Rams fans, stood and paid a deafening tribute to the quarterback who had guided the Browns to four All-America Football Conference championships, six straight American Conference championships and three NFL titles in 10 years.

Graham destroyed the Rams by completing 14 of 25 passes for 202 yards, including a 50-yard TD strike to Dante Lavelli and a 35-yarder to Ray Renfro. His touchdown runs, both in the third quarter, covered one and 15 yards.

Dwarfed by Graham's heroics was a Browns' defensive effort that produced one fumble recovery and seven interceptions.

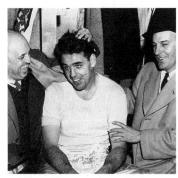

Cleveland quarterback Otto Graham, who scored two touchdowns and threw for two more in his final NFL game, is congratulated by Otto Graham Sr. (left) and Browns Coach Paul Brown (right).

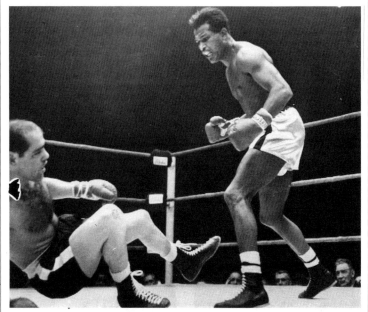

Bobo Olson hits the canvas and Sugar Ray Robinson becomes world middleweight champion for the third time.

# Dodgers finally defeat Yankees

Johnny Podres pitched an eight-hit shutout and Sandy Amoros, a defensive replacement in left field, made a game-saving catch as the Brooklyn Dodgers defeated the New York Yankees, 2-0, in the seventh game of the World Series.

The victory snapped the Dodgers' Series losing streak at seven. They had won pennants in 1916, 1920, 1941, 1947, 1949, 1952 and 1953, but had lost the Series on each occasion, the last five to the Yankees.

It didn't appear that 1955 would be any different as the Yanks won the first two games. But Podres got Brooklyn back on track with an 8-3 win and the Dodgers won the next two games, giving them two shots to win the Series at Yankee Stadium. New York ace Whitey Ford, however, answered with a 5-1, four-hit victory.

The Dodgers were leading 2-0 in Game 7 when the critical play occurred in the sixth inning. With two Yankees on base, Amoros raced to the left-field foul line, made a spectacular catch of Yogi Berra's fly ball and quickly relayed the ball back to the infield to complete a double play.

Podres took care of the rest and the Dodgers — finally — were champions.

# 1956

## Mack dies at age 93

Connie Mack, the Grand Old Man of baseball and owner-manager of the Philadelphia Athletics for 50 years, died, February 8, of natural causes in Philadelphia at the age of 93. His death came about 15 months after his A's had been sold and transferred to Kansas City.

Mack began his professional baseball career as a catcher for Washington in 1886 and later managed the National League's Pittsburgh club. He became a prominent figure in Ban Johnson's Western League at the turn of the century and founded the Athletics as an original franchise in Johnson's new American League in 1901. An astute judge of talent and a natural leader, Mack built, tore down and rebuilt teams to win nine pennants and five World Series championships as well as finish last in the A.L. 17 times.

*Two baseball giants in 1955: Connie Mack (left) and Branch Rickey.*

The fatherly, soft-spoken Mack, best remembered for the way he stood in the dugout, waving his scorecard to signal his players on the field, was one of baseball's first Hall of Fame electees.

## Who was that guy?

The only sure thing about the end of the January 2 Rose Bowl game between second-ranked Michigan State and fourth-ranked UCLA was the final score: Michigan State 17, UCLA 14. Certain details of how that victory was achieved had to be explained in the dressing room after the game.

The Spartans had scored early in the fourth quarter on Clarence Peaks' 67-yard touchdown pass to John Lewis to take a 14-7 lead, but UCLA fought back to tie on Ronnie Knox's passing and a two-yard run by Doug Peters. Michigan State got the ball back in the waning moments on a short Bruin punt

and moved to the 31-yard line, from where Coach Duffy Daugherty elected to try a field goal.

The 41-yard kick was good with seven seconds remaining and the public address announcer and nationwide radio broadcasters hailed Gerry Planutis as the hero of the moment. But, as it turned out, Planutis, who had missed two earlier field-goal attempts, had been passed over in favor of Dave Kaiser, a Notre Dame transfer who had never made a college field goal.

Kaiser made this one and he eventually got his due — about 20 minutes or so after the fact.

## Unbeaten Dons win 2nd NCAA in a row

Bill Russell scored 26 points, grabbed 27 rebounds and held high-scoring Iowa center Bill Logan to 12 points, March 24, as the San Francisco Dons staked their claim as the best team in college basketball history with an easy 83-71 victory in the finals of the NCAA Tournament at Evanston, Ill.

The victory was the 29th of the season for Coach Phil Woolpert's Dons and their record 55th straight over two years. San Francisco is the third team to win consecutive NCAA titles and the first to win with an unbeaten record.

The Dons were forced to play without K.C. Jones, their captain and floor leader who had been declared ineligible for the postseason. But sophomore Gene Brown stepped right in and San Francisco's pattern of lopsided regular-season wins (no team came closer than seven points) carried into NCAA play.

One by one, the nation's top-ranked teams took their best shot at Russell and company and were blown away. Iowa at least had the distinction of running up an early 15-4 lead before being forced to surrender to the full wrath of San Francisco's defensive intensity and the intimidating presence of Russell in the middle.

*High-flying Bill Russell, the center of attention for two-time NCAA champion San Francisco.*

Good news for overmatched contenders: Undefeated heavyweight champion Rocky Marciano has decided to retire his two powerful fists.

# Undefeated Marciano retires from ring

Rocky Marciano, the iron-fisted son of a New England shoe factory worker who rose to the heights of the boxing profession, relinquished his world heavyweight championship, April 27, with the announcement that he will retire from the ring.

The 31-year-old Marciano, who has never lost in 49 professional fights, wants to devote more time to his family in Brockton, Mass. He is the first heavyweight champ to retire undefeated and he promises not to make the same mistake of previous retirees who were persuaded into unsuccessful comebacks.

"I thought it was a mistake when Joe Louis tried a comeback," said Marciano. "No man can say what he will do in the future. But, barring poverty, the ring has seen the last of me."

Marciano broke into professional fighting in 1947 and has knocked out 43 of his 49 opponents. He suffered his first professional knockdown when he won the heavyweight championship in 1952 from Jersey Joe Walcott and he went down again in his final title defense, last September against the veteran Archie Moore.

Marciano is the fourth heavyweight to retire with the title. Of James J. Jeffries, Gene Tunney and Louis, only Tunney stayed retired, however.

# A big leap forward

Charley Dumas, a freshman at Compton (Calif.) Junior College, became the first high jumper ever to clear the 7-foot barrier, June 29, when he went over the bar at 7-0½ while competing in the U.S. Olympic trials at Los Angeles.

Dumas thrilled a crowd of 50,000 fans with his record-breaking jump after missing on his first attempt. He could have made another jump, but decided to pass it up.

Dumas' previous career best, a jump of 6-foot-10¼ was recorded last year during an Amateur Athletic Union meet at the Coliseum. He had cleared only 6-foot-10 this year.

Charley Dumas, the first 7-foot high jumper.

## ★ SPORTS WATCH ★

**FEB:** Figure skaters Hayes Jenkins and Tenley Albright won the only two American gold medals in the Winter Olympic Games at Cortina d'Ampezzo, Italy.

**APR:** The Montreal Canadiens broke Detroit's run of regular-season titles at seven and then skated past the Red Wings in a quick five-game Stanley Cup series.

**APR:** The Philadelphia Warriors wiped out the Fort Wayne Pistons in five games and won their second NBA championship.

**MAY:** Pittsburgh's Dale Long connected against Dodger pitcher Carl Erskine, homering in his record-setting eighth consecutive game.

# Swaps races to a world record

Swaps, a loser last August to Nashua in the $100,000 winner-take-all match race at Chicago's Washington Park, raced to a record-setting victory, June 23, in the $52,250 Inglewood Handicap at Hollywood Park in Los Angeles. Swaps, with Bill Shoemaker in the saddle, completed the 1¹⁄₁₆-mile distance in the world record time of 1:39.

Swaps broke his own record of 1:39³/₅ set last year in the Broward Handicap at Miami's Gulfstream Park. The 1955 Kentucky Derby winner finished three lengths in front of Mister Gus with Bobby Brocato third. Bobby Brocato set the tone of the race when he broke out hard and continued his fast pace with Swaps and Mister Gus a length behind. Swaps passed Bobby Brocato at the quarter pole and never was threatened.

Swaps was timed at 1:32³/₅ for the mile, well below the record (1:33¹/₅) he had established at that distance two weeks earlier.

# 1956

## Babe Zaharias dies of cancer at age 42

Babe Didrikson Zaharias, the greatest female athlete of the half century, died on September 27, after a long bout with cancer. She was 42 years old.

Zaharias was a master of many sports, but she spent the biggest part of her legendary career posting victories on the women's golf tour. The three-time winner of the U.S. Women's Open helped found the Ladies Professional Golf Association in the late 1940s and then proceeded to dominate the tour, winning 31 titles in eight years — almost one-third of the LPGA events played during that period.

Zaharias vaulted into national prominence when she set three track and field records in the 1932 Olympics at Los Angeles. She finally settled on golf as a profession and was an instant success, winning the U.S. Amateur in 1946 on her first try.

Married to professional wrestler George Zaharias, Babe underwent her first cancer operation in 1953. Ten months later she won the Serbin Women's Open and then completed her inspiring comeback by winning the 1954 U.S. Women's Open. Cancer was discovered again in 1955 and her condition steadily deteriorated.

*Former athletic great Babe Didrikson with husband George Zaharias.*

## Masterful Burke is king of the comeback

*Jack Burke (right) accepts congratulations from Ken Venturi, the man he came from behind to beat in the Masters tournament.*

Jack Burke will not be sneaking up on anybody in the near future. Not after his sudden run of success that includes come-from-behind victories in the Masters and the PGA Championship at Blue Hills Country Club in Canton, Miss.

Burke snuck through the back door to claim his first career major and his first tour win since the Inverness Open in 1953. Trailing amateur Ken Venturi by eight strokes after three rounds of the Masters, Burke fired a closing 71 while Venturi was soaring to a final-round 80 and Cary Middlecoff was shooting a 77. The 33-year-old Burke had an improbable one-stroke victory.

His PGA chances looked just as bad in the semifinal match against Ed Furgol when he

## Mantle captures Triple Crown

New York Yankee center fielder Mickey Mantle has joined an elite group of major league players who have won Triple Crowns. His .353 average, 52 home runs and 130 runs batted in mark him as the 12th big-league player to accomplish the feat.

Boston's Ted Williams, who performed the trick in both 1942 and '47, was the last Triple Crown winner and fifth in the

A.L. Mantle also became the A.L.'s first 50-homer man since 1938, when Hank Greenberg belted 58 for Detroit. One of Mantle's blasts, his 19th of the season on May 30, carried special significance.

It came within 18 inches of becoming the first fair ball ever to be hit out of Yankee Stadium. Hitting lefthanded against Washington's Pedro Ramos, Mantle hit a mammoth drive to right field that hit just below the cornice high above the third deck. The drive was estimated at 370 feet from home plate and 117 feet above the ground. There is no telling how far the ball might have traveled had it managed those 18 inches to clear the facade.

trailed 5-down after 14. But Burke rallied to beat Furgol on the 37th and hole then defeated Ted Kroll in the final, 3 and 2.

Kroll led 3-up after 19, but Burke one-putted nine greens in the afternoon and closed out the match on the 34th hole.

# Sooner streak hits 40

Oklahoma's 53-0 victory over Oklahoma A&M completed another perfect season and earned the Sooners another national championship as they stretched their record-shattering winning streak to 40 games.

The 10-0 Sooners, in capturing their second straight national title and third of the decade, outscored opponents, 466-51, including six shutouts. Only Colorado, a 27-19 loser, gave them any kind of a test. Among their victims were Texas (45-0) and Notre Dame (40-0).

Oklahoma's success is a reflection of its coach, Bud Wilkinson, who has compiled a 94-8-3 record and .910 winning percentage in 10 years. The Sooners tied for the Big Six Conference championship with Kansas in 1947, Wilkinson's first season, but have won the Big Seven title outright for nine years in a row.

Leading the way for Oklahoma were Clendon Thomas, who led the nation with 18 touchdowns, halfback Tommy McDonald and center Jerry Tubbs.

World Series perfect game principals (left to right): Yankee pitcher Don Larsen, umpire Babe Pinelli and Yankee catcher Yogi Berra.

Coach Bud Wilkinson (front) and his happy Sooners after Oklahoma had stretched its winning streak to 40 games.

★ SPORTS WATCH ★

**SEP:** New York Yankee Yogi Berra hit his 236th career home run, tying the record for catchers held by former Chicago Cub Gabby Hartnett.

**SEP:** Cincinnati's Frank Robinson tied the N.L. record for home runs by a rookie with his 38th in an 11-5 victory over the New York Giants.

**SEP:** Veteran Shirley Fry earned her first singles titles at Wimbledon and in the U.S. championships at Forest Hills.

**NOV:** Brooklyn's Don Newcombe was named recipient of baseball's first Cy Young Award.

**DEC:** The Soviet Union amassed 98 medals, 24 more than the second-place United States, at the Summer Olympic Games in Melbourne, Australia.

**DEC:** Illinois ambushed two-time NCAA champion San Francisco, 62-33, ending the longest winning streak in college basketball history at 60.

# Larsen's perfecto

New York's Don Larsen, a 27-year-old righthander who was roughed up by Brooklyn in Game 2, pitched the first no-hitter and perfect game in World Series history, October 8, in a 2-0 victory over the Dodgers at Yankee Stadium.

The eyes of 64,519 fans were focused on 39-year-old Dodger starter Sal Maglie, who retired the first 11 Yanks he faced in Game 5. But No. 12, Mickey Mantle, rifled a home run into the right-field stands near the foul pole.

Larsen, using a no-windup style, didn't stop at 11. Three up, three down was the unfailing pattern as the game reached the seventh, the eighth, the ninth inning with the Yankees enjoying a 2-0 edge.

Carl Furillo opened the ninth by flying out and Dodger catcher Roy Campanella hit an easy grounder. Now only pinch-hitter Dale Mitchell stood between Larsen and perfection. With the count 1 and 2, he threw his 97th pitch and umpire Babe Pinelli signaled strike three. Catcher Yogi Berra rushed to the mound and jumped into Larsen's arms to celebrate.

Following that lead, Brooklyn's Clem Labine shut out the Yankees, 1-0, the next day and New York's Johnny Kucks threw a three-hit shutout in Game 7, a 9-0 Series-deciding Yankee victory.

# Jim Brown runs wild

Fullback Jim Brown put on a show that Syracuse fans will not soon forget, running for 197 yards and scoring a major college record 43 points in the Orangemen's 61-7 victory over Colgate, November 17, at Syracuse's Archbold Stadium.

Brown, playing the final regular-season game of his collegiate career, scored on touchdown runs of one, 15 and 50 yards in the first quarter and rumbled eight yards for a second-quarter score. Syracuse owned a 27-7 halftime lead and the talented senior had scored all of the Orange's points.

Brown ran 19 yards for a third-period TD and one yard for a fourth-quarter score to cap his six-touchdown effort. He kicked seven conversions to give him 43 points, one more than Mississippi's A.L. (Showboat) Boykin had scored (on seven TD runs) in a 1951 game against Mississippi State.

Brown finished off his college career with a three-touchdown, 21-point effort against Texas Christian University in the Cotton Bowl. TCU edged Syracuse, 28-27.

# 1957

## Tar Heels win NCAA

It took six overtimes in two nights and a well-devised strategy by Coach Dick McGuire to neutralize Kansas and 7-foot sophomore Wilt Chamberlain, but North Carolina persevered and capped an undefeated season, March 23, with its first NCAA Tournament title.

The title game, played at Kansas City's Municipal Auditorium, was a classic. The 31-0 Tar Heels, who had outlasted Michigan State the night before in a triple-overtime semifinal thriller, opened with a psychological shot. McGuire set 5-foot-11 guard Tommy Kearns to jump center against Chamberlain, a creative move that helped his North Carolina players relax.

The Tar Heels came out firing on all cylinders, building an early 19-2 lead and a 29-22 half-time margin on the strength of 64.7 percent shooting from the floor. North Carolina's outside success drew Chamberlain out of the middle and opened the way for high-scoring Lennie Rosenbluth to work inside.

But the Jayhawks fought back and regulation ended with the teams knotted at 46-46. Both teams scored one basket in the first overtime and no points in the second extra session. The third overtime eventually came down to Tar Heel center Joe Quigg's two free throws with six seconds left. He made both and the Tar Heels owned a 54-53 victory.

Chamberlain scored a game-high 23 points, but balanced North Carolina got 20 points from Rosenbluth while out-rebounding the Jayhawks, 42-28.

*North Carolina had to deal with dominating Kansas big man Wilt Chamberlain.*

## Unbeaten Tennessee is upset by Baylor

Eleventh-ranked and twice-beaten Baylor put a damper on Tennessee's season with a convincing 13-7 upset victory over the second-ranked and undefeated Volunteers in the New Year's Day Sugar Bowl classic at New Orleans.

The hard-hitting and opportunistic Bears, trailing 7-6 in the fourth quarter, capitalized on All-America tailback Johnny Majors' fumble at the Tennessee 15-yard line to take the lead. Six plays after Reuben Saage's recovery, quarterback Buddy Humphrey scored from one yard out and Donnel Berry kicked the extra point.

That was a relief for Berry, who had missed on a second-quarter conversion following Baylor's first score — a 12-yard TD pass from Bobby Jones to Jerry Marcontell. When Ten-

*Tennessee's All-America running back Johnny Majors.*

nessee scored in the third quarter on Majors' one-yard run and converted the extra point, it looked as if that might be the difference.

A rain-drenched crowd of 81,000 watched Baylor lift its final record to 9-2 while ending Tennessee's streak at 10.

## Bradley tames Tigers

Shellie McMillon converted a three-point play with 30 seconds remaining to give Bradley an 84-83 victory over Memphis State in the nationally televised National Invitation Tournament final at New York's Madison Square Garden.

Bradley, which trailed the smaller, quicker Tigers by 10 points with six minutes to play, rallied for a 77-77 tie before falling behind in the waning moments, 83-81. But McMillon, Bradley's center, tapped in a rebound and was fouled by the Tigers' Bob Swander. He hit the free throw to give Bradley the lead.

The Tigers worked the ball for a final shot, but Swander's one-hander with five seconds remaining bounced off the rim and the Braves had their first-ever postseason title after three runnerup finishes in the NCAA (two) and NIT.

The 11,327 fans watched Memphis State's Win Wilfong score 31 points and capture outstanding player honors.

# Celtics struggle to 1st NBA title

Professional basketball took a giant step forward on April 13, when the Boston Celtics defeated the St. Louis Hawks, 125-123, in a double-overtime classic that gave Boston its first NBA championship. The seventh game of the title series, witnessed by a national television audience and 13,909 fans at Boston Garden, showcased the streamlined, 24-second professional game and a high-profile Celtic team that could be on the verge of greatness.

Coach Red Auerbach pulled off a major coup over the summer when he traded Ed Macauley and young Cliff Hagan to St. Louis for its second draft pick. He used it to snap up Bill Russell, the high-flying San Francisco center, and then nabbed Holy Cross forward Tom Heinsohn with his regular pick.

With Bob Cousy and Bill Sharman directing traffic and triggering an explosive running game, the Celtics reeled off a league-best 44-28 record this season. They swept Syracuse in the Eastern Conference finals and appeared to be a lock in the title series against St. Louis.

The Hawks won Games 1, 3 and 6 of the championship series to force the issue. And then, every time Boston appeared on the verge of blowing them away in Game 7, they fought back. Bob Pettit, who led all scorers with 39 points, hit two free throws in the closing seconds of regulation to force overtime and Jack Coleman's long one-hander forced a second extra session.

Again Boston took the lead and again St. Louis mounted a comeback. But luck finally ran out on the Hawks. After Jim Loscutoff's free throw had given the Celtics a 125-123 lead, Pettit fired a desperation shot that bounced off the rim.

Heinsohn led Boston with 37 points while Russell had 19 points and 32 rebounds.

The foundation for a dynasty: Boston Celtics co-owners Walter Brown (left) and Lou Pieri oversee the signing of former San Francisco star Bill Russell.

## ★ SPORTS WATCH ★

**MAR:** Philadelphia sharpshooter Paul Arizin captured his second NBA scoring title with a 25.6-point average.

**MAR:** Detroit winger Gordie Howe won his fifth Art Ross Trophy with 89 points and was named recipient of the NHL's Hart Trophy for the third time.

**MAR:** Montreal's Doug Harvey earned his third consecutive Norris Trophy, given annually to the NHL's top defenseman.

**APR:** The Montreal Canadiens recorded four quick victories over the Boston Bruins to win their second straight Stanley Cup.

**MAY:** Sam Hanks averaged a track-record 135.601 in his Belond Exhaust Special and won the Indianapolis 500 by 21 seconds over Jim Rathmann.

**JUN:** California defeated Penn State, 1-0, to win the College World Series at Omaha, Neb.

# A first: American breaks 4 minutes

Dave Bowden, a 6-foot-3, 160-pound junior at the University of California, became the first American runner to break the four-minute mile barrier, June 1, when he ran 3:58.7 in the Pacific Amateur Athletic Union meet in Stockton, Calif.

Bowden was seven-tenths of a second off the world record set in 1954 by Australian John Landy. The previous best American time was the 4:00.5 recorded by Wes Santee of Kansas during the Texas Relays three years ago.

Bowden knocked over 10 sec off his previous best of 4:09.9.

Dave Bowden, the first American to break the four-minute mile barrier.

# School teacher wins marathon

John J. Kelley, a 5-foot-6, 127-pound school teacher from Groton, Conn., completed the Boston Marathon in 2:20.05, April 20, becoming the first American to win the historic race since John A. Kelley (no relation) turned the trick in 1945.

Competing against a strong 143-man field that included most of the top marathoners from around the world, Kelley took command at the 15-mile mark and never really was threatened. Finland's Veiko Karvonen, winner of the race in 1954, finished second, three minutes and 49 seconds behind Kelley.

Kelley, who was runnerup last year to another Finn, Antti Viskari, received plenty of encouragement and a big welcome home from the estimated 250,000 fans who turned out for the 26-mile, 385-yard race.

# 1957

Dodgers Owner Walter O'Malley (left) and Giants Owner Horace Stoneham (right) with New York Mayor Robert F. Wagner after conferring about the teams' proposed moves to the West Coast.

## West Coast shifts shock New Yorkers

The late-summer announcements that the New York Giants are moving to San Francisco and the Brooklyn Dodgers to Los Angeles for the 1958 season shocked the puzzled fans of New York City.

Those fans were not exactly blindsided. Rumors had been circulating for months. But still the official news was greeted with disbelief. How could two of baseball's most glamorous, tradition-steeped franchises run out on their faithful fans?

The answer, of course, is money. The old bottom line.

The Giants had a 52,000-seat stadium (the Polo Grounds), but they also had a parking problem and were feeling the pinch of a population shift to the suburbs. After drawing 1.15 million fans in their championship season of 1954, attendance skidded to 629,179 in 1956.

The Dodgers had a different

kind of problem. They had the fan support and population, but they did not have an adequate facility. Aging Ebbets Field seated only 32,000 and that simply was not enough. The perennial pennant contenders regularly have drawn 1 million fans to their games, but that figure might easily have doubled in a more spacious stadium.

Dodger President Walter O'Malley had made no secret of his dissatisfaction and even transferred seven 1956 home games to Roosevelt Stadium in Jersey City.

Among the lures extended to the Giants was the promise of a new stadium, already approved by a voter referendum. Until that park is built, the Giants will play their games in 22,500-seat Seals Stadium, which had seen plenty of action as home of the Pacific Coast League Seals for 27 seasons.

## Gibson breaks through in U.S. tennis

It has been an amazing summer for Althea Gibson. In July she became the first black player to win a singles title at Wimbledon. In August she became the first black player to compete on the United States Wightman Cup team. And in September she became the first black player to capture a U.S. singles championship.

The talented 30-year-old capped her successful run with a 6-3, 6-2 victory over former U.S. champion Louise Brough, September 8, at the West Side Tennis Club in Forest Hills. She was in top form the entire tournament, never losing a set and only allowing one opponent to

Althea Gibson, queen of American tennis.

take four games from her in a set.

After using her power attack to destroy Brough, she was presented her championship trophy by U.S. Vice President Richard M. Nixon. Ironically, it was a Brough-Gibson match in 1950 that broke the color barrier in the U.S. championships. Gibson lost a heart-breaker to the then defending Wimbledon champ.

---

### ★ SPORTS WATCH ★

**JUL:** Floyd Patterson became the undisputed world heavyweight champion when he defeated Tommy Jackson in the 10th round at New York's Polo Grounds.

**JUL:** Minnie Minoso's ninth-inning, bases loaded, two out running catch saved the A.L.'s 6-5 All-Star Game victory over the N.L. at St. Louis' Busch Stadium.

**AUG:** 12-year-old Angel Macias pitched a perfect game to lead his Monterrey Mexico team past Le Mesa for the championship of the Little League World Series at Williamsport, Pa.

**OCT:** Montreal's Rocket Richard scored his NHL-record 500th career goal in a 3-1 Canadiens' win over Chicago at the Montreal Forum.

**DEC:** Poll disagreement: AP picked 10-0 Auburn as its college football national champion while UPI opted for 8-1 Ohio State.

---

The Dodgers have not yet decided on a stadium, although they have three under consideration. They are Wrigley Field, a

minor league facility in Los Angeles, the Rose Bowl in Pasadena and the 90,000-seat Los Angeles Coliseum.

# Burdette pitches Braves past Yankees

Lew Burdette scattered seven hits and Eddie Mathews keyed a four-run third inning with a

two-run double as the Braves toppled the New York Yankees, 5-0, October 10, at Yankee Stadium to give Milwaukee its first World Series championship.

Burdette's third victory of the Series and second straight shutout came at the expense of Yankee starter Don Larsen, the hero of the 1956 fall classic. Larsen, whose Game 7 start against the Braves came one year and two days after his 1956 perfect game against Brooklyn, lasted only $2^1/_3$ innings before giving way to Bobby Shantz. By then, the damage had been done and catcher Del Crandall provided eighth-inning insurance with a solo home run.

Burdette's first victory, a 4-2 decision in Game 2, had evened the Series at a game apiece and

*Somewhere in the middle of this body mass is Milwaukee pitcher Lew Burdette, who pitched the Braves to a seventh-game World Series win over the Yankees.*

his 1-0 win in Game 5 gave the Braves a three games to two advantage. Veteran lefthander Warren Spahn pitched 10 innings in Game 4 to earn a 7-5 triumph, the winning blow a two-run homer by Mathews.

The Braves' offensive star, however, was Hank Aaron, who batted .393 with three homers and seven RBIs. It was a fitting conclusion for the Braves who had drawn a league-record 2,215,404 fans to Milwaukee.

# Irish end Oklahoma's streak at 47 games

Notre Dame, coming off consecutive losses to Navy and Michigan State, ended the longest winning streak in college football history, November 16, when it knocked off the No. 1-ranked Oklahoma Sooners, 7-0, in Norman, Okla.

The Fighting Irish, 18-point underdogs and a sure bet to become the 48th notch in the Sooners' five-season victory streak, pulled off their stunning upset with the aid of Dick Lynch's three-yard run and a stifling defense that held the Sooners to total 145 yards.

Coach Terry Brennan's Fighting Irish, who had suffered through a 2-8 1956 campaign, entered this matchup with a 4-2 record. Oklahoma had bulldozed seven straight opponents this year in their search for a third straight national championship.

But the Irish put a damper on

that idea. The game was decided when Notre Dame embarked on a fourth-period 80-yard march that culminated with Lynch's three-yard run. When all was said and done, the statistics verified that the Irish victory was no fluke. Notre Dame posted 17 first downs to nine for Bud Wilkinson's Sooners. They outrushed Oklahoma, 169-98, and also outpassed the Sooners, 79-47.

*Notre Dame's Dick Lynch (25) heads for the end zone and the touchdown that would end Oklahoma's record winning streak at 47.*

# Dick Christy rescues Wolfpack

Dick Christy's 36-yard field goal with the game clock showing zeroes gave 15th-ranked North Carolina State a 29-26 victory over South Carolina, November 23, in Columbia, S.C. Or maybe the score should read: Christy 29, South Carolina 26.

Christy had already scored on four touchdown runs (one of

two yards and three one-yarders) and kicked two extra points when he lined up for the first field-goal attempt of his college career.

The sequence leading to Christy's kick was wild. After South Carolina's Alex Hawkins had fired a 16-yard touchdown pass to Julius Derrick to tie the

game with just over a minute to play, the Wolfpack tried to come back. Tom Katich's long pass was intercepted by Hawkins, but the referee called the Gamecocks for pass interference and gave the ball back to the Wolfpack on the South Carolina 30 for one last play. That was all Christy needed.

# 1958

## Sugar Ray wins crown for record 5th time

Sugar Ray Robinson has done it again. The 37-year-old scored a 15-round split decision over Carmen Basilio, March 25, at Chicago Stadium to win the world middleweight boxing crown for the fifth time.

Robinson, who had lost the title to Basilio last September, was all business as he went about the task of outpointing his 31-year-old opponent. He controlled the tempo of the fight and closed the champ's left eye during a seventh-round barrage. But he could neither put Basilio down nor avoid the body punishment the former Marine was determined to dish out.

Only once did either fighter appear on the verge of going down. Robinson made a big effort to end the fight in the 15th round and actually had Basilio staggering. The decision gave Robinson his 141st career victory against six losses and two draws.

Kentucky players John Crigler (32), Johnny Cox (24) and Don Mills (54) surround Seattle's Jerry Frizzell (with ball) during action in the NCAA Tournament's final game at Louisville, Ky.

## Campanella paralyzed

Catcher Roy Campanella, three-time Most Valuable Player of the Brooklyn Dodgers, suffered a broken neck and paralysis from his shoulders down when the car he was driving, January 28, overturned on a slippery road in Glen Cove, N.Y.

Campanella was driving a rental car to his Glen Cove home at 3:34 a.m. after making a television appearance in New York. About a mile and a half from his home, the 1957 sedan skidded on wet pavement, turned on its right side and crashed into a telephone pole. Campanella was pinned in the car for about 30 minutes as rescuers worked to pry open the doors.

The burly 5-foot-9, 225-pounder was rushed to Community Hospital where a four-hour, 15-minute operation was performed to repair two fractured vertebrae in his neck. Campanella had some move-

Former Dodger catcher Roy Campanella after his career-ending car accident.

ment in both arms after the surgery, but none in his fingers or the lower part of his body.

Campanella joined the Dodgers in 1948 and proceeded to compile a .276 average with 242 home runs in his 10 major league seasons. He was scheduled to move with the Dodgers to Los Angeles for the 1958 campaign, but that move, along with everything else in Campy's life, now is on hold.

## Kentucky's comeback too much for Seattle

Vern Hatton scored 30 points and Johnny Cox added 24 as Adolph Rupp's Kentucky Wildcats rallied to defeat Seattle, 84-72, in the March 22 final of the NCAA Tournament which took place at Louisville, Ky.

Seattle used the offensive play of All-America Elgin Baylor to race to an early 29-18 lead, but the Chieftains ran into trouble when their star forward picked up his third foul midway through the first half. To protect Baylor, who also was playing with a rib injury, Seattle Coach John Castellani switched to a zone defense and slowed the game down.

The Chieftains escaped the first half with a 39-36 lead, but Baylor picked up his fourth foul early in the second half. With Baylor losing much of his aggressiveness, the door swung open. Kentucky finally caught the Chieftains at 56-56 and took its first lead at 61-60. It was all Wildcats after that.

Baylor finished with 25 points, but his efforts were not enough to prevent Rupp's "Fiddlin' Five" from capturing the school's fourth NCAA championship and first since 1951. The Wildcats finished 23-6 while Seattle fell to 24-7.

> ## "SPORTS TALK"
>
> "What do I care about statistics and points? You give me the championships and you can have the all-star teams."
>
> **RED AUERBACH**
> Boston Celtics Coach

# 50-point outburst by Pettit buries Celtics

Bob Pettit scored 50 points, including the winning basket with 16 seconds remaining, to give the St. Louis Hawks a 110-109 victory over the Boston Celtics and a six-game verdict in the National Basketball Association championship series.

Pettit thrilled 10,218 fans at St. Louis, April 12, as he scored 19 fourth-quarter points and almost singlehandedly staved off every Boston rally. After the Hawks went ahead to stay, 95-93, the Celtics managed to cut the margin to one on three different occasions, only to see Pettit score another basket.

Pettit's 50-point outburst was a record for a regulation playoff game. He connected on 19 of 30 field-goal attempts and 12 of 19 free throws. Boston's Bob Cousy scored 50 points in a 1953 playoff contest against Syracuse, but that game lasted four overtimes.

The championship was the first for the Hawks and spoiled the Celtics' bid to win their second straight.

*St. Louis Hawks 50-point man Bob Pettit.*

# Giants, Dodgers are victorious in West Coast home debuts

It seemed only fitting that the Dodgers and Giants should be opponents when West Coast fans got their first taste of major league baseball. And it seemed only right that the home teams should prevail.

Such was the case on April 15, when 23,448 turned out at Seals Stadium to watch the home-town San Francisco Giants pound the Dodgers, 8-0, behind the six-hit pitching of Ruben Gomez. Hall of Famer Ty Cobb was on hand for the historic game, as was Mrs. John McGraw, widow of the late, great Giants manager. The opening-day atmosphere was festive, especially when the Giants jumped on Dodger starter Don Drysdale and two relievers in an eight-hit attack that included a two-run single by Willie Mays and a home run by rookie Orlando Cepeda.

*Opening day ceremonies at San Francisco's Seals Stadium, prior to the first major league game on the West Coast.*

The Dodgers, for their part, enthralled a single-game and National League-record crowd of 78,672, April 18, when they jumped to a 5-2 lead and then held off the Giants for a 6-5 victory in the first game at the massive Los Angeles Coliseum.

# Palmer captures 1st major title

Arnold Palmer shot a final-round 73 and then waited two hours to see if his 284 total would hold up in the Masters golf tournament, April 6. When Doug Ford and Fred Hawkins both failed to sink birdie putts on the 18th green, the 28-year-old former amateur champion had a one-stroke victory and his first major title.

Palmer did not exactly tame the famed Augusta National monster, but neither did anybody else. Ford's 70 was one of only two sub-par rounds on the day, thanks to an all-night thunderstorm that left the course soggy and slow.

Palmer, known for his attacking, aggressive style, took control at the par-5 13th hole when he boomed his second shot within 18 feet of the pin. He sank the putt for an eagle and then coasted home for his long wait. Palmer's victory was not a surprise, especially to the second-place Ford.

"If I don't win today," Ford had said after the third round, "Palmer will. He's strong enough for this big course. He'll never tire. He's got a game like steel."

---

**★ SPORTS WATCH ★**

**JAN:** The NCAA passed a new rule giving college football teams the option of trying for a two-point run or pass conversion after scoring touchdowns.

**FEB:** Boston's Ted Williams became the highest paid player in baseball history when he signed a contract for $135,000.

**APR:** The NHL's Montreal Canadiens made it look easy, running over Boston in six games and winning their third straight Stanley Cup championship.

**MAY:** St. Louis' Stan Musial became the eighth player in big-league history to collect 3,000 career hits, doubling as a pinch-hitter off Moe Drabowsky at Chicago's Wrigley Field

**JUN:** Wilt Chamberlain, passing up his final year of eligibility at Kansas, signed a one-year, $65,000 contract to play for the Harlem Globetrotters.

# 1958

## Soviets, Americans meet in historic event

*Rafer Johnson, the decathlon's reigning king.*

The historic two-day dual track meet between athletes from the United States and Soviet Union ended without a hitch on July 28, with the Russians claiming a slim 172-170 point victory.

Those point totals will remain unofficial, however, because it was agreed when the event was negotiated early in the year as part of a cultural exchange program between the countries that the meet would be treated in two parts — a men's program and a women's program. The American men captured 13 firsts in 21 events to beat the Russian men, 126-109. But the American women won only four of 10 events and were beaten by their Soviet counterparts, 63-44. Five points were awarded for a first, three for a second, two for a third and one for a fourth.

The highlight of the meet was the battle between Rafer Johnson and Russian star Vasily Kuznetsov in the decathlon. Johnson came to Russia as the recognized world record-holder with a score of 7,985 points, but Kuznetsov had unofficially broken that mark with a recent score of 8,013. The crowd of 30,000 attending the second-day events at Lenin Stadium really got behind their star.

But the mad cheering for Kuznetsov seemed to inspire Johnson, who was looking to reinforce his status as the world's best all-around athlete. Johnson outdueled Kuznetsov and set another world record, compiling 8,302 points and winning the affection of a crowd that now cheered and mobbed him affectionately.

That seemed to be the atmosphere of the entire competition. There was a lot of hugging between athletes from both sides and the meet was run beautifully from start to finish. The coach of the men's team, George Eastment of Manhattan College, expressed the sentiments of most of the coaches and athletes involved.

"I've had lots of thrills in my life, but I kind of think this is it," he said. "The United States against Russia — this one was important and we did it."

They will do it again next July because the governments of the two countries have agreed to a return engagement to take place in Philadelphia.

## Gibson wins, retires

Althea Gibson lobbed her way to a 3-6, 6-1, 6-2 victory over Darlene Hard in the singles final of the U.S. championships and then told 11,000 fans at the West Side Tennis Club that she is retiring from tennis for a year.

The 31-year-old Gibson, who has swept both the Wimbledon and Forest Hills singles titles each of the last two years, said she will concentrate on her singing career and promotion of a new book that details her rise from the slums of Harlem.

She did not exactly cruise to victory over the unheralded Hard. She dropped the opening set and appeared to be in serious danger of losing the match. But she started using her lob, negating Hard's speed and forehand skills, and the strategy worked. Hard was forced to stay back and she expended a lot of energy chasing down Gibson's overhead shots.

The men's final also featured a repeat winner. Australian Ashley Cooper survived a fifth-set ankle injury and finished out his 6-2, 3-6, 4-6, 10-8, 8-6 comeback victory over fellow countryman Mal Anderson.

*Award winners Herb Elliott, the record-setting miler, and Althea Gibson, who has won both the Wimbledon and U.S. singles titles for two straight years.*

### ★ SPORTS WATCH ★

**JUL:** Yankee Gil McDougald's single drove in the deciding run as the A.L. edged the N.L., 4-3, in the All-Star Game at Baltimore's Memorial Stadium.

**AUG:** Heavyweight boxing champion Floyd Patterson scored a 13th-round technical knockout over Roy Harris in a title bout at Los Angeles.

**DEC:** Bill Shoemaker won his record fourth national riding championship when he rode four winners at California's Santa Anita Park to bring his season total to 300.

**DEC:** Cleveland Browns second-year man Jim Brown set a single-season NFL rushing record with 1,527 yards.

# Ameche's touchdown ends NFL classic

Alan Ameche's one-yard touchdown run 8 minutes and 15 seconds into the National Football League's first sudden-death overtime game gave the Baltimore Colts a 23-17 victory over the New York Giants, December 28, in the most dramatic and riveting championship contest ever played.

The 64,185 at Yankee Stadium and a national television audience were treated to a titanic battle between some of the game's most glamorous players. The Giants, who needed a 10-0 playoff win over Cleveland to get to the title game, had to rally from a 14-3 halftime deficit, created by a two-yard Ameche run and a 15-yard TD pass from Johnny Unitas to Raymond Berry.

The Giants succeeded, scoring touchdowns on a one-yard Mel Triplett burst and a 15-yard pass from Charley Conerly to Frank Gifford. The Giants led, 17-14, and the Colts, starting from their own 20, had 1:56 left to get something done. This time it was Unitas' turn.

The Colts' quarterback, who completed 26 of 40 passes for 349 yards, threw 11 yards to Lenny Moore and fired three consecutive strikes to Berry covering 62 yards. Steve Myhra's 20-yard field goal knotted the score.

*Baltimore's Alan Ameche bulls into the end zone.*

The overtime was all Baltimore. Moving 80 yards on 13 plays, the Colts brought an end to the struggle with Ameche's short burst. Baltimore had its first championship and the NFL had garnered much-needed national respect.

# Yankee comeback stymies Braves

First baseman Bill Skowron capped a four-run eighth-inning rally with a three-run homer, October 9, as the New York Yankees defeated the Milwaukee Braves, 6-2, in Game 7 of the World Series at Milwaukee. The Yankees became only the second team in history to successfully recover from a three games to one Series deficit.

Bob Turley, pitching six innings of two-hit, one-run baseball, picked up his second win of the Series, having shut out the Braves, 7-0, in Game 5. The big Yankee offensive weapons in the final three victories were Gil McDougald, Skowron and Hank Bauer. McDougald batted .321 with a pair of homers in the Series, while Bauer batted .323 and crashed four home runs.

The Series victory was the Yankees' sixth of the decade and seventh in the last 10 years.

*More Yankee World Series heroes (left to right): Elston Howard, Bob Turley and Gil McDougald.*

# Olmedo produces Davis Cup shocker

Alejandro (Alex) Olmedo, a 22-year-old Peruvian studying at the University of Southern California, shocked 18,500 Australians at Brisbane's Milton Tennis Stadium by dominating Aussie national champion Ashley Cooper in a four-set victory on December 31, that clinched the Davis Cup for the United States.

In one of the biggest upsets in Cup history, Olmedo beat Cooper, 6-3, 4-6, 6-4, 8-6 to give the U.S. an insurmountable 3-1 lead and only its second win in nine years. Olmedo was a principal in all three American victories, beating Mal Anderson in singles, 8-6, 2-6, 9-7, 8-6, and teaming with Ham Richardson in doubles to beat Anderson and Neale Fraser, 10-12, 3-6, 16-14, 6-3, 7-5.

There was controversy about whether a non-American citizen should compete for a U.S. international team, but Olmedo rewarded his supporters. He convincingly outplayed Cooper, the reigning Wimbledon, Australian and U.S. singles champion, as the crowd watched in stunned silence. Cooper did not help himself by commiting 11 double faults.

# 1959

## JANUARY-JUNE

# Daytona's mad dash

The new Daytona International Speedway got exactly what it wanted, February 22, for its inaugural 500-mile stock car race — a thrilling side-by-side dash to the finish by two steel-nerved drivers. But it also got something it didn't want — a controversy that wouldn't be settled until three days after the race.

The end of the first Daytona 500 turned into a classic duel between Johnny Beauchamp's Thunderbird hardtop sedan and Lee Petty's Oldsmobile. For the last 15 laps around the 2½-mile asphalt course, the duo thrilled the 60,000 spectators with a bumper-to-bumper battle.

But the strategy changed on the last three laps as the two cars ran side by side. When they finally crossed the finish line, it was too close to call. Bill France, president of NASCAR and the Daytona Speedway, made an on-the-spot decision, declaring Beauchamp the winner. But after checking still pictures and

*Lee Petty's car No. 42 and Johnny Beauchamp's car No. 73 hit the finish line in a dead heat in the first Daytona 500. Joe Weatherly's car No. 48 was one lap behind.*

movies over the next two days, the decision was reversed.

Petty, the 44-year-old Randleman, N.C., product was awarded the $19,000 first prize and credited with an average speed of 135.42 mph, the highest ever achieved by an American-built stock car.

# 173-139 NBA record

The 12,315 fans who attended a February 27 game at Boston Garden were treated to an unprecedented National Basketball Association offensive show. The Boston Celtics defeated Minneapolis, 173-139, in a game that produced the most combined points ever scored while setting seven league records.

The Celtics produced four of those marks: most points by one team (173), most points in a half (90), most points in one quarter (52) and most field goals in a game (72). The Lakers, who had

won five of their last six outings, set the record for most points by a losing team (139).

The combined 312 points broke the previous mark of 282 set in 1957 when the St. Louis Hawks beat Syracuse, 146-136. The final record was set by Boston guard Bob Cousy, who dished out 28 assists.

The score was 83-64 at halftime and the Celtics led 121-95 after three quarters.

Boston's Tom Heinsohn led all scorers with 43 points while Cousy added 31 and Bill Sharman 29.

# Cal tip-in wins NCAA

Denny Fitzpatrick scored 20 points and Darrall Imhoff's tip-in with 15 seconds remaining sealed the verdict as California hung on to defeat West Virginia, 71-70, and win the NCAA Tournament championship, March 21, at Louisville, Ky.

California's low-profile no-namers, looking for their 25th win of the season, held a commanding 13-point lead midway through the second half, but the Mountaineers staged a furious rally, led by Jerry West, that fell just short. West is considered one of the top two players in the country. The other is Oscar Robertson of Cincinnati, who was on the losing end of a 64-58 California semifinal victory.

Robertson, the nation's leading scorer for the second year in a row with a 32.6-point average, managed only 19 against the Golden Bears. But West scored 28 in West Virginia's final loss.

*California Coach Pete Newell and player Al Buch hold the Golden Bears' hard-earned NCAA championship trophy as Bob Dalton (left) and Bernie Simpson (right) look on.*

## ★ SPORTS WATCH ★

**MAR:** He-e-e's Ba-a-ck: Bill Veeck bought 54 percent of the Chicago White Sox franchise from the Comiskey family.

**MAR:** St. John's went overtime to defeat Bradley, 76-71, in the final of the NIT at New York's Madison Square Garden.

**MAR:** Montreal goaltender Jacques Plante was awarded his fourth straight Vezina Trophy by the NHL.

**APR:** Four straight: The Canadiens blasted Toronto in a five-game final to run their streak of NHL Stanley Cup victories to four.

**JUN:** Cleveland's Rocky Colavito joined an elite group when he hit four straight home runs in an 11-8 win over the Orioles at Baltimore's Memorial Stadium.

**JUN:** Mickey Wright defeated Louise Suggs by two strokes at Pittsburgh and became the first golfer to win back-to-back U.S. Women's Open titles.

*A disconsolate Harvey Haddix after pitching 12 perfect innings, only to lose in the 13th.*

# Perfect Haddix falls in crazy 13th inning

Pittsburgh's Harvey Haddix was perfect, May 26, against the Milwaukee Braves, but that was not good enough. For 12 incredible innings at Milwaukee County Stadium, the little left-hander set down the Braves 1-2-3, and for 12 innings his teammates failed to score a run against Lew Burdette.

Haddix's bubble finally burst in the bottom of the 13th, after Burdette had retired the Pirates in the top of the inning. Felix Mantilla broke Haddix's string of retiring 36 straight batters by reaching first base on a throwing error by Pittsburgh third baseman Don Hoak. Mantilla was sacrificed to second and Hank Aaron was walked intentionally. Big Joe Adcock followed with a drive over the right-center-field fence.

That normally would have ended the game with a final score of 3-0, but Aaron complicated matters by leaving the basepaths before scoring and Adcock was ruled out for having passed his teammate. When the dust cleared, Milwaukee was declared a 1-0 winner and Adcock's hit was a double, not a home run.

But the bottom line was still the same. Harvey Haddix had pitched the first extra-inning perfect game in baseball history — and lost.

---

## "SPORTS TALK"

*"If I had as much money as Casey, I wouldn't finish my sentences either."*

**BIRDIE TEBBETTS**
on Yankee Manager Casey Stengel

*"I only did what I said I would do. I always said it. Why is everybody so surprised?"*

**INGEMAR JOHANSSON**

---

# Johansson triumphs

Ingemar Johansson, a 26-year-old Swede with a powerful right hand, knocked down Floyd Patterson seven times in the third round and scored a technical knockout over the world heavyweight champion in a June 26 title bout at New York's Yankee Stadium. The upset was witnessed by 30,000 fans who were excited by the suddenness of Johansson's flurry and the game but futile efforts of Patterson to last out the third round.

"When I throw my right it moves so fast that no one can see it," Johansson had bragged before the fight, and those words proved prophetic early in the third round when Patterson dropped his guard and the Swede dropped him with a looping right to the jaw. The champion rose at nine and was immediately dropped again. So it continued until referee Ruby Goldstein ended the fight with 57 seconds remaining in the round.

Johansson, who has won 22 professional fights without a loss, is the first Scandinavian-born boxer to win the heavyweight crown and the first foreign champion since Italy's Primo Carnera in 1934.

*Ingemar Johansson stands over Floyd Patterson, who has just hit the canvas for the seventh and final time in the third round.*

---

# Snead shoots 59 on home course

Slammin' Sammy Snead took honors in his own golf tournament, May 16, when he shot an incredible 59 to take an eight-stroke lead after three rounds of the Sam Snead Festival played on his home course at White Sulphur Springs, W. Va.

That score, over a par-70 layout, was fashioned in a non-PGA sponsored event. Snead and six others had managed 60s in PGA tournament play, but nobody had ever broken that magic barrier in such a competitive forum.

Snead's round included nine birdies and one eagle. He one-putted 11 greens and took 25 putts overall. He recorded birdies at the 12th, 13th, 14th, 16th and 18th holes and an eagle at 15 to come home with a back-nine 28.

The 46-year-old Snead capped his incredible run with a final-round 63 and an 11-stroke win over Mike Souchak. Snead's 259 total was two strokes higher than the PGA record for a four-round score but his 36-hole count of 122 was four strokes under the record.

# 1959

## Dodgers win playoff

Gil Hodges scored the winning run in the 12th inning on a wild throw by second baseman Felix Mantilla and Los Angeles defeated Milwaukee, 6-5, to sweep a two-game playoff for the National League pennant.

The victory completed the Dodgers' rise from seventh in 1958 to a first pennant in Los Angeles. But it was not easy.

First the Dodgers had to sweat out a three-way battle with San Francisco and Milwaukee, finally tying the Braves for first place with an 86-68 mark. Then they had to come from behind to win the opener of a best-of-three playoff series in Milwaukee, 3-2. When the series shifted west, the Braves again took a seemingly secure lead into the ninth, 5-2 this time.

But singles by Wally Moon, Duke Snider and Hodges loaded the bases with nobody out. Norm Larker drove in two runs with a single and pinch-hitter Carl Furillo's sacrifice fly tied the game.

The Dodgers earned the right to play the American League-champion Chicago White Sox in the World Series when Hodges walked with two out in the 12th, moved to second on Joe Pignatano's single and scored on Mantilla's bad throw.

*Alex Olmedo, the United States' 1959 Davis Cup hero, was not so heroic in the National Clay Court tennis tournament.*

## Olmedo gets the boot

Alex Olmedo, the hero of the United States' 1958 Davis Cup victory and the reigning Wimbledon and Australian singles champion, was barred from the doubles segment of the National Clay Court tennis tournament on July 17 by angry officials who cited his sloppy, listless play in a July 16 singles match.

At issue was a match in which the 23-year-old Peruvian lost to South African Abe Segal, 6-2, 6-1, 6-0. Olmedo stayed back on the baseline, refused to charge the net, committed many unforced errors and appeared totally disinterested. The crowd began taunting and booing and Olmedo's play got worse. When the match ended, he stalked off.

Olmedo was contrite but could not explain his behavior. He pointed out that he had to play three singles matches and a doubles match in one day to catch up after arriving in Chicago two days late because of a schedule conflict.

But that explanation did not appease the Suburban River Forest Tennis Club officials who sent a report to the United States Lawn Tennis Association stating their belief that Olmedo "threw" the match and should be disciplined.

*Gil Hodges, Duke Snider and Carl Furillo, key performers in the Dodgers' two-game playoff sweep of Milwaukee.*

## Nicklaus announces his arrival

Jack Nicklaus, a brash, aggressive 19-year-old with nerves of steel, dropped an eight-foot birdie putt on the 36th hole to defeat defending champion Charley Coe, 1-up, in a dramatic conclusion to the U.S. Amateur golf championships, September 19, at the Broadmoor Golf Club in Colorado Springs.

The husky Nicklaus, a junior at Ohio State University, shot an afternoon-round 69 to wipe out Coe's 2-up morning lead and outplayed the veteran when the pressure mounted. Nicklaus did not get his first lead until the 32nd hole and lost that on the 35th. On the final hole, Coe was just off the fringe in two shots while Nicklaus was eight feet from the cup. Coe's chip shot came up an inch short and Nicklaus drilled his putt.

Nicklaus, at 19 years, 8 months, became the second youngest player ever to win the event. Robert A. Gardner of Chicago won in 1909 at 19 years, 5 months.

LSU's Billy Cannon on his way to a game-winning 89-yard punt return against Mississippi.

Right: Lamar Hunt, founder and moving force behind the American Football League.

# New AFL to begin operation in 1960

Texas oilman Lamar Hunt, founding father of the American Football League, says that his new professional circuit is not interested in starting a bidding war with the established National Football League. Hunt's comment came, December 2, after his league's eight teams had selected 425 players in its first college draft.

"We're not interested in high bidding for the name players," Hunt said after drafting 53 players for his Dallas Texans franchise. "We're not looking for individuals. We're looking for 33 players to build a team."

Despite Hunt's denial, nobody doubts that the price of talent will go up. That is the natural result any time a new league tries to butt heads with a strong, established predecessor. The NFL has fought this war before, most recently with the All-America Football Conference in the late 1940s.

The AFL was introduced with the August 14 announcement out of Chicago that franchises were being formed in New York, Dallas, Denver, Houston, Los Angeles and Minneapolis-St. Paul. Buffalo and Boston have since been added.

Among the league's owners are oilman K.S. (Bud) Adams in Houston, Hunt and Barron Hilton, son of hotel owner Conrad N. Hilton, in Los Angeles.

While Hunt and the other owners have publicly disdained the idea of a bidding war, they have promised competitive bidding for key college players and they set the league's minimum salary 10 percent higher than the NFL minimum.

The AFL will play 14 league games and four exhibitions in 1960.

# Cannon explodes and LSU triumphs

The Mississippi Rebels, ranked third by both wire-service polls, had their sights focused squarely on Louisiana State's No. 1 ranking when the teams met at Baton Rouge, La., on October 31, in a midseason game that conceivably could have decided a national championship.

LSU, the defending national champion, was 6-0 and had not allowed a touchdown all season. Mississippi also was 6-0 and had allowed only seven points. Everybody was geared for a fierce defensive battle. And they got it.

The Rebels took advantage of a first-quarter fumble by Billy Cannon, LSU's All-America halfback, to set up Ed Khayat's 22-yard field goal. They carried that lead into the fourth quarter and only 10 minutes remained when disaster struck. Or, more accurately perhaps, Cannon fired.

Mississippi's Jake Gibbs punted and the ball took a high bounce toward LSU's goal line. Cannon fielded it on his own 11 and began an arduous journey the other way. He absorbed numerous blows at the beginning of his run before breaking into the clear. His 89-yard touchdown return gave the Tigers a 7-3 lead.

Mississippi tried to come back but could not and LSU's No. 1 ranking was safe—for another week at least.

# THE 1960s

*After a whirlwind courtship in the 1950s, television executives made a solid commitment to sports programming as the new decade dawned. It was a sensible, mutually profitable marriage, a business arrangement that made plenty of dollars and sense.*

The premise was simple. The various sports would generate millions of dollars through long-term TV contracts and the television networks would provide coast-to-coast coverage of their events while acquiring a national viewer base that would attract advertising dollars. And as this formula proved wildly successful, hungry network executives began clamoring for more while the various professional leagues began scrambling for a larger piece of the pie.

Amid a backdrop of civil unrest, the unpopular Vietnam war and three shocking political assassinations, franchise shifts and expansion set the tone for North American sports in the 1960s. No longer heeding the passionate cries of jilted fans, sports officials began playing musical cities while searching for the ultimate television markets. Growing metropolises lobbied for, and usually attracted, their own major league sports. By the end of the decade, all four of the major professional leagues had expanded by at least six teams, with the National Football League growing from 14 to 26 members because of a merger with the 10-year-old American Football League that was made in television heaven. The AFL had

*UCLA big man Lew Alcindor.*

survived because of TV money, which was used to attract such talented athletes as Joe Namath and Billy Cannon.

A sports world in transition was not without its memorable moments. The decade opened with a World Series-winning home run by Pittsburgh's Bill Mazeroski and ended with Namath passing the AFL's New York Jets to a major upset over the NFL's powerful Baltimore Colts in Super Bowl III. Sandwiched between were such historic moments as Roger Maris' record-breaking 61st home run in 1961, Cassius Clay's shocking upset of heavyweight champion Sonny Liston, the 100-point

game of Philadelphia big man Wilt Chamberlain, the pitching feats of Sandy Koufax, Don Drysdale, Bob Gibson and Denny McLain and the incredible 29-foot-2½-inch long jump of Bob Beamon during the 1968 Summer Olympic Games at Mexico City.

Two of sports' greatest dynasties came to an end while another took center stage. As

## ROLL OF HONOR

### AUTO RACING

#### INDIANAPOLIS 500

| Year | Winner | Speed |
|---|---|---|
| 1960 | Jim Rathmann | 138.767 mph |
| 1961 | A.J. Foyt | 139.131 mph |
| 1962 | Rodger Ward | 140.293 mph |
| 1963 | Parnelli Jones | 143.137 mph |
| 1964 | A.J. Foyt | 147.350 mph |
| 1965 | Jim Clark | 150.686 mph |
| 1966 | Graham Hill | 144.317 mph |
| 1967 | A.J. Foyt | 151.207 mph |
| 1968 | Bobby Unser | 152.882 mph |
| 1969 | Mario Andretti | 156.867 mph |

### GOLF

#### MASTERS / US OPEN

| | MASTERS | | US OPEN |
|---|---|---|---|
| Year | Winner | Year | Winner |
| 1960 | Arnold Palmer | 1960 | Arnold Palmer |
| 1961 | Gary Player | 1961 | Gene Littler |
| 1962 | Arnold Palmer | 1962 | Jack Nicklaus |
| 1963 | Jack Nicklaus | 1963 | Julius Boros |
| 1964 | Arnold Palmer | 1964 | Ken Venturi |
| 1965 | Jack Nicklaus | 1965 | Gary Player |
| 1966 | Jack Nicklaus | 1966 | Billy Casper |
| 1967 | Gay Brewer | 1967 | Jack Nicklaus |
| 1968 | Bob Goalby | 1968 | Lee Trevino |
| 1969 | George Archer | 1969 | Orville Moody |

#### PGA CHAMPIONSHIP / US WOMEN'S OPEN

| | PGA CHAMPIONSHIP | | US WOMEN'S OPEN |
|---|---|---|---|
| Year | Winner | Year | Winner |
| 1960 | Jay Herbert | 1960 | Betsy Rawls |
| 1961 | Jerry Barber | 1961 | Mickey Wright |
| 1962 | Gary Player | 1962 | Murle Breer |
| 1963 | Jack Nicklaus | 1963 | Mary Mills |
| 1964 | Bobby Nichols | 1964 | Mickey Wright |
| 1965 | Dave Marr | 1965 | Carol Mann |
| 1966 | Al Geiberger | 1966 | Sandra Spuzich |
| 1967 | Don January | 1967 | Catherine LaCoste |
| 1968 | Julius Boros | 1968 | Susie Berning |
| 1969 | Ray Floyd | 1969 | Donna Caponi |

*Detroit Red Wings star Gordie Howe.*

## HORSE RACING

### KENTUCKY DERBY

| Year | Winner | Jockey |
|---|---|---|
| 1960 | Venetian Way | Bill Hartack |
| 1961 | Carry Back | John Sellers |
| 1962 | Decidedly | Bill Hartack |
| 1963 | Chateaugay | Braulio Baeza |
| 1964 | Northern Dancer | Bill Hartack |
| 1965 | Lucky Debonair | Bill Shoemaker |
| 1966 | Kauai King | Don Brumfield |
| 1967 | Proud Clarion | Bobby Ussery |
| 1968* | Forward Pass | Ismael Valenzuela |
| 1969 | Majestic Prince | Bill Hartack |

*Dancer's Image finished first but was disqualified after traces of prohibited medication were found in his system.

### PREAKNESS STAKES

| Year | Winner | Jockey |
|---|---|---|
| 1960 | Bally Ache | Bobby Ussery |
| 1961 | Carry Back | John Sellers |
| 1962 | Greek Money | John Rotz |
| 1963 | Candy Spots | Bill Shoemaker |
| 1964 | Northern Dancer | Bill Hartack |
| 1965 | Tom Rolfe | Ron Turcotte |
| 1966 | Kauai King | Don Brumfield |
| 1967 | Damascus | Bill Shoemaker |
| 1968 | Forward Pass | Ismael Valenzuela |
| 1969 | Majestic Prince | Bill Hartack |

### BELMONT STAKES

| Year | Winner | Jockey |
|---|---|---|
| 1960 | Celtic Ash | Bill Hartack |
| 1961 | Sherluck | Braulio Baeza |
| 1962 | Jaipur | Bill Shoemaker |
| 1963 | Chateaugay | Braulio Baeza |
| 1964 | Quandrangle | Manuel Ycaza |
| 1965 | Hail to All | John Sellers |
| 1966 | Amberoid | William Boland |
| 1967 | Damascus | Bill Shoemaker |
| 1968 | Stage Door Johnny | Gus Gustines |
| 1969 | Arts and Letters | Braulio Baeza |

## BASEBALL

### WORLD SERIES

| Year | Winner | Pennant Winner (series score) |
|---|---|---|
| 1960 | Pittsburgh Pirates | (New York Yankees, 4-3) |
| 1961 | New York Yankees | (Cincinnati Reds, 4-1) |
| 1962 | New York Yankees | (San Francisco Giants, 4-3) |
| 1963 | Los Angeles Dodgers | (New York Yankees, 4-0) |
| 1964 | St. Louis Cardinals | (New York Yankees, 4-3) |
| 1965 | Los Angeles Dodgers | (Minnesota Twins, 4-3) |
| 1966 | Baltimore Orioles | (Los Angeles Dodgers, 4-0) |
| 1967 | St. Louis Cardinals | (Boston Red Sox, 4-3) |
| 1968 | Detroit Tigers | (St. Louis Cardinals, 4-3) |
| 1969 | New York Mets | (Baltimore Orioles, 4-1) |

## BASKETBALL

### NBA CHAMPIONSHIP

| Year | Winner | Finalist (series score) |
|---|---|---|
| 1960-61 | Boston Celtics | (St. Louis Hawks, 4-1) |
| 1961-62 | Boston Celtics | (Los Angeles Lakers, 4-3) |
| 1962-63 | Boston Celtics | (Los Angeles Lakers, 4-2) |
| 1963-64 | Boston Celtics | (San Francisco Warriors, 4-1) |
| 1964-65 | Boston Celtics | (Los Angeles Lakers, 4-1) |
| 1965-66 | Boston Celtics | (Los Angeles Lakers, 4-3) |
| 1966-67 | Philadelphia 76ers | (San Francisco Warriors, 4-2) |
| 1967-68 | Boston Celtics | (Los Angeles Lakers, 4-2) |
| 1968-69 | Boston Celtics | (Los Angeles Lakers, 4-3) |
| 1969-70 | New York Knicks | (Los Angeles Lakers, 4-3) |

### NCAA TOURNAMENT FINAL

| Year | Winner | Finalist (score) |
|---|---|---|
| 1960 | Ohio State | (California, 75-55) |
| 1961 | Cincinnati | (Ohio State, 70-65 OT) |
| 1962 | Cincinnati | (Ohio State, 71-59) |
| 1963 | Loyola Chicago | (Cincinnati, 60-58 OT) |
| 1964 | UCLA | (Duke, 98-83) |
| 1965 | UCLA | (Michigan, 91-80) |
| 1966 | Texas Western | (Kentucky, 72-65) |
| 1967 | UCLA | (Dayton, 79-64) |
| 1968 | UCLA | (North Carolina, 78-55) |
| 1969 | UCLA | (Purdue, 92-72) |

## FOOTBALL

### NFL CHAMPIONSHIP

| Season | Winner | Finalist (score) |
|---|---|---|
| 1960 | Philadelphia Eagles | (Green Bay Packers, 17-13) |
| 1961 | Green Bay Packers | (New York Giants, 37-0) |
| 1962 | Green Bay Packers | (New York Giants, 16-7) |
| 1963 | Chicago Bears | (New York Giants, 14-10) |
| 1964 | Cleveland Browns | (Baltimore Colts, 27-0) |
| 1965 | Green Bay Packers | (Cleveland Browns, 23-12) |

### AFL CHAMPIONSHIP

| Season | Winner | Finalist (score) |
|---|---|---|
| 1960 | Houston Oilers | (Los Angeles Chargers, 24-16) |
| 1961 | Houston Oilers | (San Diego Chargers, 10-3) |
| 1962 | Dallas Texans | (Houston Oilers, 20-17 OT) |
| 1963 | San Diego Chargers | (Boston Patriots, 51-10) |
| 1964 | Buffalo Bills | (San Diego Chargers, 20-7) |
| 1965 | Buffalo Bills | (San Diego Chargers, 23-0) |

### SUPER BOWL

| Season | Winner | Finalist (score) |
|---|---|---|
| 1966 | Green Bay Packers | (Kansas City Chiefs, 35-10) |
| 1967 | Green Bay Packers | (Oakland Raiders, 33-14) |
| 1968 | New York Jets | (Baltimore Colts, 16-7) |
| 1969 | Kansas City Chiefs | (Minnesota Vikings, 23-7) |

## HOCKEY

### STANLEY CUP

| Year | Champion | Finalist (series score) |
|---|---|---|
| 1960-61 | Chicago Black Hawks | (Detroit Red Wings, 4-2) |
| 1961-62 | Toronto Maple Leafs | (Chicago Black Hawks, 4-2) |
| 1962-63 | Toronto Maple Leafs | (Detroit Red Wings, 4-1) |
| 1963-64 | Toronto Maple Leafs | (Detroit Red Wings, 4-3) |
| 1964-65 | Montreal Canadiens | (Chicago Black Hawks, 4-3) |
| 1965-66 | Montreal Canadiens | (Detroit Red Wings, 4-2) |
| 1966-67 | Toronto Maple Leafs | (Montreal Canadiens, 4-2) |
| 1967-68 | Montreal Canadiens | (St. Louis Blues, 4-0) |
| 1968-69 | Montreal Canadiens | (St. Louis Blues, 4-0) |
| 1969-70 | Boston Bruins | (St. Louis Blues, 4-0) |

## TENNIS

### US OPEN

| Year | Men's Winner | Women's Winner |
|---|---|---|
| 1960 | Neale Fraser | Darlene Hard |
| 1961 | Roy Emerson | Darlene Hard |
| 1962 | Rod Laver | Margaret Smith |
| 1963 | Rafael Osuna | Maria Bueno |
| 1964 | Roy Emerson | Maria Bueno |
| 1965 | Manuel Santana | Margaret Smith |
| 1966 | Fred Stolle | Maria Bueno |
| 1967 | John Newcombe | Billie Jean King |
| 1968* | Arthur Ashe | Virginia Wade |
| 1968* | Arthur Ashe | Margaret Smith-Court |
| 1969* | Stan Smith | Margaret Smith-Court |
| 1969* | Rod Laver | Margaret Smith-Court |

*Amateur and Open championships held in 1968 and '69. Became an exclusively Open championship in 1970.

*New York Jets quarterback Joe Namath.*

the Yankees' star faded after a 60-year stranglehold on baseball and the Boston Celtics grew old after winning 11 NBA championships in 13 years, a college basketball monster reared its head in the West. UCLA, first with speed and pressure and then with the dominating play of 7-foot-1 center Lew Alcindor, captured five NCAA Tournaments in six years and was well on its way to another as the decade closed.

One of the decade's biggest breakthroughs came in 1968 during an historic meeting in Paris. That's when members of the International Lawn Tennis Federation voted unanimously to open tournaments to both professionals and amateurs, a decision that would carry the sport to unimaginable prosperity.

# 1960

## The Team of Destiny

*Ecstatic members of the U.S. Olympic hockey team mob goalie John McCartan after their surprising 3-2 victory over the Russians.*

In one of the more improbable upsets in Olympic history, the United States hockey team, alias the Team of Destiny, defeated the co-favorite Canadians and Soviets before completing their gold-medal run with a 9-4 victory over Czechoslovakia during the Winter Games at Squaw Valley, Calif.

The Americans used a four-goal third period to knock off the Czechs, 7-5, in their opener and then followed with victories over Australia (12-1), Sweden (6-3) and Germany (9-1). That set the stage for back-to-back games with Canada and the Soviet Union.

With goalie Jack McCartan stopping 39 shots and Bob Cleary and Paul Johnson scoring goals, the U.S. upset Canada, 2-1. Two days later, the U.S. recorded its first-ever hockey victory over a Soviet team when the Christian brothers, Billy and Roger, combined for a third-period goal that resulted in a 3-2 victory.

There was one more hill to climb and the Americans did that the next day when they exploded for six third-period goals to beat the Czechs and complete their impossible dream.

*Cozy Ebbets Field, once the pride of Brooklyn, under the spell of a wrecking ball.*

## The end of an era

It had been the home of Leo, Zack, Dazzy, Dixie, Campy, Jackie, Pee Wee, Duke and many other zany characters. It was where super fan Hilda Chester clanged her cowbell and the Sym-Phony Band stayed out of tune for two decades. When Dem Bums fell short, Brooklyn fans always could "wait till next year."

Thousands of fond memories were violated, February 23, when demolition began on Ebbets Field, home of the Brooklyn Dodgers for 44 daffy years. In a brief pre-demolition ceremony conducted at home plate, Lucy Monroe sang the national anthem and Al Helfer, former Dodger broadcaster, introduced guests that included former players Roy Campanella, Carl Erskine and Ralph Branca.

Campy, now confined to a wheelchair because of a 1958 auto accident, was presented with three treasures-his old No. 39 uniform, his old locker and a pot of dirt from the area where he squatted for 10 seasons behind home plate.

## Palmer's finishing rush wins U.S. Open

In one of the greatest finishing rushes ever seen in a major tournament, Arnold Palmer wiped out a seven-stroke deficit with a final-round 65, June 18, and vaulted over 14 golfers to win the U.S. Open at Cherry Hills Country Club in Denver, Colo.

Palmer delighted his huge gallery with a four-birdie opening rush en route to a front-nine 30. He then coasted home with four pars for a two-stroke victory over Jack Nicklaus, a 20-year-old junior at Ohio State University.

Nicklaus couldn't keep up with Palmer, but his 282 total was the lowest ever recorded by an amateur in the U.S. Open. Third-round leader Mike Souchak, who ballooned to a 75, was one of six golfers tied at 283.

The victory, worth $14,400, was carved out with the usual zest and flair that has made Palmer the top attraction on the professional tour. His U.S. Open finish was reminiscent of his April 10 birdie-birdie finish to win the Masters by one stroke over Ken Venturi.

When the ceremonies ended, the group retired to the park rotunda and watched sadly as the wrecking ball, painted white with stitches to resemble a baseball, smashed a hole in the roof of the visitors' dugout. So began the 10-week slaughter of a revered baseball shrine. The end of an era.

# Patterson reclaims lost heavyweight title

Floyd Patterson, knocked down seven times in one round by Ingemar Johansson during a title fight a year ago, got his revenge, June 20, when he knocked out the previously undefeated Swede in the fifth round of a bout at New York's Polo Grounds and became the first fighter ever to regain the heavyweight championship.

Patterson, avoiding Johansson's powerful right hand, measured and outboxed the champion through the first four rounds before connecting with a left hook early in the fifth. Johansson tumbled to the canvas, but rose back to his feet at the count of nine. Patterson began stalking his opponent and soon landed another left hook to his jaw. Johansson went down for the count and Patterson leaped in joy around the ring.

The victory, watched on closed-circuit television in 160 cities throughout the United States and Canada, raised Patterson's career record to 36-2.

*Floyd Patterson (left) and Ingemar Johansson trade punches during their second heavyweight title fight.*

# Lakers head west

The National Basketball Association, following the lead of professional football and baseball, is expanding to the West Coast. And it is doing so in style, sending one of its most glamorous franchises.

Meet the new Los Angeles Lakers, who dominated the NBA through the first half of the 1950s as representatives of Minneapolis. The Lakers will open the 1960-61 campaign in its new home, the Los Angeles Memorial Sports Arena.

Lakers Owner Bob Short received approval for the move from the NBA Board of Governors at its annual meeting at New York's Hotel Roosevelt. Short already had secured exclusive pro basketball rights at the 14,000-seat Arena from the Los Angeles Coliseum Commission. Los Angeles basketball fans will be getting a team with a rich tradition.

The Lakers will find themselves in competition with a Los Angeles entry from the new American Basketball League, a six-team circuit that was formed last week and will begin play in 1961-62. Harlem Globetrotters founder Abe Saperstein is the commissioner of the new circuit.

# Buckeyes roll over California in NCAA

Center Jerry Lucas led the charge as all five regulars scored in double figures and the Ohio State Buckeyes romped past California, 77-55, in the March 19 NCAA Tournament final at San Francisco.

The game had been billed as the perfect matchup, Ohio State's national-best offense (the Buckeyes had averaged 90.4 points per game) against California's nation-leading defense (the Golden Bears had yielded only 49.5). Something had to give. That something was Cal's vaunted defense.

The Buckeyes played an inspired first half and made a remarkable 16 of 19 shots from the field. Lucas hit five of six. Larry Siegfield, Mel Nowell and Joe Roberts combined to make nine of nine. The Bucks led at the half, 37-19, and the Bears Coach Pete Newell was put in the position of having to abandon his patient offense.

California chipped into the lead briefly in the second half, but Ohio State began solving the Bears' press and getting easy baskets. The Buckeyes coasted the rest of the way to their first national championship and an impressive final 25-3 record.

Only two Golden Bears reached double figures and Dick Doughty was high man with 11. The loss was only California's second against 28 victories during the season.

# 1960

## Soviets capture gold, but U.S. stars shine

The Soviet Union's powerful Olympic team dominated the medal count (103-71) at the Summer Olympic Games in Rome, but the United States had its share of top performers. The most notable were Wilma Rudolph, a triple-gold winner in women's track, and decathlete Rafer Johnson, who piled up an Olympic-record 8,392 points.

Rudolph, prematurely born and sickly as a youngster before developing into a world-class runner, dominated the sprint events, winning the 100-meter dash in 11.0 seconds and the 200-meter dash in 24.0 before anchoring the world record-setting 4 X 100-meter relay team's 44.4-second run.

The spotlight in the boxing segment belonged to light heavyweight Cassius Clay, a Louisville, Ky., youngster who talked as well as he fought. Clay, who conversed and joked with everybody he met throughout the Games, earned a gold medal by decisioning three-time European champion Zbigniew Pietrzykowski of Poland in the final.

The most dominating American effort was turned in by the basketball team. Featuring such stars as Jerry Lucas, Oscar Robertson, Jerry West and Walt Bellamy, the U.S. averaged 102 points while holding the opposition to 59.5. No team came closer than 24 points.

*Wilma Rudolph crosses the finish line in the 100-meter sprint at the Rome Olympic Games, winning one of her three gold medals.*

## Rawls wins 4th Open

Betsy Rawls, who trailed by seven strokes after two rounds, made up the deficit with a blistering 68 in the morning and then survived a shaky 75 in the afternoon to win her record fourth U.S. Women's Open golf championship.

Rawls, who had won the prestigious title in 1951, '53 and '57, cruised around the 6,137-yard Worcester (Mass.) Country Club course in the morning, recording six birdies and displaying some pretty fancy putting. Rawls dropped a 50-footer and two 25-footers in tying the previous low round in Open play.

The 68 also tied her with two-time defending champion and second-round leader Mickey Wright. But Wright soared to an 82 in the afternoon and Rawls' chief challenger became Joyce Ziske, who enjoyed a two-stroke lead after nine holes. Ziske, however, missed a four-foot putt on 18 that could have forced a playoff.

*Four-time U.S. Women's Open winner Betsy Rawls.*

# Maz buries Yankees

Second baseman Bill Mazeroski stood waving his bat as 36,683 hopeful Pirates fans sat on the edge of their seats at Pittsburgh's Forbes Field. New York Yankee righthander Ralph Terry fidgeted on the mound. The score was 9-9 in the bottom of the 10th inning of Game 7 of the World Series.

Terry fired and Mazeroski connected, sending a resounding smash over the left-field wall. Yankee players bowed their heads in disappointment as Maz danced around the bases to the mob of teammates that awaited him at home plate. A nation of fans rejoiced in the realization that they had just witnessed one of the classic moments in baseball history.

The 1960 World Series had been a classic even before the dramatic fireworks of Game 7. The Yankees had bludgeoned the Pirates in winning three times. The Bucs had used finesse to garner their three victories. The American League Yankees had outscored their National League rivals, 46-17, and outhit them, 78-49.

Recapping, the Pirates won the opener 6-4 behind the pitching of Vern Law while the Yanks reeled off 16-3 and 10-0 drubbings, Mickey Mantle homering twice and driving in five runs in Game 2 and Bobby Richardson hitting a grand slam and a record six runs in Game 3.

And so the pattern continued. Pittsburgh won the next two games, 3-2 and 5-2. New York answered, 12-0, behind Whitey Ford.

Nobody knew what to expect in Game 7. But nobody was disappointed. Pittsburgh jumped on Yankee starter Bob Turley for four runs in the first two innings, but New York's Bill Skowron hit a solo homer in the fifth and Yogi Berra's three-run homer in the sixth gave the Yanks a 5-4 lead. New York stretched the lead to 7-4 with two eighth-inning runs, but the Pirates answered with five in the bottom of the inning to take a 9-7 lead. The key blow was a three-run homer by reserve catcher Hal Smith.

Not to be denied, the Yankees scratched out two ninth-inning runs to tie the game. That set the stage for Mazeroski, who wrote the perfect ending and gave Pittsburgh its first Series win in 35 years.

*Pittsburgh coaches, teammates and fans await the jubilant Bill Mazeroski as he heads for home after hitting his World Series-winning home run against the New York Yankees.*

# Hot Baylor scores 71

Elgin Baylor, a fast-shooting forward with every move in the book, exploded for a National Basketball Association record 71 points, November 15, to lead the Los Angeles Lakers to a 123-108 victory over the New York Knicks in the second game of a doubleheader at Madison Square Garden.

A crowd of 10,132, which had just watched the Detroit Pistons down the Boston Celtics in a 115-114 overtime thriller, received a different kind of treat in the second game. Baylor, scoring in every manner imaginable, made 28 field goals and 15 free throws and bettered his own 64-point record.

The 6-foot-5 former Seattle star connected on 15 of 20 field goal attempts in the first half while piling up 34 points. He added 37 more after the intermission, breaking his old record with 1:35 left in the game. He left to a standing ovation.

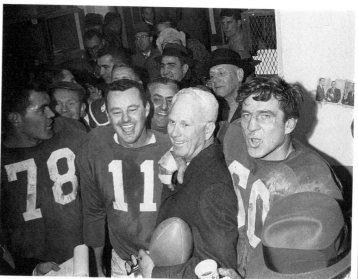

*Philadelphia quarterback Norm Van Brocklin (11) and two-way star Chuck Bednarik (60) flank Coach Buck Shaw after the Eagles' championship game victory over Green Bay.*

# Eagles rally to win NFL championship

Halfback Ted Dean set up his own five-yard touchdown run with a 58-yard fourth-quarter kickoff return as the Philadelphia Eagles rallied to a 17-13 victory over Green Bay, December 26, in the National Football League's championship game at Franklin Field in Philadelphia.

The Packers, making their first appearance since 1944, had retaken the lead when quarterback Bart Starr culminated a 12-play, 80-yard drive with a seven-yard scoring pass to Max McGee.

The Eastern Conference champion Eagles fell behind in the first half on two Paul Hornung field goals, but fought back to grab a halftime lead on a 35-yard touchdown pass from Norm Van Brocklin to Tommy McDonald and a 15-yard field goal by Bobby Walston. Hornung had set an NFL season-record with 176 points—15 touchdowns, 15 field goals and 41 extra points.

The Packers, under second-year Coach Vince Lombardi, almost came back to pull it out at the end. A frantic push ended at the Eagles' 9-yard line as time expired.

# golf

## The father of modern golf

*Arnold Palmer: the inspirational crowd-pleaser who set off golf's television and big-money explosion*

*With Jack Nicklaus in 1962.*

Everything about the man stirs emotion, whether he's riding a tractor on the television screen or hitting a golf ball over the scenic ponds and azalea bushes at Augusta National. His dark, finely-chiseled features have given way to lines and creases and he no longer is able to successfully challenge the world's best golf courses, but Arnold Palmer's legacy lives on.

Need proof? Just check out one of those PGA Senior events when the legend decides to tee it up with his Tour contemporaries. But if you do, be prepared to push, shove and fight your way for position with other members of Arnie's Army. Yes, the biggest golf spectator force on record still exists. It is not quite as demanding or as ornery to opponents as it once was, but it is maddeningly loyal. And it still grimaces, moans or celebrates with every shot.

Palmer, the man who ushered in golf's economic golden age, created his legacy with a perfectly blended mixture of talent, style and personality. The talent was effective if not refined. The style was bold and aggressive.

The personality was attractive and contagious.

The Palmer story began in Latrobe, Pa., in 1929. Arnold's father, Deacon, was the greenkeeper at Latrobe Country Club and he gave the youngster his first golf club at age 3. When his father later became club professional during the Depression, Palmer was allowed course privileges. He also spent hours on the practice tee and benefited from his father's instruction.

The long hours paid off when Arnold went off to Wake Forest University and became a three-time Atlantic Coast Conference champion. It paid

off again in 1954 when the confident 24-year-old won the U.S. Amateur championship at the Country Club of Detroit, defeating veteran Robert Sweeny on the final hole.

Palmer immediately turned professional and spent a quiet, non-winning first year on the PGA Tour. He won his first pro tournament (the Canadian Open) in 1955, captured two titles in '56 and four more in '57. But he did not capture the public eye until the spring of 1958, when he recorded a one-stroke victory in the Masters.

Arnie's gallery was but a small platoon on that April day when Palmer donned the first

of four green jackets. It grew into an army two years later on another April day when Palmer, already a four-time winner for the year, charged to a birdie-birdie finish and a Masters victory over Ken Venturi.

Arnie's Army was born that day on the 17th fairway at Augusta. A rag-tag throng of happy and excitable sports watchers gathered along the fairway and around the green in curiosity, to see if this young charger could pull off a miracle finish. They cheered

### "Most of us would still be caddies [without Palmer]."

**CHI CHI RODRIGUEZ**

enthusiastically when he belted a long drive, they yelled when he dropped his approach shot 35 feet from the pin and they let out a mighty roar when he rolled the putt home for a tying birdie.

Then they pushed and shoved their way to the 18th tee as Palmer, shirttails

*Arnie's Army was in full force during the U.S. Open at Oakmont (Pa.) Country Club in 1962.*

anging out, hair uncombed and cigarette in hand, prepared for the final battle. Another army of fans surged down from the elevated 18th green and trained against the gallery ropes for a view.

Palmer's drive was safe left and he hit a high-arching 6-iron shot that rolled to within six feet of the pin. Another roar. Palmer, just trying "to imagine I was having a nice day in the country," rolled in the putt and bedlam broke out. The gallery celebrated the beginning of a long, intense love affair.

The object of affection was a charismatic, friendly, caution-to-the-wind *everyman* who held running conversations with his gallery and spent exhaustive hours signing autographs. His appeal knew no boundary and he attracted presidents and CEOs as well as laborers and beer chuggers. Palmer made golf a game for the masses and part of his charm was his unpredictability. He might hit a 200-yard approach that would make your mouth water, or he might mess up a 20-foot chip like a weekend hacker. An athletic god or a humble mortal? You never knew what to expect and the crowd loved him for it. Palmer was living, breathing suspense and every agonizing grimace or satisfying smile from his expressive face evoked a similar emotion from his fans.

Palmer also was *fun* to watch. While many of his contemporaries stoically played with machine-like swings and precise, conservative strategy, Palmer attacked the difficult tour courses like a fighter with a chip on his shoulder. He was a puncher, not a jabber, a brawler who aimed every shot at the pin. His crouching, lunging swing looked like a bushman hacking his way through the African jungle.

It was at the 1960 U.S. Open at Cherry Hills Country Club in Denver that Palmer "charged" into the national spotlight. For three rounds he

*British Open champ in 1961.*

had whaled away and achieved little, trailing leader Mike Souchak by seven strokes. Between the first and second Saturday rounds Palmer had a now-famous conversation with sportswriter Bob Drum.

"What would happen if I shot a 65?" Palmer mused.

"Nothing," replied Drum. "You're out of it."

"The hell I am," Palmer shot back. "A 65 would give me 280, and that's a score that wins Open championships."

"Well," said Drum, "if you

went out and drove the first green maybe you could make a hole-in-one."

Palmer stomped out to the first tee and drove the green on the par-4 first hole. He opened with six birdies on the first seven holes and cruised to a 65, winning the championship.

As the boisterous galleries grew larger with every tournament, so did Palmer's victory resume. Between 1958 and 1964, he won seven of the 25 majors he entered and finished in the top 10 on 12

other occasions. He took his show to England and Scotland, winning British Open titles in 1961 and '62 after finishing second in '60. It was love at first sight for British golf fans.

Palmer went on to finish his career with 61 victories, led the money-winning list four times, won the Vardon Trophy for low scoring average four times and became the first to top $1 million career earnings.

But, more importantly, it was Palmer who single-handedly triggered golf's golden-age television and big-money explosion. With huge galleries hanging on his every move, opportunistic TV executives jumped on the bandwagon and altered the economics of professional golf. Purses that had totaled $600,000 when Palmer joined the tour in 1954 quadrupled over the next decade.

"Every golfer who makes his living off the game should thank the Lord daily that Arnold Palmer came along," said long-time rival Chi Chi Rodriguez. "Most of us would still be caddies."

While Palmer was performing his miracles in the 1960s, he also was suffering some major disappointments—particularly in his attempts to win a second U.S. Open. He lost in a 1962 playoff to a youngster named Jack Nicklaus and he incredibly blew a seven-stroke lead with nine holes to play in the 1966 Open at San Francisco. But there were many charges and collapses in a career that only produced occasional victories after 1967.

Through it all, Palmer became a one-man corporation that produced and endorsed a galaxy of products. His manager, Cleveland lawyer Mark McCormack, saw to that and kept Palmer's face and name in the public eye. It was not difficult. For while Nicklaus came along to surpass Palmer's golf supremacy in the 1960s, nobody ever approached his popularity.

*Palmer en route to the U.S. Amateur title in 1954.*

# 1961

## Goalby sees birdies

Bob Goalby knows how to turn a two-stroke deficit into instant victory. Just fire eight consecutive birdies.

That's the strategy the 30-year-old Belleville, Ill., native used, March 19, and his record-setting birdie binge resulted in a final-round 65 and a three-stroke victory over Ted Kroll in the St. Petersburg (Fla.) Open golf tournament. Trailing by two strokes after seven holes on the final day, Goalby used some sterling iron play and putting to birdie holes 8 through 15 and checked in with an impressive four-round total of 261.

Kroll settled for second place while South African Gary Player, the PGA tour's leading money-winner, was third. The previous record for consecutive birdies, seven, was shared by Tommy Bolt, Warren Smith and Don Bisplinghoff.

## Oilers win AFL title

George Blanda threw three touchdown passes and kicked an 18-yard field goal, January 1, to lead the Houston Oilers to a 24-16 victory over the Los Angeles Chargers and the first championship of the new American Football League.

The title game was played before 32,183 fans at Houston's Jeppesen Stadium. The partisan Oiler supporters watched as the Western Division champion Chargers took the lead on two first-quarter Ben Agajanian field goals.

But the 33-year-old Blanda was too much for the Chargers. He threw a 17-yard touchdown pass to Dave Smith and kicked his field goal in the second quarter. He connected with Bill Groman for seven yards and Billy Cannon for 88 in a 14-point second half.

The best Los Angeles could do was pull within a point (17-16) early in the fourth quarter.

Houston Owner K.S. (Bud) Adams congratulates Billy Cannon after the halfback had helped lead the Oilers to the first AFL championship.

## Russian eclipses high jump standard

High jumper John Thomas prepares to go up and over during competition in the Boston Athletic Association Games.

As he prepared to compete in the January 28 Boston Athletic Association Games, John Thomas, a 19-year-old Boston University student and the world indoor and outdoor high jump record holder, was informed that Valeri Brumel, an 18-year-old Russian student, had added two inches to his indoor mark earlier in the day during a track meet in Leningrad. Brumel had soared 7-foot-4½, bettering the 7-foot-2½ Thomas had recorded last March in Chicago.

"It must have been quite a jump," said Thomas, who then proceeded to clear 7-foot-1 on his first jump, 7-foot-2 on his second and 7-foot-3 on his third after two bad misses. Everybody was bracing to see if Thomas, the outdoor record holder at 7-foot-3¾, could go any higher. But on the advice of his coach, he decided to call it a night.

So the day ended with two jumpers reaching heights never before attained, Thomas indoors and Brumel either indoor or out. Brumel is a relative newcomer to the 7-foot level, but Thomas has cleared that height 56 times.

### ★ SPORTS WATCH ★

**FEB:** Charles O. Finley purchased the outstanding 48 percent of the Kansas City Athletics stock to become sole owner of the team.

**MAR:** In a battle of Ohio basketball powers, Cincinnati surprised favored Ohio State, 70-65, in the final of the NCAA Tournament at Kansas City.

**MAR:** Jockey Johnny Longden rode his record 5,500th career winner, aboard Spring Victory at Golden Gate Fields in Albany, Calif.

**APR:** San Francisco's Willie Mays became the ninth player in big-league history to hit four home runs in one game, also driving in eight runs in the Giants' 14-4 victory at Milwaukee.

**MAY:** Baltimore's Jim Gentile became the fourth player in major league history to hit grand slams in consecutive innings, performing the feat during a 13-5 Oriole victory over Minnesota.

**JUN:** Eddie Gaedel, the midget who appeared in a 1951 baseball game for the St. Louis Browns, died in Chicago at age 36.

A.J. Foyt in Victory Lane after winning the Indianapolis 500 by a slim five seconds over Eddie Sachs.

# Foyt wins Indy duel

A.J. Foyt, a 26-year-old crew-cut Texan, drove his Bowes Seal Fast Special to a thrilling five-second victory over Eddie Sachs' Dean Van Lines Special in the May 30 Indianapolis 500.

More than 200,000 spectators crowded into the Indianapolis Motor Speedway for the 50th anniversary of the Memorial Day event and nobody was disappointed. Foyt and Sachs staged an intense duel for the final 300 miles of a race that produced a surprise ending.

After exchanging the lead with his opponent for more than 100 laps, Foyt pulled ahead by four seconds with 25 miles to go. But suddenly he pulled into the pits for repair of a faulty fuel hose. Sachs had clear sailing— or so everyone thought.

With three laps to go, Sachs saw a warning strip break on a tire and had to pit. When the tire change was complete, Sachs zipped back onto the track— just as a surprised Foyt was moving back into the lead.

Foyt averaged an Indy-record 139.131 mph and collected more than $125,000. Sachs, the pole-sitter after qualifying at 147.481 mph, was the victim in the second closest race in Indianapolis 500 history.

# Records fall as Wilt hits the charts

You do not have to see 7-foot-1 Philadelphia center Wilt Chamberlain play too many times before realizing it will not be long before he owns virtually every offensive record in the books. With the exception of Boston defensive ace Bill Russell, Chamberlain simply dominates everybody in the National Basketball Association.

In the just-completed 1960-61 campaign, Chamberlain shattered 10 offensive records, eight of which were marks he had broken the year before in his rookie season. The most visible records were the 38.3-point scoring average and 3,033 total points he produced in 79 games.

But he also set records for field goals attempted (2,479), field goals made (1,251), free throws attempted (1,054), field goal percentage (.505), rebounds (2,149), rebound average (27.2 per game), minutes played (3,773) and games scoring 50 or more points (8).

Despite Chamberlain's dominance, Most Valuable Player honors went to Russell. The Boston big man led the Celtics to a 57-22 regular-season record and their third straight NBA championship, which was decided in a five-game final series against the St. Louis Hawks.

Chicago goalie Glenn Hall deflects a Detroit shot away from the net during Game 6 action in the Stanley Cup finals.

# Streaking Chicago ends long NHL Cup drought

Reg Fleming's shorthanded goal in the second period tied the game and Chicago added four more goals en route to a 5-1 April 16 victory over Detroit that earned the Black Hawks their first Stanley Cup title in 23 years.

The first period of Game 6 at Detroit belonged to the Red Wings, who held a 1-0 advantage on the strength of Parker MacDonald's goal. But midway through the second period, Fleming wrecked a Detroit power-play opportunity by stealing a pass in the Red Wing zone and firing the puck past goalie Hank Bassen. Ab McDonald scored another second-period goal to give the Black Hawks the lead. Third-period goals by Eric Nesterenko, Jack Evans and Ken Wharram sealed the verdict.

The victory capped an unlikely postseason surge during which the Black Hawks snapped Montreal's five-year Stanley Cup reign with a six-game semifinal victory. Top honors in that series belonged to goaltender Glenn Hall, who recorded 3-0 shutouts in the fifth and sixth games.

# 1961

## Maris tops the Babe

"Move over Babe Ruth." So said Roger Maris, a later-edition New York Yankee outfielder, with one swing of his bat on October 1. Maris propelled a pitch from Boston righthander Tracy Stallard into the right-field bleachers at Yankee Stadium for his record-breaking 61st home run, ending his torturous season-long chase of Ruth's 60-homer ghost.

But the historic home run did not end the controversy. For a variety of reasons—such as the incredible popularity of Ruth and the unfair perception of Maris as insensitive and inconsiderate—many fans cringed at the thought of this new-era Yankee supplanting the great Bambino. And as it became obvious that Maris was making a run at one of baseball's most cherished records, they made that point clear, even prompting Commissioner Ford Frick to jump into the fray with his famous "asterisk" ruling.

This declared that a player who sought to displace Ruth in the record book would have to hit his 61st home run before his team played its 155th complete game. Anything after 154 games would receive second billing because Ruth had produced his 60 home runs while playing a 154-game schedule in 1927. Maris was playing under a new 162-game format, the product of American League expansion.

Most of the season was a fascinating home run duel between Maris and teammate Mickey Mantle. Maris, a 27-year-old lefthander, did not hit his first homer until the Yankees' 11th game—the same day Mantle hit his sixth and seventh. But Maris soon found his groove. By the end of May, Mantle had 14 and Maris 12. As June came to a close, Maris led, 27 to 25. On July 31, Maris had 40 to Mantle's 39. As August closed, Maris had 51 homers, Mantle 48.

Soon, however, Maris was on his own. Illness plagued Mantle throughout September and he finished with 54 homers. Maris entered the Yankees' 155th game (it would count against the asterisk because of an early-season tie) with 58, needing two to tie Ruth's mark. He got one, off Baltimore righthander Milt Pappas. No. 60 came against Baltimore's Jack Fisher on September 26, and Maris

New York Yankee record chasers Roger Maris (left) and Mickey Mantle.

entered the final game of the season needing one more. He got it, in the fourth inning against Stallard, giving the Yankees a 1-0 victory. Maris was in the record book—with an asterisk, of course.

The Yankees went on to record a five-game victory over the Cincinnati Reds in the World Series, with Maris hitting one home run.

Arnold Palmer blasts out of the sand on the eighth hole during second-round play in the British Open at Birkdale, England.

## Palmer charges on

Arnold Palmer, pulling off another of his patented late surges, shot a final-day 69 and 72, July 15, and claimed a one-stroke victory in the British Open at Birkdale, England. The triumph was the first by an American since Ben Hogan won in 1953.

But it wasn't easy. After a sunny first day in which Palmer shot a 70, rain and high winds plagued the tournament, damaging the course and even postponing play for one day. When morning play opened for the third round, rain was falling and there was some question

whether the tournament would be canceled.

It was under those conditions that Palmer heated up, covering the front nine in 32 strokes and turning a one-stroke deficit into a one-stroke lead. The sun broke out in the afternoon and Palmer coasted home with a 72 for a four-round total of 284, one stroke better than Dai Rees of Wales.

Rees teed off on the par-5 18th needing an eagle to force a playoff. He hit a beautiful second shot that stopped seven feet short of the pin and he rolled in his putt for a birdie.

# Expansion Mets hire Stengel as manager

The Old Perfessor is back in baseball. That was the big news in New York, October 2, when it was announced that former Yankee boss Casey Stengel has agreed to come out of retirement and manage the expansion New York Mets in their first National League season.

Stengel, 71, a popular figure who is sure to attract fans to the ball park, is known for his colorful language, fractured syntax, off-beat humor and comical behavior. Casey will need a good sense of humor with the Mets, who figure to struggle through their formative years. It certainly will not be like it was with the Yankees, who captured 10 American League pennants and seven World Series under Stengel's 12-year leadership.

Stengel was unceremoniously replaced last year by Ralph Houk when the Yankees announced a manadatory age 65 retirement policy.

---

## ★ SPORTS WATCH ★

**JUL:** Hall of Famer Ty Cobb, baseball's all-time hit leader, died of cancer in Atlanta at age 74.

**AUG:** Milwaukee lefty Warren Spahn became baseball's 13th 300-game winner when he pitched the Braves to a 2-1 victory over the Chicago Cubs.

**AUG:** The Philadelphia Phillies' modern National League-record 23-game losing streak came to a merciful end when John Buzhardt beat Milwaukee, 7-4, in the second game of a doubleheader.

**SEP:** Young Jack Nicklaus defeated H. Dudley Wysong, 8 and 6, at Pebble Beach, Calif., to win his second U.S. Amateur golf title in three years.

**SEP:** Darlene Hard captured her second straight U.S. singles championship, beating Ann Haydon in the Forest Hills final, 6-3, 6-4.

**OCT:** The New York Mets selected catcher Hobie Landrith and the Houston Colt .45s opted for shortstop Eddie Bressoud as first picks in the expansion draft to stock their new teams. Both players came off San Francisco's roster.

**DEC:** Philadelphia center Wilt Chamberlain exploded for an NBA-record 78 points in a triple-overtime game against the Los Angeles Lakers.

**DEC:** Heavyweight champion Floyd Patterson retained his title with a fourth-round knockout of Tom McNeeley at Toronto.

**DEC:** Defense was the order of the day as Houston outlasted San Diego 10-3 in the American Football League championship game, a match riddled with turnovers.

*Ecstatic Green Bay fans celebrate the Packers' NFL championship game victory over the New York Giants at City Stadium.*

## Hornung's 19 points key Green Bay romp

Paul Hornung, on leave from Army duty, scored 19 points and the Green Bay Packers captured their seventh National Football League championship, December 31, by thrashing the New York Giants, 37-0, on a bitterly cold afternoon at City Stadium in Green Bay.

Hornung scored on a six-yard touchdown run early in the second quarter and kicked three field goals and four conversions to spark the Packer victory. Ron Kramer caught touchdown passes of 14 and 13 yards from quarterback Bart Starr and Boyd Dowler took a 13-yard Starr pass for the remaining Green Bay points.

Billed as an even matchup, the West Division-champion Packers (11-3 during the regular season) were never even challenged by the Giants (10-3-1 in the East). Flanker Kyle Rote dropped two sure first-half touchdown passes, but the New Yorkers never threatened otherwise. Coach Vince Lombardi's opportunistic defense forced five turnovers and kept the Giants bottled up all day.

When the game ended, 39,029 fans surged onto the field and began a celebration that lasted long into the night. Green Bay, the smallest city in the NFL, would be known henceforth as "Titletown, U.S.A."

---

# 1962

## JANUARY - JUNE

## Marine vaults 16 feet

John Uelses, the world's first 16-foot pole vaulter, after his victory in the Milrose Games.

John Uelses, a 24-year-old crewcut corporal in the U.S. Marine Corps, soared into the 'record books, February 2, when he became the first athlete ever to clear the magical 16-foot barrier in the pole vault during competition in the 55th Milrose Games at New York's Madison Square Garden.

Uelses missed on his first two tries at 16-foot-0¼ but easily cleared the bar on his final vault, topping his week-old 15-foot-10¼ indoor mark. George Davies of Oklahoma State cleared 15-foot-10¼ last May in an outdoor meet and still is waiting official certification. Davies' vault would stand as the world record because only outdoor marks are officially recognized.

Uelses, born in Berlin but raised in Florida, used a new fiberglass pole. The 6-foot-1, 170-pounder had preceded his record with vaults of 14-foot-6, 15-foot-0, 15-foot-4, and 15-foot-8.

"I just can't believe it," he said. "Even when I was pounding down the runway I was thinking I'll never make it."

## Bearcats repeat upset

Paul Hogue scored 22 points, grabbed 19 rebounds and put a defensive blanket on high-scoring Ohio State center Jerry Lucas, March 24, as Cincinnati repeated its 1961 upset by beating the favored Buckeyes, 71-59, in the NCAA Tournament final at Louisville, Ky.

It was a sweet victory for the Bearcats, who listened all summer to talk that their 70-65 overtime win over the previously unbeaten Buckeyes in the 1961 final had been a fluke, an upset they could not hope to pull off two years in a row. Their critics were forced to eat their words.

With Hogue setting the tone at both ends of the court, the 28-2 Bearcats methodically built a 37-29 halftime lead and then stretched the margin to 18 points in the second half. Tom Thacker gave Hogue plenty of offensive help with 21 points and Ron Bonham held high-scoring John Havlicek to 11.

Lucas, who had wrenched his knee during Ohio State's 84-68 semifinal victory over Wake Forest, played the final with his leg heavily taped and finished with 11 points.

Boston's Frank Ramsey reaches in to strip the ball from Los Angeles' Rudy LaRusso, who is more concerned about how he is going to shoot over Bill Russell (6) during NBA Finals action.

## Celtics triumph again

Sam Jones and Bill Russell combined to score nine of Boston's 10 overtime points, April 18, and the Celtics hung on to defeat the Los Angeles Lakers, 110-107, and win their record fourth consecutive National Basketball Association championship.

With a packed house of 13,909 home fans cheering them on in Game 7 of the championship series, the Celtics lost a fourth-quarter lead before recovering in the extra session. The Lakers' Frank Selvy scored the final two baskets of regulation to tie the game 100-100.

The Celtics made it look easy in overtime, rolling to a 110-102 advantage that sealed the verdict. Russell, the NBA's Most Valuable Player for the second year in a row, capped his big season with a 30-point, 44-rebound performance against the Lakers. Elgin Baylor (41) and Jerry West (35) combined for 76 Los Angeles points.

The Lakers missed their big chance when they lost a 119-105 Game 6 decision at home.

The Bearcats of Cincinnati have that No.1 feeling after upsetting Ohio State for the second straight year in the NCAA Tournament final.

# Nicklaus overcomes Palmer, hostile fans

Jack Nicklaus, a husky 22-year-old looking for his first professional victory, withstood the taunts of a hostile gallery and the patented charge of crowd favorite Arnold Palmer to win an 18-hole playoff and the U.S. Open golf championship at Oakmont Country Club in Pennsylvania.

It was a difficult situation for the two-time U.S. Amateur champion because Palmer is from nearby Latrobe, Pa., and the tournament drew record galleries—most of whom came to follow Arnie's drive for a second Open title. Arnie's Army was loud in support of its hero.

The record crowd of 24,492 was getting just what it wanted in the final round with Palmer leading by three strokes over Nicklaus at the ninth hole. But Arnie inexplicably stubbed a chip shot and took a double bogey, letting Nicklaus back into the contest. The rookie shot a 69 for a 283 total, forcing the Monday playoff.

The 11,000 fans who showed up for the extra round continued their vociferous support of Palmer. But they were stunned when Nicklaus jumped to a four-stroke lead after six holes and refused to fold. Nicklaus, putting like a veteran, came home with a 71, three strokes better than Palmer.

*Jack Nicklaus chips out of a hazard during his U.S. Open playoff round against Arnold Palmer.*

---

# Paret's death studied

A three-day public hearing was conducted by a legislative committee set up to determine the future of boxing in New York state in the wake of Benny (Kid) Paret's death as the result of injuries suffered in a March 24 welterweight title fight at Madison Square Garden. Emile Griffith, the winner of that fight and current welterweight champion of the world, testified May 22.

Paret died on April 3, after going to the canvas two minutes into the 12th round. The 23-year-old Griffith, who had controlled most of the fight, put the champion away with a relentless flurry of 25 blows after backing him against the ropes. Paret was helpless during the assault and appeared out on his feet, well before referee Ruby Goldstein stopped the onslaught.

Paret tumbled to the canvas and was carried unconscious to the dressing room. An ambulance took him to the hospital where an emergency operation was performed to relieve pressure on his brain. The 25-year-old Cuban never regained consciousness.

---

# Chamberlain explodes

Wilt Chamberlain, the Philadelphia Warriors' 7-foot-1 scoring machine, nicked the Knicks for 100 points, March 2, as the Warriors blasted the New Yorkers, 169-147, in a game at Philadelphia.

The Knicks could not slow down the one-man demolition crew. He scored a record 36 field goals and 28 free throws. His 100-point outburst broke the one-game record of 78, a mark he set last December against Los Angeles.

The combined point total of 316 also was an NBA record, breaking the mark set in 1959 when Boston beat Minneapolis, 173-139. The Knicks, with Richie Guerin scoring 39, Cleveland Buckner 33 and Willie Naulls 31, scored the most points ever for a losing team.

Chamberlain, who also grabbed 25 rebounds in his 100-point game, went on to finish the season with 4,029 points, an amazing 50.4 average, and set 10 offensive records. He scored 50 or more points 44 times in the Warriors' 80 games.

---

## ★ SPORTS WATCH ★

**JAN:** After leading in the three previous Daytona 500 races, Glenn (Fireball) Roberts won the fourth running in a world-record average of 152.529 mph.

**JAN:** A new mile record: New Zealand's Peter Snell lowered the world mark to 3:54.4.

**MAR:** Chicago Black Hawks star Bobby Hull scored his 50th goal in a 4-1 victory over the New York Rangers, tying the record of Rocket Richard and Bernie Geoffrion.

**APR:** Eddie Arcaro, one of the greatest jockeys in horse racing history, retired after 31 years and 4,779 winning rides.

**MAY:** St. Louis Cardinals slugger Stan Musial broke Honus Wagner's National League record when he collected career hit No. 3,431.

**JUN:** A two-run homer by Jack Reed, his first major league round-tripper, gave the New York Yankees a 9-7 win over Detroit after seven hours and 22 innings. The teams combined for 16 straight scoreless innings.

# 1962

## Chamberlain takes show to West Coast

The National Basketball Association's off season of musical franchises has resulted in the sale and shift of the Philadelphia Warriors to San Francisco and the dumping of the Cleveland Pipers from the league's expansion plan, only a few weeks after Commissioner Maurice Podoloff had welcomed the first-year American Basketball League champion to the fold.

West Coast basketball will be eagerly awaiting the arrival of the Warriors and their one-man wrecking machine, 7-foot-1 center Wilt Chamberlain. The former Kansas star's amazing 1961-62 season included a 50.4 scoring average and a 100-point game against the New York Knicks. The Warriors franchise was purchased by a New York syndicate for a record $850,000.

The Pipers, believing that the ABL was on the verge of folding, had petitioned for admission into the NBA for the coming season. But when the ABL decided, July 30, to play another season with six teams, Commissioner Abe Saperstein threatened a lawsuit if the NBA went ahead with its plans.

That threat, plus the team's inability to meet financial requirements, resulted in the NBA deciding to remain in its present nine-team alignment.

## U.S. falls to Mexico in tennis shocker

*Rafael Osuna reaches for a Jon Douglas shot while leading Mexico to a shocking Davis Cup victory over the United States.*

Unheralded Rafael Osuna, exhausted and seemingly on the verge of collapse during his August 6 match with Jon Douglas, came back to life in a surprising fifth set to defeat the American and give Mexico a shocking victory over the United States in Davis Cup play at Mexico City.

Osuna's 9-7, 6-3, 6-8, 3-6, 6-1 victory insured the Mexicans' first win over an American team in 16 meetings dating back to 1928.

Osuna had run out of gas and was taking oxygen while trying to cope with the 7,800-foot altitude. But with a standing-room-only crowd of 3,200 wildly cheering him on at the Chapultepec Sports Center, Osuna suddenly came to life and stormed past his startled opponent. Douglas simply could not cope with the revived Mexican or the vociferous crowd.

Chuck McKinley had defeated Osuna in the opener of the series, 6-2, 7-5, 6-3, but Douglas fell to Mario Llamas in a four-set second match. Osuna teamed with Antonio Palafox to stun the heavily-favored U.S. doubles team of McKinley and Dennis Ralston in a five-set marathon.

*Sonny Liston lands a long left to the head of Floyd Patterson during his first-round knockout of the heavyweight champion.*

## Liston claims title

Sonny Liston, a dour, unsmiling knockout machine, needed only 2 minutes, 6 seconds, September 25, to pound out a victory over Floyd Patterson in a heavyweight championship fight at Chicago's Comiskey Park.

The crowd of 26,000 had barely settled in when the 214-pound Liston backed the 189-pound champion into a corner and hit him with a left to the body that doubled him over, a left hook to the head that straightened him up and a devastating right that sent him to the canvas for the count.

**SEP:** A tennis Grand Slam: Australian lefthander Rod Laver won the Wimbledon, French, Australian and U.S. singles championships.

**SEP:** Washington's Tom Cheney set a major league record by striking out 21 Orioles in the Senators' 16-inning, 2-1 win at Baltimore.

**OCT:** New York Giants quarterback Y.A. Tittle tied an NFL record with seven touchdown passes in a 49-34 victory over Washington at Yankee Stadium.

**DEC:** The Dallas Texans overcame the Houston Oilers after 2 minutes, 54 seconds of the second overtime period, 20-17, and claimed the American Football League championship in the longest professional football game ever played.

It was the 24th knockout of Liston's nine-year career. The new champ has won 34 of 35 pro bouts.

Patterson has lost the heavyweight crown twice after winning it originally when he knocked out Archie Moore on November 30, 1956. He lost to Ingemar Johansson in 1959 and defeated the Swede in a rematch a year later.

# San Francisco rally comes up inches short

The entire season had been an uphill battle for the San Francisco Giants. They caught the Los Angeles Dodgers on the last day to force a pennant playoff. They needed a four-run ninth-inning rally to produce a 6-4 win in Game 3 of the playoff and earn a trip to the World Series.

And here they were, down 1-0 in the bottom of the ninth of Game 7 of the fall classic, with runners stationed at second and third and big Willie McCovey standing at the plate. Could the Giants do it again?

As McCovey stood at the plate waving his bat like a toothpick, New York Yankee ace Ralph Terry stood nervously on the mound. He had been in this situation before. In Game 7 of the 1960 fall classic, Pittsburgh's Bill Mazeroski had connected for a spectacular 10th-inning Series-winning home run off the righthander.

Hero or goat. Those were the choices that whipped through Terry's mind as he went into his windup and delivered his third pitch to the Giants slugger.

Terry cringed as McCovey sent a wicked shot toward right field. Yankee second baseman Bobby Richardson moved slightly to his left, lifted his glove and snared the ball. The Yankees had won their second straight World Series and the unlucky Giants had come up inches short—literally.

The early part of the Series, like the season and playoff for the Giants, was a test of talent and endurance. Bad weather and two open dates thrown in for coast-to-coast travel meant the Series was contested over a 13-day period.

But it was worth the wait. The teams swapped victories from beginning to end, Whitey Ford recording a 6-2 Yankee win in the opener and Jack Sanford shutting out the Bronx Bombers, 2-0, in the second game. So it continued until Game 7, when Terry, a 5-3 winner in Game 5, matched up against Sanford. The decisive run came in the fifth inning when Bill Skowron scored on Tony Kubek's double-play grounder.

New York Yankee pitcher Ralph Terry gets a victory ride after shutting out San Francisco in Game 7 of the World Series.

# Wills steals the show

Maury Wills, the man who lights the fuse for the Los Angeles Dodgers' offense, was named National League Most Valuable Player, November 23.

The speedy shortstop enjoyed a banner season in which he batted .299 and tied for the league lead in triples. But his biggest accomplishments came on the basepaths and helped the Dodgers win numerous games.

Wills became the first player ever to top the 100 mark in steals, swiping 104 and breaking Ty Cobb's one-season record of 96. Wills tied and broke Cobb's record in a 12-2 loss to St. Louis, stealing second in both the third and seventh innings.

Wills' final two steals came during Game 3 of the Dodgers' pennant playoff against San Francisco. He singled with one out in the seventh and swiped second. One out later, he stole third and continued home when catcher Bob Bailey's throw skipped into left field.

# Green Bay repeats

Jerry Kramer kicked three field goals and Jim Taylor scored on a seven-yard run as the Green Bay Packers braved a slicing, cold 35-mph wind to record a 16-7 National Football League championship game victory at New York's Yankee Stadium.

With 64,892 freezing fans braving the elements, the Packers displayed machine-like efficiency in handing the Giants a title-game loss for the second straight year. Kramer opened the scoring with a 26-yard field goal in the first quarter and he added another in both the third and fourth quarters. Sandwiched between was a Taylor scoring run that was set up by a New York fumble.

The only Giants' points came shortly after halftime when rookie Jim Collier recovered a blocked Green Bay punt in the end zone for a touchdown.

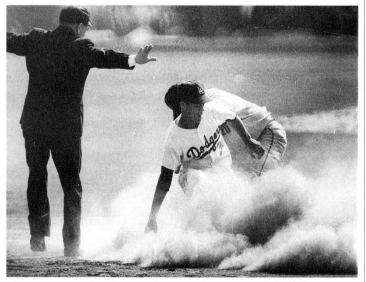

The umpire signals safe as Dodger speedster Maury Wills slides into third base with record steal No. 104 during a playoff game against San Francisco.

# 1963

## JANUARY-APRIL

## Wisconsin's frantic rally falls just short

Southern Cal, out to prove that its final No. 1 ranking was well deserved, did just that through three quarters of its Rose Bowl matchup with No. 2 and once-beaten Wisconsin at Pasadena, Calif. The Trojans rolled to a 42-14 lead behind four Pete Beathard touchdown passes.

But in the final period the Badgers and quarterback Ron VanderKelen cranked up their offense, and Southern Cal's safe lead turned into a frantic race against the clock.

With 11 minutes, 41 seconds remaining, Wisconsin reduced the deficit on Lou Holland's 13-yard touchdown run. Vander-Kelen's four-yard touchdown pass to Gary Kroner with 8:32 left and a bad Trojan snap that resulted in a safety with 2:40 to go cut the lead to 42-30. VanderKelen, who completed 33 of 48 passes for 401 yards in the game, then hit Pat Richter for the 11th time with a 19-yard TD pass, cutting the margin to 42-37 with 1:19 remaining.

After an unsuccessful onside kick, Southern Cal ran three plays and punted. As Vander-Kelen desperately tried to set up for one last play, the final gun sounded. The Trojans had held on—barely.

## ABL calls it quits

The American Basketball League, submerged in red ink, suspended operations on January 1, after a season and a half, throwing about 100 players into the open market as free agents.

The announcement by Commissioner Abe Saperstein sent officials from the National Basketball Association scurrying to the telephones. The names that drew most of the early attention were Connie Hawkins, the ABL's scoring leader in its only full campaign, Dick Barnett and Bill Bridges. Former University of Cincinnati star Jerry Lucas had signed to play with the ABL's Cleveland Pipers, but was forced to sit out when the Pipers withdrew from the ABL after winning the league's first championship, only to be denied permission to join the NBA.

Saperstein, who said that not one of the six teams (Kansas City, Long Beach, Pittsburgh, Oakland, Philadelphia and Chicago) was operating in the black, declared Kansas City (22-9) the second-year champion.

*The furious Rose Bowl rally of Wisconsin and quarterback Ron VanderKelen (15) came up five points short.*

*Former Cleveland Coach Paul Brown.*

## Paul Brown is fired

Paul Brown, the man who formed the Cleveland Browns and molded them into the biggest success story in professional football history, was relieved of his general manager and coaching duties, January 9, by team owner Art Modell.

The shocking announcement reflects the extent that relations between the two have been strained. Modell had privately expressed growing dissatisfaction and reportedly had been contemplating a "reorganiza-tion" for some time. Brown, the only coach in the 17-year history of the franchise, has been asked to serve out the remaining six years of his contract as a team vice president.

Brown's record speaks for itself. His teams compiled a 47-4-3 record and won all four championships in the now-defunct All-America Football Conference. When the Browns joined the National Football League in 1950, they either won or tied for the Eastern Confer-ence crown in eight of their first nine seasons and won three NFL titles. Browns' NFL coach-ing record is 111-44-5.

### "SPORTS TALK"

*"Statistics don't mean a thing. When they can measure heart, when they can measure what a player does in the clutch, then I'll start believing in statistics. Otherwise, they're just a lot of numbers."*

**RED AUERBACH**
Boston Celtics Coach

# Rozelle suspends Karras, Hornung

Green Bay halfback Paul Hornung and Detroit defensive tackle Alex Karras, two of the premier players in the National Football League, were suspended indefinitely, April 17, for betting on league games and associating with and passing information to gamblers.

Hornung, the golden boy from Notre Dame, was penalized for "his pattern of betting and transmission of specific information concerning NFL games for betting purposes," according to Pete Rozelle, the NFL Commissioner. Rozelle said Karras had made at least six significant bets on games since 1958.

But Rozelle also emphasized that there was no evidence of players betting against their own team or giving less than 100 percent during games.

The Commissioner also fined Detroit players John Gordy,

*Detroit defensive tackle Alex Karras, one of two NFL stars suspended indefinitely for betting on games.*

Gary Lowe, Sam Williams, Joe Schmidt and Wayne Walker $2,000 apiece for their alleged gambling activities.

# Toronto rolls in Stanley Cup final

Eddie Shack scored on a deflection in the third period and Dave Keon scored twice, once into an empty net, April 18, to give Toronto a 3-1 victory over Detroit and its second straight Stanley Cup.

A capacity home crowd cheered on the Maple Leafs, who closed out the five-game series much like they started it —on a roll. Toronto's Dick

Duff had scored twice within the first 68 seconds of Game 1 and the Leafs cruised to a 4-2 victory—one of three 4-2 wins they would record in the series.

Game 5 was easily the most intense. Keon scored in the first period, but Alex Delvecchio answered for the Red Wings in the second. Shack received credit for the game-winner when a Kent Douglas

shot caromed off a Detroit player, hit Shack's stick and bounced behind goaltender Terry Sawchuk.

Toronto, which needed only five games to dispose of Montreal in the semifinal round, thrived in the postseason even though Frank Mahovlich, their top player while winning the regular-season championship, did not score.

## ★ SPORTS WATCH ★

**JAN:** Baseball rule change: The expanded strike zone will now be from the top of the shoulders to the bottom of the knees.

**FEB:** American Jim Beatty set a world indoor mile record when he was clocked at 3:58.6.

**FEB:** Tiny Lund drove his Ford to victory in the Daytona 500, averaging 151.566 mph.

**MAR:** Providence defeated Canisius, 81-66, to win its second NIT title in three years.

**APR:** After 11 big-league at-bats, Cincinnati infielder Pete Rose finally broke into the hit column with a triple off Pittsburgh righthander Bob Friend.

**APR:** After Boston had dispatched the Los Angeles Lakers for the Celtics' record sixth straight NBA championship, veteran guard Bob Cousy announced his retirement.

# Loyola pulls shocker

Loyola of Chicago, a longshot to even make the NCAA Tournament, erased a 15-point Cincinnati lead in the final 12 minutes of regulation and scored a dramatic 60-58 overtime victory in the March 23 title game at Louisville, Ky.

Cincinnati, the top-ranked team in the country and a heavy favorite to win its record third straight NCAA title, gave high-scoring Loyola a quick defensive lesson, forcing the Ramblers to miss 13 of their first 14 shots. Top scorer Jerry Harkness did not get a point in the first half and Cincinnati held a 29-21 lead.

The second half looked like an easy stroll, especially when

Cincinnati extended its lead to 45-30. But the battle-hardened Bearcats crumbled in the face of Loyola's furious press and a national television audience witnessed one of the most thrilling comebacks in college basketball history.

With Cincinnati turnovers and fouls starting to pile up, the Ramblers cut the deficit— 48-39, 48-43 and, with 2:42 left, 50-48. The comeback was completed when Harkness tied the game at 54-54 with time running out in regulation. Loyola's improbable victory was sealed with one second remaining in the extra session when Vic Rouse grabbed an offensive rebound and layed it in.

*Chicago Mayor Richard Daley (right) shakes hands with Loyola Coach George Ireland at the airport after the Ramblers had arrived home with the NCAA championship trophy, held by high-scoring Jerry Harkness.*

# 1963

## MAY - AUGUST

## Davis dies of leukemia

Former Syracuse All-America running back Ernie Davis, who in 1961 became the first black to win college football's Heisman Trophy, died of leukemia at a Cleveland hospital, May 18, at age 23.

Davis was first diagnosed as having the disease at the College All-Star camp last July, shortly after signing an $80,000 contract to play with the National Football League's Cleveland Browns.

Forced to sit out the 1962 NFL season, Davis got good news in October when doctors announced that the leukemia was in remission and gave him the okay to resume his training program. But six weeks ago, his blood began deteriorating.

Apparently unaware of the seriousness of his condition, Davis continued working as a salesman for a soft-drink distributor in addition to conducting a film study for the Browns. When he entered the hospital, May 15, he told Cleveland officials he probably would be out in a couple of days.

Davis arrived at Syracuse two years after the great Jim Brown had graduated and broke all his rushing records, compiling 2,386 yards on 360 carries while scoring 220 points.

Bob Hayes hits the tape with a new world record (9.1 seconds) in the 100-yard dash.

## Hayes dashes to glory

Bob Hayes, a 20-year-old at Florida A&M University, staked his claim as the world's fastest human, June 21, when he set a world record by running the 100-yard dash in 9.1 seconds in the Amateur Athletic Union championships at St. Louis.

Hayes made his historic run in a semifinal heat and then duplicated it in the finals. The first run was well within the allowable wind conditions, but the second was not.

Hayes put his football experience—he plays halfback—to good use during his dash to glory. With elbows out and knees kicking high, he broke out of the blocks into the lead and really turned on the burners in the middle 50 yards. He was pushed by an excellent field and just finished ahead of Johnny Gilbert, who matched the previous world mark of 9.2 held by Frank Budd of Villanova and Harry Jerome of Canada.

## Jones holds on, wins first Indianpolis 500

Californian Parnelli Jones, driving an Agajanian Willard Battery Special with a traditional Offenhauser-powered engine, set an Indianapolis 500 speed record and held off the late charge of Jim Clark's new streamlined Lotus-Ford to win the Memorial Day race at the Indianapolis Motor Speedway.

Jones averaged 143.137 mph for the race, finishing 34 seconds ahead of Clark, a Scot who has dominated recently on the Grand Prix tour. Jones, who collected more than $450,000, survived a late scare when his car began leaking oil with only 50 miles remaining and Clark right on his bumper.

Clark skidded on the slicked track and he dropped back to a safer margin. Eddie Sachs, holding down fourth place, spun out. Officials prepared to disqualify Jones from the race, but suddenly changed their minds, evidently convinced that the leak had stopped.

After the race, Sachs complained that Jones had jeopardized the life of every driver. The next day, at a post-race luncheon, the two racers got into a fight that started when Jones punched Sachs.

Parnelli Jones and his Agajanian Willard Battery Special en route to victory in the Indianapolis 500.

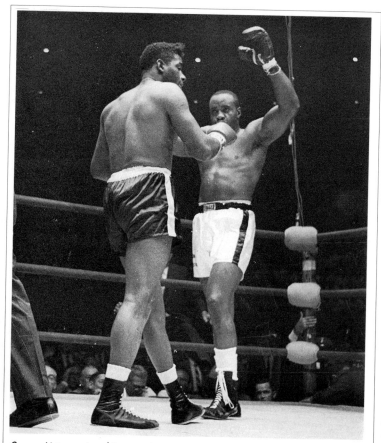

Sonny Liston raises his arms in victory as a groggy Floyd Patterson offers congratulations.

# Another Sonny day

The only bright spot for Floyd Patterson after his July 22 Las Vegas fight against heavyweight champion Sonny Liston was that he lasted longer than the first time the two met. In that bout, Patterson was knocked out in 2 minutes, 6 seconds. This time, it was over at the 2-minute, 10-second mark.

Liston dominated again and the 7,816 fans at Convention Hall had just barely settled into their seats when Patterson hit the canvas for the first time. He rose at two and was dropped again almost as fast. He jumped up quickly again and was put away by a crushing right that left him groggy and disoriented well after he had been counted out.

It was the 35th victory in 36 fights for the champion. But he barely had time to raise his hand in triumph when another contender, young and brash former Olympic champion Cassius Clay, jumped into the ring and showboated for the crowd. He had been regaling ringside patrons all evening with such pronouncements as "I'm the champ, the uncrowned champ," and "Liston is the tramp, I'm the champ."

# Green Bay bombed

Ron VanderKelen fired a 74-yard touchdown pass to former Wisconsin teammate Pat Richter, August 2, and the College All-Stars, winless against the defending National Football League champions for the last five years, held off a late Green Bay rally and pulled off a monumental 20-17 upset at Chicago's Soldier Field.

VanderKelen and the All-Stars faced a third-and-four situation in the fourth quarter as they tried to hold their precarious 13-10 lead. VanderKelen spotted Richter on a short sideline pattern and the receiver made the catch, ducked cornerback Jesse Whittenton and had clear sailing to take the ball into the end zone.

The play delighted the 65,000 crowd, mainly Chicago Bears fans. They naturally pulled against conference rival Green Bay, a loser of only one game in 1962. The Packers, who looked disinterested for much of the contest, came back to score on Jim Taylor's second short TD run, but that was it.

John Pennel sails up and over, becoming the first vaulter ever to clear 17 feet.

# Pennel clears 17-foot barrier

John Pennel, a 23-year-old competing in front of his hometown fans, became the first pole vaulter ever to clear 17 feet, August 24, when he broke his own world record during competition in the Florida Gold Coast Amateur Athletic Union meet in Miami.

Pennel, who had cleared 16-foot-10¼ on August 5, easily soared over the bar at 17-foot-0¾ on his first try at that height. He then attempted 17-foot-3⅞, but failed on all three tries.

"I wanted that," a smiling Pennel said. "I knew that one of these days everything was going to be just right and 17 wasn't going to look too high at all. This was the day."

Pennel, who uses a fiberglass pole, has now broken the world record six times since March 23, when he became the first to vault 16-foot-3. The fall of the 17-foot barrier came only a year and a half after John Uelses became the first to clear 16 feet.

# 1963

## Dodger pitchers key World Series sweep

Sandy Koufax, Don Drysdale, Johnny Podres and Ron Perranoski slammed the door on the New York Yankees' vaunted power machine and the Los Angeles Dodgers, looking for their third World Series victory in nine tries, recorded a stunning four-game sweep of their old nemesis.

Koufax pitched two complete games and allowed three runs —and he was high man. Podres allowed one run and Drysdale and Perranoski were both unscored upon in the Series, contributing to a team 1.00 ERA.

The Dodgers did not exactly pound the Yankees into submission, but they scratched and clawed for more than enough

Game 2 victory with the relief help— the final two outs—of Perranoski, and Drysdale threw a 1-0 shutout in Game 3.

*Sandy Koufax (left) and catcher John Roseboro celebrate after the Los Angeles Dodgers' surprising World Series sweep of the New York Yankees.*

runs to support their pitching. Koufax, a 25-game winner during the regular season, struck out 15 Yankees and beat the New Yorkers 5-2 in the October 2 Series opener at Yankee Stadium and he stopped the Bronx Bombers 2-1 in the October 6 clincher at Dodger Stadium. Podres recorded a 4-1

## Texans flex muscles, overpower Sooners

The second-ranked Texas Longhorns, anxious to improve their national championship aspirations, took a giant step forward, October 12, when they overpowered Oklahoma, 28-7, before 75,504 fans at the Cotton Bowl in Dallas.

The Sooners, who were coming off an upset of No. 1-ranked Southern Cal, were slight favorites going into this annual clash. Nobody was shocked by the Texas victory, but few expected it to be so easy. The Longhorns rolled up 239 rushing yards against an excellent Oklahoma defense.

Texas took the opening kick-off and marched 68 yards on 13 plays for a touchdown. Quarter-back Duke Carlisle did the honors from two yards out.

Tommy Ford's 12-yard run and Phil Harris' three-yard blast increased the score to 21-0 before Oklahoma finally got on the scoreboard. Second and third-stringers wrapped up the Longhorns' fourth straight victory with a fourth-quarter touchdown.

The victory was the sixth straight for Texas Coach Darrell Royal over his old boss, Oklahoma's Bud Wilkinson.

## Speedy Scot cruises

Speedy Scot, too durable and too fast for the rest of the field, cruised to an easy straight-heat victory in the 67th Kentucky Futurity, October 4, becoming only the second standardbred in history to win the Triple Crown of trotting.

The pride of Castletown Farm follows Scott Frost, the 1955 winner of the Yonkers Futurity, the Hambletonian and the Kentucky Futurity—the three legs of the Triple Crown

for 3-year-olds. And with Ralph Baldwin in sulky, Speedy Scot won the heats with the two fastest times ever recorded on the Lexington, track.

First the son of Speedster and Scotch Love trotted to victory in 1:57$^{1}/_{5}$. Then, one hour later, he came back with a 1:57$^{2}/_{5}$ clocking. The previous record was established in 1961 when Caleb finished in 1:58$^{1}/_{5}$.

Speedy Scot has recorded 12 victories in 14 outings this year.

*Speedy Scot and entourage in the winner's circle after capturing the Kentucky Futurity and the trotting Triple Crown.*

# U.S. recaptures Cup

Chuck McKinley outlasted John Newcombe in a tension-filled December 29 match at Adelaide, Australia, giving the United States its first Davis Cup victory since 1958 and snapping the Aussies' latest victory streak at four.

McKinley survived four set points in a marathon opening set, but lost 10-12. The Missourian showed plenty of heart, fighting back for a 6-2, 9-7, 6-2 victory that gave the U.S. a final 3-2 edge. The turning point came in the third set when Newcombe thought he had boomed a second service for an ace, but

the umpire overruled and called it a double fault. He seemed to lose his poise after that.

It was the second loss for Newcombe, who also fell to Dennis Ralston in a five-set Cup opener. Roy Emerson tied the series when he beat McKinley in a four-set second match and the U.S. doubles team of Ralston and McKinley beat Emerson and Neale Fraser in four sets. The Australians tied it again on the final day when Emerson beat Ralston, 6-2, 6-3, 3-6, 6-2.

The Cup victory was the 19th for the U.S.

*Dennis Ralston serves during competition in the United States' Davis Cup victory over Australia.*

# Brown's rushing mile

*New NFL rushing leader Jim Brown of Cleveland.*

Jim Brown continued his assault on the National Football League record books, becoming the first player ever to go over a mile in one season while claiming the career mark for rushing yardage.

The talented running back finished his big year, December 16, with a 125-yard performance in the Browns' season-ending 27-20 victory over the Redskins at Washington. That brought his one-season record total to 1,863 yards and his career total to 9,322 yards, ahead of former San Francisco and Baltimore star Joe Perry (1950-62), who gained 8,378. Brown also surpassed former NFL great Ollie Matson's career record for all-purpose running, 11,801-11,317.

Another record was set on December 16 when New York Giants' quarterback Y.A. Tittle threw three touchdown passes in a 33-17 victory over Pittsburgh at Yankee Stadium. That brought Tittle's record one-season TD total to 36, three more than he threw in 1962.

# NFL plays while nation mourns

Thousands of football fans, enraged by the National Football League's decision to play its regular Sunday schedule in the wake of President John F. Kennedy's November 22 assassination in Dallas, swamped team switchboards, the league office, newspapers and offices of politicians with calls to express their indignation.

Many sports events were cancelled on Friday night and

Saturday as the nation went into mourning. Some NBA and NHL teams cancelled games. Most horse racing tracks were shut down.

The American Football League followed suit and cancelled its four Sunday games, extending its regular season by one week. But NFL Commissioner Pete Rozelle, saying "football was Mr. Kennedy's game," announced the Sunday

schedule would be unaffected.

Callers expressed shock and shame that the NFL would not show respect. But the unhappiness was not limited to fans.

"Simply and flatly, the (Washington-Philadelphia) game is being played by order of the Commissioner," said Eagles President Frank McNamee, who added that he would miss his team's game for a Kennedy memorial service.

# 1964

## Floating Clay stings Liston, takes crown

Brash, loud-mouthed Cassius Clay, "floating like a butterfly and stinging like a bee," out-talked, out-danced and out-boxed Sonny Liston, February 25, and pulled off one of the most shocking upsets in boxing history. The 22-year-old Clay became heavyweight champion of the world when Liston, unable to continue because of a shoulder injury, failed to answer the bell for the seventh round.

When the technical knockout was announced, Clay danced a jig in the middle of the ring, looked at the newsmen covering the fight and yelled, "Eat your words."

Clay had been regaling everybody with his poetry and boasts ("I am the greatest") leading up to the fight. But nobody took the former light heavyweight Olympic champion seriously, especially the writers, most of whom had predicted an early Liston knockout. From the opening bell, however, it

**" SPORTS TALK "**

*"Whatcha gonna say now? I won't last one round? He'll be out in two? How many heart attacks were there? Oh, am I pretty!"*

**CASSIUS CLAY**
chastising reporters after upsetting Sonny Liston for the heavyweight title

became apparent there was more to this youngster than met the ear.

Clay kept his hands perilously low but avoided Liston jabs with quick feints while circling around the champion's devastating left hooks. He fired away with jabs and quick combinations that opened a gash under Liston's left eye and another cut on his left cheek.

After six rounds a tired, bleeding Liston threw in the towel. His injury later was verified by a team of eight doctors.

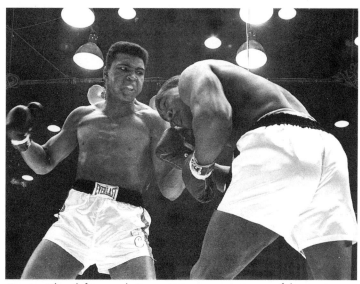

*Cassius Clay (left) pounds Sonny Liston en route to one of the most stunning heavyweight upsets in history.*

## Baseball star Hubbs dies in plane crash

Ken Hubbs, the slick-fielding Chicago Cubs second baseman who won National League Rookie of the Year honors two years ago, died, February 13, when the plane he was flying crashed on a frozen lake near Provo, Utah. He was 22.

Hubbs and a companion, 23-year-old Dennis Doyle, were en route from Provo to their home in Colton, Calif., after participating in a basketball tournament at Brigham Young University, where both had attended college. Hubbs, who had just secured his pilot's license two weeks earlier, took off in his new red and white plane despite bad weather and low visibility. The crash occurred moments later.

Hubbs set a major league fielding record in his rookie season when he played errorless ball for 78 consecutive games while handling 418 chances. He batted .262 that season and followed that with a .235 average in 1963.

*Players and coaches of the Chicago Cubs observe a moment of silence for former teammate Ken Hubbs before a spring training game in Arizona.*

## Struggling AFL gets television windfall

The struggling American Football League received a major financial assist, January 29, when NBC agreed to pay $36 million over the next five years for the rights to televise its games. The agreement assures each of the league's eight teams a $900,000 yearly payment from 1965 through '69—a much-needed shot in the arm.

NBC's decision came after CBS won a bidding war for the rights to National Football League regular-season games. CBS outbid both NBC and ABC and signed a $28.2 million, two-year contract with the NFL. The CBS schedule will call for telecasts on 14 Sundays, two Saturdays and one game on Thanksgiving Day. The network plans to do as many as seven regional telecasts on Sundays.

The CBS package more than tripled the $9.3 million it had paid the NFL under a two-year contract that expired last month. Likewise, the NBC package triples ABC's current AFL contract that runs through 1964.

# Bruins press Duke, capture NCAA title

The UCLA Bruins, working their devastating 2-2-1 zone press to perfection, ran over and around the taller Duke Blue Devils, March 21, at Kansas City and won their first NCAA Tournament championship.

Coach John Wooden's over-achievers raced to a 98-83 victory that provided the perfect cap to a 30-0 season. In becoming only the third team ever to win an NCAA title with an unbeaten record, the Bruins defeated each of the other Final Four teams (Kansas State, Michigan and Duke) at least once.

UCLA's tallest starters are 6-foot-5 Fred Slaughter and Keith Erickson, but that appears to make little difference. The Bruins relentlessly pressure their opponents into mistakes and, invariably, will make an explosive run at some point during the game. The time of reckoning came for Duke with 7:14 remaining in the first half and

*UCLA Coach John Wooden and his NCAA Tournament champion Bruins.*

the Blue Devils leading, 30-27. Two minutes and 16 points later, UCLA had a 43-30 lead and never looked back.

UCLA's top gun, lefty Gail Goodrich, scored 27 points while Kenny Washington came off the bench to score 26. Bruin point guard Walt Hazzard earned tournament outstanding-player honors.

## ★ SPORTS WATCH ★

**JAN:** Texas punctuated its 1963 national championship with a 28-6 rout of No. 2 Navy and Heisman Trophy-winning quarterback Roger Staubach in the Cotton Bowl.

**JAN:** The San Diego Chargers won their first AFL championship by pounding Boston, 51-10, in the 1963 title game.

**FEB:** The Soviet Union edged Canada, 3-2, in the final to win the hockey gold medal in the Winter Olympic Games at Innsbruck, Austria.

**APR:** With his record fourth victory in the Masters, Arnold Palmer became the first golfer to pass $500,000 in career earnings.

**APR:** Houston's Ken Johnson became the first major league pitcher to lose a nine-inning no-hitter when an error by second baseman Nellie Fox allowed Cincinnati to escape with a 1-0 victory.

**APR:** In the first game at New York's new Shea Stadium, the Pittsburgh Pirates recorded a 4-3 victory over the Mets.

# Maple Leafs survive, win 3rd straight Cup

Andy Bathgate scored a first-period goal and Dave Keon, Red Kelly and George Armstrong added third-period scores, April 25, as the Toronto Maple Leafs, behind the 33-save goaltending of Johnny Bower, captured their third straight Stanley Cup with a 4-0 victory over Detroit.

The Game 7 triumph, recorded before 14,571 screaming home fans, was an impressive display of hockey. The Leafs forechecked well throughout the game and peppered Detroit goalie Terry Sawchuk with shots.

The Leafs had teetered on the verge of elimination after Detroit's 4-3 victory in Game 5, but Bob Baun's overtime goal at Detroit won Game 6.

The Cup victory was Toronto's 10th, tying the Leafs with the Montreal Canadiens at the top of the all-time list. Toronto had finished third in the regular-season standings, the Red Wings fourth.

*Detroit's Ed Joyal (21) leans over Toronto goaltender Johnny Bower during Stanley Cup final action in Toronto.*

# Russell leads Celtics

Bill Russell put the defensive squeeze on Wilt Chamberlain and the Boston Celtics proved they still are the class of the National Basketball Association, April 26, when they defeated the San Francisco Warriors, 105-99, and captured their sixth straight championship.

The Celtics' five-game victory delighted the 13,909 fans who showed up at Boston Garden hoping to watch their team become the first in professional sports to win six consecutive titles. The New York Yankees in baseball and Montreal Canadiens in hockey had both matched Boston's five-title streak.

Russell held Chamberlain scoreless in the first six minutes and to 30 points overall. The Celtics built an 11-point third-quarter lead but had to hold off the Warriors' late charge. When the victory was complete, fans stormed the court and lifted Coach Red Auerbach and various players to their shoulders in celebration.

Tom Heinsohn led Boston's balanced scoring with 19 points. Sam Jones and Frank Ramsey added 18 apiece.

# 1964

## MAY-AUGUST

## The perfect ending

Philadelphia righthander Jim Bunning dazzled the New York Mets, June 21, and became the first National League pitcher in 84 years to throw a perfect game.

Bunning set down 27 straight Mets in a 6-0 Phillies victory in the first game of a doubleheader at New York's Shea Stadium. When the 32-year-old struck out pinch-hitter John Stephenson to end the game, he received a long standing ovation from appreciative Mets fans.

Bunning needed 86 pitches and two good defensive plays to carve his niche in the history books. Second baseman Tony Taylor made a diving stop and threw out Jesse Gonder in the fifth inning and shortstop Cookie Rojas made a leaping catch of Amado Samuel's line drive in the third.

The former Detroit Tiger Bunning is the first pitcher in the modern era to throw no-hitters in both leagues (he no-hit the Boston Red Sox in 1958) and the eighth major leaguer to throw a perfect game.

Ken Venturi, hot, tired and happy, gives a half-hearted victory salute after winning the U.S. Open.

## Venturi sizzles in U.S. Open win

Ken Venturi, close to heat exhaustion after an outstanding morning round of 66, shot a final-round 70 over the Congressional Country Club course at Washington D.C. and won the U.S. Open by four strokes over Tommy Jacobs.

Venturi fired a front-nine 30 in the morning round and was on his way home at the 16th tee when he was overcome by the 100-degree heat and high humidity. He looked over at Ray Floyd, his playing partner, and said, "I don't know if I can make it in."

He did, but it was questionable that he would make it back out after the allotted 45-minute rest period. Under doctor's orders Venturi rested and soon was ready to tee off, trailing Jacobs by two strokes with 18 holes remaining.

With the doctor accompanying him carrying salt tablets and iced tea, Venturi slowly carved out a 70, good for a four-round total of 278. Jacobs, who had tied a record with a blistering second-round 64, ballooned to a 76 for a 282.

The badly-needed victory was the first for Venturi in four years as a pro.

Philadelphia's Jim Bunning, Mr. Perfect, strikes out New York's John Stephenson to complete his masterpiece.

## Foyt wins tragic Indy

A.J. Foyt averaged a record 147.350 mph to win his second Indianapolis 500, May 30, but his victory was overshadowed by the deaths of fellow drivers Eddie Sachs and Dave MacDonald in a second-lap crash.

MacDonald's Allstates Special spun and ricocheted off the wall. His full tank of gas exploded into flames and Sachs' rear-engine Ford slammed into MacDonald's flaming wreckage. Five more cars joined the fray. Sachs was killed instantly and MacDonald, helicoptered to a nearby hospital, died a few hours later.

For the first time in 48 runnings, the race was stopped because of a crash and the debris was cleared away. It restarted one hour and 45 minutes later, with the Lotus-Ford entries of Jim Clark, Bobby Marshman and Dan Gurney apparently in control. But they all experienced mechanical problems and it came down to a race between Foyt's Sheraton Thompson Special and Rodger Ward's Kaiser Aluminum Special.

Foyt eventually pulled away to a one-lap victory that earned him $153,650.

# Johnny on the spot

Philadelphia outfielder Johnny Callison hit the first pitch from fireballing Boston reliever Dick Radatz for a dramatic two-out, three-run homer in the bottom of the ninth inning, July 17, to give the National League a come-from-behind 7-4 victory over the American League in the All-Star Game at New York's Shea Stadium.

Callison's blast capped a four-run rally that began with a walk to San Francisco's Willie Mays. Willie stole second base and scored the tying run on Giants teammate Orlando Cepeda's bloop single and Yankee first baseman Joe Pepitone's throwing error.

After St. Louis' Ken Boyer fouled out, Radatz walked Cincinnati's Johnny Edwards intentionally to set up a double play. Hank Aaron struck out, setting the stage for Callison.

The A.L. had tied the game in the sixth inning on a two-run triple by Baltimore's Brooks Robinson and took the lead on a seventh-inning sacrifice fly by the Angels' Jim Fregosi.

The N.L. victory evened the series at 17-17-1.

*All-Star Game hero Johnny Callison of Philadelphia is mobbed by happy National League teammates.*

---

# Wright wins 4th Open in playoff

Mickey Wright, the dominant player on the women's professional tour, added another trophy to her case, July 12, when she defeated Ruth Jessen in an 18-hole playoff and became the second golfer to record four victories in the U.S. Women's Open championship, emulating Betsy Rawls.

Wright fired a playoff-round 70 over the San Diego Country Club course to defeat Jessen by two strokes. Wright previously had won in 1958, '59 and '61 and she also earned a record four LPGA Championship titles during that same span.

Wright recorded four birdies and one bogey in the playoff while Jessen parred 17 holes and suffered one bogey. Wright's birdie at the 10th gave her a two-stroke advantage that Jessen could not overcome.

The playoff became necessary when Jessen birdied the 72nd for a 290 score. Wright, needing a par to tie, blasted her third shot out of a bunker to within three feet and putted out.

---

# 2 Chicago Bears die in car crash

Willie Galimore and John Farrington, starters last year for the National Football League-champion Chicago Bears, died July 26, when the car Galimore was driving crashed on a county road 2½ miles from Rensselaer, Ind. The Bears are conducting their summer training camp at St. Joseph's College in Rensselaer.

Galimore, a 29-year-old, 187-pound running back who gained 2,985 yards in seven seasons, was driving his Volkswagen about 55 mph at 10:25 p.m. when it went off the road. The players, trying to beat an 11 p.m. curfew, were thrown out of the top of the car, which then pinned them. They died instantly.

The 28-year-old Farrington was a 217-pound end who caught 21 passes for 335 yards and two touchdowns last season. The Prairie View (Tex.) College product owns the team record for longest TD catch—a 98-yarder in 1961.

Galimore, a Florida A&M graduate, was trying to come back from surgery that sidelined him for much of 1963.

## ★ SPORTS WATCH ★

**MAY:** Defensive lineman Alex Karras, reinstated by the NFL along with Green Bay's Paul Hornung from a year-long gambling-related suspension, signed a two-year contract with the Detroit Lions.

**MAY:** The San Francisco Giants prevailed over the New York Mets, 8-6, in the second game of a doubleheader—a 7-hour, 22-minute marathon that was decided in the 23rd inning.

**JUN:** Northern Dancer, ridden by the great Bill Hartack, finished third in the Belmont Stakes after winning the Kentucky Derby and Preakness Stakes.

**JUL:** Young Kansas City shortstop Bert Campaneris became the second player since 1900 to hit two home runs in his first major league game, connecting twice against Minnesota.

**JUL:** The U.S.-Russia annual track meet: American men won, 139-97, while the Russian women triumphed, 57-48, in competition at Los Angeles.

**AUG:** Billie Jean Moffitt and Karen Susman defeated the Australian team of Margaret Court-Smith and Lesley Turner, 3-6, 6-2, 6-4, to win the U.S. doubles championship at Forest Hills, N.Y.

*John Farrington, one of two Chicago Bears killed in an Indiana car accident.*

# Marshall's wrong turn

Rekindling memories of the wrong-way run of California defender Roy Riegels in the 1929 Rose Bowl, Minnesota Vikings defensive end Jim Marshall picked up a fourth-quarter 49ers' fumble and rambled 60 yards to his *own* end zone in an October 25 game at San Francisco's Kezar Stadium.

"I thought they were cheering me on," Marshall said, referring to the frantic coaches and players on the Viking sideline. "About the 5-yard line, I looked around and things just didn't seem right. Fran (Tarkenton) was yelling at me from the sidelines and pointing in the opposite direction. I couldn't think of anything else to do, so I threw him the ball."

Marshall's *throw* went out of bounds in the end zone and the 49ers were awarded a safety. But Minnesota held on for a 27-22 National Football League victory, saving Marshall from the fate that befell Riegels—a one-point loss to Georgia Tech and everlasting regret.

The Vikings had built their lead on an eight-yard run by quarterback Tarkenton and a 45-yard right-way fumble return by Carl Eller.

*Minnesota's Jim Marshall scoops up a fumble (above) and heads for the wrong goal line (below left). The embarrassed Marshall got a warm greeting (below right) from San Francisco's Bruce Bosley.*

*The Phillies' overworked aces, Jim Bunning (left) and Chris Short.*

# The Philadelphia story

The Philadelphia Phillies, owning a comfortable 6½-game lead over Cincinnati with 12 to play in the National League regular season, returned home for a seven-game home stand, confident and poised to wrap up the team's first pennant in 14 years.

But a funny thing happened on the way to the World Series. The Phillies' express was derailed by a puzzling collapse that was aided by a curious piece of strategy implemented by Manager Gene Mauch.

The Reds stormed into Philadelphia and swept three games cutting their deficit to 3½ games. The St. Louis Cardinals, hot on Cincinnati's heels, split two with the New York Mets. With Milwaukee coming into town next for a four-game series, Mauch revised his pitching rotation so that aces Jim Bunning and Chris Short would work on two days rest, rather than their normal three.

The strategy backfired. Milwaukee won all four games, two of them with heartbreaking rallies in the final inning and another when Bunning was bombed in a 14-8 defeat. The Phillies' seventh straight loss came on a day when Cincinnati swept a doubleheader from the Mets, running its winning streak to nine and taking over first place by one game. The Cardinals, in the midst of an eight-game streak, were 1½ games behind the Reds in third place. Three straight losses in St. Louis dropped the Phillies 2½ back with two games to play. St. Louis now was in first place by half a game over the Reds.

The Phillies finally broke their 10-game losing streak with a 4-3 victory over the Reds and the Mets made things interesting by winning two straight from the Cardinals. Going into the final day, St. Louis and Cincinnati were tied for first with Philadelphia one game back. The Phillies beat the Reds, 10-0, and awaited the result of the Cardinals-Mets game in St. Louis. The final report, an 11-5 pennant-clinching victory for the Cardinals, turned the Phillies' agony into despair.

St. Louis, 54-29 in the second half, went on to record a seven-game World Series victory over the New York Yankees.

## " SPORTS TALK "

*"It's the most champagne I've had in four years. I'd rather beat the Yankees than any other team in baseball."*

**BRANCH RICKEY**

82-year-old special consultant for the Cardinals, after St. Louis had beaten the New Yorkers in a seven-game World Series

# Swimmer Schollander leads U.S. gold rush

Don Schollander became the first swimmer ever to win four gold medals at one Olympic Games and Bullet Bob Hayes retained his 100-meter title as the United States recorded a 90-36 medal-count victory over the Soviet Union in a strong showing in the Summer Games at Tokyo.

Schollander edged Great Britain's Robert McGregor by six inches in winning the 100-meter freestyle and then won the 400-meter freestyle in a world record 4:12.2. The 18-year-old capped his grand slam by anchoring the 4 X 100-meter and 4 X 200-meter freestyle relay teams, both of which produced world records.

Hayes, who ran a 9.9 wind-aided 100-meter semifinal heat, bolted away from a strong field in the final to win by seven feet —the widest margin in Olympic history—tying his own world record of 10.0 seconds in the process.

Other highlights: Joe Frazier won boxing's Super Heavy-

*Record-breaking swimmer Don Schollander took the victory stand four times during the Summer Olympic Games in Tokyo.*

weight gold medal—despite fighting with a broken right hand; Al Oerter set an Olympic record by throwing the discus 200 feet, 1 inch, and the men's basketball team, featuring such stars as Bill Bradley, Jeff Mullins, Walt Hazzard and Mel Counts, remained undefeated in Olympic competition.

# Howe sweet it is: Gordie sets record

Detroit right winger Gordie Howe's breakaway goal in the November 14 game at the Montreal Forum wiped away the last major career record of Maurice (Rocket) Richard and made him the most prolific goal scorer in National Hockey League history.

Howe picked up a loose puck at center ice, skated in alone on Charlie Hodge and beat the Montreal goaltender with a backhander. The goal was Howe's 627th—569 in the regular season and 58 in the playoffs. Richard scored 544 regular-season goals and a record 82 in playoff competition.

The crowd gave Howe a long ovation, even though the record was not announced. Montreal followed with three first-period goals, however, and went on to a 4-2 victory.

*Detroit's Gordie Howe (9), the most prolific scorer in NHL history, works for a shot against the Toronto Maple Leafs.*

★ SPORTS WATCH ★

**OCT:** The New York Yankees, coming off a season of dissension and a World Series loss to St. Louis, fired Manager Yogi Berra.

**OCT:** Johnny Keane, manager of the St. Louis Cardinals, resigned his job and accepted the managerial opening with the Yankees.

**OCT:** Ayres became the third trotter to win a Triple Crown, capturing the Yonkers Trot, the Hambletonian and the Kentucky Futurity.

**NOV:** St. Louis Hawks star Bob Pettit became the first NBA player to go over 20,000 career points.

**NOV:** British Columbia won its first Grey Cup title defeating Hamilton in the CFL championship game, 34-24.

**DEC:** Buffalo captured its first AFL championship with a 20-7 victory over San Diego at Buffalo, while Cleveland rolled over Baltimore, 27-0, to win the NFL championship.

# Trojans' rally stuns unbeaten Notre Dame

No. 1 ranked Notre Dame, holding a 17-0 halftime lead in its season-ending game at Southern Cal, watched its hopes for an undefeated season and national championship slip away on November 28, when the Trojans rallied for a dramatic 20-17 victory before 83,840 fans.

Notre Dame, playing under new Coach Ara Parseghian, was 30 minutes away from its 10th straight victory and first unbeaten record since 1949. Taking the second-half kickoff, the Trojans drove 66 yards, with halfback Mike Garrett scoring from the 1.

After the Irish had failed to convert two scoring opportunities, Southern Cal set off on a 10-play, 88-yard fourth-quarter drive that culminated with Craig Fertig's 23-yard scoring pass to Fred Hill. The comeback was completed with 1:33 left to play when Fertig fired a 15-yard TD pass to sophomore Rod Sherman.

Notre Dame quarterback John Huarte, named Heisman Trophy winner four days earlier, completed 18 of 29 passes for 272 yards and a touchdown. But he couldn't stop the 30-minute collapse, which resulted in the Irish finishing third in the polls behind Alabama and Arkansas.

# No. 1 Alabama falls

Alabama might rank as the official 1964 college football national champion in the minds of the Associated Press and United Press International pollsters who determine this distinction at the end of every regular season. But Arkansas emerged as the *real* No. 1 team by virtue of two after-the-poll results in New Year's Day bowl games.

First the Razorbacks, undefeated and ranked No. 2, scored a fourth-quarter touchdown and escaped with a 10-7 victory over sixth-ranked Nebraska in the Cotton Bowl. Then that night, the Crimson Tide, also 10-0, fell short in its comeback attempt against Texas, losing a 21-17 thriller in the Orange Bowl. The fifth-ranked Longhorns had lost only once—a 14-13 decision to Arkansas.

Arkansas thrilled 75,504 Cotton Bowl fans with a gutty 80-yard fourth-quarter drive that culminated with a three-yard run by reserve tailback Bobby Burnett. The touchdown, which came with 4:41 left to play, was set up by Fred Marshall, who completed four passes and ran 10 yards for a key first down.

The young Nebraska defensive line completely shut down Arkansas' running game, allowing the Hogs only 45 rushing yards, 39 less than Harry Wilson gained for the Cornhuskers. Wilson scored Nebraska's only touchdown in the second period on a one-yard run.

Texas shocked 72,647 Orange Bowl fans by jumping to a 21-7 halftime lead, Ernie Koy setting the tone with a 79-yard first-quarter touchdown sprint. But the second half belonged to Alabama and quarterback Joe Namath.

The strong-armed Namath, who had missed most of the season with a knee injury, took over in the second quarter and completed 18 passes for 255 yards

*Jerry Welch jumps on Arkansas teammate Bobby Burnett after Burnett had scored the game-winning touchdown in the Cotton Bowl.*

and two touchdowns. He pulled Alabama to within four points in the final period and then drove the Tide toward a winning score in the final moments. Alabama reached the Texas 1, but Namath was stopped short on a fourth-down sneak.

# AFL's Jets pull off major coup, sign Joe Namath, John Huarte

The New York Jets, looking for a high-profile quarterback to strengthen their credibility in the country's biggest football market, pulled off a major coup by signing the top *two* signal-callers from the college ranks.

The biggest victory was the signing of Alabama quarterback Joe Namath on January 2. Namath, generally considered the prize of the college draft, is a 6-foot-2, 195-pound thrower with a quick release and uncanny accuracy. He completed 203 of 374 passes for 2,713 yards and 25 touchdowns during his career under Coach Bear Bryant at Alabama.

Namath did not come cheaply or without risk. His contract is believed to be in the three-year, $400,000 range—

the biggest ever awarded to a rookie athlete. But the youngster has a history of knee problems. The Jets have been assured that the knee will heal.

On January 9, one week after Namath was introduced to the New York press, Notre Dame quarterback and Heisman Trophy winner John Huarte was signed to a contract believed to be in the $200,000 range. Huarte passed for 2,062 yards and 16 touchdowns in an outstanding college career.

Namath's draft rights were held by the National Football

*Alabama quarterback Joe Namath and Crimson Tide Coach Paul (Bear) Bryant.*

League's St. Louis Cardinals and Huarte's by the Philadelphia Eagles.

# Houston opens "Dome"

Houston's Harris County Domed Stadium, otherwise known as the Astrodome and the Eighth Wonder of the World, opened, April 9, with U.S. President Lyndon B. Johnson, Texas Governor John Connally and 47,876 curious fans gazing upon its splendor. They did so with plenty of oohs and aahs through the course of major league baseball's first indoor game—an exhibition between the New York Yankees and Astros.

For the record, Yankee great Mickey Mantle got the park's first hit (a first-inning single to center field) and its first home run (a 400-foot drive to right-center field in the sixth) and the Astros won, 2-1, in 12 innings.

But the game was almost incidental. Most of the fans spent the game gazing at the 3½ acres of Tiffany Bermuda grass, specially imported from Georgia; the 474-foot scoreboard with a half-acre surface; the massive dome that rose 208 feet—18 stories—at its highest point, and numerous other innovative wonders.

The highlight of the night was when the scoreboard ran through its 45-second pyrotechnic display, which will be used to celebrate Astro home runs.

The scoreboard goes through its 45-second pyrotechnic display as Houston's Leon McFadden circles the bases after hitting a home run during an April 11 exhibition game at Houston's new Astrodome.

## ★ SPORTS WATCH ★

**JAN:** San Francisco traded Wilt Chamberlain to the Philadelphia 76ers for $150,000 and three players—Connie Dierking, Lee Shaffer and Paul Neumann.

**JAN:** Once-beaten and fourth-ranked Michigan pounded Oregon State, 34-7, in the Rose Bowl on New Year's Day.

**FEB:** Fred Lorenzen averaged 141.539 in his Ford to win the rain-shortened (332-mile) Daytona 500.

**MAR:** St. John's defeated Villanova, 55-51, at Madison Square Garden to become the first four-time winner of the NIT.

**APR:** The Boston Celtics, winners of a record 62 games during the regular season, captured their seventh straight championship with a five-game victory over the Los Angeles Lakers in the NBA Finals.

# Goodrich scores 42 as UCLA wins again

UCLA guard Gail Goodrich gets a victory ride after scoring 42 points in the Bruins' NCAA Tournament final victory over Michigan.

UCLA guard Gail Goodrich, taking a cue from Princeton forward Bill Bradley, scored a title-game-record 42 points, March 20, and led the Bruins to a 91-80 victory over Michigan and their second straight NCAA Tournament championship.

After Bradley had scored a Final Four-record 58 points in Princeton's 118-82 rout of Wichita State in the third-place game at Portland, Ore., the Bruins outplayed the No. 1-ranked Wolverines in every way possible. After trailing early, 20-13, UCLA used its vaunted 2-2-1 press to overtake Michigan and build a 47-34 halftime lead.

Goodrich hit 12 of 22 shots from the floor and 18 of 20 free throws. The 6-foot-1, 170-pound lefthander single-handedly fouled out three Michigan defenders. But as outstanding as Goodrich was, Bradley took individual honors on this night.

Playing his final college game, he hit 22 of 29 field-goal attempts and 14 of 15 free throws while collecting 17 rebounds and dishing out four assists.

# Nicklaus sets record

Jack Nicklaus, playing imposing Augusta National like it never before had been played, shot a final-round 69, April 11, to win the Masters by a record nine strokes while shooting a four-round record 271.

"The victory by Jack Nicklaus in the Masters today was the greatest tournament performance in golf history," said Bobby Jones, the man who helped design the 6,980-yard Masters layout.

"One of the finest 72 holes of golf ever played," marveled Arnold Palmer, who tied for second with South African Gary Player at 280.

Nicklaus' performance was not as spectacular as it was steady, relentless and mistake free. He shot rounds of 67, 71, 64 and 69, including 19 birdies and five bogeys, while using

only 123 putts in the tournament. Nicklaus' 64 gave him a five-stroke advantage and he cruised through the final round unchallenged.

The 271 broke the record of Ben Hogan, who shot a 274 in winning the 1953 Masters.

# 1965

## MAY-AUGUST

# Clay's "phantom punch" rocks Liston in first

Cassius Clay, who had scored a technical knockout over Sonny Liston 15 months earlier, retained his title, May 25, with a controversial punch that produced the fastest knockout in heavyweight boxing history.

Just how fast Clay's knockout really was is open to debate. Maine boxing officials scored the knockout at 1 minute. Radio and television observers timed it at 1:42. Referee Jersey Joe Walcott officially declared Clay the winner at 2:17.

No matter. The real question is whether the short right that Clay delivered to Liston's head really had enough snap to produce a knockout. Many of the 4,280 fans in attendance at Lewiston, Maine, didn't think so and began yelling, "Fake! Fake! Fake!" Members of the press sarcastically labeled the winning blow as the "phantom punch."

Clay called it his anchor punch and said it was part karate and part corkscrew. When he delivered it, Liston certainly dropped like an anchor, laying on his stomach as Clay danced over him, waving and taunting.

Officials, who spent the next day viewing film, said the blow was indeed a damaging one. ABC showed the fight from different angles and speeds on its Wide World of Sports program a few days later.

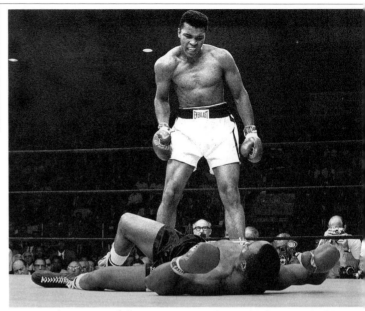

*Cassius Clay taunts a fallen Sonny Liston during the first round of their heavyweight title fight.*

*Liston stays down and Clay does a victory dance around the ring.*

# The expansion war

The American Football League voted, on June 7, to expand to 10 teams by 1966—and 12 by 1968—a move forced by the June 3 decision of the rival NFL to expand from 14 to 16 teams.

The expansion war, touched off by economic considerations and the NFL's hopes to gain a strong foothold in the South, brings an abrupt end to hopes for an AFL-NFL merger. Buffalo Owner Ralph C. Wilson Jr. said talks that had been going on for three months have collapsed in the wake of the expansion scramble. A merger could have resulted in interleague play, a common draft and a championship game as early as 1966.

The AFL announced, June 8, that it would award an expansion franchise to Atlanta. But officials who hold the purse strings for the new $18 million Atlanta Fulton County Stadium have refused to give the AFL a lease, saying they want to hear from the NFL first. The war for Atlanta could be tense and bitter, although the warm-weather sites of Miami and New Orleans also have some attraction.

> ## "SPORTS TALK"
>
> *"It's been my cross to bear that I've been singled out as a villain ever since I started to play. I've learned to live with it, but sometimes it still hurts. It's the old story that no one likes Goliath."*
> **WILT CHAMBERLAIN**

# NHL adds six teams

The National Hockey League, slow in following the lead of the other professional sports, voted, June 25, to expand to 12 teams and awarded new franchises to interests in St. Louis and Los Angeles.

The vote, taken during a meeting of the NHL board of governors in New York, calls for the league to double in size by 1968.

The six new teams will be set up in a separate division and the current 70-game schedule will be raised to 74. Each new team will be required to pay $2 million and each will get 20 players from a special dispersal draft.

The decision to expand was prompted by increasing attendance and the NHL's desire to land a lucrative television contract. Baltimore, Houston, Vancouver, Philadelphia, Pittsburgh and San Francisco are some of the other cities being considered for new teams.

# Marichal goes crazy

San Francisco pitcher Juan Marichal touched off a 14-minute brawl, August 22, when, while hitting against Los Angeles lefthander Sandy Koufax, he suddenly turned around and attacked catcher John Roseboro with his bat.

The ugly incident occurred in the third inning of a game at Candlestick Park and resulted in both dugouts emptying onto the field. Fighting was minimal, however, as everybody seemed horrified by the nature of the attack.

Marichal connected twice on Roseboro's head before Koufax and other peacemakers arrived on the scene. The catcher suffered a two-inch cut that was more ugly than dangerous and Marichal, who later was suspended for eight playing days and fined $1,750, was ejected from the game. He said he attacked because Roseboro's throws back to the pitcher were coming perilously close to his head.

After peace was restored, the rest of the game (won 4-3 by the Giants) was played without incident in a subdued atmosphere.

Peacemakers arrive to stop San Francisco pitcher Juan Marichal's bat attack on Los Angeles catcher John Roseboro.

Cincinnati's Jim Maloney en route to his second 10-inning no-hitter of the season.

# Maloney no-hits Cubs

Hard-throwing Jim Maloney fired his second 10-inning no-hitter of the season on August 19—and this time he actually won the game.

The Cincinnati righthander shut down the Cubs at Wrigley Field, but it was far from a work of art. Maloney struggled through 187 pitches, went to a three-ball count on 15 batters, issued 10 walks and hit one batter. He loaded the bases in both the third and ninth innings.

But Maloney, who struck out 12 and did not allow a ball to be hit out of the infield through seven innings, persevered. And Leo Cardenas rewarded him by hitting a 10th-inning home run that made a tough-luck loser of Chicago's Larry Jackson.

Maloney had not been so fortunate, June 14, when he no-hit the Mets for 10 innings at New York, only to lose in the 11th when Johnny Lewis touched him for a game-winning homer. Maloney walked only one batter in that outstanding performance and struck out 18.

# Stengel ends managerial career

Casey Stengel, who as a major league manager in New York went from the height of Yankee glory to the depth of Mets ineptitude, ended his 56-year baseball career, August 29, announcing his retirement for health reasons at age 75.

Stengel, who is recovering from a broken hip he suffered on July 25, said he will turn his managerial duties over to Wes Westrum and perform some scouting duties for the Mets in his home state of California.

After leading the Yankees to 10 pennants and seven World Series victories in 12 years (1949-60), Stengel was forced out by management because of his age. He was hired by the expansion Mets and directed the team through an Amazin' four years. The Mets, 175-404 under Casey, won the hearts of their fans with their bumbling and inept play.

By contrast, the machine-like Yankees were 1,149-696 under Stengel's leadership. Earlier managerial stints with Brooklyn and the Boston Braves produced a 602-767 record.

# 1965

## SEPTEMBER-DECEMBER

# Dodgers catch Twins

A three-hit, 10-strikeout performance by Sandy Koufax and a fourth-inning home run by Lou Johnson gave the Los Angeles Dodgers a 2-0 victory over the Minnesota Twins in the seventh and deciding game of the World Series, October 14, at Metropolitan Stadium in Minneapolis.

The shutout, his second of the Series, was the perfect ending for Koufax's outstanding season. The fireballing lefthander had finished the regular campaign with a 26-8 record, a National League-best 2.04 earned-run average and a major league-record 382 strikeouts.

But the exploits of Koufax and his 6-foot-6 pitching partner, 23-game winner Don Drysdale, didn't seem to mean much to the slugging Twins when the Series opened. Minnesota, getting home runs from Don Mincher and Zoilo Versalles and solid pitching from ace righthander Jim (Mudcat) Grant, roughed Drysdale up for seven runs in 2²/₃ innings and cruised to an easy 8-2 Game 1 triumph. The Twins followed with a surprising 5-1 victory over Koufax behind the seven-hit pitching of Jim Kaat.

Minnesota was in the driver's seat as the Series shifted to Los Angeles. But not for long. Claude Osteen shut out the Twins on five hits for a 4-0 victory, Drysdale came back strong in a 7-2 Dodger win and Koufax was virtually untouchable in a four-hit, 7-0 victory.

Grant reprieved the Twins in Game 6, pitching a six-hitter and hitting a three-run homer, but Koufax, pitching on two days rest, was masterful in the finale.

Maury Wills, who stole 94 bases for the Dodgers during the regular season, batted .367 in the Series and Ron Fairly hit .379 with a pair of home runs.

---

### "SPORTS TALK"

*"We were beaten by a great pitcher, and he had to be great to beat us. He's the best I've seen."*
**SAM MELE**
Minnesota Manager on Dodger ace Sandy Koufax

---

*Los Angeles' Lou Johnson connects for his Game 7 World Series home run against Minnesota.*

# Koufax is masterful

Los Angeles Dodgers left-hander Sandy Koufax, in one of the most overpowering performances in baseball history, retired all 27 Chicago Cubs he faced, September 29, and became the first pitcher in major league history to record four career no-hitters.

Koufax's 1-0 perfect-game victory before 29,139 fans at Dodger Stadium was a work of art. He allowed only seven balls to be hit to the outfield and there were no tough chances for his defense. He struck out 14 Cubs, including the last six he faced. His final victim was pinch-hitter Harvey Kuenn, a former American League batting champion.

The eighth perfect game in big-league history came at the expense of Chicago lefthander Bob Hendley, who retired the first 12 batters he faced and pitched a one-hitter. The Dodgers scored in the fifth when Lou Johnson walked, was sacrificed to second, stole third and came home on catcher Chris Krug's wild throw. Johnson later got the game's only hit, a seventh-inning bloop double to right field.

Koufax, who has pitched a no-hitter in each of the last four years, joins Pittsburgh's Harvey Haddix (who lost in 13 innings in 1959) and Philadelphia's Jim Bunning (1964) as National Leaguers who have thrown perfect games this century. Larry Corcoran, Cy Young and Bob Feller are three-time no-hit pitchers.

*Sandy Koufax during his perfect game against the Chicago Cubs.*

# Innovator Rickey dies at 83

Branch Rickey, an innovative baseball executive who broke baseball's color barrier when he signed Jackie Robinson, died, December 9, in Columbia, Mo., at age 83. Rickey had suffered a heart attack, November 13, while giving a speech and never regained consciousness.

After spending his early years as a lawyer, baseball scout and manager, Rickey became president of the St. Louis Cardinals. In 1919, he created baseball's first farm system, a device for acquiring and training young players. This revolutionary idea eventually became a permanent method of operation in the game.

Rickey was an astute judge of talent and his Cardinals won six National League pennants and four World Series. He left St. Louis to become president of the Dodgers in 1942 and they soon enjoyed similar success.

Rickey's most notable contribution came in October 1945, when he signed Jackie Robinson to a professional contract. He brought the talented infielder to the major leagues in '47, a move that opened the door for scores of other black athletes.

Rickey later worked in the Pittsburgh Pirates front office and did some consulting work for the Cardinals.

# Clay mocks Patterson

Like a little boy pulling the wings off a butterfly, Cassius Clay battered, mocked, humiliated and punished Floyd Patterson for most of 12 rounds, November 22, before the referee stepped in and halted the heavyweight title fight at the Las Vegas Convention Center.

With most of the 7,402 fans in attendance pleading with Clay to put the former champion out of his misery, the 23-year-old Kentuckian seemed intent on inflicting as much damage on Patterson's dignity as his body. Younger, faster and stronger, he danced around the ring, waving, taunting and screaming as he jabbed and hit almost at will.

The late rounds were especially pitiful as Clay toyed with a Patterson who was unable to offer much resistance. When the referee stopped the contest he was doing everybody a favor.

The bout might well have been the last for Patterson, the only fighter in history to have won the heavyweight championship twice. He lost it in 1959 to Ingemar Johansson and regained it from the Swede a year later.

*Gale Sayers, Chicago's six-touchdown man.*

# Bears' rookie Sayers scores 6 touchdowns

Chicago rookie halfback Gale Sayers scored six touchdowns, December 12, and tied a National Football League record as the Bears pounded San Francisco, 61-20, at Wrigley Field.

Sayers, who rushed nine times for 113 yards, tied the record first set in 1929 by the Chicago Cardinals' Ernie Nevers and matched in 1951 by Cleveland's Dub Jones. Sayers scored on an 80-yard pass from Rudy Bukich in the first quarter, 21 and 7-yard runs in the second period, 50 and 1-yard runs in the third period and on an 85-yard punt return in the final quarter. Nevers scored all of his touchdowns on runs while Jones scored on four runs and two pass receptions.

Ironically, on this same afternoon, Green Bay's Paul Hornung scored five touchdowns in a 42-27 victory over Baltimore. Hornung tallied on runs of 2, 9 and 3 yards and pass receptions of 50 and 65 yards.

*Heavyweight champion Cassius Clay toying with former champ Floyd Patterson during their one-sided title fight.*

# 1966

## Bowl game upsets open door for Tide

Fate and the wire-service polls have been kind to Alabama over the last two seasons. And that's why Crimson Tide boss Bear Bryant now ranks as one of five coaches to win back-to-back national championships.

In 1964, Alabama and Arkansas finished the regular season 10-0. Both the Associated Press and United Press International opted for the Crimson Tide as their No. 1 team. The final selections, made before the New Year's Day bowl games, were official, even though Alabama was upset by Texas in the Orange Bowl while Arkansas beat Nebraska in the Cotton Bowl.

To avoid such controversy, AP decided to wait until after the bowl games to decide its 1965 champion. Smart move.

Going into New Year's Day, Michigan State, Arkansas and Nebraska, all undefeated, ranked 1 through 3, with 8-1-1 Alabama fourth. But an amazing sequence of upsets changed things drastically.

In the day's first game, Arkansas' 22-game winning streak ended when Louisiana State pounded out a 14-7 Cotton Bowl victory. Michigan State was next, falling to UCLA, 14-12, in the Rose Bowl.

The underdog Bruins, who had lost to the Spartans by 10 points in their season opener, scored a pair of first-half touchdowns on one-yard sneaks by quarterback Gary Beban and then held on. Michigan State, shut out through 3½ quarters, scored twice in seven minutes but both 2-point conversion

*UCLA's Bob Stiles moves in for the tackle against Michigan State ballcarrier Dwight Lee during New Year's Day Rose Bowl action.*

attempts failed—the second with 31 seconds left to play.

Having seen these two results, Nebraska players were understandably eager to claim the suddenly wide-open No. 1 ranking. All they would have to do is beat Alabama in the Orange Bowl. But. . . .

With Crimson Tide quarterback Steve Sloan completing 20

passes for 296 yards, Alabama rolled up 512 total yards and recorded a 39-28 upset of the Cornhuskers. Ray Perkins, who pulled in a pair of touchdown passes, made a record 10 catches for 159 yards.

Final AP standings: 1. Alabama. 2. Michigan State. 3. Arkansas. 4. UCLA. 5. Nebraska.

*Green Bay's Paul Hornung follows his blocker through the mud during action in the NFL championship game against Cleveland.*

## Packers back on top of the NFL mountain

Don Chandler kicked three field goals and Paul Hornung's 13-yard third-quarter touchdown run broke open a tight contest as the Green Bay Packers returned to the top of the National Football League with a 23-12 championship game victory over the Cleveland Browns, January 2, at Green Bay's Lambeau Field.

The game was played on a sloppy, slippery surface and resulted in a run-oriented, defensive battle—the type of game the Packers play so well.

Green Bay, which made it to the title game by virtue of its 13-10 overtime victory over Balti-

more in a Western Conference playoff game, scored quickly when quarterback Bart Starr crossed up the Browns by firing a 47-yard touchdown pass to Carroll Dale on a third-and-one play. But Cleveland struck back on a 17-yard Frank Ryan-to-Gary Collins TD pass and two field goals by Lou Groza. Two Chandler field goals gave the Packers a 13-12 halftime lead.

The Packer defense shut down the Browns in the second half while Hornung and Chandler provided a comfortable cushion. The Packers limited Jim Brown to 50 yards rushing and Ryan to 128 passing yards.

Texas Western guard Bobby Joe Hill drives toward the basket as Kentucky's Tommy Kron tries to keep up during the title game.

# Miners stun Kentucky

It was as simple as black and white. The unusual all-black starting five of Texas Western was quicker, faster and stronger than the all-white starters of top-ranked Kentucky. The result was a 72-65 upset, March 19, in the finals of the NCAA Tournament at College Park, Md.

The unheralded Miners parlayed their quickness and defensive intensity into an inspiring Cinderella story. Don Haskins' team, 27-1 but underrated because of a weak regular-season schedule, posted a 34-31 halftime lead, stretched it out midway through the second half and forced the Wildcats to foul. The Miners, playing with a quick, three-guard lineup, helped their cause by making 28 of 34 free-throw attempts.

The victory was especially sweet because Texas Western had been totally overlooked. Most attention was focused on a semifinal battle that pitted No. 1 Kentucky against No. 2 Duke, a game that everybody figured would decide the national championship. The Wildcats prevailed, 83-79, but could not keep up with the Miners in suffering only their second loss in 29 games.

Guard Bobby Joe Hill led Western with 20 points while 6-foot-7 David (Big Daddy)

Lattin added 16 points and grabbed nine rebounds.

# Celtics win 8th straight NBA title

The Boston Celtics won one for the Gipper, so to speak. In this case the Gipper was Arnold (Red) Auerbach, the architect of the greatest sports dynasty ever constructed.

When Auerbach lit his traditional victory cigar with 25 seconds remaining in Boston's 95-93 win over the Los Angeles Lakers, April 28, it punctuated the Celtics' record eighth consecutive National Basketball Association championship and signaled the end of Red's 16-year coaching tenure. The record is phenomenal considering that no other professional team has ever won more than five straight championships.

The 48-year-old Auerbach had announced his plan to give up coaching and concentrate on his front-office duties on April 18. He also made a more

Boston's Red Auerbach, coaching his last NBA game.

historic announcement—the selection of Bill Russell as his successor. The 6-foot-10 center, the heart and soul of the Celtics for 10 years, will become the NBA's first black coach.

It was no accident, of course, that Auerbach's timing coincided with Boston's 133-129 overtime loss to the Lakers in the opening game of the title series, inspiring the Celtics to reel off three straight victories. The Boston express hit a snag with losses in Games 5 and 6, but Russell's 25 points, 32 rebounds and outstanding defensive play in the finale sealed the verdict.

Boston players lauded the selection of Russell as the franchise's fourth coach. Although the scowling big man can be militant in his views, he is an intelligent take-charge individual, respected by his peers. Russell, who holds the NBA record with 19,761 career rebounds, will continue to play while performing his bench duties.

The Celtics have now won nine of the last 10 NBA championships (losing to the St. Louis Hawks in 1958) and Russell is the only player to have been there for each one. Up until this year when Boston finished second in the Eastern Division to Philadelphia, the Celtics had won every title since 1957.

# 1966

## AFL, NFL announce merger agreement

Seven years of war came to an end, June 8, when the National Football League and American Football League announced a merger agreement that eventually will result in a 26-team, 25-city circuit with a unified schedule and a common draft.

The merger will not be fully implemented until 1970, when the two leagues' multi-million dollar television contracts expire. They will maintain their present identities while working toward unification.

The first big step toward that goal will be a "world championship" game that will be contested next January and pit the champions from the two leagues. The first common draft, which should eliminate costly bidding wars, also will be held next year, as will interleague preseason games.

Under terms of the agreement, each of the nine AFL teams will pay $2 million to the existing NFL over a 20-year period; NFL Commissioner Pete Rozelle will continue in that role with jurisdiction over both leagues, and all existing franchises will be retained and each league will add one new member by 1968.

## Casper wins as Palmer collapses twice

*Billy Casper does a little jig after sinking a birdie putt on the 11th hole during his U.S. Open playoff victory over Arnold Palmer.*

In one of the biggest turnarounds in sports history, Billy Casper made up seven strokes in eight holes on the back nine to force a playoff, June 19, and then pulled off another stirring comeback the next day to win the U.S. Open golf tournament at San Francisco's Olympic Country Club.

The victim in this unlikely scenario was Arnold Palmer, who appeared to be well on his way to a second U.S. Open title when he turned with a 32 and a seven-stroke lead over Casper in the final round. But to the utter astonishment of the gallery, Palmer's game suddenly fell apart and Casper's came alive.

After dropping two shots on the first five holes of the back nine, Palmer still owned a five-stroke advantage. But Palmer bogied 15, 16 and 17, and Casper went birdie, birdie, par. Just like that, the match was even. Casper's final-round 68 and Palmer's 71 resulted in a 278 tie.

Palmer took a two-stroke lead in the playoff after a front-nine 33, but again he fell apart on the closing holes. He finished with a 73, four strokes behind Casper, who claimed his second U.S. Open title and the $25,000 top prize.

## Overtime goal caps Montreal's comeback

Henri Richard's goal at 2:20 of overtime gave Montreal a 3-2 victory over Detroit, May 5, and completed the Canadiens' comeback from a two-game deficit in the National Hockey League's Stanley Cup series.

Richard's goal at Detroit's Olympia Stadium erased the Red Wings' hopes of becoming only the second fourth-place team to win the Cup. But it was hardly a work of art. Richard scored when he was tripped in the Detroit zone by a Red Wing defenseman, fell on Dave Balon's pass, rolled through the crease and inadvertently knocked the puck in the net past a startled Roger Crozier.

"It just hit my leg and went in," Richard admitted. "I didn't even know I had scored until I heard everyone screaming."

The Canadiens won their four straight games after dropping 3-2 and 5-2 decisions at the Montreal Forum.

*Claude Provost (14) and Jean Beliveau (right) get front-row looks at the Stanley Cup as other happy Montreal Canadiens look on.*

# Pitcher smashes two slams

Atlanta's Tony Cloninger, doing his best impression of Superman, hit two grand slams and a run-scoring single *and* pitched the Braves to a 17-3 victory over the Giants in a July 3 game at San Francisco's Candlestick Park.

Cloninger became only the fifth player in major league history and the first National Leaguer to hit two bases-loaded homers in the same game. The first, off Bob Priddy, sailed over the center-field wall and capped a seven-run Atlanta first inning. The second was an opposite-field line drive off lefthander Ray Sedecki in the fourth.

The nine runs batted in were the most ever by a pitcher, beating the seven by Vic Raschi in 1953. They raised Cloninger's season total to 19 RBIs, 18 of which have come in his last four games. Cloninger also enjoyed a two-homer, five-RBI game against the New York Mets on June 16.

The 6-foot, 200-pound righthander did take time out from his offensive heroics to do a little pitching. He set down the Giants on seven hits, improving his record to 9-7.

*Milwaukee pitcher-turned-slugger Tony Cloninger.*

*Jim Ryun hits the tape with the fastest mile in history, a 3:51.3 clocking in the All-America invitation meet at Berkeley, Calif.*

## ★ SPORTS WATCH ★

**MAY:** The St. Louis Cardinals christened new Busch Memorial Stadium with a 12-inning, 4-3 victory over the Atlanta Braves.

**JUN:** Minnesota's Rich Rollins, Zoilo Versalles, Tony Oliva, Don Mincher and Harmon Killebrew stunned Kansas City with the first five-home run inning in baseball history en route to a 9-4 victory.

**JUL:** Cleveland's Jim Brown, the NFL's all-time career leading rusher with 12,312 yards, announced his retirement.

**AUG:** San Francisco's Willie Mays moved into second place on the all-time home run list when he hit No. 535 off St. Louis' Ray Washburn.

# Ryun runs 3:51.3 mile, sets a world record

Jim Ryun, a 19-year-old freshman miler at the University of Kansas, clipped more than two seconds off the world record on July 17, when he broke the tape at 3:51.3 during competition in the All-America invitation meet at Berkeley, Calif.

Ryun, the first American to hold the world record in the mile since Glenn Cunningham ran a 4:06.8 in 1934, covered the first quarter in 57.7, the half mile in 1:55.4 and the three-quarters in 2:55 before sprinting the final quarter in 56.3. He was clocked at 3:36.1 at 1,500 meters, one-half second off the world record.

Ryun, whose previous best time of 3:53.7 was recorded, June 4, during the Compton Games, broke the record of 3:53.6 set June 9, 1965, by Frenchman Michel Jazy. He was pushed by University of Texas stars Tom von Ruden and Richard Romo, who set a blistering pace.

The 6-foot-2, 165-pound Kansan was third at the quarter-mile mark, second at the half mile and first at three-quarters.

# Billie Jean King wins first major

Billie Jean King, a perky Californian, worked over Maria Bueno with an assortment of lobs, volleys and pinpoint passing shots, July 2, and recorded a 6-3, 3-6, 6-1 victory over the three-time champion in the Wimbledon singles finals.

The 22-year-old King, who finally won her first major tournament, played out her game plan to perfection. She served to Bueno's forehand, chopped her returns to the Brazilian star's shoetops and, after she drew her to the net, finessed the baseline with high lobs.

King broke service in the fourth game of the first set, losing only six points on her own punishing serve. After dropping the second set and opening at 1-1 in the third, she played masterfully the rest of the way.

King had upset defending champion Margaret Smith in a straight-set semifinal match.

# 1966

## Baltimore pitchers too much for Dodgers

The Baltimore Orioles, giving the pitching-rich Los Angeles Dodgers a taste of their own medicine, fired a series of blanks at the National League champions and recorded a surprising four-game sweep in the World Series.

Dave McNally's four-hit, 1-0 victory over Dodger right-hander Don Drysdale, October 9, at Baltimore was a fitting conclusion to a quick-and-easy fall classic. After McNally and Moe Drabowsky defeated the Dodgers, 5-2 in the opener, Jim Palmer fired a four-hit, 6-0 shutout and Wally Bunker allowed six hits in a 1-0 triumph. McNally's final-game gem ended the Dodgers' offensive misery.

The Dodgers set Series-record lows in runs (2), hits (17), batting average (.142) and consecutive scoreless innings (33).

After getting a third-inning run in Game 1 on a bases-loaded walk, the Dodgers did not score again. The four Baltimore pitchers who saw duty compiled a 0.50 earned-run average.

The Orioles batted only .200 themselves, but that was more than adequate. Frank Robinson, the American League Triple Crown winner (a .316 average, 49 home runs and 122 RBIs), hit two home runs, the second a fourth-game winner.

### "SPORTS TALK"

*"I know all the other National League teams were looking at us and saying, 'Why don't you play that way against us?'"*
**MAURY WILLS**
Los Angeles shortstop after the World Series

*Baltimore third baseman Brooks Robinson leaps for joy toward pitcher Dave McNally, who completed a World Series sweep of the Dodgers with a 1-0 shutout.*

## Passing fancy Unitas sets 2 NFL records

Baltimore Colts quarterback Johnny Unitas, rewriting the National Football League's passing records, got two of the big ones during recent games against the Minnesota Vikings and Los Angeles Rams.

When Unitas connected with John Mackey for a 26-yard scoring strike on September 18, in Bloomington, Minn., he moved past Y.A. Tittle on the all-time touchdown pass list. That was one of four that Unitas threw in the Colts' 38-23 victory over the Vikings. He also hit Mackey with an 83 yarder and fired four yard TD passes to Raymond Berry and Tom Matte.

Milestone No. 2 occurred October 30, during Baltimore's 17-3 victory over Los Angeles when Unitas completed a 31 yard pass to Berry and moved past Tittle on the all-time passing yardage list. Tittle threw for 28,339 yards while Unitas finished the game with 28,375.

*Baltimore quarterback Johnny Unitas releases his record-setting 26-yard touchdown pass to John Mackey.*

## Yankee ship sinks

It is official. The incredible New York Yankee dynasty has crumbled and, like Humpty Dumpty, it appears doubtful that it can ever be put back together again.

From first place and the World Series in 1964 to last place in 1966—the fall was steep and distressing. The Yankees lost 16 of their first 20 games this season and fired Manager Johnny Keane. Ralph Houk went from the front office back to the dugout but, confronted by injuries to key players like Mickey Mantle, Roger Maris and Whitey Ford, he could not halt the skid. The Yankees fell to a 70-89 record, finishing a game and a half behind ninth-place Boston and 26½ games behind pennant-winning Baltimore.

The realization that the Yankees indeed are mortal comes as a major shock to a franchise that won 29 American League pennants and captured a record 20 World Series titles in a 44-year period from 1921-64. The Yankees, simply, were better than everybody else and if they faltered, they made prudent signings or one-sided trades.

But no more. Last year's Bronx Bombers fell to sixth place and this year's team dropped into the basement.

# Koufax ends career

Los Angeles Dodger lefthander Sandy Koufax, the most overpowering pitcher in the major leagues over the last half decade, shocked the baseball world, November 18, when he announced his retirement because of a fear that he might permanently injure his arthritic left elbow.

The talented 30-year-old told reporters at a Los Angeles press conference that the pain has grown progressively worse in the three seasons since it began. He requested the Dodgers put him on the voluntarily retired list. This means Koufax will forfeit his $125,000-per-year salary.

Pain or no pain, Koufax has been phenomenal. Over the last four years, he has recorded a 97-27 record, including 26-8 in 1965 and 27-9 this year. He has won five consecutive earned-run average titles, a major league record, and three Cy Young Awards. He has pitched a record four no-hitters, including a perfect game last year, and he set a one-season strikeout mark of 382. His ERAs of 1.88 (1963), 1.74 (1964), 2.04 (1965) and 1.73 (1966) can be topped only by his 0.95 ERA in eight World Series games.

*The 1-2 Dodger punch of Sandy Koufax (right) and Don Drysdale dazzled hitters through the first half of the decade.*

*Notre Dame Coach Ara Parseghian (left) and Michigan State Coach Duffy Daugherty share their thoughts after the Irish and Spartans had fought to a controversial 10-10 tie.*

# A no-win proposition

In the much-anticipated, winner-take-all "Game of the Decade" between top-ranked Notre Dame (8-0) and No. 2 Michigan State (9-0), November 19, at East Lansing, Mich., there was no winner to take anything. The Battle of the Titans ended in a 10-10 tie and the battle for No. 1 was left in the hands of the pollsters.

There was, however, a loser. That was Fighting Irish Coach Ara Parseghian, who was roundly criticized after the game by millions of television viewers and many of the 80,011 fans who attended the contest at Spartan Stadium. At issue was Parseghian's decision to preserve the tie by running out the clock rather than trying for a victory in the waning moments. "It's all over and we're still Number 1," he told sportswriters after the game.

Michigan State had jumped to a 10-0 second-quarter lead on Regis Cavender's four-yard run and Dick Kenney's 47-yard field goal. But the Irish responded with Coley O'Brien's 34-yard TD pass to Bob Gladieux and Joe Azzaro's 28-yard field goal to open the fourth quarter. Azzaro later missed a 41-yarder.

When Notre Dame got the ball on its own 30-yard line with 1:24 left to play, everybody expected one last thrust for a victory. But Parseghian ordered four straight running plays that produced a first down and the game ended without any attempt to score.

The strategy left a bitter taste in the mouths of Michigan State players and fans.

"I respect them, but I resent them for what happened," said Spartan halfback Clint Jones. "We should be No. 1 now because we played to win."

United Press International evidently agreed, ranking Michigan State No. 1 in its next poll while the Associated Press stuck with the Irish. But the final AP and UPI polls, taking note of Notre Dame's season-ending 51-0 victory over Southern Cal, supported Parseghian's strategy by awarding the Irish a national championship.

# 1967

## Packers given scare

The 1966 National Football League championship game, which would decide the participant in the inaugural Super Bowl, was a battle between the old, traditional Green Bay dynasty and the young, exciting Dallas Cowboys. The 74,152 fans who jammed Dallas' Cotton Bowl on January 1 got their money's worth.

The Cowboys, making their first championship appearance, were shocked when the Packers took the opening kickoff and drove 76 yards for a touchdown, and stunned when Packer Jim Grabowski recovered a fumble on the ensuing kickoff and returned it 18 yards for another score. Dallas was behind 14-0—before its offense had even taken the field.

But the Cowboys showed heart and fought back. They trailed 21-20 in the third quarter before Bart Starr fired TD passes to Boyd Dowler and Max McGee, apparently putting the game out of reach.

But Dallas quarterback Don Meredith suddenly connected with tight end Frank Clarke on a 68-yard fourth-quarter TD strike and then dramatically drove the Cowboys downfield for a possible tying touchdown. Trailing 34-27, Dallas had a first down on the Packer 2-yard line.

But Green Bay held and Meredith was pressured on a fourth-down pass play by linebacker Dave Robinson. In desperation, he threw wildly and Green Bay's Tom Brown intercepted in the end zone.

## Green bay is "Super"

Max McGee, an unlikely hero who was filling in for injured starter Boyd Dowler, caught seven passes for 138 yards and two touchdowns, January 15, to lead the Green Bay Packers to a 35-10 victory over the Kansas City Chiefs in the first championship game ever contested between the AFL and NFL.

The Super Bowl, a nickname coined by Kansas City Owner and AFL founder Lamar Hunt, was contested at the Los Angeles Coliseum and played to rave reviews. A crowd of 61,946 attended the historic game and an estimated 60 million more watched on television, where advertisers paid up to $85,000 for one-minute commercial spots.

When the bands, baton twirlers and choral groups had finished their pre-game revelry, 4,000 pigeons were released from the floor of the stadium to signal the start of the game. And the Packers, heavy favorites as NFL champions, struck first when quarterback Bart Starr hit McGee with a 37-yard touchdown pass to cap a six-play, 80-yard drive.

But the Chiefs, 12-2-1 in the regular campaign and a winner over Buffalo in the AFL title contest, tied the game in the second period on Len Dawson's seven-yard TD pass to Curtis McClinton. A 14-yard run by Green Bay's Jim Taylor and a 31-yard field goal by Kansas City's Mike Mercer gave the Packers a slim 14-10 halftime lead.

The second half belonged to Green Bay. Playing a stifling defense that allowed the Chiefs only one penetration into Packer territory, Coach Vince Lombardi's troops capitalized on a 50-yard Willie Wood interception return that set up Elijah Pitts' five-yard TD run, a 13-yard Starr-to-McGee bomb and a one-yard run by Pitts.

*Dallas quarterback Don Meredith, in the grasp of Green Bay linebacker Dave Robinson, threw a desperation pass that was intercepted by Tom Brown, sealing the Packers' 1966 championship game victory.*

*Green Bay's Max McGee gathers in his second touchdown pass during the Packers' 35-10 victory over Kansas City in the first Super Bowl.*

# 76ers end Celtic reign

The Philadelphia 76ers, with 7-foot-1 center Wilt Chamberlain scoring less and enjoying it more, brought a screeching halt to the eight-year reign of the Boston Celtics as National Basketball Association champions while carving their own niche in the league's record books.

Simply, the 76ers of 1966-67 were awesome. And much of the credit has to go to Chamberlain, who gave up his seven-year stranglehold on the NBA scoring title to upgrade his defense and other offensive contributions. The big man dominated, leading the league in rebounding (24.2 per game) while finishing third in assists (7.8) and scoring (24.1). But it was his stifling Bill Russell-type defense that made the real difference.

With Chamberlain playing a more team-oriented role, Coach Alex Hannum's supporting cast of Hal Greer, Billy Cunningham, Chet Walker, Wally Jones and Lucious Jackson really blossomed. Philadelphia won 45 of its first 49 games and finished with a 68-13 record, the best in the history of the NBA and eight games ahead of Boston.

The 76ers quickly dispatched Cincinnati in the first round of the playoffs, stopped the Celtics in a five-game semifinal series and completed their barrage with a six-game championship series victory over San Francisco—bringing their final season record to an unprecedented 79-17.

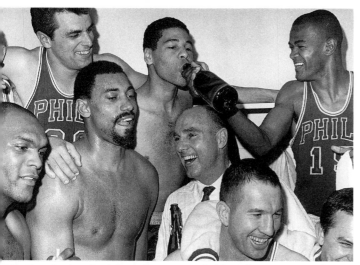

*Wilt Chamberlain (with beard) is surrounded by a happy group of 76ers after Philadelphia's victory over San Francisco in the NBA Finals.*

# NBA faces challenge

The American Basketball Association has set up shop as an alternative major league, determined to avoid the short-lived fate of the American Basketball League.

The ABA, which became official on February 2 when it introduced the world's tallest commissioner, 6-foot-10 former NBA great George Mikan, will challenge the 21-year-old National Basketball Association with an 11-team configuration, playing a 78-game schedule. The Eastern Division will include New York, Pittsburgh, Minnesota, Indianapolis and Louisville. Oakland, Anaheim, Denver, Dallas, Houston and New Orleans will make up the Western Division.

The ABA, which held its first draft, April 15, a month before the NBA's annual draft, plans to experiment with such innovations as a red, white and blue ball and a three-point field goal.

# Alcindor shines as UCLA wins again

*UCLA sophomore Lew Alcindor jumped into the national spotlight and led the Bruins to another NCAA Tournament championship.*

"At times, he frightens me." So said UCLA basketball Coach John Wooden after watching his Bruins destroy Dayton in the March 25 NCAA Tournament final at Louisville, Ky., and close out a 30-0 season. Wooden, of course, was referring to his 7-foot-1 sophomore center, Lew Alcindor, who had averaged 29 points while dominating the college game like nobody before him.

With a talented supporting cast that included guards Mike Warren and Lucius Allen and forwards Lynn Shackelford and Ken Heitz, the Bruins ran roughshod over everybody they played. The only way to compete was to hold the ball and keep it out of Alcindor's hands for as long as possible. Once he got hold of it, the talented, graceful big man proved to be virtually unstoppable.

So the Flyers found out in their 79-64 title-game loss. They crowded the middle and held Alcindor to 20 points, but Allen and Warren combined for 36 and the Bruins led 70-46 late in the game when Wooden removed his last starter. UCLA had its third NCAA championship title in four years—with the promise of more to follow.

## ★ SPORTS WATCH ★

**JAN:** Kansas City rolled to a 31-7 victory over Buffalo in the AFL title game played at Buffalo's War Memorial Stadium, qualifying as the league's representative for the Super Bowl.

**JAN:** San Diego interests were awarded the NBA's 12th franchise, which will begin play in the 1967-68 campaign.

**FEB:** Mario Andretti averaged 149.926 mph in his Ford and captured the ninth running of the Daytona 500 at Daytona Beach, Fla.

**MAR:** Chicago winger Bobby Hull scored 52 goals, topping the 50-goal barrier for the second straight year and third time in his career.

**APR:** Gay Brewer shot a final-round 67 to defeat Bobby Nichols by one stroke in the 31st Masters golf tournament at Augusta.

**APR:** Former Princeton basketball star Bill Bradley signed a four-year, $500,000 contract to play with the NBA's New York Knicks.

# boxing

## "The most famous person on earth"

*Brash, boastful, black and beautiful, Muhammad Ali dominated the boxing scene in the 1960s and '70s, enchanting and frustrating his followers in equal measures*

The kid threw his arms skyward in exultation and began dancing a little center-ring jig as 8,297 fans at Miami Beach's Convention Center watched in stunned silence. The former heavyweight champion of the world sat stoically in his corner, the kid's handlers rushed the ring in jubilation and press-row typewriters clicked off the urgent, incredulous words that would describe this major sports development on front pages of newspapers around the country.

Loud, brash, sassy and arrogant, Cassius Clay was indeed "the greatest," as he had been proclaiming to the world for weeks leading up to his February 25, 1964, championship fight with Sonny Liston. The 22-year-old, a veteran of only 19 professional bouts, had bypassed more deserving challengers by baiting Liston with a nonstop flurry of insults and boasts. The stonefaced, powerful, relentless champion could not wait to silence his tormentor.

It never happened. As promised, the poetic Clay "floated like a butterfly and stung like a bee" while staying away from Liston's powerful left and right hooks. He was too fast, too clever for the man who had recorded two first-round knockouts over former champion Floyd Patterson. He fought one round by Braille while blinded by an unknown foreign substance and he methodically wiped away "the Ugly Bear's" aura of invincibility. When the champion failed to answer the

*Clay after beating Liston, 1964.*

bell for the seventh round because of an injured shoulder, a new era dawned.

The era of Cassius Clay. Cassius X. Muhammad Ali. The "prettiest, fastest, smoothest, greatest" heavyweight champion of all time.

The Clay story began in

Louisville, Ky., where he was raised by a sign painter and a loving mother who described him as a "talker, right from the start. Like lightning he'd talk." The youngster took up boxing at age 12, became a Golden Gloves champion in both 1959 and '60 and blossomed into an international celebrity at the Rome Olympic Games, where he walked away with a gold medal in the light-heavyweight division after captivating everybody with his friendly, gregarious personality.

By the time he pulled his shocking upset of Liston (he was a 7-1 underdog) to lift his pro record to 20-0, Clay was in the process of making other changes in his life—changes that would have a profound effect on his boxing career. The first blockbuster came just days before the bout, when he announced to the world that he was converting from the Baptist religion to the teachings of Islam, joining the Black Muslims and changing his name to Muhammad Ali.

White America was shocked. The Muslims were perceived as angry, sinister militants who preached violence and hatred. But the youngster pressed on, dropping his white backers and putting his career into the hands of Elijah Muhammad while actively promoting black power issues.

Suddenly the youngster who had amused the boxing world with his colorful epithets, knockout predictions and poetry was not so amusing anymore. His first-round phantom-punch knockout of Liston in a May 1965 fight did nothing to endear him to a

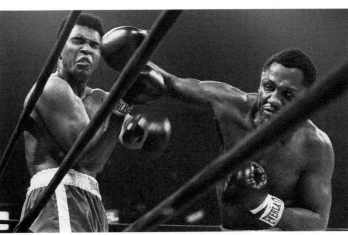

*Ali takes a right during his 1971 loss to Joe Frazier.*

boxing public that cried "fix," and his brutal battering of Patterson later that year in a 12-round match he could have finished much earlier was widely viewed as diabolical.

But his biggest blow was to the central fiber of America and it came in 1966, shortly before a title fight against Ernie Terrell. Reclassified 1-A by the Louisville draft board as the United States fought its war in Vietnam, Ali told the world, "I ain't got no quarrel with them Viet Cong," and then signed his name "Cassius X" when he was called to the induction center, where he flunked the mental aptitude test.

## "How many times I got to prove to you how great I am?"

### MUHAMMAD ALI
*On regaining his world title from George Foreman in 1974*

Shortly after he knocked out Zora Folley in his ninth title defense in the spring of 1967, Ali received his draft notice. Refusing induction into the Army on religious grounds, Ali was dragged into court and convicted of draft evasion. He also lost his title—to the various boxing commissions, which did what no boxer had been able to accomplish. At age 25, Ali's career would be put on hold for more than three years.

Branded a coward and threatened with imprisonment, Ali was finally cleared in 1970 when the U.S. Supreme Court reversed his conviction. Many Americans, who had discovered they did not have a quarrel with "them Viet Cong," either, drifted back into his corner.

After 43 idle months, Ali returned to the ring in 1970, surprising skeptics by carving up Jerry Quarry in a convincing three-rounder in

*Ali punches champ George Foreman in 1974 at Zaire.*

*Ali and Frazier during their 1975 "Thrilla in Manila."*

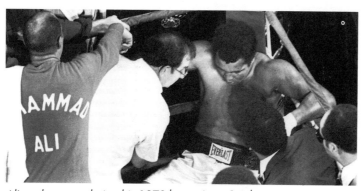

*Ali on the ropes during his 1978 loss to Leon Spinks.*

Atlanta. Ali was back. But there was a new force to be reckoned with in the heavyweight division, a fighting machine named Joe Frazier.

Ali got his first chance to regain his long-lost title in March 1971 when he squared off against undefeated Smokin' Joe at New York's Madison Square Garden. The so-called "Fight of the Century" was everything it was supposed to be—and more.

For $2.5 million guarantees, the fighters battered each other mercilessly for 15 rounds. Ali had predicted a victory in six, but Frazier secured the decision when he sent his challenger to the canvas in the 15th. Both ended up in the hospital with a begrudging respect for each other.

"Was he human that night?" Ali asked. "No human could take the punishment he took. But I guess I took some, too. I

felt he'd taken after me with a baseball bat."

Ali defeated Frazier in a 1974 return match, but there was no title to go with his victory. Frazier had fallen a year earlier in a second-round technical knockout to George Foreman in Jamaica. Ali got his first shot at Big George and his second title chance in October 1974, in Kinshasa, Zaire.

No longer able to float like a butterfly at age 32, Ali concocted a curious strategy for that fight. In what he later called "rope-a-dope," Ali laid back against the ropes in the early rounds and covered up as Foreman flailed away. Soon the champion was exhausted and Ali knocked him out in the eighth round.

"How many times I got to prove to you how great I am?" Ali lectured after his Foreman victory.

Back on top at last, Ali stayed there through 10 title defenses, including another tough battle with Frazier. Ali won that "Thrilla in Manila" ("It was like death," he said), but his reign ended suddenly in February 1978 when Olympic star Leon Spinks scored a stunning 15-round split decision at Las Vegas. Undaunted, Ali pounded out a unanimous decision over Spinks seven months later to win the heavyweight crown for an unprecedented third time and promptly announced his retirement.

The self-proclaimed "most famous person on earth" made two ill-advised returns to the ring, losing to Larry Holmes at age 38 in a 1980 title fight and to Trevor Berbick in a 1981 non-title bout. But those losses did not tarnish an outstanding career that produced a 56-5 final record with 37 knockouts.

Although opinion varies on Ali's place among the all-time best fighters, there's no doubt his ring flair and magnetism were unmatched. He truly was, in that regard, "the greatest."

# 1967

## MAY-AUGUST

## Nicklaus sets Open record, beats Palmer

Jack Nicklaus rolled in a 22-foot birdie putt on the 18th green, June 18, to beat Arnold Palmer by four strokes in the final round of the U.S. Open at the tough Baltusrol Golf Club in Springfield, N.J. Nicklaus' final-round 65 gave him a U.S. Open-record four-round total of 275.

After the 27-year-old Columbus, Ohio, native shot a front-nine 31 to open a four-stroke advantage, it became a battle of Nicklaus versus Baltusrol. Ben Hogan's 1948 score of 276 at the Riviera Country Club in Los Angeles stood as the lowest total ever recorded in the 67 U.S. Open championships that

had been contested, and Nicklaus clearly had a shot at the record.

He faltered at the 10th hole with a rare bogey, but birdied three of the last eight holes and recorded his double triumph.

Nicklaus, Palmer and Billy Casper all trailed 23-year-old amateur Marty Fleckman by one stroke after three rounds, but Fleckman ballooned to a final-round 80, Casper struggled through a tough round and Palmer, despite an excellent 69, could not keep up with Nicklaus. The Open title was the second for Nicklaus, who defeated Palmer in a 1962 playoff.

## NHL stocks 6 teams

The 50-year-old National Hockey League officially became a 12-team circuit, June 6, when six expansion teams stocked their rosters with a draft of 120 players.

The Los Angeles Kings opened the proceedings by picking Toronto goaltender Terry Sawchuk. By the time the draft had ended, the Kings, St. Louis Blues, Philadelphia

Flyers, Pittsburgh Penguins, Minnesota North Stars and California Seals had each selected 20 players, mainly second-rate veterans or untried youngsters. The general feeling was that the six established teams did not give the newcomers much in the way of quality for their $2 million league entry fee.

The teams will begin play in the 1967-68 campaign.

## Foyt wins third Indy

A.J. Foyt, chasing the dust of Parnelli Jones' turbine engine STP Oil Treatment Special for 197 laps, zoomed to victory in the Indianapolis 500 on May 31, when Jones was forced out of the race by a broken ball-bearing holder with three laps to go.

The victory was Foyt's third in the Memorial Day classic, tying him with Louis Meyer, Mauri Rose and Wilbur Shaw for that distinction. He averaged a record 151.207 mph in his Coyote-Ford.

Foyt's chances looked gloomy as Jones, with an innovative Pratt-Whitney designed engine, sailed toward victory, 45 seconds ahead of the Texan's over-matched piston engine. But suddenly a $6 part in the car's gear box broke and Foyt had a clear run to the finish line. Well,

almost. As he cleared the No. 4 turn on the final lap, he had to weave his way to the checkered flag through a five-car tangle of spinning and smoking debris.

The race, scheduled for May 30, was stopped after 18 laps because of a rainstorm and restarted the next day. It marked the first time the race ever had to be run over a two-day period.

*Jack Nicklaus waves to the gallery after sinking a 22-foot birdie putt on 18 and winning the U.S. Open with a record-breaking 275.*

*A.J. Foyt heads for the Indianapolis 500 finish line after weaving his way through a five-car wreck on the homestretch.*

# Ryun sets another world record

Jim Ryun, already holder of the mile world record, sped through a record-shattering performance in the 1,500 meters, July 8, during competition in the United States-British Commonwealth track and field meet at the Los Angeles Coliseum.

Ryun finished the race in 3:33.1, 2.5 seconds faster than Australian Herb Elliott's 3:35.6 record run in the 1960 Olympic Games at Rome. The 7-year-old record fell in the final 300 meters when Ryun flew across the finish line with an unbelievable 38.1-second kick.

Ryun, who lowered his own world record for the mile to 3:51.1 two weeks ago in the national Amateur Athletic Union meet, ran lap fractions of 60.9, 1:57.5 and 2:55, covering

*1,500-meter record holder Jim Ryun, a Kansas University sophomore.*

the last 400 meters in 54.1.

The 20-year-old Kansan beat Kip Keino by 35 yards after letting the Kenyan set the pace through three laps. Ryun's record time is the equivalent of a 3:48 mile.

# Perez's homer ends All-Star marathon

Cincinnati's Tony Perez belted a Catfish Hunter pitch over the left-field fence with one out in the 15th inning, July 12, giving the National League a 2-1 All-Star Game victory over the American League.

Perez's home run before 46,309 fans at California's Anaheim Stadium ended a masterful display by 12 pitchers representing both leagues. The N.L. scored a second-inning run on a homer by Philadelphia third baseman Richie Allen and the A.L. tied the game on a sixth-inning solo homer by Baltimore third baseman Brooks Robinson. It is the longest game in the event's 35-year history.

The N.L. combination of Juan Marichal, Ferguson Jenkins, Bob Gibson, Chris Short, Mike Cuellar, Don Drysdale and Tom Seaver allowed eight hits while striking out 17. Los Angeles' Drysdale, who pitched two shutout innings, was credited with his league's fifth straight All-Star victory.

A.L. pitchers Dean Chance, Jim McGlothlin, Gary Peters, Al Downing and Hunter allowed nine hits while striking out 13. Perez was a 10th-inning replacement for Allen, meaning all three homers were hit by third basemen.

*All-Star Game hero Tony Perez of Cincinnati.*

# January wins playoff

Don January shot a playoff-round 69 and posted a two-stroke victory over Don Massengale, July 24, in an unlikely conclusion to the PGA Championship at Columbine Country Club in Littleton, Colo.

January and Massengale were paired in the playoff when third-round leaders Dan Sikes (209), Jack Nicklaus (211) and Arnold Palmer (213) all faltered, allowing January (213) and Massengale (215) to jump over them. Massengale blazed around the 7,437-yard course early with a 66 and then waited to see if anybody could match his four-round total of 281.

January finally did, but it took four birdies between the 12th and 17th holes and a par on 18. That forced Monday's 18-hole playoff and January took control of that round with a 30-foot birdie putt on 10 and an excellent wedge shot on 15 that resulted in another birdie.

# Boston's dream ends

*Happy Cardinals mob pitcher Bob Gibson (without cap) after the St. Louis ace had pitched a three-hitter to defeat Boston in Game 7.*

The Boston Red Sox were awakened from their "impossible dream," October 12, by the strong arm and determination of St. Louis ace Bob Gibson.

The big righthander fired a Game 7 three-hitter at Boston's Fenway Park, which gave the Cardinals a 7-2 victory and registered their eighth World Series championship.

The Red Sox, ninth-place finishers in 1966, survived a torrid four-team American League pennant race under rookie Manager Dick Williams. Boston won 92 times and finished one game ahead of Detroit and Minnesota and three games in front of the Chicago White Sox, thanks largely to the Triple Crown hitting heroics of Carl Yastrzemski and the 22-victory

performance of righthander Jim Lonborg.

But with two Gibson victories offsetting a one-hit, 5-0 Lonborg shutout in Game 2, the Cardinals jumped to a 3-1 Series lead and appeared to have the fall classic well in hand. Boston, however, rallied behind Lonborg in Game 5 for a 3-1 victory

and tied the Series with an 8-4 win in Game 6. The finale pitted Gibson against Lonborg.

Gibson allowed only three hits in his third Series triumph and even hit a home run off Lonborg. The big blow, however, was second baseman Julian Javier's three-run blast in the sixth.

---

# Billie Jean is King

Billie Jean King, controlling the temper that held her back for six years, has moved to the forefront of women's tennis. The bespectacled, peppery 23-year-old dismissed any lingering doubts, September 10, when she defeated Ann Haydon Jones in straight sets at Forest Hills,

becoming the first American to win the U.S. singles championship since 1961.

King defeated her British rival, 11-9, 6-4, just as she had in July in the Wimbledon singles final. Billie Jean also combined with Rosie Casals and Australian Owen Davidson to win

the women's doubles and mixed doubles at both Wimbledon and Forest Hills, making her the first to accomplish that sweep since Alice Marble in 1939.

King, who did not lose a set at Forest Hills, overcame Jones with her speed and volleying skills. Jones was playing with a bad hamstring that hobbled her throughout the match and caused her to fall in pain during the second set. King rushed the length of the court to help her fallen rival, but Jones pronounced herself fit to continue.

*Billie Jean King returns a backhand en route to a straight-set victory over Ann Haydon Jones in the U.S. Open final.*

---

# A day to remember

Sometimes you have it, sometimes you don't. On October 27, Texas-El Paso quarterback Brooks Dawson had it.

Playing in a game against New Mexico in Albuquerque, Dawson started his day inauspiciously when he threw three straight incompletions. Later in the first quarter, he connected with Bob Wallace on a 25-yard touchdown pass.

Dawson's second completion also came in the first quarter—a 10-yard touchdown pass to Larry McHenry. Volley Mur-

phy caught Dawson's third completion, a 74-yard touchdown strike. Paul White got in on the act in the second quarter, catching Dawson's fourth completion for an 83-yard touchdown and Murphy added 86 and 52-yard TD catches in the second and third quarters, respectively.

Six completions, six touchdown passes. Dawson only completed three other passes in UTEP's 75-12 victory over the Lobos, but he finished the game with 376 passing yards, averaging 41.8 yards per completion.

# Simpson's run beats top-ranked UCLA

A dazzling 64-yard run by Southern California halfback O.J. Simpson wiped out a six-point fourth-quarter deficit, November 18, and Rikki Aldridge's extra-point kick allowed the Trojans to defeat the No. 1-ranked UCLA Bruins, 21-20, in a titanic struggle at the Los Angeles Coliseum.

With a Rose Bowl bid and a possible national championship on the line, Simpson took a handoff and faked right before sailing around left end. He cut to the middle at about the Bruins' 40-yard line and, with teammate Earl McCullouch blocking downfield, outran the secondary.

UCLA had broken a 14-14 tie moments earlier when Dave Nuttall caught a 20-yard TD pass from Gary Beban. But Zenon Andrusyshyn's conversion kick sailed wide—a mistake that would come back to haunt the Bruins.

Simpson, who ran 30 times for 177 yards, also scored a second-period touchdown on a 13-yard carry and Pat Cashman returned a Beban interception 55 yards for a first-quarter TD. UCLA scored first-half touchdowns on Greg Jones' 12-yard run and George Farmer's 53-yard reception.

The victory lifted Southern Cal's final record to 9-1.

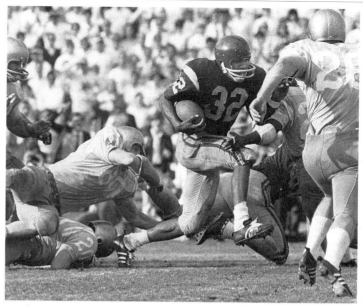

*Southern Cal's O.J. Simpson eludes UCLA defenders en route to a 13-yard second-quarter TD run.*

# N.L. will go along with A.L. expansion

National League owners, saying they did not want to be stampeded into expansion, nevertheless voted unanimously to add two new teams by no later than 1971, agreeing to go along with the American League's decision to add franchises in Kansas City and Seattle in 1969.

The vote, taken December 1, on the final day of the Winter Meetings at Mexico City, avoided conflict over the A.L.'s decision to let Charles O. Finley move his Athletics to Oakland and the junior league's accelerated expansion program. The Athletics will compete with San Francisco for the Bay Area dollar.

The N.L. announcement attracted applications from six hungry U.S. and Canadian cities: Milwaukee, Dallas-Fort Worth, Montreal, Toronto, Buffalo and San Diego. A committee has been set up to screen the applicants.

The A.L. already has announced that it will divide its 12 teams into two divisions for 1969 with the two division winners meeting in a playoff to determine a participant for the World Series.

# Packers put Dallas on ice

Green Bay's Bart Starr dived into the end zone on a quarterback sneak with 13 seconds remaining, December 31, to give the Packers a 21-17 victory over the Dallas Cowboys and the right to meet Oakland in Super Bowl II.

The Packers' third straight National Football League championship and fifth in six years was decided before 50,861 Green Bay fans on a frozen Lambeau Field in a minus 13-degree temperature with a 14-knot wind that made it feel like minus 35. Starr's winning sneak was a third-down win-or-lose

*Green Bay quarterback Bart Starr confers with Coach Vince Lombardi (left) before scoring the winning touchdown in the Ice Bowl*

gamble—the Packers, having moved from their own 31-yard line, had no timeouts remaining.

From the start, the "Ice Bowl" was a dramatic test of nerves and endurance.

Green Bay took a 14-0 lead on two Starr TD passes to Boyd Dowler. Dallas countered on a seven-yard fumble return by George Andrie and Danny Villanueva's 21-yard field goal. The Cowboys appeared to have the game in hand when quarterback Don Meredith made a fourth-quarter pitchout to Danny Reeves, who fired a 50-yard pass to Lance Rentzel.

# 1968

## NHL player dies

Bill Masterton, a Minnesota North Stars center, died of a massive internal brain injury, January 15, at Bloomington, Minn., approximately 30 hours after he cracked his head on the ice during a 2-2 tie with the Oakland Seals.

The 29-year-old Winnipeg native, the first player in the 51-year history of the National Hockey League to die as a result of a game-related injury, was upended about 25 feet in front of the Oakland goal, fell backward and hit his head on the ice. He was not wearing a helmet. Masterton was rushed to Fairview-Southdale Hospital, where he remained until his death.

Masterton returned to hockey last year after a four-year retirement. With more jobs available because of expansion, the former Canadien hooked on with the new North Stars. He had four goals and seven assists.

NHL officials and top players, gathered in Toronto for the NHL All-Star Game, expressed shock over Masterton's death. They also discussed the possibility of league legislation to make the wearing of helmets mandatory.

## Packers triumph in "Super" contest

*Green Bay's Donny Anderson breaks free for a two-yard TD run in Super Bowl II.*

Don Chandler kicked four field goals and quarterback Bart Starr's precision passing carved up Oakland's defense, January 14, as Green Bay won its second straight Super Bowl with a 33-14 victory over the Raiders at Miami's Orange Bowl.

The Packers, only 9-4-1 during the regular National Football League season, were too disciplined and poised for the 14-1 Raiders. Starr, capitalizing on every Oakland mistake, got Chandler in position for three first-half field goals and connected with Boyd Dowler on a 62-yard touchdown pass as Green Bay forged a 16-7 lead.

As they did in Super Bowl I against Kansas City, the Packers really took control after intermission. A two-yard run by Donny Anderson, another Chandler field goal and Herb Adderley's 60-yard interception return stretched the margin to 33-7 before the Raiders got a consolation touchdown on Daryle Lamonica's 23-yard pass to Bill Miller.

*UCLA's Lew Alcindor (33) battles Houston's Elvin Hayes for the opening tip in a much-anticipated battle of unbeatens at the Astrodome.*

## Hayes, Houston end UCLA's win streak

Houston forward Elvin Hayes hit two free throws with 28 seconds remaining, January 20, and the Cougars held on to post a 71-69 victory over powerful UCLA in a much-ballyhooed battle of unbeatens at Houston's Astrodome.

The victory, Houston's 49th straight on its home court and 18th straight overall, ended UCLA's 47-game winning streak, the second longest in college basketball history. It also put the No. 2-ranked Cougars in position to supplant the Bruins as the nation's top team.

With a basketball-record crowd of 52,693 fans and a national television audience looking on, the 6-foot-8 Hayes put on quite a show. He scored 39 points, connecting on 17 of 25 field goal attempts, grabbed 15 rebounds and blocked four shots. He also helped put the defensive squeeze on 7-foot-1 UCLA center Lew Alcindor who had sat out UCLA's previous two games with a scratched eyeball and was obviously off form, scoring only 15 points overall.

The Bruins trailed almost the entire game, managing to force ties on three occasions. The final came at 69-69 with 44 seconds remaining when guard Lucius Allen, high scorer with 25 points, dropped in two free throws.

### " SPORTS TALK "

*"It has to be the greatest thrill of my life. I was scared to death all the time. In the last 12 seconds, I told them to get the ball to (Elvin) Hayes."*

**GUY LEWIS**
Houston basketball coach

# A costly mistake

Happy-go-lucky Roberto de Vicenzo did the giving rather than the receiving on his 45th birthday, April 14, when he signed an incorrect scorecard and forfeited his chance for a victory in the Masters.

The Buenos Aires native had just gone around the Augusta National course in 65 strokes, tying Bob Goalby for the lead at 277 and forcing a playoff. He glanced over his scorecard at the official scorer's table by the 18th green, signed it and turned it in. He was notified later that his playing partner, Tommy Aaron, had put down the wrong score at the 17th hole (a 4 instead of a birdie 3) and his total strokes added up to 66 instead of 65. Golf rules specifically dictate that the 66 would have to stand.

Goalby, suddenly the outright winner, received $20,000 for his efforts. De Vicenzo, now second, won $15,000, a sad culmination to what had started as a glorious day. The Argentinian opened the final round by holing his approach shot for an eagle and dropping birdie putts at the second and third holes.

Goalby shot a final-round 66 to win.

Roberto de Vicenzo and Masters winner Bob Goalby, after the scorecard controversy.

## ★ SPORTS WATCH ★

**JAN:** Two NBA newcomers: Milwaukee and Phoenix were awarded expansion franchises.

**FEB:** Players and owners ratified baseball's first Basic Agreement.

**FEB:** Peggy Fleming won the hearts of Americans and a figure skating title, the only U.S. gold, at the Winter Olympic Games in Grenoble, France.

**MAR:** Lew Alcindor scored 34 points and UCLA raced past North Carolina, 78-55, to win its second straight NCAA Tournament and fourth in five years.

**APR:** Hot-shooting Louisiana State sophomore Pete Maravich set a single-season college basketball scoring record, averaging 43.8 points per game.

**APR:** The Naismith Memorial Basketball Hall of Fame opened on the Springfield (Mass.) College campus where the game was invented by Dr. James Naismith in 1891.

# Frazier beats Mathis

Former Olympic champion Joe Frazier claimed a piece of boxing's heavyweight championship, March 4, when he battered big Buster Mathis, recording an 11th-round technical knockout at New York's Madison Square Garden.

Frazier, giving away almost 40 pounds, bloodied Mathis' nose in the opening round and then went to work with a savage body assault. By round 5, Mathis' white trunks were turning red.

The body attack brought Mathis' hands lower and lower and Frazier put the 243-pound giant away in the 11th round with a short right to the chin and a left hook to the temple.

Mathis fell backward through the ropes onto the canvas apron and barely struggled to his feet by the count of 10. The referee waved his arms, signaling Frazier's 20th professional victory without a loss.

However, Frazier will be recognized as heavyweight champion only in New York, Illinois and Massachusetts. He will meet the winner of the World Boxing Association tournament bout between Jerry Quarry and Jimmy Ellis later in the year. The New York State Athletic Commission and WBA stripped Muhammad Ali (the former Cassius Clay) of the heavyweight crown last year when he was convicted for draft evasion.

Big Buster Mathis (white trunks) feels the brunt of Joe Frazier's power.

# Open tennis prevails

Sixty-six representatives from 47 nations attending an extraordinary general meeting of the International Lawn Tennis Federation in Paris made history on March 30, when they voted to endorse open tennis.

The controversial, long-debated issue was forced to a vote when Great Britain announced late last year that it was opening the 1968 Wimbledon championships to both professional and amateur players, regardless of the consequences. The British, well aware that the Federation had adamantly voted down all previous attempts for open tennis, were anticipating expulsion from the international organization.

Instead, they were praised for their leadership role. Not one dissenting voice was heard and the vote drew wild applause.

Bob Kelleher, president of the USLTF, said the American organization would meet soon to decide the future course of tennis in this country. The ILTF decision leaves the issue to the various national associations.

# 1968

## MAY-AUGUST

## Stingy Drysdale streaks to record

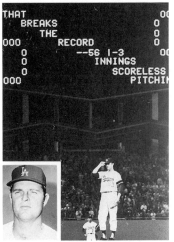

The scoreboard tells the story as Los Angeles pitcher Don Drysdale listens to the ovation of the Dodger Stadium crowd.

Los Angeles righthander Don Drysdale streaked past Hall of Famer Walter Johnson into the baseball record books, June 8, running his scoreless-inning count to 58 before finally surrendering a run to Philadelphia.

Drysdale received a standing ovation from the 50,060 fans at Dodger Stadium when he edged past Johnson's record (55⅔ innings) in the third inning against the Phillies. He stretched the record to 58 before the Phillies finally broke through in the fifth, scoring on Tony Taylor and Clay Dalrymple singles and Howie Bedell's sacrifice fly.

Drysdale began his streak on May 14 against the Chicago Cubs with a 1-0 victory and then followed with shutouts against St. Louis, Houston twice, San Francisco and Pittsburgh.

Philadelphia scored two more runs against Drysdale: in the sixth on Bill White's home run and in the seventh on Cookie Rojas' single. He was relieved in that inning but still got credit for his eighth victory in 11 decisions.

## Dancer's Image loses

Dancer's Image, the colt that thrilled the racing world with his last-to-first Run for the Roses in the May 4 Kentucky Derby, was dropped from first to last, May 7, after chemical tests disclosed that he had run with a pain-killing drug in his system.

The shocking announcement made a winner of Forward Pass, the Derby favorite that finished a length and a half behind Dancer's Image over the 1¼-mile Churchill Downs course in Louisville, Ky. The Calumet Farm entry wins $122,600; Dancer's Image gets nothing.

News that the chemist for the Kentucky State Racing Commission had discovered a pain-killing drug in a urine sample seemed to stun owner Peter Fuller and trainer Lou Cavalaris. Both said they were "mystified" and suggested that maybe some samples got switched. It was the first disqualification in 94 runnings of America's most prestigious race for 3-year-olds.

Dancer's Image, with Bobby Ussery in saddle, had thrilled 100,000 spectators with a dramatic run to victory along the rail after sitting in 14th place for much of the race.

## Trevino fires 69, captures U.S. Open

Celebration time for Lee Trevino, a first-time winner of the U.S. Open golf tournament.

Lee Trevino, a fast-talking "Texican" from Horizon City, Tex., fired a final-round 69, June 16, and cruised to a four-stroke victory in the U.S. Open at Rochester, N.Y. Trevino, a first-time winner on the professional tour, tied the four-round Open record of 275 set last year by Jack Nicklaus.

The 28-year-old Trevino, trailing Bert Yancey by one stroke after three rounds, turned the tables on the front nine and led by one at the turn. He picked up a stroke on each of the next four holes with two birdies and two pars and coasted the rest of the way.

Yancey finished with a 76 and 281, yielding second place to Nicklaus. The defending champion finished at 279.

Trevino became the first golfer to play all four rounds of the U.S. Open under par and the third to make the Open his first pro tournament victory. Nicklaus did it in 1962 and Jack Fleck in 1955.

### "SPORTS TALK"

*"My goal is to play as good as I can for as long as I can. I'm going to keep practicing and playing until I get about 100 years old."*
**LEE TREVINO**

### ★ SPORTS WATCH ★

**MAY:** The Pittsburgh Pipers won the first ABA championship in a seven-game thriller against the New Orleans Buccaneers.

**MAY:** Oakland's Catfish Hunter threw the first A.L. perfect game in 46 years, shutting out the Minnesota Twins, 3-0, and driving in all of the A's runs.

**MAY:** Montreal and San Diego were awarded teams that will play next season as N.L. expansion franchises.

**MAY:** Montreal Coach Toe Blake, after watching his Canadiens sweep St. Louis for their eighth Stanley Cup title in 13 years, announced his retirement.

**JUL:** Julius Boros shot a final-round 69 and recorded a one-stroke victory in the PGA Championship at the Pecan Valley Country Club in San Antonio, Tex.

**JUL:** Billie Jean King captured her third straight Wimbledon singles title, beating Judy Tegart, 9-7, 7-5, in the finals.

# Unhappy 76ers trade Chamberlain to L.A.

The Philadelphia 76ers, disillusioned after being upset in the National Basketball Association playoffs and unwilling to meet Wilt Chamberlain's salary demands, traded the 7-foot-1 center to the Los Angeles Lakers, July 5, for three players and an undisclosed amount of cash.

Chamberlain, who had led the 76ers to their first NBA title in 1966-67, helped them win 62 regular-season games and repeat as Eastern Division champions last year. But Philadelphia fell to Boston in a tough seven-game semifinal series, Alex Hannum resigned as coach and jumped to Oakland of the American Basketball Association and Chamberlain demanded a million-dollar contract and a say in naming the team's new coach.

Philadelphia owner Irv Kosloff gave Wilt his answer by shipping him to Los Angeles for Darrell Imhoff, Archie Clark, Jerry Chambers and cash. The Lakers need a big man to complement talented Elgin Baylor and Jerry West and owner Jack Kent Cooke thinks Chamberlain may be just the answer.

JoAnne Carner hugs the trophy after winning her fifth U.S. Women's Amateur golf title.

## Carner wins 5th title

JoAnne Carner, the robust long-hitter from Seeconk, Mass., defeated "good friend and golfing buddy" Ann Quast Welts, 5 and 4, August 17, at Birmingham, Mich., winning her fifth U.S. Women's Amateur golf title. She is now one victory behind 1920s and '30s great Glenna Collett.

Outdriving her smaller opponent by an average of 40 yards, Carner led 2-up after nine. But Welts fought back to even the match early in the afternoon round. Carner pulled away with four birdies in the next 11 holes.

The morning round started on a Birmingham Country Club course that had been soaked overnight by a torrential downpour. Puddles stood in the fairways, water had to be pumped out of bunkers and repair work continued on the 18th green as the two golfers approached, courtesy of a creek that overflowed. But the course had dried considerably by afternoon and Carner cruised.

New Los Angeles Lakers center Wilt Chamberlain.

## NFL settles strike, opens training camps

National Football League owners reached agreement with the striking NFL Players' Association on a new contract, July 14, clearing the way for the opening of training camps and averting a potentially costly cancellation of preseason and regular-season games.

NFL President and Cleveland Browns owner Art Modell made the announcement at a joint news conference with players' head John Gordy, an offensive tackle for the Detroit Lions. The agreement came after a 5-hour, 23-minute bargaining session at New York's Waldorf-Astoria Hotel.

Under the new pact, owners will contribute $3 million to an upgraded pension fund. They also will upgrade medical insurance benefits, raise the minimum pay for second-year players to $12,000 and provide additional financial incentives.

The opening of training camps has been delayed for more than a week. The exhibition season opens August 1 when Washington plays Houston and August 2 when the world champion Green Bay Packers compete in Chicago's annual College All-Star Game.

# 1968

## McLain gets 30th win

Detroit righthander Denny McLain, bidding to become baseball's first 30-game winner in 34 years, watched from the dugout, September 14, as his Tiger teammates rallied for two ninth-inning runs and a 5-4 triumph over the Oakland A's at Tiger Stadium.

The victory lifted McLain's record to 30-5 and made the righthander the first pitcher to reach the select 30 club since Dizzy Dean. He struck out 10 batters and allowed six hits, two of them home runs by Reggie Jackson.

Detroit's winning rally started when Diego Segui walked Al Kaline and then gave up a single to Mickey Stanley. Kaline scored on an error by first baseman Danny Cater and Stanley scored the winner when Willie Horton lined a one-out hit over left fielder Jim Gosger's head.

McLain finished the season at

*Detroit's Al Kaline (left) escorts Denny McLain (with towel) out of the dugout after Willie Horton's ninth-inning single had given the righthander his 30th victory.*

31-6, earned one World Series victory and walked away with both the American League Cy Young and Most Valuable Player awards. His classy 1.96 earned-run average and six shutouts were indicative of his domination.

---

### ★ SPORTS WATCH ★

**SEP:** Boston's Carl Yastrzemski, the A.L.'s only .300 hitter, won his second straight batting championship with a .3005 mark, the lowest winning average in history.

**SEP:** Arthur Ashe became the first black male to win the U.S. singles championship, beating Dutchman Tom Okker in a tough five-set final.

**SEP:** Giants ace Gaylord Perry pitched a no-hitter against St. Louis, September 17, but Cardinal pitcher Ray Washburn returned the favor the next day by throwing a no-hitter against San Francisco.

**NOV:** Southern California running back O.J. Simpson was awarded the Heisman Trophy.

**DEC:** The United States ended Australia's four-year reign as Davis Cup champion with a 4-1 victory at Adelaide, Australia.

---

# Mexico City Olympics

From black power protests to one of the most incredible athletic feats ever performed—the Summer Olympic Games at Mexico City had controversy and excitement.

The protests, thrust upon an international audience by American sprinters Tommie Smith and John Carlos, occurred early in the track and field segment and evoked reactions ranging from support to indignation and embarrassment. Smith had just won the 200-meter final and Carlos had finished third. They took their places on the victory stand wearing black scarfs and one black glove each.

After receiving their medals, both raised their gloved hands with fists clenched and kept their heads deeply bowed during the playing of the national anthem and the raising of the American flag.

The United States Olympic Committee was divided on how the matter should be handled, but the International Olympic Committee made its feelings perfectly clear: Either discipline Smith and Carlos, or the entire American contingent might be banned from competition.

On October 18, Smith and Carlos were suspended and told they must leave the Olympic Village and their credentials were taken away. Other black athletes were stung by the action and many threatened to drop out of the Games.

It was amid this political turmoil that Bob Beamon, another black athlete, performed one of the greatest athletic achievements in history. On his first attempt in the long jump final Beamon soared an incredible 29 feet, 2½ inches, breaking the previous world record by 21¾ inches. The 28-foot barrier, akin to the first sub 4-minute mile, was totally bypassed.

From a competition standpoint, the U.S. enjoyed an excellent Olympics, piling up 45 gold medals and 107 overall to the Soviet Union's 29 golds and 91 total medals. Such athletes as sprinters Lee Evans, Jim Hines and Wyomia Tyus, pole vaulter Bob Seagren, swimmer Debbie Meyer and the members of the U.S. basketball team, were outstanding.

But the 1968 Games will be best remembered for the demonstration of Smith and Carlos and the grandaddy of all records, Beamon's incredible long jump.

*Bob Beamon breaking the long jump record during the Summer Olympic Games at Mexico City.*

# Gibson's big season

*St. Louis ace Bob Gibson (right) with coach Red Schoendienst.*

It was not surprising, November 13, when St. Louis ace Bob Gibson was selected as the National League's Most Valuable Player, an award that fits nicely with his already earned Cy Young. Gibson staged one of the most dominating pitching performances in baseball history.

He recorded a 22-9 record in the regular season and posted the lowest earned-run average in N.L. history. Allowing only 38 earned runs and 198 hits in 305 innings, Gibson finished with a 1.12 ERA and threw 13 shutouts. His pitching was a big reason behind the Cardinals' run to their second straight pennant.

The fun did not end there. In Game 1 of the World Series, Gibson squared off against Denny McLain, Detroit's 31-game winner. Gibson fired a 4-0 shutout and struck out a World Series-record 17 Tigers.

He allowed only five hits in posting a 10-1 victory in Game 4, but his luck ran out in the seventh game. Gibson shut out the Tigers for six innings, until a misjudged fly ball by Cardinal center fielder Curt Flood led to three Tiger runs. Detroit went on to win, 4-1.

*St. Louis' Red Berenson (7) exploded for six goals in one NHL game.*

# Red Berenson scores six goals in one game

St. Louis center Red Berenson broke his goal-scoring slump in style, November 7, when he burned Flyers goaltender Doug Favell six times in the Blues' 8-0 National Hockey League victory at Philadelphia.

Berenson's explosion was the best single-game goal-scoring effort in 24 years, matching the 1944 performance of Detroit's Syd Howe. Quebec's Joe Malone set the NHL record with seven goals in a 1920 contest and six-goal games were accomplished four times in the 1920 and '21 seasons, when the NHL still was in its formative years.

Berenson, held scoreless for more than a week and credited with only three goals all season, beat Favell at 16:42 of the opening period and then tied another NHL record when he blasted home four goals in the second stanza. He scored again in the third and just missed a seventh goal late when Favell kicked out a low slapshot. He topped off his big day with a third-period assist on Camille Henry's 270th career goal.

# The Heidi maneuver

Hundreds of fans, irate over missing a whirlwind ending to a November 17 football game when NBC switched to its regularly scheduled programming, deluged the network with complaints and reacted so vehemently that NBC promised to avoid such future plug-pulling.

At issue was the final 61 seconds of an American Football League game between the Oakland Raiders and the New York Jets. The Jets, featuring "Broadway" Joe Namath at quarterback, had just taken a 32-29 lead. The Raiders, featuring "Mad Bomber" Daryle Lamonica, had the ball on their own 22-yard line.

Promptly at 7 p.m. (Eastern time) with the tension building, NBC switched to a production of *Heidi*, a children's drama about a Swiss mountain girl.

While fans were fuming, Lamonica moved the Raiders quickly downfield and connected with Charlie Smith on a 43-yard TD pass. As if that wasn't bad enough, the Jets fumbled the ensuing kickoff and Oakland's Preston Ridlehuber recovered in the end zone.

Final: Raiders 43, Jets 32, NBC 0.

# 1969

# Underdog Jets fulfill Namath's prophecy

The New York Jets, fulfilling the prophecy of Joe Namath, shocked the nation, January 12, by beating the powerful Baltimore Colts, 16-7, at Miami's Orange Bowl and giving the 9-year-old American Football League its first Super Bowl victory.

In one of the greatest sports upsets of all time, the 18- to 23-point underdog Jets didn't just beat the Colts, they dominated them. Some of the credit should go to Namath, who performed flawlessly after "guaranteeing" a Jets victory three days earlier. Some should go to a Jets defense that controlled the line of scrimmage and hurried Baltimore quarterbacks Earl Morrall and Johnny Unitas into four damaging interceptions and numerous other bad throws.

But most of all it was the team's overall poise, especially during a shaky first quarter dur-

ing which the Colts missed two excellent scoring chances. The first came after a 54-yard drive when Lou Michaels was wide on a field goal. The second came after Baltimore had recovered a fumble on the Jets' 12-yard line and Randy Beverly intercepted a Morrall pass in the end zone.

It was all Jets from that point on. The New Yorkers moved quickly downfield on the passing of Namath and running of Matt Snell. They scored midway through the second quarter on Snell's four-yard run and Jim Turner's extra-point conversion.

Things deteriorated for the Colts after halftime. Tom Matte fumbled on the first series, leading to a 32-yard Turner field goal, and Turner added a 30-yarder minutes later for a 13-0 lead. Turner's 9-yard kick in the fourth quarter gave the Jets a

*New York Jets quarterback Joe Namath winds up to throw as Baltimore's Bubba Smith leaps up in the air during action in Super Bowl III.*

commanding 16-0 advantage.

By this time, Baltimore Coach Don Shula had replaced Morrall with the veteran Unitas. The great Johnny U. engineered a late touchdown drive capped by Jerry Hill's one-yard run, but he otherwise was treated much like his predecessor by the uncompromising Jets.

True to his word, Namath had delivered an important victory for the AFL. The pain of watching Green Bay destroy Kansas City and Oakland in the first two Super Bowls had been

wiped away and AFL believers finally could begin talking with some justification about parity.

# No. 1 Buckeyes win

Ohio State, determined to justify its No. 1 ranking, spotted second-ranked Southern California a 10-point lead and then roared back for a 27-16 Rose Bowl victory before a New Year's Day crowd of 102,063 at Pasadena, Calif.

After being stung by an early field goal and an 80-yard second-quarter touchdown run by Heisman Trophy winner O.J. Simpson, the Buckeyes settled down and took control.

Quarterback Rex Kern directed two second-quarter drives that produced a 10-10 halftime tie and then took

advantage of two costly Trojan fumbles by throwing two short fourth-quarter touchdown passes to Leophus Hayden and Lonnie Gillian.

Southern Cal scored again on Steve Sogge's 19-yard pass to Sam Dickerson, but the game was already out of reach. The Trojans outgained the Buckeyes, 366 yards to 361, but turnovers made the difference.

Simpson, the nation's leader in rushing and all-purpose yards for two straight years, completed his final college game with 171 yards on 28 carries and eight receptions for 85 yards.

*Southern Cal's O.J. Simpson slips through the Ohio State defense en route to an 80-yard touchdown run during Rose Bowl action.*

# Alcindor ends career with 3 championships

The Lew Alcindor era came to a glorious conclusion, March 22, when the UCLA big man scored 37 points in 36 minutes and led the Bruins to a 92-72 victory over Purdue and their unprecedented third straight NCAA Tournament championship.

The 7-foot-1 Lew Alcindor destroyed the Boilermakers' man-to-man defense and closed out his career with an amazing 88 victories in 90 games. His first UCLA team finished 30-0, last year's team went 29-1 and this year's squad, losing only to Southern California in its final regular-season game, posted another 29-1 record.

Unlike its 85-82 victory over Drake in a semifinal game, UCLA was never really threatened by Purdue. One reason was the defensive play of Ken Heitz on high-scoring Rick Mount, who missed 24 of 36 shots and fell five points below his average.

The championship was the fifth in six years for UCLA Coach John Wooden.

*Lew Alcindor shares a moment with his father after leading UCLA to victory in the NCAA Tournament final.*

# Alcindor spurns ABA, signs with Milwaukee

Lew Alcindor, the 7-foot-1 three-time All-America who led UCLA to three straight NCAA Tournament championships, agreed to a five-year contract with the National Basketball Association's Milwaukee Bucks, April 2, ending the rival American Basketball Association's hopes of landing its second "franchise" player.

Alcindor and his agent, Sam Gilbert, had announced that they would accept one sealed bid from each league. The ABA, anxious to get another marquee player to go along with Oakland's Rick Barry, assigned his rights to the New York Nets (Alcindor's home state) and put together a package with all teams sharing the costs.

It was not enough. The talented big man signed with Milwaukee for a reported $1.4 million. The ABA rushed back with a higher offer (believed to be in the $3.2 million range), but Alcindor stuck to his promise.

The signing virtually assures that the Bucks will become instant title contenders. They finished the 1968-69 season with a 27-55 record.

# Baseball does Canada

The expansion Montreal Expos, resilient if not overly talented, captured the heart of a city, April 14, when they put on a spirited rally that produced an 8-7 victory over the defending National League-champion St. Louis Cardinals in the first major league regular-season game contested on foreign soil.

The Expos gave 29,184 fans at Jarry Park a taste of what to expect in the team's inaugural season. They scored six quick runs, five of them on a three-run homer and two-run triple by Mack Jones, and then helped the Cardinals to seven runs in the fourth by committing four errors. Reliever Dan McGinn eventually drove in the winning run with a single in the seventh and shut out the Cardinals for the win.

More than 200 newsmen were on hand for the historic contest and the crowd was enthusiastic. Everything, from pregame introductions to starting lineups, was done twice—in both French and English.

Montreal had been without baseball since the 1961 departure of the Montreal Royals, a longtime Dodgers Triple-A farm club.

*Montreal catcher John Bateman during opening-day ceremonies for the first regular-season major league game played outside the United States.*

# basketball

## The run-and-gun Celtics

*Coach Red Auerbach creates a sledgehammer of a team that leaves the shamrock indelibly imprinted on the NBA*

He was a flamboyant, fast-talking, fiery, cigar-smoking son of a Russian immigrant who was dedicated, above all else, to the creation of a basketball monster. And when 39-year-old Arnold (Red) Auerbach emerged from his Boston laboratory in 1956, he was convinced he finally had discovered the formula that would turn his run-and-gun Celtics into the terror of the National Basketball Association.

Step 1 required the Boston coach to give up Ed Macauley and the rights to 1953 draft choice Cliff Hagan to St. Louis for the Hawks' second overall draft position. Step 2 required Auerbach to use that selection on 6-foot-10 University of San Francisco center Bill Russell, an exceptional leaper and defensive-minded athlete who was unrefined and suspect at the offensive end of the court.

But Auerbach was not concerned about offense. Since 1951 he had watched his teams lead the league in scoring while giving up tons of points. What he needed was a center, a rebounder who could clean the boards and make the quick outlet pass to guards Bob Cousy and Bill Sharman while playing solid defense. He had never seen Russell play, but the youngster came highly recommended.

"I had to have somebody who could get me the ball," Auerbach recalled years later. "Bill Reinhart (Auerbach's college coach) said Russell was the greatest defensive player and greatest rebounder he'd ever seen."

It took $24,000 and a lot of talking to get Russell to spurn an offer from the Harlem Globetrotters and sign his first professional contract. And it took a waiver allowing him to play for the United States Olympic team, meaning Russell would not be available until December. But when he joined the Celtics and a lineup that already included Cousy, Sharman, Jim Loscutoff, swingman Frank Ramsey and Tom Heinsohn, another talented rookie, a dynasty was born.

"Russell," marveled Auerbach in the mid-1960s, "is the greatest basketball center who ever lived. The defense he plays is fantastic. He has a wonderful sense of timing. He may not be the greatest rebounder of all time, but he's the greatest in the clutch. When you really need the ball, Russell will get it for you."

With Russell "getting the ball" and providing the quick outlet to Cousy and Sharman, Boston's running game accelerated into full gear. Forwards Loscutoff and Heinsohn discovered they could box out their men, let Russell grab the defensive rebound and release on the fast break.

On the defensive end, Russell's presence in the middle intimidated shooters

*The sign tells the story.*

league-wide. Never had anybody witnessed a shotblocking force like this youngster and the other Celtics were able to take defensive gambles, knowing Russell could cover their mistakes.

## "He doesn't know what it means to play on a loser."

**RED AUERBACH**
*on Celtics center Bill Russell*

With the scowling, intense Russell forming the centerpiece to Auerbach's new-look juggernaut, the Celtics rolled to a 44-28 record in 1956-57 and finished six games ahead of Syracuse in the Eastern Division. Russell averaged 14.7 points and 19.6 rebounds per game, Cousy captured NBA Most Valuable Player honors and Heinsohn earned the Rookie of the Year citation.

But best of all, the Celtics fulfilled Auerbach's dream and won their first NBA championship. It wasn't easy, the Celtics needed seven games and two tough overtimes in the final series against St. Louis, but it was rewarding. And it

*A champagne shower for Coach Red Auerbach after the 1960 championship.*

*Tom Heinsohn (left), Auerbach (center) and Bill Russell (right), 1964.*

was the first step toward basketball immortality.

The 1957-58 Celtics added another talented star, guard Sam Jones, but stumbled in the NBA Finals against the Hawks and fired-up scorer Bob Pettit. The Celtics, forced to play much of the series without Russell (a sprained ankle), fell in six games. It was their last misstep for eight glorious years.

With Russell's former San Francisco teammate, guard K.C. Jones, now available after military duty, the Celtics reached the Finals again in 1958-59 and swept the Minneapolis Lakers. They won a record 59 regular-season games the next year and defeated the Hawks in a tough seven-game Finals. Another year and 57 victories later, Boston won its third straight title with a five-game victory over St. Louis.

As the championship banners hanging from the rafters above Boston Garden's parquet floor multiplied, so did the mystique surrounding Celtic pride. Here was a team, a near-perfect blend of playmaking (Cousy), shooting (Sharman, Sam Jones, Heinsohn), rebounding (Russell) and defense (Russell, K.C. Jones, Tom Sanders), that played unselfishly and with one goal—winning. The players genuinely liked each other and pulled together, both on and off the court.

"I like my teammates,"

*Auerbach passed the Celtic coaching mantle on to Russell in 1966.*

Russell said. "I look around and I say to myself, 'Bill, you're playing with the greatest bunch of guys in the world'."

It was onward and upward in 1961-62 as Auerbach directed his troops to a regular-season record 60 victories and a rugged seven-game Eastern Conference championship victory over Philadelphia and young center Wilt Chamberlain. The Celtics' fourth straight Finals victory was forged during overtime of Game 7 at Boston against the Lakers and another young superstar, Elgin Baylor.

Title No. 5, a six-game Finals victory over the Lakers, came in Cousy's farewell season and the rookie campaign of John Havlicek, a former Ohio State star. It matched the records of excellence compiled by baseball's New York Yankees, who won five World Series

from 1949-53, and hockey's Montreal Canadiens, who won Stanley Cups from 1955-56 to 1959-60.

But the Celtics did not stop there. With a retooled fast break and offensive game, Boston stretched its NBA mastery to a professional record seven straight championships with victories over San Francisco in 1963-64 and the Lakers again the following year. Boston's eighth straight title came in Auerbach's final season as

*Russell (6) won many of his battles with the great Wilt Chamberlain.*

coach and it required seven tough games against the Lakers. After losing to Los Angeles in Game 1, Auerbach provided a psychological spark by telling his players they would be guided the following

season by Russell—the first black coach in NBA history.

All good things must end, however, and the Celtics' championship string unraveled in 1966-67 as the Philadelphia 76ers, led by Chamberlain, put together a record-breaking 68-win regular season and ousted Boston, a 60-game winner, in the Eastern Conference Finals. But the reign was not over.

Two more championships, Boston's 10th and 11th in an incredible 13-year period, came at the expense of the frustrated Lakers. The 1969 NBA Finals marked the last appearance for Russell, who retired at age 35, and it marked the end of an unparalleled period of success in professional team sports.

It was no coincidence that the Celtics' reign began in 1956 with the arrival of Russell and ended in 1969 with his departure. Cousy, Sharman, Heinsohn, Sam Jones, K.C. Jones, Havlicek . . . all were vital cogs in the basketball machine that fashioned a .705 winning percentage over 13 seasons, but Russell was the mechanic that made it go.

"Pride," Auerbach once said, emphasizing what Celtic basketball is all about. "Bill has great pride. He is proud of his team and proud of his own personal skills. He doesn't know what it means to play on a loser."

*Los Angeles' Elgin Baylor drives as Celtics (left to right) Satch Sanders, Russell and Sam Jones look on.*

# 1969

## MAY-AUGUST

## Frazier rocks Quarry

Joe Frazier extended his claim on the world heavyweight boxing title, June 23, when he scored a technical knockout over Jerry Quarry in a seven-round bout at New York's Madison Square Garden.

Frazier, recognized as champion in six states, opened an inch-long cut under the 24-year-old Californian's right eye with a savage left hook near the end of the third round. Quarry was examined by a doctor and allowed to continue, but it soon became apparent that his vision was impaired and the doctor told the referee to stop the fight after the seventh round.

"The eye was completely swollen," said Dr. Harry Kleiman of the New York State Athletic Commission. "He had no sight in it and he was not as alert as before. It was my business to prevent a slaughter."

Quarry had come out strong in the first round, but the rest of

*Joe Frazier rocks Jerry Quarry with a hard left during their bout at Madison Square Garden.*

the fight belonged to the 25-year-old Frazier. Quarry's swollen, bloody face and eight-stitch cut told the tale of Smokin' Joe's 24th consecutive professional victory.

It is likely that Frazier's next bout will be against Jimmy Ellis, the recognized World Boxing Association champion.

## NFL sets new format

It took 36 hours of bargaining, May 9 and 10, but the Pittsburgh Steelers, Baltimore Colts and Cleveland Browns finally agreed to move from the newly-designated National Football Conference to the American Football Conference when the NFL-AFL merger is completed in 1970.

The three-club switch will even the count at 13 teams apiece and permit a six-division setup and an elaborate playoff formula to decide the participants in the Super Bowl.

Cleveland will be placed in a division with Pittsburgh, Cincinnati and Houston. Baltimore, the NFL's defending champion, will join Boston, Buffalo, Miami and New York Jets. The third division will feature Kansas City, Oakland, Denver and San Diego.

The three transferring teams were enticed by incentives and an estimated payoff of $2 to $3 million each. The NFC alignment will be decided later.

### ★ SPORTS WATCH ★

**MAY:** The Oakland Oaks ran away with the ABA's second championship, disposing of the Indiana Pacers in a five-game final series.

**JUN:** John Pennel set a world outdoor pole vault record when he cleared the bar at 17-foot-10$\frac{1}{4}$.

**JUN:** Orville Moody carved out a 281 total and one-stroke victory in the U.S. Open on the Cypress Creek Course at Houston, Tex.

**AUG:** Los Angeles righthander Don Drysdale, the last active holdover from the Brooklyn Dodgers, retired because of a shoulder injury.

## Montreal wins 9th Cup in 14 years with four-game sweep of St. Louis

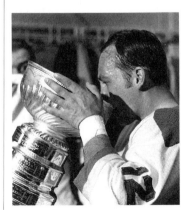

*Montreal's Yvan Cournoyer's Cup runneth over after the Canadiens' four-game finals sweep of the St. Louis Blues.*

Goals by Ted Harris and John Ferguson within a 2:20 span of the third period, May 4, carried the Montreal Canadiens to a 2-1 victory over the St. Louis Blues and their ninth Stanley Cup title in 14 years.

A noisy crowd of 16,126 at the St. Louis Arena were convinced that the Blues, leading 1-0 entering the final stanza, were about to avoid a four-

game Montreal sweep. St. Louis had outhustled and outskated the Canadiens up to that point and led on a second-period goal by Terry Gray.

But in the opening minute of the third period, Harris drilled a screened 50-foot slapshot past 37-year-old goaltender Glenn Hall and Ferguson connected on a 10-footer 2½ minutes later. Rogatien Vachon, filling in for

injured Gump Worsley in the Canadiens' goal, stopped the Blues the rest of the way, finishing with 32 saves.

The victory made a winner out of rookie Coach Claude Ruel, who took over when Toe Blake retired after leading Montreal to eight titles in 13 years. The Canadiens now have won the Stanley Cup 16 times in their 52-year history.

# Celtics great Russell retires

*Boston General Manager Red Auerbach and Coach Bill Russell after the Celtics' seven-game NBA Finals victory over Los Angeles.*

Bill Russell, the 6-foot-10 defensive giant who led Boston to 11 National Basketball Association titles in 13 years, retired as both coach and player, July 30, almost three months after the Celtics' surprising seven-game championship series victory over the Los Angeles Lakers.

The 35-year-old Russell, the heart and soul of the Celtics since he arrived in Boston, has been bothered by arthritic knees for the last two seasons. His departure will leave a major void on the Boston roster, both

on the floor and the bench. He has served as player-coach for three seasons, compiling a cumulative 162-83 record.

The aging Celtics struggled to a 48-34 record and a fourth-place finish in the Eastern Division this year. But once the playoffs started, it was just like

old times. With Russell intimidating high-scoring opponents in the middle, Boston polished off Philadelphia in five games, the New York Knicks in six and the Lakers and Wilt Chamber-

lain with a pair of victories after falling behind three games to two.

Russell finishes his career with a 15.1-point regular-season scoring average.

# Namath agrees to sell nightclub

New York Jets quarterback Joe Namath ended his retirement, July 18, after resolving his differences with National Football League Commissioner Pete Rozelle by agreeing to sell his interest in Bachelors III, a New York restaurant.

Namath's decision ends six weeks of turmoil that began in early June when Rozelle ordered him to divest himself of the property because of

allegedly "undesirable" customers that frequent the establishment. Namath responded to the commissioner's order by announcing his retirement.

Much has been written since then, attempting to link the hero of Super Bowl III to the mafia. Namath, saying he was tired of the situation and "just wanted to play football," met with the commissioner at Rozelle's Park Avenue office and announced the decision about an hour later.

The always colorful quarterback, dressed in a two-tone beige sports shirt, black bell-bottom slacks with white stripes and gray sneakers, said he was a victim of "guilt by association" and stressed that he had done nothing wrong.

# O.J. signs with Bills

Running back O.J. Simpson, one of the most prized collegians in professional football history, signed a four-year contract with Buffalo, August 9, ending speculation that the Bills would be unable to meet his lofty price.

Although terms of the contract were not divulged, Bills Owner Ralph Wilson did say that the contract was the highest given to a rookie since the American Football League and National Football League began holding a common draft in 1967. That means the pact is worth no less than $80,000 per year, probably a lot more.

The 6-foot-2, 204-pound Simpson, the No. 1 overall pick in the draft this year, could become pro football's next great running back. The 22-

year-old led the nation last year with 1,709 rushing yards on 355 carries, scored 22 touchdowns for Southern California and was awarded the Heisman Trophy. He should provide instant offense for the lowly Bills, who finished 1-12-1 last season.

*Recent Buffalo signee O.J. Simpson checks signals with quarterback Jack Kemp before training camp.*

# 1969

## SEPTEMBER–DECEMBER

## Amazing Mets win World Series

From expansion and ineptitude in 1962 to the top of the baseball world in 1969. From ninth in 1968 to 100 victories and first in the National League East Division this season. A three-game sweep of Atlanta in the N.L.'s first Championship Series. A five-game victory over powerful Baltimore in the World Series.

This is the story of the Amazing Mets. They were so amazing that, when all was said and done, nobody was quite sure what they had just witnessed.

They weren't given much chance when they matched up their inoffensive lineup and young pitching staff against a Baltimore team that had won 109 regular-season games and boasted a potent blend of pitching and power. And nobody was surprised when Baltimore outfielder Don Buford slammed Tom Seaver's second pitch of Game 1 for a home run and the American Leaguers went on to capture a 4-1 victory behind the six-hit pitching of Mike Cuellar.

But Manager Earl Weaver and his Orioles were in for a big surprise. Big boppers Frank Robinson, Brooks Robinson and Boog Powell batted a combined .171 in the Series and the Mets made all the right plays at all the right times.

Jerry Koosman and Ron Taylor combined on a two-hitter in Game 2, the Mets scoring a ninth-inning run on light-hitting Al Weis' single for a 2-1 victory.

*Relief ace Tug McGraw gets a champagne shower from Ed Kranepool after the New York Mets had disposed of Baltimore in five World Series games.*

Game 3 at New York belonged to center fielder Tommie Agee, who made two outstanding catches and hit a home run to back up the pitching of Gary Gentry and Nolan Ryan in a 5-0 shutout. Game 4 belonged to Seaver and right fielder Ron Swoboda, who made a game-saving catch in the ninth inning of a 2-1, 10-inning triumph.

The Mets wrapped up their unlikely championship on October 16, in front of the home fans when they rallied from a 3-0 deficit for a 5-3 victory. Don Clendenon's two-run sixth-inning homer and a seventh-inning blast by Weis tied the game and the Mets won with a two-run rally in the eighth.

### "SPORTS TALK"

*"Some people still might not believe in us, but then some people still think the world is flat."*

**CLEON JONES**
New York Mets outfielder

## Laver repeats slam

Rod Laver, a 5-foot-9, 155-pound lefthander with a rocket serve, became the first player in any sport to win two grand slams when he defeated fellow Australian Tony Roche, 7-9, 6-1, 6-2, 6-2, September 8, in the singles final of the U.S. Open at Forest Hills.

Laver's wins in the Australian, French, Wimbledon and U.S. championships matched his 1962 feat and the 1938 accomplishment of Don Budge. Maureen Connolly (1953) is the only woman to win all four majors in the same year. This slam was especially impressive considering the major events now are open to all comers, not just the top amateurs.

In Roche, the 31-year-old Laver was matched against a young opponent who had beaten him five times in seven tries. And he was playing on a soft, slick grass surface that had to be dried by a helicopter after

*Australian Rod Laver completing his second grand slam during play in the U.S. Open final against Tony Roche.*

a morning's rain.

But after Roche had won the first set, Laver took command. He rolled to victory in the second set and then easily disposed of his 24-year-old opponent in the third after a 30-minute rain delay. One more quick set and Laver was $16,000 richer—the highest singles payoff in tennis history.

# Toomey sets record

If at first you don't succeed, try, try again. That success formula finally paid dividends for Bill Toomey, December 11, when the 1968 Olympic champion broke the world record for the decathlon.

Toomey, in his tenth attempt of the year for the world mark, reached his goal in his final meet of 1969. He scored 8,417 points during competition in the Southern Pacific Amateur Athletic Union event at UCLA, breaking the 2-year-old record of 8,319 points set by West Germany's Kurt Bondlin.

The 6-foot-1, 195-pounder, representing the Southern California Striders, compiled 4,448 points in the first-day events and collected 3,969 the following day, far outdistancing second-place finisher John Warkentin's 7,440-point total.

Toomey recorded career bests in the pole vault (14-0¼) and the shot put (47-2¼) and ran the 100 meters in 10.3 seconds.

*Bill Toomey breaks the tape in the 1,500-meter run and sets a decathlon world record with 8,417 points.*

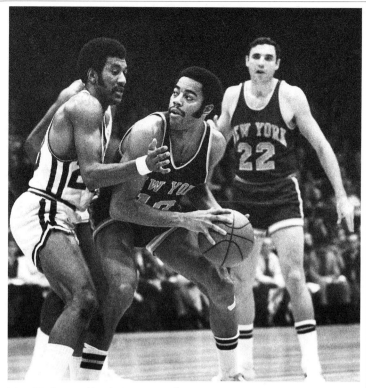

*New York guard Walt Frazier works against Cincinnati's Norm Van Lier during the Knicks' NBA-record 18th consecutive victory.*

# Knicks go on a binge, win 18 straight games

The New York Knicks, 16 seconds away from having their winning streak snapped by Cincinnati, November 28, shocked the Royals with a six-point burst that pulled out a 106-105 victory, their record 18th win in a row.

The Knicks were trailing the Royals 105-100, and their hopes of bettering the 17-game one-season win streak of Boston in 1959 were slim and none. But two free throws by Willis Reed, a steal and layup by Dave DeBusschere and another steal by Walt Frazier put the Knicks in position to win.

Frazier misfired on a jumper with two seconds left but was fouled. He made both free throws and the Knicks had their record-setting victory and 23rd triumph in 24 season-opening games.

The euphoria didn't last long, however. New York returned home to Madison Square Garden the next night and lost 110-98 to the struggling Detroit Pistons—their first loss since October 23.

# Longhorns slip past Arkansas

Texas quarterback James Street, with the Southwest Conference title, a Cotton Bowl bid and a possible national championship on the line, rallied the No. 1-ranked and unbeaten Longhorns to a 15-14 victory over arch-rival Arkansas, December 5, in a drama-packed fourth quarter at Fayetteville, Ark.

With his team facing a 14-0 deficit before 44,000 screaming fans, as well as President Richard M. Nixon and a national television audience, Street set off on a dramatic 42-yard scramble which ended with a touchdown on the first play of the final quarter and then ran for a two-point conversion.

The backbreaker came with 4:47 remaining when Street, a wishbone quarterback facing a fourth-and-three at his own 43-yard line, shocked the Arkansas defense by throwing deep to receiver Randy Peschel at the Arkansas 13. Jim Bertelsen ran two yards for the touchdown two plays later and Happy Feller's conversion kick gave Texas the lead with 3:58 to play.

The unbeaten Razorbacks, who had built their earlier advantage on a one-yard touchdown run by Bill Burnett in the first quarter and a 29-yard Bill Montgomery-to-Chuck Dicus TD pass in the third quarter, drove quickly to the Texas 39, but defensive back Tom Campbell picked off a Montgomery pass to seal the Longhorns' 19th consecutive victory.

# THE 1970s

*The television-induced prosperity of the 1960s continued to escalate as the new decade dawned. But unforeseen developments complicated the economic picture and changed the course of North American sports, both in reality and perception.*

The biggest complications were the athletes who had suddenly gained a national celebrity status that bordered on adoration. The television cameras captured their feats and performances and viewers coast-to-coast watched in fascination. It followed naturally that as the television pie grew larger, the athletes began demanding a bigger piece.

As a result, 1970 ushered in the decade of litigation, strikes, free agency and escalating salaries. Discovering the power of the courtroom and organized labor unions, athletes challenged owners in every way imaginable. Facing what seemed like a never-ending stream of lawsuits and threatened work stoppages, the owners grudgingly gave ground. But it was

the collapse of baseball's reserve clause and pro football's so-called "Rozelle Rule" that really opened the vault doors.

Especially in baseball. With the advent of free agency in 1976, impact players became available and greedy owners could hardly contain themselves. The result was mind-boggling contracts that shot through the ceiling. Pete Rose, who had signed for $105,000 per year with Cincinnati in 1970, was handed an $850,000 contract by Philadelphia in 1978. Houston made Nolan Ryan a million-dollar man a year later.

Nothing was sacred. Even the

*Golfer Jack Nicklaus.*

journeyman free agent could expect a sizable—and lengthy—contract. And adding to the spiraling salaries were the rene-

*Baseball home run king Hank Aaron.*

## ROLL OF HONOR

### AUTO RACING

**INDIANAPOLIS 500**

| Year | Winner | Speed |
|------|--------|-------|
| 1970 | Al Unser | 155.749 mph |
| 1971 | Al Unser | 157.735 mph |
| 1972 | Mark Donohue | 162.962 mph |
| 1973 | Gordon Johncock | 159.036 mph |
| 1974 | Johnny Rutherford | 158.589 mph |
| 1975 | Bobby Unser | 149.213 mph |
| 1976 | Johnny Rutherford | 148.725 mph |
| 1977 | A.J. Foyt | 161.331 mph |
| 1978 | Al Unser | 161.363 mph |
| 1979 | Rick Mears | 158.899 mph |

### GOLF

**MASTERS**

| Year | Winner |
|------|--------|
| 1970 | Billy Casper |
| 1971 | Charles Coody |
| 1972 | Jack Nicklaus |
| 1973 | Tommy Aaron |
| 1974 | Gary Player |
| 1975 | Jack Nicklaus |
| 1976 | Ray Floyd |
| 1977 | Tom Watson |
| 1978 | Gary Player |
| 1979 | Fuzzy Zoeller |

**OPEN**

| Year | Winner |
|------|--------|
| 1970 | Tony Jacklin |
| 1971 | Lee Trevino |
| 1972 | Jack Nicklaus |
| 1973 | Johnny Miller |
| 1974 | Hale Irwin |
| 1975 | Lou Graham |
| 1976 | Jerry Pate |
| 1977 | Hubert Green |
| 1978 | Andy North |
| 1979 | Hale Irwin |

**PGA CHAMPIONSHIP**

| Year | Winner |
|------|--------|
| 1970 | Dave Stockton |
| 1971 | Jack Nicklaus |
| 1972 | Gary Player |
| 1973 | Jack Nicklaus |
| 1974 | Lee Trevino |
| 1975 | Jack Nicklaus |
| 1976 | Dave Stockton |
| 1977 | Lanny Wadkins |
| 1978 | John Mahaffey |
| 1979 | David Graham |

**US WOMEN'S OPEN**

| Year | Winner |
|------|--------|
| 1970 | Donna Caponi |
| 1971 | JoAnne Carner |
| 1972 | Susie Berning |
| 1973 | Susie Berning |
| 1974 | Sandra Haynie |
| 1975 | Sandra Palmer |
| 1976 | JoAnne Carner |
| 1977 | Hollis Stacy |
| 1978 | Hollis Stacy |
| 1979 | Jerilyn Britz |

gade leagues that sparked expensive bidding wars with their established competitors.

The American Basketball Association, like the American Football League a decade earlier, stubbornly refused to die and finally forced a merger with the National Basketball Association in 1976, after nine expensive seasons. Likewise, the World Hockey Association battled for seven tough years before finally reaching agreement with the National Hockey League in 1979.

Through all the maneuvering, the spirit of competition survived. Some notable team accomplishments: The Miami Dolphins capped the National Football League's first perfect season with a victory in Super Bowl VII and won again the next year, while the Pittsburgh Steelers captured four Super Bowls in six seasons; the Oakland A's won three consecutive World Series before passing the baton to the Big Red Machine of Cincinnati; UCLA completed its incredible run of NCAA Tournament championships in 1975, having won 10 in 12 years, and the Montreal Canadiens won six Stanley Cups, including four straight to close out the decade.

Individual honors: Hank Aaron became baseball's greatest home run hitter in 1974; Buffalo's O.J. Simpson went on a rushing odyssey that produced 2,003 yards in 1973; Ohio State's Archie Griffin and Pittsburgh's Tony Dorsett, a pair of talented running backs, assaulted the NCAA record books; swimmer Mark Spitz won a record seven gold medals at the tragedy-marred 1972 Summer Olympic Games at Munich, and young stars like Jimmy Connors, Chris Evert, Martina Navratilova and John McEnroe emerged to escort tennis into the big-money stratosphere.

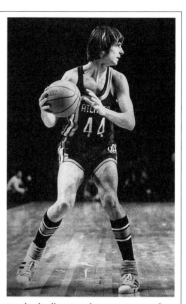

*Basketball's Pistol Pete Maravich.*

# HORSE RACING

## KENTUCKY DERBY

| Year | Winner | Jockey |
|------|--------|--------|
| 1970 | Dust Commander | Mike Manganello |
| 1971 | Canonero II | Gustavo Avila |
| 1972 | Riva Ridge | Ron Turcotte |
| 1973 | Secretariat | Ron Turcotte |
| 1974 | Cannonade | Angel Cordero |
| 1975 | Foolish Pleasure | Jacinto Vasquez |
| 1976 | Bold Forbes | Angel Cordero |
| 1977 | Seattle Slew | Jean Cruguet |
| 1978 | Affirmed | Steve Cauthen |
| 1979 | Spectacular Bid | Ron Franklin |

## PREAKNESS STAKES

| Year | Winner | Jockey |
|------|--------|--------|
| 1970 | Personality | Eddie Belmonte |
| 1971 | Canonero II | Gustavo Avila |
| 1972 | Bee Bee Bee | Eldon Nelson |
| 1973 | Secretariat | Ron Turcotte |
| 1974 | Little Current | Miguel Rivera |
| 1975 | Master Derby | Darrel McHargue |
| 1976 | Elocutionist | John Lively |
| 1977 | Seattle Slew | Jean Cruguet |
| 1978 | Affirmed | Steve Cauthen |
| 1979 | Spectacular Bid | Ron Franklin |

## BELMONT STAKES

| Year | Winner | Jockey |
|------|--------|--------|
| 1970 | High Echelon | John Rotz |
| 1971 | Pass Catcher | Walter Blum |
| 1972 | Riva Ridge | Ron Turcotte |
| 1973 | Secretariat | Ron Turcotte |
| 1974 | Little Current | Miguel Rivera |
| 1975 | Avatar | Bill Shoemaker |
| 1976 | Bold Forbes | Angel Cordero |
| 1977 | Seattle Slew | Jean Cruguet |
| 1978 | Affirmed | Steve Cauthen |
| 1979 | Coastal | Ruben Hernandez |

# BASEBALL

## WORLD SERIES

| Year | Winner | Pennant Winner (series score) |
|------|--------|-------------------------------|
| 1970 | Baltimore Orioles | (Cincinnati Reds, 4-1) |
| 1971 | Pittsburgh Pirates | (Baltimore Orioles, 4-3) |
| 1972 | Oakland Athletics | (Cincinnati Reds, 4-3) |
| 1973 | Oakland Athletics | (New York Mets, 4-3) |
| 1974 | Oakland Athletics | (Los Angeles Dodgers, 4-1) |
| 1975 | Cincinnati Reds | (Boston Red Sox, 4-3) |
| 1976 | Cincinnati Reds | (New York Yankees, 4-0) |
| 1977 | New York Yankees | (Los Angeles Dodgers, 4-2) |
| 1978 | New York Yankees | (Los Angeles Dodgers, 4-2) |
| 1979 | Pittsburgh Pirates | (Baltimore Orioles, 4-3) |

# BASKETBALL

## NBA CHAMPIONSHIP

| Year | Winner | Finalist (series score) |
|------|--------|-------------------------|
| 1970-71 | Milwaukee Bucks | (Baltimore Bullets, 4-0) |
| 1971-72 | Los Angeles Lakers | (New York Knicks, 4-1) |
| 1972-73 | New York Knicks | (Los Angeles Lakers, 4-1) |
| 1973-74 | Boston Celtics | (Milwaukee Bucks, 4-3) |
| 1974-75 | Golden State Warriors | (Washington Bullets, 4-0) |
| 1975-76 | Boston Celtics | (Phoenix Suns, 4-2) |
| 1976-77 | Portland Trail Blazers | (Philadelphia 76ers, 4-2) |
| 1977-78 | Washington Bullets | (Seattle SuperSonics, 4-3) |
| 1978-79 | Seattle SuperSonics | (Washington Bullets, 4-1) |
| 1979-80 | Los Angeles Lakers | (Philadelphia 76ers, 4-2) |

## NCAA TOURNAMENT FINAL

| Year | Winner | Finalist (score) |
|------|--------|------------------|
| 1970 | UCLA | (Jacksonville, 80-69) |
| 1971 | UCLA | (Villanova, 68-62) |
| 1972 | UCLA | (Florida State, 81-76) |
| 1973 | UCLA | (Memphis State, 87-66) |
| 1974 | North Carolina State | (Marquette, 76-64) |
| 1975 | UCLA | (Kentucky, 92-85) |
| 1976 | Indiana | (Michigan, 86-68) |
| 1977 | Marquette | (North Carolina, 67-59) |
| 1978 | Kentucky | (Duke, 94-88) |
| 1979 | Michigan State | (Indiana State, 75-64) |

# FOOTBALL

## SUPER BOWL

| Season | Winner | Finalist (score) |
|--------|--------|------------------|
| 1970 | Baltimore Colts | (Dallas Cowboys, 16-13) |
| 1971 | Dallas Cowboys | (Miami Dolphins, 24-3) |
| 1972 | Miami Dolphins | (Washington Redskins, 14-7) |
| 1973 | Miami Dolphins | (Minnesota Vikings, 24-7) |
| 1974 | Pittsburgh Steelers | (Minnesota Vikings, 16-6) |
| 1975 | Pittsburgh Steelers | (Dallas Cowboys, 21-17) |
| 1976 | Oakland Raiders | (Minnesota Vikings, 32-14) |
| 1977 | Dallas Cowboys | (Denver Broncos, 27-10) |
| 1978 | Pittsburgh Steelers | (Dallas Cowboys, 35-31) |
| 1979 | Pittsburgh Steelers | (Los Angeles Rams, 31-19) |

# HOCKEY

## STANLEY CUP

| Year | Champion | Finalist (series score) |
|------|----------|-------------------------|
| 1970-71 | Montreal Canadiens | (Chicago Black Hawks, 4-3) |
| 1971-72 | Boston Bruins | (New York Rangers, 4-2) |
| 1972-73 | Montreal Canadiens | (Chicago Black Hawks, 4-2) |
| 1973-74 | Philadelphia Flyers | (Boston Bruins, 4-2) |
| 1974-75 | Philadelphia Flyers | (Buffalo Sabres, 4-2) |
| 1975-76 | Montreal Canadiens | (Philadelphia Flyers, 4-0) |
| 1976-77 | Montreal Canadiens | (Boston Bruins, 4-0) |
| 1977-78 | Montreal Canadiens | (Boston Bruins, 4-2) |
| 1978-79 | Montreal Canadiens | (New York Rangers, 4-1) |
| 1979-80 | New York Islanders | (Philadelphia Flyers, 4-2) |

# TENNIS

## US OPEN

| Year | Men's Winner | Women's Winner |
|------|--------------|----------------|
| 1970 | Ken Rosewall | Margaret Smith-Court |
| 1971 | Stan Smith | Billie Jean King |
| 1972 | Ilie Nastase | Billie Jean King |
| 1973 | John Newcombe | Margaret Smith-Court |
| 1974 | Jimmy Connors | Billie Jean King |
| 1975 | Manuel Orantes | Chris Evert |
| 1976 | Jimmy Connors | Chris Evert |
| 1977 | Guillermo Vilas | Chris Evert |
| 1978 | Jimmy Connors | Chris Evert |
| 1979 | John McEnroe | Tracy Austin |

# 1970

## Super Chiefs scalp defenseless Vikings

Quarterback Len Dawson carved up Minnesota's vaunted defense with pinpoint passing and Kansas City's defense ran roughshod over the Vikings and quarterback Joe Kapp as the Chiefs recorded another emphatic victory for the American Football League with a 23-7 triumph in Super Bowl IV.

Millions of television viewers and the 80,562 fans at Tulane Stadium in New Orleans were shocked as the Chiefs dominated their National Football League rivals, emulating the 1969 performance of the AFL's New York Jets in their Super Bowl III upset of the Baltimore Colts. Minnesota was prohibitive favorite because of a defense that had allowed less than 10 points per game in compiling a 12-2 regular-season record.

Dawson, who had suffered through a difficult Super Bowl week when his name came up in a Detroit gambling investigation, completed 12 of 17 passes, including a third-quarter 46-yard touchdown strike to Otis Taylor. He had previously driven the Chiefs to three Jan Stenerud field goals and a second-quarter TD capped by Mike Garrett's five-yard run.

The Chiefs, 11-3 in the regular campaign and a title-game winner over Oakland, punctuated their victory when Aaron Brown recorded a fourth-quarter sack that knocked Kapp out of the game.

### « SPORTS TALK »

*"The best thing about this game is that we don't have to answer for it for the next three years like we did the last time. This time we're the champions."*

**LEN DAWSON**
Kansas City quarterback

*Kansas City quarterback Len Dawson picking apart Minnesota's outstanding defense in Super Bowl IV.*

## Longhorns win late

*The scoreboard tells the story as Texas Coach Darrell Royal and quarterback James Street discuss late-game Cotton Bowl strategy.*

Billy Dale's one-yard touchdown run with 68 seconds remaining, set up by an acrobatic fourth-down pass reception by Cotton Speyrer, capped a desperation Texas rally and gave the No. 1-ranked Longhorns a 21-17 New Year's Day Cotton Bowl victory over Notre Dame and college football's national championship.

Undefeated Texas, which had survived an equally tough encounter with Southwest Conference rival Arkansas, had fallen behind earlier in the final period when Fighting Irish quarterback Joe Theismann threw his second touchdown pass of the game, a 24-yarder to Jim Yoder.

Quarterback James Street quickly drove the Longhorns 66 yards to the Notre Dame 10, where Texas faced a fourth-and-two situation. Longhorns Coach Darrell Royal opted for a pass, which Street underthrew at the 2. But Speyrer made a desperate grass-level catch and Dale won the game.

Texas defender Tom Campbell sealed his team's 11th victory by intercepting a Theismann pass at the Longhorn 14. Notre Dame, making its first bowl appearance in 45 years, finished 8-2-1.

## Frazier pounds Ellis

Joe Frazier unleashed a furious assault on Jimmy Ellis and claimed the undisputed heavyweight championship in a February 16 bout at New York's Madison Square Garden.

Frazier, recognized as heavyweight champion in six states entering the fight, knocked down the World Boxing Association champion two times with brutal left hooks in the fourth round and was battering the 29-year-old at will. Ellis' trainer, Angelo Dundee, kept his fighter on his stool as the bell sounded to open the fifth round.

Ellis, a former sparring partner for deposed heavyweight champion Muhammad Ali, came out fast in the opening round, but the rest of the fight belonged to Frazier. Smokin' Joe rocked Ellis with two left hooks to the jaw in Round 3 and moved in for the kill in the following round.

Frazier, 25-0 with 22 knockouts as a professional boxer, announced after the fight that he might retire unless Muhammad Ali returns.

# Maravich signs rich Atlanta contract

The National Basketball Association's Atlanta Hawks signed Pistol Pete Maravich, the most prolific scorer in college basketball ever, to possibly the richest contract in NBA history, March 26.

Maravich, the three-time Louisiana State All-America who scored a career-record 3,667 points (44.2 per game), signed a five-year pact believed to be in the $1.5 million range. The sharpshooting, ball-handling wizard of Baton Rouge was the object of an intense bidding war between Atlanta Owner Tom Cousins and Jim Gardner, owner of the American Basketball Association's Carolina Cougars.

The signing was announced at an Atlanta dinner in Maravich's honor and the youngster spent much of a news conference denying he had backed out of an earlier decision to play for the Cougars.

Maravich, who played under his father, Press Maravich, at LSU, set a national scoring record by averaging 43.8 points per game as a sophomore, 44.2 as a junior and 44.5 as a senior last season, when the Tigers played in the National Invitation Tournament.

*Pistol Pete Maravich, the most prolific scorer in college basketball history.*

# South Africa banned from Davis Cup play

The International Lawn Tennis Federation, representing 34 Davis Cup nations, banned South Africa from this year's Cup competition at a special meeting in London, March 23.

The decision was made in response to international outcries over South Africa's policy of apartheid. The committee expressed concern that South Africa's presence would turn the competition into a political football.

The special meeting was triggered when Arthur Ashe, the only male world-class black tennis player, applied for a visa to play in the South African Open. Ashe, the former U.S. Open champion who had become the first black to win the Australian Open on January 27, was refused, based on his views on apartheid. The decision was immediately branded as racial discrimination and South Africa's participation in Davis Cup competition was questioned.

Ashe admitted that he intentionally tried to force the issue.

*Tennis star Arthur Ashe, center of the South African apartheid storm.*

Either he would play in a stadium full of white South Africans or the country's policy would come under an international microscope.

# Seaver ties strikeout mark against Padres

Tom Seaver struck out 19 Padres, including the last 10 in succession, to give the New York Mets a 2-1 victory over San Diego, April 22, at Shea Stadium.

Seaver, in winning his 13th straight game over two seasons, tied the nine-inning strikeout record set last September by St. Louis lefthander Steve Carlton, who dropped a 4-3 decision to the Mets. But the 25-year-old righthander broke the major league record for most consecutive strikeouts (eight, shared by four players).

Seaver's 136-pitch performance was marred only by two hits—a second-inning home run by Al Ferrara and a fourth-inning single by Dave Campbell off third baseman Joe Foy's glove. He retired the last 16 Padres consecutively, beginning his final strikeout flourish by getting Ferrara with two out in the sixth and ending the game by fanning Ferrara again.

Mike Corkins was the tough-luck loser for San Diego, allowing one run on a Ken Boswell double in the first and another on Bud Harrelson's third-inning triple. Seaver, a 25-game winner in 1969, had received his Cy Young Award in ceremonies before the game.

# 1970

## Orr score kills Blues

Defenseman Bobby Orr's acrobatic goal 40 seconds into overtime, May 10, gave the Boston Bruins a 4-3 victory over the St. Louis Blues and their first Stanley Cup title since 1941.

The Bruins completed their four-game sweep before 14,835 fans at Boston Garden when Orr took Derek Sanderson's pass in the St. Louis zone, was sent flying by a Larry Keenan check and somehow managed to knock the puck past startled Blues goaltender Glenn Hall while in midair.

Keenan had given the Blues a 3-2 lead in the first minute of the final period, but John Bucyk forced overtime at 13:28.

The game, witnessed by a national television audience, was the only close one of the series. The victory was the fourth straight for East Division teams and the loss was the third straight sweep suffered by the Blues.

*Boston defenseman Bobby Orr (left) whoops it up after scoring a Stanley Cup-winning overtime goal against St. Louis.*

## Frazier helps Knicks win first NBA title

Walt Frazier scored 36 points and handed out 17 assists and big man Willis Reed, playing with a painful leg injury, provided inspiration as the New York Knicks defeated the Los Angeles Lakers, 113-99, to capture their first National Basketball Association championship.

The seventh-game victory at New York's Madison Square Garden was an exhibition of precision and efficiency. The Knicks jumped out to a 38-24 first-quarter lead, stretched their margin to 51-31 and closed the door on the Lakers. While Frazier, Dick Barnett (21 points) and Dave DeBusschere (18 points, 17 rebounds) provided the firepower, Reed provided the mental spark.

The talented center was injured in New York's Game 5 victory. He sat out Game 6 and the New Yorkers suffered a crushing defeat in Los Angeles. Aided by several pain-killing injections, Reed limped through the final game, managing only four points and three rebounds. But he inspired his teammates and occupied Lakers' center Wilt Chamberlain defensively.

The loss was the seventh in nine years for Los Angeles in the championship final, the previous six to the Boston Celtics.

*New York Knicks guard Walt Frazier fires a jump shot over the Lakers' Jerry West during NBA Finals action.*

## Players fight merger

The 24-year-old National Basketball Association and the 3-year-old American Basketball Association agreed to a merger on June 18, but the agreement faces two major obstacles—a U.S. District Court injunction on behalf of the NBA Players' Association and approval of Congress.

The players, claiming that a merger would eliminate competition for their services and represent a violation of antitrust laws, have vowed to fight the move with all the force they can muster. The merger of the American Football League and National Football League received Congressional approval in 1966 as a rider to an appropriations bill, but it was not opposed.

The primary reason for a merger would be to eliminate the costly bidding war for players through a common draft. That's exactly what the players are trying to stop. The agreement provides for 28 franchises in 27 cities, a championship playoff, interleague play and, eventually, a single league schedule. Each ABA team would pay $1.25 million to the NBA over 10 years.

NBA teams voted 13-4 in favor of the merger, but the player opposition could make some owners reconsider.

# Rose, N.L. winners in All-Star collision

Cincinnati's Pete Rose, playing before his home fans in new Riverfront Stadium, July 14, bowled over Cleveland catcher Ray Fosse in a violent home-plate collision and scored the winning run with two out in the bottom of the 12th inning, bringing an end to a dramatic All-Star Game.

Rose scored from second base on a single to center by Chicago's Jim Hickman and his football-style body block on Fosse was prompted by a strong throw from Kansas City outfielder Amos Otis. As Fosse lay dazed on the ground, Rose and his National League teammates celebrated their eighth consecutive All-Star victory over the American League.

Through eight innings, it appeared that the A.L. would end its midseason classic misery. An RBI single by Boston's Carl Yastrzemski, one of his four hits, a sacrifice fly by Fosse and a two-run triple by Baltimore's Brooks Robinson had forged a 4-1 lead and Oakland ace Catfish Hunter was on the mound to close things out.

But the N.L. magic of recent years was alive and well. San Francisco's Dick Dietz opened the ninth with a home run and New York's Bud Harrelson and Houston's Joe Morgan followed with singles. The Giants' Willie McCovey singled in one run and Roberto Clemente tied the game with a sacrifice fly, forcing extra innings for the sixth time in All-Star Game history.

The winning rally off California's Clyde Wright was set up by two-out singles by Rose and the Dodgers' Billy Grabarkewitz. Claude Osteen of the Dodgers pitched three scoreless innings for the victory.

*Dave Stockton chips onto the seventh green en route to a PGA Championship victory.*

*Cincinnati's Pete Rose crashes into Cleveland catcher Ray Fosse, bringing the All-Star Game to a painful conclusion.*

# Stockton takes PGA

Dave Stockton, a 28-year-old Southern Californian in search of his first career major, built up a big lead early in the final round of the PGA Championship and then struggled to a two-stroke victory over Arnold Palmer and Bob Murphy in the hundred-plus degree heat of Tulsa, Okla.

Stockton, a three-time winner in six years on the tour, was paired with Palmer and faced the prospect of battling one of golf's all-time greats as well as his ever-present Army of fans. But he jumped off to a fast start over the 6,962-yard Southern Hills Country Club course and really took control on the 7th, when he sank a 120-yard wedge for an eagle 2. At that point, Stockton owned a seven-stroke advantage over Palmer and a nine-stroke edge over Murphy.

But he could not stand prosperity and shot a double bogey on 8. The rest of the round was an adventure. With five bogeys over the final six holes, he finished with a final-round 73 and a one-under-par total of 279.

The early deficit, however, was just too much for Palmer and Murphy to overcome. Once again, Palmer failed to win the only major that has eluded him. And for the third time, he finished in a second-place tie. Palmer finished the day with a 70, Murphy with a 66.

Stockton set up his victory with a scorching third-round 66, good for a three-stroke lead over Ray Floyd and a five-stroke advantage over Palmer.

# 1970

## Coaching legend Lombardi dies at 57

*Former Green Bay Packers and Washington Redskins Coach, the incomparable Vince Lombardi.*

Vince Lombardi, the man who led the Green Bay Packers into national prominence in the 1960s and generally considered one of the greatest coaching minds in the history of football, died, September 3, of intestinal cancer at Georgetown Hospital in Washington, D.C. He was 57 years old.

Lombardi, who guided the Packers to six division titles, five National Football League championships and two Super Bowl victories in nine seasons, symbolized toughness and dedication in sports. He retired after the 1967 season to concentrate full time on his duties as Green Bay general manager, but he missed the sideline and was lured back after one season by a lucrative offer from Washington. He coached the Red-

skins to a 7-5-2 record last year, bringing his career coaching mark to 141-39-4.

Lombardi, the son of an immigrant Italian butcher in Brooklyn, attended Fordham University and played guard on the Rams' famed "Seven Blocks of Granite" line. He began his coaching career at the high school level and later worked as an assistant at Fordham, Army and with the New York Giants before taking the Green Bay job.

### ★ SPORTS WATCH ★

**SEP:** The United States swept past West Germany, 5-0, to win its third straight Davis Cup title.

**SEP:** After playing an N.L.-record 1,117 consecutive games, Chicago Cubs outfielder Billy Williams took a day off.

**OCT:** The powerful Baltimore Orioles swept aside the Minnesota Twins in the A.L. Championship Series and then dispatched Cincinnati in a five-game World Series.

**NOV:** Montreal recorded its first Grey Cup victory since 1949, dispatching the Calgary Stampeders, 23-10.

**DEC:** Rod Laver became the first tennis player ever to top $200,000 in winnings in one year.

## Ali returns in style

Muhammad Ali, still floating like a butterfly and stinging like a bee, returned to boxing after a 3½-year exile, October 26, and quickly dispatched Jerry Quarry with a three-round technical knockout in Atlanta.

The 28-year-old Ali, fighting a younger man for the first time in his 30-fight, unbeaten professional career, dominated the nine minutes the bout lasted. He came out dancing and jabbing, frequently stepping in for quick left-right combinations that seemed to befuddle his 25-year-old opponent.

The decisive blow was a jab that opened a long gash over Quarry's left eye—a cut that later required 11 stitches to close. When the third round was over, Teddy Bentham, Quarry's trainer, asked referee Tony Perez to stop the fight. He did and Ali was back on top—at least in the minds of many boxing fans.

"I'm just glad to be back, to clear up all this mess," said Ali, who was stripped of the heavyweight championship because of his refusal to be inducted into the armed services on religious grounds.

*Muhammad Ali, returning to the ring after a 3½-year exile, delivers a right to the head of Jerry Quarry.*

## Kuhn versus McLain

Denny McLain who took baseball by storm in 1968 when he won 31 games for the Detroit Tigers, was suspended, September 9, for the third time this year by Commissioner Bowie Kuhn.

McLain's troubles began when Kuhn announced on April 1 that the two-time Cy Young Award winner would be suspended for three months because of his alleged involvement with Detroit bookmaking activities. He struggled to a 3-5 record and 4.65 earned-run average after his return and further complicated matters last week when he dumped a bucket

of ice water on two Detroit sportswriters, an act that cost him another stint on the suspended list.

McLain still was serving that suspension when Kuhn announced in New York that it would continue for at least the rest of the season. Kuhn would only say that the decision concerned the righthander's lack of respect toward Detroit management and information that McLain has carried a gun on occasion.

McLain, who in 1968 became the first 30-game winner in 34 years, won 24 last year.

# Dempsey gets kicks

When Errol Mann kicked an 18-yard field goal with 11 seconds remaining to give Detroit a 17-16 lead over the Saints in a game at New Orleans, he set in motion a whirlwind finish that would rival any in National Football League history. Those fans who stayed to the end were rewarded—and then some.

New Orleans took the kick-off to its own 28 and quarter-back Billy Kilmer completed a pass to Al Dodd, who stepped out of bounds at the Saints' 45 with two seconds on the clock. To everybody's surprise, out came the field-goal unit. Holder Joe Scarpati received the snap and placed the ball at the Saints' 37. Tom Dempsey, who was born with half a right foot and wore a special kicking shoe approved by the league,

stepped into the ball and sent it sailing toward the goal posts— 63 yards away.

"I saw the referee's hands go up and heard everybody start yelling and I knew it was good," Dempsey said. "I'm still shook up."

The 63-yard field goal, his fourth, was seven yards longer than Bert Rechichar's 1953 record kick for Baltimore.

A scuffed helmet, cleats and other strewn equipment tell the sad story of the Colorado plane crash that killed 14 Wichita State football players and their coach.

New Orleans kicker Tom Dempsey follows through on his game-winning record-breaker against Detroit.

# Two schools stunned by airplane crashes

A chartered airliner carrying the Marshall University football team and coaching staff crashed, November 14, in the Appalachian Mountains, about a mile outside Huntington, W. Va., near the Tri-State Airport.

All 75 passengers were killed in the crash of the twin-jet DC-9 owned by Southern Airways in Atlanta. The plane went down at 7:40 p.m. as the team was returning from its game against East Carolina at Kinston, N.C. The dead included 37 players, Marshall's entire coaching staff, a West Virginia assemblyman and members of the Big Green Boosters Club.

The disaster is the second of the year involving a college football team. On October 2, 31 persons, including 14 Wichita State players and Coach Ben Wilson, died when a chartered twin-engine Martin 404 crashed in the Colorado Rockies near Denver. There were 11 survivors in that crash, which was transporting half of Wichita State's team to a game against Utah State in Logan, Utah.

# Bickering factions sign truce

International Lawn Tennis Federation officials, trying to deal with the splintering of their sport into professional factions, signed a truce, December 8, with World Championship Tennis, guaranteeing the participation of the world's top players in their major events.

After a week of negotiations, it was announced that the WCT's 32 contract professionals can play in the U.S., French and Wimbledon championships as well as the Federation's Grand Prix events. A feud had developed over the WCT's demand for guaranteed participation payments.

Top pros including Rod Laver, Ken Rosewall, John Newcombe, and Arthur Ashe have signed with Lamar Hunt's WCT, which has organized a 20-city tour for 1971 offering $1 million in prize money.

The situation is equally confusing in women's tennis. Upset over the ratio of women's prize money to men's, top female players boycotted a recent USLTA tournament in Los Angeles.

The group, led by Billie Jean King and Gladys Heldman, publisher of World Tennis magazine, has formed an independent tour, excluding the four major tournaments, that will draw sponsorship from the Virginia Slims cigarette company.

# 1971
## JANUARY-APRIL

# Colts kick Cowboys

Rookie Jim O'Brien kicked a 32-yard field goal with five seconds remaining, January 17, to give Baltimore a 16-13 victory over Dallas in Super Bowl V. It was the culmination of the National Football League's first season with the two-conference alignment and victory thus went to one of the three NFL teams who had joined the American Football Conference.

A crowd of 79,205 fans in Miami's Orange Bowl witnessed the most exciting Super Bowl ending yet staged. But the rest of the game was far from a football masterpiece. The teams combined to commit 10 turnovers, the Colts losing three fumbles and three interceptions and the Cowboys fumbling once and having three passes picked off. Both teams missed great scoring opportunities.

The comedy of errors started early when Baltimore's Ron Gardin fumbled a punt at the Colts' 9-yard line and the Cowboys converted it into a 14-yard field goal. Dallas stretched its lead to 6-0 early in the second quarter when Mike Clark kicked his second field goal, a 30-yarder.

The Colts struck back when Johnny Unitas threw a pass that was deflected by Dallas defensive back Mel Renfro into the waiting arms of John Mackey, who ran 75 yards for a touchdown. But O'Brien's attempt

*Baltimore placekicker Jim O'Brien (80) exults after booting the winning field against Dallas in Super Bowl V.*

at the conversion kick was blocked.

Dallas, taking advantage of a Unitas fumble, regained the lead on a seven-yard pass from Craig Morton to Duane Thomas and then made a brilliant goal-line stand after the Colts had moved to a first-and-goal at the 2.

The game's key play occurred shortly after intermission when the Cowboys drove to the Baltimore 2, only to lose the ball

on a Thomas fumble. Rich Volk's fourth-quarter interception and 30-yard runback to the Dallas 3 set up Baltimore's game-tying touchdown, a two-yard run by Tom Nowatzke, and linebacker Mike Curtis picked off another Morton pass with less than two minutes remaining to set up O'Brien's winning kick.

The victory was vindication for the Colts, who lost in Super Bowl III to the New York Jets.

★ SPORTS WATCH ★

JAN: Two relic quarterbacks, Baltimore's 37-year-old Johnny Unitas and Oakland's 43-year-old George Blanda, combined for 516 passing yards and three touchdowns in the Colts' 27-17 AFC title-game victory over the Raiders.

FEB: Chicago star Bobby Hull moved into second place on the NHL's all-time scoring list when he notched his 546th career goal.

MAR: Jack Nicklaus recorded a two-stroke victory over Billy Casper in the PGA Championship, becoming the first golfer to win all four majors two times.

MAR: Center Steve Patterson scored 29 points and UCLA defeated Villanova, 68-62, at Houston to win its fifth straight NCAA Tournament championship.

APR: Atlanta's Hank Aaron became the third member of baseball's 600-homer club with a blast against San Francisco.

APR: The Philadelphia Phillies christened new Veterans Stadium with a 4-1 victory over Montreal.

# Nebraska beats LSU, claims No. 1

The No. 3-ranked Nebraska Cornhuskers, knowing that top-ranked Texas and second-ranked Ohio State already had lost their New Year's Day bowl games, scored a fourth-quarter touchdown and then held off Louisiana State in a 17-12 Orange Bowl victory before 80,699 fans at Miami.

The Cornhuskers laid claim to the Associated Press national championship with 8:50 remaining when quarterback Jerry Tagge smashed over from the 1-yard line, wiping out a 12-10

deficit. LSU had taken the lead on the final play of the third quarter when Al Coffee caught a 31-yard TD pass from Buddy Lee.

Nebraska's game-winning drive started with a 16-yard keeper by Tagge, who then completed a six-yard pass to Dan Schneiss, a nine-yarder to Johnny Rodgers and a 17-yarder to Jeff Kinney, setting up a first-and-goal at LSU's 5.

The victory lifted Coach Bob Devaney's Huskers to 11-0-1 and put them in position to vault

over Texas and Ohio State in AP's final rankings. The Longhorns, UPI's national champions by virtue of their 10-0 final regular-season record, fell to sixth-ranked Notre Dame, 24-11, in the Cotton Bowl, ending their winning streak at 30 games. Ohio State dropped a 27-17 Rose Bowl decision to Stanford.

*Nebraska tight end Jerry List (85) just misses connections on an Orange Bowl touchdown pass over an LSU defender.*

# Offensive Bruins go on record goal binge

When the Boston Bruins were upset by Montreal, April 18, in a seven-game first-round series of the National Hockey League playoffs, the glitter of a season-long, record-smashing offensive display was lost in the disappointment. Lost, maybe, but not forgotten.

Boston, the most powerful scoring machine in NHL history, rolled to a record 57 wins and a best-ever 121 points. En route the Bruins established records for goals (399), assists (697), points (1,096) and intimidation.

Leading the offensive charge were center Phil Esposito and defenseman Bobby Orr. The 29-year-old Esposito scored an amazing 76 goals, 18 more than Bobby Hull's 1968-69 record for Chicago, and totaled a record 152 points, 26 more than his own mark of 126 in 1968-69.

The 22-year-old Orr was just as devastating, setting a one-season record for assists (102) and goals by a defenseman (37). His 139 points are the second most in history.

*Boston's Phil Esposito, who set NHL scoring records with 76 goals and 152 points.*

# Frazier clips Ali's butterfly wings

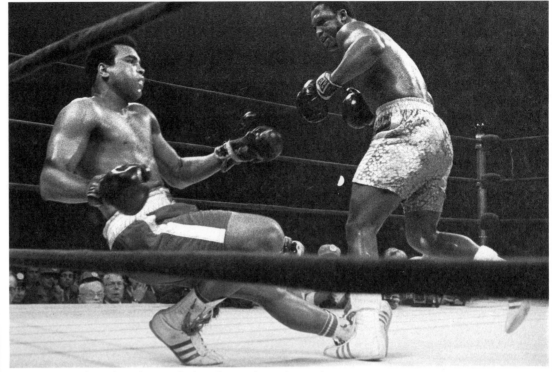

*Joe Frazier's left sends Muhammad Ali reeling in the 15th round.*

In a classic 15-round display of boxing and showmanship, Joe Frazier clipped the floating butterfly wings of Muhammad Ali by scoring a unanimous 15-round decision in a March 8 championship fight at New York's Madison Square Garden, solidifying once and for all his hold on the world heavyweight crown.

Frazier had ascended to his throne without going through Ali. But Frazier silenced his skeptics by unleashing a relentless body attack on the former champ and controlling the tempo of the fight. He capped his performance with a 15th-round knockdown, courtesy of one of his patented left hooks to Ali's jaw. Ali jumped up and took the mandatory eight count, but for all practical purposes his comeback hopes were dashed.

Ali, seeking to make Frazier his 32nd straight victim, spent much of the early fight dancing and taunting the champion. Frazier did a little taunting of his own later on, sticking out his chin and showing that he could take Ali's best shot.

After the fight, Ali dashed off to have his swollen jaw X-rayed. The interview room was strangely quiet.

# Haywood controversy finally ends

Spencer Haywood has been cleared to play next season for the National Basketball Association's Seattle SuperSonics. After months of bickering and court-room red tape, all obstacles have been removed for the youngster to become a full-fledged NBA superstar.

Haywood signed a professional contract with Denver of the American Basketball Association after his sophomore season at the University of Detroit.

After leading the league in scoring his first season, Haywood decided to accept an offer from Seattle. Since his college class had not yet graduated and he had not gone through an NBA draft as prescribed by league rules, other NBA teams protested and Haywood was ruled ineligible.

The Sonics and Haywood responded by filing an antitrust suit against the NBA in Federal District Court in Los Angeles and they gained a temporary injunction that allowed him to play the last 33 games of the season (he averaged 20.6 points).

An out-of-court settlement was finally reached, March 26, and all litigation in the case was dropped. But not before a federal judge had ruled in a landmark decision that the NBA's four-year college draft rule was improper, forcing the league to introduce a hardship draft for underage players.

# 1971

**MAY-AUGUST**

## Bucks cap big season

The Milwaukee Bucks, with 24-year-old Lew Alcindor scoring 27 points and 32-year-old Oscar Robertson contributing 30 points and nine assists, completed their drive to the National Basketball Association championship, April 30, with a 118-106 victory over Baltimore.

The Bucks' four-game sweep capped an amazing season that included a record 20-game winning streak, a scoring championship for Alcindor (31.9 points per game) and one of the best season records ever compiled (78-18, including playoffs).

Milwaukee, playing only its third NBA campaign after joining the league as an expansion franchise in 1968-69, rolled to a 66-16 regular-season record and first-place finish in the Midwest Division. Contributing to that record, the second best ever recorded (the 1966-67 Philadelphia 76ers were 68-13), was the 20-game streak that surpassed the New York Knicks' year-old record of 18.

With Robertson pulling the offensive strings, the Bucks were unstoppable. Alcindor, flanked by forwards Bob Dandridge and Greg Smith, led Milwaukee to five-game victories over San Francisco and Los Angeles and the Bucks beat the Bullets by margins of 10, 19, 8 and 12 points.

*Milwaukee guard Oscar Robertson (1) puts a hand in the face of Bullets' guard Earl Monroe during NBA Finals action in Baltimore.*

## Dryden saves the day

*Montreal's Henri Richard eyes Chicago goalie Tony Esposito as he prepares to fire his third-period Stanley Cup winner into the net.*

The Montreal Canadiens, getting outstanding goaltending from young Ken Dryden and two clutch goals from veteran Henri Richard, defeated the Chicago Black Hawks, 3-2, May 18, in the seventh game of the Stanley Cup finals at Chicago Stadium.

Dryden, who played in his first National Hockey League game near the end of the regular season, made 31 saves against the Black Hawks and was spectacular at times, just as he had been throughout the playoffs in victories over Boston and Minnesota.

Montreal, which finished third in the East Division behind Boston and the New York Rangers, needed Dryden's fine work after falling behind 2-0 midway through the second period on goals by Dennis Hull and Danny O'Shea. Jacques Lemaire cut the deficit in half and Richard, a 35-year-old veteran, tied the score late in the second period.

Richard, who has played on 10 Stanley Cup winners, swooped in front of Chicago goaltender Tony Esposito early in the final stanza and lifted the game-winner into the net.

The victory was Montreal's 16th since the foundation of the NHL in 1917 and 11th in the last 19 years.

### "SPORTS TALK"

*"This was the biggest goal of my life and of the 10 Stanley Cup winners I've been on, this is the best because we were the underdogs."*
**HENRI RICHARD**
after scoring the game-winning goal in the Stanley Cup final series

## Connors wins NCAA

Jimmy Connors, a brash young lefthander attending UCLA, became the first freshman ever to win the NCAA tennis championships, June 19, when he defeated Stanford's Roscoe Tanner, 6-3, 4-6, 6-4, 6-4, at the Notre Dame campus in South Bend, Ind.

Connors, the No. 1-ranked junior player in the country and 14th in the men's national rankings, dropped service only one time in 19 games en route to winning for the eighth time in the week-long event. He had to defeat his UCLA teammate, Haroon Rahim, in the semifinal round. Another Bruin, defending champion Jeff Borowiak, fell to Tanner in the semifinals.

Tanner, also a lefthander and a member of the U.S. Junior Davis Cup team, double faulted seven times. Tanner also fell in the finals last year.

# A.L. flexes its muscle in All-Star slugfest

Home runs by American Leaguers Reggie Jackson, Frank Robinson and Harmon Killebrew produced six runs, two more than homers by National Leaguers Johnny Bench, Hank Aaron and Roberto Clemente, as the junior circuit broke an eight-game All-Star Game losing streak, July 13, with a 6-4 win at Detroit's Tiger Stadium.

Like two heavyweight boxers slugging it out, the two leagues delighted a national television audience with an unexpected power display. The fireworks started in the second inning when Cincinnati catcher Bench touched Oakland lefthander Vida Blue for a two-run homer and continued in the third when Atlanta slugger Aaron hit a solo shot off Blue.

But Boston shortstop Luis Aparicio led off the bottom of the third with a single and Oakland outfielder Jackson, batting for Blue, put the A.L. back on track—emphatically. Reggie connected with a delivery by Pittsburgh's Dock Ellis and sent a mammoth shot soaring toward the outer reaches of Tiger Stadium. The ball struck a light tower on the roof in right-center field, traveling an estimated 520 feet. Jackson stood at the plate admiring his work before circling the bases.

Baltimore's Robinson added another two-run shot in the inning and Minnesota's Killebrew belted a two-run homer off Chicago righthander Ferguson Jenkins in the sixth. Pittsburgh's Clemente closed out the scoring with a solo blast in the eighth before Tiger lefty Mickey Lolich closed the door in the ninth.

American League power sources (left to right) Frank Robinson, Harmon Killebrew and Reggie Jackson.

# Trevino shows poise in British Open win

Lee Trevino, leading by three strokes with two holes to play, took a near-disastrous 7 on the 17th hole and had to birdie the 18th to hold on and win the 100th British Open, July 13, giving him a four-week sweep of the U.S., Canadian and British championships.

Trevino's 72-hole total of 278 on the Royal Birkdale course in Southport, England, was one stroke better than Liang Huan Lu, a polite little Formosan with a toothy grin. The self-described Merry Mex birdied three of the first four holes on the final round and made the turn in a blistering 31, good for a five-stroke lead. But Lu refused to give up and cut the margin to one after Trevino's problems in the rough on 17. Both birdied the par 5 18th to close out an exciting round.

The inexhaustable Trevino, who had entered the closing round with a one-stroke advantage over Lu and Tony Jacklin, was attempting to become only the fourth golfer in history to win both the U.S. Open and British Open in the same year. Bobby Jones did it in 1930, Gene Sarazen in 1932 and Ben Hogan in 1953.

Trevino had captured his second U.S. Open title, June 21, at the tough Merion course in Ardmore, Pa., following a playoff against Jack Nicklaus. Trevino, who had let victory slip away from him in regulation with an 18th-hole bogey, jokingly tossed a rubber snake at his rival on the first tee before the playoff and then shot a 68, good for a three-stroke victory.

He followed that with another playoff-round win, over Art Wall in the Canadian Open at Richelieu Valley.

Lee Trevino hits out of the Royal Birkdale rough en route to his victory in the British Open.

# 1971

## Pirate slugs Giants

With the booming bat of Willie Stargell having gone strangely silent, the Pittsburgh Pirates got a Ruthian-type lift in their National League Championship Series battle with the San Francisco Giants from first baseman Bob Robertson.

With the Pirates trailing 1-0 in the series and 2-1 in Game 2 at Candlestick Park on October 3, Robertson, who had doubled and scored Pittsburgh's only run in the second inning, tied the game with a solo home run off John Cumberland in the fourth. In the seventh he belted a three-run homer off Ron Bryant and added a solo ninth-inning shot off Steve Hamilton.

Robertson's three-homer performance matched the post-season record set by Yankee great Babe Ruth, who enjoyed three-homer games in both the 1926 and '28 World Series. Robertson's 14 total bases set a postseason single-game record and his five RBIs propelled the Pirates to a 9-4 victory and a five-game Series triumph. He finished the Series with four homers and a .438 average. Stargell, a 48-homer man during the regular season, went hitless in 14 at-bats.

*Pittsburgh Championship Series star Bob Robertson.*

## Americans get sweep

Second-seeded Stan Smith defeated unseeded Czech Jan Kodes and top-seeded Billie Jean King blitzed No. 2 seed Rosemary Casals, September 15, in the finals of the U.S. Open championships at Forest Hills, giving the tournament its first American sweep of the singles titles in 16 years.

The 6-foot-4 Smith, getting time off from his two-year hitch with the Army, dispatched the 25-year-old Kodes, 3-6, 6-3, 6-2, 7-6, to capture his first major open championship. After drop-ping the first set, Smith took control with his power game.

But Kodes refused to die. He extended Smith to a nine-point fourth-set tiebreaker and took a 3-1 lead. Smith, the Wimbledon runnerup, showed his poise with a match-closing rally.

King, who has defeated Casals eight times in nine matches this year, rolled to a 6-4 first-set victory but, like Smith, needed a tiebreaker to close out the match. She out-pointed Casals, 5-2, for her second U.S. championship.

### ★ SPORTS WATCH ★

**SEP:** Baltimore slugger Frank Robinson joined the 500-homer club when he connected in each game of a doubleheader with Detroit.

**SEP:** Washington Owner Bob Short received A.L. permission to move his Senators to Arlington, Tex.

**SEP:** Detroit's Gordie Howe, probably the greatest player in the history of the NHL, retired after 25 seasons and a record 786 career goals.

**OCT:** The United States edged past Romania, 3-2, and captured its fourth straight Davis Cup title.

**NOV:** Oakland's Vida Blue won the A.L. Cy Young and MVP awards after compiling a 24-8 record, 301 strikeouts and a league-leading 1.82 ERA.

**NOV:** Grey Cup final: Calgary 14, Toronto 11.

**DEC:** Willie Ellison of the Los Angeles Rams set an NFL single-game rushing record when he picked up 247 yards against New Orleans.

## Blass shuts down O's

Steve Blass fired a four-hitter and Roberto Clemente hit a solo home run, leading the underdog Pittsburgh Pirates to a 2-1 victory over Baltimore in Game 7 of the World Series. It was the second Series victory for Blass and Clemente closed out his second fall classic with a .414 batting average and a 14-game Series hitting streak.

Pittsburgh's chances did not look bright when the Series opened at Baltimore. Dave McNally and Jim Palmer, half of a record-tying starting rotation that featured four 20-game winners in 1971, pitched the Orioles to 5-3 and 11-3 victories.

But when the Series moved to Pittsburgh, the momentum shifted. Blass pitched the Pirates to a 5-1 victory, Bruce Kison provided stellar long relief in a 4-3 come-from-behind win and Nelson Briles fired a 4-0 Game 5 shutout. Firepower was provided by Clemente and first baseman Bob Robertson, who homered in the third and fifth games.

Baltimore's 3-2, 10-inning Game 6 victory set up a Game 7 pitching duel between Blass and Mike Cuellar.

*Steve Blass gets a victory hug from Bob Robertson.*

208

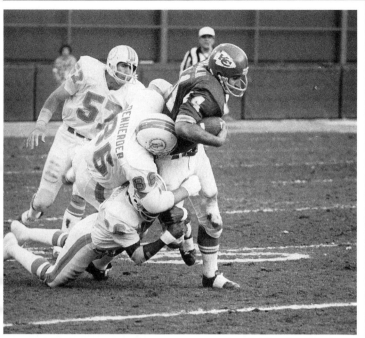

Miami defenders gang tackle Kansas City's Ed Podolak, who netted 350 yards during the Dolphins' marathon playoff victory over the Chiefs.

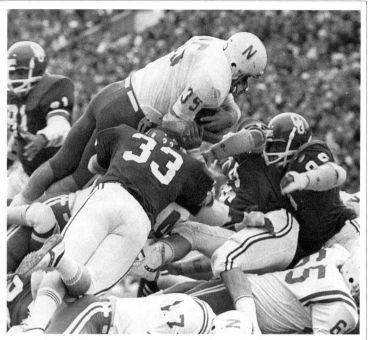

Nebraska's Jeff Kinney goes over the top for a Thanksgiving Day touchdown against Oklahoma.

# Dolphins outlast Chiefs in marathon

Garo Yepremian kicked a 37-yard field goal with 7:40 remaining in the second overtime period, giving the Miami Dolphins a 27-24 victory over the Kansas City Chiefs in an American Football Conference divisional playoff matchup. It ended the longest game in professional football history.

The marathon encounter, played Christmas Day at Kansas City's Municipal Stadium, lasted 4 minutes, 46 seconds longer than the previous longest contest—a 1962 American Football League championship game between the Dallas Texans and Houston Oilers. Yepremian's winning kick, his second field goal of the game, was set up by a 29-yard run by fullback Larry Csonka.

The Chiefs appeared to have victory within their grasp numerous times, but could never put the Dolphins away. Kansas City led 10-0 early and held a 24-17 advantage with 1:36

remaining when Miami's Marv Fleming caught a five-yard game-tying TD pass from Bob Griese. Jan Stenerud missed a 31-yard field goal with 35 seconds left in regulation and had a 42-yard try blocked in the first overtime.

Lost in the shuffle was the outstanding performance of Chiefs' running back Ed Podolak, who scored twice and netted 350 total yards—85 rushing, 110 receiving and 155 on kick returns.

# WHA will begin play

The World Hockey Association, a new rival to the 54-year-old National Hockey League, named its first 10 franchises, November 1, and announced that the circuit would begin play in October of 1972.

Teams will be located in New York, Dayton, Chicago, Miami, Los Angeles, San Francisco and St. Paul in the United States and Winnipeg, Edmonton and Calgary in Canada. WHA President Gary Davidson said two more sites will be selected.

Davidson also announced that the WHA will offer player contracts without reserve or option clauses, hoping to make

the league attractive to both established stars and youngsters coming up through the Junior ranks. A player choosing to change teams within the WHA will need the approval of a three-man arbitration board and his new team will have to give up a draft choice.

# Nebraska triumphs in classic matchup

Jeff Kinney, capping a dramatic 74-yard drive with 1:38 left to play, ran two yards for his fourth touchdown and No. 1-ranked Nebraska outlasted second-ranked Oklahoma, 35-31,

in a "Game of the Century" that lived up to expectations.

The Thanksgiving Day matchup at Norman, Okla., witnessed by a national television audience, was a classic: 9-0 Oklahoma's 45-point-per-game wishbone offense against a Cornhusker defense that had surrendered only 6.4 points per contest in 10 straight victories.

With Kinney running for 174 yards on 30 carries and quarterback Jerry Tagge directing Nebraska's 38.9-point-per-game offense, the Cornhuskers moved over, around and through Oklahoma as expected. However, the Sooners dented Nebraska's previously impregnable defense for 467 yards in total offense, scored in every period and managed leads of 17-14 (halftime) and 31-28 (midway through the fourth quarter).

Both of Oklahoma's leads came on unexpected passes from quarterback Jack Mildren to Jon Harrison (24 and 16 yards). Mildren also ran for a pair of touchdowns.

Another Cornhusker star was Johnny Rodgers, who bolted for a first-quarter touchdown on a 72-yard punt return and made a fingertip reception on the winning drive.

# 1972

## JANUARY - APRIL

## Nebraska explodes, destroys Alabama

Nebraska exploded for three touchdowns in a four-minute stretch of the first half against second-ranked Alabama to cap its second straight national championship with a resounding 38-6 New Year's Day victory before 78,151 fans in Miami's Orange Bowl classic.

The Cornhuskers, considered by many the greatest college football team ever assembled, put the lock on their 23rd straight victory and a 32-game unbeaten streak with an imposing first-half performance against one of the nation's top defenses. Multi-talented Johnny Rodgers keyed the charge by returning a first-quarter punt 77 yards for a touchdown, and Nebraska built a 28-0 halftime lead while amassing 225 yards and taking advantage of numer-

*Nebraska quarterback Jerry Tagge laterals to Jeff Kinney as he is tackled in the Orange Bowl.*

ous Crimson Tide mistakes.

The result was the most lopsided loss in the long coaching career of Alabama's Bear Bryant and confirmed the popular suspicion that the two best teams in the nation, Nebraska and Oklahoma, had played in a Thanksgiving Day classic won by the Huskers, 35-31.

The Associated Press pollsters evidently agreed, voting Nebraska No. 1, the 11-1 Sooners No. 2 and 10-2 Colorado No. 3—a Big Eight Conference trifecta—in their final rankings.

## Freshmen are eligible

In a surprise move that is sure to create a lot of controversy in the coming months, the National Collegiate Athletic Association announced, January 8, that freshmen will be eligible to play football and basketball at major colleges and universities this fall.

The unexpected action was taken at a business meeting that concluded the NCAA's annual convention in Hollywood, Fla. As a result, first-year students now will be eligible for varsity competition in football and basketball. The freshman restrictions were removed from all other sports two years ago.

The question of freshman eligibility in basketball was passed by a strong voice vote, but a count had to be taken on the football issue. It passed, 94-67. The new rule is not mandatory, so individual schools and conferences may decide to take their own action on the issue.

### ★ SPORTS WATCH ★

**FEB:** Los Angeles center Wilt Chamberlain became the first NBA player to reach 30,000 points when he scored during a 110-109 Laker victory at Phoenix.

**FEB:** The newest NHL expansion team, playing out of Long Island, N.Y., will be called the Islanders.

**FEB:** Texan A.J. Foyt, a three-time Indianapolis 500 winner, won his first Daytona 500 in a Mercury, averaging a Daytona International Speedway-record 161.550 mph.

**MAR:** Former NBA center Wayne Embry became professional sports' first black general manager, taking the reins for the champion Milwaukee Bucks.

**MAR:** Franchise transfer: The Cincinnati Royals have become the Kansas City-Omaha Kings.

**APR:** New York Mets Manager Gil Hodges died of a heart attack just after leaving a West Palm Beach, Fla., golf course near the end of spring training.

## Dallas sinks Dolphins

Duane Thomas rushed for 95 yards and a touchdown and Roger Staubach fired two scoring passes, January 16, as the Dallas Cowboys shook off years of frustration and claimed football's biggest prize with a 24-3 victory over Miami in Super Bowl VI at Tulane Stadium in New Orleans.

The Cowboys, bridesmaids to Green Bay in the 1966 and '67 NFL championship games and to Baltimore in last year's Super Bowl, dominated the offensive and defensive lines, controlled

the tempo of the game and turned Miami's only two turnovers into 10 points.

The first break came on Miami's second possession when fullback Larry Csonka fumbled and Dallas recovered at its own 46-yard line. The Cowboys quickly moved into position for a Mike Clark field goal and then added to their lead in the second quarter on a seven-yard Staubach-to-Lance Alworth TD pass.

Garo Yepremian gave Miami fans a flicker of hope just before

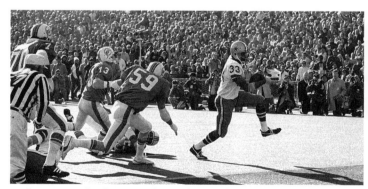

*Dallas running back Duane Thomas breaks free for a third-quarter Super Bowl touchdown against Miami.*

halftime with a 31-yard field goal, but Thomas ran three yards for a touchdown on Dallas' first series of the second half and Staubach, who completed 12 of 19 passes, ended the scoring with a seven-yard toss to tight end Mike Ditka.

# Walton dominates as UCLA reloads

Major college basketball had survived the Lew Alcindor era at UCLA. Now Sidney Wicks, Curtis Rowe and Steve Patterson were gone. Surely the Bruins would require a rebuilding period, maybe take a year or two off.

Not so.

When opposing coaches got their first glimpse of the Walton Gang, it was not hard to see that UCLA would be difficult to beat for at least three more years. Three talented sophomores—6-foot-11 Bill Walton, smooth and versatile forward Keith Wilkes and guard Greg Lee—joined holdovers Henry Bibby and Mike Farmer in a starting lineup that was nothing less than formidable.

With the multi-talented Wal-

Keith Wilkes, a charter member of UCLA's Walton Gang, takes a tumble under Florida State pressure during the NCAA Tournament championship game.

ton leading the charge, the new-look Bruins blitzed their way through an unbeaten regular season and then pulverized the competition through one round after another of the NCAA Tournament. Their final test was probably their stiffest, although they never were seriously threatened in an 81-76 victory over Florida State.

The title, won before 15,063 fans at the Los Angeles Sports Arena, March 25, was UCLA's sixth consecutively and eighth in the last nine seasons. Walton led the way with a typical 24-point, 20-rebound performance. Leading the charge for the 23-6 Seminoles was Ron King, who scored 27 points.

---

# Adolph Rupp retires

Adolph Rupp, the grand baron of Kentucky basketball for 42 years, was forced to the sideline, March 28, by a Kentucky state law that requires mandatory retirement at age 70.

Kentucky coaching legend Adolph Rupp retired with 875 career victories and tons of memories.

Rupp, whose teams have compiled an 875-190 record while winning four NCAA Tournaments and one NIT championship, turned 70 last September 2, just as his final basketball team was preparing to begin a campaign that would result in a 21-7 final record, a co-Southeastern Conference championship and a trip to the finals of the NCAA Tournament's Mideast Regional. The Wildcats have won or shared 27 SEC titles, including the last five in a row, under Rupp.

Rupp was a Kansas youngster who attended the University of Kansas and played basketball for the Jayhawks under legendary Phog Allen. He coached his first game at Kentucky in 1930, his Wildcats beating Georgetown (Ky.) College, 67-19. The victories piled up as Rupp kept his Wildcats in the national spotlight and they captured consecutive NCAA championships in 1948 and '49 and then added titles in '51 and '58.

In 1967, Kentucky defeated Notre Dame, giving Rupp his 722nd career victory and allowing him to pass Allen as the all-time winningest college basketball coach.

---

# Baseball strike ends

The first general strike in baseball history ended in its 13th day, April 13, when players and owners agreed to start the season without making up any of the 86 cancelled games.

The settlement was reached with the 24 owners gathered in Chicago and the player representatives in New York, where they had been meeting for the last three days. The issue that caused the strike, an increase in the players' pension fund, had been settled on April 11, but it could not be agreed whether players would be paid for rescheduled games.

As a result of the decision to not play the 86 games, division titles will be decided strictly on a percentage basis. All teams lost between six and nine games from their schedules.

---

# MAY · AUGUST

## Riva Ridge is upset

Bee Bee Bee, an unheralded colt, pulled off one of the biggest upsets in the long history of the Preakness Stakes, May 20, running over a sloppy Pimlico track to an unlikely victory that dashed the Triple Crown hopes of Kentucky Derby winner Riva Ridge.

The Maryland-bred Bee Bee Bee, with 44-year-old Eldon Nelson in saddle, took the lead out of the gate and never trailed in recording an impressive 1¼-length victory over No Le Hace. Key To The Mint finished third, just ahead of Riva Ridge, a prohibitive 1-5 favorite with Ron Turcotte in saddle. Bee Bee Bee's winning time was 1:55³/₅.

Riva Ridge, being touted as the first Triple Crown winner in 24 years, pulled into second place as the seven-horse field rounded the final turn and appeared to be primed for a stretch run. But Bee Bee Bee, a two-time winner in seven starts this year, was not to be denied his shock win.

*Jockey Eldon Nelson guides Bee Bee Bee through the final turn en route to his upset victory in the Kentucky Derby.*

## Lakers go on a roll

The Los Angeles Lakers, the National Basketball Association's state-of-the-art winning machine, completed its romp through the record books, May 7, with a 114-100 victory over the New York Knicks, closing the books on a glorious 81-16 campaign and a long-awaited league championship.

The five-game victory over the Knicks brought Los Angeles its first NBA title after losses in seven of the last 10 final series. En route to the championship, the Lakers recorded an astounding 33-game winning streak, won a record 69 regular-season games and romped through the playoffs with a 12-3 mark, giving them a final 81-16 ledger that eclipsed the 79-17 record compiled by the 1966-67 Philadelphia 76ers.

Nothing can top that championship feeling, but the Lakers' 33-game winning streak—the longest ever compiled by a professional sports team—came close. Featuring a lineup of Wilt Chamberlain, Happy Hairston, Jim McMillian, Jerry West and Gail Goodrich, Los Angeles won its game of November 5 and proceeded to go unbeaten for more than two months. The streak ended, January 9, in Milwaukee when the Bucks, led by Kareem Abdul-Jabbar's 39 points, pulled away in the fourth quarter for a 120-104 victory that *dropped* the Lakers' record to 39-3.

---

### "SPORTS TALK"

*"I don't want a pro job. I don't want to coach somebody who makes more money than I do."*
**AL McGUIRE**
Marquette basketball Coach

## NHL star Bobby Hull Jets off to Winnipeg

Bobby Hull, the National Hockey League's 33-year-old Golden Jet, shocked the hockey world on June 27 when he announced that he was joining the new World Hockey Association's Winnipeg Jets for a contract package worth at least $2.5 million.

Hull, the Chicago Black Hawks left winger who ranks second on the NHL's all-time goal-scoring charts with 604, will serve as a player-coach in the fledgling league while providing a much-needed identity focus. All 12 WHA teams banded together to raise the $1 million up-front bonus that Hull accepted in St. Paul, Minn.

Later, he hopped in a chartered plane and flew to Winnipeg, where he signed a 10-year contract with the Jets. He reportedly will receive $200,000 annually for the first five years and $100,000 per year as a coach or front-office employee for the remainder of the contract.

Hull topped the 50-goal plateau five times with Chicago.

*Bobby Hull, player-coach of the World Hockey Association's Winnipeg Jets.*

# Colbert has a blast

San Diego slugger Nate Colbert, who entered the game with a .233 batting average, lit up the Atlanta sky with a dazzling power display, August 1, hitting five homers and driving in 13 runs in the Padres' 9-0 and 11-7 doubleheader sweep of the Braves.

Colbert started quickly, blasting a three-run, first-inning home run off Ron Schueler. He added a solo shot in the seventh off Mike McQueen and singled twice, driving in another run.

But Colbert saved his best for the nightcap. First he belted a second-inning grand slam off Pat Jarvis, then he hit two-run homers off Jim Hardin in the

*San Diego slugger Nate Colbert.*

seventh and Cecil Upshaw in the ninth.

Colbert's 13-RBI explosion set a doubleheader record and his five home runs tied the twin bill mark set by St. Louis' Stan Musial in 1954.

★ SPORTS WATCH ★

**MAY:** The high-scoring Boston Bruins captured their second Stanley Cup in three years, beating the New York Rangers in a six-game final series.

**JUN:** Hank Aaron's career homer No. 649, his N.L. record-tying 14th grand slam, moved him past Willie Mays and into second place on the all-time list.

**JUN:** The U.S. Supreme Court, by a 5-3 vote, upheld baseball's exemption from antitrust laws and the validity of the reserve clause when it confirmed lower-court rulings against former baseball star Curt Flood.

**AUG:** Detroit shortstop Ed Brinkman's errorless streak ended after 72 games and 331 chances.

**AUG:** Gary Player shot a four-round total of 281 and beat Jim Jamieson and Tommy Aaron by one stroke in the PGA Championship at Oakland Hills Country Club in Birmingham, Mich.

# Trevino wins again

Lee Trevino, obviously disgusted with the way he had played Muirfield's 17th hole in the final round of the July 15 British Open, quick-hit a chip shot from an embankment just off the green and then watched in amazement as it dropped into the hole for a par-saving 5, the decisive shot in his one-stroke victory over Jack Nicklaus.

Trevino, the first back-to-back British Open winner since Arnold Palmer in 1961 and '62, ended Nicklaus' hopes of a grand slam. Nicklaus had already won the Masters and U.S. Open, but he entered the

final day at Muirfield six shots back.

But the Golden Bear recorded six birdies in the first 11 holes. Suddenly he led by a stroke. Trevino and Tony Jacklin, playing together two groups behind Nicklaus, answered with birdies of their own and regained the lead when Nicklaus bogeyed 16. They were tied when they teed off on 17 and Trevino pulled his drive into a deep bunker. He exploded out and hit his third shot into a heavy rough. He rolled his fourth shot over the green, setting up his winning chip.

# King, Smith triumph

Billie Jean King captured her fourth Wimbledon title with a straight-set victory over Evonne Goolagong, July 7, and Stan Smith made it an American sweep two days later when he dispatched Ilie Nastase in a five-set classic and became the first American winner of the men's championship since 1963.

King, atoning for a semifinal loss to the 20-year-old Goolagong in last year's Wim-

bledon, rolled to a 6-3, 6-3 victory. The smooth Australian is a notoriously slow starter and the relentless King had the match by the throat before she could ever get going.

Smith's 4-6, 6-3, 6-3, 4-6, 7-5 victory was much tougher. It was the tall American's power game against the quickness, finesse and concentration lapses of Nastase, a volatile Rumanian.

The contrast was magnified

*American Wimbledon champion Stan Smith.*

in the final set. Three times Smith had Nastase at match point and three times he made beautiful returns on seemingly

impossible shots. But on match point No. 4, Nastase muffed an easy return at the net to give Smith his first Wimbledon title.

# sports trends

## The heroines of sports

*Women athletes successfully challenge the prejudices of the male-dominated sports establishment*

Today's woman athlete is a determined, intense, state-of-the-art mechanic who performs before large crowds in high-stakes, pressure-filled competitions. She is healthy, wealthy and wise. She is strong, smart and talented. Her rewards for victory can be immense; her failures devastating.

Such a description 20 years ago would have evoked chauvinistic snickers from a male-dominated sports society. Sure the women's sports movement had come a long way from the early days of the century, but its leaders were still fighting to remove the Neanderthal shackles and social restrictions of yesteryear. "State-of-the-art" and "high-stakes" did not compute as adjectives associated with women athletes.

But help was on its way. In 1972, Title IX, an amendment to a civil rights act passed by Congress in the previous decade, brought equality in participation and funding to amateur athletics at educational institutions. And in 1973, Billie Jean King, a product of the 1960s feminist revival and leading advocate for women's rights in professional sports, defeated Bobby Riggs in a "Battle of the Sexes" tennis match that generated incredible attention for women's liberation.

Simply stated, Title IX requires equality of opportunity, facilities, practice time, coaching, travel and *funding* in every high school and college in America. The legislation was fought bitterly by the National Collegiate Athletic Association, the primary men's governing body, but, given the green light at

*The great Babe Didrikson gained prominence in the 1932 Olympics.*

long last, women's athletics flourished. Basketball became an amateur showcase event, but everything on the NCAA agenda, from softball and volleyball to track and field, was affected.

That became especially apparent in the Olympic Games of the 1980s when U.S. women began showcasing their long repressed talents and competing on an equal level with the once-dominant Eastern-bloc athletes. Women like Florence Griffith-Joyner and Jackie Joyner-Kersee rose to the forefront of track and field competition in 1988 at Seoul, South Korea, as did swimmer Janet Evans.

What Title IX did for amateur sports, Billie Jean did for professionals. In the late 1960s, King parlayed her standing as one of the world's top women athletes and her passion for liberation into a battle against the tennis establishment. She talked other top players into boycotting

tournaments, fought for equality in pay and helped found the Virginia Slims women's tour that began operating independently in 1971.

The women proved they could draw crowds, they increased their purses and eventually shared prize money equally with men at the major events. In the process, King, a

*Glenna Collett, early trend-setter.*

*Helen Wills in the 1930s.*

six-time Wimbledon and four-time U.S. Open champion, became the first woman to win $100,000 in a season.

"In a way," said tennis star Chris Evert, "Billie Jean did for our sport what Arnold Palmer did for golf."

The biggest breakthrough, however, was that 1973 battle in Houston's Astrodome between the "Libber and the Lobber." It was showbiz, theater, hype and hustle all rolled into one neat package. But it also was an important step for women's sports into the consciousness of a worldwide audience.

That fact was not lost on King, who had ignored the chauvinistic jibes of the 55-year-old Riggs, a pre-World War II Wimbledon and U.S. Open champion who boasted that he could defeat the best women's player in the world despite his age disadvantage. But when Margaret Court accepted Riggs' challenge and suffered an embarrassing Mother's Day defeat, King reconsidered.

"I had to play Bobby for a lot of reasons," King said. "The Slims tour was still on shaky ground and needed all the support it could get. After Riggs beat Margaret Court so handily, everything was on the line . . . The credibility of the women's circuit was at stake."

King entered the arena on a litter hoisted high by four muscular men. Riggs entered on a rickshaw pulled by six well-endowed models in tight outfits. Riggs presented King with a huge all-day sucker. King gave Riggs a baby pig, a fitting gift for any chauvinist. The largest crowd ever for a tennis match (30,492), a national television audience and fans from 36 foreign countries watched King destroy her tormentor, 6-4, 6-3, 6-3.

"I like him and I hate him," King said, referring to Riggs. "I think he's been great for tennis. He makes people notice the game and that's good. But most

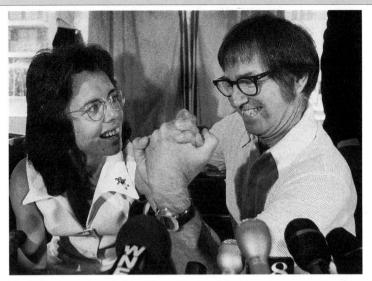

The Billie Jean King–Bobby Riggs "Battle of the Sexes" gave tennis a big national boost in 1973.

of the things he says about women are ridiculous.

"After the match, women came up to me and told me I'd changed their lives. They said I'd helped them gain a whole new confidence in themselves."

It is ironic that a tennis match between an over-the-hill male and a 29-year-old women's champion in the prime of her career could generate such interest and serve as a springboard for the feminist movement. It was the kind of equality battle the women athletes of yesteryear could never have envisioned.

The women athletes of early-century America played pitty-pat tennis in their long, socially acceptable dresses on the amateur courts of the United States and Wimbledon and a few rebellious souls bucked social mores by swinging golf clubs in public. Basketball was popular among college and high school girls, but it was far from the game we know today and was acceptable only in a social, non-competitive forum.

It wasn't until after World War I that the shackles loosened and women began to show they had more to offer than a pretty face. The trigger was the Constitution's 19th amendment, which granted women the right to vote.

While this news did not exactly touch off an equality-

in-athletics movement, it did set the stagnant evolutionary process in motion. Pioneer athletic heroines suddenly began to emerge and catch the attention of a sports community heretofore consumed with its more accomplished male sports heroes. Athletes such as Glenna Collett in golf, Helen Wills in tennis and Gertrude Ederle, the first woman to swim the English Channel,

Florence Griffith-Joyner winning the Olympic 100-meter dash.

were trend setters in their fields. But the biggest influence of the first half-century was Mildred (Babe) Didrikson, the greatest all-round athlete of her time.

Didrikson generated unprecedented attention for women's sports. Not only could this marvelous athlete dominate the top females of her era, she also could compete with many of the more revered male competitors. This was both a blessing and a curse.

> ## "After the match, women came up to me and told me I'd changed their lives."
>
> **BILLY JEAN KING**
> *On the "Battle of the Sexes"*

She emerged as a three-medal track and field winner in the 1932 Olympic Games at Los Angeles (setting one Olympic and two world records) and then gravitated to swimming, basketball, baseball and golf. She excelled at every sport she attempted, often competing against males in exhibitions. Didrikson finally settled on golf as a career choice, never having played the sport before the 1932 Olympics. But she hit the tour in 1940 and proceeded to win 34 of the 88 tournaments she entered, 22 of them between 1944 and '47.

She also paid a price for her success. Throughout her career she was dogged by critics who questioned her femininity. She dressed like a man, acted like a man and competed like a man. Even after she married wrestler George Zaharias and began making efforts to be more feminine, an American public, obviously not ready for this curious prodigy, continued its unrelenting assault. She died of cancer in 1956, probably not realizing just how far-reaching her impact on the feminist sports movement had been.

# 1972

*Mark Spitz, floating like a butterfly en route to his seventh gold medal.*

# Spitz discovers gold

American sensation Mark Spitz captured his record-setting seventh gold medal, September 4, when he swam the butterfly leg for the 400-meter medley relay team on the final day of the swimming competition in the Summer Olympic Games at Munich, West Germany.

Spitz turned a tight race against the East Germans into a rout when he completed the butterfly leg two body lengths ahead of his nearest competitor and turned matters over to anchor man Jerry Heidenreich. The freestyle specialist finished the race in a world-record time of 3:48.16.

The 22-year-old Spitz finished the Olympic competition with four individual golds (the 100- and 200-meter freestyle and the 100- and 200-meter butterfly) and three relay golds. Every one of his seven final races resulted in world records.

Spitz, a Californian, led an American charge to 10 victories in 15 events. The previous best individual gold-medal count of five had been achieved three times.

## "SPORTS TALK"

*"He's so hyperextended that he can kick six inches deeper than anyone else. His legs are like a bow. When he puts on a pair of pants, the stripes on the seam go in different directions."*

**JERRY HEIDENREICH**
on the build of teammate
Mark Spitz

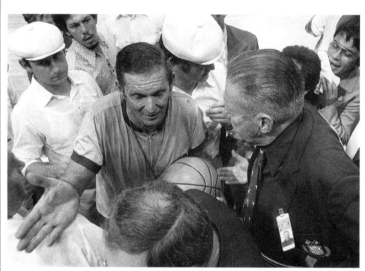

*American Coach Henry Iba (right) angrily pleads his case with an Olympic basketball referee near the end of the controversial gold-medal loss to the Russians.*

# Russians shock U.S.

In one of the most chaotic finishes ever witnessed in international sports competition, the Soviet Union snapped the United States' 63-game Olympic win streak with a controversial 51-50 victory in the finals of the basketball competition.

Down by eight points with 6:07 remaining, the U.S. rallied to pull within one point, and with three seconds left, Doug Collins hit two free throws to give the U.S. its first lead. The Soviets inbounded the ball from under their own basket, the pass was deflected and the horn sounded ending the game. Or so the Americans thought.

The celebration was interrupted by a ruckus at the scorer's table. American Coach Henry Iba was angrily stalking the officials after learning that Robert Jones, secretary-general of the International Amateur Basketball Federation, had ruled the Soviets had called a timeout prior to the inbounds pass. Three seconds were restored to the clock and a long pass was rifled downcourt toward burly Aleksander Belov, who grabbed the ball, knocked two American defenders to the floor and scored a layup that gave the Russians their unlikely victory.

Iba filed a protest, but a five-member committee rejected it and the Soviet victory stood. The shocked and disappointed U.S. players refused to accept their silver medals.

# Terrorist attack kills 11 Israelis at Munich

The festive and competitive mood at the Munich Olympics took a somber twist on the morning of September 5, when eight Palestinian terrorists invaded the Olympic Village dormitory of the Israeli athletes and started a killing spree that eventually claimed 17 lives.

Two Israelis were killed during the attack and nine others were taken hostage. The terrorists demanded that Israel release 200 prisoners and that the West Germans provide safe passage to the Middle East.

The 22-hour drama came to a bloody conclusion in the early hours of September 6, when the German police lured the terrorists and their hostages to a military airport and engaged in a gun battle. All nine hostages were killed, as was one German policeman and five Palestinians. Three terrorists were captured.

A memorial service was held in the main Olympic stadium and the Games were suspended for 34 hours. When they continued, many athletes found they had lost their desire to compete.

# Steelers nip Oakland on amazing touchdown

Pittsburgh running back Franco Harris picked a deflected Terry Bradshaw fourth-and-10 pass off his shoetops and raced 60 yards for a touchdown with five seconds remaining as the Steelers posted a stunning 13-7 victory over the Oakland Raiders in a December 23 American Conference divisional playoff game.

Harris' "Immaculate Reception" occurred less than a minute after Raiders reserve quarterback Ken Stabler had run 30 yards for the touchdown that gave Oakland a 7-6 advantage and silenced the capacity crowd at Pittsburgh's Three Rivers Stadium. Bradshaw quickly moved the Steelers to their own 40-yard line on two short passes, but threw three straight incompletions.

With 22 seconds remaining, Bradshaw dropped back and looked for Preston Pearson, his primary receiver. Pearson was covered so Bradshaw fired toward running back Frenchy Fuqua, who was streaking downfield. Raiders' defensive back Jack Tatum got to Fuqua at the same time as the ball and knocked it away, apparently foiling Pittsburgh's last gasp.

But the ball sailed backward and Harris snatched it in full flight at the Oakland 42. He headed toward the end zone, fought off a desperation shove from defensive back Jimmy Warren and scored the game-winning touchdown.

*Pittsburgh's Franco Harris is surrounded by delirious Steeler fans after his Immaculate Reception.*

## ★ SPORTS WATCH ★

**SEP:** Wimbledon champion Billie Jean King won her third U.S. Open title, beating Australian Kerry Melville, 6-3, 7-5, at Forest Hills, N.Y.

**OCT:** Oakland catcher Gene Tenace tied a World Series record with four home runs and the A's recorded a seven-game victory over the Cincinnati Reds.

**OCT:** Former Brooklyn Dodger great Jackie Robinson, the man who broke major league baseball's color barrier in 1947, died of heart disease at age 53.

**NOV:** Lefthander Steve Carlton, whose 27 victories were 46 per cent of the last-place Philadelphia Phillies' 59 wins, captured the N.L. Cy Young Award.

**DEC:** Jack Nicklaus finished the year with a record $320,542 in money winnings.

**DEC:** New York Jets receiver Don Maynard caught seven passes in a game against Oakland and brought his record-setting career reception total to 632 in 15 seasons.

## Davis dazzles Irish

Southern California's Anthony Davis dazzled Notre Dame with a sensational six-touchdown performance, December 2, and the Trojans handed the Fighting Irish a 45-23 setback at the Los Angeles Coliseum.

Davis took the opening kickoff and sprinted 97 yards for a score, before going on scoring runs of one and five yards in the opening quarter and four yards in the third period as the Trojans built 19-3 and 25-10 leads.

But Notre Dame, behind the passing of quarterback Tom Clements, fought back to trail, 25-23. Clements hit Willie Townsend on a five-yard scoring pass, Gary Diminick on an 11-yarder and Mike Creaney on a 10-yarder.

The Irish came no closer. Taking the kickoff after Creaney's score, the elusive halfback raced 96 yards for a touchdown late in the third quarter. Davis capped his 99-yard rushing day with an eight-yard TD dash in the final period.

## Clemente dies in crash

Pittsburgh outfielder Roberto Clemente, a four-time National League batting champion and 12-time All-Star, died on December 31, when a cargo plane that was carrying relief supplies to earthquake victims in Nicaragua crashed in the ocean moments after takeoff from San Juan International Airport.

Clemente, the most popular sports figure in the history of his native Puerto Rico, was the leader of his country's efforts to help the Nicaraguan quake victims. He was aboard the flight because he wanted to make sure that the supplies would get to the neediest cases. The DC-7, carrying a crew of three and one other passenger, crashed in 100 feet of water.

The 38-year-old Clemente, a sure-bet baseball Hall of Famer, had collected his 3,000th hit just before the season ended. His .317 career average was highest

*Pittsburgh's Roberto Clemente after collecting his 3,000th hit, almost three months before his death in a plane crash.*

among active players and he led the Pirates to World Series championships in 1960 and '71. The 18-year veteran also was an excellent right fielder with a powerful throwing arm.

# Dolphins finish 17-0

The Miami Dolphins staked their claim as the most perfect football machine ever assembled, January 14, when they defeated the Washington Redskins, 14-7, in Super Bowl VII and completed their perfect 17-0 season.

The Dolphins, the first team in the 53-year history of the National Football League to go through a season undefeated and untied, put on an impressive show for the crowd of 90,192 fans at the Los Angeles Coliseum. They ground out the clock offensively and completely dominated the Redskins with their "No-Name Defense." Only a crazy play involving placekicker Garo Yepremian allowed Washington to cross the Miami goal line.

The Dolphins were leading

14-0 when Yepremian attempted a 42-yard field goal. But the kick was blocked by onrushing lineman Bill Brundige and the ball bounced back toward Yepremian. Instead of falling on it, the little man from Cyprus picked it up, saw several big defenders closing in and frantically tried to pass. When the ball slipped out of his hand, Washington's Mike Bass grabbed it and ran 49 yards for a touchdown.

The sudden reversal of fortunes was short-lived, however. Washington did get the ball back with 1:14 remaining, but Miami's defense swarmed all over Redskins quarterback Billy Kilmer.

Miami scored its first touchdown in the opening quarter on Bob Griese's 28-yard pass to

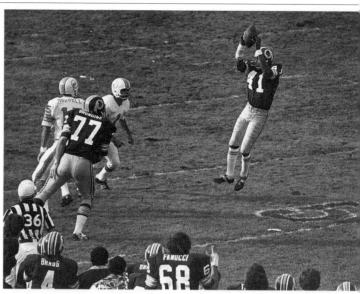

Washington's Mike Bass (41) catches a desperation pass from Miami kicker Garo Yepremian (1). Bass ran 49 yards for a Super Bowl VII touchdown.

Howard Twilley and added a second score on Jim Kiick's one-yard run in the second period. Griese's 8-of-11 passing, fullback Larry Csonka's 112

rushing yards and Jake Scott's two interceptions, one in his own end zone, kept the Dolphins in control of the clock and their own destiny.

# Foreman batters Frazier in upset

Heavyweight boxing champion George Foreman.

Big George Foreman startled a Jamaican crowd of 36,000 at Kingston's National Stadium, January 22, by battering Joe Frazier to the canvas six times en route to a second-round technical knockout and the undisputed world heavyweight championship.

Foreman, unbeaten in 37 fights since winning the Super Heavyweight gold medal at the 1968 Olympic Games in Mexico City, fended off Frazier's early charge with his long reach and then stunned the champion with

a strong left hook to the body. Suddenly Foreman began moving forward with left-right combinations and he sent Frazier sprawling with a right uppercut. The champion hauled himself to his feet and took the mandatory eight count.

The champion went back on the attack and his big challenger nailed him with another uppercut that sent him to his knees. A straight right hand put Frazier on his back for a third time as the bell sounded.

After 1:35 of the second round and three more knockdowns, referee Arthur Mercante stopped the fight with Frazier wobbling on his feet, unable to stop the attack.

"I started to fight back when I should have bobbed and weaved," said a disappointed Frazier after his first loss in 30 professional outings. "I was anxious to get at him. I should have held back and let my head clear."

The title defense was Frazier's 10th since winning a piece of the title by beating Buster Mathis in 1968 and his third since outpointing Muhammad Ali almost two years ago.

# Walton puts on show

Bill Walton put on one of the most dominating offensive shows ever witnessed on a basketball court, March 26, and the UCLA Bruins rolled to an 87-66 victory over Memphis State and their seventh consecutive NCAA Tournament championship at the St. Louis Arena.

Controlling the game from start to finish, Walton connected on 21 of 22 shots from the field and two of five free throws for a championship game-record 44 points. He iced his big night with 13 rebounds and some excellent defense. Walton's numbers could have been even more dazzling had he not sat out more than four min-utes of the first half with foul trouble and the last 2½ minutes with a sprained ankle.

Scoring on short jumpers, lobs from guard Greg Lee and offensive rebounds, Walton staked the Bruins to a 37-30 lead. But when he went to the bench with three fouls, Memphis State (24-6) rallied to lead 41-39, early in the second half. However, UCLA stormed out to a big lead and cruised to its NCAA-record 75th straight victory.

Forward Keith Wilkes added 16 points to the Bruin cause, while Larry Kenon and Larry Finch combined for 49 of Memphis State's points.

UCLA's Bill Walton soared for 44 points and UCLA beat Memphis State to win its seventh straight NCAA Tournament championship.

# Underdog is master

Tommy Aaron, a 36-year-old journeyman, fired a final-round 68, April 9, and held off J.C. Snead and defending champion Jack Nicklaus for a one-stroke victory in the Masters at Augusta.

Aaron, the first native Georgian to wear the prized green jacket, began the final round four strokes behind Englishman Peter Oosterhuis and blistered the Augusta National course with four front-nine birdies. He dropped a stroke to par on the 10th and 11th holes, but fought back with birdies at 13 and 15 that put him into position to win for the third time in 12 years as a touring professional.

While Oosterhuis was struggling to a 74, Snead and Nicklaus were in hot pursuit of the leader. Snead was in good position until he found the water at the par-3 12th hole and took a 5. Nicklaus, a four-time winner of this prestigious event, stormed into contention with a final-round 66 that moved him from 15th place after three rounds to a final tie for third, two strokes behind Aaron (283) and one behind Snead.

# DH experiment begins

The American League introduced its new designated hitter rule, April 6, when New York Yankee Ron Blomberg stepped to the plate with the bases loaded in the first inning and drew a walk off Boston's Luis Tiant in a season-opening game at Fenway Park.

So began a noble experiment with the most significant baseball rule change in many years. The A.L. voted unanimously at last year's winter meetings to give the rule a three-year test before deciding whether to adopt it permanently. The rule allows each A.L. team to replace weak-hitting pitchers in the lineup with hitters who will bat without playing the field.

Blomberg collected one hit in three-at-bats as baseball's pioneer designated hitter, but Boston DH Orlando Cepeda went hitless in six at-bats, even though the Red Sox pounded the Yankees, 15-5.

New York's Ron Blomberg, baseball's first designated hitter.

# 1973

## MAY-AUGUST

## Secretariat romps

*Secretariat roars around the final turn at Belmont Park en route to an awesome 31-length victory and horse racing's Triple Crown.*

Secretariat, bidding to become the first Triple Crown winner in 25 years, roared to a 31-length victory over Twice a Prince in the June 9 Belmont Stakes, electrifying 69,138 fans with one of the most incredible performances in horse racing history.

The Meadow Stable colt, with Ron Turcotte in saddle, sped to a track-record time of 2:24, the fastest dirt-course mile and a half ever run in America. And he did it without being pushed.

Secretariat, the son of Bold Ruler and Somethingroyal, was expected to get a test from Sigmund Sommer's Sham, the second-place finisher in both the Kentucky Derby and Preakness Stakes. And, indeed, Sham did threaten early.

But Secretariat took control at the three-quarter pole and ran away from the pack almost like it was standing still. The big crowd gasped in awe as he hit the finish line.

It was his 12th victory in 15 races, making him the ninth Triple Crown winner and the first since Citation in 1948.

*Hockey's Howe boys, Mark (left), Marty (center) and Gordie, in 1977 as members of the Hartford Whalers.*

## Howe boys will join forces in the WHA

The World Hockey Association, groping for recognition and box-office appeal, dipped into the National Hockey League's past, June 19, when it signed former Detroit Red Wings great Gordie Howe to a four-year, $1 million contract with the Houston Aeros.

It was not really the money that lured the NHL's all-time leading goal-scorer out of retirement. It was the chance to play on the same team with his two sons, Marty and Mark, both of whom had recently signed four-year contracts of their own.

The 45-year-old Howe, whose 1,687 games, 786 goals and 1,023 points all rank as NHL records, probably will be positioned on a line with Mark. Marty is a defenseman.

## Rain, deaths mar Indy

Gordon Johncock, a 150-pound veteran driving for Andy Granatelli's STP team, steered his Eagle-Offenhauser to victory, May 30, in a rain-shortened, tragedy-marred Indianapolis 500 at the Indianapolis Motor Speedway.

The race, delayed two days because of rain, was brought to an early conclusion when rain began falling again and track officials pulled out the red flag, ending the classic after 332.5 miles. Johncock, one of 11 drivers still on the track at that point, won by a little more than a minute over Billy Vukovich's Sugaripe Prune Special Offenhauser with an average speed of 159.014 mph.

The ill-fated event was marred by three deaths, one during qualifying and two in the race. Veteran Art Pollard died when he crashed his Cobre Special on the first turn while traveling 190 mph during qualifying. Disaster struck 54 minutes into the race when Swede Savage's Eagle-Offenhauser crashed into the inner wall of the fourth turn, exploded and burst into flames. Savage died on the way to a hospital. Also killed was a member of Graham McRae's pit crew, who was struck by an emergency vehicle rushing to aid Savage.

The race was red-flagged to a stop while debris and fuel was cleaned off the track and resumed one hour and 15 minutes later.

### ★ SPORTS WATCH ★

**MAY:** The New England Whalers became the first champions of the WHA defeating the Bobby Hull-coached Winnipeg Jets in five games.

**MAY:** The Montreal Canadiens captured their 17th Stanley Cup and second in the last three years with a six-game victory over Chicago.

**JUN:** Johnny Miller shot a course-record 63 in the final round of the U.S. Open at Oakmont (Pa.) Country Club and beat John Schlee by a single stroke.

**JUL:** California fireballer Nolan Ryan pitched his second no-hitter of the season, beating Detroit 6-0 and striking out 17 Tigers in a game at Tiger Stadium.

**AUG:** The NHL announced that it will expand to 20 teams before the 1974-75 season and split into a four-division format.

**AUG:** New York Mets slugger Willie Mays hit home run No. 660, the last of his outstanding career, against Cincinnati lefthander Don Gullett.

*The scoreboard tells the story as Hank Aaron touches home plate with another milestone homer.*

# Aaron blasts No. 700

Atlanta Braves slugger Hank Aaron, entering the home stretch in his chase of Babe Ruth's home run record, belted career homer No. 700, July 21, off Philadelphia lefthander Ken Brett during a game at Atlanta Stadium.

The 39-year-old veteran connected on a 1-1 pitch in the third inning with a man aboard, sending a towering 400-foot blast into the left-center field bleachers. The home run gave the Braves a 4-2 lead, but the Phillies eventually won 8-4.

The ball was retrieved by 18-year-old Atlantan Robert Winborne, who presented Aaron with the ball after the game and received 700 silver dollars for his efforts. Hammerin' Hank received a long standing ovation and was pushed out of the dugout for two curtain calls. Champagne was passed around the Atlanta locker room.

The home run pulls Aaron to within 14 of Ruth's all-time record. Aaron was 5 months old in 1934 when the Babe connected for No. 700.

---

## "SPORTS TALK"

*"I don't feel any special thrill. It's just a number. The only real one is THE one."*

**HANK AARON**
after hitting career home run No. 700

---

# King humbles Evert

Billie Jean King, looking for her second straight Wimbledon singles title and fifth in eight finals, played a near-perfect first set and then held off the challenge of 18-year-old Chris Evert, July 7, for a 6-0, 7-5 victory.

King's 17-minute first-set blitz was a flawless exhibition of tennis. Abandoning her normal aggressive style to compensate for Evert's pinpoint shotmaking and baseline game, she stayed back and showed a little shotmaking of her own. She only came to the net when she caught her young opponent off-balance and when she did, her volleying skills produced sure winners.

"Billie Jean would have made anybody look like a beginner," Evert said.

"It's the best set I've ever played," King admitted.

After winning the first two games of the second set, however, Evert fought back to take 4-3 and 5-4 leads. But with the scored tied 15-all in the next game, King served two aces and hit a low volley winner for 5-all, broke Evert's service for the next game and then served out to clinch the championship.

---

# Dwight Stones soars to high jump record

Dwight Stones, a 19-year-old California jumping jack, leaped over a bar set at 7 feet, $6\frac{1}{2}$ inches, July 11, during the West German-U.S. dual track meet at Munich, breaking the world high jump record by a quarter of an inch.

Returning to the Olympic Stadium where he had earned a high jump bronze medal in last year's Summer Games, Stones electrified a crowd of 25,000 when he cleared the record height on his third attempt. He had previously cleared 7-foot-$5\frac{1}{2}$ to win the competition, but asked officials to take the bar up another inch.

On his record leap, Stones galloped to the bar in a wide curve and flung himself over using the flop technique. He brushed the bar, jumped to his feet and begged with clenched fists for it not to fall. When it didn't, Stones went on a wild sprint around the stadium to a standing ovation.

The 6-foot-5, 170-pounder bettered the 7-foot-$6\frac{1}{4}$ set by Pat Matzdorf in July of 1971.

*American Dwight Stones soars to a world record during high jump competition at Munich.*

# 1973

## King outclasses Riggs in "Battle of Sexes"

Billie Jean King, striking a blow for women everywhere, crushed Bobby Riggs, 6-4, 6-3, 6-3, September 20, in their $100,000 winner-take-all "Battle of the Sexes" tennis match at Houston's Astrodome.

Playing in a circus atmosphere that represented a complete departure from traditional tennis events, the 29-year-old King brought an end to the bizarre story of the 55-year-old hustler who had jumped into the national spotlight with his blunt putdowns of women's tennis and the role of today's female.

A crowd of 30,492, paying up to $100 per seat, watched the five-time Wimbledon champion make short work of Riggs, the 1939 Wimbledon and U.S. singles champ. Millions more watched on television and 36 foreign countries picked it up via satellite.

King used a classic serve-and-volley game to embarrass Riggs. She controlled the tempo of the match, dominated the net and moved him around the baseline to the point of near exhaustion.

It was clear from the beginning that this was not going to be an ordinary sports event. King entered the arena first on a Cleopatra-style gold litter that was held aloft by four muscular athletes. Riggs entered in a gold-wheeled rickshaw pulled by "Bobby's Bosom Buddies," six female models in tight red and gold outfits.

A band blared march music and costumed characters from Astroworld entertained. Large banners were on display, and the crowd cheered, taunted and sipped champagne.

It was a vast departure from the first "Battle of the Sexes," a

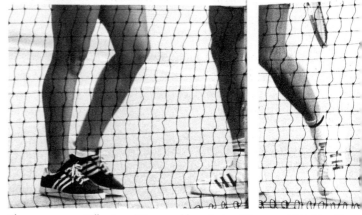

*The conquerer, Billie Jean King, and her victim, 55-year-old Bobby Riggs*

Mother's Day match between Margaret Court and Riggs that the self-proclaimed hustler won in straight sets at a make-shift arena seating 3,000 in Ramona, Calif.

## Bickering A's capture 2nd straight Series

*Oakland second baseman Mike Andrews makes one of his two critical errors in Game 2 of the World Series against the New York Mets.*

Home runs by Reggie Jackson and Bert Campaneris and the combined eight-hit pitching of Ken Holtzman, Rollie Fingers and Darold Knowles lifted the Oakland A's to a 5-2 seventh-game victory over the New York Mets, October 21, and a second consecutive World Series.

The A's triumphed as expected, but not before being pushed by a surprising Mets team that had finished only three games over .500 during the regular season and had squeezed past Cincinnati in an intense National League Championship Series.

The A's got a Series jump when Holtzman, Fingers and Knowles combined to shut down the Mets in a 2-1 victory. But New York fought back to win a wild second game, 10-7, in 12 innings. Aiding the Mets' four-run 12th-inning outburst were two errors by second baseman Mike Andrews, who quickly became the center of a World Series controversy.

Oakland Owner Charlie Finley announced the next day that he was deactivating Andrews, in effect "firing" him. But when he tried to place the 30-year-old on the disabled list, he was stopped by Commissioner Bowie Kuhn,

who stepped in and said, "No".

Oakland reclaimed the advantage with a 3-2 Game 3 victory at New York's Shea Stadium, but the Mets won Games 4 and 5 behind the pitching of Jon Matlack and Jerry Koosman and the hitting of Rusty Staub. The A's came back in Game 6 for a 3-1 victory.

# 2,003: A rushing odyssey for O.J.

Running back O.J. Simpson, needing just 61 yards in Buffalo's final game to become the National Football League's leading single-season rusher, ripped the New York Jets' defense for 200 yards, December 16, and ended his incredible campaign with 2,003.

Running behind a fired-up offensive line (the Electric Company) on a snow-covered Shea Stadium field, Simpson passed former Cleveland great Jim Brown's 1963 record (1,863 yards) on his eighth carry of the game—a six-yard gain in the first quarter.

*O.J. Simpson, professional football's first 2,000-yard rusher.*

Suddenly the magic 2,000-yard mountain did not seem too high. Carrying 26 more times, the Juice scaled that peak with seven minutes remaining in a 34-14 Bills' victory. His final game: 34 attempts for 200 yards. His season: 332 attempts for 2,003 yards.

Simpson topped the 200-yard barrier three times.

# Irish turn Tide, 24-23

In a national championship-deciding classic that rivaled the 1971 Oklahoma-Nebraska Thanksgiving Day shootout for excitement and intensity, Notre Dame squeezed out a 24-23 victory over top-ranked Alabama in the December 31 Sugar Bowl game at New Orleans.

This battle of unbeaten powerhouses featured six lead changes and was not decided until the final three minutes when Fighting Irish quarterback Tom Clements, facing a third-and-eight from his own 2-yard line, backed up into the end zone and fired a daring 35-yard pass to tight end Dave Weber that allowed Notre Dame to run out the clock.

Notre Dame struck first on a one-yard Wayne Bullock run, but Alabama answered with a six-yard Randy Billingsley scamper. Al Hunter's 93-yard kickoff return again gave the Irish the lead, but the Crimson Tide fired back on a 39-yard Bill Davis field goal and Wilbur

Jackson's five-yard run. After Eric Penick's 12-yard third-quarter TD run thrust Notre Dame back into the lead, Alabama moved ahead 23-21 on a halfback pass from Mike Stock to quarterback Richard Todd.

A 19-yard Bob Thomas field goal with 4:26 to play gave Notre Dame its 11th victory and in the process locked up Coach Ara Parseghian's third national title in 10 years.

*The Notre Dame defense converges on Alabama quarterback Gary Rutledge, who wisely pitches the ball away during second-quarter Sugar Bowl action.*

# Everybody loses in Big Ten tie

When No. 1-ranked Ohio State traveled to Ann Arbor to play fourth-ranked Michigan, November 25, in a battle of unbeatens, a Big Ten championship, a Rose Bowl berth and, conceivably, a national championship were on the line. What the Buckeyes and Wolverines got was a costly 10-10 black eye.

The game itself was not exactly a testimonial for diverse offenses. Running the ball on every play, Coach Woody Hayes' Buckeyes scored 10 first-half points and made them stand up until a fourth-quarter rally by the Wolverines tied the game. The Buckeyes did not throw their first pass until 1:06 remained and it resulted in an interception by Michigan's Tom Drake. But Mike Lantry missed a 44-yard field goal that could

have won the game for them.

Big Ten athletic directors voted the next day to award the Rose Bowl berth to Ohio State, a decision that brought a charge of "petty jealousies" from Wolverine Coach Bo Schembechler. Michigan's Rose Bowl hopes had been dashed, the two teams had to share the Big Ten title and both dropped out of the national picture.

# 1974

## Dolphins super again

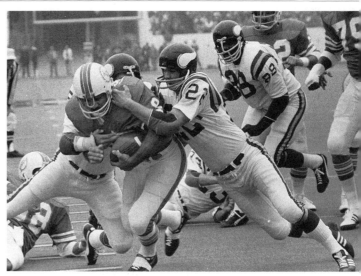

*Miami fullback Larry Csonka drags Vikings into the end zone and scores the Dolphins' first Super Bowl VIII touchdown.*

The Miami Dolphins, dominating the Minnesota Vikings both offensively and defensively, cruised to an efficient 24-7 victory in Super Bowl VIII, January 13, at Houston's Rice Stadium, becoming only the second team to win football's biggest prize two years in a row.

The Vikings became the first team to lose two Super Bowls. And it was evident almost from the opening kickoff that Minnesota was in for a long afternoon.

Starting from his own 38-yard line, Dolphins quarterback Bob Griese quickly drove his team for a touchdown. Mixing runs by Larry Csonka and Mercury Morris with passes to Jim Mandich and Marlin Briscoe, Griese carved up Minnesota's famed "Purple People Eaters" defense. Miami's defense held the Vikings without a first down until the final play of the first quarter and pressured quarterback Fran Tarkenton relentlessly.

Csonka, a 1,003-yard rusher during a 12-2 regular season that followed the Dolphins' perfect 1973 campaign, scored Miami's first and last touchdowns on runs of five and two yards, and he finished the day with a Super Bowl-record 145 yards. Minnesota could not score until the fourth quarter when Tarkenton rolled four yards around right end.

## UCLA's streak ends

*Notre Dame's Dwight Clay heads downcourt as UCLA players give chase during the final moments of the Fighting Irish's great upset victory.*

Dwight Clay hit a jump shot from the corner and Notre Dame survived five missed UCLA shots in the final 21 seconds to record one of the biggest upsets in basketball history, a 71-70 thriller that broke the Bruins' record three-year, 88-game winning streak.

The Fighting Irish slayed college basketball's grand dragon on January 19 with an amazing rally that stunned the crowd of 11,343 fans at the Athletic and Convocation Center in South Bend, Ind. The Bruins had controlled play for more than 36 minutes and owned a comfortable 70-59 lead with 3 minutes, 32 seconds left to play.

But then the weapon that has been so good to UCLA Coach John Wooden over the years struck back at him. Notre Dame went into a full-court press and the Bruins fell apart. On its next five possessions, UCLA committed five turnovers—and the Irish converted each one into points. The culmination of the drive came with 29 seconds to play when Clay dropped his bomb from the right corner.

After a timeout with 21 sec-

onds left, UCLA's Tommy Curtis missed a shot from 25 feet, Dave Meyers missed a tip attempt and a rebound was knocked out of bounds by an Irish defender. With six seconds to go, the Bruins got the ball to Walton, who missed a 12-footer. Two more Bruins missed follow-up attempts.

Ironically, the loss, the first in the varsity careers of Walton, Curtis, Greg Lee and Keith Wilkes, occurred on the same court where UCLA last lost three years ago. And it happened in a game in which the Walton Gang shot 70 percent while rolling up a 17-point first-half lead.

As a result of the upset, the unbeaten and second-ranked Irish most likely will replace UCLA atop the polls. But that reign could be short-lived. Notre Dame must travel to Los Angeles for a January 27 rematch.

Walton led UCLA, winner of seven straight NCAA Tournament championships, with 24 points and nine rebounds. Gary Brokaw topped the Irish scoring list with 25 points.

# Wolfpack brakes UCLA's title run

N.C. State's David Thompson outduels UCLA's Bill Walton for a rebound.

North Carolina State, playing before a partisan crowd of 15,829 in Greensboro, N.C., ended UCLA's seven-year reign as NCAA Tournament champion, March 23, when it rallied for an 80-77 double-overtime victory in a Final Four semifinal matchup.

In a classic confrontation, the teams battled to a 35-35 halftime tie, a 65-65 regulation standoff and a 67-67 overtime deadlock. But in the second 5-minute overtime period, the Bruins jumped out to a 74-67 lead and prospects looked bleak for the top-ranked Wolfpack.

N.C.-State rallied, with high-flying David Thompson scoring six points, 7-foot-4 Tom Burleson three and 5-foot-5 guard Monte Towe four more. UCLA had pounded the Wolfpack, 84-66 (their only defeat), during an early-season meeting.

Bill Walton, winding down his UCLA career, scored 29 points. But Thompson's 28-point effort and 20 from Burleson were enough to offset Walton and insure that a new champion would be crowned for the first time since 1966.

Two days later the Wolfpack defeated Marquette in the championship game, 76-54.

## ★ SPORTS WATCH ★

**FEB:** Richard Petty, averaging 140.894 mph in his Dodge, won his record fifth Daytona 500, a race that was shortened to 450 miles because of the national energy crisis.

**FEB:** Tony Waldrop set a mile indoor world record of 3:55 during competition in the San Diego Indoor Games.

**MAR:** George Foreman retained his world heavyweight championship by scoring a second-round technical knockout over Ken Norton at Caracas, Venezuela.

**MAR:** Purdue captured its first National Invitation Tournament championship with a 97-81 victory over Utah at Madison Square Garden in New York.

**MAR:** American race car driver Peter Revson was killed when his Ford UOP Shadow crashed during a practice run for the South African Grand Prix at Johannesburg.

# Aaron passes Ruth

Hank Aaron, answering the pressure of an unprecedented media blitz, belted career home run No. 715, April 8, in his first game of the season at Atlanta Stadium and staked his claim as the greatest slugger in baseball history.

The record-setting blast came on a one-ball pitch from left-hander Al Downing in the fourth inning of a game against the Los Angeles Dodgers. Aaron, who had walked on his first at-bat, deposited a fastball into the Braves' left-field bullpen with teammate Darrell Evans on base, tying the game at 3-3. He calmly circled the bases with an escort from two overexuberant fans and was greeted at the plate by a monster hug from his elderly mother. The game was delayed 10 minutes while fans and officials showered their praise on the new home run champion.

The Hammer had tied the 714 career record of former New York Yankee great Babe Ruth on April 4 in Cincinnati, when he blasted a Jack Billingham pitch over the left-center field wall on his first swing of the new season. He sat out the Braves' second game in Cincinnati and went hitless in the third, setting the stage for his royal homecoming.

New home run king Hank Aaron gets a triumphant hug from his mother.

# WFL signs 3 Dolphins

The new World Football League gained credibility, March 31, when Toronto Northmen Owner John Bassett Jr. announced that Larry Csonka, Jim Kiick and Paul Warfield, players from Miami's defending Super Bowl champions, have agreed to contracts that will cost him about $3 million.

The trio will play one more season with the Dolphins before joining the Northmen for the 1975 campaign. That will allow them to play out the option year in their Miami contracts. Agent Ed Keating negotiated the guaranteed deals that will make his clients the highest-paid players in football.

The biggest loss for Miami will be Csonka, a 240-pound fullback who has rushed for 5,157 yards and scored 32 touchdowns in six seasons. Kiick, a running back, lost his starting job last year to Mercury Morris. Warfield is a 31-year-old wide receiver with 344 catches for 7,165 yards in a nine-year career with Cleveland and Miami.

# 1974

## 100-yard record falls

Ivory Crockett, a slightly built 24-year-old Southern Illinois University graduate, shattered the 100-yard dash world record set by Bob Hayes 11 years ago, flashing to victory in 9 seconds flat during competition in the May 11 Tom Black Classic Track Meet at the University of Tennessee in Knoxville.

The 5-foot-7, 150-pound Crockett, whose previous best clocking in the 100 was 9.2, shaved a tenth of a second off Hayes' mark. Five others had tied the record.

The event was sanctioned by the NCAA and there was virtually no wind. The artificial track was slightly wet from an earlier rain.

Crockett, who works as a computer firm marketing representative in Peoria, Ill., was running for the AAU Philadelphia Pioneers Club. Reggie Jones of Tennessee finished second at 9.2.

*World record setter Ivory Crockett hits the 100-yard dash finish line.*

## Parent leads Flyers

Philadelphia's Broad Street Bullies, the rough-and-tumble bad boys of the National Hockey League, showed that they can skate as well as fight, May 19, when they defeated the high-scoring Boston Bruins 1-0 to win the Stanley Cup.

The Flyers' Game 6 victory at the Philadelphia Spectrum closed out a rugged series that was dominated by the outstanding play of goaltender Bernie Parent. Whereas the first five games featured numerous fights and push-and-shove tactics by both teams, the finale was a free-skating affair that should have been more to the Bruins'

liking. But it didn't matter. Parent was spectacular and Rick MacLeish's first-period power-play goal provided him with all the offense he needed.

The Bruins, who led the NHL with 349 regular-season goals, managed only 13 in its six games against Parent. Their two big guns, Phil Esposito and Bobby Orr, scored only two apiece.

The Flyers and their fans were inspired before the game when singer Kate Smith, their good-luck charm, performed a stirring rendition of "God Bless America." The Flyers are 37-4 when Smith sings that song before their games.

## Nets climb ABA peak

*New York's Julius Erving works for a shot against Utah's Willie Wise during Game 3 of the ABA championship series.*

The New York Nets, featuring the aerial act of Julius Erving, completed their rise to prominence, May 10, when they defeated the Utah Stars, 111-100, and captured their first American Basketball Association championship.

Erving scored 20 points and grabbed 16 rebounds and Larry Kenon contributed 23 points and 11 rebounds to the Nets' Game 5 victory before 15,934 fans at Nassau Coliseum in Uniondale, N.Y. The Stars, who had managed an eight-point victory in Salt Lake City in Game 4, were otherwise overmatched by a team that averaged only 23 years of age and less than three years of professional experience per man.

The Nets' championship ended a long trip from nowhere. Starting as the New York Americans, they played in small arenas unfit for big-league basketball. Nobody paid much

attention, at least not until Erving's arrival from the Virginia Squires, the drafting of such players as Kenon and John Williamson and the hiring of Coach Kevin Loughery. The team really began to jell near the end of the season and won 22 of its last 25 games, including 12 of 14 in the playoffs. The exciting Erving was the ABA scoring champion, averaging 27.4 points per game.

# The Jimmy-Chris show

It seemed only fitting, July 5 and 6, when 21-year-old Jimmy Connors and 19-year-old Chris Evert were crowned king and queen of Wimbledon. Fitting because these two rising stars are planning to be married in November.

Evert, the sweet-swinging Floridian with a composure beyond her tender years, held up her end first, blitzing Russian Olga Morozova, 6-0, 6-4, in a one-hour women's final that made her the youngest Wimbledon winner since 17-year-old Maureen Connolly in 1952.

Evert, winner of the Italian Open and French Open earlier this year, cruised through the first set. Morozova fought to 4-all in the second, but Evert stepped up her volleys and closed out the match.

Connors took center stage the next day and crushed Australian veteran Ken Rosewall, 6-1, 6-1, 6-4, in a 93-minute final. Rosewall had rebounded from a two-set match-point deficit to defeat Stan Smith in the semi-final round.

But Connors outran, outhit and outplayed his 39-year-old opponent. He stayed back early, hitting hard and deep while swinging the ball from side to side, and then rushed the net later to close out his first Wimbledon victory.

*Wimbledon king and queen: Jimmy Connors and fiancée Chris Evert.*

# Hot Miller wins 6th tourney of year

Johnny Miller, still riding an incredible hot streak that started with last year's U.S. Open victory, fired a final-round 67, August 25, and recorded a two-stroke victory in the Westchester Classic, his sixth PGA tour win of the year.

Miller, who led Tom Weiskopf by two strokes entering the final round, carved out a four-day total of 269 over the 6,614-yard Westchester Country Club course, two strokes better than Don Bies and three ahead of Weiskopf. The $50,000 first prize brought his yearly earnings to $256,383 and put him in position to challenge Jack Nicklaus' one-year record of $320,542 (1972).

The 27-year-old Californian's hot streak began last June at Oakmont (Pa.) Country Club when he shot a record-setting 63 for a one-stroke victory over John Schlee. He began 1974 by winning the tour's first three tournaments, added two more titles and then missed three events because of the birth of his third child. He is the fifth golfer in the last 20 years to win six or more events.

*Johnny Miller and caddy watch a long putt during action in the Westchester Classic.*

# Youngster reaches for the Stars

Moses Malone found the promised land, August 29, and the Utah Stars found a 6-foot-11 body for the middle of their lineup. In a landmark signing, the American Basketball Association Stars gave a seven-year contract with a potential value of $3 million to a 19-year-old just out of high school.

When the Stars drafted the Petersburg, Va., youngster, everybody thought it was a publicity stunt. But James A. Collier, Utah owner, was dead serious and proved it by making Malone the first basketball player ever to go straight from high school to the pro ranks.

Malone, acclaimed as the country's top high school player last year, was offered scholarships by more than 300 colleges. He signed a letter-of-intent with the University of Maryland, but his college plans were washed away by the Utah offer.

Malone reportedly will make between $150,000 and $200,000 per year in base salary.

# 1974

## Brock runs to record

St. Louis Cardinals outfielder Lou Brock ran into baseball's record books on September 10 when he stole two bases against the Philadelphia Phillies and broke the one-season mark set by Maury Wills 12 years ago.

The 35-year-old Brock singled in the first inning off Dick Ruthven and immediately swiped second base for his record-tying 104th steal. When he singled again in the seventh, the crowd of 27,285 at St. Louis' Busch Stadium began buzzing with anticipation.

They didn't have to wait long. After one pitch and two pickoff attempts, he took off again and catcher Bob Boone's throw was late. Steal No. 105 was greeted by confetti, streamers, firecrackers and a thundering ovation as players from both teams crowded around second base.

*Single-season base-stealing champion Lou Brock (left) with Hall of Famer Cool Papa Bell.*

Brock, whose previous one-season high was 74 in 1966, was honored with an 11-minute ceremony. The two steals also made him the top National League career base-stealer of all time with 740, two more than Max Carey's former mark.

### ★ SPORTS WATCH ★

**SEP:** Detroit veteran Al Kaline joined the 3,000-hit club when he stroked a double off Baltimore's Dave McNally in a 5-4 Tiger victory.

**SEP:** California's Nolan Ryan fired his third career no-hitter and struck out 15 batters in a 4-0 Angels' victory.

**SEP:** Jimmy Connors beat Ken Rosewall in straight sets to capture his first U.S. Open at Forest Hills, N.Y.

**NOV:** Los Angeles ironman Mike Marshall, who appeared in a major league record 106 games, became the first relief pitcher to win a Cy Young Award.

**NOV:** Baseball Commissioner Bowie Kuhn suspended New York Yankees Owner George Steinbrenner for two years because of his conviction for illegal political campaign contributions.

**DEC:** The first World Bowl: Birmingham beat the Florida Blazers, 22-21, for the championship of the WFL.

## Ali outlasts Foreman

Using one of the most bizarre strategies ever concocted, Muhammad Ali stayed against the ropes for seven rounds, October 29, and let George Foreman punch him at will before knocking out his arm-weary opponent in the eighth round and recapturing the heavyweight boxing crown that had been stripped from him more than seven years earlier.

The 32-year-old Ali, fighting before 60,000 in Kinshasa, Zaire, lived up to his prediction that Foreman would fall from exhaustion by the end of the 10th round. He disdained his butterfly tactics for his "rope-a-dope," a strategy in which he remained against the ropes, allowing Foreman to flail away.

The champion, who had won his three previous title bouts in a total of 11:35, could not deliver the big blow. In fact, he never even appeared to hurt Ali. When Foreman began stumbling in the eighth round, obviously exhausted, Ali jumped in with a big left-right combination that sent him spinning to the canvas.

The victory made Ali only the second fighter to win a heavyweight title for the second time.

### « SPORTS TALK »

*"I didn't dance. I wanted to make him lose his power. He punches like a sissy."*
**MUHAMMAD ALI**
after dethroning George Foreman

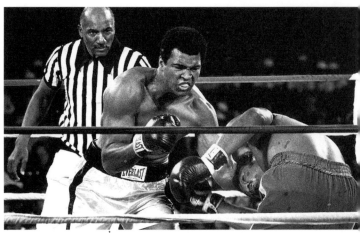

*Muhammad Ali delivers a left as George Foreman ducks away during their heavyweight championship fight in Kinshasa, Zaire.*

## Rudi homer lifts A's

The feuding and fighting Oakland A's rode a seventh-inning Game 5 home run by Joe Rudi to a 3-2 victory over Los Angeles and their third consecutive World Series championship, October 17, at Oakland.

With the score tied 2-2 and reliever Mike Marshall pitching for the Dodgers, the game was delayed 15 minutes when fan debris had to be cleaned off the field. Marshall served up Rudi's Series-winning homer on his first pitch after the game resumed.

The victory ended an A's season that included players bickering with Owner Charlie Finley and Manager Alvin Dark while fighting, sometimes physically, among themselves.

Reggie Jackson got the A's off to a fast start against the Dodgers with a second-inning home run in Game 1. The A's won that game 3-2, lost the second 3-2 and then won Games 3 and 5 by the same score. The only deviation from that pattern was a 5-2 win in Game 4.

# Yankees land Catfish

The New York Yankees won the most celebrated bidding war in American sports history, December 31, when they signed former Oakland A's pitching ace Jim (Catfish) Hunter to a five-year contract estimated at $3.75 million.

The 28-year-old righthander, winner of 88 games over the last four seasons and the ace of a staff that triumphed in the last three World Series, had been declared a free agent by arbitrator Peter Seitz, December 13, after Hunter charged A's Owner Charles O. Finley with breach of contract.

The race to sign baseball's top pitcher began in the law offices of Cherry, Cherry and Flythe in Ahoskie, N.C., near Hunter's home town. Numerous team officials paraded into the city and made their lucrative offers to the most attractive free agent in baseball history.

The Yankees landed a Catfish who finished the 1974 season 25-12 and captured the American League Cy Young Award.

*Members of the Yankee delegation introduce free-agent signee Catfish Hunter to the New York media.*

# "Rozelle Rule" illegal

In a sweeping decision that is almost certain to ignite a long succession of appeals and litigation, Federal District Judge William T. Sweigert in San Francisco ruled that the National Football League's contract and player reserve system is illegal.

The decision is a result of the antitrust suit filed more than four years ago by former Minnesota quarterback Joe Kapp. The judge's ruling declared both the so-called Rozelle Rule and the league's draft system "patently unreasonable and illegal" because they allow the NFL to exert excessive control over a player's employment.

The Rozelle Rule was a major issue in the summer strike that shut down NFL training camps. It allows the commissioner's office to decide compensation due when a free agent signs a contract with another league team. Kapp complained that this gives Commissioner Pete Rozelle the power to restrain signings.

The decision means that unless the NFL can get a quick stay of the opinion, a new era of uncompensated and unrestricted free agency is at hand.

# 55 points, 17 minutes

Trailing 24-0 with less than one minute remaining in the first half, Southern California was being embarrassed by Notre Dame in a November 30 game at the Los Angeles Memorial Coliseum. And the 8-1-1 Trojans faced the prospect of mounting a comeback against the No. 1-ranked defensive team in the nation, a team that had allowed only nine touchdowns in a 9-1 campaign.

But tailback Anthony Davis, who had blitzed the Irish in a six-touchdown performance two years earlier, caught a seven-yard pass from Pat Haden just before halftime, igniting an incredible rally.

Davis started the sequence by returning the second-half kickoff 100 yards. He then scored on a six-yard run and a four-yard sprint, adding in a two-point conversion run that gave the Trojans a 27-24 lead. But the story did not end there.

J.K. McKay, son of USC Coach John McKay, caught 18 and 45-yard TD passes from Haden in the third quarter, Shelton Diggs caught a 16-yard fourth-quarter TD strike and

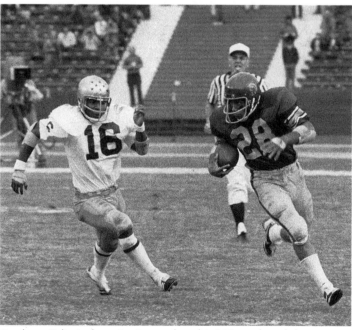
*Southern Cal's Anthony Davis completes his 100-yard touchdown return of the second-half kickoff against Notre Dame.*

Charles Phillips returned an interception 58 yards for a touchdown. Southern Cal 55, Notre Dame 24.

The Trojans had stung the best defensive team in the country for 49 second-half points and 55 in 17 minutes of game action.

# 1975

## Record breaking Miller is carving up PGA tour

Johnny Miller, winner of eight tournaments and a record $353,021 on the 1974 PGA tour, continued to sizzle through the opening weeks of the 1975 campaign, shaving 49 strokes off par and winning the Phoenix Open and Tucson Open by a combined total of 23 strokes.

First he cruised around the Phoenix Country Club course with rounds of 67-61-68-64, completing the 72-hole tournament, January 12, with a 24-under-par 260 that ranked as the second-best four-round total ever compiled. His 14-stroke margin over second-place Jerry Heard was the biggest ever in a PGA-sponsored event.

The following week Miller blistered the 7,200-yard Tucson

*Everything was 'okay' for Johnny Miller after his 25-under-par 263 in the Tucson Open.*

National Golf Club for rounds of 66-69-67-61 to finish 25 under par with a tournament-record 263, nine strokes ahead of John Mahaffey.

Miller's 11-under 61 in the final round bordered on the unbelievable. He birdied five of the first seven holes and recorded an eagle on 11, finishing with sub-par scores on 10 of the 18 holes. And he missed birdie putts inside of 15 feet on the remaining eight. His 61 beat his own Tucson course record of 62, set last year during a similar Arizona sweep.

## Larrieu sets record

Francie Larrieu, America's 22-year-old queen of distance running, added the metric mile (1,500 meters) to her long list of indoor world records, February 14, completing the race in 4:10.4 during the Maple Leaf Indoor Games at Toronto.

Larrieu, who holds world indoor records in the mile, two-mile, 1,000-meters and 3,000-meters, knocked six-tenths of a second off the previous mark while outdistancing second-place Glenda Reiser, Canada's top woman miler. Larrieu's fast pace included clockings of 64.9 seconds for the first quarter-mile and 2:11.7 for a half mile. Her 1,500-meter time was the equivalent of a 4:30 mile.

Larrieu, who trains with the UCLA men's track team, is the only female member of the Pacific Coast Club of Long Beach, Calif.

### ★ SPORTS WATCH ★

**FEB:** Jimmy Connors became the first player to win three consecutive national indoor tennis titles with a 5-7, 7-5, 6-1, 3-6, 6-0 victory over Vitas Gerulaitis at Salisbury, Md.

**FEB:** More than 11,000 spectators turned out to witness a first at Madison Square Garden: Immaculata versus Queens in women's college basketball.

**MAR:** Martina Navratilova, an 18-year-old Czech, defeated Evonne Goolagong, 6-2, 4-6, 6-3, to win the national women's indoor tennis title at Boston.

**APR:** Larry O'Brien was named to succeed Walter Kennedy as the new commissioner of the National Basketball Association.

**APR:** Pole vaulter Steve Smith set a world indoor record when he cleared the bar at 18-foot-4 in a professional meet sponsored by the International Track Association.

**APR:** Jack Nicklaus shot a four-round total of 276 to outdistance Johnny Miller and Tom Weiskopf and win his fifth Masters title at Augusta.

## Steelers win 1st title

The Pittsburgh Steelers ended 42 years of frustration for Owner Art Rooney, January 12, when they put the defensive clamps on the Minnesota Vikings en route to a 16-6 victory in Super Bowl IX at Tulane Stadium in New Orleans.

The Steeler defense, led by linemen Joe Greene and L.C. Greenwood, smothered the Vikings' running game and pressured quarterback Fran Tarkenton into three interceptions. By game's end,

Minnesota had managed only 119 yards, 17 on the ground.

Pittsburgh, 10-3-1 during the regular season, controlled the ball offensively, thanks to the Super Bowl-record 158-yard rushing performance by 230-pound Franco Harris, who scored the Steelers' first touchdown on a nine-yard run in the third quarter.

The Steelers led by an unlikely score of 2-0 at halftime, the points coming courtesy of a Minnesota fumble that Tarken-

ton recovered in his own end zone. After Harris' TD increased the lead to 9-0, Minnesota scored on a blocked punt that Terry Brown recovered in the end zone. A four-yard pass from Terry Bradshaw to tight end Larry Brown closed out the scoring and gave Rooney his long-awaited first championship.

*Pittsburgh Owner Art Rooney, clutching the Super Bowl trophy and a game ball, poses with Commissioner Pete Rozelle after watching his Steelers capture their first NFL championship.*

# Robinson debuts as 1st black manager

Photographers surround Frank Robinson, baseball's first black manager, as he kneels in the on-deck circle during his historic debut.

Frank Robinson, the first black manager in baseball history, got his new career off to a rousing start on April 8, when he guided the Cleveland Indians to a 5-3 opening-day victory over the New York Yankees before a history-witnessing crowd of 56,204 at Cleveland's Municipal Stadium.

Not only did Robinson pull the managerial strings that produced a victory, he also contributed a dramatic home run playing as Cleveland's designated hitter. Robinson's 575th career homer came off Yankee starter Doc Medich with one out in the first inning. It stirred up the big crowd and evoked a celebration in the Indians' dugout.

Robinson had been waiting more than six months for this occasion, after breaking the managerial color barrier last October 3 with the announcement by General Manager Phil Seghi at a news conference. Robinson had been the focus of the media's spotlight throughout spring training as he prepared his young team for battle.

Fittingly, Rachel Robinson, the widow of Jackie Robinson, the man who broke the color barrier as a player in 1947 for the Brooklyn Dodgers, was accorded the honor of throwing out the first pitch.

---

# Wooden era ends with 10th NCAA title

The UCLA Bruins won one for the Wizard, March 31, defeating Kentucky, 92-85, at the San Diego Sports Arena and giving retiring Coach John Wooden his 10th NCAA Tournament championship.

The architect of the greatest dynasty in college basketball history had announced his intentions to his players after their dramatic 75-74 semifinal conquest of Louisville in overtime. The decision reportedly was health related.

Thus inspired, the Bruins set their sights on another title. Kentucky is a strong, physical inside team, and this UCLA squad, not one of Wooden's most talented, relies more on finesse and execution.

With Richard Washington and Dave Meyers doing most of the scoring, the Bruins jumped to a 43-40 halftime lead and pushed it to 10 points midway through the second half. But the Wildcats closed to 76-75. The turning point came when Meyers was called for a technical after fouling Kentucky's Kevin Grevey. The Wildcat star missed two free throws, Kentucky turned the ball over and the Bruins raced to their 10th NCAA victory in 12 years.

The win brought Wooden's 27-year record to 620-147, an .808 winning percentage.

---

# Connors takes big-money match

Jimmy Connors, solidifying his position as the world's top male player and, possibly, its richest, defeated Australian John Newcombe, 6-3, 4-6, 6-2, 6-4, April 26, in a million-dollar match staged by Caesar's Palace in Las Vegas.

Connors, who had defeated Australian Rod Laver in a similar battle 12 weeks ago, collected $500,000 and brought his four-year tennis earnings to well over $1 million. The 22-year-old had picked up $150,000 for his four-set victory over Laver.

The match against Newcombe was surprisingly undramatic, failing to produce the crowd excitement or inspired play of the Connors-Laver battle. Newcombe's serve was unreliable and the 30-year-old three-time Wimbledon champ could not seem to win key points. He worked his way to 11 break points in the first two sets, but was successful only once.

Connors took control of the match in the third set when he ran off 10 consecutive points.

Jimmy Connors en route to a $500,000 victory over John Newcombe.

**"SPORTS TALK"**

*"Connors is like Henry Aaron. If you keep giving him the same thing, he'll hit it out of the park."*
**JOHN NEWCOMBE**
Australian tennis star on Jimmy Connors

# 1975

## MAY - AUGUST

# Flyers bully Buffalo, drink from Cup again

Third-period goals by Bob Kelly and Bill Clement and the sturdy goaltending of Bernie Parent gave the Philadelphia Flyers a 2-0 victory over Buffalo, May 27, and a second consecutive Stanley Cup championship.

The Game 6 victory at Buffalo removed all doubt about the talent level of the "Broad Street Bullies." After their six-game victory over Boston last year, critics said the Flyers had triumphed through a combination of luck and intimidation.

The Flyers certainly rank among the most physical—and most penalized—teams in hockey history. With such intimidators as Kelly, Dave Schultz and Don Saleski patrolling the ice, there's never a dull moment. And in a violent year marked by the much-publicized stick attack of Boston's Dave Forbes on Minnesota's Henry Boucha, it seems only fitting that this team should win.

Philadelphia's game is based on defense. Parent did not allow more than one goal in any of the Flyers' four victories.

*Philadelphia goalie Bernie Parent and teammate Bobby Clarke (16) show off the Stanley Cup after skating to a 2-0 Game 6 victory over Buffalo.*

*Jockey Jacinto Vasquez storms to victory aboard Foolish Pleasure in the 101st running of the Kentucky Derby.*

# Confused? Derby won by Foolish Pleasure

What was the name of that horse? That's the question asked by many of the 113,324 race enthusiasts at Louisville's Churchill Downs and millions of viewers on ABC-TV after the 101st running of the May 3 Kentucky Derby.

That horse was Foolish Pleasure, the race favorite who made a nice stretch run with Jacinto Vasquez in saddle to overtake Avatar and win by 1¾ lengths. But track announcer Chick Anderson called the leader all the way to the finish line as Prince Thou Art before suddenly discovering his mistake. The Churchill Downs crowd and a national television audience listened in amazement as Anderson said, ". . . at the wire, Prince Thou . . . now Foolish Pleasure." Prince Thou Art finished well back in the 15-horse pack.

Foolish Pleasure, the son of What a Pleasure and Fool Me Not, stayed at the middle of the pack early and moved up to fourth by the final turn. In the stretch run of the 1¼-mile event, John Greer's colt shot past Diablo and Avatar and claimed his 11th victory in 12 career races.

# Milwaukee trades Kareem to Lakers

In a deal that is sure to change the balance of power in the National Basketball Association, the Milwaukee Bucks traded talented 7-foot-1 center Kareem Abdul-Jabbar to the Los Angeles Lakers, June 16.

Abdul-Jabbar was dealt along with backup center Walt Wesley for center Elmore Smith, guard Brian Winters and two prime draft picks—UCLA's Dave Meyers and Louisville's Junior Bridgeman.

The 28-year-old Abdul-Jabbar immediately returns the Lakers to contender status after a disastrous 1974-75 season that saw them tumble to last place in the Pacific Division (30-52) and miss the playoffs for the first time since moving from Minneapolis to Los Angeles.

The Bucks, knowing they would lose their unhappy superstar to free agency in two years, agreed to his trade request. It came down to New York, Abdul-Jabbar's hometown, or Los Angeles, his college home (UCLA).

Abdul-Jabbar transformed the Bucks when he arrived six years ago and he led them to an NBA championship in 1970-71. But the Bucks fell on hard times last season (38-44) when their big man missed 17 games because of an injury.

# Ruffian destroyed

Ruffian, an outstanding filly unbeaten in 10 races, was destroyed by injection, July 7, eight hours after she had pulled up with a broken leg during a $350,000 match race against Kentucky Derby winner Foolish Pleasure at Belmont Park.

The Kentucky-bred 3-year-old, a 2-5 race favorite, had a slight lead after 3½ furlongs of the 1¼-mile race when she pulled up lame. As jockey Jacinto Vasquez guided her to the side of the track, Braulio Baeza guided Foolish Pleasure to victory and $225,000 for Owner John Greer.

Ruffian was taken to the equine hospital across the street, where a team of doctors operated on the sesamoids in her right ankle for 3½ hours. The ankle was fitted with a cast and a special shoe to keep it from slipping. But when Ruffian awoke from the anesthesia, she fought hard, pulling out all the nails in the shoe. Owner

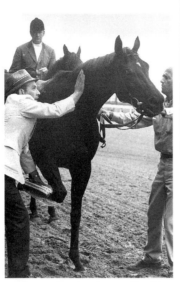

*Ruffian is fitted with an inflatable splint minutes after breaking her leg during a Belmont Park match race against Foolish Pleasure.*

Stuart Janney had no choice but to have her put to sleep.

Ruffian, daughter of Reviewer and Shenanigans, had run mostly stakes races in her career. She was buried on the infield of Belmont Park.

# American racer dies

Mark Donohue, a winner of 57 major titles and more than $1 million of prize money in an outstanding auto racing career, died, August 19, as a result of brain injuries suffered two days earlier during a practice run before the Austrian Grand Prix near Graz, Austria.

The 38-year-old former Indianapolis 500 winner (1972) was driving his Formula One racer 160 mph when a tire blew out. As the car rocketed through four wire fences and several roadside billboards, Donohue was hit on the head by flying debris. It was first believed he had suffered a concussion, but later tests revealed a blood clot on the brain and he never regained consciousness after a three-hour operation.

Ironically, Donohue came out of an eight-month retirement last year to drive for longtime boss Roger Penske after Peter Revson was killed in a practice run before the South African Grand Prix. He had retired in 1973 with a Can-Am championship, three Trans-Am titles and victories in numerous stock car races.

## ★ SPORTS WATCH ★

**JUN:** Brazilian soccer great Pele signed a three-year, $7 million contract to play for the New York Cosmos of the NASL.

**JUN:** California's Nolan Ryan tied the record set by former Dodger Sandy Koufax when he pitched his fourth career no-hitter, stopping Baltimore, 1-0.

**JUN:** Lou Graham fired a playoff-round 71 and defeated John Mahaffey by two strokes in the U.S. Open at Medinah Country Club in Medinah, Ill.

**JUL:** Sandra Palmer defeated amateur Nancy Lopez by four strokes and won her first U.S. Women's Open golf title at Northfield, N.J.

**AUG:** New Zealand's John Walker became the first runner to break the 3:50 mile barrier, clocking 3:49.4 in a meet at Goteborg, Sweden.

# Ashe slows Connors

*Arthur Ashe, celebrating his slow-but-sure Wimbledon victory over Jimmy Connors.*

Veteran Arthur Ashe derailed the Jimmy Connors express, July 5, when he confounded the 22-year-old basher with a steady diet of junk and became the first black male ever to win a Wimbledon singles championship.

Ashe's 6-1, 6-1, 5-7, 6-4 victory stunned the packed Centre Court crowd. The lefthander had appeared almost unbeatable for more than a year, winning the 1974 Wimbledon and U.S. Open titles, capturing his record third straight national indoor title and dominating both Rod Laver and John Newcombe in big-money matches in Las Vegas.

But Ashe found the winning formula—a slowdown game. The 31-year-old former U.S. Open champ chipped and dinked, lobbed and dropped while serving consistently and working to Connors' backhand. Connors won the first game of the match, but Ashe ran off nine consecutive points to take control.

Ashe joins Althea Gibson (1957 and '58) and Evonne Goolagong (1971), an Australian aborigine, as the only black winners of the world's most prestigious tennis event.

# 1975

## Reds outlast Boston in spellbinding Series

Joe Morgan looped a ninth-inning single to center field off Boston reliever Jim Burton, October 22, scoring Ken Griffey and giving the Cincinnati Reds a 4-3 victory in Game 7 of one of the most exciting World Series ever staged.

Morgan's hit at Boston's Fenway Park completed the Reds' comeback from a 3-0 final-game deficit and punctuated one of the most spellbinding scripts ever written.

Even this exciting conclusion paled in comparison to the events of Game 6, however. With the Reds leading the Series three games to two, the Red Sox rallied to win an unforgettable contest.

Everything was normal enough through 7½ innings as the Reds built a 6-3 lead and moved within six outs of a World Series victory. But the fireworks started in the eighth when pinch-hitter Bernie Carbo tied the game with a clutch three-run homer.

Boston nearly won it in the ninth, but the Reds escaped a bases-loaded, nobody-out jam and sent the game into extra innings. The Red Sox did some escaping of their own in the 11th when right fielder Dwight Evans made a leaping, one-handed grab to rob Morgan of a home run.

After Boston reliever Rick Wise escaped a two-on, one-out situation in the top of the 12th, Red Sox catcher Carlton Fisk brought the game to a dramatic conclusion with a towering drive off the left-field foul pole.

The buildup to that game had been exciting enough. Luis Tiant shut out the Reds in the opener, 6-0, Cincinnati answered in Game 2 with a two-run ninth-inning rally that produced a 3-2 victory and the Reds took the Series lead by winning Game 3 in the 10th inning, 6-5, with the help of a controversial umpire's call.

*It's a happy World Series homecoming for Boston catcher Carlton Fisk, who belted a dramatic 12th-inning Game 6 home run to keep the Red Sox's hopes alive against Cincinnati.*

The Series was delayed 72 hours by a drenching New England rain after the teams had split the fourth and fifth games in Cincinnati, but the wait proved worthwhile.

## Ali overcomes Frazier in "Thrilla in Manila"

Muhammad Ali retained his heavyweight boxing championship, October 1, when old rival Joe Frazier failed to answer the bell for the 15th round of a brutal confrontation in the Philippines.

The "Thrilla in Manila," witnessed by 25,000 fans and Philippine President Ferdinand Marcos, came to a sudden halt when Eddie Futch, Frazier's Manager, threw in the towel. Frazier had been battered by the 33-year-old Ali through the previous three rounds and his right eye was swollen shut. He also was exhausted and any continuation would have put him at serious risk.

It's unlikely that Frazier's early retirement made any difference. Ali was well ahead on points and in full control.

Disdaining his normal dancing style and refraining from the clowning that had marked his career, Ali slugged it out with Frazier and dominated the early rounds. But the 31-year-old challenger, relentless as ever, came back to take control in the middle rounds before tiring. Ali, getting his second wind, took over again in the 12th and finished the fight with his usual flourish.

The victory was Ali's second in three fights with Frazier.

*Muhammad Ali bends down Joe Frazier with a strong left hook while defending his heavyweight championship during the 'Thrilla in Manila.'*

**SEP:** Chris Evert's first U.S. Open victory came at the expense of Evonne Goolagong-Cawley, 5-7, 6-4, 6-2, at Forest Hills.

**OCT:** Unable to sustain itself without a television contract or season-ticket support, the World Football League folded 11 weeks into its second season.

**OCT:** Casey Stengel, one of the most colorful figures in baseball history, died of cancer at age 85 in Glendale, Calif.

**OCT:** Texas A&M kicker Tony Franklin booted a pair of record-setting field goals—64- and 65-yarders—in a game against Baylor.

**NOV:** The expansion Seattle Seahawks and Tampa Bay Bucs were aligned in the NFC West and AFC West Divisions, respectively, for 1976.

**NOV:** Boston's Fred Lynn, .331 batting average, 21 homers and 105 RBIs, became the first rookie to win an MVP award.

# Griffin honored again

Archie Griffin, the little big man of Ohio State's undefeated and top-ranked football team, made history, December 2, when he became the first man to win the Downtown Athletic Club's coveted Heisman Trophy two times.

The 5-foot-8, 184-pound tailback, who has helped carry the Buckeyes to a 40-5-1 record, four Big Ten championships and four Rose Bowl appearances in his four college seasons, outpolled California back Chuck Muncie 1,800-730 in voting by 888 sportswriters and broadcasters.

Griffin finished his career with an NCAA-record 5,176 yards and a record 33 100-yard games, 31 of these coming consecutively.

The talented youngster last year became the fifth junior to win the award, joining Army's Doc Blanchard, SMU's Doak Walker, Ohio State's Vic Janowicz and Navy's Roger Staubach.

*Ohio State's Archie Griffin, the first two-time winner of college football's coveted Heisman Trophy.*

# Staubach playoff prayer is answered

Dallas quarterback Roger Staubach's prayer was answered, December 28, and the Cowboys escaped with an unlikely 17-14 National Football Conference divisional playoff victory over Minnesota at Metropolitan Stadium in Bloomington, Minn.

"I guess it's a 'Hail Mary' pass," Staubach said with a smile after connecting with Drew Pearson on 50-yard touchdown play in the final minute. "You throw it up and pray he catches it."

The Vikings appeared to be in control after Brent McClanahan's one-yard TD run had given them a 14-10 advantage with 5:24 to play in the fourth quarter. Their famed Purple People Eaters defense had given the Cowboys fits all day and Dallas' last thrust, from its own 25-yard line, was on the verge of dying.

*Dallas receiver Drew Pearson (88) answered Roger Staubach's prayer and scored the winning touchdown in a playoff victory over Minnesota.*

But Staubach completed a 25-yard pass to Pearson on a fourth-and-16 play. Then, after an incompletion, he threw it up and prayed for Pearson to somehow pull it down.

The pass was underthrown and Pearson had to come back for it. He snatched it away from defenders Nate Wright and Terry Brown and rolled into the end zone with 24 seconds left. The Cowboys were alive to play another day.

# Ruling rocks baseball

In a ruling that could topple major league baseball's reserve system, labor arbitrator Peter Seitz handed pitchers Andy Messersmith and Dave McNally their unqualified free agency, December 23.

The landmark decision puts owners in a precarious position in their never-ending battle to preserve the status quo. Twice in the last half-century they have received favorable rulings from the Supreme Court on the system that binds an athlete to his team until he is traded or retires. But more players are testing the question and Seitz's ruling is a clear-cut victory for the Major League Players' Association.

Management has two options. It can either go to court and challenge Seitz's decision, or it can modify the system through collective bargaining. Ironically, the current Basic Agreement expires December 31.

The 31-year-old Messersmith, a two-time 20-game winner during his eight-year career with California and Los Angeles, should prosper tremendously. He instigated the decision by filing a suit claiming that he had completed his option year with the Dodgers and should be a free agent.

McNally, a 33-year-old former Baltimore star, retired last year midway through his first season with Montreal.

# 1976

## JANUARY - APRIL

# Flyers mug Russians

The Philadelphia Flyers, setting back detente 10 years with what Russian Coach Konstantin Loktev called an exhibition of "animal hockey," bullied their way to a 4-1 victory over the Soviet Central Army team, January 11, in an international matchup that almost ended in forfeit.

The stylish Soviets, one of two Russian teams making an eight-game tour of NHL cities, were visibly upset with the Flyers' intimidating tactics early in the contest at the Philadelphia Spectrum. The situation grew ugly when defenseman Ed Van Impe belted Valery Kharlamov, the Soviets' top player, with a vicious hit from behind midway through the opening stanza. When no penalty was signaled, Loktev called his goalie off the ice.

The referee handed the Russians a delay of game penalty and Loktev sent his team to the dressing room. But after a conference between NHL officials and members of the Soviet delegation, Loktev was overruled and his team returned to the ice—16 minutes after he had ordered its walkoff.

It took only 17 seconds for Reggie Leach to score on a power play and the Flyers went on to an easy victory.

*A referee tries to help fallen Soviet star Valery Kharlamov after a vicious hit from Philadelphia defenseman Ed Van Impe.*

# Steel Curtain drops

Terry Bradshaw threw a pair of touchdown passes, Roy Gerela kicked two field goals and Pittsburgh's "Steel Curtain" defense shut down miracle worker Roger Staubach in the final minute as the Steelers carved out a 21-17 victory over Dallas, January 18, in Super Bowl X at Miami's Orange Bowl.

Pittsburgh's second straight victory was sealed by 14 fourth-quarter points—a blocked-punt safety, Gerela's field goals and a 64-yard TD bomb from Bradshaw to Lynn Swann. But the Cowboys answered with a 34-yard Staubach-to-Percy Howard touchdown pass with just under two minutes remaining.

Dallas held defensively and Staubach came in for one last shot at victory. The former Navy star had beaten Minnesota in a divisional playoff game with a 50-yard "Hail Mary" pass and then had thrown four TD passes in a 37-7 upset of the Los Angeles Rams in the NFC championship game. But it was not to be this time as safety Glen Edwards intercepted and dashed the Cowboys' hopes.

# Pearson chugs to win

As five-time Daytona 500 winner Richard Petty watched helplessly in his stalled Dodge less than 50 yards from the finish line, long-time rival David Pearson's battered Mercury chugged to victory, February 15, in a bizarre conclusion to stock car racing's most prestigious event.

Petty and Pearson, the top two career winners on the Grand National circuit, had waged an intense battle through most of the first 499 miles and they made the final turn side by side, Petty holding a slight advantage. With about a quarter of a mile to go, however, Petty's Dodge slid into Pearson's Mercury and sent it spinning into a concrete wall at 180 mph.

As 130,000 fans at the Daytona International Speedway watched in horror, the Mercury bounced off the wall and collided again with the Dodge, which went spinning along the wall. Petty's car finally slid down the high bank and came to rest on the infield, not far from the Mercury.

Both drivers frantically tried to get their cars running and Pearson finally succeeded. He made it onto the apron and crossed the finish line at 20 mph for his first Daytona 500 victory.

*David Pearson's Mercury (top right) sits on the infield as Richard Petty's Dodge spins off the track after a final-lap accident in the Daytona 500.*

# "Perfect" Hoosiers overcome Michigan

Scott May, Kent Benson and Quinn Buckner combined to score 36 of 38 points in a second-half burst and the almost-mechanical Indiana Hoosiers defeated Big Ten Conference rival Michigan, 86-68, in the March 29 NCAA Tournament final at the Spectrum in Philadelphia.

In becoming the seventh team to make it through the NCAA finals undefeated (32-0), the Hoosiers were relentless practitioners of Coach Bob Knight's team-first work ethic. They usually operated at a level just short of perfection and they needed "perfect" in the second half against Michigan, a team they had beaten twice during the regular season.

Led by speedy guard Rickey Green, the Wolverines had sprinted to a 35-29 halftime lead. But the Hoosiers came out and quickly nullified Green— by scoring every time they touched the ball. During a 14-minute stretch that began less than three minutes into the second half, Indiana went from four points down (37-33) to 14 points up (73-59) and was never threatened again.

May finished with 26 points and Benson, a 6-foot-11 inside force, added 25.

*Happy Hoosiers (left to right) Coach Bob Knight, Scott May and Quinn Buckner after Indiana's NCAA final victory over Michigan.*

# Floyd wins Masters

Ray Floyd, a six-time winner in 13 years on the PGA tour, carved up the demanding Augusta National Golf Club course for four days with a record-tying 271 and recorded an impressive eight-stroke victory in the Masters.

Floyd's final-round 70 on April 11 finished off a 65-66-70-70 blitz that destroyed the field and tied Jack Nicklaus' 1965 Masters record. He was one of only two golfers to play the fourth round under par on a windy Augusta day. The other was Ben Crenshaw, who checked in with a 67 and grabbed second-place money.

Floyd, only the fifth golfer to lead the Masters from beginning to end, was never challenged after grabbing a five-stroke second-round lead over Nicklaus. It was like the

*Easy Masters winner Ray Floyd.*

Miami pro was playing in one tournament and the rest of the field in another. He was cool and confident, especially when playing Augusta's par-5s.

He recorded one eagle, 12 birdies and three pars on those holes to account for 14 of the 17 strokes he finished under par.

# Pitcher accepts lifetime contract

Andy Messersmith, the talented righthander who became a free agent in December last year on arbitrator Peter Seitz's historic decision, signed a "lifetime contract" with Atlanta Braves Owner Ted Turner, April 10, in San Diego.

Although the principals would not release figures, the contract is believed to be in the $1.75 million range for three years, with renewal clauses to be exercised as long as the 31-year-old Messersmith can pitch. "He'll never be traded. He'll be a Brave as long as I am," Turner promised.

That statement was ironic. Messersmith filed suit last year because his option had run out with the Los Angeles Dodgers and he did not think it was right that he should be bound to one team forever. The ruling that supported his free-agency contention has been upheld twice in the courtroom.

Messersmith, a two-time 20-game winner who won 19 last year for the Dodgers, was in San Diego to talk to the Padres. Turner and the Braves were in town for a three-game series.

# football

## The phenomenon of the Super Bowl

*The ultimate sporting extravaganza — a party, a ritual, a mission, a religious experience*

**W**ith his simple words, "The Jets will win on Sunday, I guarantee it," brash, irreverent and cocky New York quarterback Joe Namath stunned the staid, conservative rulers of professional football. The boast was unprecedented, its logic baffling considering that the American Football League's Jets were 18- to 23-point underdogs to the National Football League's powerful Baltimore Colts in the days leading up to Super Bowl III.

### "The Jets will win on Sunday, I guarantee it."

**JOE NAMATH**
*New York quarterback before Super Bowl III*

But the flamboyant Namath did not stop there. In interviews conducted poolside with a pretty blonde at his side or at one of his favorite nightspots, Namath named five AFL quarterbacks he thought were better than Baltimore's Earl Morrall and he baited the Colts at every opportunity. He strutted around Miami and Fort Lauderdale like a colorful peacock in his hip, eye-catching

clothes and then pranced around the football field in his low-cut white cleats while delivering on his promise—a 16-7 Jets' victory.

That win gave the AFL its first satisfying dose of credibility and Namath gave the fledgling league a personality. More importantly in the long run, Broadway Joe brought a star quality to the Super Bowl and almost single-handedly turned it into a media-crazed event, a spectacular, a happening that would grow beyond *everyone's* wildest dreams.

The Super Bowl was but a sketchy fantasy of AFL founder Lamar Hunt when his Dallas Texans began play in the new league in 1960. It was a difficult season in which AFL teams bathed in deep rivers of scorn, ridicule and red ink. But an early television contract with ABC-TV kept the league afloat and a $36 million, five-year 1964 pact with NBC guaranteed the AFL perseverance beyond the staying power of previous rival circuits.

It also led to a 1966 merger agreement under which all nine AFL teams would be absorbed into the National Football League. This agreement could

*Green Bay Coach Vince Lombardi in 1967, after his Packers had won the first Super Bowl.*

*New York Jets quarterback Joe Namath before Super Bowl III.*

not be fully implemented until 1970, after the leagues' multi-million dollar television contracts with CBS and NBC expired, but several facets of it would take effect immediately. There would be a common draft in 1967—and a "world championship" game to follow the '66 campaign. After six years of vying for players, fans, television contracts and newspaper headlines, the fighting would be done where it really counted—on the field.

That first title playoff

between the winners of the two leagues was a semi-Super Bowl, a curiosity piece for football fans. Officially designated as "The AFL-NFL World Championship Game," the alternative title of "Super Bowl" (a product of Hunt's imagination) was offered but not pushed too hard because nobody knew just how super it was going to be.

As everyone expected, the powerful Green Bay Packers were too much for the Kansas City Chiefs and carried the NFL banner high while rolling to a lopsided 35-10 victory at the Los Angeles Coliseum. The game aroused a lot of curiosity, but very little emotional involvement. Only 61,946 fans, less than two-thirds capacity at the Coliseum, turned out for the contest, and 60 million-plus watched on CBS or NBC, which broadcast simultaneously.

There was plenty of pre-game hoopla, but most of it took place on the field in the form of bands, baton twirlers, choral groups, musicians and thousands of fluffy white pigeons that were released from the arena floor.

Super Bowl II was more of the same and Vince Lombardi, who viewed every football game as a life and death struggle, directed his Packers to another easy victory—a 33-14 triumph over the Oakland Raiders. That set the stage for Namath in Super Bowl III and curiosity turned to passion.

What has happened since almost defies explanation. The Super Bowl has turned into a media monster, created and programmed in the laboratories of former NFL

Commissioner Pete Rozelle and hungry television executives. It has become a ritual, a mission, a party, a time out from life, a religious experience. Everything stops on Super Sunday and both fans and semi-fans spend a glorious few hours in football heaven.

Advertisers who spent from $75,000 to $85,000 for a one-minute commercial spot during the first Super Bowl were willing to dish out $800,000 for a 30-second spot in 1991. There were 110 million viewers in 1983, but the 1991 silver anniversary contest played to a television crowd of 750 million *worldwide*. The game has been watched from outer space and by soldiers fighting a foreign war. It has become a "Where were you during Super Bowl . . . ?" point of reference.

There has traditionally been a two-week gap between the conference championship games and the Super Bowl, a gearing-up period filled with celebration and hype. For the fans, the host city offers parties, parades, more parties, shows and even more parties. For the players and coaches, there are interviews, practices, more interviews, strategy sessions and even more interviews. Every inch of the city is dissected by hungry fans, always wearing their respective

*A "Super" ride for Oakland Coach John Madden after Super Bowl XI.*

team colors and always looking for a good time. Every inch of the teams' playbooks and every player strength and weakness is dissected by the hungry media.

The game itself almost has become an afterthought. Even once it does get underway, the television cameras scan for celebrities, well-choreographed halftime shows go on and on, and the game's Most Valuable Player announces that he's going to Disney World. Many of the games have resulted in disappointing blowouts, but the Super Bowl has also produced

golden memories:

Like Baltimore's Jim O'Brien jumping up and down after kicking the game-winning field goal against Dallas in Super Bowl V, and the Cowboys' Jackie Smith rolling around the end zone in frustration after dropping a Roger Staubach touchdown pass against Pittsburgh in Super Bowl XIII.

Like quarterbacks Jim Plunkett of Oakland and Doug Williams of Washington gaining vindication and relighting the fires of their

fading careers, and Minnesota's Fran Tarkenton, Denver's John Elway and Miami's Dan Marino losing the starry luster of theirs.

Like the Steelers and 49ers, four-time Super Bowl winners, and the Vikings and Broncos, four-time losers. Like the beautiful spirals of Pittsburgh's Terry Bradshaw and San Francisco's Joe Montana, and the end-over-end desperation of Miami kicker Garo Yepremian.

Like the grace and artistry of Pittsburgh's Lynn Swann, Los Angeles' Marcus Allen and Dallas' Tony Dorsett, and the raw power of Washington's John Riggins and Miami's Larry Csonka. Like the animated coaching of Kansas City's Hank Stram and Oakland's John Madden, and the stone-faced silence of Minnesota's Bud Grant and the Cowboys' Tom Landry.

The Super Bowl is all this and more . . . and more. The Super Bowl is excess. It is gaudy. It is overkill. The Super Bowl is a marching band on your front sidewalk, an elephant stampede through your living room. Yet it has that special something that makes you come back for more . . . and more.

It is, simply, the greatest sports show on earth.

*Dallas' Jackie Smith's frustration (left) after dropping a TD pass in Super Bowl XIII. Washington bruiser John Riggins (right) in XVII.*

# 1976

## MAY · AUGUST

# ABA accepts merger

American Basketball Association owners, unwilling to throw in the towel through nine costly seasons, finally admitted defeat, June 17, and accepted merger terms of the rival National Basketball Association.

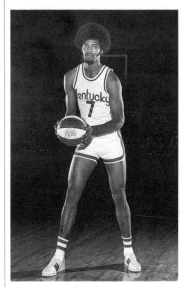

*Kentucky Colonels center Artis Gilmore, one of the ABA's brightest stars.*

Under the agreement, four of the six existing ABA franchises will be absorbed into the NBA, bringing its membership to 22. The New York Nets, Indiana Pacers, Denver Nuggets and San Antonio Spurs all will pay $3.2 million up front to the NBA for the right to begin competition in the 1976-77 season. The Kentucky Colonels and St. Louis Spirits will fold.

Kentucky and St. Louis players will be dispersed in a special draft open to all 22 teams. The Chicago Bulls, getting the first selection because of their league-worst 24-58 record last year, are expected to grab 7-foot-2 Colonels center Artis Gilmore.

The ABA, which opened as an 11-team league in 1967-68, started the 1975-76 campaign with 10 members. But the Baltimore Claws, San Diego Sails, Utah Stars and Virginia Squires all folded in fast succession,

★ SPORTS WATCH ★

**MAY:** The Montreal Canadiens ended the two-year reign of Philadelphia's Broad Street Bullies with a four-game sweep of the Flyers in the Stanley Cup final series.

**JUN:** Bobby Orr, probably the greatest defenseman ever to play hockey, left the Boston Bruins for a free-agent contract with the Chicago Black Hawks.

**JUL:** Milwaukee's Hank Aaron belted the 755th—and last—home run of his major league career off California righthander Dick Drago.

**JUL:** Johnny Miller's 279 over the Royal Birkdale course in England was good enough to hold off Jack Nicklaus and Seve Ballesteros in the British Open.

**AUG:** Dave Stockton won his second PGA Championship, holding off Ray Floyd and Don January at the Congressional Country Club in Bethesda, Md.

leaving the final count at six. Many observers doubted the circuit could have survived another season.

Throughout its colorful existence, the ABA battled courageously. There were unstable ownerships, bad debts, transient franchises, never-ending litigation (including the unsuccessful merger bid by the same parties in 1970) and a failure to land a national television contract. But there also were innovations and some excellent players.

The most exciting were Julius Erving, George McGinnis, Gilmore, Moses Malone, David Thompson, Spencer Haywood, Connie Hawkins, Rick Barry, Billy Cunningham and George Gervin. They played with a funny colored ball, a 30-second clock and a three-point shooting line.

Indiana captured three ABA championships, the Nets two (including the finale) and Kentucky, Utah, Pittsburgh and Oakland one apiece.

# Celtics dim Sunshine

The Boston Celtics officially wrapped up their 13th National Basketball Association championship in 20 years on June 6 when they defeated Phoenix, 87-80, in a slow-paced sixth game at the Suns' Memorial Coliseum. But the series actually was decided two days earlier in a dramatic triple-overtime thriller at Boston Garden.

The Celtics prevailed in that heart-stopper, 128-126. But that's only part of the story. The Suns refused to be intimidated under difficult circumstances and twice hit desperation shots to tie the contest before finally running out of gas in the third

extra session of the game.

Boston seemed to have the game in hand when John Havlicek hit a running jumper to give the Celtics a 111-110 lead with two seconds left in the second overtime. Fans poured onto the court and the situation became tense for the referees and Phoenix players. But order was finally restored, the fans were pushed to the edges of the court and Boston was given a technical shot because the Suns had called an illegal timeout.

Jo Jo White, Boston's leading scorer with 33 points, hit the free throw and the Suns threw the ball inbounds to Garfield

*John Havlicek, a big gun in the Celtics' NBA Finals victory, was a popular man when the team made its triumphant return to Boston.*

Heard. He sank a long, desperation jumper for another tie.

As the fans, still at close quarters, harrassed the Suns, Boston

jumped to a six-point lead in the third overtime. Phoenix fought back with two late baskets, but the Celtics prevailed.

# Jenner is top U.S. Olympic performer

While the Montreal Summer Olympic Games might not have been the United States' best in terms of medal count, it did provide memorable moments. The Soviet Union had 31 more medals and the East Germans had six more golds, but the U.S. had Bruce Jenner.

The young decathlete had a sound strategy as he began competition: stay within 200 points of Russian Nikolai Avilov and German Guido Kratschmer through the first day, which contained Jenner's weakest events. He was surprised when the first day ended and he was only 35 points behind Kratschmer and 17 behind Avilov.

It was no contest the rest of the way. Jenner piled up points, and when he finished the 1,500-meter run he owned a world record with 8,631.

American boxers unexpectedly laid claim to five gold medals. Michael and Leon Spinks, the first brothers to triumph in the same boxing Olympics, claimed two, Michael in the middleweight division and Leon as a light heavyweight. Other gold winners were stylish light welterweight Sugar Ray Leonard, lightweight Howard Davis and flyweight Leo Randolph.

# Carner captures see-saw playoff

JoAnne Carner took advantage of her superior strength on the final two holes and defeated defending champion Sandra Palmer in a see-saw 18-hole playoff for the U.S. Women's Open at Springfield, Pa.

Carner led her 5-foot-1 opponent by four strokes after 13 holes. But she could not stand prosperity and Palmer fought back to take a one-stroke lead after 16. The closing holes, both par 5s, belonged to the five-time U.S. Amateur champion.

Carner birdied 17 and parred 18 while Palmer struggled to a pair of bogeys. The three-stroke swing (actually, eight strokes were gained or lost over five holes) gave Carner a 76-78 win and her second Open title.

The victory, worth $9,000, raised Carner's 1976 winnings to $64,891—second only to Judy Rankin's record-setting total of $100,614.

Middleweight gold medal winner Michael Spinks salutes the crowd during an awards ceremony at the Montreal Olympic Games.

# Stones is back on top

Dwight Stones sails safely over the bar and into the record book with a 7-foot-7¼ high jump during a meet in Philadelphia.

Dwight Stones, disappointed with his bronze-medal performance in the Olympic Games four days earlier, broke his own world high jump record, August 4, when he soared 7-foot-7¼ in the Bicentennial Meet of Champions at Philadelphia.

Stones, heavily favored for the Olympic gold medal, failed three times to clear 7-foot-3¾ on a wet runway at Montreal's Olympic Stadium. But working on a dry runway, Stones cleared the bar on his first attempt at the record-breaking height.

The crossbar quivered slightly as Stones watched anxiously. When it held, he jumped out of the pit, raised both arms and pointed back at the bar.

"Things didn't happen the way I would have liked in Montreal," Stones admitted. "But as long as the surface is dry, nobody can beat me."

Stones, who cleared a world record 7-foot-7 two months ago, made successful first jumps at 6-foot-10, 7-foot-0, 7-foot-2 and 7-foot-3. It took him two tries to clear 7-foot-4¼.

# 1976

## SEPTEMBER-DECEMBER

## 76ers acquire Dr. J

The New York Nets, evidently in need of money to finance their entry into the National Basketball Association, were forced to sell their most valuable commodity, the high-flying forward Julius Erving, to the Philadelphia 76ers for a reported $3 million on October 21.

Philadelphia Owner F. Eugene Dixon, fast putting together a talented team capable of winning an NBA championship, made the deal with Nets Owner Roy Boe and then signed "Dr. J" to a six-year, $3.5 million contract on the eve of the 76ers' 1976-77 season opener.

Erving, who captured three American Basketball Association scoring titles and led the Nets to two ABA champion-ships, will join a high-salaried nucleus of George McGinnis, Doug Collins, Fred Carter, Caldwell Jones and Darryl Dawkins in Philadelphia. Long lines formed at the Spectrum's ticket windows minutes after the purchase was announced.

Erving averaged 29.3 points last season and 35 through the playoffs. He had refused to report to the Nets' training camp this year because of a dispute over renegotiation of his contract.

## Chambliss kills Royals

*A policeman tries to protect Yankee first baseman Chris Chambliss from a delirious New York crowd after his pennant-winning homer against Kansas City.*

A dramatic ninth-inning home run by Chris Chambliss vaulted the New York Yankees to their first American League pennant since 1964 and touched off one of the wildest mob scenes in the history of American sports.

The October 14 shot off Kansas City relief ace Mark Littell leading off the ninth broke a 6-6 deadlock in the decisive fifth game of the A.L. Championship Series. As the ball cleared the right-field fence, thousands of fans rushed onto the Yankee Stadium field. By the time Chambliss reached first base, he was surrounded by spectators. When he reached second, the bag already had been removed by a souvenir collector. He never reached third, retreating to the New York clubhouse for his own safety.

All players and umpires escaped without injury, but Yankee Stadium sustained $100,000 in damage. It was a wild conclusion to a closely-contested series and final game.

The Yankees appeared to be in control of the finale as they entered the eighth inning with a 6-3 lead. But Royals third baseman George Brett blasted a game-tying three-run homer off reliever Grant Jackson. The score remained at 6-6 until Chambliss stepped to the plate and belted Littell's first pitch.

## Big Red Machine rolls over Phillies, Yankees

Cincinnati's Big Red Machine, finely tuned and operating at peak efficiency, took its place among baseball's greatest teams with an impressive seven-game sprint through the playoffs and World Series.

First the Reds gave the Philadelphia Phillies a lesson in winning baseball during the National League Championship Series. They won the first game, 6-3, prevailed in the second, 6-2, and rallied for three runs in the ninth inning to win Game 3. The Reds tied it on back-to-back George Foster and Johnny Bench home runs and won it on Ken Griffey's single.

The World Series—the New York Yankees' first appearance in a fall classic since 1964—was even easier. With seven regulars hitting over .300 and Bench supplying a pair of homers and six RBIs, Cincinnati rolled to 5-1, 4-3, 6-2 and 7-2 victories. Reds' pitchers compiled a 2.00 earned-run average.

That brought Cincinnati's two-year totals to 210 regular-season victories, a 6-0 NLCS record and World Series wins over Boston and New York.

*Cincinnati's Johnny Bench connects with an Ed Figueroa pitch for a home run in the Reds' machine-like World Series sweep of the New York Yankees.*

# Pitt runs over Lions

Tony Dorsett sped over, around and through Penn State's defense, November 26, capping his record-setting season with 224 yards and a pair of touchdowns in Pittsburgh's 24-7 victory over the Nittany Lions at Three Rivers Stadium.

Dorsett, who finished his outstanding regular-season career as the most prolific rusher and scorer in college football history, helped the Panthers end the regular campaign with an 11-0 record and the No. 1 ranking in both polls. Only a January 1 Sugar Bowl date with Georgia stands between Coach Johnny Majors' team and a national championship.

After Penn State took a 7-0 first-quarter lead, the game became a Tony Dorsett showcase. First he ran six yards for the tying touchdown in the second quarter. Then he burst 40 yards for the game-deciding score in the third quarter en route to a 173-yard second half.

When the dust had cleared, the talented 22-year-old owned records for career rushing (6,082), career scoring (356 points), most seasons getting 1,000 or more yards (4) and most seasons getting 1,500 or more yards (3). He tied former Army great Glenn Davis for career touchdowns (59) and former Ohio State star Archie Griffin for most career games gaining 100 or more yards (33).

Dorsett was named Heisman Trophy winner to November 30.

University of Pittsburgh record-setter Tony Dorsett.

# Baseball holds 1st re-entry draft

Free agency became an accepted part of baseball, November 4, when team owners gathered at New York's Plaza Hotel for the first re-entry draft to determine bargaining rights for 26 players who have played out their option.

The draft, as specified by the new Basic Agreement hammered out by Players' Association executive director Marvin Miller and owners in July in the wake of the 1975 Andy Messersmith free-agency ruling by arbitrator Peter Seitz, allows teams to select those players they wish to bid for.

Teams can pick as many players as they want, but a particular player can only be drafted 12 times. Those players drafted by one team or none at all are free to bargain with any team. Teams that stand to lose a player can retain negotiating

New York Yankee free-agent acquisition Reggie Jackson tries on his new cap.

rights if they choose.

When the draft began, Baltimore second baseman Bobby Grich was the first player chosen. But Oakland catcher Gene Tenace was the first to be taken off the board after a dozen selections. The Chicago White Sox drafted the most players with 18, the Cincinnati Reds refused to take part.

What it all means is that a lot of players are going to get rich quick. Officials from several of the more high-profile teams said they would go after their choices with open pocketbooks.

The Red Sox drew first blood with the November 6 signing of 28-year-old Minnesota reliever

Bill Campbell to a four-year, $1 million contract. The Yankees pulled off one of the draft's biggest plums—30-year-old Baltimore slugger Reggie Jackson. The New Yorkers gave a five-year, $2.9 million contract to the former Oakland and Baltimore right fielder on November 29.

## "SPORTS TALK"

*"It was like trying to hustle a girl in a bar. . .the reason I'm a Yankee is that George Steinbrenner outhustled everybody else."*

**REGGIE JACKSON**

# 1977

## JANUARY·APRIL

## Erving steals show

Julius Erving, the former ABA aerial artist who has sacrificed flair for teamwork through 55 games with the Philadelphia 76ers, opened up his vast offensive arsenal, February 13, and put on a dazzling show during the National Basketball Association All-Star Game at Milwaukee Arena.

Dr. J opened plenty of eyes with a 30-point, 12-rebound effort in 30 minutes. He scored 13 of those points in the fourth quarter when the Eastern Conference stars staged a dramatic rally that fell just short in a 125-124 loss. The game ended when the East's Pete Maravich was stripped of the ball as he drove for what could have been the winning basket.

Win or lose, this game belonged to Erving, the game's MVP. His big moment came on a fast break when he beat Golden State's Rick Barry downcourt, drove the lane and

NBA Commissioner Larry O'Brien presents Philadelphia's Julius Erving with the All-Star Game MVP trophy.

slammed one home over 7-foot-1 Los Angeles center Kareem Abdul-Jabbar, bringing 10,938 amazed fans to their feet.

Erving received plenty of help from New York Knicks forward Bob McAdoo, who also scored 30 points. Abdul-Jabbar led the West with 21.

## Pitt leashes Bulldogs

Pittsburgh completed its perfect season for departing Coach Johnny Majors and running

back Tony Dorsett concluded his near-perfect career as the Panthers ran over Southeastern Conference-champion Georgia, 27-3, in the New Year's Day Sugar Bowl classic at New Orleans.

The Panthers left nothing to the imagination as they rolled up a 21-0 halftime lead while holding the Bulldogs to 25 total yards. In the middle of the action was Dorsett, the NCAA's all-time rushing leader and scorer who ran for a Sugar Bowl-record 202 yards on 32 carries.

Dorsett, a holder of 18 NCAA records, scored his

## Raiders sack Vikings

If at first you don't succeed, try, try again. So reads the philosophy of the Minnesota Vikings, four times a bridesmaid in pro football's biggest game after their 32-14 loss to Oakland, January 9, in Super Bowl XI.

As 103,438 fans looked on in the Rose Bowl at Pasadena, Calif., the Raiders scored 16 second-quarter points and rolled to their first Super Bowl victory. It was the fourth Super Bowl loss in eight years for the Vikings and the third time they had been beaten by a first-time winner.

The key play occurred early. After Minnesota's Fred McNeill had blocked a Ray Guy punt

and recovered on the Oakland 3-yard line, running back Brent McClanahan fumbled and linebacker Willie Hall recovered. Given a reprieve, the Raiders exploded behind the passing of quarterback Ken Stabler, the sure hands of receiver Fred Biletnikoff and the running of Clarence Davis and Mark van Eeghen.

A 24-yard field goal by Errol Mann, a one-yard touchdown reception by Dave Casper and Pete Banaszak's one-yard run in the second quarter gave Oakland all the points it really needed. Coach John Madden's Raiders coasted the rest of the way.

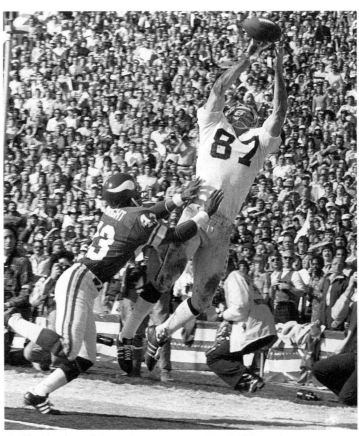

Oakland tight end Dave Casper snags a Ken Stabler end zone pass, setting the Raiders on course for a Super Bowl victory over Minnesota.

team's third TD on an 11-yard run. Pitt quarterback Matt Cavanaugh accounted for the first two, scoring on a six-yard keeper and throwing a 59-yard pass to Gordon Jones.

The victory, Pittsburgh's 12th

straight, wrapped up its first national championship since 1937. It also was the last game for Majors, who officially became head coach at Tennessee, his Alma Mater, the day after the game.

# Warriors win NCAA

The Marquette Warriors, one of the last teams added to the NCAA Tournament field, gave retiring Coach Al McGuire a going-away present, March 28, when they upset North Carolina, 67-59, in the Final Four championship game at Atlanta.

As the Warriors connected on their last 12 free throws and closed out their unlikely run to the school's first national championship, McGuire, the street-smart, fast-quipping alley-fighter, stood sobbing at courtside, overwhelmed by the enormity of the moment. A few feet away, his players were dancing and celebrating.

Marquette was fortunate to even be in the tournament, much less the championship game. The Warriors' up-and-down season had produced seven losses. But now they were on a roll and it continued through a surprising first half against North Carolina during which speedy guard Butch Lee dictated a Marquette tempo that resulted in a 39-27 lead.

The Tar Heels fought back after intermission. A Walter Davis jumper tied the game at 41-41 and the teams traded baskets to forge a 45-45 tie.

With 12:45 remaining, however, North Carolina Coach Dean Smith decided to go to his feared four-corner offense, a slowdown, ball-protecting maneuver that had unnerved Nevada-Las Vegas in an 84-83 semifinal victory. With playmaking guard Phil Ford at the controls, the four-corners would milk the clock, test the patience of the opponent and usually result in defensive breakdowns that produced easy baskets.

But the Warriors refused to fall under its magic spell. After killing off more than two minutes against Marquette, Ford fed teammate Bruce Buckley, who drove for a basket. He missed. At the other end, Jim Boylan scored to give Marquette the lead. McGuire went into a delay game of his own, the Carolina players fouled and the Warriors were deadly from the line, clinching the school's first basketball championship and giving McGuire reason for tears.

Lee led Marquette with 19 points while Boylan and Bo Ellis chipped in with 14 apiece. Davis led the 28-5 Tar Heels with 20 points.

*Marquette Coach Al McGuire celebrates his team's NCAA title game victory over North Carolina with player Bernard Toone.*

## ★ SPORTS WATCH ★

**JAN:** Chicago's Norm Van Lier scored only two points in an NBA game against San Antonio and they came on a desperation 84-foot hook shot.

**FEB:** Rosalyn Bryant completed her winter track schedule with five world records—the 200-, 300-, 400- and 500-meter runs as well as the 500-yard sprint.

**FEB:** Cale Yarborough, averaging 153.218 mph in his Chevrolet, won his second Daytona 500 at the Daytona International Speedway.

**MAR:** Pistol Pete Maravich, averaging 31.1 points for the New Orleans Jazz, won his first NBA scoring title.

**MAR:** St. Bonaventure won its first major basketball championship, beating Houston 94-91 in the NIT finals at Madison Square Garden.

**MAR:** Delta State earned its third straight women's basketball championship, knocking off LSU 68-55 in the AIAW Finals.

**APR:** The Philadelphia Phillies ruined Montreal's debut in Olympic Stadium, beating the Expos 7-2.

# Blue Jays win 1st A.L. game in Canada

American League baseball arrived in Canada, April 7, when the Toronto Blue Jays, one of the circuit's two new expansion teams, outslugged the Chicago White Sox, 9-5, before 44,649 curious fans at Toronto's Exhibition Stadium.

The Blue Jays follow in the footsteps of the Montreal Expos, the first franchise to field a team on foreign soil. The Expos joined the National

*First baseman Doug Ault helped get Toronto's new franchise off to a roaring start.*

League as an expansion team in 1969.

Playing on a frigid afternoon in their first-ever game, the Blue Jays exploded for 16 hits and wiped out an early 4-1 deficit. Leading the charge was first baseman Doug Ault, who belted a solo home run in the first inning off Ken Brett, a two-run homer in the third and a run-scoring single in the eighth.

Also contributing to the cause was Al Woods, who became the 10th man to hit a home run in his first major league at-bat. Jerry Johnson received credit for the victory with 2²/₃ innings in relief of starter Bill Singer.

The Seattle Mariners opened their first season, April 6, at Seattle's Kingdome, but did not fare as well. The Mariners dropped a 7-0 decision to California and lefthander Frank Tanana before 57,732 fans.

# 1977

## Geiberger shoots 59

Al Geiberger, a soft-spoken, slow-moving 39-year-old tour veteran, made professional golf history, June 10, when he shot an incredible 59 over the 7,193-yard Colonial Country Club course during the second round of the Memphis Golf Classic.

Geiberger's 13-under-par effort (11 birdies and an eagle) set a competitive record for a PGA-sponsored event and represented a golf breakthrough equivalent to Roger Bannister's first sub-4-minute mile.

Geiberger, starting his round on the 10th tee, covered his first nine holes in 30 strokes and his second nine in 29. Over a seven-hole stretch beginning at 15, the lanky veteran fired six birdies and an eagle, gaining eight strokes on par. He entered the record books when he rolled in a 10-foot putt on the final hole.

Several golfers had recorded 59s, but never in a PGA-sponsored event. Sam Snead performed the trick in 1959 during a non-PGA tournament. Six golfers, including Snead, had shot 60s in PGA events, but they were all in the 1950s on shorter courses.

Geiberger, ironically, went on to record a three-stroke victory without shooting another round under 70.

## Slew runs to record

Seattle Slew, a heavy favorite to become horse racing's first undefeated Triple Crown winner, led from start to finish on June 11 in the 109th running of the Belmont Stakes and recorded a four-length victory over Run Dusty Run.

The dark-brown, Kentucky-bred colt negotiated the muddy 1½-mile course in a relatively slow 2.29³/₅. When Seattle Slew closed to within 20 yards of victory, jockey Jean Cruguet stood up in the stirrups and waved his whip at the crowd of 70,229.

Seattle Slew, the son of Bold Reasoning and My Charmer, broke away quickly and set a moderate pace. When the field completed a mile in a slow 1:38⁴/₅, everyone knew the race belonged to Slew, a noted fast closer. True to form, the Kentucky Derby and Preakness champion pulled away from Run Dusty Run on the stretch

*Seattle Slew charges toward the Belmont Park finish line and a place in horse racing history.*

to become racing's 10th Triple Crown winner.

Seattle Slew is 9-0 in a career that has been cautiously choreographed by owners Karen and Mickey Taylor and trainer Billy Turner. The last Triple Crown winner was Secretariat in 1973.

## Female drives in Indy

A.J. Foyt captured his record fourth Indianapolis 500, May 29, but this Memorial Day classic is most likely to be remembered for Janet Guthrie's debut as the race's first female driver.

Foyt, a winner in 1961, '64 and '67, benefited most when the engine of Gordon Johncock's Wildcat DGS blew out at the beginning of the 185th lap, less than 40 miles from the finish line. The Texan coasted his Coyote-Foyt to victory, 28 seconds ahead of Tom Sneva's McLaren-Cosworth. Two-time winner Al Unser was third in a Parnelli-Cosworth.

Guthrie, a 39-year-old New Yorker who had made history when she qualified her Bryant Heat-Cool Vollstedt/O at better than 187 mph, was plagued by engine trouble. She had to make eight pit stops and completed only 27 laps, good for 29th place in the 33-car field.

Johncock led 128 of the 200 laps and Foyt only 46. But the 42-year-old grandfather was there at the end, averaging 161.331 mph.

*Janet Guthrie (left) with her racing team and the car she used to qualify for the Indianapolis 500.*

### ★ SPORTS WATCH ★

**MAY:** The powerful Montreal Canadiens recorded their second straight four-game sweep in the Stanley Cup finals, rolling over the Boston Bruins.

**JUN:** The Portland Trailblazers, led by 6-foot-11 center Bill Walton, cruised past Philadelphia in six games to win their first NBA championship.

**JUN:** Hubert Green shot a final-round 70 to beat Lou Graham by a single stroke and win the U.S. Open golf tournament at Tulsa, Okla.

**JUL:** Four first-inning runs proved to be too much for the A.L. as the N.L. won its sixth straight All-Star Game and 14th in 15 years with a 7-5 victory at Yankee Stadium.

**AUG:** Lanny Wadkins defeated Gene Littler on the third hole of a sudden-death playoff and captured the PGA Championship at Pebble Beach, Calif.

# Brock passes Cobb

St. Louis speedster Lou Brock carved another niche in baseball's record books, August 29, when he swiped two bases against San Diego and supplanted Hall of Famer Ty Cobb as the modern game's all-time greatest basestealer.

Leading off a contest against the Padres at San Diego, Brock drew a walk off starter Dave Freisleben and took off for second base on the righthander's next pitch. He slid in safely with record-tying steal No. 893 and went to third on catcher Dave Roberts' throwing error.

The Cardinals' 38-year-old left fielder got the record-breaker in the seventh when he reached first on a fielder's choice and again set sail on Freisleben's first pitch, beating Roberts' wide throw. He was mobbed by teammates and presented with the second base bag. Brock was removed from the lineup in a game eventually won, 4-3, by the Padres.

Brock, who stole a single-season record 118 bases in 1974, compiled his record total in 2,376 career games. Cobb played in 3,033 over 24 years.

*Tom Watson celebrates his dramatic British Open victory over Jack Nicklaus after sinking his final putt at Turnberry, Scotland.*

# Watson tops Nicklaus

In a stirring head-to-head battle of golf heavyweights, Tom Watson erased a three-stroke final-round deficit to Jack Nicklaus, July 9, and recorded a one-stroke victory in the British Open golf tournament at Turnberry, Scotland.

Watson, who had defeated Nicklaus in similar fashion at the Masters earlier this year, chipped in from the fringe for a birdie on 15, dropped a monster 60-foot putt for a birdie on 16 to pull even and took the lead on the par-5 17th with another birdie.

Watson hit the fairway with his drive on 18, but Nicklaus pushed his behind a shrub.

# Borg edges Connors

Wimbledon's 100-year celebration ended in a blaze of glory on July 2, when 21-year-old Bjorn Borg defeated 24-year-old Jimmy Connors, 3-6, 6-2, 6-1, 5-7, 6-4 in a classic match that ranks among the best ever played in this storied event.

The Centre Court battle lasted three hours and 14 minutes. The young Swede, changing speeds to neutralize Connors' power, appeared to be in control after three sets. Connors seemed to have momentum after the fourth. The outcome was up in the air right up to the final stroke.

Borg raced to a 4-0 fifth-set lead, but Connors amazingly battled back to 4-all. When he broke Borg to tie the set, the American pumped his fist and exhorted himself to keep up the pressure. He did for one more point, but suddenly double-faulted. As the crowd derisively cheered, Connors made an obscene gesture and then proceeded to lose three straight points and the game. Borg held service for the victory.

*Wimbledon winner Bjorn Borg kisses his prize cup after outlasting Jimmy Connors in a five-set singles final.*

Nicklaus recovered nicely, however, hitting the green and leaving himself a 32-foot putt. Watson answered by hitting his approach two feet from the pin.

All over, right? Wrong. Nicklaus stepped up to his putt and drilled it home, putting pressure on Watson. But the 27-year-old came through, winning his second British Open in three years and his fourth tournament of 1977.

This was strictly a two-way battle for the last two rounds—and Watson and Nicklaus put on quite a show. Both recorded third-round 65s and Watson came home with a final-round 65 to a 66 for Nicklaus.

# Yankees win Royally

The New York Yankees, who defeated Kansas City in the 1976 American League Championship Series on Chris Chambliss' ninth-inning Game 5 home run, employed a similar script, October 9, when they captured their second straight pennant with a 5-3 victory at Royals Stadium.

As in 1976, the two A.L. division winners had battled evenly — and bitterly — while splitting the first four games of the ALCS. But the Royals had the

advantage in Game 5, thanks to a two-run first inning keyed by George Brett and Hal McRae and the strong pitching of Paul Splittorff over seven innings.

The game tightened in the eighth, however, when Reggie Jackson, benched by Yankee Manager Billy Martin because of his 1-for-14 performance through four games, stroked a pinch-hit single to cut Kansas City's lead to 3-2 and set the stage for another ninth-inning comeback. That rally started with Paul Blair's bloop single off Dennis Leonard and a walk to pinch-hitter Roy White.

The big hit came when Mickey Rivers singled to right off Larry Gura, scoring Blair and tying the game. Willie Randolph's sacrifice fly and Brett's error sent the Yankees to another World Series.

*New York relief ace Sparky Lyle leaps into the arms of catcher Thurman Munson after wrapping up the Yankees' come-from-behind Championship Series victory over Kansas City.*

# Reggie's power show

Reggie Jackson, displaying his uncanny flair for the dramatic and enhancing his reputation as Mr. October, blasted the Los Angeles Dodgers into oblivion, October 18, with three mighty swings that lifted the New York Yankees to their first World Series championship since 1962.

Jackson, signed as a free agent after playing out his option with Baltimore in 1976, had belted 32 homers and driven in 110 runs in his first New York season. It had not been a happy one, however, as the 31-year-old slugger fought and squabbled continuously with fiery Manager Billy Martin.

But October is showtime for Jackson and the World Series

his stage. When he stepped to the plate in the fourth inning of Game 6 with the Yankees leading the fall classic three games to two but trailing in this contest, 3-2, he owned a .317 career Series batting average in 17 games (12 with Oakland) with four home runs and 10 runs batted in. He had, in fact, homered in his last official at-bat of Game 5 and walked in the second inning of this game.

On Burt Hooton's first pitch, Jackson blasted a rocket into the right-field stands for a two-run homer. With two out and Willie Randolph on base in the fifth, Jackson stroked another first-pitch homer, this time off Elias Sosa. Then, facing Charlie Hough leading off the eighth,

*Yankee slugger Reggie Jackson watches the flight of his second Game 6 World Series home run against the Los Angeles Dodgers.*

Jackson hit a monster shot over the center-field fence — on another first pitch.

Pandemonium reigned in Yankee Stadium as 56,407 fans paid tribute to one of the most memorable World Series performances in history. Jackson's three blasts, which lifted the New Yorkers to an 8-4 Series-

closing victory, gave him a record five for the classic and an unprecedented four in successive official at-bats.

Taking a backseat to Jackson were righthander Mike Torrez, who won two Series games, including the clincher, and catcher Thurman Munson, a .320 hitter.

# Little Stevie Wonder

Steve Cauthen, horse racing's 17-year-old bionic jockey, took another ride into uncharted territory, December 10, when he became the first person to top $6 million in purses in one year.

Stevie Wonder became the Six Million Dollar Man in the sixth race at Aqueduct when he rode Little Happiness to a victory worth $15,000. The youngster's 475th win of the year triggered a standing ovation from the crowd of 19,103 and a trophy presentation in the winner's circle.

The money total is phenom-enal when you consider that no jockey had ever passed the $5 million mark before Cauthen did in October. The farmboy from Walton, Ky., didn't stop there, continuing an incredible victory pace that included three programs of six winners, four of five winners and 13 four-winner cards. And Cauthen missed a month with injuries.

Half of Cauthen's $6 million-plus winnings came during the first five months of the year when he was a 16-year-old apprentice with a weight allowance.

*Steve Cauthen, horse racing's Six Million Dollar Man.*

## ★ SPORTS WATCH ★

**SEP:** Three in a row: Chris Evert defeated Wendy Turnbull, 7-6, 6-2, in the U.S. Open singles final at Forest Hills.

**SEP:** Defending champion Jimmy Connors was upset by Guillermo Vilas in a tough four-set U.S. Open final at Forest Hills.

**OCT:** The Los Angeles Dodgers finished the season with four 30-homer men: Steve Garvey (33), Reggie Smith (32), Ron Cey (30) and Dusty Baker (30).

**NOV:** Chicago's Walter Payton broke O.J. Simpson's single-game NFL rushing record by two yards when he rushed for 275 against the Minnesota Vikings.

**DEC:** Gordie Howe, now playing for the WHA's New England Whalers, scored his 1,000th career goal.

**DEC:** Texas fullback Earl Campbell outpolled Oklahoma State's Terry Miller to claim the Heisman Trophy.

# Evansville basketball team killed in crash

A chartered DC-3 airplane carrying the University of Evansville basketball team crashed shortly after takeoff in a dense fog, December 13, killing all 29 persons aboard.

The air tragedy was the first involving a sports team since 1970, when members of the Marshall and Wichita State football squads were killed in separate air crashes. In this crash, 14 players, first-year Coach Bobby Watson and other members of the school's athletic department perished.

The team, scheduled to play a December 14 game in Murfreesboro, Tenn., against Middle Tennessee State, waited several hours at Dress Regional Airport in Evansville, Ill., for the weather to clear. Shortly after a foggy takeoff, the plane went down in a cornfield about 1½ miles from the airport.

Evansville, a five-time Division II national champion, had just moved up to Division I play this year. The Aces were 1-3.

# NBA fighter punished

Kermit Washington, the Los Angeles Lakers' burly power forward who sent Houston's Rudy Tomjanovich to the hospital with a roundhouse punch during a December 9 National Basketball Association game in Los Angeles, was fined $10,000 and suspended for at least 60 days by Commissioner Larry O'Brien, December 12.

The suspension and fine, believed to be the largest in sports history, served as a warning to other NBA players that the recent upsurge in fighting will not be tolerated. Washington, who will not be paid during his suspension, stands to lose $50,000.

Tomjanovich was actually an innocent bystander. Early in the third quarter, the 6-foot-8, 240-pound Washington traded punches with 7-foot Houston center Kevin Kunnert, knocking him to the floor. As Tomjanovich rushed toward his fallen teammate, Washington whirled around and smashed him in the jaw. Tomjanovich, also 6-foot-8, fell backward and hit his head on the floor.

Tomjanovich, the Rockets' captain and the NBA's 15th leading scorer, suffered a double fracture of his jaw, a broken nose, facial cuts and a concussion. He spent several days in intensive care. An operation will be required when the swelling on his jaw subsides, and his basketball future is in doubt.

*Houston Rockets forward Rudy Tomjanovich.*

# 1978

## JANUARY-APRIL

## Spinks surprises Ali

Muhammad Ali's second reign as heavyweight champion came to an end on February 15, when young Leon Spinks, bucking incredible odds, bashed his way to a 15-round split decision in a title fight at Las Vegas.

Spinks, a real-life Rocky who rose from poverty in East St. Louis to become an Olympic champion at the 1976 Montreal Summer Games, was the aggressor from the opening bell and never slowed down his attack. Ali danced, taunted and used both his peek-a-boo and rope-a-dope defenses. But

nothing slowed down the former Marine Corporal. Ali's taunts were answered with a big, toothless grin.

The 36-year-old Ali, tired of taking punishment while hoping that his 24-year-old opponent would punch himself out, finally resorted to good old-fashioned boxing and jolted Spinks in the 10th and 11th rounds. But still he came. The 15th round was a classic donnybrook, both fighters realizing the score was close and looking for a knockout.

As it turned out, Ali was the one who needed it.

Leon Spinks exults after his shocking upset of Muhammad Ali.

## A wild day of upsets

Fifth-ranked Notre Dame upset previously undefeated and top-ranked Texas, 38-10, in the January 2 Cotton Bowl and claimed the national championship on a wild day of major bowl upsets.

The Fighting Irish were able to leapfrog four teams when Arkansas stunned No. 2 Oklahoma, 31-6, in the Orange Bowl, Washington shocked No. 4 Michigan, 27-20, in the Rose

Bowl and finally third-ranked Alabama beat a lower-ranked Ohio State team in the Sugar Bowl. Notre Dame, Alabama, Arkansas, Texas, Penn State and Kentucky all finished the season with one loss.

The Irish finished No. 1 by virtue of their impressive romp over the Longhorns, scoring on all five Texas turnovers inside its own 35-yard line. Vagas Ferguson posted three TDs.

The Arkansas win was amazing. Coach Lou Holtz had dismissed three key players for disciplinary reasons and the Razorbacks entered the game as 18-point underdogs. But a ferocious defense against the top-rushing team in the nation and the Orange Bowl-record 205-yard, two-touchdown performance of Roland Sales baffled the oddsmakers.

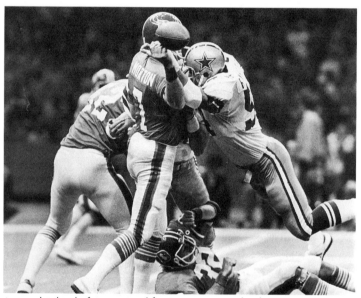

It was this kind of Super Bowl for Denver quarterback Craig Morton, who was harassed all day by Randy White and other Dallas defenders.

## Cowboys ride Broncos

An aggressive and relentless Dallas defense forced seven first-half turnovers and the Cowboys overpowered the Denver Broncos, 27-10, January 15, in Super Bowl XII at the New Orleans Superdome.

With end Harvey Martin and tackle Randy White harassing

former teammate Craig Morton into four first-half interceptions and the defense forcing three fumbles, the Cowboys took control of the game early. One interception led to a three-yard Tony Dorsett touchdown run in the first quarter and Efren Herrera kicked a pair of field goals

> ## "SPORTS TALK"
>
> *"If he was 6-2, he'd be an All-America. Of course if he was 6-2, he'd be at Southern California."*
>
> **BILL YEOMAN**
> University of Houston Coach
> on 5-9 quarterback Randy Gomez

that gave the Cowboys a 13-0 halftime lead. This came despite an off-day for Herrera, who managed to miss three field-goal attempts.

Denver, held to 72 yards of total offense and three first downs in the opening half, scored early in the third quarter

on a 47-yard Jim Turner field goal, and made it through the second half without another turnover. But a 45-yard TD pass from Roger Staubach to Butch Johnson and a 29-yard halfback pass from Robert Newhouse to Golden Richards finally sealed the verdict.

# Givens destroys Duke

Lefthanded sharpshooter Jack Givens fired holes in Duke's 2-3 zone and Rick Robey dominated play inside, March 27, as the Kentucky Wildcats captured their first NCAA Tournament championship in 20 years with a 94-88 victory over the Blue Devils at St. Louis.

With Duke sagging down low to stop Robey and big Mike Phillips, Givens kept finding defensive holes on the baseline and at the free throw stripe. Hitting nine of 12 shots and scoring 23 points, he lifted the Wildcats to a 45-38 halftime lead.

Duke quickly cut the margin to three early in the second half, but a long shot by Truman Claytor, two free throws by Macy and Robey's dunk raised the difference to nine and ended the suspense. With Givens continuing his bombardment, the Blue Devils were overmatched down the stretch.

Givens finished his college career with 41 points while Robey scored 20 and grabbed 11 rebounds. Duke got balanced scoring from Gene Banks (22), Jim Spanarkel (21) and Mike Gminski (20).

Coach Joe B. Hall's Wildcats finished with a 30-2 record.

Kentucky sharpshooter Jack Givens, wearing the spoils of the Wildcats' NCAA championship game victory over Duke.

# Gervin prevails in shootout

San Antonio's George Gervin.

In a wild conclusion to the National Basketball Association's regular season, April 9, Denver's David Thompson scored 73 points in an afternoon game and San Antonio's George Gervin answered with 63 in a night game to win the closest scoring race in league history.

With Thompson slightly behind Gervin entering the final day of the season and the Nuggets having already clinched the Midwest Division title, Denver players fed the ball to Thompson.

The acrobatic forward played 43 minutes in the game won 139-137 by the Pistons, connecting on 20 of 23 shots in a 53-point first half and 28 of 38 in the game. Thompson's single-game total tied for third on the all-time list.

When the Central Division-champion Spurs tipped off at New Orleans that night, they knew Gervin needed 59 points to win the title. He scored 20 in the first quarter and exploded for a record 33 in the second. He reached his goal early in the third quarter and sat out much of the second half. He made 23 of 49 field goals and 17 of 20 free throws in a 153-132 loss.

Final averages: Gervin 27.22, Thompson 27.15.

## ★ SPORTS WATCH ★

**JAN:** Flamboyant quarterback Joe Namath, the star of Super Bowl III, announced his retirement at age 34.

**JAN:** Dick Buerkle set a world indoor record for the mile when he was clocked at 3:54.8 during competition in the National Invitation meet at the University of Maryland.

**JAN:** Roberto Duran became undisputed lightweight boxing champion when he knocked out Esteban DeJesus in the 12th round at Las Vegas.

**APR:** South African Gary Player shot a 72-hole total of 277 and won his third Masters title at Augusta, Ga.

**APR:** A miscue by Cincinnati second baseman Joe Morgan against San Francisco ended his major league-record errorless streak at 91 games.

# Buffalo trades Simpson to 49ers

O.J. Simpson, the most prolific one-season rusher in National Football League history and second on the NFL's all-time charts, was granted his wish, March 24, when the Buffalo Bills traded him to the San Francisco 49ers.

It will be a homecoming for the 30-year-old Simpson, who was frustrated with Buffalo's futility (43-81-2 in his nine seasons). He had requested a trade to the West Coast, preferably to his native San Francisco. The Bills, looking to rebuild after a 3-11 season, dealt their star for five draft choices.

The 49ers, looking for an offensive spark to complement a respected defense, were delighted with the acquisition of a sure box-office favorite as well as a 10,183-yard career rusher. Simpson played in only seven games last year because of a knee injury, rushing for 557 yards.

# 1978

## Bullets hit their mark

The National Basketball Association's Cinderella Series came to a fitting conclusion on June 7, when the experienced Washington Bullets defeated the young and sassy Seattle SuperSonics, 105-99, in Game 7 at the Seattle Coliseum.

The Bullets' victory erased memories of four-game losses to Milwaukee in 1971 and Golden State in 1975 in their only previous NBA finals appearances. It also was a fitting addendum to the 10-year career of 6-foot-7 center Wes Unseld, who sealed the final victory with a pair of late free throws.

The Bullets, trying to become only the third NBA team to win a seventh game on the road, led from the first quarter and never let go. But Seattle, sparked by rookie Jack Sikma and Marvin Webster, pulled to within 101-99 in the final minute after Unseld missed two free throws.

Washington's Wes Unseld (left) and Elvin Hayes chase a loose ball during Game 7 action.

Big Wes was fouled again, however, and this time he came through.

Washington had trailed the Sonics 2-1 and 3-2 in the series. But Seattle, a team that had opened the season 5-17 before surging under new Coach Lenny Wilkens, watched its hopes wash away when the Bullets posted a Finals-record 35-point victory in Game 6.

## Canadiens rule again

The Montreal Canadiens, showing why they have ruled the National Hockey League recently, got four points from two seldom-used youngsters, May 25, and closed out Boston in the decisive sixth game of the Stanley Cup finals with a 4-1 victory at Boston Garden.

Mario Tremblay, a 21-year-old right winger playing in just his fifth playoff game, scored two goals and Pierre Mondou, a 22-year-old center, assisted on two scores. Mondou was taking a regular shift only because veteran Doug Risebrough had injured his back in the first period.

With Boston covering Montreal star Guy Lafleur like a blanket, that offensive splurge was welcome. But the game was really won by Montreal's stifling defense, led by Larry Robinson, Guy Lapointe and Andre Savard. Boston, which scored the first goal early on a Brad Park shot, was checked relentlessly and limited to 16 shots total, making life easy for goaltender Ken Dryden.

The championship is the third straight for Scotty Bowman's Canadiens. Montreal had swept Philadelphia and the Bruins in the previous two finals and led this one, 2-0, before Boston rallied to equalise by winning the third and fourth games.

## Affirmed joins elite

Affirmed fought off Alydar in a brilliant stretch duel and claimed his place alongside 10 other Triple Crown winners in the Belmont Stakes, July 10.

Covering the $1\frac{1}{2}$-mile test in $2:26\frac{4}{5}$, the third fastest time in Belmont history, Affirmed beat Alydar by a head. The two 3-year-olds pulled away from the pack on the backstretch and ran the final half mile side by side, faster than it had ever been run before. When they hit the finish line, Affirmed jockey Steve Cauthen stood up in his stirrups, sure of his victory.

Affirmed, owned by Louis and Patrice Wolfson, has won seven of nine career races against Alydar and most have been close. Affirmed won the Kentucky Derby by $1\frac{1}{2}$ lengths over the Calumet Farm product and then edged him by a neck in the Preakness Stakes.

Affirmed hits the Belmont Stakes finish line just ahead of Alydar, becoming horse racing's 11th Triple Crown winner.

### ★ SPORTS WATCH ★

**MAY:** Cincinnati third baseman Pete Rose's single off Montreal's Steve Rogers was career hit No. 3,000.

**JUN:** San Francisco slugger Willie McCovey became the 12th member of baseball's 500-home run club when he connected off Atlanta's Jamie Easterly.

**JUN:** Larry Holmes claimed the WBC heavyweight championship with a 15-round split decision over Ken Norton in a fight at Las Vegas.

**JUL:** A single and triple by Los Angeles first baseman Steve Garvey propelled the National League to a 7-3 All-Star Game victory at San Diego.

**JUL:** Sweden's Bjorn Borg won his third straight Wimbledon singles title and second straight over Jimmy Connors, 6-2, 6-2, 6-3.

**JUL:** Jack Nicklaus became the first golfer to win all four majors at least three times when he captured another British Open title at St. Andrew's, Scotland.

# Martina's comeback too much for Evert

Martina Navratilova, who left her parents and homeland three years ago, rallied from a third-set deficit to overcome two-time champion Chris Evert, July 7, in the Wimbledon singles final.

The 21-year-old lefthander rebounded after losing the first set and trailing 2-4 in the finale for a 2-6, 6-4, 7-5 victory. As her final volley landed for a winner, Navratilova raised her arms triumphantly and put her hands to her face as tears welled in her eyes.

She had traveled a long road from her native Czechoslovakia where, as a schoolgirl, she had dreamed of winning the world's most prestigious tennis title.

Wimbledon champion Martina Navratilova fights her emotions and gets a congratulatory pat from Chris Evert, her final-round opponent.

She defected three years ago during the U.S. Open and has become one of the world's top players.

Navratilova appeared nervous in the first set before gaining her composure. Trailing 4-5 in the third set, Martina held with four powerful serves, broke Evert in the next game and then held service again to close out her first major victory.

---

# Braves end Rose hit streak at 44

Atlanta rookie Larry McWilliams and veteran reliever Gene Garber combined, August 1, to end the National League record-tying 44-game hitting streak of Cincinnati third baseman Pete Rose.

The 31,159 fans at Atlanta's Fulton-County Stadium had plenty to cheer as their Braves pounded out a 16-4 victory and Rose attempted to inch closer to Joe DiMaggio's 1941 major league-record 56-game streak.

Rose walked in the first inning and hit a blistering line drive in the second that was picked off ankle high by McWilliams. He grounded out next time up and lined into a double play in the seventh facing Garber.

When Rose stepped to the plate in the ninth for what obviously would be his last chance to extend the streak, the crowd gave him a long ovation. He bunted Garber's first offering foul and then took two balls. He fouled off the fourth pitch before swinging at strike three.

Over the streak that began June 14, Rose batted .385. He had tied Willie Keeler's 81-year-old N.L. record on July 31.

---

Former Patriots' receiver Darryl Stingley, 10 years after his paralyzing football accident.

# Stingley paralyzed during an NFL game

New England wide receiver Darryl Stingley was paralyzed from the head down, August 12, when he was tackled by Raiders defensive back Jack Tatum in the second quarter of a National Football League exhibition game at the Oakland Coliseum.

Patriots quarterback Steve Grogan fired a short pass to Stingley over the middle late in the half. Stingley dived futilely for the ball and was drilled by Tatum. He fell to the ground and lay motionless for about five minutes before being carried gingerly off the field.

It later was announced that Stingley had suffered a fracture dislocation of his cervical spine and a one-hour operation was performed at an Oakland hospital to realign his vertabrae and reduce pressure on his spine.

Doctors now fear the 26-year-old will be paralyzed permanently. The 6-foot, 195-pound Purdue product caught 110 passes for 1,883 yards and 14 touchdowns in a five-year NFL career. He led the Patriots last season with 39 receptions for 657 yards and five touchdowns.

# 1978

## The Yankee Express

*Yankees Roy White (6) and Chris Chambliss (10) greet Bucky Dent at home plate after the little shortstop's division playoff home run.*

The light-hitting double-play combination of Bucky Dent and Denny Doyle combined for five runs batted in and slugger Reggie Jackson added a two-run seventh-inning homer, October 17, as the New York Yankees defeated Los Angeles, 7-2, in the decisive sixth game of the World Series.

The game at Dodger Stadium completed a four-straight blitz by the Yankees after dropping the first two games and capped an incredible season full of stirring comebacks. The fun really began back on July 19, when the New Yorkers appeared hopelessly out of the American League East Division race,

buried 14 games behind the first-place Boston Red Sox.

Despite the distraction of Manager Billy Martin being forced into a tearful resignation in late July and unfamiliarity with new boss Bob Lemon, the Yankees went on a tear that produced a 52-21 record to the end of the regular season and allowed them to catch the Red Sox. No A.L. team had ever come from 14 games behind, but the Yankees pulled even over the weekend of September 7, 8, 9 and 10 when they staged the infamous "Boston Massacre" at Fenway Park.

The Yankees outscored the Red Sox, 42-9, and outhit them, 67-21, in the four-game series. The teams stayed even the rest of the way, forcing a one-game divisional playoff.

Again the Yankees had to come back. Trailing 2-0 with two out and two runners on base in the seventh inning, Dent hit a dramatic home run that propelled his team to a 5-4 victory and gave Ron Guidry his 25th win. Guidry's marvelous 25-3

campaign, featuring the best winning percentage ever for a 20-game winner, included a 1.74 earned-run average and nine shutouts.

But the talented lefthander was not through. He pitched the Yankees to a 2-1 pennant-clinching victory over Kansas City in the fourth game of the A.L. Championship Series and a third-game win over the

Dodgers after the New Yorkers had fallen behind by two games in the World Series.

It all added up to the Yankees' record 22nd championship and second straight after a 14-year dry spell. Lemon also became the first manager in A.L. history (the third in baseball) to win a pennant after starting the season with another team (the Chicago White Sox).

---

### "SPORTS TALK"

*"You don't put those numbers on the board by accident. You don't buy them in the supermarket."*

**REGGIE JACKSON**

on Yankee teammate Ron Guidry after his 25-3, 1.74-ERA season

---

## Ali reclaims lost title

Muhammad Ali, floating like a 36-year-old butterfly, danced and jabbed his way to a unanimous decision over Leon Spinks, September 16, becoming the first fighter to win the heavyweight championship for a third time.

With the crowd at the New Orleans Superdome chanting, "Ali, Ali," the challenger avenged his February 15 loss to the 25-year-old. Ali moved well, jabbed consistently and battered Spinks with hooks and short

rights. The result was a one-sided decision that returned Ali to the heavyweight throne.

Spinks was a completely different fighter than the one that defeated Ali with a relentless stalking attack at Las Vegas. Making his first title defense, the youngster looked like a helpless amateur.

After the bout, Ali hinted that he might retire. "Thank God it's over," he said. "That's my last one. . .I don't think I'll ever fight again."

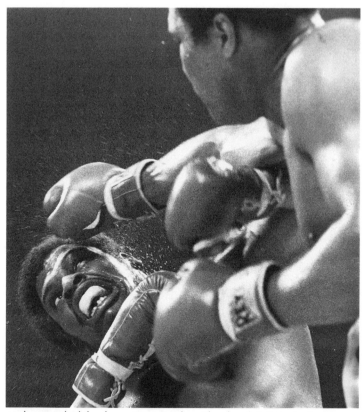

*Muhammad Ali backs up Leon Spinks with a hard right to the head during their return match at New Orleans.*

# Nancy Lopez honored

Nancy Lopez, the 21-year-old phenom from Roswell, N.M., became the first golfer to be named best player and top rookie in the same year when the LPGA honored her at a December 11 awards dinner in New York.

It was the perfect conclusion to an incredible debut season for the talented youngster. Lopez won nine tournaments, including an LPGA-record five in a row, and earned a tour-record $161,235. Her winnings even surpassed Jerry Pate's rookie record for earnings on the more lucrative men's tour.

The highlight of the year came on June 18, when Lopez shot a final-round 69 to make up five shots on leader Jane Blalock and capture the LPGA

*LPGA sensation Nancy Lopez shoulders arms.*

tournament at the Locust Hill Country Club in Rochester, N.Y. She blitzed the front nine with an LPGA-record 32 en route to her fifth consecutive victory. That broke the women's record of four straight held by Mickey Wright, Kathy Whitworth and Shirley Englehorn.

# Phillies' future Rosey

The wildest auction in baseball history ended, December 5, when the Philadelphia Phillies won the Pete Rose sweepstakes, signing the 16-year Cincinnati star to a four-year contract calling for an $800,000 annual salary.

The announcement was made at a packed news conference in Orlando, Fla., site of baseball's winter meetings. It brought to an end an innovative sales job by the 37-year-old veteran, who jetted around the country and invited free-agent offers from various major league teams. Those offers reportedly reached as much as $1 million per year from Atlanta and similar amounts from the New York Mets, Pittsburgh and Kansas City.

But Rose opted for Philadelphia, which in the light of bigger bids had dropped out of the bidding a week earlier before revising its offer. The Phillies get a .310 career hitter noted for his hustling style on the field and his clubhouse leadership. Rose is coming off a season in which he collected his 3,000th hit and compiled a National League record-tying 44-game hitting streak.

The contract makes Rose the highest-paid player in baseball, surpassing Yankee pitcher Catfish Hunter's $650,000 yearly salary.

# Buckeyes fire Hayes

*Ohio State player Ken Fritz, trying to restrain Buckeye Coach Woody Hayes, gets a left to the jaw for his trouble.*

Woody Hayes, the gruff, temperamental football coach at Ohio State University for 28 successful years, was fired, December 30, the morning after he punched Clemson linebacker Charlie Bauman in a sideline incident near the end of the Gator Bowl at Jacksonville, Fla.

Bauman had intercepted a pass, sealing a 17-15 Clemson victory with 1:58 left to play. When he was knocked out of bounds near the Ohio State bench, he was attacked by a swinging Hayes. Ken Fritz tried to restrain his coach but was punched in the face.

Hayes stormed off the field at the end of the game under police escort and refused to be interviewed. When Athletic Director Hugh Hindman asked him to resign the next morning, the coach refused, making his dismissal the only option left.

The 65-year-old Hayes coached the Buckeyes to a 205-61-10 record in 28 seasons dating back to 1951. His 1954 and '68 squads captured national championships and he was named Coach of the Year in 1957 and '75. However, his behaviour had progressively come under fire in recent years for various sideline incidents, off-hand statements and conflicts with coaches at other Big Ten Conference schools.

# 1979

## Soviets dazzle NHL

*A happy Soviet delegation poses with the Challenge Cup it won in a three-game series against a surprised team of NHL All-Stars.*

The Soviet National hockey team put on a dazzling display of speed and finesse, February 11, and stunned a crowd of 17,545 fans at Madison Square Garden with a decisive 6-0 victory over a National Hockey League All-Star squad in the rubber game of the first Challenge Cup series.

The Soviets, using four efficient lines and getting outstanding goaltending from Vladimir Myshkin, swarmed all over the Canadian-dominated All-Star team in 60 minutes of up-tempo hockey. The NHL stars were not used to this style and they appeared overmatched.

Boris Mikhailov and Viktor Zhluktov scored second-period goals for the Soviets. The frustrated NHL stars answered back with ferocious checks, but the strategy did not faze the Soviets. They took everything that was dished out and exploded for four more goals in a 6:02 span of the final period.

The loss exploded the NHL's superiority complex. Some of the NHL players were cocky after winning the series opener, 4-2, but that changed when the Soviets rallied from a 4-2 deficit for a 5-4 Game 2 victory.

## Steelers' record is super

Pittsburgh quarterback Terry Bradshaw passed for 318 yards and four touchdowns and the Steelers became the first three-time Super Bowl winner, January 21, with an exciting 35-31 victory over Dallas at Miami's Orange Bowl.

The Steelers' first two scores came on 28 and 75-yard strikes to wide receiver John Stallworth. Bradshaw also threw a seven-yard TD pass to running back Rocky Bleier and his 18-yard pass to Lynn Swann gave the Steelers a 35-17 advantage with 2½ minutes remaining.

But quarterback Roger Staubach marched the Cowboys downfield, throwing seven yards to Billy Joe DuPree for the score. Dallas then recovered an onside kick and Staubach passed four yards to Butch Johnson for a touchdown.

Now trailing by only four points with 22 seconds remaining, the Cowboys tried another onside kick that failed.

*Pittsburgh quarterback Terry Bradshaw signals what everybody already knows: the Steelers are No. 1 for a record third time.*

## Tide rolls over No. 1 Penn State

Alabama upset top-ranked Penn State, 14-7, in the Sugar Bowl on New Year's Day, but that sterling effort only earned the Crimson Tide half a national championship. The other half went to Southern Cal, a 17-10 Rose Bowl winner over Michigan.

Alabama finished the regular season as the AP's second-ranked team. But UPI disagreed, assigning its No. 2 ranking to the Trojans. Both teams had one loss, but Southern Cal had defeated the Crimson Tide, 24-14, during the regular season.

Alabama built its 14-7 Sugar Bowl lead on Jeff Rutledge's 30-yard second-quarter touchdown pass to Bruce Bolton and an eight-yard Major Ogilvie TD run in the third quarter. But a dramatic fourth-quarter defensive stand decided the issue.

The Nittany Lions, looking for their first national championship under Coach Joe Paterno, drove to the Alabama 1-yard line. With two downs to get the tying touchdown, both fullback Matt Suhey and tailback Mike Guman were stopped.

The Tide defense intercepted four Chuck Fusina passes and sacked the Penn State quarterback five times.

# Fuzzy is "Masterful" in playoff

Fuzzy Zoeller, a cheerful 27-year-old who enjoys exchanging wisecracks with the gallery, won the 43rd Masters golf tournament on April 15 when he defeated Tom Watson and Ed Sneed on the second hole of a sudden-death playoff at Augusta National Golf Club.

The three golfers were tied after completing regulation with eight-under-par 280s. But Zoeller dropped an eight-foot putt on the second extra hole to claim the prestigious green jacket in his first appearance at Augusta, the first to do so since Gene Sarazen in 1935.

The title appeared to belong to Sneed. He led Watson by five strokes and Zoeller by six entering the final day and held a six-stroke advantage over Zoeller with 13 to play. But Sneed bogeyed 16, 17 and 18 to finish with a 76, allowing Watson (71) and Zoeller (70) to force the playoff. Watson was hurt by his putter, missing seven birdie chances from within 12 feet.

*Fuzzy Zoeller does a victory jig after sinking a birdie putt in a sudden-death playoff to win his first Masters championship.*

# Peace: NHL absorbs four WHA franchises

The costly seven-year war between the National Hockey League and World Hockey Association came to an end, December 30, when the NHL agreed to absorb four WHA franchises.

The owners of the New England Whalers, Winnipeg Jets, Edmonton Oilers and Quebec Nordiques will pay $6 million to join the NHL as expansion teams. They will be able to protect two skaters and two goaltenders on their current rosters. The remainder will be made available to the existing 17 NHL teams and an expansion draft will be held in June.

The move is being treated as expansion rather than a merger to avoid difficulties with the players' union. Two franchises, Birmingham and Cincinnati, will be dissolved.

With the addition of four new teams, the NHL did some division shuffling. Washington will move from the Norris to the Patrick Division with the Whalers joining the Norris, the Nordiques being placed in the Adams and the Jets and Oilers going into the Smythe.

# Like Magic, Spartans capture NCAA title

Earvin (Magic) Johnson scored 24 points, Greg Kelser added 19 and Michigan State grounded high-scoring Larry Bird as the Spartans handed Indiana State its first loss of the season, 75-64, in the March 26 NCAA Tournament championship game.

Bird, the talented 6-foot-9 senior forward who had carried Indiana State to a 33-0 record, was the object of unwelcome attention. Every time he touched the ball, there was a man in his face. Every time he dribbled, he ran into two defenders.

The result was an ineffective 7-for-21 shooting night, leaving the Sycamores increasingly vulnerable. Michigan State raced to a 37-28 halftime advantage.

With Terry Donnelly hitting long jump shots at the beginning of the second half, the Spartans stretched their lead to 50-34. But Indiana State refused to die, clawing back to within six points with 10:10 remaining. Johnson, Michigan State's multi-talented 6-foot-8 guard, then scored seven quick points and reestablished control.

The rest of the game was a parade to the free-throw line and Michigan State's 26th victory was punctuated with a perfect lead pass from Johnson to Kelser for an emphatic game-ending slam dunk.

*Indiana State's Larry Bird is trapped by Michigan State's Jay Vincent (31) and Magic Johnson during action in the NCAA Tournament championship game.*

# 1979

## Montreal wins again

Montreal's five-game Stanley Cup conquest of the Cinderella New York Rangers was a predictable ending to an overused plot. The Canadiens won their fourth straight Cup, their 15th in 24 years and their National Hockey League-record 21st overall.

But for Montreal fans, this one was special. For the first time since 1968, the Canadiens actually won the Cup at the Montreal Forum. With less than a minute remaining in the Canadiens' 4-1 Game 5 victory over the Rangers, the palace of hockey kings erupted into a wild frenzy that was fed by the appearance of the Stanley Cup on the ice and ecstatic players tossing their equipment into the crowd.

Montreal had lost the series opener to a New York team that finished third in the Patrick Division during the regular season. But Coach Scotty Bowman's Canadiens stormed back to take control. After playing New York to a 1-1 first-period tie in the clincher, the Canadiens allowed the Rangers only seven more shots on goal while getting two goals from Jacques Lemaire and another from Bob Gainey.

## 23-22: A windy story

*Three-homer Chicago slugger Dave Kingman.*

What happens when you combine Chicago's Wrigley Field with an 18-mph wind blowing to left? The answer, on May 17, was an 11-homer, 50-hit slugfest that resulted in a 23-22 Philadelphia win over the Cubs.

Phillies' third baseman Mike Schmidt decided the issue when he hit a Bruce Sutter pitch out of the park in the 10th inning for his second home run of the game. Dave Kingman blasted three home runs for Chicago.

The 45 combined runs fell four short of the major league record set by the same two teams at Wrigley Field in 1922. The Cubs won that ERA-bruiser, 26-23. The 11 home runs tied a record and the 50 total hits were two short of the National League record for an extra-inning contest.

The Phillies scored seven runs in the first inning while building a 17-6 advantage. Chicago scored six in the first, seven in the sixth and finally caught the Phillies at 22-22 with a three-run eighth.

Bob Boone drove in five runs for the Phillies while Chicago got seven RBIs from Bill Buckner and six from Kingman. Rawly Eastwick, the Phillies' fifth pitcher, fired two shutout innings for the victory.

---

### ★ SPORTS WATCH ★

**MAY:** Outspoken center Bill Walton, unhappy in Portland, signed a seven-year free-agent contract with the San Diego Clippers.

**JUN:** The Seattle SuperSonics turned the tables on 1978 champion Washington with a five-game NBA Finals victory over the Bullets.

**JUN:** The NBA voted to experiment with the three-point field goal, setting the distance at 22 feet along the baseline and 23 feet, 9 inches at the top of the key.

**JUL:** Lee Mazzilli's bases-loaded walk scored the winning run for the N.L.'s eighth straight All-Star Game victory, a 7-6 decision at Seattle's Kingdome.

**AUG:** St. Louis' Lou Brock got his 3,000th hit, a single off Chicago's Dennis Lamp, during a 3-2 victory over the Cubs.

---

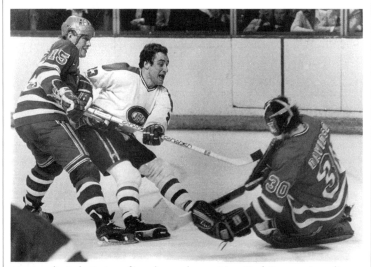

*Montreal's Bob Gainey fires the puck past New York Rangers' goalie John Davidson, giving the Canadiens a 2-1 lead in the Stanley Cup series finale at Montreal.*

## Striking umps reach contract agreement

Order returned to major league baseball, May 19, as 52 umpires went back to work after a bitter strike that resulted in the first month and a half of the season being played under the sometimes wild and crazy dictates of amateur and minor league arbiters.

A new agreement was hashed out on May 17, after a 14-hour negotiating session in New York. The umpires, represented by Richie Phillips, unanimously approved a contract that will give them an average $7,000 salary increase, raise the maximum salary from $40,000 to $50,000 after 20 years and provide for a two-week vacation during the season.

The vacation concession means that both the American and National leagues will have to hire an extra crew of four umpires. The big question will be whether the newcomers should come from the so-called "scab umpires" or those who honored the strike.

# Yankee Munson dies in air crash

Thurman Munson, the New York Yankees' 32-year-old catcher and captain, died, August 2, when the plane he was piloting crashed short of the runway at the Akron-Canton Airport in Ohio.

Munson, the American League's Rookie of the Year in 1970 and its Most Valuable Player in 1976, was trying to land his Cessna Citation twin-engine jet when it clipped the tops of some trees, crashed and came to rest about 200 feet from the runway. The plane lost its wings and burst into flames.

David Hall and Jerry D. Anderson, two passengers with Munson, both survived the crash and were reported in fair condition at a local hospital. The two men tried to rescue Munson, but the intense flames finally thwarted their efforts. Munson was a native of Canton and often flew home during the season to be with his wife and three children.

An intense competitor, he owned a .292 career average and topped the .300 mark five times. He helped lead the Yankees to three pennants and two World Series titles during his 10-year career.

# Cardinal J.V. Cain collapses, dies

*Members of the St. Louis Cardinals football team carry the casket of J.V. Cain, their former teammate who collapsed on the practice field and died two hours later at a hospital.*

The football world was stunned, July 22, by the news that St. Louis Cardinals tight end J.V. Cain had collapsed during a summer workout session and died two hours later at St. Joseph Hospital in St. Charles, Mo.—on his 28th birthday.

Cain, who had caught 76 passes for 1,014 yards and nine touchdowns in four National Football League seasons, had run a pass pattern during an evening workout at The Lindenwood Colleges. He turned and took two steps toward the huddle before he collapsed to the ground. Team trainer John Omohundro and Dr. Bernard Garfinkel worked hard to revive Cain, and he was rushed to the emergency room by a team of paramedics.

The cause of death remains a mystery. Doctors ruled out cardiac arrest, they said the 90-degree heat was not a factor and they determined that he was not on drugs. He was in excellent physical shape after rehabilitating an Achilles' tendon injury that sidelined him for the entire 1978 season.

The 6-foot-4, 221-pounder was the Cardinals' first-round draft choice out of Colorado in 1974. He became a starter in 1975 and enjoyed his best season two years later, catching 25 passes for 328 yards and two touchdowns.

# Mile mark is broken by Decker

*Colorado sophomore Mary Decker, the fastest woman miler in the United States.*

Mary Decker, a 20-year-old Colorado sophomore, outsprinted Francie Larrieu over the last quarter and set an American record of 4:23.5 for the women's mile in the Brooks Meet of Champions at Philadelphia's Franklin Field.

The 5-foot-6, 110-pounder fell short of the 4:22.1 world record set by Rumanian Natalia Maracescu last January. But Decker thinks it is only a matter of time.

"I'm disappointed because I missed the world record, but that leaves me the opportunity to break it another day," she said. "I have no doubt that I can break it."

Susan Vigil and Jan Merrill set the early pace with Decker and Larrieu right behind. Decker took the lead at the bell and opened up a 25-yard margin of victory. Larrieu, former American record holder, finished second with a personal-best of 4:27.6.

# 1979

## SEPTEMBER-DECEMBER

# Austin, McEnroe get 1st Open wins

Youth was served in the finals of the U.S. Open championships, September 9, when 16-year-old Tracy Austin stopped Chris Evert-Lloyd and 20-year-old John McEnroe beat Vitas Gerulaitis to claim their respective titles for the first time.

Austin's victory was the most startling. The California high school junior defeated Martina Navratilova in straight sets in the semifinal round and then ended Evert-Lloyd's four-year reign as U.S. Open queen with a convincing 6-4, 6-3 victory. She became the youngest U.S. Open winner in history, three months younger than Maureen Connolly in 1951.

It was not a pretty match. Of the first 46 points played, 38 were decided on errors, most of them unforced. The battle of the baseline actually was decided by a lot of missed returns. Austin trailed 0-30 in the final game, battled back to deuce and then won when Evert-Lloyd hit a weak volley.

McEnroe had to get past Ilie Nastase and Jimmy Connors en route to becoming the youngest men's champion in 31 years. The final pitted the always-aggressive serve-and-volley style of McEnroe against fellow New Yorker Gerulaitis, a speed-and-finesse man.

McEnroe applied pressure from both the net and baseline. He seemed to break service easily and he outplayed his 25-year-old opponent in every phase of

*High schooler Tracy Austin does a victory dance after beating Chris Evert-Lloyd in the U.S. Open final.*

his 7-5, 6-3, 6-3 victory.

That brought Gerulaitis' record against McEnroe, Connors and Bjorn Borg, tennis' classic power players, to 2-31.

# Strong "Family" ties

*'Family' leader Willie Stargell gets a hug from Omar Moreno after hitting a two-run Game 7 World Series homer that helped the Pirates beat Baltimore.*

Willie Stargell's two-run homer gave Pittsburgh a sixth-inning lead and relievers Grant Jackson and Kent Tekulve made it stand up as the Pirates closed out the World Series with a 4-1 Game 7 victory over Baltimore on October 17 at Baltimore's Memorial Stadium.

The victory climaxed a dramatic Pittsburgh comeback from a three-games-to-one deficit and provided one more

shining moment for the 38-year-old Stargell, known affectionately in the Pirates' clubhouse as "Pops." Stargell was the unofficial head of Pittsburgh's "family" and the glue that pulled everyone together when the chips were down.

They couldn't have been more down following Game 4 at Pittsburgh, after the Orioles had rallied from a 6-3 deficit with a six-run eighth-inning burst to a 9-6 victory and a 3-1 Series advantage. The O's were seriously testing the Pirates' family structure.

However, shortstop Tim Foli drove in three runs and Jim Rooker and Bert Blyleven combined on a six-hitter, giving Pittsburgh the fifth game, 7-1. John Candelaria and Tekulve combined on a seven-hit 4-0 shutout in Game 6 tying the Series, and the cast of Jim Bibby, Don Robinson, Jackson and Tekulve silenced the Oriole bats in Game 7. Baltimore had managed only two runs in the final 28 innings of the Series.

"Pops," of course, was the offensive ringleader, batting .400 and hitting three home runs, but four other Pirates (Dave Parker, Phil Garner, Omar Moreno and Foli) collected 10 or more hits. The family unit, at least in Pittsburgh, was alive and well.

---

## ★ SPORTS WATCH ★

**SEP:** Boston's Carl Yastrzemski became the first A.L. player to collect 3,000 hits and 400 home runs when he singled off New York's Jim Beattie during a 9-2 Red Sox victory.

**SEP:** Cardinal Lou Brock's 938th stolen base, the last of his major league career, moved him one ahead of 19th Century speedster Billy Hamilton.

**SEP:** WBC heavyweight champion Larry Holmes retained his title for the third time in 1979 with a TKO of Earnie Shavers.

**NOV:** Edmonton became the first Canadian Football League team in 10 years to retain the Grey Cup, defeating Montreal, 17-9.

**DEC:** John McEnroe and Vitas Gerulaitis helped the United States to its second straight Davis Cup with a 5-0 romp over Italy.

**DEC:** Southern Cal tailback Charles White outpolled Oklahoma running back Billy Sims to win the Heisman Trophy.

# Leonard perseveres in battle with Benitez

Sugar Ray Leonard, the stylish Olympic champion with lightning-quick hands, captured the world welterweight boxing championship, November 30, when he stopped undefeated Wilfred Benitez six seconds before the final bell of their bruising 15-round fight at Las Vegas.

Referee Carlos Padilla stopped the bout with the 21-year-old Puerto Rican having

struggled to his feet after being knocked down by a left hook in the 15th round. It was Leonard's second knockdown of the fight and all three judges had him well ahead on points.

"We threw punches that would have rocked a volcano," said Leonard, a winner of 26 straight fights since turning professional. And, indeed, both Benitez (37-1-1) and his 23-year-old challenger delivered their share of punishment.

The fight started off slowly, but Leonard suddenly floored Benitez with a left hook in the third round. The champ jumped to his feet and both fighters became more active, Benitez landing with overhands and Leonard scoring with quick combinations. So it went until the final round, when Leonard removed any doubts about the outcome.

*Sugar Ray Leonard sends Wilfred Benitez to the canvas during the 15th round of their welterweight championship fight at Las Vegas.*

---

*Quarterback Marc Wilson, Brigham Young's top offensive weapon.*

# Indiana wins 38-37 thriller over BYU

Cornerback Tim Wilbur picked up a punt fumbled by his own teammate and raced 62 yards for a fourth-quarter touchdown, December 21, giving underdog Indiana a 38-37 Holiday Bowl victory over Brigham Young in one of the most exciting post-season games of recent years.

BYU, undefeated and featuring quarterback Marc Wilson, the nation's offensive leader with 3,720 passing yards, had taken a 34-31 lead with 1:42 left in the third quarter on a 15-yard Wilson-to-Eric Lane touchdown pass and stretched its advantage to six on a 38-yard Brent Johnson field goal.

Wilbur was in the right spot

# Boxer dies after bout

Willie Classen, a 29-year-old middleweight from Santurce, P.R., died, November 28, from injuries he suffered five days earlier during a Madison Square Garden bout against Wilford Scypion.

Classen, knocked out in the 10th round by a powerful Scypion combination, was taken from the ring on a stretcher and never regained consciousness. He died in a New York hospital of cardiac arrest, complicated by brain-stem failure and subdural hematoma.

Classen had taken a lot of punishment in the ninth round and was examined by a doctor before the 10th. Pronounced fit to continue, Classen answered the bell slowly and was greeted by a left hook and a right to the chin by Scypion. He fell backward through the lower rope and two doctors worked over him for 15 minutes before calling for a stretcher.

This was the worst ring tragedy since Benny (Kid) Paret died after a welterweight bout against Emile Griffith in 1962.

when Steve Rohe fumbled a Clay Brown punt. He picked it up, broke several tackles and scored the game-winning touchdown. BYU fought back in the final minutes, but Johnson missed a 27-yard field goal with seven seconds remaining.

Wilson, who threw for 380

yards and two touchdowns while scoring two himself, directed the Cougars to six leads. The 8-4 Hoosiers, with quarterback Tim Clifford running for two touchdowns and throwing for another, held the lead three times before the exciting climax.

# THE 1980s

*The decade opened with one of the great upsets in sports history and a nationwide rush of patriotic fervor.*

*Boston Celtics star Larry Bird.*

When a ragtag group of American Olympic hockey players pulled off a shocking victory over the poised and polished "professionals" of the Soviet Union and went on to win a gold medal at Lake Placid, N.Y., the country experienced an emotional outpouring of patriotism unmatched since the end of World War II.

But, alas, this interlude into reality was all too brief. Soon, it was business as usual with the off-field battles of big business, strikes, litigation and drugs, testing the patience of fans.

Not long after the Miracle on Ice, President Jimmy Carter, responding to the Soviet Union's aggression in Afghanistan, called for—and got—an American boycott of the Summer Olympic Games in Moscow. This unwelcomed intrusion of politics into the sports arena was disappointing, but no more than some of the intrusions that were to follow.

In 1981, baseball fans endured a seven-week strike. In 1982, National Football League players sat out 57 days. The issue in both cases was money, and as television revenues shot into the billions of dollars, sports salaries skyrocketed beyond every player's greatest fantasy. Reggie Jackson, one of baseball's original free agents in 1976, accepted a five-year, $2.9 million deal with the New York Yankees. In 1991, free agent Bobby Bonilla signed a five-year, $29 million contract with the New York Mets.

As owners wrestled with spiraling salaries, they also had to deal with the intrusion of drugs into their locker rooms. Players like Maryland basketball star Len Bias and Cleveland Browns defensive back Don Rogers died from cocaine usage and others fell under its spell, spending time on suspended lists and in rehabilitation. In 1988, Canadian sprinter Ben Johnson was sent home in disgrace and stripped of his 100-meter world record and Olympic gold medal after testing positive for steroids.

There were some positive developments.

The Los Angeles Lakers captured five NBA titles in the 1980s and became the first repeat champions in 19 years; the New York Islanders won four straight Stanley Cups and Edmonton captured four in five years; Villanova and North Carolina State pulled off gigantic NCAA basketball upsets, and

*Houston fireballer Nolan Ryan.*

## ROLL OF HONOR

### AUTO RACING

**INDIANAPOLIS 500**

| Year | Winner | Speed |
|------|--------|-------|
| 1980 | Johnny Rutherford | 142.862 mph |
| 1981 | Bobby Unser | 139.084 mph |
| 1982 | Gordon Johncock | 162.029 mph |
| 1983 | Tom Sneva | 162.117 mph |
| 1984 | Rick Mears | 163.612 mph |
| 1985 | Danny Sullivan | 152.982 mph |
| 1986 | Bobby Rahal | 170.722 mph |
| 1987 | Al Unser | 162.175 mph |
| 1988 | Rick Mears | 149.806 mph |
| 1989 | Emerson Fittipaldi | 167.581 mph |
| 1990 | Arie Luyendyk | 185.981 mph |
| 1991 | Rick Mears | 176.457 mph |

### GOLF

| MASTERS | | US OPEN | |
|------|--------|------|--------|
| Year | Winner | Year | Winner |
| 1980 | Seve Ballesteros | 1980 | Jack Nicklaus |
| 1981 | Tom Watson | 1981 | David Graham |
| 1982 | Craig Stadler | 1982 | Tom Watson |
| 1983 | Seve Ballesteros | 1983 | Larry Nelson |
| 1984 | Ben Crenshaw | 1984 | Fuzzy Zoeller |
| 1985 | Bernhard Langer | 1985 | Andy North |
| 1986 | Jack Nicklaus | 1986 | Ray Floyd |
| 1987 | Larry Mize | 1987 | Scott Simpson |
| 1988 | Sandy Lyle | 1988 | Curtis Strange |
| 1989 | Nick Faldo | 1989 | Curtis Strange |
| 1990 | Nick Faldo | 1990 | Hale Irwin |
| 1991 | Ian Woosnam | 1991 | Payne Stewart |

| PGA CHAMPIONSHIP | | US WOMENS OPEN | |
|------|--------|------|--------|
| Year | Winner | Year | Winner |
| 1980 | Jack Nicklaus | 1980 | Amy Alcott |
| 1981 | Larry Nelson | 1981 | Pat Bradley |
| 1982 | Ray Floyd | 1982 | Janet Anderson |
| 1983 | Hal Sutton | 1983 | Jan Stephenson |
| 1984 | Lee Trevino | 1984 | Hollis Stacy |
| 1985 | Hubert Green | 1985 | Kathy Baker |
| 1986 | Bob Tway | 1986 | Jane Geddes |
| 1987 | Larry Nelson | 1987 | Laura Davies |
| 1988 | Jeff Sluman | 1988 | Liselotte Neumann |
| 1989 | Payne Stewart | 1989 | Betsy King |
| 1990 | Wayne Grady | 1990 | Betsy King |
| 1991 | John Daly | 1991 | Meg Mallon |

quarterback Joe Montana led San Francisco to four Super Bowl victories.

Outstanding career milestones were reached by baseball's Pete Rose and Nolan Ryan, NBA all-time scoring leader Kareem Abdul-Jabbar and NFL career rushing leader Walter Payton. Michael Jordan soared to new NBA heights, Wayne Gretzky rewrote the NHL record books and Tom Watson hit golf shots heard 'round the world.

*Tennis great Martina Navratilova.*

There were sad notes. The 1989 World Series was interrupted by a devastating earthquake in San Francisco and Rose, who was banned from baseball for his alleged gambling activities, spent much of 1990 in jail for tax evasion. A shock only slightly less in intensity than the earthquake was felt in 1991 when Lakers star Magic Johnson announced his retirement from professional basketball after testing positive for HIV, the virus that causes AIDS.

# HORSE RACING

### KENTUCKY DERBY

| Year | Horse | Jockey |
|------|-------|--------|
| 1980 | Genuine Risk | Jacinto Vasquez |
| 1981 | Pleasant Colony | Jorge Velasquez |
| 1982 | Gato Del Sol | Eddie Delahoussaye |
| 1983 | Sunny's Halo | Eddie Delahoussaye |
| 1984 | Swale | Laffit Pincay |
| 1985 | Spend A Buck | Angel Cordero |
| 1986 | Ferdinand | Bill Shoemaker |
| 1987 | Alysheba | Chris McCarron |
| 1988 | Winning Colors | Gary Stevens |
| 1989 | Sunday Silence | Pat Valenzuela |
| 1990 | Unbridled | Craig Perret |
| 1991 | Strike the Gold | Chris Antley |

### PREAKNESS STAKES

| Year | Winner | Jockey |
|------|--------|--------|
| 1980 | Codex | Angel Cordero |
| 1981 | Pleasant Colony | Jorge Velasquez |
| 1982 | Aloma's Ruler | Jack Kaenel |
| 1983 | Deputed Testamony | Donald Miller |
| 1984 | Gate Dancer | Angel Cordero |
| 1985 | Tank's Prospect | Pat Day |
| 1986 | Snow Chief | Alex Solis |
| 1987 | Alysheba | Chris McCarron |
| 1988 | Risen Star | Eddie Delahoussaye |
| 1989 | Sunday Silence | Pat Valenzuela |
| 1990 | Summer Squall | Pat Day |
| 1991 | Hansel | Jerry Bailey |

### BELMONT STAKES

| Year | Winner | Jockey |
|------|--------|--------|
| 1980 | Temperence Hill | Eddie Maple |
| 1981 | Summing | George Martens |
| 1982 | Conquistador Cielo | Laffit Pincay |
| 1983 | Caveat | Laffit Pincay |
| 1984 | Swale | Laffit Pincay |
| 1985 | Creme Fraiche | Eddie Maple |
| 1986 | Danzig Connection | Chris McCarron |
| 1987 | Bet Twice | Craig Perret |
| 1988 | Risen Star | Eddie Delahoussaye |
| 1989 | Easy Goer | Pat Day |
| 1990 | Go and Go | Michael Kinane |
| 1991 | Hansel | Jerry Bailey |

# BASEBALL

### WORLD SERIES

| Year | Winner | Pennant Winner (series score) |
|------|--------|-------------------------------|
| 1980 | Philadelphia Phillies | (Kansas City Royals, 4-2) |
| 1981 | Los Angeles Dodgers | (New York Yankees, 4-2) |
| 1982 | St. Louis Cardinals | (Milwaukee Brewers, 4-3) |
| 1983 | Baltimore Orioles | (Philadelphia Phillies, 4-1) |
| 1984 | Detroit Tigers | (San Diego Padres, 4-1) |
| 1985 | Kansas City Royals | (St. Louis Cardinals, 4-3) |
| 1986 | New York Mets | (Boston Red Sox, 4-3) |
| 1987 | Minnesota Twins | (St. Louis Cardinals, 4-3) |
| 1988 | Los Angeles Dodgers | (Oakland Athletics, 4-1) |
| 1989 | Oakland Athletics | (San Francisco Giants, 4-0) |
| 1990 | Cincinnati Reds | (Oakland Athletics, 4-0) |
| 1991 | Minnesota Twins | (Atlanta Braves, 4-3) |

# BASKETBALL

### NBA CHAMPIONSHIP

| Year | Winner | Finalist (series score) |
|------|--------|-------------------------|
| 1980-81 | Boston Celtics | (Hounston Rockets, 4-2) |
| 1981-82 | Los Angeles Lakers | (Philadelphia 76ers, 4-2) |
| 1982-83 | Philadelphia 76ers | (Los Angeles Lakers, 4-0) |
| 1983-84 | Boston Celtics | (Los Angeles Lakers, 4-3) |
| 1984-85 | Los Angeles Lakers | (Boston Celtics, 4-2) |
| 1985-86 | Boston Celtics | (Houston Rockets, 4-2) |
| 1986-87 | Los Angeles Lakers | (Boston Celtics, 4-2) |
| 1987-88 | Los Angeles Lakers | (Detroit Pistons, 4-3) |
| 1988-89 | Detroit Pistons | (Los Angeles Lakers, 4-0) |
| 1989-90 | Detroit Pistons | (Portland Trail Blazers, 4-1) |
| 1990-91 | Chicago Bulls | (Los Angeles Lakers, 4-1) |

### NCAA TOURNAMENT FINAL

| Year | Winner | Finalist (score) |
|------|--------|------------------|
| 1980 | Louisville | (UCLA, 59-54) |
| 1981 | Indiana | (North Carolina, 63-50) |
| 1982 | North Carolina | (Georgetown, 63-62) |
| 1983 | North Carolina State | (Houston, 54-52) |
| 1984 | Georgetown | (Houston, 84-75) |
| 1985 | Villanova | (Georgetown, 66-64) |
| 1986 | Louisville | (Duke, 72-69) |
| 1987 | Indiana | (Syracuse, 74-73) |
| 1988 | Kansas | (Oklahoma, 83-79) |
| 1989 | Michigan | (Seton Hall, 80-79 OT) |
| 1990 | UNLV | (Duke, 103-73) |
| 1991 | Duke | (Kansas, 72-65) |

# FOOTBALL

### SUPER BOWL

| Season | Winner | Finalist (score) |
|--------|--------|------------------|
| 1980 | Oakland Raiders | (Philadelphia Eagles, 27-10) |
| 1981 | San Francisco 49ers | (Cincinnati Bengals, 26-21) |
| 1982 | Washington Redskins | (Miami Dolphins, 27-17) |
| 1983 | Los Angeles Raiders | (Washington Redskins, 38-9) |
| 1984 | San Francisco 49ers | (Miami Dolphins, 38-16) |
| 1985 | Chicago Bears | (New England Patriots, 46-10) |
| 1986 | New York Giants | (Denver Broncos, 39-20) |
| 1987 | Washington Redskins | (Denver Broncos, 42-10) |
| 1988 | San Francisco 49ers | (Cincinnati Bengals, 20-16) |
| 1989 | San Francisco 49ers | (Denver Broncos, 55-10) |
| 1990 | New York Giants | (Buffalo Bills, 20-19) |
| 1991 | Washington Redskins | (Buffalo Bills, 37-24) |

# HOCKEY

### STANLEY CUP

| Year | Champion | Finalist (series score) |
|------|----------|-------------------------|
| 1980-81 | New York Islanders | (Minnesota North Stars, 4-1) |
| 1981-82 | New York Islanders | (Vancouver Canucks, 4-0) |
| 1982-83 | New York Islanders | (Edmonton Oilers, 4-0) |
| 1983-84 | Edmonton Oilers | (New York Islanders, 4-1) |
| 1984-85 | Edmonton Oilers | (Philadelphia Flyers, 4-1) |
| 1985-86 | Montreal Canadiens | (Calgary Flames, 4-2) |
| 1986-87 | Edmonton Oilers | (Philadelphia Flyers, 4-3) |
| 1987-88 | Edmonton Oilers | (Boston Bruins, 4-0) |
| 1988-89 | Calgary Flames | (Montreal Canadiens, 4-2) |
| 1989-90 | Edmonton Oilers | (Boston Bruins, 4-1) |
| 1990-91 | Pittsburgh Penguins | (Minnesota North Stars, 4-2) |

# TENNIS

### US OPEN

| Year | Men's Winner | Women's Winner |
|------|--------------|----------------|
| 1980 | John McEnroe | Chris Evert-Lloyd |
| 1981 | John McEnroe | Tracy Austin |
| 1982 | Jimmy Connors | Chris Evert-Lloyd |
| 1983 | Jimmy Connors | Martina Navratilova |
| 1984 | John McEnroe | Martina Navratilova |
| 1985 | Ivan Lendl | Hana Mandlikova |
| 1986 | Ivan Lendl | Martina Navratilova |
| 1987 | Ivan Lendl | Martina Navratilova |
| 1988 | Mats Wilander | Steffi Graf |
| 1989 | Boris Becker | Steffi Graf |
| 1990 | Pete Sampras | Gabriela Sabatini |
| 1991 | Stefan Edberg | Monica Seles |

# 1980

## The Miracle on Ice

In one of the most startling and dramatic upsets in sports history, an American hockey team made up of collegians and itinerant minor leaguers defeated the powerful Soviet nationals, 4-3, in a February 22 semifinal matchup during the Winter Olympic Games at Lake Placid, N.Y.

The victory, which put the seventh-seeded Americans one step away from a gold medal, triggered an incredible outpouring of emotion. After 10,000 fans had chanted down the final seconds at the Olympic Field House, parents and friends dashed onto the ice, hugging anybody wearing red, white and blue. Those fans remaining in the stands chanted, "U.S.A. U.S.A.," and hundreds more outside waved American flags.

But the celebration did not end there. Across the nation, car horns blared, fireworks crackled and shrieks of joy sounded the excitement. Switchboards at newspapers and radio and television stations lit up as Americans expressed their surge of national pride.

The object of this affection was a ragtag group of hockey players coached by Herb Brooks. Not blessed with great talent, Brooks had instilled a sense of fierce pride and determination with the hope that this squad could spring a few upsets, perhaps even reach the medal round. Surprisingly, it did that by winning four times and tying once in the opening round. Next up: the fast-skating Soviets, probably the finest hockey team in the world.

From the first check of that semifinal encounter, the atmosphere was electric. The Americans were overmatched talent-wise, but through sheer determination and the goaltending of Jim Craig, they stayed in the game. The score was 2-2 after one period. The Soviets led 3-2 after two.

Many jaws dropped when Mark Johnson banged in a rebound early in the final period to tie the score. Shock waves rippled through the arena midway through the final stanza when Mike Eruzione connected on a 30-foot slapshot. Could it be? As the minutes counted down and the Americans continued to thwart the swarming Soviets, two nations took notice.

The victory came over a team that had captured the last four

*Bedlam broke out on the ice, in the stands and throughout the United States after the American hockey team upset the Soviet Union, 4-3, in a Winter Olympics semifinal contest at Lake Placid.*

Olympic golds and five of the last six. Ironically, the only Olympic team to defeat the Soviets since 1956 was the American squad of 1960, which captured the gold at Squaw Valley, Calif.

The Americans finished their golden journey, February 24, when they scored three third-period goals and defeated Finland, 4-2.

The 1980 version of the Miracle on Ice was complete.

## Heiden has a golden touch in Olympics

Lost in the emotion of the U.S. hockey upset was the record five-gold medal performance of Eric Heiden, the 21-year-old speed skater from Madison, Wis., who dominated his segment of the Winter Games like no athlete in Olympic history.

Heiden, a three-time world champion, completed a nine-day blitz of the world and Olympic record books, February 23, with a victory in the rugged 10,000 meters, already having raced at four different distances. He covered the 6.2-mile race in 14:28.13, knocking more than six seconds off the

*American Eric Heiden looks up at his world-record time after winning the 10,000-meter race and his fifth Olympic gold medal.*

world record.

Heiden's resounding 10,000-meter triumph followed victories in the 500, 1,000, 1,500 and 5,000-meter events. He set world records in the 1,000, 1,500 and 10,000 meters and broke Olympic marks in the other two.

# Louisville tops UCLA

High-flying Darrell Griffith scored 23 points and Louisville survived a turnover-filled battle against UCLA, March 24, beating the Bruins, 59-54, in the NCAA Tournament championship game at Indianapolis.

It was a surprisingly low score for a game that matched two young, racehorse teams. And race they did, sometimes with control of the ball, sometimes without. By the end of a 28-26 first half (UCLA's lead), the teams had combined for 16 turnovers, 11 steals and 18 fouls.

The turnovers continued after intermission, but the intensity and drama of the final minutes was worth the price of admission. Trailing by five

*Louisville's Darrell Griffith (left) and Tony Branch display the Cardinals' championship trophy.*

points with just over six minutes remaining and 54-52 with 3:26 to play, Louisville rallied to tie, took the lead on Griffith's 18-foot jump shot and stretched the margin to four on a pair of free throws by Derek Smith.

The keys to Louisville's 33rd victory and first national championship were the final-game leadership of Griffith, Coach Denny Crum's only senior starter, and a defense that held UCLA's Kiki Vandeweghe to 14 points.

## "SPORTS TALK"

*"They can put on my tombstone: 'He'd a lasted a lot longer if he hadn't played Pittsburgh six times in two years.'"*

**BUM PHILLIPS**
Houston Oilers football Coach

# U.S. boycotts Games

The Olympic dreams of hundreds of American athletes were shattered, April 12, when the United States Olympic Committee voted to endorse President Jimmy Carter's call for a boycott of the Summer Games in Moscow.

The dramatic vote came at a meeting in Colorado Springs attended by nearly 300 athletes, sports leaders and business officials who make up the committee's house of delegates. It followed hours of sometimes-angry debate and an emotional appeal for support from Vice President Walter Mondale.

The vote was a major victory for Carter, who sought the boycott to show displeasure over the Soviets' military action in Afghanistan. It was a major disappointment for athletes who had devoted four hard years to training for the Games.

---

## ★ SPORTS WATCH ★

**JAN:** The Pittsburgh Steelers won their second straight Super Bowl and fourth in six years, beating the Los Angeles Rams, 31-19, at the Rose Bowl in Pasadena, Calif.

**JAN:** The Minnesota North Stars defeated Philadelphia, 7-1, and halted the Flyers' NHL-record 35-game unbeaten streak at Bloomington, Minn.

**FEB:** The Dallas Mavericks, paying an admission price of $12 million, were accepted as the NBA's 23rd team.

**MAR:** The Whalers' 51-year-old Gordie Howe scored his record 800th regular-season NHL goal during a 3-0 victory over St. Louis in a game at Hartford.

**APR:** Seve Ballesteros shot a 72-hole total of 275 and earned his first Masters victory at Augusta.

---

# Marathon officials uncover Rosie's Ruse

Bill Rodgers became the first runner in 56 years and only the second ever to capture three straight Boston Marathons when he covered the 26-mile, 385-yard course in 2:12.11 on April 21. But the 32-year-old Rodgers' effort was overshadowed by a major controversy involving the first female finisher, a 26-year-old New Yorker named Rosie Ruiz, who staggered past the finish line in 2:31.56.

Ruiz, running only her second marathon, had gone unnoticed for most of the race. Her finishing time, the third fastest ever recorded by a woman, caught everybody by surprise

and prompted race officials to begin an investigation. She donned the traditional laurel wreath and received a medal and silver bowl for winning a race many doubted she had run.

As the investigation proceeded, evidence mounted that Ruiz's New York City Marathon finish, which qualified her for the Boston race, also was suspect. Her New York time was 25 minutes slower than her Boston time and a witness reported seeing her elsewhere while the race was being contested.

New York officials acted first, invalidating her time of 2:56.27 for that race. On April 29,

*Rosie Ruiz, wearing her championship wreath, gets a police escort after apparently winning the women's segment of the Boston Marathon.*

after a seven-day review of observers' notes and more than 10,000 photographs, Boston officials stripped Ruiz of the title and awarded it to Jacqueline Gareau of Montreal.

# MAY-AUGUST

## Islanders nip Flyers, win 1st Stanley Cup

Bob Nystrom shoved the puck past Philadelphia goaltender Pete Peeters 7 minutes, 11 seconds into overtime, May 24, giving the New York Islanders a 5-4 victory over the Flyers and their first Stanley Cup triumph.

The dramatic Game 6 victory sent the 14,995 fans at Nassau Coliseum into a frenzy. The Islanders, born eight years ago, became only the second expansion team to capture hockey's coveted prize. The Flyers did it first, winning in 1974 and '75.

The Islanders did not exactly dominate the NHL during the regular season, finishing fifth in the overall standings, but they captured 15 of 21 playoff contests and always seemed to have the answer when the chips were down. Seven times they played postseason overtime games and six times they won.

The finale was not pretty. There was plenty of drama and emotion, but there also was a lot of fighting, roughing and chippy tactics. After a 2-2 first period, the Islanders took a 4-2 lead on second-period goals by Mike Bossy and Nystrom. But the Flyers battled back to tie on goals by Bob Dailey and John Paddock.

## Johnson is Magic in Lakers' title win

It wasn't supposed to end this way. The Los Angeles Lakers held a 3-2 advantage in the NBA Finals, but Game 6 would be contested in Philadelphia, May 16, and the Lakers would be playing without the man most responsible for getting them that far—Kareem Abdul-Jabbar. The big center had sprained his ankle while scoring 40 points in the Lakers' 108-103 Game 5 victory.

But, like Magic, that became a moot point. Earvin Johnson, a 6-foot-8 sophomore guard on Michigan State's NCAA championship team last year, scored 42 points, grabbed 15 rebounds and handed out seven assists in a 123-107 series-ending Laker victory. And he played center.

Johnson was unstoppable and dominated the boards over players three inches taller. He got plenty of help from Keith Wilkes, the Lakers' forward who added 37 points.

Wilkes was the key in a 14-point Los Angeles surge to open the third period after a 60-60 halftime tie. The 76ers closed to within two points three times, but a 20-6 game-ending blitz settled the issue.

*Los Angeles rookie Magic Johnson wipes away the champagne he poured over the head of team Owner Dr. Jerry Buss.*

## Filly captures Derby

Genuine Risk, the first filly to be entered in a Kentucky Derby since 1959, outran 12 colts and won the May 3 Run for the Roses at Louisville's Churchill Downs.

In becoming the first filly to win a Derby since Regret in 1915, Genuine Risk broke from a tight pack at the top of the stretch and completed the 1¼-mile test in 2:02. With 131,859 fans watching in surprise, Rumbo came on hard but could not quite close the gap.

Genuine Risk, ridden by Jacinto Vasquez, had won six straight races before finishing third in the Wood Memorial, her first test against male horses. Trainer LeRoy Jolley said after that race that she would not be competing any more against colts.

But Jolley was overruled by owners Diana and Bert Firestone, and the move paid off. The last filly to run in the Derby was C.V. Whitney's Silver Spoon, which finished fifth.

*Jacinto Vasquez rides filly Genuine Risk across the finish line and into the Kentucky Derby record books.*

---

### ★ SPORTS WATCH ★

**MAY:** San Francisco Giants first baseman Willie McCovey belted the 521st—and last—home run of his career off Montreal righthander Scott Sanderson.

**MAY:** Chicago White Sox first baseman Mike Squires caught the final inning of an 11-1 loss to Milwaukee, becoming the first lefthanded catcher in the major leagues since Dale Long in 1958.

**JUL:** Edwin Moses broke his own world record in the 400-meter hurdles, clocking 47.3 seconds at Milan, Italy.

**JUL:** Nine in a row: Cincinnati's Ken Griffey starred as the National League continued its All-Star Game domination with a 4-2 victory at Dodger Stadium.

**JUL:** Tom Watson's four-round total of 271 was good enough to earn him a third British Open victory at Muirfield, Scotland.

# Borg beats McEnroe in Wimbledon classic

In a match that ranks among the greatest ever witnessed on Centre Court, Bjorn Borg outdueled John McEnroe, July 5, in a 3-hour, 53-minute thriller and captured his fifth straight Wimbledon singles title with a 1-6, 7-5, 6-3, 6-7, 8-6 victory.

"Electrifying" was the only way to describe a fourth set that concluded with a dramatic 34-point tiebreaker after McEnroe had fought off seven match points. Borg led 5-4 and 40-15 on his own serve but McEnroe fought back. Borg got his third match point at 6-5 in the tiebreaker. McEnroe again survived. Every other point from then on was a set or match point for somebody until McEnroe finally prevailed, 18-16.

The tiebreaker and final set both were fiercely contested battles of strong-willed competitors, who stretched, lunged and dove for every shot. The 21-year-old McEnroe stuck with his aggressive serve-and-volley style and the 24-year-old Swede played with the fluid movement and pinpoint strokes that are his trademark.

In the final set, Borg's serve made the difference, producing 19 consecutive points and his record 35th straight victory in Wimbledon matches.

Bjorn Borg celebrates after defeating John McEnroe and winning his fifth straight Wimbledon singles championship.

# Jack wins 19th major

Jack Nicklaus, in search of his 19th major golf title, coasted to a final-round 69 and captured the PGA Championship by a record seven strokes, August 10, at Oak Hill Country Club in Rochester, N.Y.

The Golden Bear, winner of his fourth U.S. Open in June, took control of this tournament with a third-round 66 and steadily increased his three-stroke lead with a safe, consistent final round. As he played conservatively, Andy Bean and Lon Hinkle battled for second place, losing strokes in the process. Nicklaus finished with a 72-hole total of 274, six under par and seven ahead of Bean.

The victory was Nicklaus' fifth PGA, to go with five Masters, four U.S. Opens, three British Opens and two U.S. Amateurs. Bobby Jones ranks second with 13 titles.

# Houston ace Richard sidelined by a stroke

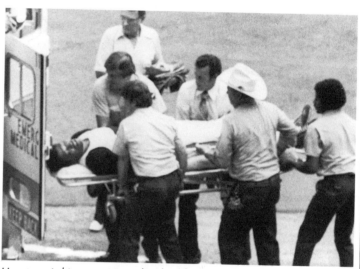

Houston pitching ace J.R. Richard is lifted into an ambulance after suffering a stroke during a workout at the Astrodome.

J.R. Richard, the intimidating 6-foot-8 fireballer of the Houston Astros, underwent successful surgery for a blocked artery in his neck, July 30, hours after collapsing during a workout at the Astrodome.

Richard, a 20-game winner in 1976 and 10-4 this season, had been complaining for several months of a fatigued arm. He entered the hospital a week ago for four days of tests. Team doctors, unable to find anything wrong physically, had suggested that Richard's problem could be emotional.

That obviously was not the case. The big righthander, with the blazing fastball and 90-mph slider, collapsed while playing catch. He was rushed to the hospital where a blood clot was detected behind his right collarbone in a main artery that provides circulation for the upper limbs. That caused him to suffer a stroke.

Richard, who had pitched for the National League in the July 6 All-Star Game, has a career record of 107-71 with a 3.15 earned-run average and 1,493 strikeouts in seven-plus seasons. It is unknown whether he will pitch again.

# Holmes batters Ali, spoils comeback bid

*Muhammad Ali (right) and Larry Holmes trade blows during their heavyweight title fight at Las Vegas.*

Larry Holmes, exhibiting the hand speed and quickness that used to be a Muhammad Ali trademark, bruised and battered the former champion, October 2, and scored a technical knockout when Ali failed to answer the bell for the 11th round of a WBC title bout at Las Vegas.

The 38-year-old Ali, trying to come back from a two-year retirement and win the heavyweight championship for a fourth time, was completely overmatched against his talented 30-year-old opponent. As Ali labored around the ring, Holmes danced and delivered a variety of punches, most of them finding their mark.

Ali appeared hopelessly beaten in the ninth round when he took a right uppercut to the chin and a left to the kidney. After taking a lot more punishment in the 10th, he called it a night.

The victory was the 36th straight for Holmes.

# Houston wins playoff

Joe Niekro pitched a six-hitter and Art Howe drove in four runs as the Houston Astros escaped with a 7-1 victory over Los Angeles in a one-game playoff that decided the National League West Division championship, October 6, at Dodger Stadium.

The confident Astros had arrived in Los Angeles on October 3, for a regular season-closing three-game showdown against the Dodgers, needing only one victory to clinch the first division title in club history.

But the Dodgers won the first game, 3-2, on Joe Ferguson's 10th-inning home run, won the second, 2-1, on Steve Garvey's fourth-inning homer and won the third, 4-3, on Ron Cey's two-run shot in the eighth inning.

The Astros needed to regain their composure—and fast. They did, scoring two unearned runs in the first inning of the playoff and increasing the lead with Howe's two-run homer in the fourth. Niekro allowed only one unearned run in picking up his 20th win.

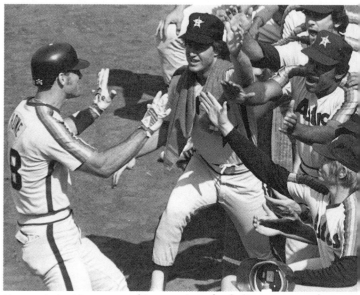

*Houston's Art Howe gets a big reception after belting a two-run homer during the Astros' N.L. West Division playoff victory over Los Angeles.*

# Phils survive Astros

Garry Maddox doubled home a run in the 10th inning and Dick Ruthven made it stand up as Philadelphia defeated Houston, 8-7, and ended a tense, topsy-turvy National League Championship Series.

The Phillies, trailing 5-2 entering the eighth inning of the October 12 game at Houston's Astrodome, rallied for five runs and a 7-5 advantage. But the Astros came back to tie, forcing the fourth extra-inning contest of the five-game series.

Only the opener, won 3-1 by Philadelphia behind Steve Carlton and Tug McGraw, was decided in regulation. Houston rallied for four 10th-inning runs and a 7-4 victory in Game 2 and then took the series lead on a 10th-inning sacrifice fly by Denny Walling that produced a 1-0 relief win for Dave Smith.

The fourth game featured a near-triple play controversy in the fourth inning that held up the contest 20 minutes. When play resumed, the Phillies wiped out a 2-0 deficit with three eighth-inning runs, Houston tied in the bottom of the inning and Philadelphia won in the 10th on RBI doubles by Greg Luzinski and Manny Trillo.

# Leonard gets revenge

Sugar Ray Leonard regained the WBC welterweight title he had lost to Roberto Duran six months earlier when he scored an eighth-round technical knockout over the champ, November 25, at the New Orleans Superdome.

The fight came to a surprising conclusion when the 29-year-old Panamanian suddenly stepped away from Leonard, turned to the referee and said, "No mas, no mas," which is Spanish for "no more." Duran said later that he conceded to his 24-year-old challenger because of stomach cramps that were getting worse every round.

Duran had captured Leonard's title last June in a brawling slugfest at Montreal. But Leonard controlled this fight from the start and led on all scorecards when Duran quit. The shuffle, crisp jabs and quick combinations that were absent in Montreal all returned and Duran appeared to lose heart.

The loss was the second in 74 career fights for Duran. Leonard is 28-1.

Roberto Duran says "No mas" and Sugar Ray Leonard celebrates his sudden victory over the man who had taken away his welterweight title.

# Brett flirts with .400

Kansas City third baseman George Brett was named American League Most Valuable Player, November 18, capping a wild and crazy season that ran the gamut from despair to ecstasy.

It started slowly, with Brett struggling for hits and fighting nagging injuries. And just when the talented lefthanded hitter heated up in early June with a 34-for-76 tear, he had the misfortune to damage his foot and missed 26 games.

But there was nothing frustrating about the rest of the regular season. Brett compiled a 30-game hitting streak, flirted with the magic .400 mark until late September and led the Royals to the A.L. West Division title. He finished under a media microscope with a .390 average, the highest in baseball since Ted Williams hit .406 in 1941, 24 home runs and 118 RBIs in 117 games.

Brett's unusual season did not end there, however. His dramatic three-run homer off Yankee relief ace Goose Gossage in Game 3 of the A.L. Championship Series gave the Royals their first-ever World Series berth and reestablished him as a baseball Superman. But an embarrassing case of World Series hemorrhoids brought him back to earth.

Brett underwent surgery after Game 2, but returned for Game 3, hitting a home run and double. But Philadelphia prevailed in six games.

Kansas City slugger George Brett jumps for joy after the final out had been recorded in the Royals' A.L. Championship Series victory over New York.

## ★ SPORTS WATCH ★

**SEP:** John McEnroe outlasted Bjorn Borg in five sets and Chris Evert-Lloyd needed three sets to beat Hana Mandlikova in an American sweep of the U.S. Open singles titles at Flushing Meadow.

**SEP:** Quarterback Richard Todd completed an NFL-record 42 passes (447 yards) in a game against San Francisco, but the 49ers posted a 37-27 victory over the Jets at New York's Shea Stadium.

**OCT:** Oakland outfielder Rickey Henderson stole 100 bases, topping Ty Cobb's 65-year-old American League single-season stolen base record of 96.

**NOV:** Illinois quarterback Dave Wilson set an NCAA single-game record of 621 yards passing in a game against Ohio State, but the Buckeyes won the contest 49-42.

**DEC:** South Carolina running back George Rogers outpolled Pittsburgh defensive end Hugh Green and captured the Heisman Trophy.

# Georgia pulls one out

Georgia quarterback Buck Belue, backed up near his own goal line with time running out and his team's chances for an undefeated season slipping away, fired a 93-yard touchdown strike to Lindsay Scott, November 8, giving the Bulldogs a dramatic 26-21 victory over arch-rival Florida at the Gator Bowl in Jacksonville, Fla.

The Gators, down 20-10 entering the final period, had rallied to take a 21-20 lead on an 11-yard touchdown run by James Jones, a two-point conversion pass from Warren Peace to Tyrone Young and Brian Clark's 40-yard field goal.

With less than two minutes remaining, Georgia received a punt on its own 7-yard line. Belue scrambled for no gain and threw an incomplete pass. On third down, he fired over the middle to Scott, who grabbed the pass at the Georgia 35, spun around and slipped through a ring of defenders. He was off to the races and the 9-0 Bulldogs were on their way to a national championship.

Georgia super freshman Herschel Walker scored on a 72-yard touchdown run and finished with 238 yards.

# 1981

## JANUARY-APRIL

## Super Raiders make Eagles go ker-plunk

*Oakland quarterback Jim Plunkett barks orders during the Raiders' 27-10 Super Bowl victory over Philadelphia.*

Jim Plunkett threw three touchdown passes and linebacker Rod Martin intercepted three Ron Jaworski passes, January 25, as Oakland became the first wild-card playoff team to win a Super Bowl with a 27-10 victory over Philadelphia at the New Orleans Superdome.

Plunkett, the former Heisman Trophy winner who had been languishing with Oakland since 1978 as a seldom-used backup,

fired a two-yard first-quarter touchdown strike to Cliff Branch and then connected a few minutes later with running back Kenny King on an 80-yarder—the longest pass play in Super Bowl history. Plunkett threw a 29-yard TD pass to Branch in the third quarter.

The veteran quarterback had taken over for injured Dan Pastorini in the Raiders' fifth game of the 1980 season and guided Oakland to an 11-5 record and a wild-card berth. The Raiders swept past Houston, Cleveland and San Diego in gaining their third Super Bowl appearance.

The Eagles, making their first, were never really in the game. Jaworski, hounded all day by the Raider pass rush, completed only 18 of 38 passes and was picked off three times by Martin.

### "SPORTS TALK"

*"When Charlie had his heart operation, it took eight hours—7½ just to find his heart."*

**STEVE McCATTY**
Oakland pitcher on A's Owner Charles O. Finley

## Lewis breaks record

Carl Lewis, a multi-talented sophomore at the University of Houston, leaped into the record books, February 20, when he set an indoor world mark for the long jump at 27-10¼ during competition in the Southwest Conference indoor track and field championships at Fort Worth, Tex.

The tall 19-year-old, the reigning NCAA long jump champion both indoor and outdoor, broke the 27-6 mark set last year by Larry Myricks of Mississippi College. Ironically, Myricks competed in a meet at San Diego, February 20, and won the long jump competition with a mediocre leap of 27-2¾. Lewis' previous best was 27-4.

He also won the 60-yard dash with the third-fastest indoor time ever recorded. Lewis was timed in 6.06 seconds, slightly off the 6.04 record set two weeks ago by Stanley Floyd in the Dallas Times-Herald meet.

## Bossy joins 50-50 club

New York Islander right winger Mike Bossy, running out of time in his quest to tie one of the National Hockey League's most enduring records, scored two goals in the final 4:10 of a January 24 game against Quebec and became the second player in history to score 50 goals in the first 50 games of a season.

Bossy, double and triple-teamed the entire game by the Nordiques, did not even manage a shot in the first two periods. As time ran down in a 4-4 game, it appeared he would fall short in his quest to tie the record set in 1944-45 by former Montreal great Maurice (Rocket) Richard.

But with 15,008 fans at Nassau Coliseum cheering his every move, Bossy finally got a chance on a power play and flicked a backhander past Quebec goaltender Ron Grahame. As the red light came on, the crowd rose en masse and roared its approval.

The record-tying goal came with 1:29 remaining when Bossy took a pass from Bryan Trottier and rifled a shot past Grahame. Bedlam broke out, both on the ice and in the stands. The Islanders won the game, 7-4.

*New York Islander Mike Bossy, the NHL's second 50-50 goal scorer.*

# Fernando continues to amaze

Los Angeles lefthander Fernando Valenzuela, the 20-year-old Mexican wunderkind, continued to baffle major league hitters, April 27, as he pitched his fourth shutout of the season and fifth straight complete game in a 5-0 whitewash of San Francisco before 49,478 roaring fans at Dodger Stadium.

Valenzuela, a stocky, awkward-looking youngster with a moon face and a devastating screwball, has taken the baseball world by storm. He broke into the big leagues late last year with 17⅔ scoreless innings in 10 relief appearances and he has allowed one earned run in his five starts this year. His earned-run average is a nifty 0.20 in 1981, 0.14 in 62⅔ career innings. He currently is working on a scoreless string of 28⅔ innings.

But that is only part of the story. Valenzuela, the youngest player in the National League, also can swing a bat, as evidenced by the seven hits he has collected in his last 11 at-bats. He was 3-for-4 against the Giants and singled in the Dodgers' four-run fourth inning.

*Los Angeles lefthander Fernando Valenzuela, baseball's newest wunderkind.*

**JAN:** Frank Robinson, baseball's first black manager with Cleveland in 1975, signed to manage the San Francisco Giants.

**JAN:** Georgia wrapped up the 1980 college football national championship with a 17-10 Sugar Bowl victory over Notre Dame.

**FEB:** Richard Petty, averaging 169.651 mph in his Buick, won his record seventh Daytona 500.

**MAR:** Houston's Calvin Murphy broke Rick Barry's consecutive free throw record of 60 in February and went on to make 78 straight.

**APR:** Edmonton whiz kid Wayne Gretzky became hockey's first two-points-per-game scorer, totaling 55 goals and a record 109 assists for 164 points.

**APR:** Larry Holmes retained his world heavyweight championship with a unanimous 15-round decision over Trevor Berbick in a bout at Las Vegas.

**APR:** Former boxing great Joe Louis, heavyweight champion for almost 12 years, died of cardiac arrest at age 66 in Las Vegas.

# Watson holds on to win Masters

Tom Watson held off the challenges of Jack Nicklaus and Johnny Miller, April 12, and captured his second Masters tournament at Augusta National Golf Club.

Watson's two-stroke victory was forged on a final-round 71 that required three tricky par-saving escapes. He sank a tough eight-foot putt on 12 after rolling his first putt past the pin, he recovered on the par-5 13th after dropping his second shot into Rae's Creek, and he aggressively blasted out of a sand trap on 17 to within four feet of the pin.

With a birdie on 15 sandwiched into the equation, Watson finished at 280. Nicklaus, trailing Watson by one stroke after three rounds, struggled to a 72 and Miller, five strokes behind, came home with a 68. The fast greens and devilish pin placements made the going tough for everybody.

In winning the fifth major championship (two Masters and three British Opens) and 23rd tournament of his outstanding career, the talented Watson never was tied in the final round and he never led by more than two strokes.

# Sophomore triggers Hoosiers

*NCAA Tournament MVP Isiah Thomas (left) of Indiana gets a friendly hug from North Carolina's Al Wood after the Hoosiers' 63-50 victory.*

Indiana sophomore Isiah Thomas, a 6-foot-1 basketball prodigy, destroyed North Carolina during a seven-minute stretch of the second half, March 30, and Coach Bob Knight's Hoosiers went on to record a 63-50 victory in the NCAA Tournament championship game at Philadelphia.

With Thomas scoring 10 of his game-high 23 points, making several key steals and feeding open teammates in the first seven minutes after intermission, the Hoosiers turned a 27-26 halftime advantage into a 43-34 lead. The All-America guard went on to add nine more points and controlled play.

The game almost was postponed. Earlier in the day, President Ronald Reagan had been shot in an assassination attempt. Even after it was determined that he was out of danger and the game would be played, a somber mood pervaded the normally electric championship atmosphere.

The Tar Heels broke out to 8-2 and 16-8 leads, but the first-half shooting of Randy Wittman kept Indiana in the game until Thomas could get rolling.

# 1981

## MAY-AUGUST

## A 33-inning marathon

Two months and 33 innings after it started, the longest baseball game in history ended in just 18 minutes, June 23. The Pawtucket Red Sox scored the first time they batted in the continuation of an April 18 marathon and defeated the Rochester Red Wings, 3-2.

The International League teams had battled to an 8-hour, 7-minute 2-2 tie through 32 innings of their April encounter in Pawtucket, R.I. International League President Harold Cooper had ordered the game halted at 4:07 the morning of April 19, with 20 of the original 1,470 fans remaining in the stands.

The game, scheduled for completion on Rochester's next trip to Pawtucket, generated national headlines. When it was resumed, 54 newspapers, three television networks and numerous radio crews were crammed into little McCoy Stadium along with 5,756 fans. Broadcasters came from as far away as Great Britain and Japan.

Amid all the hoopla, Pawtucket's Bob Ojeda retired the Red Wings without incident in the top of the 33rd. But the Red Sox loaded the bases with nobody out in the bottom of the inning and Dave Koza's single brought in Marty Barrett with the winning run.

The previous longest professional game was a 29-inning Florida State League contest between Miami and St. Petersburg in 1966.

*Pawtucket's Dave Koza (left), who stroked the winning hit in the 33rd inning, hugs pitcher Bob Ojeda after the completion of the longest game in baseball history.*

## Shoemaker races on

Bill Shoemaker rode War Allied into uncharted territory, May 27, winning his record 8,000th career race during competition at Hollywood Park, Calif.

Shoemaker established the milestone in the first race on the Hollywood program, and rode three more winners, including Gam Bey in the $53,500 Happy Issue Stakes. War Allied won by three lengths and sparked a standing ovation from the crowd of 20,188.

The 49-year-old Shoemaker, who rode his first winner on April 20, 1949, had moved into second place on the all-time victory list in 1970, when he rode his 6,033rd winner and broke Johnny Longden's career record. He had won his 7,999th race, May 24, at Hollywood Park aboard Native Prospector.

The 8,000th winner brought Shoemaker's career earnings for all mounts to $81,851,276.

*War Allied carries jockey Bill Shoemaker to his record 8,000th first-place finish.*

## Celtics catch 76ers

Larry Bird tied the score with two free throws and then hit a game-winning 16-foot bank shot with 1:03 remaining to complete an incredible Boston rally and give the Celtics a 91-90 victory over Philadelphia in the May 3 seventh game of the Eastern Conference finals.

Boston's luck appeared to have run out when Philadelphia built its lead to 89-82 on Julius Erving's reverse layup with 5:23 remaining. But the 76ers suddenly began forcing shots and turning the ball over. The Celtics, never ones to waste such opportunity, outscored them 9-1 down the stretch.

That was the same collapsing pattern the 76ers had followed in blowing a 3-1 series lead. They built a 10-point advantage and lost Game 5 and then let a 17-point lead slip away in Game 6. Their lead reached 11 at one point in the finale.

But with Bird scoring 23 points and Kevin McHale doing a nice defensive job on Erving down the stretch, the Celtics won this battle of teams that had finished the regular season with 60-22 records.

Boston went on to win its 14th championship, beating Houston in the NBA Finals.

# Baseball settles lengthy strike

The longest strike in American sports history came to an end, July 31, when negotiators for baseball's owners and players reached agreement on the sticky free-agent compensation issue that had brought the season to a skidding halt seven weeks ago.

With the season fast approaching the point of no return, Marvin Miller, head of the Players' Association, hammered out agreement on a complicated pooling system for free-agent compensation with Ray Grebey, the owners' chief negotiator. The owners also agreed to restore service credit to the players for strike time in exchange for an extra year on the Basic Agreement that was signed in 1980 without resolution of the compensation problem.

The strike, which began on June 12, forced cancellation of 706 games (38 percent of the schedule) and cost players an estimated $28 million in salaries. The owners' losses were estimated at $116 million, although strike insurance will cut that deficit by a third.

With the cancellation of so many games, a plan has been formulated to divide the season into two halves. Teams that were in first place through games of June 11 will be declared first-half division winners and they will meet teams that finish in first place over the second half in a best-of-five divisional playoff to decide League Championship Series participants. The Oakland A's (A.L. West), New York Yankees (A.L. East), Philadelphia Phillies (N.L. East) and Los Angeles Dodgers (N.L. West) already have qualified as first-half champions.

The second season will kick off, August 9, with the All-Star Game in Cleveland, and teams will begin play the next day.

*With an end to the baseball strike nowhere in sight, many players, such as Yankee pitcher Ron Davis (above), tried their hands at regular jobs.*

# McEnroe stops Borg

John McEnroe capped a tumultuous two weeks at Wimbledon, July 4, by ending Bjorn Borg's 41-match winning streak and five-year reign as champion with a 4-6, 7-6, 7-6, 6-4 victory.

Johnny Mac, playing under the threat of a $10,000 fine and lengthy suspension because of his stormy conduct throughout the prestigious event, showed against Borg that he can play championship tennis without the tantrums and off-colored theatrics that have earned him an international reputation. Keeping his temper under wraps and controlling his sometimes-erratic first serve, the 22-year-old New Yorker earned his first Wimbledon title.

McEnroe won 82 of 104 points played off his first serve, an impressive 79 percent. He used that serve as an effective weapon in both tiebreakers, which he dominated by scores of 7-1 and 7-4. Borg had four set points in the third set, but McEnroe controlled service on each occasion.

The match lacked the excitement and drama of last year's five-set classic and those who showed up to see McEnroe's temperamental act were disap-

*John McEnroe gives the choke sign to a Wimbledon linesman during action in his tumultuous semifinal match against Rod Frawley.*

pointed. He had been particularly unruly in his semifinal match with Rod Frawley and the tournament committee of the All England Club recommended a fine and suspension for "consistently arguing over line decisions, bad language and verbal abuse of referees, umpires and linesmen."

McEnroe's victory completed an American singles sweep. Chris Evert-Lloyd beat Hana Mandlikova, 6-2, 6-2, for her third Wimbledon title.

## ★ SPORTS WATCH ★

**MAY:** The New York Islanders defeated Minnesota, 5-1, in Game 5 of the Stanley Cup finals, wrapping up their second straight title.

**MAY:** On a rainy night in Cleveland, Indians' righthander Len Barker thrilled 7,290 fans by pitching the 13th perfect game in modern major league history, beating Toronto, 3-0.

**JUL:** Pat Bradley captured her first U.S. Women's Open golf title with a one-stroke victory over Beth Daniel at La Grange (Ill.) Country Club.

**AUG:** On the first day back after the strike, Philadelphia's Pete Rose became the all-time N.L. hits leader when he singled during a game against St. Louis.

**AUG:** Sebastian Coe of Great Britain lowered the mile world record to 3:47.33 during a meet at Brussels, Belgium.

## The artful Dodgers

It was a come-from-behind kind of year for the Los Angeles Dodgers, who performed their postseason magic against Houston in the strike-forced divisional playoff, Montreal in the National League Championship Series and the New York Yankees in the World Series.

The Dodgers, first-half N.L. West Division winners, appeared to be headed for an early playoff exit as they succumbed to the Astros in the first two divisional playoff games. But strong pitching performances by Burt Hooton, Fernando Valenzuela and Jerry Reuss propelled them into the Championship Series against the Expos.

Again Los Angeles fell behind, this time two games to one. But Steve Garvey triggered a 7-1 triumph and Rick Monday's ninth-inning home run in Game 5 gave the Dodgers a clinching 2-1 victory.

Los Angeles fell behind again as the New Yorkers swept the first two World Series games at Yankee Stadium. But the Dodger comeback pattern continued. With Pedro Guerrero, Ron Cey, Steve Yeager and Garvey providing the offensive punch, Los Angeles rolled to four straight wins and its third Series victory in 11 tries against the Yankees.

*Los Angeles Manager Tom Lasorda (arms straight up) leads a victory rush after the comeback Dodgers had defeated the Yankees in Game 6 of the World Series.*

## Unser wins—finally

Bobby Unser, the first driver in the 65-year history of the Indianapolis 500 to lose a first-place finish on an official ruling, was reinstated as winner of the May 24 race on October 8 by a three-man panel of the United States Auto Club.

The panel, hearing the appeal of the Roger Penske Racing team, voted 2-1 to restore Unser as the winner, stating the one-lap penalty imposed on him after the race was too harsh. Unser instead was fined $40,000 for violations on lap 149, when he ignored pre-race instruction and improved his position under a yellow caution flag.

Unser drove his Penske PC-9B to a slim five-second victory over Mario Andretti, averaging 139.084 mph for the 200-lap race. He celebrated his third Indy win in Victory Lane before learning the next morning that race stewards had penalized

*Bobby Unser celebrates his third Indianapolis 500 win in Victory Lane—a win taken away and given back over the next 4 1/2 months.*

him one lap and awarded the victory to Andretti.

The decision by the USAC panel gave the Penske team a winning purse of $262,424, $93,750 more than Andretti's Patrick Racing team received for second place.

## Sugar Ray rallies to defeat the Hit Man

Sugar Ray Leonard, behind on all three official scorecards and operating with his eye almost swollen shut, stunned Thomas (Hit Man) Hearns with a sudden rally that resulted in a 14th-round technical knockout, September 13, in a welterweight title fight at Las Vegas.

Hearns appeared fresh and in full control entering the 13th round. But he suddenly was stunned by a right cross and Leonard quickly followed with a flurry of punches that landed and knocked him to his knees. Hearns went down again

moments later after another barrage, but made it to the bell.

When the 14th round opened, Leonard charged in and landed three solid lefts. The referee stopped the fight at 1:45.

The victory gave Leonard control of both the WBC and WBA welterweight crowns. It was the first time the two rival factions had a common division champion since Roberto Duran beat Esteban DeJesus in a 1978 lightweight bout.

The victory was the 31st in 32 fights for Leonard. Hearns is 32-1 with 30 knockouts.

# Bear gets 315th win

His record 315th coaching victory neatly tucked away, Alabama Coach Bear Bryant and Crimson Tide players fight through the crowd.

Alabama Coach Paul (Bear) Bryant etched his name in the NCAA record books, November 28, when he guided his Crimson Tide to a regular season-closing 28-17 victory over arch-rival Auburn—the 315th win of his storied career.

The 68-year-old Bryant moved past Amos Alonzo Stagg, who coached 314 victories in 57 years at Springfield (Mass.) College, Chicago and Pacific. Bryant has compiled his 315-80-17 record in 37 seasons at Maryland, Kentucky, Texas A&M and Alabama.

Joe Namath and many other former Alabama players were among the 78,170 fans who packed Legion Field in Birmingham, Ala., for the annual showdown. Bryant, wearing his familiar houndstooth cap, watched as the favored Crimson Tide fumbled and stumbled through three quarters. The Tigers held a 17-14 lead and it was beginning to look like Bryant would have to wait another year to put his name in the record books.

But Walter Lewis threw a 38-yard touchdown pass to Jesse Bendross and Linnie Patrick scored on a 15-yard run to turn the Tide and insure Alabama's ninth win of the season.

# Trojans' star wins Heisman Trophy

Southern Cal's Marcus Allen.

Southern Cal's Marcus Allen, the first man to top 2,000 yards rushing in a single season, capped his big year, December 5, by outpolling Georgia's Herschel Walker and record-setting Brigham Young quarterback Jim McMahon in voting for the Heisman Trophy.

Allen, who led the nation in all-purpose running as a junior, came back this year to rush for 2,342 yards. He averaged 5.81 yards on 403 carries, scored 23 touchdowns and either set or tied 12 NCAA records. He smashed the previous mark of 1,948 yards set by Pittsburgh's Tony Dorsett in 1976.

The 6-foot-2, 202-pounder finished his final regular season on a big note, November 20, rushing for 219 yards and two touchdowns in the Trojans' 22-21 victory over arch-rival UCLA. That marked the record eighth time this season he had topped 200 yards in a game.

McMahon became the NCAA's all-time passing leader on the same day when he threw for 565 yards and four touchdowns in a 56-28 victory over Utah. McMahon finished his regular-season career with a record 9,535 passing yards.

## ★ SPORTS WATCH ★

**SEP:** Houston righthander Nolan Ryan became the only man in baseball history to throw five career no-hitters when he stopped Los Angeles, 5-0.

**SEP:** John McEnroe beat Bjorn Borg in four sets and Tracy Austin stopped Martina Navratilova in three to win the U.S. Open singles titles at Flushing Meadow.

**NOV:** Ace Milwaukee reliever Rollie Fingers (28 saves, 1.04 ERA) captured both the American League MVP and Cy Young awards.

**DEC:** Muhammad Ali, loser of a unanimous decision to Trevor Berbick, announced his retirement from the ring.

**DEC:** The United States won its third Davis Cup title in four years with a 3-1 decision over Argentina at Cincinnati.

# Eskimos' Moon rises

Edmonton quarterback Warren Moon, coming back strong after a difficult first half, scored two touchdowns and drove the Eskimos to a winning field goal in a 26-23 victory over Ottawa in the November 22 Grey Cup final at Montreal.

The victory, Edmonton's 15th of the season and record fourth straight in the Canadian Football League's championship game, was not the blowout that was expected. In fact, the heavily favored Eskimos trailed 20-1 at halftime to a team that had finished its regular season at 5-11 — the worst record ever for a team reaching the Grey Cup final.

Moon, who completed only one pass in the opening 30 minutes and was removed from the game at one point, returned to direct three second-half touchdown drives, two of which ended with him sneaking into the end zone. After the third score, Moon passed to Marco Cyncar for a two-point conversion that tied the game with 4:05 remaining.

When Edmonton got the ball back on its own 51 with 1:22 left, Jim Germany carried four times for 29 yards to set up Dave Cutler's 27-yard winning kick.

# 1982

## Chargers edge Miami

*San Diego tight end Kellen Winslow picks up yardage after one of his 13 receptions during a dramatic playoff game against Miami.*

In a game that tested the physical and emotional limits of every player and coach involved, the San Diego Chargers survived a big Miami comeback and defeated the Dolphins, 41-38, in a dramatic, January 2, American Conference divisional playoff matchup at Miami's Orange Bowl.

The game had everything: big plays, misplays, unusual plays and a wild Dolphin comeback from a 24-0 first-quarter deficit. The Chargers appeared to be headed for a rout when they scored on a 32-yard Rolf Benirschke field goal, a 56-yard Wes Chandler punt return, a one-yard run by Chuck Muncie

and an eight-yard pass from Dan Fouts to James Brooks.

But when Coach Don Shula replaced quarterback David Woodley in the second quarter with Don Strock, the Dolphins roared back. Strock drove Miami to a field goal and then threw three touchdown passes (two in the second period and one early in the third) that tied the game.

Fouts answered with a 25-yard scoring toss to tight end Kellen Winslow. But Miami tied again on Strock's 50-yard pass to Bruce Hardy and took a 38-31 lead on Tony Nathan's 12-yard run early in the final period. San Diego forced over-

time when Fouts hit Brooks for a nine-yard touchdown with 58 seconds left in regulation.

The emotional roller-coaster continued as Miami kicker Uwe von Schamann had field goals blocked at the end of regulation and in overtime, and Benirschke missed a 27-yard overtime kick.

The marathon ended when Benirschke connected on a 29-yarder 13 minutes, 52 seconds into the extra period.

Fouts threw for 433 yards and three touchdowns, while Strock passed for 403 yards and four TDs. Winslow caught 13 passes for 166 yards.

## 49ers get their kicks, win first Super Bowl

San Francisco turned three first-half Cincinnati turnovers into 17 points and Ray Wersching kicked four field goals as the 49ers won the battle of Super Bowl first-timers, January 24, with a 26-21 victory at the Pontiac (Mich.) Silverdome.

The first two turnovers occurred deep in 49er territory. A Dwight Hicks interception at the 5 triggered an 11-play 49er drive that ended with quarterback Joe Montana diving into the end zone, and a Lynn Thomas fumble recovery at the 8 sparked another drive that ended with Montana's 11-yard pass to Earl Cooper.

Wersching's 22-yard field goal with 18 seconds left in the half made the score 17-0 and, when Cincinnati failed to cover the ensuing kickoff and the 49ers recovered, Wersching

added a 26-yarder with three seconds remaining.

That cushion was too much for the Bengals. They did cut the margin to six when quarterback Ken Anderson ran five yards for a third-quarter touchdown and then passed four yards to tight end Dan Ross in the fourth quarter, but two more Wersching field goals sealed the verdict.

The victory capped a dramatic turnaround for the 49ers under Coach Bill Walsh. After finishing 6-10 in 1980, they rolled to a 13-3 record in 1981—the best in the NFL. The highlight of their Super Bowl drive was a 28-27 victory over Dallas in the NFC championship game —the result of a leaping touchdown catch by Dwight Clark on a six-yard throw by Montana with 51 seconds left.

*San Francisco quarterback Joe Montana celebrates Ray Wersching's third field goal in the fourth quarter of the 49ers' Super Bowl victory over Cincinnati.*

# Jordan ruins Hoyas

Freshman Michael Jordan hit a 16-foot jump shot with 15 seconds remaining and James Worthy made a key steal 10 seconds later to insure North Carolina's 63-62 victory over Georgetown in the March 29 NCAA Tournament championship game at the New Orleans Superdome.

Georgetown used the dominating inside defense and scoring of 7-foot freshman Patrick Ewing to forge a 32-31 halftime advantage and set up an outstanding second half during which neither team could manage more than a four-point lead. Eric Smith and Sleepy Floyd provided offensive support for Ewing; Jordan's jump shooting and Worthy's drives paced the Tar Heels.

Floyd gave the Hoyas their last lead, 62-61, on a short jumper with 57 seconds remaining. North Carolina killed 25 seconds and called a timeout to set up a play. Everybody expected Worthy, a junior, to get the call, but North Carolina Coach Dean Smith opted for Jordan, who calmly drilled home the game-winning shot.

The Hoyas had 15 seconds left to score, but their hopes were dashed when Fred Brown

*With only 17 seconds remaining, North Carolina's Michael Jordan releases the jump shot that ruined Georgetown's NCAA championship hopes.*

fired an errant pass right into Worthy's chest, sealing Carolina's 32nd victory in 34 games.

Worthy led all scorers with 28 points. Ewing had 23 for Georgetown.

# "The Walrus" Masters Pohl in golf playoff

Craig Stadler, known affectionately on the PGA tour as The Walrus because of his rotund build and thick mustache, won his first Masters tournament, April 11, when he parred the first hole of a sudden-death playoff and Dan Pohl missed a six-foot putt for a bogey.

That turnaround must have only seemed fair to Stadler, who had bogeyed four of the last seven regulation holes and missed a six-foot putt of his own that could have won the tournament on 18. While the long-hitting Pohl, playing in his first

Masters, was carving out a final-round 67, Stadler was struggling home with a 73 and watching his six-stroke advantage disappear.

It was under those difficult circumstances that Stadler teed off against Pohl on the par-4 10th hole in the playoff. Both hit good drives, but Pohl pushed his 7-iron shot to the right fringe, 40 feet from the pin. Stadler hit his second shot 35 feet from the hole and putted to within a foot for a tap-in. Pohl's pitch was six feet short and he missed his par-saving putt, giving Stadler his second victory of the year.

# Gretzky scores amazing 212 points

Wayne Gretzky, Edmonton's 21-year-old scoring machine, assisted on a goal by Jari Kurri in the Oilers' final game of the season and finished with an incredible 212 points, 51 more than his own National Hockey League one-season record.

Among Gretzky's records were goals (92), assists (120), total points, hat tricks (10), point average per game (2.65) and quickest 50 goals (39 games). The previous record for goals in one season belonged to former Boston great Phil Esposito, who scored 76 in 1970-71. Gretzky broke his own assist record of 109 (1980-81).

Not surprisingly, the Oilers rode Gretzky's performance to 111 points and the second best overall record in the NHL. The Great One scored five goals in one game against St. Louis and

*Wayne Gretzky, Edmonton's 21-year-old scoring machine.*

enjoyed three four-goal efforts. He was held scoreless only eight times.

## ★ SPORTS WATCH ★

**JAN:** Clemson wrapped up the Atlantic Coast Conference's first college football national championship in 28 years by defeating Nebraska, 22-15, in the Orange Bowl classic on New Year's Day.

**JAN:** Carl Lewis became the first long jumper to surpass 28 feet when he soared 28-1 in the U.S. Olympic Invitational meet.

**FEB:** The Pittsburgh Penguins stopped the New York Islanders' NHL-record 15-game winning streak with a 4-3 victory at Pittsburgh.

**FEB:** Bobby Allison averaged 153.991mph in his Buick to capture his second Daytona 500 victory.

**MAR:** San Antonio defeated Milwaukee, 171-166, in a three-overtime marathon that set an NBA record for most combined points—337.

**APR:** The Atlanta Braves set a major league record by opening the season with 13 victories.

# hockey

## The "Greatest" show on earth

### *Hockey's national treasure becomes an American art form and leaves Canada in mourning*

The news raged across the isolated prairies of Alberta like an uncontrollable brush fire, leaving tears and grief in its wake. Within minutes, a country was in mourning and a continent was in shock. A sports entrepreneur from the United States had heisted Canada's most revered and beloved national treasure and spirited it off to Los Angeles.

Wayne Gretzky, No. 99, The Great One, would take his incomparable hockey skills to Tinseltown in a Hollywood-like script that didn't make sense to anybody north of the U.S. border. Gretzky cried and newsmen gasped when Edmonton Oilers Owner Peter Pocklington somberly dropped his August 9, 1988 bomb—Gretzky, Mike Krushelnyski and Marty McSorley were being traded to Bruce McNall's Kings for Jimmy Carson, Martin Gelinas, three first-round draft picks—and $14.4 million.

So ended one of the most glorious and kingly reigns in sports history—but not without repercussions. "It's like ripping the heart out of the city," moaned Edmonton Mayor Laurence Decore, and outraged Oilers fans burned Pocklington in effigy outside of Northlands Coliseum while others began organizing boycotts against two of his businesses.

Many fans incorrectly

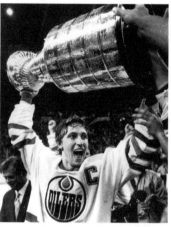

*Wayne Gretzky and Edmonton's first Stanley Cup.*

blamed Gretzky's wife of 24 days, American actress Janet Jones, and compared her to Yoko Ono, who was often blamed for the breakup of the Beatles because of her relationship with John Lennon. Headlines in newspapers across Canada referred to Jones with such descriptive adjectives as "witch" and "Jezebel." Pocklington, stung by the reaction, deflected blame for the trade to Gretzky, saying The Great One had demanded the deal and "Wayne has the ego the size of Manhattan." But evidence later surfaced to refute that claim.

Nothing, however, could refute the bottom line— Gretzky, the greatest hockey player of all time, holder of 43 individual scoring records and the heart and soul of a team that had won four of the last five Stanley Cups, was gone. Edmonton did have its memories of nine amazing seasons, seven straight scoring titles and eight straight Most Valuable Player awards, but that hardly seemed enough. At 27, Gretzky was in his prime.

*The Great One first topped the 200-point barrier in 1983-84.*

For Gretzky, parting was sweet sorrow. His Edmonton years were gratifying, his teammates were like brothers and the fans treated him like a king. When he and Jones were married, all of Canada had tuned in to its version of a royal wedding and his bride was welcomed into the family with open arms.

But Los Angeles offered a new world to conquer. It was glitter and shine, a fitting atmosphere for a player with the skills of Gretzky. His greatest tasks would be to turn a city onto hockey and turn a traditionally downtrodden team into a winner. It was a challenge he relished.

## "It's like ripping the heart out of the city."

**LAURENCE DECORE**
*The Mayor of Edmonton bemoans Gretzky's departure*

From the time he was accepted in his hometown of Brantford, Ontario, as a 6-year-old hockey prodigy, Gretzky had been taking up challenges. At age 6, he played against 10-year-olds, scoring one goal, and as a 7-year-old he scored 27. He tallied 104 the next year against 13-year-olds and 196 goals and 316 points the following campaign at age 9. The 4-foot-4, 70-pound Gretzky scored an amazing 378 goals in 82 games at age 10.

By age 15, Gretzky already was playing major junior hockey. At age 17, he was signed to his first professional contract by the World Hockey Association's Indianapolis Racers and was traded later that year to the WHA's Oilers. He scored 43 goals in his first full professional season (1978-79) and added 61 assists for 104 points. But hockey fans hadn't seen nuttin' yet.

When the National Hockey League accepted Edmonton in its 1979 merger-expansion agreement, Gretzky turned his

*Gretzky and Janet Jones during their 1988 royal wedding.*

game up a notch. In his first NHL season, the 19-year-old became the youngest player to score 50 goals (51) and 100 points (137) while walking away with his first Hart Trophy as the player most valuable to his team. He followed with a 55-goal, 164-point 1980-81 campaign and then performed what most hockey insiders had labeled impossible—a 200-point season.

"That's like rushing for 3,000 yards or hitting 80 home runs in a season," said Oilers assistant coach Billy Harris after Gretzky's 212-point effort in 1981-82.

"To me, the fact he's now got 90 goals (he finished with 92) is the unbelievable thing," said teammate Dave Lumley. "And they say his shot can't break a pane of glass."

Nothing about Gretzky as a physical specimen would suggest greatness. He has a longish nose, floppy hair and a slight 6-foot, 170-pound frame that makes him an inviting target for hard checkers and goons. He is not strong, he is not particularly fast and his shot does not drive fear into opposing goaltenders.

But Gretzky does have an uncanny, instinctive hockey

sense and quickness that produces split-second shots and pinpoint passes. He never seems to take a direct hit. Gretzky is a hunchback skater who darts up and down the ice and handles the puck like a sleight-of-hand spider, ready to pounce on his careless prey.

Gretzky pounced on opponents for 196 points in 1982-83 and 205 the next year, helping Edmonton win its first Stanley Cup. He followed with seasons of 208, 215, 183 and 149 as the Oilers, boasting such supporting stars as Paul Coffey, Jari Kurri, Mark Messier and goaltender Grant Fuhr, dominated the league.

Gretzky's scoring feats were spectacular and amazing. He scored 50 goals in the first 39 games of the 1981-82 season and set another record in 1983-84 by scoring in 51 consecutive games. He was the youngest and fastest player to reach 500 and 1,000 points, set one-season records for goals, assists and points, set numerous playoff scoring records and won just about every award imaginable. Simply put, he played on a different level than his competitors.

"There's nothing left to say about him that already hasn't

been said," marveled Philadelphia veteran Bobby Clarke in 1983. "And nothing that has been said is adequate."

It was not surprising that Gretzky took Los Angeles by storm and helped the Kings record their best record in history. Playing before average crowds of 14,875 (more than 3,000 better than the previous year) in 1988-89, Gretzky won his eighth Hart Trophy while scoring 54 goals and 168 points. The Kings finished with a 42-31-7 record, the fourth best in the NHL and a 12-win improvement over the previous campaign. Gretzky, however, was supplanted in the scoring race for the second straight year by Pittsburgh's Mario Lemieux, the league's newest wizard.

It was back to the top, however, in 1989-90 and 1990-91 and he added an important record while helping the Kings remain among the NHL's elite

*The "King" of L.A.*

teams. On October 15, 1989, Gretzky surpassed the great Gordie Howe (1,850) in career points during a game in *Edmonton*. And he did it with his typical flair, scoring a game-tying goal with 53 seconds left in regulation and the game-winner with 1:36 remaining in overtime in a 5-4 victory.

"If there is a hockey god," said Pocklington, "he was smiling on Wayne tonight." And Wayne, as always, smiled back.

# 1982

## USFL to begin play

The National Football League, which has survived the challenges of numerous outlaw circuits over the years, will have another to contend with in 1983. The United States Football League will begin play as a 12-team loop with an unusual March to July schedule.

Peter B. Spivak, the league's acting chairman, said that the USFL's owners have pledged to commit more than $100 million over the next two years to insure success. Investors have been working for months to get their teams ready for a 16-game schedule next spring.

Teams tentatively will be operating in Boston, Birmingham, Chicago, Denver, Detroit, Los Angeles, New York, Philadelphia, San Diego, San Francisco, Tampa and Washington. Among the owners will be David F. Dixon, the USFL's founder, and John F. Bassett, a key figure from the defunct World Football League that operated in 1974-75.

## Johncock captures thrilling Indy win

In the most frantic wheel-to-wheel finish ever witnessed at the Indianapolis Motor Speedway, Gordon Johncock drove his Wildcat-Cosworth across the finish line 16-hundredths of a second ahead of Rick Mears' Penske PC-10 and captured his second Indianapolis 500 Memorial Day race.

Johncock's car was losing steam and becoming harder to handle over the final laps and Mears closed fast. Down by 12 seconds with 13 laps to go, Mears pulled to within 1.8 seconds with three to go and less than one second a lap later. When the two drivers took the white flag signaling the final lap, Mears was looking for a chance to pass.

He never found it. Johncock gave it everything he had and the cars finally pulled side by side down the final stretch. Johncock held on—barely.

The beginning of the race was

### "SPORTS TALK"

*"I think I've got the best job in America. If I wasn't doing this for a living, I'd probably be playing a couple nights a week at a 'Y' someplace and I'd end up with all these bumps and bruises for free."*

**JULIUS ERVING**
Philadelphia basketball star

## Drug use in NFL?

*Don Reese, pictured tackling Raiders quarterback Ken Stabler in 1979, told a sordid story of NFL drug use in a July issue of* Sports Illustrated.

Don Reese, a former defensive end for three teams in the National Football League, asserted in the July 14 issue of *Sports Illustrated* that cocaine "now controls and corrupts" the game because so many players are hooked on it.

Reese, who played with Miami (1974-76), New Orleans (1978-80) and San Diego (1981), was sentenced in 1977 to a year in prison for selling the drug. The *Sports Illustrated* story, presented under the byline of Reese with staff writer John Underwood, accuses the NFL of ignoring a problem that is growing like a cancer.

"Cocaine can be found in quantity throughout the NFL," Reese said. "It's pushed on players, often from the edge of the practice field. Sometimes it's pushed by players. Prominent players.

"A cocaine cloud covers the entire league. I think most coaches know this or have a good idea. Except the dumb ones. . . ."

Reese told of using cocaine with many players and said that he and other Saints indulged in free-basing. He also said he currently owes drug dealers $30,000 and has been threatened several times.

The NFL instituted a program two years ago to allow players with drug or alcohol problems to find help. Seventeen players have taken advantage of the program.

*Gordon Johncock's Wildcat-Cosworth hits the finish line 16-hundredths of a second ahead of Rick Mears' Penske PC-10 in a tight Indianapolis 500 finish.*

almost as exciting as the ending. Four cars, including Mario Andretti's, were eliminated from competition in a pace lap accident. Johncock averaged 162.026 mph.

# Henderson passes Lou Brock

Oakland speedster Rickey Henderson passed Lou Brock and claimed baseball's one-season basestealing record, August 27, when he swiped four bases during a 5-4 loss to the Brewers at Milwaukee.

The record-breaking steal (No. 119) came in the third inning after Henderson had drawn a walk from Doc Medich. The Brewers' righthander tossed to first four times and then threw a pitchout to catcher Ted Simmons as Henderson took off. Simmons' throw to shortstop Robin Yount was on target, but Henderson slid under the tag and was called safe.

Members of both teams surrounded Henderson, who pulled the base out of the ground and held it high in a triumphant gesture. As the 41,600 fans at County Stadium stood and applauded, American League President Lee MacPhail and Brock, the former St. Louis

*Oakland speedster Rickey Henderson, having eclipsed the one-season record of 118 steals set by former St. Louis Cardinal Lou Brock (left), celebrates as newsmen huddle at County Stadium in Milwaukee.*

great who was on hand for the event, went onto the field for a brief ceremony.

But Henderson, who set the record in 127 games, 26 fewer than Brock needed to steal 118 bases in 1974, didn't stop at 119. He stole second in the sixth and he swiped second and third in the eighth.

# Mary's record assault

Mary Decker-Tabb continued her assault on the women's record book, July 16, when she ran the 10,000-meter race in a world-record 31:35.30 at Hayward Field in her hometown of Eugene, Ore.

It was the first time she had ever run that race on a track and she made it look easy, topping the 32:17.19 set last year by Russian Yelina Sipatova. The distance had been dominated by Soviet women, who owned the world's nine fastest times before Decker-Tabb's performance.

One week earlier, at an international meet in Paris, Decker-Tabb had set a world record for the mile, turning in a 4:18.08 clocking. She won by 13 seconds, beating the 4:20.89 record held by another Soviet runner, Lyudmila Veselkova.

The 23-year-old also owns world records in the 5,000-meter run (15:08.26) and 3,000 meters (8:29.71).

# Watson "Opens" up

Tom Watson, fresh from his dramatic U.S. Open victory over Jack Nicklaus one month earlier, added a fourth British Open to his impressive resume, July 18, with a one-stroke win over Nick Price and Peter Oosterhuis at Troon, Scotland.

Watson trailed Price by two strokes after 14 holes and appeared to be in a tight race for second-place money. But the South African suffered a double bogey at 15 and a bogey at 17.

Except for an eagle 3 at 11, it was an uneventful round for the talented Missourian, one of only nine golfers to break par on the difficult, wind-blown course. He had one birdie and one bogey for a final-round 70 and 284 total. It was a far different approach to victory than he had used in winning his first U.S. Open at Pebble Beach.

Tied with Nicklaus at the 17th hole, Watson broke the deadlock by dropping a chip shot from the rough next to the green. He followed with a birdie at 18 to insure a dramatic two-stroke victory.

*Tom Watson watches a bunker shot during British Open action.*

# 1982

## Brewers beat the odds and California

*Happy Milwaukee Brewers celebrate their comeback A.L. Championship Series triumph over California.*

Cecil Cooper's two-run seventh-inning single completed an unprecedented Milwaukee comeback, October 10, and gave the Brewers a 4-3 victory over California and their first American League pennant.

Cooper's bases-loaded single capped the Brewers' rally from a 3-1 Game 5 deficit and a 2-0 deficit in the A.L. Championship Series, a comeback feat never before accomplished. The Angels had rolled to 8-3 and 4-2 victories, but could not close the door on the franchise's first World Series berth.

Milwaukee started its comeback with a 5-3 win in Game 3 and rode the 3-for-4, three-RBI Game 4 performance of seldom-used Mark Brouhard to a 9-5 victory. The Angels built their Game 5 lead on two RBI singles by Fred Lynn and one by Bob Boone.

The game ended with Milwaukee reliever Peter Ladd retiring seven-time A.L. batting champion Rod Carew with the tying run on second base.

## Moses to lead 76ers

The Philadelphia 76ers, looking for that final piece to their championship puzzle, signed 6-foot-10 free-agent center Moses Malone to a six-year $13.2 million free-agent deal, September 2.

The prospect of putting the National Basketball Association's reigning Most Valuable Player in the middle of his lineup was too much for Philadelphia Owner Harold Katz to pass up. Frustrated by his team's inability to win an NBA championship and its loss to Los Angeles in the 1982 Finals, he traded center Darryl Dawkins to New Jersey last week and began negotiations with Malone, a 31.1-point scorer last season for Houston.

The Rockets matched the Philadelphia offer sheet and then traded Malone to the 76ers for Caldwell Jones and a 1983 first-round draft choice.

Despite his eight years of professional experience, Malone is only 27 years old. He joined the ABA's Utah Stars right out of high school in 1974.

## Cardinals win Series

A two-run sixth-inning single by Keith Hernandez tied the game and George Hendrick's RBI single gave St. Louis a lead it never relinquished as the Cardinals rolled to a 6-3 victory over Milwaukee, October 20, in the seventh game of the World Series at St. Louis.

The speed, defense and pitching of the Cardinals beat Milwaukee's raw power. But when the Series opened the Brewers rapped out 17 hits in support of Mike Caldwell's three-hit pitching in a 10-0 Milwaukee victory. The Cardinals rebounded to win the next two games, 5-4 and 6-2, Willie McGee providing the Game 3 spark with two home runs and a pair of outstanding catches in center field.

When Harvey's Wallbangers (they had hit a record 216 regular-season home runs for Manager Harvey Kuenn) bounced back to post 7-5 and 6-4 decisions, the Cardinals answered 13-1 at St. Louis.

Manager Whitey Herzog's Redbirds overcame a 3-1 deficit with their sixth-inning rally and Joaquin Andujar and reliever Bruce Sutter made the lead stand up, giving St. Louis its ninth World Series crown.

*Fireworks signal victory and St. Louis fans pour onto the Busch Stadium field after the Cardinals' seventh-game World Series win over Milwaukee.*

# Leonard retires because of injury

Welterweight champion Sugar Ray Leonard, one of the most popular boxers in ring history, ended his outstanding 5½-year, 33-fight career, November 9, because of a partially detached retina that required surgery last May.

Leonard made his announcement in a ring at the Baltimore Civic Center, where he began his career in 1977. Among the 10,000 spectators on hand were Muhammad Ali and middleweight champion Marvin Hagler.

Leonard earned more than $37 million while compiling an impressive 32-1 record with 22 knockouts. He won the welterweight title twice, the second time from Roberto Duran, the only man to defeat him, and he

Welterweight champion Sugar Ray Leonard tells a Baltimore Civic Center crowd of 10,000 that his fighting days are over.

also held the junior middleweight title at one time. His toughest bouts were against Duran, Wilfred Benitez and Thomas Hearns.

Dr. Ronald Michels, the ophthalmologist who performed the surgery on Leonard's left eye, gave him the green light to fight again—while strongly advising against it. The 26-year-old former Olympic champion listened.

# Football strike ends

The 57-day strike that has crippled the National Football League season came to an end, November 16, when players and owners reached agreement on a new five-year contract.

The settlement, worth more than $1.3 billion to the players, opens the door for workouts to begin immediately and the season to resume November 20. Each team will play nine regular-season games, including the two that were played before the strike began, September 21, and the season will end on January 2, a week later than planned. Sixteen teams will qualify for the playoffs, six more than usual.

The agreement ends the longest strike in sports history. It lasted seven days longer than last year's baseball strike and cost the league an estimated $240 million in gate and television receipts as well as 112 games. It was the first time players had interrupted the regular-season schedule.

The agreement extends through 1986 and brings the players $60 million in bonus money for 1982 and $1.313 billion in salaries and benefits for 1983-86.

# Cal beats the band

When California lined up to receive a Stanford kickoff with four seconds remaining in a November 20 game at Berkeley, Calif., nothing short of a touchdown return would be good enough. The Cardinal had just taken a 20-19 lead on Mark Harmon's 35-yard field goal and needed only to make one tackle to secure victory. But . . .

Cal's Kevin Moen took the squib kick at the Golden Bears' 43, advanced about 10 yards and rifled an overhand lateral near the left sideline. Richard Rogers caught the ball and made another short advance before lateraling to Dwight Garner, who caught the ball and, while falling, flipped it back to Rogers at the Stanford 48-yard line.

Rogers cut toward the middle of the field and let fly with another lateral, this one to Mariet Ford, who raced downfield before encountering Cardinal defenders at the 25. Ford, running at full speed, tossed the ball blindly over his right shoulder, hoping somebody in a Cal uniform might be there.

Somebody was. Moen caught the ball and headed for the end zone. He was aided by the Stan-

ford band, which had marched prematurely onto the field and provided a corridor of sorts by screening off potential tacklers. Moen burst through the band, knocking a trombone player to the ground, and scored an incredible five-lateral touchdown. Final: California 25, Stanford 20.

California's Kevin Moen dances through the Stanford band with the winning touchdown in one of the wildest college football finishes ever witnessed.

# 1983

## The Lions roar—finally

Curt Warner ran for 117 yards and two touchdowns, quarterback Todd Blackledge executed a flawless game plan and the Penn State defense contained explosive Georgia running back Herschel Walker as the Nittany Lions shook off 96 years of frustration and captured their first national championship with a 27-23 Sugar Bowl victory over the Bulldogs at the New Orleans Superdome.

The New Year's Day showdown between No. 1-ranked Georgia (11-0) and second-ranked Penn State (10-1) was everything it was expected to be. Blackledge marched the Lions up and down the field in a first half that produced an early 20-3 lead and a comfortable 20-10 at intermission.

But the Bulldogs fought back, scoring early in the third quarter on a one-yard Walker run and forcing Penn State's defense to buckle down. It did, and Blackledge reestablished control by throwing a 47-yard touchdown pass to Gregg Garrity early in the final period.

The victory was sweet for Penn State Coach Joe Paterno, who had produced three unbeaten and untied teams since taking over in 1966 but always lost out in the polls. His 1978 squad was ranked No. 1 and unbeaten before falling to Alabama in the Sugar Bowl.

Herschel Walker, the Heisman Trophy winner and owner of 10 NCAA rushing records, was restricted to only 103 yards and one touchdown.

*Penn State's Curt Warner circles left end for 23 of his 117 rushing yards during the Nittany Lions' Sugar Bowl victory over Georgia.*

## Generals sign Walker

Georgia tailback Herschel Walker signed a precedent-setting contract with the New Jersey Generals of the new United States Football League, February 23, and instantly became the highest-paid performer in football history.

The contract, reportedly for $1.5 million or more per year, dwarfs the estimated $700,000 that Chicago's Walter Payton earns as the highest-paid player

in the National Football League. The guaranteed three-year deal brings the USFL some instant credibility.

To get Walker, who had just completed his junior season, the Generals went against the USFL's stated policy that it would not go after any player whose class was not due to graduate the following spring. The NFL has always operated by that rule and the NCAA was not pleased.

The signing ended a week-long controversy in which Walker signed a tentative agreement, tried to back out and then was ruled ineligible by an NCAA investigation. The 5,259-yard career rusher and owner of 10 NCAA records was left with no choice but to sign for the Generals.

## Crimson Tide's Bear dies of heart attack

Paul (Bear) Bryant, the legendary Alabama boss who retired 37 days earlier as the winningest coach in college football history, died, January 26, of a massive heart attack at a Tuscaloosa, Ala., hospital at age 69.

Bryant had ended his colorful 38-year career with a 323-85-17 record that included stints at Maryland, Kentucky and Texas A&M before 25 years at Alabama, his alma mater. Six of his teams either won or shared national championships.

Bryant, who got his nickname

for wrestling a bear in a circus sideshow, developed such quarterbacks as Joe Namath, George Blanda, Babe Parilli, Ken Stabler and Richard Todd. Among his former players who went on to coaching success were Jerry Claiborne (Kentucky), Howard Schnellenberger (Miami), Jackie Sherrill (Texas A&M), Pat Dye (Auburn) and Steve Sloan (Duke).

Bryant coached his final victory, December 29, when Alabama beat Illinois, 21-15, in the Liberty Bowl.

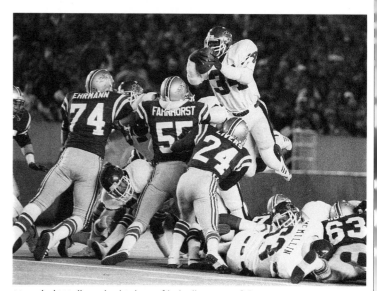

*Herschel Walker, the high-profile ballcarrier of the USFL's New Jersey Generals.*

# Phi Slama Jama gets grounded by Wolfpack

It was Houston's high-flying, rim-shaking Phi Slama Jama fraternity against the Cardiac Pack of North Carolina State. A mismatch, everyone agreed. The Cougars would roll to the NCAA Tournament championship, April 4, in Albuquerque.

That prognosis was based on Houston's 31-2 record, 26-game winning streak, top ranking in both polls and gravity-defying exploits. It also was based on N.C. State's shaky 25-10 record and NCAA Tournament struggles against Pepperdine (two overtimes) and Virginia (a 63-62 squeaker).

Houston's Phi Slama Jama reputation had been even further enhanced during a hair-raising 94-81 semifinal win over second-ranked Louisville. Over the final 20 minutes of that game, Akeem Olajuwon, Clyde Drexler, Benny Anders and Michael Young literally held a party above the rim. Houston slammed home 11 stylish dunks, scored 58 second-half points and left everybody with their mouths hanging open.

"I've never seen anything like that in my 16 years of coaching college basketball," marveled Wolfpack Coach Jim Valvano. "We'll try to handle their team by playing, shall I say, a slower tempo. If we get the opening tip, we may not take a shot until Tuesday morning."

Valvano was exaggerating— slightly. With guards Dereck Whittenburg and Sidney Lowe handling the ball, N.C. State quickly showed it was more than capable of controlling the pace. And a tightly-packed zone limited Houston's dunk opportunities and helped the Wolfpack forge a surprising 33-24 halftime lead.

But a 17-2 surge by Houston at the beginning of the second half put N.C. State into an ominous hole. That hole disappeared when Houston Coach Guy Lewis surprisingly ordered his team to spread the court and force the Wolfpack to change defense.

N.C. State took advantage of the strategy and pulled within four, 52-48. Two long jumpers by Whittenburg tied the game. When Houston freshman Alvin Franklin misfired on a one-and-one free throw attempt, the Wolfpack had the ball with a chance to win.

With time running out, Whittenburg grabbed a deflected ball and let go a desperation 30-foot shot that came up short. But 6-foot-7 Lorenzo Charles was in the right place at the right time, catching the ball in midair and slamming it home with one second remaining.

Lorenzo Charles (43), the man who scored the winning basket, celebrates with his North Carolina State teammates after the Wolfpack's shocking NCAA Tournament victory over Houston.

## "SPORTS TALK"

*"You go into the paint against him and he'll mess up your digestive tract. You'll be passing leather for two days."*

**SHELBY METCALF**
Texas A&M basketball Coach
on Houston shot-blocker
Akeem Olajuwon

Defending champion Craig Stadler lends a traditional assist to Seve Ballesteros, who is putting on the green jacket for a second time.

# Ballesteros triumphs

Seve Ballesteros blazed into the lead with a birdie-eagle-par-birdie start, April 11, and coasted to his second Masters victory in four years at Augusta National Golf Club.

Ballesteros trailed co-leaders Craig Stadler and Ray Floyd by one stroke when the final round opened, but he quickly took control. The key to his four-hole blitz was a 4-wood shot on the par-5 second hole that hit the green and stopped 18 feet from the pin. He sank the eagle putt and suddenly led by two.

Ballesteros played steady through the next six holes and negotiated the difficult Amen Corner (holes 11, 12 and 13), losing only one stroke to par. He capped his final-round 69 by chipping in for par on 18.

The four-stroke victory over Ben Crenshaw and Tom Kite was worth $90,000 to the Spaniard, who finished with a total of 280.

## ★ SPORTS WATCH ★

**JAN:** Washington fullback John Riggins rushed for 166 yards and a touchdown to lead the Redskins to a 27-17 Super Bowl XVII victory over Miami in the Rose Bowl at Pasadena, Calif.

**FEB:** Edmonton's Wayne Gretzky scored four goals and led the Campbell Conference to a 9-3 victory over the Wales in the NHL All-Star Game at Nassau Coliseum in Uniondale, N.Y.

**FEB:** Cale Yarborough averaged 155.979 mph in his Pontiac and earned his third victory in the Daytona 500.

**APR:** San Diego first baseman Steve Garvey played in his 1,118th consecutive game, breaking the National League record held by former Chicago Cub Billy Williams.

**APR:** Southern Cal captured the NCAA women's basketball title with a 69-67 victory over defending champion Louisiana Tech at Norfolk, Va.

**APR:** Luther Bradley of the Chicago Blitz intercepted six passes in a 42-3 USFL victory over the Tampa Bay Bandits at Tampa Stadium.

# 1983

## Islanders win again

The New York Islanders joined the Montreal Canadiens in the record books, May 17, when they completed their four-game sweep of Edmonton with a 4-2 victory and won their fourth consecutive Stanley Cup title.

The Islanders became only the second National Hockey League team to win four titles in a row and they did it by throwing a defensive blanket over the high-scoring Oilers and Wayne Gretzky, who had scored 71 goals and 196 points during the regular season. The Oilers were held to six goals in the final series and failed to score off goaltender Billy Smith in seven of the 12 periods. Bryan Trottier and Butch Goring shadowed Gretzky and held him to four assists.

In the clincher at the Nassau Coliseum, Trottier, Mike Bossy and John Tonelli scored first-period goals and Edmonton got second-period scores from Jari Kurri and Mark Messier.

The Islanders, sixth in the overall regular-season standings, have to win one more title to match the five straight by Montreal from 1956-60.

New York's Denis Potvin holds the Stanley Cup high as the Islanders celebrate their status as only the second team to win four straight NHL championships.

## Chiefs' star drowns

Joe Delaney, a 1,121-yard rusher as a rookie for Kansas City two years ago, drowned, June 29, when he jumped into a pond while trying to rescue three floundering youngsters in his hometown of Monroe, La.

The 24-year-old Delaney, a 5-foot-10, 184-pound running back from Northwestern (La.) State, was sitting in a public park near a water-filled hole left by construction workers. Three wading youths stepped into deep water and cried for help.

One 11-year-old boy drowned, another was hospitalized in critical condition. The other boy safely reached the side of the two-acre pond.

Delaney, a Division I-AA All-America and track performer in college, was selected

Former Kansas City running back Joe Delaney.

by Kansas City in the second round of the 1981 draft. He was outstanding as a rookie, earning a trip to the Pro Bowl, but a detached retina limited his 1982 action to eight games.

---

### ★ SPORTS WATCH ★

**JUN:** Jack Dempsey, heavyweight champion of the world from 1919-26, died of a heart ailment at age 87 in New York.

**JUL:** Tom Watson's four-round total of 275 at the Royal Birkdale course in England produced his fifth British Open championship.

**JUL:** Evelyn Ashford set a women's world record for the 100-meter run when she was clocked in 10.79 during competition in the National Sports Festival at Colorado Springs.

**AUG:** Jan Stephenson defeated JoAnne Carner and Patty Sheehan by one stroke and captured her first U.S. Women's Open championship at Cedar Ridge Country Club in Tulsa, Okla.

---

## Malone leads way as 76ers win title

Moses Malone, Philadelphia's 13-million-dollar man, helped the 76ers complete their journey to the Promised Land, May 31, when he scored 24 points and grabbed 23 rebounds in a 115-108 victory over Los Angeles that completed a four-game sweep of the National Basketball Association's championship series.

Malone, acquired before the season to provide the last piece for the 76ers' championship puzzle, did exactly that as he averaged 24.5 points per game and an NBA-leading 15.3 rebounds. He intensified his efforts in the playoffs, averaging 25.8 points and 18.5 rebounds.

That's just what long-frustrated Philadelphia Owner Harold Katz had in mind when he handed a $13.2 million contract to the 6-foot-10 center. Combining with Julius Erving, Malone led the 76ers to a record 12-1 playoff blitz followed by four stunning victories over the defending champions.

Los Angeles, playing at home, used the Magic of Earvin Johnson (27 points, 13 assists) to build a 65-51 halftime lead and a 93-82 third-quarter advantage in Game 4. But Malone took control in the fourth quarter and Erving scored seven critical points down the stretch as Philadelphia caught the Lakers and pulled away to its first title since 1967.

# Lynn's slam helps end A.L. All-Star drought

California slugger Fred Lynn capped a record seven-run third inning with the first grand slam in All-Star Game history and propelled the American League to a 13-3 victory over the National League, ending the junior circuit's embarrassing 11-game losing streak in the mid-summer classic.

The first A.L. victory since 1971 came on the 50th anniversary of the showcase event, which was staged on the same field where it was originally contested in 1933 — Chicago's Comiskey Park. The American Leaguers won that inaugural game, too, but with nothing like the pitiless vengeance they showed, July 6, in their record 13-run onslaught against seven pitchers.

After spotting the N.L. an unearned first-inning run, the A.L. tied the game in the bottom of the inning, took the lead in the second and exploded against San Francisco lefthander Atlee Hammaker in the third.

Boston's Jim Rice led off the inning with a solo homer and two more runs scored before Hammaker issued a two-out intentional walk to Milwaukee's Robin Yount to load the bases for Lynn. On a 2-2 pitch, Lynn drove a pitch into the right-field bleachers. The A.L. added two runs in both the eighth and ninth innings to complete the scoring.

*California's Fred Lynn raises his fist in triumph as he circles the bases after hitting the first grand slam in All-Star Game history.*

# Royals win infamous encounter

In an uneventful conclusion to one of the most controversial major league games ever played, the Kansas City Royals posted a 5-4 victory over New York, August 18 — 25 days after the first 8⅓ innings of the contest had been played at Yankee Stadium.

There was nothing unusual about the July 18 game through the first eight innings. The Yankees held a 4-3 lead as Kansas

City batted in the ninth with two out and nobody on base. But a single by U.L. Washington brought up George Brett, who promptly hit a Goose Gossage fastball for a home run — or so everybody thought.

After Brett had circled the bases, Yankee Manager Billy Martin protested that the Royals third baseman had used an illegal bat. The umpires examined the bat, conferred, measured the stick against home plate and conferred again before Tim McClelland signaled "out."

Brett went into a rage and charged McClelland, only to be intercepted and grabbed around the neck by umpiring crew chief Joe Brinkman. In the confusion that followed, Kansas City pitcher Gaylord Perry sneaked out of the dugout and swiped the bat, only to have security men retrieve it before it could be secreted away to the Royals' clubhouse.

The point in question was a sticky substance called pine tar, used by many players to enhance their grip. The rule book allows the substance to extend 18 inches up the bat from the handle, a distance that clearly was violated by Brett. But the Royals protested to A.L. President Lee MacPhail on the basis of intent, arguing that the substance does not enhance a player's hitting ability. MacPhail agreed and ruled that the game resume from the point of stoppage, with the Royals leading.

Resumption of the game occurred on an open date for both teams. With 1,245 fans on hand, Kansas City's Hal McRae made the final out in the top of the ninth and the Yankees went down in order in the bottom of the inning.

*Umpire Joe Brinkman restrains an enraged George Brett after the Kansas City third baseman's ninth-inning game-winning homer at Yankee Stadium had been disallowed because of an illegal bat.*

# 1983

## Martina wins easily

Martina Navratilova, reaffirming her claim as the top woman player in the world, gave six-time champion Chris Evert-Lloyd a 63-minute tennis lesson, September 10, and captured her first U.S. Open singles title.

Navratilova's 6-1, 6-3 victory was a study in domination. Her strategy was simple and effective: rush the net after every serve and don't let Evert-Lloyd get set up on the baseline. The result startled the National Tennis Center's 20,819 fans—and Chris.

"I think this was one of the matches where I was beaten the worst," she said.

The victory earned the former Czech defector $120,000 and a $500,000 bonus from Playtex. The bonus was for winning major titles on three different surfaces: Wimbledon on grass, the Hilton Head, S.C., event on clay and the U.S. Open on a hard, fast surface. That brought her career winnings to $6,089,756 — more than any player in history, male or female.

The victory was Martina's 66th in her last 67 singles matches.

Martina Navratilova jumps for joy after brushing aside Chris Evert-Lloyd and winning her first U.S. Open singles championship.

## Chicago's Papa Bear dies at age 88

Papa Bear George Halas, coach of the Chicago Bears in 1950.

George Halas, a pioneer of professional football, founder of the National Football League's Chicago Bears and the team's owner and coach for over half a century, died, October 31, at Chicago. The 88-year-old Papa Bear had been ill with heart disease and other ailments.

From 1920 when he founded the Bears as the Chicago Staleys until his retirement from coaching in 1968 at age 73, Halas ruled as the absolute baron of Chicago sports. He helped pioneer the NFL from rags to riches, he created the famed "Monsters of the Midway" teams that dominated in the early years and he directed his Bears to a record 321 victories.

Halas coached seven NFL championship teams and his alumni list includes such names as Red Grange, Bronko Nagurski, Jack Manders, Sid Luckman, George McAfee, Johnny Lujack, Gale Sayers and Mike Ditka. As a coach, he used fundamental strategy and the T-formation.

The former baseball and football star (he played right end for the Staleys) was the last survivor of a group that founded the NFL at a Canton, O., automobile agency under the name of American Professional Football Association.

## Murray, McGregor help O's win Series

The big bat of Eddie Murray, silent through the first four games of the World Series, crashed two home runs to back the five-hit pitching of Scott McGregor, giving Baltimore a 5-0 victory over Philadelphia and the team's first championship since 1970.

The October 16 triumph at Philadelphia completed a four-game Baltimore blitz after the Orioles had dropped a 2-1 opening-game decision to the Phillies and starter John Denny. That game was decided by an eighth-inning Garry Maddox home run—on McGregor's first pitch after waiting five minutes while President Ronald Reagan was being interviewed on television.

Rookie Mike Boddicker evened the Series with a three-hit shutout in Game 2, Baltimore scored an unearned run in the seventh inning to capture a 3-2 Game 3 win and Rich Dauer drove in three runs to spark a 5-4 fourth-game victory.

That set the stage for Murray and McGregor in the decisive fifth game.

# Veterans clean up in "Skins"

Gary Player and Arnold Palmer, two players past their competitive prime, walked away with a combined $310,000 in winnings, November 27, after competing in The Skins Game, a new high-stakes golf match devised for television.

The 48-year-old Player won $170,000 and the 54-year-old Palmer won $140,000 of the $360,000 purse. Jack Nicklaus, designer of the 7,099-yard Desert Highlands course that hosted the event in Scottsdale, Ariz., won $40,000 and Tom Watson earned $10,000.

The concept was simple. Each of the first six holes were worth $10,000, the middle six $20,000 and the final six $30,000. If one golfer won a hole, he would win the money. But if two tied for low, all four stayed alive and the money would carry over.

That's why Player picked up $150,000 with one birdie putt on 17. The four previous holes had been tied and the money had built up. Palmer got $100,000 for a 40-foot birdie putt that dropped on 12.

*Arnold Palmer does a $100,000 victory jig after sinking a 40-foot birdie putt on the 12th green during The Skins Game.*

*A judge put Willie Wilson's baseball career on hold with a three-month prison sentence for attempting to purchase cocaine.*

# Gretzky extends scoring streak

Wayne Gretzky made another assault on the record books, November 13, but his effort on this occasion was lost in the ominous shadow cast by the four-time defending champion New York Islanders in a game at Nassau Coliseum in Uniondale, N.Y.

The Great One dished out one assist and notched a goal to stretch his scoring streak to a National Hockey League-record 31 straight games, but a four-goal outburst by Butch Goring stole the show and sparked the Islanders to an 8-5 win over the Edmonton Oilers.

The Islanders won all three regular-season games against Edmonton last year before sweeping the Oilers in the Stanley Cup finals. They won twice this year, deflating the Oilers' 21-7-3 league-best record.

Mike Bossy scored two goals within the first three minutes and Goring scored once in the first period, twice in the second and once more in the third. The Islanders led 5-1 after one period and 7-2 after two.

Gretzky broke his own record of 30 straight scoring games when he assisted on Willy Lindstrom's goal early in the final stanza. He later added a goal, the 300th of his NHL career.

# 3 Royals in drug violations

Willie Wilson, Willie Aikens and Jerry Martin, three members of last year's Kansas City Royals, became the first active baseball players ever to be sent to prison for drug violations, November 17, when a federal magistrate handed them a three-month sentence for attempting to purchase cocaine.

United States Magistrate J. Milton Sullivant, noting a professional athlete's "special place in our society," also fined Wilson and Aikens the maximum $5,000 and Martin $2,500. He later pronounced the same sentence and fine on Vida Blue, a former Royals pitcher who pleaded guilty to possession of cocaine in the same case.

Wilson, Aikens and Martin all pleaded guilty after being caught trying to buy the drug during a federal investigation centered in Kansas City. Martin, Aikens and Blue all have been released by the Royals. The 28-year-old Wilson, the Royals' starting center fielder and a former American League batting champion, still is a member of the organization.

Commissioner Bowie Kuhn followed by suspending the four players for one year.

# 1984

## U.S. skiers strike gold

American success in Winter Olympic Games competition, normally limited to ice skating venues, took a dramatic turn at Sarajevo, Yugoslavia, when U.S. skiers captured three of the six events usually dominated by the European Alpine power-houses.

The most dramatic victory was turned in, February 16, by 23-year-old Bill Johnson, a cocky Californian who became the first American ever to capture a gold medal in a men's downhill race. Johnson negotiated the 3,066-meter course in 1:45.59, 27-hundredths of a second faster than Peter Mueller of Switzerland. He caught and passed Mueller with a sizzling burst to the finish line.

Johnson's rousing performance was sandwiched between 1-2 American finishes in the women's giant slalom and the men's slalom. Debbie Armstrong won the giant slalom gold medal and Christin Cooper the silver on February 13. Twin brothers Steve and Phil Mahre swept down the icy slopes to their dramatic gold-silver victory on the final day of the Games.

*Californian Bill Johnson, moments after becoming the first American ever to win an Olympic downhill gold medal.*

## Raiders set records as Allen runs for 191

Marcus Allen ran for two touchdowns and a record 191 yards and the Los Angeles defense produced two big first-half defensive plays that resulted in scores as the Raiders pounded out a lopsided 38-9 victory over defending champion Washington, January 22, in Super Bowl XVIII at Tampa Stadium.

In the first quarter Derrick Jensen blocked a punt by Jeff Hayes, chased the ball into the end zone and fell on it for a touchdown. After Cliff Branch had caught a 12-yard touchdown pass from quarterback Jim Plunkett early in the second quarter, linebacker Jack Squirek picked off a Joe Theismann pass and ran it back five yards for another score.

The Raiders stretched their 21-3 halftime lead into a third-quarter rout. Allen's five-yard TD run offset a one-yard plunge by Washington's John Riggins and his 74-yard touchdown dash provided icing for the cake.

The Raiders' 38 points and 29-point margin of victory were Super Bowl records.

## Miami's Hurricane destroys Nebraska

Defensive back Ken Calhoun turned in the biggest play in Miami football history, January 2, knocking away a Nebraska two-point conversion pass attempt with 48 seconds remaining to preserve a 31-30 Orange Bowl victory over the top-ranked Cornhuskers and the Hurricanes' first-ever national championship.

Calhoun's defensive gem thwarted a furious Nebraska rally from a 31-17 deficit with 4:44 remaining. Jeff Smith, a third-quarter replacement for injured running back Mike Rozier, capped a 76-yard Nebraska drive with a one-yard run and then scored on a 24-yard run with the Huskers facing fourth-and-eight. Coach Tom Osborne, knowing that his team probably needed only a tie to clinch the national championship, elected to go for the victory. His gamble failed.

The Hurricanes, 10-1 and ranked fourth (UPI) and fifth (AP) in the two major polls, jumped out to a 17-0 lead on the strength of two Bernie Kosar touchdown passes. But Nebraska, an 11-point favorite riding a 22-game winning streak, tied the game in the third period before Miami pulled away again.

Miami's championship hopes were aided by Georgia's upset of second-ranked Texas in the Cotton Bowl and UCLA's lopsided win over Illinois (ranked fourth by AP) in the Rose Bowl. No. 3 Auburn recorded an unimpressive win over Michigan in the Sugar Bowl.

*Miami running back Alonzo Highsmith goes over a pack of defenders to score the Hurricanes' third Orange Bowl touchdown against Nebraska.*

# Kareem gets record

Los Angeles center Kareem Abdul-Jabbar floated a 12-foot skyhook over two helpless Utah defenders, April 5, and entered the record book as the most prolific scorer in NBA history during the Lakers' 129-115 victory over the Jazz at Las Vegas.

Abdul-Jabbar's historic basket, scored with 8:53 remaining, allowed the 7-foot-2 star to pass the record set 11 years ago by another basketball giant — Wilt Chamberlain. Wilt scored 31,419 career points in 14 seasons before retiring after the 1972-73 campaign. Abdul-Jabbar tallied his 31,421 points in 15 seasons, playing 121 more games than Chamberlain.

Abdul-Jabbar entered the final quarter needing only three points. He dunked to tie Chamberlain and hit his record-breaker over Utah center Mark Eaton and guard Rickey Green.

After a prolonged ovation and a brief ceremony, Abdul-Jabbar was removed from the contest with 22 points. The game was one of 11 Utah home games scheduled for Las Vegas.

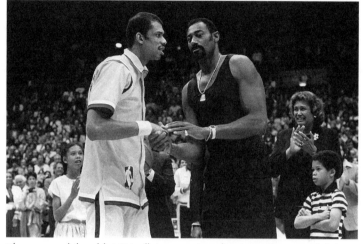

The new and the old: NBA all-time scoring champion Kareem Abdul-Jabbar is congratulated by former champ Wilt Chamberlain before a Los Angeles Lakers game at the Forum in Inglewood, Calif.

# Colts "sneak" away

In a clandestine operation that left Baltimore city officials and fans in a state of shock, a fleet of moving vans commissioned by Colts Owner Robert Irsay cleaned out the team's training facility in the dead of night and headed for the club's new home in Indianapolis.

"The Colts are coming to Indianapolis," declared William Hudnut, the city's mayor, on March 29. The news had first been announced by a spokesman for the Indianapolis Capital Improvement Board, the organization that controls the still-unfinished 60,000-seat Hoosier Dome where the Colts will play their National Football League games.

Irsay, unhappy with his Memorial Stadium lease and declining ticket sales in Baltimore, had negotiated with Indianapolis officials for several months. But his sudden move caught everybody by surprise — which is evidently what he wanted.

With everything already moved to Indianapolis, there is not much Maryland officials can do by way of legal action. And the NFL, stung recently by the Federal Court ruling that allowed the Oakland Raiders to move to Los Angeles, has taken a hands-off posture.

# Hoyas claim 1st title

Freshmen Reggie Williams and Michael Graham combined for 33 points and Georgetown wore down Houston with a tight man-to-man defense, April 2, as the Hoyas claimed their first national championship with an 84-75 victory over the Cougars in the NCAA Tournament final at Seattle's Kingdome.

What had been billed as a battle of the 7-foot titans, Georgetown's Patrick Ewing versus Houston's Akeem Olajuwon, actually took shape as a battle of supporting casts. Coach John Thompson's Hoyas were the clear winners.

With Michael Young hitting three quick jump shots, Houston pulled out to a 14-6 lead. But that was the only highlight for the run-and-gun Cougars. Georgetown caught them at 14, pulled out to a 28-22 lead and reached halftime with a 40-30 advantage. When Olajuwon picked up his fourth foul 23 seconds into the second half, the Cougars were in trouble.

Sophomore guard Alvin Franklin did his best to keep Houston in the game, scoring 14 of his team's next 20 points, but the Cougars could pull no closer than three. With Williams and Graham combining for 11 of the Hoyas' 15 second-half field goals, Georgetown pulled away to its 34th victory in 37 games.

Georgetown center Patrick Ewing blocks a shot by Houston's Rickie Winslow.

# 1984

## MAY - AUGUST

## Oilers end Islanders' four-year Cup reign

*Edmonton's Wayne Gretzky celebrates after scoring the first of his two final-game goals.*

Mixing defense and determination with the highest-scoring offense in National Hockey League history, the Edmonton Oilers rolled to a 5-2 victory over the Islanders, May 19, and snatched the Stanley Cup after its four-year stay in New York.

The decisive fifth-game victory at Edmonton's Northlands Coliseum was spearheaded by Wayne Gretzky, who scored two goals and an assist as the Oilers built a 4-0 lead. Pat LaFontaine provided the Islanders with momentary hope

when he scored twice within the first 35 seconds of the third period, but Edmonton put out a defensive blanket to insure victory.

It was only fitting that Gretzky, the league's leading scorer for four straight years, should light the offensive fuse. The Great One scored 87 goals and 205 points in 1983-84 and set an NHL record by scoring in an incredible 51 consecutive games. The Oilers' good defense was the result of a lesson well learned during the Islanders' 1983 sweep of Edmonton in the Cup finals.

The Oilers scored an NHL-record 446 goals during the regular season.

*It was love at first sight for Fuzzy Zoeller when he was handed the U.S. Open championship trophy after his 18-hole playoff victory over Greg Norman.*

## U.S. Open goes Fuzzy

Fuzzy Zoeller shook up Australian Greg Norman with a 68-foot birdie putt on the second hole of a June 18 playoff round and then stormed to an eight-stroke victory and his first U.S. Open golf championship.

Zoeller, who had watched from the fairway when Norman dropped a 40-foot putt on the

18th hole of regulation to force a tie, burned up the 6,930-yard Winged Foot course (Mamaroneck, N.Y.) for a playoff-round 67 while Norman struggled to a 75. As Zoeller was scoring his birdie at the second hole, Norman was taking three putts for a double bogey 6. Norman three-putted again on the third and fifth holes.

As the two golfers neared the end of their round, they were joking. When Zoeller putted on 18, Norman pulled a white towel out of his bag and waved it in surrender—the same as Zoeller had done at 18 the day before.

Zoeller, who had finished regulation with a 4-under 276, won his only other major in 1979 when he beat Tom Watson and Ed Sneed in a sudden-death Masters playoff.

## Celtics close out Lakers in seven

Boston's starting front line of Cedric Maxwell, Larry Bird and Robert Parish combined for 36 rebounds—three more than the entire Los Angeles team—and the Celtics bulled their way to a 111-102 seventh-game victory over the Lakers in the NBA Finals at Boston Garden.

The June 12 win wrapped up

Boston's 15th NBA title and kept intact the Celtics' record of never having lost in the seventh game of the league's title series. Boston has lost only once in 16 championship series and has now beaten the Lakers eight times without losing in the finals.

The Celtics owned a whopping 52-33 edge in rebounding

and converted that into victory. Boston led most of the way and broke open a 105-102 contest with six game-ending points.

Maxwell scored 24 points and Bird added 20 to lead the Celtics, while Kareem Abdul-Jabbar topped Los Angeles with 29. The Lakers' big man sparked a 17-6 fourth-quarter surge that made the game close.

# U.S. gymnasts excel

In one three-day period, six male athletes and one female wiped out decades of American gymnastics frustration by winning gold medals in the men's team competition and the women's individual all-around at the Los Angeles Summer Olympic Games.

Aided by the absence of the boycotting Soviets, the American team of Peter Vidmar, Bart Conner, Mitch Gaylord, Tim Daggett, Jim Hartung and Scott Johnson rose to an inspiring performance that produced a slim 591.40 to 590.80 victory, August 1, over a world champion Chinese team that had been labeled unbeatable.

With five of the six events completed, the Americans had built a slim lead. It would take everything they could muster to hold on and capture the first gold medal in American history.

But first a decision would have to be made. Should the American team play it safe with more conservative routines and less challenging dismounts? Or should it take a chance with the riskier stunts that usually generate higher scores? They decided to go for broke.

Johnson led off and his bad dismount added to the pressure. But Gaylord performed his sensational Gaylord II somersault and scored a 9.95, Conner turned in a 9.90, Vidmar a 9.95 and Daggett a perfect 10. The Americans prevailed.

As if that victory wasn't emotional enough, a 4-foot-9, 94-pound bundle of energy named

*America's newest sweetheart, Mary Lou Retton, performs on the balance beam en route to her all-around gymnastics gold medal.*

Mary Lou Retton stepped into the role of America's sweetheart two days later. After helping the women to a second-place finish in the team competition, Retton worked her way through the first five events of the individual all-around in a tight duel for first with Romanian Ecaterina Szabo.

Szabo had finished when Retton prepared for her final event—the vault. Mary Lou would need a near-perfect 9.95 to tie, a 10 to win.

The 16-year-old's takeoff was good, she performed a full back somersault in layout position with a full twist and she landed perfectly. She got her 10 and became the first woman to win a gymnastics gold medal.

She didn't need her second vault, but did it anyway. Another 10. Her final margin over Szabo was 79.175 to 79.125.

# Carl Lewis captures four golds

*Carl Lewis adds a touch of patriotism to his celebration after winning the 100-meter dash during competition in the Los Angeles Olympic Games.*

Carl Lewis, matching the feat performed by Jesse Owens 48 years earlier, captured four gold medals and established himself as the top individual performer at the Los Angeles Summer Olympic Games.

The 23-year-old Lewis recorded victories in the 100-meter and 200-meter dashes and the long jump before anchoring a world record-setting effort by the 4 x 100-meter relay team. Those were the same events Owens won in 1936.

Lewis opened his assault, August 3, when he came from behind and recorded an impressive 9.99 victory in the 100-meter, beating Sam Graddy by eight feet. His winning long jump (28-0¼) came on his first try and he passed the final four rounds to preserve energy. He won the 200-meter race in 19.80.

Graddy, Ron Brown, Calvin Smith and Lewis combined in the 4 x 100-meter relay, August 11, and produced the only track and field world record. The winning time was 37.83.

# 1984

## SEPTEMBER-DECEMBER

## 357-yard explosion a record for Mayes

Washington State running back Rueben Mayes exploded for 357 yards during the Cougars' 50-41 victory over Oregon, October 27, breaking the single-game rushing record set six years earlier by Georgia Tech's Eddie Lee Ivery.

Mayes' performance included three touchdowns and came on the heels of a 216-yard, five-touchdown performance against Stanford on October 20. His 357-yard game beat Ivery's performance by one yard and his 573-yard two-game total set a major college record.

Mayes rushed nine times for 41 yards in the first quarter, 11 times for 156 in the second,

*Washington State's Rueben Mayes, the most prolific one-game rusher in NCAA history.*

seven times for 73 in the third and 12 times for 87 in the fourth. His record-breaking run came with a minute left in the game.

The visiting Cougars compiled 663 yards in total offense, while the Ducks gained 478 yards overall. There were 58 passes attempted in the game with only one interception.

## Payton passes Brown

Chicago's Walter Payton took a third-quarter pitch from quarterback Jim McMahon, October 7, and ran into the National Football League record book. His six-yard gain in a game against New Orleans moved him past former Cleveland great Jim Brown and into first place on the career rushing charts.

Payton's run, which moved him beyond Brown's career record of 12,312, came early in his 10th NFL campaign. Brown compiled his yardage from 1957 through 1965, when the Browns were a dominant NFL force.

The game was delayed after Payton's historic run so officials could present him with the ball. After the 30-year-old veteran received congratulations from both teammates and opponents, the Bears went on to win 20-7.

Payton finished the day with 154 yards and a career total of 12,400. The 100-yard game was the record-setting 59th of his career, surpassing Brown.

## Tigers conclude a dream season

Kirk Gibson hit two upper-deck homers and drove in five runs, October 14, at Tiger Stadium as Detroit recorded an 8-4 victory over San Diego and brought a fitting conclusion to the World Series and a season of domination.

The 1984 Tigers were quick-strike artists. They won a record 35 of their first 40 games and 104 overall while leading the American League East Division from first day to last. They swept Kansas City in the A.L. Championship Series and put down the Padres in a five-game World Series. In four games of the fall classic, two San Diego starters failed to get through the first inning, one could not make it past the second and another could not survive the third.

The only Padre starter to last more than three was Mark Thurmond, who pitched five innings in the opener and dropped a 3-2 decision to Jack Morris. The first World Series game ever contested in San Diego was decided by a two-run fifth-inning homer by Larry Herndon.

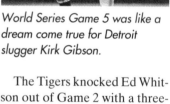

*World Series Game 5 was like a dream come true for Detroit slugger Kirk Gibson.*

The Tigers knocked Ed Whitson out of Game 2 with a three-run outburst in the first inning, but Padre relievers Andy Hawkins and Craig Lefferts pitched brilliantly and San Diego rebounded for a 5-3 victory. That was it, however, for the Padres. The Tigers won the third game 5-2, won the next day, 4-2, and finished off their dream season in Game 5.

---

### ★ SPORTS WATCH ★

**SEP:** St. Louis relief ace Bruce Sutter tied Dan Quisenberry's 1-year-old record for single-season saves when he recorded No. 45 in a 7-3 win over the New York Mets.

**SEP:** California's Mike Witt joined select company on the final day of the season when he pitched a perfect-game 1-0 win over Texas, striking out 10 and throwing just 97 pitches.

**NOV:** Detroit relief ace Willie Hernandez capped his 32-save, 1.92-ERA season by capturing both the American League Cy Young and MVP awards.

**NOV:** The Winnipeg Blue Bombers won their first Grey Cup in 22 years with a 47-17 thrashing of the Hamilton Tiger-Cats.

**DEC:** Miami quarterback Dan Marino shredded the NFL record book, passing for 48 touchdowns and 5,084 yards on 362 completions.

# Rams' Dickerson overtakes O.J.

Los Angeles Rams running back Eric Dickerson completed his record-setting season, December 14, when he ran for 98 yards in a game against San Francisco and finished with 2,105 for the season, 102 more than O.J. Simpson gained in 1973 for the Buffalo Bills.

Dickerson's rushing feat was accomplished in 16 games, two more than Simpson played when he became the first to break the 2,000-yard barrier in one season. Dickerson finished his 14th game with 1,792 yards on 326 carries and moved past O.J. with a 215-yard effort against Houston the next week.

The record-breaker came before his home fans at Anaheim Stadium on Dickerson's 27th and last carry of the day— a nine-yard run that boosted his output for the season to 2,007.

Simpson topped the 200-yard barrier three times during his record season while Dickerson made it twice.

*Los Angeles Rams running back Eric Dickerson (right) gets a hug from teammate Norwood Van after breaking O.J. Simpson's one-season rushing record during a game against Houston.*

# Flutie's TD bomb destroys Miami

Doug Flutie dropped a 48-yard last-play touchdown bomb on Miami and a stunned Orange Bowl audience, November 23, and Boston College escaped with a wild 47-45 victory in one of the most exciting passing duels ever staged.

The Eagles appeared out of luck when Miami's Melvin Bratton scored his fourth touchdown on a one-yard run with 28 seconds left. But Flutie moved Boston College to the Miami 48-yard line with time enough remaining for one more play. The strategy was simple.

"You put the ball in the end zone," Flutie said. "We've got a couple guys down there, they've got a couple guys down there, (and) you see who comes up with it."

*Boston College quarterback Doug Flutie dropped a touchdown bomb on the Miami Hurricanes.*

Flutie fired the "Hail Mary" pass 64 yards in the air and Boston College's Gerard Phelan "came up with it," making his 11th and most important catch of the day. It was a fitting conclusion to a wild and crazy game that matched up two of college football's top guns.

Flutie and Miami's Bernie Kosar put on quite a show. Flutie completed a remarkable 34 of 46 passes for 472 yards and three touchdowns; Kosar connected on 25 of 38 attempts for 447 yards and two TDs.

# Bosco TD passes lift BYU to victory

Brigham Young quarterback Robbie Bosco, playing with a painful leg injury and limping noticeably through most of the game, threw a pair of fourth-quarter touchdown passes, December 21, and rallied the Cougars to a 24-17 Holiday Bowl victory over Michigan that cemented their claim to the 1984 college football national championship.

With their top ranking in both polls and 12-0 record on the line, the Cougars marched 80 yards early in the final quarter and tied the game, 17-17, on a seven-yard pass from Bosco to Glen Kozlowski. Bosco then drove BYU 83 yards in the final 4:30, connecting on a 13-yard strike to tight end Kelly Smith with 1:23 remaining.

The victory over the 6-5 Wolverines left Brigham Young as the only undefeated major college team in the nation. The prospect of staying that way appeared questionable in the first quarter when Bosco was decked by a late hit and the nation's total offense leader had to be carried from the field. He returned in the second quarter, however, and limped his way through the rest of the game.

# 1985

## Montana leads 49ers

*The Joe Montana (16)-Roger Craig (33) connection was lethal for San Francisco in Super Bowl XIX.*

Joe Montana threw for three touchdowns and ran for another, January 20, carrying San Francisco to a 38-16 victory over Miami in Super Bowl XIX at Stanford Stadium in Palo Alto, Calif.

Montana connected with Carl Monroe for 33 yards in the first quarter and Roger Craig on touchdown passes of eight and 16 yards in the second and third periods. He also ran six yards for a second-quarter score and finished the game with 59 rush-ing yards. Montana completed 24 of 35 passes for a Super Bowl-record 331 yards and out-dueled record-setting Miami quarterback Dan Marino.

The 49ers' defense made life difficult for Marino, rushing him into premature passes and recording two interceptions. Marino completed 29 of 50 attempts for 318 yards and one touchdown, but he was Miami's only offensive weapon.

Montana received first-class support from running backs Wendell Tyler (65 yards) and Craig (58 rushing yards and seven receptions for 77 yards). When the Dolphin pass rush pressured Montana, he simply outran the pursuit and picked up some valuable yardage himself.

The Super Bowl victory was the second in four years for Coach Bill Walsh's team and Miami's second loss in the last three years.

## Knight throws a chair

Indiana Coach Bob Knight closed another chapter in his stormy career, February 24, when he formally apologized for throwing a chair across the floor during Purdue's 72-63 victory over the Hoosiers at Bloomington, Ind.

In the apology, Knight said his action was an "embarrass-ment to the university," and added that it was prompted by his frustration over officiating in the Big Ten.

The frustration first surfaced in a home loss to Illinois (66-50), during which Knight broke a chair in a moment of rage and allegedly made an obscene ges-ture toward referee Jim Bain. Early in the Purdue game, Knight picked up a chair and hurled it across the court as the Boilermakers' Steve Reid was preparing to shoot a technical foul shot. He was ejected.

Knight is well known for his on-court tantrums and verbal assaults. His most infamous tirade occurred in 1979 when he created an international inci-dent by hitting a policeman in Puerto Rico. Knight, coaching the United States team during the Pan American Games, later was tried in absentia and sen-tenced to six months in jail.

*Stock car driver Bill Elliott recorded his biggest career victory at Daytona Beach, Fla.*

## Elliott roars to Daytona victory

Bill Elliott, driving a powerful red, white and blue Thunder-bird, gained the biggest victory of his Grand National stock car racing career, February 17, when he held off Neil Bonnett's late challenge in the Daytona 500 at Daytona International Speedway.

Elliott, starting from the pole position after setting a stock car qualifying record of 205.114 mph, dueled Cale Yarborough early in the race before the defending champion dropped out with engine trouble. Elliott was in control through lap 161, when a yellow caution allowed Bonnett's Chevrolet Monte Carlo to catch up.

Elliott was forced to pit for new tires with six laps remain-ing and Bonnett took over the lead. But the Thunderbird roared back, passed Bonnett on the 195th lap and cruised to vic-tory. Bonnett spun out.

# Hagler decks Hearns

Marvin Hagler, chasing Thomas Hearns around the ring like an angry bull, scored a third-round technical knockout over the challenger, April 15, in a breathtaking middleweight championship fight at Las Vegas.

Hagler, a notoriously slow starter, rushed to the center of the ring at the opening bell and began pummeling away. Hearns pummeled back and the frantic pace continued for the next eight minutes and one second. By that time, the fighters had landed nearly 200 punches, the last one a right by Hagler that dropped Hearns on his back.

Hearns barely beat the count, but referee Richard Steele looked into his glassy eyes and called off the fight. Hearns was helped to his corner while Hagler enjoyed a victory ride around the ring.

The win was Hagler's 11th successive title defense, three shy of Carlos Monzon's middleweight record, and it improved his career mark to 61-2-2. Hearns, the reigning super-welterweight champion, is 41-2.

Hearns opened two cuts, one above Hagler's right eye and another on his forehead. Steele stopped the fight briefly in the third round to have a doctor examine the cuts.

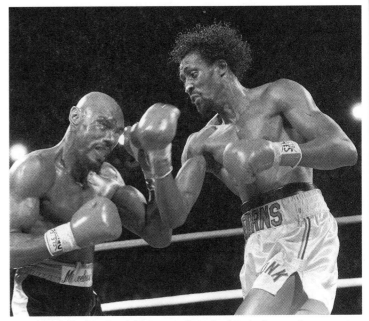

*Thomas Hearns (right) delivers a right to the head of Marvelous Marvin Hagler during second-round action in their middleweight title fight.*

# A Villanova shocker

Villanova Coach Rollie Massimino knew there was only one way to beat big bad Georgetown in the finals of the NCAA Tournament at Rupp Arena in Lexington, Ky. His Wildcats would have to play their usual tenacious defense while at the same time keeping offensive mistakes to a minimum.

But not even he could have imagined just how mistake-free the Wildcats would be on the night of April 1. Playing an outstanding first half and an even better second half, Villanova slayed the giant, 66-64.

*Villanova center Ed Pinckney shows the NCAA championship trophy during a downtown Philadelphia rally celebrating the Wildcats' shocking upset of Georgetown.*

Georgetown, led by dominating 7-foot center Patrick Ewing, had followed its first NCAA title with an impressive 35-2 run to the championship game. Villanova had lost two times to its Big East Conference rival and 10 times overall.

But it's hard to argue with near perfection. When Harold Pressley hit a basket at the end of the first half to give the Wildcats a 29-28 lead, the crowd rose in tribute. Villanova had connected on 13 of its first 18 shots and handled Georgetown's relentless full-court pressure. The Wildcats had hounded the Hoyas with defensive intensity.

But as good as they were in the first half, the Wildcats were better in the second. With point guard Gary McLain committing just two turnovers against a defense that contested every dribble, Villanova rode a second-half surge to a 38-32 lead. Hounding high-scoring Hoyas Reggie Williams and Ewing relentlessly, the Wildcats played methodically and under control.

Georgetown fought back to four one-point leads, but Villanova regained control each time and finally went into its delay. The Hoyas fouled and the Wildcats converted 11 of 14 foul shots down the stretch. That complemented their nine-of-10 second-half shooting from the field and 22-of-28 shooting (.786) for the game.

Dwayne McClain (five-of-seven and 17 points) and Harold Jensen (five-of-five and 14 points) were two of the top guns for Villanova, but a lot of credit went to center Ed Pinckney, who scored 16 points and outplayed Ewing.

# 1985

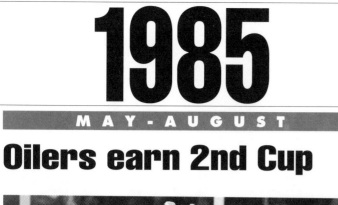

## Oilers earn 2nd Cup

*Three key members of Edmonton's prolific scoring machine (left to right): Charlie Huddy, Paul Coffey and Jari Kurri.*

Defenseman Paul Coffey scored two goals and Wayne Gretzky added a goal and three assists as the Edmonton Oilers speeded, finessed and checked their way to a second straight Stanley Cup with an 8-3 Game 5 victory over Philadelphia.

The May 30 clincher at Edmonton's Northlands Coliseum was decided early. Jari Kurri opened the scoring in the first period with his playoff record-tying 19th goal and Willie Lindstrom gave the Oilers a two-goal advantage only 35 seconds later.

Coffey connected twice within a 2:26 span later in the period and another two-goal blitz in the second stanza increased the lead to 6-1. Gretzky, who finished the series with a playoff-record 47 points (17 goals, 30 assists), scored the team's seventh goal in the final period.

Taking the brunt of this assault was goaltender Bob Froese, who had to step in for injured Pelle Lindbergh. Edmonton goalie Grant Fuhr finished the playoffs with a 15-3 record.

## Lakers wipe out jinx

Wiping out a jinx that extended back to 1959 and the team's final years in Minneapolis, the Los Angeles Lakers finally defeated Boston in a National Basketball Association championship series and ruined the Celtics' bid to become the league's first repeat champion since 1969.

With 38-year-old Kareem Abdul-Jabbar scoring 29 points and James Worthy adding 28 in

a 111-100 Game 6 triumph at Boston Garden on June 9, the Lakers ended a frustrating string of eight straight losses to the Celtics in NBA Finals play over 26 years. The title was the second in four years for the Lakers and the loss was only the second ever for Boston in 17 final series.

After a 55-55 halftime standoff, Los Angeles came out in the third period and hit its first six

## North finds Opening

Andy North, who had not won a PGA tournament since his surprise victory in the 1978 U.S. Open, survived a final-round 74 and outlasted three competitors to record a one-stroke victory in the U.S. Open at Oakland Hills Country Club in Birmingham, Mich.

North's June 16 victory was aided by the final-round collapse of third-round leader Tze-Chung Chen. Chen, a 26-year-old Taiwanese, held a commanding four-stroke lead after four holes, but he took a quadruple bogey 8 on the fifth and bogeyed six, seven and eight to put himself into a hole.

Chen regained a share of the lead with North and Dave Barr at 13, but a bogey at 14 dropped him back for good. Barr bogeyed 17 and 18 to offset North's 18th-hole bogey.

North's 74, one of the poorest final rounds for an Open champion in history, gave him a

*Andy North shows off the U.S. Open championship trophy he won with a not-so-pretty final-round 74.*

72-hole total of 279, one better than Chen, Barr and Denis Watson. Chen, who closed with a 77, had made history in the opening round when he sank a 255-yard 3-wood shot on the par-5 second hole for a double eagle.

### ★ SPORTS WATCH ★

**MAY:** Danny Sullivan drove his Miller American Special to victory in the Indianapolis 500, averaging 152.982 mph.

**MAY:** High-flying Michael Jordan averaged 28.2 points per game and captured NBA Rookie of the Year honors.

**JUN:** Edmonton's Wayne Gretzky topped the 200-point barrier for the third time and won his sixth consecutive Hart Trophy as the NHL player most valuable to his team.

**JUL:** Houston's Nolan Ryan became the first pitcher to record 4,000 strikeouts when he fanned Danny Heep in the sixth inning of a 4-3 win over the New York Mets.

**AUG:** On the same day, Chicago White Sox righthander Tom Seaver became the 17th player in major league history to win 300 games and California's Rod Carew became baseball's 16th 3,000-hit man.

shots to take control. The goggled Abdul-Jabbar connected on three critical baskets in the final 2½ minutes to hold off a late Boston comeback attempt.

Kevin McHale's 32 points

and Larry Bird's 28 were not enough to offset poor shooting by guards Dennis Johnson and Danny Ainge (a combined 6 for 31) and center Robert Parish (5 for 14).

# Women's mile mark broken in Zurich

Mary Decker-Slaney held off a late challenge by Rumanian Maricica Puica, August 21, and broke Puica's world record in the women's mile with a clocking of 4:16.71 in the Weltklasse track and field meet at Zurich, Switzerland.

Decker-Slaney, undefeated outdoors this season, took over from Diana Richburg at the halfway mark and never trailed again. She was challenged, however, by Puica, who had set the previous mile record (4:17.44) two years ago. Puica got close on the homestretch, but could not catch up.

*Mary Decker-Slaney holds a slight lead over Zola Budd as she heads for a world record in the mile.*

Ironically, Puica also beat her former record with a 4:17.33 second-place clocking while South African Zola Budd, running under British colors, was third at 4:17.52. The loss was Puica's first in major outdoor competition this year.

# A night of fireworks

There were plenty of fireworks on the night of July 4 at Atlanta's Fulton-County Stadium, but the real ones didn't come until 4 the next morning. It was a bizarre ending to one of the more bizarre games in history.

With Braves officials ready to unleash a fireworks display after the game as a holiday celebration, the New York Mets and Atlanta fought to an 8-8 tie. The Mets finally broke through for two runs in the 13th inning, but the Braves tied it in the bottom of the frame with two of their own. The score remained 10-10 until the 18th, when New York scored a single run.

It appeared to be showtime when, with two out and nobody on base, pitcher Rick Camp was forced to bat for himself because Atlanta had run out of non-pitchers to pinch-hit. But Camp, an .060 career hitter, hit a game-tying home run.

Undeterred, the Mets scored five runs in the top of the 19th. Again the Braves came back, but this time their rally fell short and the game ended 16-13—at 3:55 a.m., six hours and 10 minutes after it started.

So at 4 a.m., the few remaining Braves fans got their fireworks show—and the locals got an early wakeup call.

# McEnroe upset at Wimbledon

Kevin Curren, a 27-year-old South African with a monster serve, pulled a Wimbledon shocker, July 3, when he ousted top-seeded and defending champion John McEnroe, 6-2, 6-2, 6-4, in a quarterfinal match.

It was McEnroe's most lopsided loss since he became the No. 1 player in the world in 1981 and it was his earliest elimination from the Wimbledon tournament in six years. It also meant that, for the first time since 1979, the tournament's final would be played without its top seed.

McEnroe was never really in the match. The sixth-seeded Curren consistently mixed hard groundstrokes with a lob and a looping forehand that caught McEnroe at the net. His booming serves to the body kept McEnroe jumping back.

The 26-year-old McEnroe, called "McNasty" by the British tabloids because of his volatile temper and well-publicized on-court tantrums, accepted the loss stoically and said he felt weary. He also said he was going to begin a period of self-examination. McEnroe had defeated Curren in their seven previous meetings.

*John McEnroe argues with officials as Kevin Curren works to maintain concentration during quarterfinal action at Wimbledon.*

# 1985

**SEPTEMBER · DECEMBER**

# Michael Spinks upsets a lackluster Holmes

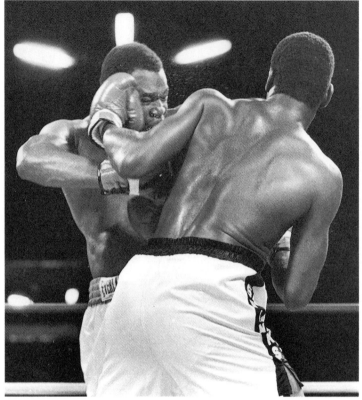

Michael Spinks, en route to a major heavyweight boxing upset, lands a solid left to the head of Larry Holmes.

## Rose gets record hit against San Diego

Pete Rose salutes the Riverfront Stadium crowd after collecting record-breaking hit 4,192.

When San Diego pitcher Eric Show delivered a 2-1 pitch, September 11, a familiar figure uncoiled from his familiar crouch and lined a familiar single into left field. Cincinnati player-manager Pete Rose had career hit No. 4,192, ending his long, relentless chase of Ty Cobb's ghost.

The record-breaking moment occurred 57 years to the day after Cobb had played his last major league game. The 44-year-old Rose rounded first base with his usual vigor and paused as flashing cameras turned Riverfront Stadium into a light show. He returned to the bag and pandemonium broke loose.

Rose's 15-year-old son Petey led the surge from the dugout as teammates and opponents gath-

ered to congratulate him. A bright red Corvette with license plate "PR 4192" was presented by Reds Owner Marge Schott.

Suddenly, Rose found himself standing alone as the ovation began to vibrate through the stadium. Tears streamed down his face as emotion took over. Rose went on to score both runs and hit a triple in the Reds' 2-0 victory.

International Boxing Federation heavyweight champion Larry Holmes, bidding to win his record-tying 49th consecutive professional fight, was upset, September 21, by light-heavyweight champion Michael Spinks in a unanimous 15-round decision at Las Vegas.

Holmes' first loss came 30 years to the day after Rocky Marciano had won his record 49th straight fight, beating Archie Moore—the reigning light-heavyweight champion. The 35-year-old Holmes became the first heavyweight

champion ever to be dethroned by a light-heavyweight.

The fight figured to be a mismatch. But Holmes, weighing 21½ more pounds than his challenger, appeared lackluster and disinterested. He did all of his scoring with his left jab, seldom even trying to throw a right.

The 29-year-old Spinks was little better, getting the edge early and clinching the decision with one mad flurry in the 15th round. Spinks becomes the second half of the first brother team to claim the heavyweight crown. Leon upset Ali in 1978.

## A Royal celebration

Darryl Motley hit a two-run homer and Bret Saberhagen pitched a five-hitter, October 27, as Kansas City pounded out an 11-0 seventh-game victory over the cross-state rival St. Louis Cardinals in the World Series. But this fall classic actually was decided a day earlier, in Game 6 at Kansas City.

The Cardinals, carrying a three games to two lead into that contest, finally broke through against Royals starter Charlie Leibrandt for a 1-0 lead on an eighth-inning bloop

single by pinch-hitter Brian Harper. With relief ace Todd Worrell on the mound in the ninth, the Redbirds appeared ready for champagne heaven.

But pinch-hitter Jorge Orta led off with a grounder to first baseman Jack Clark, who tossed to Worrell dashing for the bag. Television cameras showed Worrell definitely beat Orta, but umpire Don Denkinger called the runner safe. The Cardinals argued vehemently . . . and then unraveled.

Clark inexplicably let Steve

Balboni's foul popup drop and Balboni promptly singled to left. One out and one passed ball later, pinch-hitter Dane Iorg singled home two runs to win the game and give the Royals the momentum they needed to complete their long journey back from a three games to one deficit.

# Flyers' goalie dies in crash

Pelle Lindbergh, the Philadelphia Flyers' outstanding 26-year-old goaltender, died November 12, two days after an automobile accident in Somerdale, N.J., had left him brain dead with no hope of recovery.

Lindbergh was rushed to the hospital when the red Porsche he was driving failed to negotiate a turn and skidded into a concrete wall. The 1984 Vezina Trophy winner suffered severe brain and spinal cord injuries, a fractured skull and broken legs. Lindbergh was put on a life-support system.

Two days later, the young Swede died when doctors, with permission from his parents, performed a five-hour operation to remove his organs for transplant. Doctors later said that his blood had shown a high level of intoxication.

Lindbergh, the Flyers' MVP last year, compiled a 40-17-7 record while leading Philadelphia all the way to the Stanley Cup final series, where it lost to Edmonton. He was 12-6 in the playoffs with three shutouts.

Two passengers in the car, Ed Parvin and Kathy McNeal, were in stable condition with multiple injuries.

*Philadelphia goaltender Pelle Lindbergh during the 1985 season.*

**SEP:** Cincinnati lefthander Tom Browning became the first rookie to win 20 games in one season since 1954 when he posted a 20-9 mark for the Reds.

**SEP:** Hana Mandlikova pulled off a U.S. Open shocker when she beat Martina Navratilova, 7-6, 1-6, 7-6, in the finals at Flushing Meadow.

**OCT:** New York Yankee veteran Phil Niekro recorded his 300th career victory on the final day of the season when he shut out Toronto, 8-0.

**NOV:** Second-year New York Mets fireballer Dwight Gooden, 24-4 with an N.L.-leading 1.53 ERA, earned his first Cy Young Award.

**DEC:** Auburn running back Bo Jackson outpolled Iowa quarterback Chuck Long in voting for the Heisman Trophy.

**DEC:** Former New York Yankee Roger Maris, the man who broke Babe Ruth's one-season home run record with 61 in 1961, died of cancer at age 51.

*Well-wishers surround Grambling's Eddie Robinson after his record-breaking 324th victory.*

# Robinson passes Bryant

When Grambling closed its regular season, November 23, with a 29-12 victory over Southern University at New Orleans, Eddie Robinson, the newly crowned king of football coaches, owned a 329-109-15 career record. He had shoved former Alabama coaching great Paul (Bear) Bryant into a backup role.

The history-making victory came, October 5, before 36,652 fans and more than 500 journalists at Dallas' Cotton Bowl. The Tigers pounded Prairie View A&M, 27-7, to give Robinson his 324th win in his 45th year of coaching. Bryant had retired with 323 career victories.

"I did a lot of crying tonight —with my coaches, with my players," Robinson said. "Later on, I'll cry for the man whose father was a sharecropper, and who's amazed that so much attention should come his way."

In the fourth quarter the Grambling sideline looked like one continuous celebration. When the game ended, Robinson was mobbed by players, friends and well-wishers. Photographers swarmed.

Robinson's Tiger teams now have compiled 26 straight winning seasons.

# Backup stars in Lions' Cup win

Ned Armour, a former track star who never played college football, caught two touchdown bombs from Roy Dewalt and sparked British Columbia to a 37-24 victory over Hamilton in the November 24 Grey Cup game at Montreal's Olympic Stadium.

Armour, who had appeared in only one regular-season game, was a replacement for star receiver Mervyn Fernan-dez, the Canadian Football League's Most Valuable Player who was sidelined with a thigh injury. Armour did not waste his opportunity, scoring first-half touchdowns on 84 and 59-yard throws by Dewalt.

British Columbia took a 13-0 first-quarter lead on Armour's 84-yard catch and two field goals by Lui Passaglia. But Hamilton took a 14-13 lead in the second period on a 35-yard TD pass from Ken Hobart to Ron Ingram and a second touchdown that was set up by Hobart's 61-yard run.

But Armour put the Lions back in front with his second touchdown and Passaglia's third field goal stretched the lead to 23-14. British Columbia put the game out of reach in the third quarter when Jim Sandusky hauled in a 66-yard deflected pass for a touchdown.

# 1986

## Sooners tame Lions

Freshman quarterback Jamelle Holieway stunned Penn State with a 71-yard touchdown pass to tight end Keith Jackson and Oklahoma's defense intercepted four passes to key a 25-10 Orange Bowl victory over the top-ranked and previously unbeaten Nittany Lions.

The New Year's Day victory put Oklahoma in line to claim its sixth AP national championship and fifth UPI title. The 10-1 Sooners, ranked second by UPI and third by AP behind Miami, benefitted when the Hurricanes were pounded by Tennessee in the Sugar Bowl, 35-7.

Penn State's game plan was aimed at stopping Oklahoma's vaunted wishbone, which had ground out 335.8 rushing yards per game through the regular season. And the Lions were surprisingly successful, holding the Sooners to 31 first-half yards while grabbing an early 7-0 lead.

But Oklahoma fought back on Tim Lashar's 26-yard field goal, and Holieway's long strike to Jackson, one of three passes

*Oklahoma quarterback Jamelle Holieway signals No. 1 as he celebrates with teammate Darin Berryhill during the closing minutes of the Sooners' Orange Bowl victory over Penn State.*

he completed on the day. The Sooner defense took care of the rest, making life miserable for Penn State quarterbacks John Shaffer and Matt Knizner. Sophomore Lydell Carr sealed the verdict when he ran 61 yards for a fourth-quarter touchdown.

## Baseball fights drugs

Baseball Commissioner Peter Ueberroth, facing a rapidly growing drug problem, handed out one-year suspensions, February 28, to seven players, all of whom he said had used drugs themselves or facilitated the spread of drugs in baseball.

The New York Mets' Keith Hernandez, the Yankees' Dale Berra, Oakland's Joaquin Andujar, Cincinnati's Dave Parker, San Francisco's Jeffrey Leonard, Kansas City's Lonnie Smith and Los Angeles' Enos Cabell all were suspended without pay. But Ueberroth did offer an alternative.

The players can have their suspensions lifted if they agree to certain conditions, including contribution of 10 percent of their salaries this year to drug-prevention programs, a willing submission to drug tests for the remainder of their careers and participation in up to 200 hours of community service over the next two years.

The seven either testified or were implicated last year in Pittsburgh during the investigations and trials of seven men charged with cocaine distribution. None of the players were charged in the cases, but everybody except Andujar gave incriminating testimony and Andujar was named by several players as having used cocaine.

Ueberroth also handed out lesser penalties to 14 others.

## Bears claw Patriots

The Chicago Bears, hoping to leave their mark as one of the outstanding teams in National Football League history, crushed New England, 46-10, January 26, in Super Bowl XX at the New Orleans Superdome and completed their 18-1 season with a look of invincibility.

The Bears, who had scored 456 points while allowing a league-low 198 during a dominating regular season, simply ran roughshod over the Patriots. Quarterback Jim McMahon directed a near-perfect offensive plan that produced 408 yards and 37 points. End Richard Dent led a defensive charge that produced nine points while limiting New England to seven rushing yards.

One touchdown was scored by defensive back Reggie Phillips, who returned a Steve Grogan interception 28 yards, and the Bears tackled Grogan in the end zone for a fourth-quarter safety. McMahon scored twice on short runs and Kevin Butler kicked three Chicago field goals.

*Chicago Coach Mike Ditka gets a victory ride after the Bears' crushing Super Bowl victory over New England.*

---

**★ SPORTS WATCH ★**

**JAN:** The Islanders' Mike Bossy scored his 500th career goal in a 7-5 New York victory over Boston.

**FEB:** Despite losing his arbitration case, Boston third baseman Wade Boggs still walked away with a one-year contract calling for $1.35 million.

**MAR:** Ohio State captured its first NIT basketball championship with a 73-63 victory over Wyoming at Madison Square Garden.

**APR:** The NCAA adopted the three-point field goal for use in basketball games beginning next winter.

**APR:** At the age of 46, Jack Nicklaus shot a 279 and won his sixth Masters title at Augusta.

# Clemens sets record at Mariners' expense

Boston's Roger Clemens staged an awesome pitching performance, April 29, when he struck out a record 20 Seattle Mariners in a 3-1 Red Sox victory at Boston's Fenway Park.

Clemens broke the nine-inning strikeout record of 19 shared by Charles Sweeney (Providence, 1884), Steve Carlton (St. Louis, 1969), Tom Seaver (New York Mets, 1970) and Nolan Ryan (California, 1974). The big righthander, who had undergone shoulder surgery eight months earlier, lived up to his nickname (the Rocket) with a fastball clocked at 98 mph.

Clemens threw 138 pitches and did not walk a batter. He struck out each hitter in the Seattle starting lineup at least once and fanned Phil Bradley four times. Eight batters took called third strikes and he struck out the side in the first, fourth and fifth innings. He matched the American League record of eight consecutive strikeouts from the fourth to sixth.

Bradley became his 20th victim with two out in the ninth, after Spike Owen had struck out to lead off the frame. The Mariners, who managed only three hits, scored on a seventh-inning home run by Gorman Thomas.

Roger Clemens, on his way to a major league record 20 strikeouts during a game against Seattle, gets a glad hand from a teammate in the Boston dugout.

# Freshman carries Louisville to title

Freshman center Pervis Ellison scored a game-high 25 points and pulled down 11 rebounds to lead Louisville to a 72-69 victory over Duke in the March 31 NCAA Tournament final at Dallas.

The Cardinals trailed 61-55 with 7:19 remaining when the 6-foot-9 Ellison, known as "Never Nervous Pervis," stepped into the national spotlight. As the Blue Devils went through an untimely cold-shooting stretch, Ellison scored, grabbed rebounds and swatted away shots, as Louisville inched ahead.

The Cardinals were up by one with 48 seconds remaining when Duke's tenacious defense forced guard Jeff Hall to make an off-balance shot. Ellison went up, grabbed the airball and laid it in for a 68-65 lead. When Duke's David Henderson missed a shot at the other end, Ellison grabbed the rebound, was fouled and calmly sank both free throws to insure Louisville's 32nd victory and second NCAA championship under Coach Denny Crum.

Duke's Johnny Dawkins fends off Louisville's Pervis Ellison (43) and Milt Wagner as he chases a loose ball during action in the NCAA Tournament championship game.

While Ellison stole the spotlight, Duke guard Johnny Dawkins scored 24 points, played outstanding defense and single-handedly kept the Blue Devils (37-3) in the game.

# Holmes falls again in Spinks rematch

Michael Spinks, silencing critics who claimed that his September victory over Larry Holmes was a fluke, defeated the former champion again, April 20, and retained his heavyweight crown on a split decision at Las Vegas.

Displaying patience, Spinks warded off a furious Holmes attack in the early going and took control of the fight in the middle rounds with a left hook that scored repeatedly and relentless body punches.

Holmes charged out in a first-round rage and wrestled Spinks to the canvas, yelling, "Come on, get up." The 36-year-old fought like a crazy man for four rounds as Spinks stayed back and let him flail away.

Gradually, Spinks' left hooks began taking their toll. In the eighth round, the 29-year-old champion stepped up the tempo and took control. Holmes, appearing to lose steam, did stagger Spinks in the 14th, but he did not have enough left to press the issue. Spinks, who had moved up from the light-heavyweight ranks for his first fight against Holmes, held on for his 29th straight career victory. Holmes is 48-2, both losses against Spinks.

# 1986

# Longshot takes Derby

Ferdinand, a 17-1 longshot ridden by a 54-year-old jockey and handled by a 73-year-old trainer, ran to the roses, May 3, at Louisville's Churchill Downs and captured a slow Kentucky Derby by 2¼ lengths over Bold Arrangement.

Ferdinand might have been even more of a longshot if not for the presence of Bill Shoemaker, horse racing's all-time winningest jockey. Shoemaker attracted a lot of bettors and lived up to their confidence by guiding his unsung mount from last to first in becoming the oldest jockey to win horse racing's most prestigious event.

Weaving through traffic on the homestretch, Ferdinand covered the 1¼-mile test in 2:02⁴⁄₅. Early favorites Snow Chief and Badger Land finished out of the money.

The victory was especially sweet for Charlie Whittingham, who had never trained a Derby winner in his illustrious career. Ferdinand, the son of Najinsky II, is owned by Elizabeth and Howard Keck of Los Angeles.

The victory was Shoemaker's fourth in the prestigious Kentucky Derby.

*Ferdinand carries 54-year-old Bill Shoemaker to an upset victory in the Kentucky Derby.*

# Rahal wins Indy sprint

Bobby Rahal made a bold inside pass with two laps to go and then won a three-car, five-mile sprint to the finish line that decided the May 31 Indianapolis 500 at the Indianapolis Motor Speedway.

Rahal was running second to Kevin Cogan and just ahead of two-time winner Rick Mears with six laps (15 miles) remaining when a yellow caution flag came out because of a minor accident. If the yellow had remained out through the duration of the race, the three drivers would have been locked into their current positions. But with two laps to go, the green flag was waved and the race was on again in earnest.

As the three March-Cosworth cars neared the start-finish line, Rahal spotted an opening and shot past Cogan on the inside. He held his lead and finished 1.4 seconds ahead of Cogan and 1.8 seconds ahead of Mears in the tightest three-car finish in the history of the prestigious event.

Rahal also finished with the fastest winning time in history, averaging 170.722 mph in the relatively accident-free race.

*March-Cosworths driven by Bobby Rahal (3), Kevin Cogan (7) and Rick Mears (4) head for a 1-2-3 finish in one of the tightest Indianapolis 500s ever run.*

# Maryland star dies after drug abuse

Len Bias, a 22-year-old Maryland All-America basketball star, collapsed and died, June 19, two days after being selected as the second overall pick in the National Basketball Association draft by the Boston Celtics. An autopsy report revealed that he died of intoxication from cocaine that he probably sniffed minutes before his death.

Bias had returned to the College Park, Md., campus the night before from Boston, where he was introduced to Celtics fans as the heir-apparent to reigning star Larry Bird. He was in his room with former teammates David Gregg and Terry Long when the tragedy occurred.

State Medical Examiner Dr. John Smialek said the intoxication interrupted the electrical activity in Bias' brain and caused the heart to beat irregularly. That in turn triggered seizures and cardiac arrest.

The 6-foot-8 Bias finished his senior season as the Atlantic Coast Conference Player of the Year and Maryland's leading career scorer (2,149 points). He averaged 23.2 points per game in his final campaign and pulled down 224 rebounds.

# Bob Tway's incredible sand shot

In an incredible finish to the PGA Championship, Bob Tway dropped a 25-foot bunker shot into the cup for a final-hole birdie and a two-stroke victory over a stunned Greg Norman, August 11, at the Inverness Country Club in Toledo, O.

As Tway jumped up and down in the sand, Norman stood near his ball on the fringe of the green staring in amazement. Moments earlier, Tway and Norman, playing in the final threesome, had teed off at 18 deadlocked at 7 under par. But after watching Tway's third shot drop in the hole, a rattled Norman took three strokes for a closing bogey.

The Australian had led through three rounds and carried a four-stroke advantage to the 11th tee. But a double bogey on that hole and a bogey on 14 allowed Tway to come back. The 27-year-old finished the day with a 70 while Norman scored a 76.

Norman had also led through three rounds in the other three majors this year, losing in the Masters and U.S. Open before winning the British Open.

Bob Tway jumps up and down moments after sinking a 25-foot, 18th-hole bunker shot that gave him a dramatic victory in the PGA Championship.

# Stunned USFL owners give up

The eight remaining team owners in the United States Football League, still reeling from an unfavorable ruling six days earlier in their antitrust suit against the National Football League, voted, August 4, to call off the 1986 season.

The USFL, which began play in 1983 with 12 teams, had decided to switch from its spring-summer schedule to the fall for 1986. But, unable to get a television contract, the league filed suit against the NFL, claiming that it monopolized the networks and prevented the USFL from getting a TV deal. The USFL had hoped to get $1.69 billion in damages.

After a lengthy trial, the jury ruled that the NFL was indeed a professional monopoly, but that it had not pressured the networks to keep the USFL off the air. Damages were awarded to the USFL—for $1.

Without a huge award or a television contract, play in 1986 was no longer feasible. Estimates place USFL losses between $150 million and $200 million over its three seasons.

## ★ SPORTS WATCH ★

**MAY:** After a six-year absence from the winner's circle, Montreal stormed past Calgary in five games and won the NHL's Stanley Cup.

**JUN:** The Boston Celtics overcame Houston and captured their 16th championship in a six-game NBA Finals.

**JUN:** California's Don Sutton became the 19th member of baseball's 300-win club when he stopped the Texas Rangers, 3-1.

**JUL:** Atlanta's Bob Horner became the 11th major leaguer to hit four home runs in a game, but the Braves lost 11-8 to Montreal.

**AUG:** New Jersey Generals running back Herschel Walker signed a five-year contract with the NFL's Dallas Cowboys.

# Joyner's heptathlon record

Jackie Joyner, a silver medalist at the 1984 Summer Olympic Games, won the hearts of the Soviets, July 7, when she set a world heptathlon record in the Goodwill Games at Moscow.

Joyner amassed 7,148 points, 202 more than the previous mark held by Sabine Paetz of East Germany. She broke the record when she ran the 800-meter race in 2:10.02 with the Soviet crowd cheering her all the way. The Soviet announcer had alerted the fans that Joyner needed to beat 2:24.64 to clinch the record.

Joyner had set a first-day record with 4,151 points in four events. She set an American heptathlon mark by running the 100-meter hurdles in 12.85 seconds, cleared 62 inches in the high jump, threw the shot put 48-5¼ and ran the 200 meters in 23 seconds.

Joyner opened her second day by setting a heptathlon world record of 23 feet in her favorite event, the long jump. She threw the javelin 163-4 before her crowd-pleasing finish in the 800 meters.

American Jackie Joyner, on her way to setting a world record in the heptathlon competition, shows off her long jump form.

# 1986

## Bo gets Royal welcome

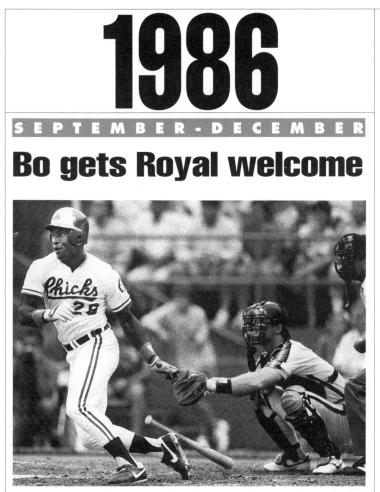

*Bo Jackson spent the first part of his first baseball season playing for the Class-AA Memphis Chicks.*

Bo Jackson's first baseball season ended, October 5, with mediocre numbers and great expectations. The Kansas City Royals certainly were not complaining.

That's because they stole this incredible physical specimen from other baseball officials who had assumed he would take his Heisman Trophy-winning talent to the National Football League. As the No. 1 selection of Tampa Bay in the NFL draft, there was a $7.6 million contract waiting for him in Florida. But the Royals' fourth-round selection in the June draft shocked everybody by opting for a three-year, $1.066 million contract to play the sport he "likes best."

He certainly has the tools: a rifle arm, world-class speed and power. But he showed quickly that his talent is raw, batting .277 with seven homers and 81 strikeouts in 53 games with the Royals' Class-AA Memphis team. And despite flashes of brilliance, he struggled through his September debut in Kansas City.

The former Auburn star batted only .207 with two homers while striking out 34 times. But one of those home runs was a 475-foot blast off Seattle's Mike Moore — the longest ball ever hit at Royals Stadium.

### "SPORTS TALK"

*"He has better raw material than anyone who's ever put on a baseball uniform. He already throws the ball harder than anyone in the league. He can run faster than anyone in the game. And who can hit the ball farther?"*

**JOHN SCHUERHOLZ**
Kansas City General Manager, talking about Bo Jackson

## An amazing comeback

What goes around comes around. That was the tough lesson the Boston Red Sox learned when they won the American League Championship Series battle but lost the World Series war.

The Red Sox were on the ropes, October 12, when they trailed the California Angels three games to one in the Championship Series and 5-4 with two out in the ninth inning of Game 5 at Anaheim. California relief ace Donnie Moore was facing Dave Henderson with one man on base.

Henderson worked the count to 2-2 and fouled off two pitches. On Moore's next delivery, the Boston outfielder belted a drive into the left-field seats. California came back to tie in the bottom of the ninth, but the Red Sox scored a run in the 11th to gain a 7-6 victory. Boston then posted 10-4 and 8-1 wins to put the shocked Angels out of their misery.

The momentum carried into the World Series as Bruce Hurst defeated the New York Mets twice and Boston bolted to a three games to two advantage. One more victory and starved Boston fans would have their first championship since 1918.

Roger Clemens was on the mound for Game 6 and the big righthander left after seven innings with the Red Sox leading, 3-2. But the Mets tied the score in the eighth against reliever Calvin Schiraldi.

Henderson struck again in the 10th, hitting a solo homer, and the Red Sox added another run. Schiraldi retired the first two Mets in the bottom of the inning.

Singles by Gary Carter and Kevin Mitchell delayed the celebration and Ray Knight followed with a looping, two-strike single to center, scoring Carter and moving Mitchell to third. Now it was up to Mookie Wilson, facing new pitcher Bob Stanley.

Wilson worked the count to 2-2 and began fouling off pitches. Stanley's seventh delivery was wild and Mitchell scored the tying run. Wilson hit Stanley's 10th pitch to first baseman Bill Buckner, who let the ball go through his legs. Knight scored the winning run.

Having now suffered the same fate as California, the Red Sox succumbed weakly in Game 7. Homers by Knight and Darryl Strawberry and clutch pitching by reliever Jesse Orosco lifted the Mets to an 8-5, Series-clinching victory.

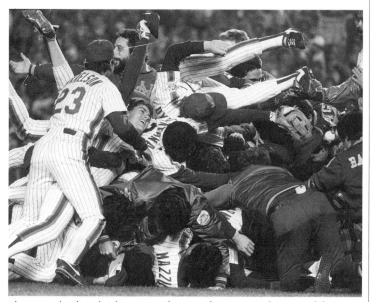

*There are bodies, bodies everywhere as the New York Mets celebrate their seven-game World Series victory over the Boston Red Sox.*

# A Grey Cup shocker

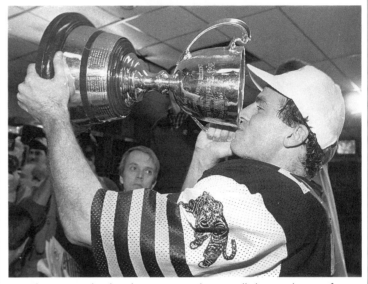

*Hamilton quarterback Mike Kerrigan takes a well-deserved swig of champagne from the Grey Cup after leading the Tiger-Cats to an upset win over Edmonton.*

The Hamilton Tiger-Cats pulled off one of the biggest upsets in Canadian sports history, November 30, when they easily defeated Edmonton, 39-15, in the Grey Cup title game at Vancouver, B.C.

Hamilton, 9-8-1 during a mediocre Canadian Football League season and a 12-point underdog to Edmonton, forced 10 Eskimo turnovers and sacked quarterbacks Matt Dunigan and Damon Allen 13 times. The Tiger-Cats scored 17 first-quarter points and never looked back in posting their lopsided victory over the CFL's regular-season champions.

Mike Kerrigan threw a 35-yard touchdown pass to Steve Stapler and defensive back Jim Rockford recovered a blocked Edmonton punt in the end zone for a touchdown, triggering Hamilton's first-quarter explosion. Kerrigan later hit Ron Ingram for a 44-yard third-quarter TD pass.

End Grover Covington led the defensive charge, recording five sacks, and linebacker Ben Zambiasi recovered two Edmonton fumbles.

The title was the 14th for Hamilton.

# Miami star shines

*Heisman Trophy winner Vinny Testaverde carved up Oklahoma with his passing during Miami's early season upset of the Sooners.*

Vinny Testaverde, the 22-year-old trigger man for Miami's explosive offense, walked away with the Heisman Trophy, December 6, in a landslide decision over Temple back Paul Palmer.

Testaverde, who completed 175 of 276 passes for 2,557 yards and 26 touchdowns this season while leading the Hurricanes to a 10-0 record, picked up 2,213 points from the voters, 1,541 more than Palmer. Only Southern Cal running back O.J. Simpson enjoyed a larger margin of victory in 1968.

There wasn't much suspense in the winning announcement. Testaverde had virtually locked up the award in Miami's third game of the season when he engineered a convincing 28-16 victory over top-ranked Oklahoma. He was outstanding in that game, completing 21 of 28 passes for 261 yards and four touchdowns. Fourteen completions were consecutive.

Testaverde will have one more test before turning professional. In a battle for the national championship, January 2, Miami and unbeaten Penn State will square off in the Fiesta Bowl.

# Tyson wins by TKO

Mike Tyson, a 20-year-old slugger from Catskill, N.Y., pounded Trevor Berbick to the canvas twice in the second round of their November 22 fight in Las Vegas and scored a technical knockout, becoming the youngest heavyweight champion in boxing history.

Tyson dropped Berbick early in the round with a series of blows that culminated with a hard left hook. But the WBC champion jumped up quickly and continued fighting defensively, trying to stave off his intimidating challenger with movement and clinching tactics.

The end came when Tyson delivered another left hook to the temple and Berbick dropped backward to the canvas, flopping around like a fish out of water as he tried to get to his feet. He did, at the count of 9, but the referee looked into his eyes and stopped the fight.

The new champion, almost two years younger than Floyd Patterson, the previous youngest heavyweight champion, is 28-0 with 26 knockouts.

# 1987

## JANUARY - APRIL

## Simms is super and so are the Giants

New York quarterback Phil Simms put on a dazzling passing display and the Giants exploded for 30 second-half points, January 25, en route to a 39-20 victory over Denver and the franchise's first Super Bowl win.

Simms completed 22 of 25 passes for 268 yards and three touchdowns. He outplayed John Elway, who was 22 of 37 for 304 yards but did most of his damage in the first half. The Broncos forged a 10-9 lead before intermission but squandered several excellent scoring opportunities, completely changing the complexion of the game. The second half

*New York Coach Bill Parcells gets his traditional Gatorade victory bath after guiding his Giants to an easy Super Bowl XXI victory over Denver.*

belonged to the vaunted New York defense and Simms.

In a picture-perfect third quarter blitz, Simms threw a 13-yard TD pass to Mark Bavaro and drove the Giants to a field goal and another touchdown on Joe Morris' one-yard run. A six-yard TD pass to Phil McConkey early in the final period stretched the lead to 33-10 and sealed away the verdict.

## Lions nip Miami in battle of unbeatens

Penn State's aggressive, blitzing defense neutralized Heisman Trophy-winning quarterback Vinny Testaverde and the Nittany Lions took advantage of seven Miami turnovers to record a 14-10 victory in a battle of unbeatens in the January 2 Fiesta Bowl at Tempe, Ariz.

The Nittany Lions picked off five passes and claimed their second national championship in five years. Both teams entered the game with 11-0 records and oddsmakers favored Miami's high-powered offense over Penn State's outstanding defense.

But the Hurricanes kept shooting themselves in the foot with turnovers and picked up nine costly penalties. Even so, they almost won.

When linebacker Shane Conlan made his second interception midway through the fourth quarter, the Lions drove for the go-ahead touchdown—a six-yard run by D.J. Dozier. But the Hurricanes mounted a desperation drive with Testaverde throwing for 32 yards on a fourth-and-six play and completing five straight passes to the Penn State 6.

On fourth down, with nine seconds left, Testaverde's final pass (he completed 26 of 50 attempts) was intercepted by linebacker Pete Giftopoulos. Despite being outgained 445 yards to 162 and outpassed 285 to 53, Penn State had prevailed.

*Penn State quarterback John Shaffer can't avoid hard-rushing Miami defender Winston Moss during a Fiesta Bowl battle of unbeaten teams.*

## ★ SPORTS WATCH ★

**JAN:** NBA Commissioner David Stern suspended Houston guards Lewis Lloyd and Mitchell Wiggins after they tested positive for cocaine.

**FEB:** Bill Elliott won his second Daytona 500 in three years, driving his Ford to victory when Geoff Bodine's Chevrolet ran out of gas with three laps remaining.

**MAR:** Woody Hayes, longtime football coaching great at Ohio State University, died at age 74 in his Columbus, O., home.

**APR:** Philadelphia slugger Mike Schmidt made his 500th career homer count, blasting a three-run ninth-inning shot off Pittsburgh's Don Robinson to give the Phillies an 8-6 victory.

**APR:** The NBA voted to expand by four teams, adding Miami and Charlotte franchises in 1988-89 and Orlando and Minnesota in 1989-90.

## NCAA penalizes SMU

The National Collegiate Athletic Association, citing Southern Methodist University's "abysmal" record of rules transgressions, barred the school from fielding a football team next fall, limited its 1988 schedule and imposed other penalties, February 25, because of improper payments to Mustang players.

The penalties were the stiffest ever handed out to a football program and put SMU in a start-from-scratch position. Scholarships and the team's coaching staff were reduced, the school was placed on probation for four years and athletes were given the right to transfer without losing eligibility.

SMU, a Southwestern Conference football power in recent years, had been placed on probation six times in the past and the newest penalties were intended to "eliminate a program that was built on a legacy of wrongdoing, deceit and rules violations."

The NCAA's seven-page report said payments had been made to as many as 13 players on a monthly basis from September 1985 to December 1986 and ranged from $50 to $725. The NCAA said the source of money was a person not officially connected to the Dallas school, but alleged that payoffs were distributed by athletic department officials.

# "Smart" Hoosiers overcome Syracuse

Indiana point guard Keith Smart swished a 16-foot baseline jump shot with five seconds remaining to give the Hoosiers a come-from-behind 74-73 victory over Syracuse in the March 30 NCAA Tournament final at the New Orleans Superdome.

With the Syracuse defense shadowing Indiana sharpshooter Steve Alford, Smart flipped the ball to burly forward Daryl Thomas, took a return pass and shot his game-winner over defender Howard Triche. The shot gave him 21 points and 12 of the Hoosiers' final 15.

The Orangemen appeared to be in control with 38 seconds remaining when they owned a 73-70 lead. But Triche missed a free throw and Smart quickly scored at the other end. When Derrick Coleman, Syracuse's 6-foot-9 freshman, missed the front end of a one-and-one, Indiana got its final shot.

Alford scored seven three-point field goals and scored 23 points for Indiana (30-4) while guard Sherman Douglas scored 20 points and Coleman grabbed an impressive 19 rebounds for Syracuse (31-7).

The championship was Indiana's third under Coach Bob Knight.

Indiana's Rick Calloway pumps his fist after watching teammate Keith Smart's jumper seal the Hoosiers' 74-73 NCAA championship game victory over Syracuse.

# Dodger VP Campanis creates racial furor

Al Campanis, the 70-year-old vice president in charge of player personnel for the Los Angeles Dodgers, resigned under fire, April 8, in the wake of a national storm caused by his comments on the April 6 segment of ABC's "Nightline".

Campanis, appearing on a show honoring the 40th anniversary of Jackie Robinson breaking baseball's color barrier, was asked by host Ted Koppel why the major leagues had no black managers, general managers or owners.

"I truly believe that they may not have some of the necessities to be, let's say, a field manager or perhaps a G.M.," replied Campanis, who had played as a minor leaguer with Robinson 41 years ago. When Koppel asked Campanis if he really believed that, the Dodger executive responded, "Well, I don't say that all of them, but they are short. How many quarterbacks do you have, how many pitchers do you have, that are black."

A moment later, Campanis added, "Why are black men or black people not good swimmers? Because they don't have any buoyancy."

The comments unleashed a storm of controversy and forced Campanis into an apology. He maintained that his statements were misconstrued and he does not believe that blacks are less intelligent than whites.

# Sugar Ray returns, takes Hagler's title

Middleweight champion Marvin Hagler ducks away from a Sugar Ray Leonard left during a title bout in Las Vegas.

Sugar Ray Leonard came out of retirement, April 6, and pounded out a 12-round split decision over WBC middleweight champion Marvelous Marvin Hagler in a title bout at Las Vegas.

Leonard, who had fought one time in five years, put on a dazzling boxing exhibition as he outpointed one of the sport's outstanding fighters. He danced, twirled and jabbed through the early rounds and then outslugged Hagler in a toe-to-toe donnybrook at the end.

The final tallies were extremely close, but Leonard got the verdict, much to the delight of 15,336 fans who chanted "Sugar Ray, Sugar Ray" when the decision was announced.

The loss was Hagler's first since 1976 and the third in a career that has produced 63 victories and 52 knockouts. The victory was the 34th in 35 fights for Leonard.

# 1987

## Moses' streak ends

*American Danny Harris clears the final hurdle in his 400-meter victory that ended Edwin Moses' 122-race winning streak.*

American Danny Harris, performing a feat unmatched by anybody since 1977, defeated Edwin Moses in the 400-meter hurdles, June 4, and ended the 31-year-old veteran's record 122-race winning streak.

The 21-year-old Harris took the lead at the fifth hurdle and outdueled Moses in the finals of an international meet at Madrid, finishing with a time of 47.56. Moses, whose last loss had been to West German Harald Schmid, hit the last hurdle and finished second at 47.69. Moses owns the world record in the event (47.02) and the next 10 fastest times.

Moses smiled as he ran a solitary lap of honor following the race and 11,000 fans chanted his name. Harris waited before shaking his hand.

"It's been a great day for me," said Harris, a former Iowa State star and three-time NCAA hurdles champion. "It makes me proud to have beaten an athlete of his caliber."

## "Old Al" wins 4th Indy

Al Unser Sr. became the oldest driver to win the Indianapolis 500 and only the second to win the prestigious race four times when he finished five seconds ahead of Roberto Guerrero, May 24, before 400,000 fans at the Indianapolis Motor Speedway.

Unser, a 47-year-old without a car or a sponsor 11 days ago, drove a March-Cosworth to victory, averaging 162.175 mph. He was replacing Danny Ongais, who suffered a concussion in a practice accident, on the Roger Penske team.

Unser ran a distant third for much of the race, behind Mario Andretti's Lola-Ilmor Chevrolet and Guerrero's March-Cosworth.

Andretti, who led 170 of the 200 laps, went out when his engine failed on No. 180, leaving Guerrero more than a lap ahead. But a rookie mistake cost the 28-year-old Colombian a victory.

Instead of putting his engine in neutral during a refueling stop, he kept the clutch engaged. When the jack was released and the car hit pavement, the engine stalled. It took his crew 55 seconds to get it running again and by that time Unser had taken the lead.

Unser, who had won previously in 1970, '71 and '78, matched A.J. Foyt's record of four victories. His 25-year-old son, Al Jr., finished fourth.

*Al Unser Sr. celebrates his record-tying fourth Indianapolis 500 victory after becoming the oldest driver to win auto racing's crown jewel.*

## Oilers ground Flyers

Jari Kurri scored the winning goal in the second period and Glenn Anderson put the game on ice with 2:24 remaining in the match as the Edmonton Oilers recorded a 3-1 victory over Philadelphia, May 31, in the seventh game of the Stanley Cup finals at Edmonton's Northlands Coliseum.

The Oilers' third Cup victory in four years was the result of an outstanding defensive effort that protected a slim lead until Anderson ripped the puck past Flyers' goaltender Ron Hextall and triggered a wild celebration. Hextall had been outstanding throughout the series, holding the high-scoring Oilers in check and giving his teammates an excellent chance to secure a surprising victory.

Down three games to one in a battle between the top overall regular-season teams, the Flyers rallied with a 4-3 victory at Edmonton in Game 5 and a 3-2 win at Philadelphia in Game 6. But Hextall didn't get much help in the final, facing 43 Oiler shots while Edmonton goalie Grant Fuhr saw only 20.

# Johnson outruns Lewis

In a classic 100-meter confrontation between the top two sprinters in the world, August 30, Canadian Ben Johnson exploded out of the blocks, beat American Carl Lewis by a step and set a world record of 9.83 seconds in the world track and field championships at the Stadio Olimpico in Rome.

"If you would have asked me before the race, could anybody run that fast, I would have said no," said Lewis.

What made Lewis marvel was his own time of 9.93, tying the previous world record set by Calvin Smith four years ago in the rarefied air of Colorado Springs, 6,000 feet above sea level. Johnson set his record and Lewis tied the previous mark in the heavier air at Rome, almost sea level.

The Jamaican-born Johnson won the race with his explosive start. He was off so fast that some observers complained he had left early—a feeling obviously not shared by Lewis, the 1984 Olympic 100-meter champion. Both were flying when they hit the finish line.

*Canadian sprinter Ben Johnson proudly displays his gold medal and waves to the crowd after setting a 100-meter world record during competition at Rome.*

# Becker outlasts McEnroe

Boris Becker survived a 6-hour, 38-minute test of endurance and determination, July 24, and recorded a 4-6, 15-13, 8-10, 6-2, 6-2 victory over John McEnroe, giving West Germany a 2-0 lead over the United States in a Davis Cup relegation match at Hartford, Conn.

The 19-year-old Becker simply outlasted his 28-year-old opponent. As the match dragged on through a 28-game second set and an 18-game third set, McEnroe began losing steam.

"I just didn't have much left," McEnroe conceded, referring to

# Bo takes up "hobby" for the winter

Just three months after reaffirming his intentions of having a baseball-only career, Bo Jackson signed a five-year contract, July 14, to play with the Los Angeles Raiders of the National Football League.

But that does not mean Bo is suddenly changing careers. The former Heisman Trophy winner from Auburn is simply adding "a hobby" to get him through those cold winter months.

Jackson's two-sport plan calls for him to join the Raiders as soon as Kansas City's baseball season is over. That would be October 4 if the Royals do not make the playoffs, the end of October if they go to the World Series. That would give the athletic phenomenon about half a football season.

For those eight or so games, he will earn approximately

*West German Boris Becker chases down a John McEnroe return during a marathon Davis Cup match at Hartford, Conn.*

the end of the match. He used most of his energy in the second and third sets, combating Becker's superior power and deep volley game with his angled volleys, strategically

placed serves and deft workmanship at the net.

During the 2-hour, 35-minute second-set marathon, he tried to distract Becker by arguing line calls, berating passersby and other tactics. But it didn't work. McEnroe missed his chance in the 20th game when he mishit a sure winner.

Becker's victory followed Eric Jelen's five-set upset of American Tim Mayotte.

## ★ SPORTS WATCH ★

**JUN:** The Los Angeles Lakers captured their fourth NBA championship of the 1980s with a six-game victory over their old nemesis, the Boston Celtics.

**JUN:** Scott Simpson's 72-hole total of 277 was one stroke better than Tom Watson in the U.S. Open at the Olympic Club in San Francisco.

**JUN:** Former New York and Kansas City Manager Dick Howser died of a brain tumor at age 51 in Kansas City.

**JUL:** Angel Cordero became the sixth jockey to ride 6,000 winners when he guided Lost Kitty to victory at Monmouth Park in Oceanport, N.J.

**JUL:** New York Yankee Don Mattingly hit a home run in his eighth consecutive game, tying the major league record set in 1956 by Pittsburgh's Dale Long.

**AUG:** Cleveland rookie John Farrell stopped Paul Molitor's 39-game hitting streak while losing a 1-0 decision in 10 innings to Milwaukee.

$500,000 to go with a $1 million up-front signing bonus. He is making approximately $300,000 in his first full season with the Royals and entered the All-Star break batting .254 with 18 home

runs and 45 runs batted it.

Jackson, the NFL's No. 1 overall draft pick in 1986, spurned a $7.6 million offer from Tampa Bay to sign with Kansas City.

# 1987

## Strike settled, but. . .

The National Football League Players' Association ended its 24-day work stoppage, October 15, without a new agreement or a collective bargaining contract. And when the players tried to go back to work, they were told they had missed the reporting deadline for Sunday's game and would have to wait another week to begin play and get paid.

The unusual developments meant that football fans would have to spend one more weekend watching games with replacement players and those regulars who crossed the picket lines before the Wednesday 1 p.m. deadline. The remaining regulars will have to report on Monday and begin play on October 25.

Players' Association chief Gene Upshaw had negotiated with the owners for 24 hours prior to the announcement. Agreement had been reached on most of the minor issues, but nobody would budge on the major questions of unrestricted free agency, drug testing and pension funding. When more and more players defected to their teams, Upshaw told the players to report Thursday.

But all were turned away because they had missed the league-imposed Wednesday deadline for Sunday competition. Upshaw, meanwhile, filed a lawsuit in Minneapolis charging that, without a bargaining agreement, the system that ties a player to his team violated Federal antitrust laws.

One week of games was lost to the strike and replacement players have played two games. The replacements receive $4,000 per contest, $10,000 less than the regulars.

*Jack Donlan, executive director of the NFL Management Council, tells the world, on October 13, that he was unable to reach agreement with the striking players during the latest round of negotiations.*

---

### ★ SPORTS WATCH ★

**SEP:** Toronto erupted for a major league-record 10 home runs in an 18-3 win over Baltimore. Ernie Whitt hit three, Rance Mulliniks and George Bell two apiece, and Lloyd Moseby, Rob Ducey and Fred McGriff one each.

**OCT:** Oakland first baseman Mark McGwire finished his first big-league season with a rookie-record 49 home runs.

**OCT:** In a complicated three-team NFL trade, Indianapolis got star running back Eric Dickerson from the Los Angeles Rams and Buffalo got the draft rights to former Alabama star Cornelius Bennett.

**NOV:** Andre Dawson, a 49-homer, 137-RBI man with the Chicago Cubs, became the first player from a last-place team ever to win MVP honors.

**NOV:** Boston righthander Roger Clemens became the first pitcher since former Baltimore ace Jim Palmer in 1975-76 to win consecutive Cy Young Awards.

**DEC:** Notre Dame flanker Tim Brown easily outpolled Syracuse quarterback Don McPherson to win the Heisman Trophy.

## No place like home

"There's no place like home. There's no place like home." With those words, the Minnesota Twins clicked together their heels and disposed of St. Louis in a seven-game World Series that had baseball purists mumbling to themselves.

Playing in the cozy Hubert H. Humphrey Metrodome, the Twins won the first two indoor games in World Series history, lost the next three in St. Louis and captured the final two in Minnesota. That was similar to the pattern they had followed in posting a mediocre 85-77 record en route to winning the American League West Division—an outstanding 56-25 mark at home, a not-so-wonderful 29-52 ledger on the road.

The Cardinals, 95-67 while winning the National League East, got their first taste of the Metrodome's teflon roof, bad lighting, ear-splitting acoustical problems and walls lined by

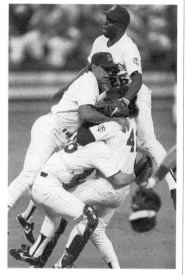

*It was celebration time in Minnesota after the Twins' 4-2 seventh-game World Series victory over the St. Louis Cardinals.*

trash bags on October 17. And the combination of the Twins' batting power (Dan Gladden hit a homer and drove in five runs) and the hanky-waving fans' lung power resulted in a 10-1 victory. Minnesota followed the next night with an 8-4 triumph.

But the bats that had produced four home runs in the first two games went silent when the scene shifted to massive Busch Stadium in St. Louis and the Cardinals rolled off 3-1, 7-2 and 4-2 victories. One more win would give Whitey Herzog's Redbirds a championship—but it would require a breakthrough at the Metrodome.

It was not to be. Trailing 5-2 in Game 6, the Twins turned on the power. Don Baylor hit a three-run homer in the fifth, Kent Hrbek hit a grand slam in the sixth and Minnesota recorded an 11-5 win.

The Game 7 clincher came when Frank Viola pitched eight strong innings and Minnesota overcame two runners being thrown out at the plate for a 4-2 victory. The powerful Twins, ironically, scored the Series-winning run on Greg Gagne's bases-loaded slow roller down the third-base line.

# Rice sets two NFL receiving records

*Record-setting San Francisco receiver Jerry Rice.*

San Francisco wide receiver Jerry Rice set two National Football League receiving records and scored three touchdowns, December 20, in the 49ers' 35-7 victory over Atlanta at Candlestick Park.

After scoring on a five-yard end-around in the second quarter, Rice caught a third-quarter 20-yard touchdown pass from quarterback Steve Young that put him in the record book. The catch broke the record of Miami's Mark Clayton for most touchdown catches in a season (19) and it marked the record 12th straight game in which Rice had scored on a reception.

Rice scored his third touchdown on a one-yard pass from Young.

Rice was not the only record-setter in the game. Sylvester Stamps of Atlanta and Joe Cribbs of San Francisco tied an NFL mark when they ran back successive kickoffs for third-period touchdowns.

# Eskimos' hot finish

Jerry Kauric kicked a 49-yard field goal with 1:10 remaining, November 29, and the Edmonton Eskimos escaped with a 38-36 victory over Toronto in the Grey Cup championship game at Vancouver.

Kauric's third field goal of the game capped an Edmonton comeback from a 24-10 halftime deficit. The spark was provided by quarterback Damon Allen, the younger brother of Los Angeles Raiders running back Marcus Allen, who replaced Matt Dunigan and threw for two touchdowns while running for another.

Allen connected on a six-yard TD pass to Marco Cyncar in the third quarter and pulled the Eskimos into a 28-27 lead with a 15-yard pass to Brian Kelly early in the fourth period. After the Argonauts had kicked a field goal, Allen scored on a 19-yard run to give Edmonton a 35-30 advantage.

Toronto regained the lead on Danny Barrett's 25-yard run with 2:36 remaining, but the Argonauts missed on a two-point conversion try.

Edmonton's Henry Williams set a Grey Cup record in the first quarter when he returned a missed field goal attempt 115 yards for a touchdown.

# Indiana fans witness another Knightmare

Indiana basketball Coach Bob Knight, a master of the international incident, pulled his Hoosiers off the floor and forfeited a November 21 game against a touring Soviet Union team at Assembly Hall in Bloomington, Ind.

Knight got into a heated discussion with one of the referees in the second half. When he was signaled for his third technical foul, he was automatically ejected and responded by calling for his team to follow him into the locker room. The officials awarded a forfeit to the Soviets, who were holding a commanding 66-43 lead anyway.

Knight, who was convicted in 1979 of hitting a Puerto Rican policeman during the Pan American Games, was contrite the next day and apologized.

"I am really apologetic to our fans for what should have been a good game, a good evening, a chance to see our players play," he said. "I got a technical foul called on me, apparently, for being out of the coach's box. From that point, I just should have walked away from it."

Knight's coaching career has been stormy and controversial. In another celebrated tantrum, he got into hot water in 1985 for throwing a chair across the court during a Purdue-Indiana game at Assembly Hall.

*Indiana Coach Bob Knight yells at a referee after being whistled for the first in a series of technical fouls that prompted him to pull his Hoosiers off the court during an exhibition game against a touring Soviet team.*

# 1988

## Olympic perfection

American athletes managed to win only two gold medals in the Winter Olympic Games at Calgary, and both winners needed near-perfect performances.

In one of the closest figure skating competitions ever staged, Californian Brian Boitano delivered a breathtaking performance in the long program after holding a slim short-program lead over Canadian crowd favorite Brian Orser. Boitano skated with emotion and flair to upbeat military music.

But Orser was almost as good. Carrying the additional pressure of representing the only gold medal hope for the host country, Orser was splendid until committing a slight glitch in his triple flip jump landing and he lost favor late in the routine when he downgraded a triple axel to a double.

Speed skater Bonnie Blair won the second U.S. gold, February 22, when she blurred to a world record 39.10-second clocking in the 500-meter sprint. Nothing less would have been enough. Two pairs earlier, Blair had watched defending Olympic champion Christa Rothenburger of East Germany shatter her own world record with a 39.12 clocking.

### "SPORTS TALK"

*"My goal on every jump is to survive. If I broke a leg, I wouldn't necessarily consider it a bad jump. If I died, that would be bad."*

**EDDIE (THE EAGLE) EDWARDS**

The British ski jumper who was the hit of the Winter Olympics

## Williams, Redskins break Broncos

*Super Bowl XXII belonged to Washington quarterback Doug Williams, who blitzed Denver with four touchdown passes.*

Washington quarterback Doug Williams threw four touchdown passes and rookie Tim Smith rushed for a Super Bowl-record 204 yards, January 31, as the Redskins dominated Denver and rolled to a comfotable 42-10 victory at San Diego's Jack Murphy Stadium.

Williams was masterful in becoming the first black quarterback ever to lead his team to an NFL championship, completing 18 of 29 passes for a Super Bowl-record 340 yards. Four of those completions produced touchdowns in a second-quarter Washington explosion that turned a 10-0 Denver lead into a 35-10 deficit. Smith added a 58-yard TD run in the period and a four-yard touchdown run in the final quarter as the Redskins posted their second Super Bowl win in six years and the National Conference's fourth straight lopsided victory.

The loss was the third in as many tries for Denver and the second straight under the leadership of golden-boy quarterback John Elway. After connecting with Ricky Nattiel for a 56-yard touchdown pass on the Broncos' first play from scrimmage, Elway threw three interceptions and completed only 14 of 38 passes.

*American figure skating gold medalist Brian Boitano is flanked by Canada's Brian Orser (left), the silver medalist, and Russian Viktor Petrenko.*

## Hurricanes pull apart Oklahoma's wishbone

The Miami Hurricanes, desperate to change their image as January chokers and win another national championship, pulled apart Oklahoma's powerful wishbone and defeated the top-ranked Sooners, 20-14, in the New Year's Day Orange Bowl classic.

After upsetting Nebraska in the 1984 Orange Bowl and winning their first national title, Hurricanes had lost three consecutive January bowl encounters to UCLA (Fiesta), Tennessee (Sugar) and Penn State (Fiesta). Victories in two of those games would have given them national championships.

But Miami (12-0) dominated the Sooners, holding an offense that had averaged 499.7 yards per game to 255. The Hurricanes got all the offense they needed from quarterback Steve Walsh, who fired touchdown passes to Melvin Bratton and Michael Irvin, and kicker Greg Cox, who connected on an Orange Bowl-record 56-yard field goal and added a 48-yarder late in the game.

Oklahoma (11-1) needed a trick play (the "Fumblerooski") to make the score close with 2:05 remaining. Guard Mark Hutson picked up an intentional fumble and, while the flow moved away from him, ran 29 yards for a touchdown.

# Underdog Jayhawks surprise Sooners

Danny Manning scored 31 points and grabbed 18 rebounds to lead underdog Kansas to an electrifying 83-79 upset of Big Eight Conference-rival Oklahoma in the April 4 final of the NCAA Tournament at Kansas City.

Coach Larry Brown's Jayhawks had lost twice to the Sooners during the regular season. And what developed was an intense, physical game that ranked high on the entertainment charts.

Both teams played the first half with relentless precision and finished in a 50-50 deadlock. Oklahoma was 7-for-11 from three-point range, Kansas 4-for-5. The Jayhawks shot 71 percent from the floor.

The expected second-half Oklahoma runaway never materialized. The Sooners did man-

Danny Manning, top gun in Kansas' NCAA upset victory over Oklahoma, lets everybody know exactly how he feels.

age a 65-60 lead with Dave Sieger hitting from the outside and Stacey King in the paint, but Kansas (27-11) refused to fold.

After Oklahoma had tied the game 71-71, Kevin Pritchard made a driving layup, Manning hit a jumper and Chris Piper hit from the corner. Oklahoma (35-4) got back to within one, but Manning hit four free throws in the final 10 seconds.

## ★ SPORTS WATCH ★

**JAN:** Chicago's Walter Payton, pro football's all-time leading rusher, played his final game when the Bears dropped a 21-17 playoff decision to Washington.

**JAN:** NBA great Pete Maravich died of a heart attack in Pasadena, Calif., at age 40 while playing in a pickup basketball game.

**JAN:** Mike Tyson scored a fourth-round technical knockout of former heavyweight champion Larry Holmes in a bout at Atlantic City, N.J.

**FEB:** Pittsburgh sensation Mario Lemieux handed out three assists and scored three goals, including the game-winner in overtime, as the Wales Conference defeated the Campbell in the NHL All-Star Game at St. Louis.

**MAR:** The NFL owners, meeting in Phoenix, approved Cardinals Owner Bill Bidwill's plan to move his franchise to that city for the upcoming season.

**APR:** Louisiana Tech earned its second women's basketball championship with a 56-54 victory over Auburn in the NCAA final at Tacoma, Wash.

# Lyle wins Masters on 18th

Sandy Lyle hit a masterful 150-yard bunker shot 10 feet from the pin on the 18th green and then sank the birdie putt to record a one-stroke victory, April 10, over Mark Calcavecchia in the Masters tournament at Augusta.

Lyle, a 30-year-old Scot, needed a comeback after almost killing his chances on Augusta National's infamous Amen Corner—holes 11, 12 and 13. He three-putted 11 for a bogey, went into the water at 12 and

## "SPORTS TALK"

*"The man has only one weakness. He can hit the ball 450 feet lefthanded, but he can hit it only 420 feet righthanded."*

**MIKE LAVALLIERE**

Pittsburgh catcher on switch-hitting teammate Bobby Bonilla

took a double bogey and saved par on 13 with an excellent bunker shot.

That cost him the lead temporarily, but he caught Calcavecchia at 16 with a 15-foot birdie putt and won at 18. The 27-year-old Calcavecchia, playing in the group just ahead of Lyle, closed with a par and a final-round 70. Lyle, the 1985 British Open champion, finished 71-281 while becoming the first British golfer ever to win the Masters.

Sandy Lyle dances across the 18th green after sinking a 10-foot birdie putt that gave him a one-stroke victory in the Masters.

# O's set futility mark

Few expected the Baltimore Orioles to finish outside the lower reaches of the American League East Division in 1988, but nobody could have predicted the depths to which this once-proud franchise would sink. And how quickly.

Two season-opening losses to Milwaukee and four to Cleveland were not as shocking as the reaction from Baltimore management. Manager Cal Ripken Sr. was fired after only six games and Frank Robinson replaced him. The Orioles responded by losing three straight home games to Kansas City and three more to the Indians. When they lost their 13th straight two days later at Mil-

waukee, the Orioles broke the major league record for most losses to open a season. But they were just getting started.

Two more losses to the Brewers and three at Kansas City raised the count to 18 and threatened the A.L. record for consecutive losses—20. Three losses at Minnesota broke that mark and now they were approaching the longest losing streak ever—23, by Philadelphia in 1961.

But with a nation watching with morbid fascination, the Orioles belted the White Sox, 9-0, in Chicago, ending the nightmare. Well, almost. They lost two more to Chicago and staggered home with a 1-23 record.

# sports trends

## The business of sports

*The all-pervasive influence of television on sports prompts franchise shifts, league restructuring, sponsorship deals and mega-buck contracts for America's sports stars*

On August 26, 1939, many Americans were glued to their radio sets, listening to the ominous rumblings of war in Europe. Nazi Germany's Adolph Hitler was bearing down on Poland, Prime Minister Neville Chamberlain was preaching impending doom to the people of Great Britain and the French government was advising its citizens to evacuate Paris.

Other Americans, believing they were in no danger from this growing Nazi cancer, might have been listening to "Your Hit Parade" or laughing at comedian Red Skelton.

It's a safe bet that not many were watching television that historic day, when innovative W2XBS, an experimental station in New York, aired the first major league baseball game. With 33,535 fans in the Ebbets Field stands, the opening contest of a doubleheader between Cincinnati and Brooklyn was telecast to a New York audience that probably numbered only several hundred watching on the city's 400 or so sets with five-, nine- and 12-inch screens.

"Keep in mind, this was the beginning of television," said Red Barber, who handled the play-by-play for that first telecast. "The director of the telecast had only two cameras —one on the ground near home plate and another right in among the fans in the upper deck above third base."

In the August 27 newspaper reports of the Reds' 5-2 victory, the event was mentioned only in passing, if at all. Only a few farsighted individuals seemed to understand that this development presaged a massive shift in the very structure, organization and philosophy of all sports. One such person was a writer for *Life* magazine, who predicted, "Reception was fuzzy . . . but no fuzziness can hide what it means to American sports. Within 10 years, an audience of 10 million sitting at home will see the World Series and Rose Bowl games."

*The good ol' days of television sports broadcasting.*

That prediction fell far short in numbers, but the impact it suggested was realized many times over. With the end of World War II, television executives began experimenting more seriously with sports programming, and by the 1950s it was becoming apparent just how far the television's antenna would extend. Like an Indian snake charmer, the one-eyed box mesmerized and seduced a nation and turned the world of fun and games into big business.

At first, television executives were drawn to the arena sports like boxing, wrestling and Roller Derby because of their concentrated action within a small ring or playing area. Cameras were unsophisticated and equipment was primitive, making the action sports of baseball and football more challenging to produce. The early 1950s were the "Golden Age of Boxing," when Gillette's Friday night fights became something of an American institution.

But that's not to say the national pastime was ignored. If Friday night belonged to boxing in the 1950s, Saturday afternoon belonged to baseball and the fractured syntax of colorful Dizzy Dean, a Hall of Fame pitcher and former member of the St. Louis Cardinals' Gas House Gang. Dean, with his country drawl and humorous anecdotes, was an instant success on the CBS Game of the Week.

Dean helped usher televised sports into the 1960s, when the genius of Commissioner Pete Rozelle helped the National Football League take center stage with a sudden burst of big-money contracts. The price went up . . . and up . . . and up. When CBS began televising NFL games in 1956, the network negotiated individual contracts with the 12 teams ranging from $35,000 to $185,000. Rozelle negotiated a combined two-year team package with CBS in 1962 for $4.5 million. In 1990, NFL officials negotiated four-year contracts with CBS, ABC, NBC, ESPN and Turner Broadcasting for a combined $3.6 billion.

Likewise, baseball received $6 million from Gillette in 1950 for the six-year rights to the World Series and All-Star Games. In 1989, officials signed a four-year deal with CBS for $1.1 billion and another with ESPN for $400 million.

The sudden infusion of big money into the sports coffers had profound effects. Once-stable franchises suddenly began shifting to larger cities with more extensive television markets, leagues expanded, new circuits popped up and the labor force, i.e. the players, became restless.

Heeding Horace Greeley's advice, Cleveland Rams Owner Dan Reeves headed west in 1946, settling in Los Angeles and broadening the sports map by half a continent. With air travel improving rapidly, the Rams were joined on the West

Red Barber interviews Leo Durocher after calling play-by-play for the first televised major league game in 1939.

Coast the same year by two members of the new All-America Football Conference —the Los Angeles Dons and the San Francisco 49ers.

In 1953, the Boston Braves shook up baseball's establishment by moving to Milwaukee—the first franchise shift in 50 years. In short order, the St. Louis Browns moved to Baltimore and the Philadelphia Athletics to Kansas City. But

Dizzy Dean turned CBS' Game of the Week into a must-see.

the real shocker occurred after the 1957 season, when the Brooklyn Dodgers and New York Giants moved to Los Angeles and San Francisco, respectively. Any lingering doubts were confirmed: money speaks louder than fan loyalty.

With dollar signs dancing in their eyes, entrepreneurs

begged for expansion franchises, rival leagues were formed to battle for television revenues and mergers were effected in a sometimes-painful period of growth—and prosperity. Baseball jumped from a 16-team configuration in 1960 to a 28-club circuit with its two-team National League expansion of 1993. The NFL, through expansion and its merger with the American

The NFL thrived, thanks to Commissioner Pete Rozelle.

Football League in 1970, jumped from 12 to 14 to 16 and finally to 28 teams. The National Basketball Association, a cozy eight-team circuit in 1960-61, now boasts 27 members. And the National Hockey League now is 22 teams strong, a far cry from its 1966-67 six-team format.

Television monies also provide important funding for collegiate sports, as proven by the College Football Association's amended 1990 five-year agreement with ABC and ESPN for $300 million. It would have been higher, but Notre Dame broke away from the group and negotiated its own TV contract: $75 million over five years for exclusive rights to the Fighting Irish football telecasts.

The big-buck maneuvering was not limited to team owners and collegiate officials, however. Players, watching all of this with hungry eyes, began demanding their fair share of the profits and used every avenue available to secure what they believed was rightfully theirs. They went out on strike, they challenged contract reserve clauses and other traditional practices in the courtroom and they jumped back and forth to rival leagues, creating some fascinating bidding wars. In the end, they were the big winners.

In 1949, New York Yankee great Joe DiMaggio became baseball's first six-figure performer. When free agency arrived in 1976, Baltimore slugger Reggie Jackson signed for an incredible $2.9 million over five years. But that was not as incredible as the contract former Pittsburgh star Bobby Bonilla signed in 1991 with the New York Mets: $29 million for five years.

The price shot up in all the sports and owners, especially in the big-market areas, ran amok in search of the perfect team. Individual sports, also fueled by television revenues that prompted big purses, prospered. The bottom line was the bottom line.

That, of course, was a big departure from sports in the first half century, but it is a fact of life that is not likely to change as the century draws to a close. Sports are fun and they are games, but first and foremost they are *business*.

# 1988

## Tyson's reign of terror continues

Iron Mike Tyson continued his reign of terror, June 27, when he scored a first-round knockout over Michael Spinks and claimed the undisputed world heavyweight championship in a bout at Atlantic City, N.J.

Tyson moved right in at the opening bell and began hammering the undefeated Spinks. When the normally resourceful Spinks had trouble dodging Tyson's big right hands, he chose to stand his ground and trade punches. That proved to be a costly mistake.

Tyson landed a right to Spinks' head and followed with a left hook that dropped the former light-heavyweight champion to his knees. Spinks got up quickly, but Tyson felled him

*Mike Tyson puts an end to Michael Spinks' reign as heavyweight champion during the first round of their fight in Atlantic City, N.J.*

again with a left hook and a right to the jaw. Spinks rolled to his side and took the 10 count at 1:31, the fourth quickest heavyweight knockout in history.

The victory was the 35th straight for Tyson, 31 by knockout. Spinks, who had never been knocked down, is 31-1. Tyson walked away with a cool $22 million—and hardly worked up a sweat.

## Filly Winning Colors wins Kentucky Derby

Winning Colors, trying to become the third filly to win a Kentucky Derby, jumped to an early lead and held off the late challenge of Forty Niner in the May 7 Run for the Roses at Louisville's Churchill Downs.

Winning Colors, the sentimental favorite if not the betting choice, took the lead out of the gate, cruised through the first mile unchallenged and carried a three-length lead into the homestretch. But the daughter of Caro, with Gary Stevens in saddle, seemed to tire and both

Forty Niner and Risen Star made a run.

Forty Niner pulled to within a neck but came up just short in the closest Derby finish in 19 years.

Winning Colors, trained by D. Wayne Lukas and owned by Eugene Klein, ran the 1¼-mile course in 2:02⅕ and followed in the hoofprints of Regret (1915) and Genuine Risk (1980), the other filly winners of America's most prestigious horse race. It was the first Derby victory for Lukas.

## Lakers fulfill promise

*Los Angeles Lakers Coach Pat Riley, having gained vindication for his repeat championship guarantee, celebrates his team's victory over Detroit.*

The Los Angeles Lakers, fulfilling the bold promise their coach had made a year earlier, outlasted Detroit, 108-105, in the seventh game of the NBA Finals, June 21, and became the first team to win back-to-back titles since the 1969 Boston Celtics.

When asked last June whether the Lakers would break the repeat jinx, Los Angeles Coach Pat Riley responded, "I'll guarantee it." It took a record 24 playoff contests and three tough seventh games, but the Lakers made Riley look like a genius. The title was their fifth of the decade and they have lost in two other NBA Finals.

The Lakers can thank their league-best 62-20 regular-season record for their playoff success. They needed the home-court advantage in tough series against Utah and Dallas and had to come back from a 3-2 deficit against the Pistons. Playing Game 7 at the Forum, Los Angeles used the first career triple-double of James Worthy (36 points, 16 rebounds and 10 assists) and a 36-point third-quarter explosion to build a 94-79 lead and then held off a late Piston charge.

Detroit, playing the finale with guard Isiah Thomas hobbled by an ankle sprain, pulled within two points three times but could never get even.

### ★ SPORTS WATCH ★

**MAY:** Cincinnati Manager Pete Rose was suspended for 30 days for an incident in which Rose shoved umpire Dave Pallone.

**MAY:** Rick Mears averaged 149.809 mph in his Penske-Chevrolet V-8 and captured his third Indianapolis 500.

**JUN:** Curtis Strange defeated Nick Faldo by four strokes in an 18-hole U.S. Open playoff at the Brookline (Mass.) Country Club.

**JUL:** Oakland catcher Terry Steinbach's home run and sacrifice fly drove in both runs in the A.L.'s 2-1 All-Star Game victory over the N.L at Cincinnati's Riverfront Stadium.

**AUG:** Art Rooney, founder and sole owner of the NFL's Pittsburgh Steelers for 55 years, died of a stroke at age 87 in Pittsburgh.

**AUG:** Jeff Sluman shot a final-round 65 at Oak Tree Country Club in Edmond, Okla., and recorded his first PGA tour victory—a three-stroke decision over Paul Azinger.

# Holdout Wrigley lights up

The sun set on day-only baseball, August 9, when the Chicago Cubs defeated the New York Mets, 6-4, in the first official night game at Chicago's Wrigley Field—the last bastion of a time-honored au naturel tradition. It was treated as a gala occasion, but there was mixed emotion among the 36,399 fans who witnessed the 74-year-old park's first explosion of artificial light.

The ceremony and clamor actually occurred on August 8, the scheduled day of the memorable event. History was made when a 91-year-old Chicago fan flipped the switch, turning on the 540 lights resting in six banks on the park's roof. But the Cubs and Philadelphia Phillies managed to play only 3½ innings before the game was postponed by a heavy thunderstorm. The Mets arrived in town the next day.

The decision to light Wrigley was made in February after years of fighting among community groups, politicians and baseball traditionalists. It also was a matter of Cubs management facing economic reality. Permission was granted with a hitch—the Cubs were limited to 18 night games per year.

*The end of a baseball tradition: lights at Chicago's Wrigley Field.*

# Oilers trade Gretzky

In what could rank as the most sensational trade in professional sports history, Edmonton Owner Peter Pocklington sent Wayne Gretzky, the universally accepted greatest player in National Hockey League history, to the Los Angeles Kings.

Gretzky and teammates Mike Krushelnyski and Marty McSorley were dispatched to Los Angeles, August 9, for center Jimmy Carson, left wing Martin Gelinas, three first-round draft choices and $14.4 million of Owner Bruce McNall's money. "It's like ripping the heart out of the city," moaned Edmonton Mayor Laurence Decore.

What really rankled distraught Oilers fans was that Gretzky had requested the trade. Gretzky, who in May led the Oilers to their fourth Stanley Cup victory in five years, married American actress Janet Jones in July, an occasion treated like a royal wedding throughout Canada.

Negative reaction by Edmonton fans was understandable. In his nine seasons with the Oilers, the 27-year-old superstar set 43 NHL scoring records, won eight straight Hart Trophies (Most Valuable Player) and seven consecutive scoring titles.

Pocklington, stung by criticism in the wake of the trade, asserted that Gretzky "has an ego the size of Manhattan" and said he cried crocodile tears at the emotional press conference announcing his departure. "He's a great actor. . .he pulled it off beautifully," Pocklington said.

*Wayne Gretzky fights back a tear at the Edmonton press conference announcing his stunning trade to Los Angeles.*

# Rozelle steps up NFL war on drugs

The National Football League escalated its war against drugs when Commissioner Pete Rozelle issued suspensions to 19 players for substance abuse.

Three of the league's premier defensive stars—Lawrence Taylor of the New York Giants, Dexter Manley of the Washington Redskins and Bruce Smith of the Buffalo Bills—were among 18 players suspended for 30 days. Indianapolis running back Tony Collins was suspended for one year.

Under the new guidelines, a player who flunks a drug test for the first time is warned and treated. A player who fails a second test receives a 30-day suspension. A third violation warrants a lifetime suspension subject to application for reinstatement for good behavior.

# 1988

## Gold winner Johnson sent home in disgrace

Ben Johnson, the Canadian sprinter who shattered the 100-meter world record on September 24, in the Summer Olympic Games, was stripped of his title three days later when his urine sample tested positive for a performance-enhancing steroid.

Johnson exploded out of the starting blocks in Seoul, South Korea, and blitzed to a stunning 9.79 finish in the 100-meter final, well ahead of second-place Carl Lewis, who ran a 9.92. It was a dramatic performance with the world's top two sprinters going head to head.

But when traces of stanozolol, an anabolic steroid banned by the International Olympic Committee, was discovered in his drug test, the Jamaican-born sprinter was barred from competing on Canada's national team for life and he was sent home in disgrace.

Johnson's disqualification gave the gold medal to Lewis, the defending Olympic champion who also captured the long jump. Lewis was a four-time gold medalist in the 1984 Games at Los Angeles.

*Ben Johnson (left) was No. 1 in the Olympic 100-meter dash until officials disqualified him for steroid use.*

## Joyners, swimmers star in Olympics

The United States finished behind the Soviet Union and East Germany in medal count at the Summer Olympic Games in Seoul, South Korea. But American athletes turned in some memorable performances.

The stars of track and field were sisters-in-law—Florence Griffith-Joyner, alias FloJo, and Jackie Joyner-Kersee. FloJo, a media sensation because of her sexy outfits and sensational performances, captured the 100-meter dash with an Olympic-record time of 10.54, set a world record in the 200 meters (21.34) and ran the third leg for the 400-meter relay team to win her third gold medal.

Joyner-Kersee set an Olympic record with a 24-3½ leap in the long jump and broke her own heptathlon world record with 7,291 points.

Two swimmers conducted their own personal gold rushes. Janet Evans, a 17-year-old dynamo, set a world record in the 400-meter freestyle and also won the 800-meter freestyle and the 400-meter individual med-

*Florence Griffith-Joyner was a media sensation and a three-gold medal winner at the Seoul, South Korea, Olympic Games.*

ley. Matt Biondi won five gold medals in men's competition and added a silver and bronze.

One of the most dramatic performances was turned in by Greg Louganis, who became the first diver to win two gold medals at consecutive Olympics. Louganis came back to win after hitting his head on the board in the preliminary round of the three-meter springboard competition, and then won the 10-meter platform event.

## Graf beats Sabatini, completes Grand Slam

Steffi Graf, a 19-year-old West German, defeated Gabriela Sabatini, 6-3, 3-6, 6-1, in the final of the U.S. Open championships, September 10, and became the fifth player and third woman ever to win tennis' Grand Slam.

Graf joins Rod Laver (1962 and '69), Don Budge (1938), Maureen Connolly (1953) and Margaret Smith-Court (1970) as the only players to win the Australian Open, French Open, Wimbledon and U.S. Open in the same calendar year. In 28 Grand Slam matches this year, Graf lost only two sets.

One of those was in Flushing Meadow, against Sabatini, the only person to beat the West German this year. After Graf broke Sabatini twice to take the first set, the Argentinian returned the favor in the second. But Graf's forehand began taking its toll in the finale and Sabatini tired quickly.

**SEP:** National League President A. Bartlett Giamatti was elected to succeed Peter Ueberroth as baseball commissioner.

**SEP:** Cincinnati lefthander Tom Browning pitched the 14th perfect game in baseball history, stopping the Dodgers 1-0 at Riverfront Stadium.

**SEP:** Oakland's Jose Canseco finished the season with 42 homers and 40 stolen bases, becoming the first player to record such a 40-40 double.

**OCT:** Columbia ended its major college-record 44-game losing streak with a 16-13 victory over Princeton at Columbia.

**NOV:** Seattle receiver Steve Largent broke the NFL record for all-time reception yardage when he reached 12,167 yards during a game against San Diego.

# Gibson, Hershiser propel Dodgers

*Los Angeles pitcher Orel Hershiser was riding high after pitching the Dodgers' Game 5 World Series clincher over Oakland.*

Veteran Los Angeles outfielder Kirk Gibson was named National League Most Valuable Player, November 15, five days after teammate Orel Hershiser had walked away with Cy Young honors. That postseason double was icing on the cake for the Cinderella Dodgers, who swept to a surprisingly easy five-game World Series victory over Oakland.

The starring role in the Dodgers' dream season went to Hershiser, the 30-year-old right-hander who was virtually unhittable over the last month and finished with 23 victories. Hershiser's incredible stretch run began without fanfare on August 30, when he pitched scoreless baseball over the final four innings of a 4-2 victory at Montreal.

In his next start, Hershiser shut out Atlanta, 3-0. He followed with a 5-0 victory over Cincinnati, a 1-0 win over Atlanta, a 1-0 triumph at Houston and a 3-0 win at San Francisco. Hershiser's scoreless-inning streak stood at 49, only nine innings away from the major league record set by former Dodger Don Drysdale 20 years ago in 1968.

In his final regular-season start, Hershiser pitched 10 shutout innings against San Diego, bringing his scoreless streak to 59. He left the game after 10 innings and the Padres eventually won in 16.

But Hershiser's dream did not end there. He pitched the Dodgers to a 6-0 victory over New York in Game 7 of the Championship Series and then won two World Series games against Oakland, including the Game 5 clincher.

Gibson did not dominate like Hershiser, but he, too, did his job with flair. After hitting .290 with 25 homers and 76 runs batted in during the regular season, the lefthanded-hitting slugger pounded a 12th-inning homer to win Game 4 of the Championship Series.

But his biggest role was to be played in a World Series in which he batted only one time because of a painful knee injury. The heavily-favored A's took a 4-3 lead into the bottom of the ninth inning of Game 1 and turned matters over to ace reliever Dennis Eckersley, who got two quick outs before walking Mike Davis.

As the Dodger Stadium crowd thundered approval, Gibson hobbled out of the dugout to pinch-hit. In obvious pain, he hung tough against Eckersley and worked the count full. On the 3-2 pitch, Gibson golfed a low breaking ball into the right-field seats for one of the most dramatic home runs in World Series history.

# Running for records

Oklahoma State running back Barry Sanders, named Heisman Trophy winner only hours earlier, rewrote two of college football's most prestigious records, December 4, as he ran for 257 yards and four touchdowns in the Cowboys' 45-42 victory over Texas Tech in Tokyo.

Sanders ran 15 yards with 2:33 remaining in the first quarter to become college football's all-time top single-season rusher, surpassing former Southern Cal back Marcus Allen's record of 2,342 yards. Sanders finished his regular season with 2,553.

He also ended with 39 touchdowns, 10 more than any player in NCAA history. Those are the kinds of numbers that Heisman Trophies are made of and Sanders was an easy winner, outpolling Southern Cal quarterback Rodney Peete by 966 points. Sanders is the eighth junior to win the award.

The 9-2 Cowboys pulled ahead and took command of the game on Mike Gundy touchdown passes of 11 and six yards to Hart Lee Dykes.

*Oklahoma State Heisman Trophy winner and record-setting rusher Barry Sanders.*

# 1989

## JANUARY - APRIL

## Waltrip wins gamble

Darrell Waltrip, a three-time Winston Cup champion, took the biggest gamble of his career, February 19, and it paid off in his most prestigious victory— the Daytona 500, crown jewel of the NASCAR circuit.

The 42-year-old Waltrip had never won the Daytona Beach, Fla., classic and was running

fourth in his Chevrolet when leaders Dale Earnhardt and Ken Schrader made quick stops for gas on lap 188. Ignoring orders from his crew to stop and refuel, Waltrip moved into second place and prepared for an all-or-nothing finish.

He took over first early on lap 197 when leader Alan Kulwicki slowed with a flat tire and from that point on, it was a simple question of how long his gas would hold out. Waltrip coasted across the finish line on fumes, having driven the final 132½ miles without refueling.

Waltrip's Chevrolet averaged 148.466mph in a race slowed for 30 laps by seven caution flags.

*Darrell Waltrip's Chevrolet, running on fumes, gets the Daytona 500 checkered flag as it coasts across the finish line.*

## Irish eyes are smiling

Tony Rice threw two touchdown passes and Notre Dame dominated both sides of the ball in posting an easy 34-21 victory over West Virginia, January 2, in the Fiesta Bowl at Tempe, Ariz.

The top-ranked Fighting Irish took control early in this battle of unbeatens, recording a 45-yard field goal on their first possession and building a 23-6 halftime margin. Third-ranked West Virginia, which had averaged 42.9 points per game in rolling up an 11-0 record, did not make its initial first down until 20½ minutes elapsed.

Part of that could be attributed to the injury suffered by quarterback Major Harris on the Mountaineers' third play. Part of it could be attributed to Notre Dame's defensive intensity.

While Harris struggled, Rice completed seven of 11 passes for 213 yards and two touchdowns. He also was the game's leading rusher with 75 yards.

The national championship was Notre Dame's first since 1977 and first under Coach Lou Holtz. West Virginia was looking for its first perfect season in 96 years.

*San Francisco's John Taylor, recipient of a 10-yard Joe Montana touchdown pass with 34 seconds remaining in Super Bowl XXIII, does a victory leap in the back of the end zone.*

## Montana rallies 49ers

Joe Montana rifled a 10-yard pass to John Taylor in the back of the end zone with 34 seconds left, capping a last-ditch San Francisco drive that resulted in a 20-16 Super Bowl XXIII victory over Cincinnati, January 22, at Miami's Joe Robbie Stadium.

Montana, who threw for a Super Bowl-record 357 yards, enhanced his reputation as one of the great pressure quarterbacks of all time. With the 49ers trailing 16-13 and 3:10 left on the clock, he started the winning drive from his own 8-yard line. Mixing passes and runs and working the clock like a master, Montana choreographed one of

the most exciting finishes in Super Bowl history.

Cincinnati had taken its lead on the strength of Stanford Jennings' 93-yard third-quarter kickoff return, three field goals by Jim Breech and staunch work by a defense that would bend but not break.

The 49ers had tied the score earlier in the final period when Montana connected with Jerry Rice on a 14-yard touchdown pass, but the Bengals regained the lead on Breech's 40-yard field goal.

The victory was San Francisco's third title-game victory in the 1980s, all under Coach Bill Walsh.

# Michigan overcomes adversity, wins NCAA

Michigan guard Rumeal Robinson sank two free throws with three seconds remaining and the Wolverines posted their first NCAA Tournament championship with an exciting one-point victory, 80-79 in overtime, over Seton Hall, April 3, at Seattle's Kingdome.

The victory culminated an unusual postseason for Michigan, which entered the tournament under the direction of interim Coach Steve Fisher. Former Coach Bill Frieder had accepted a job with Arizona and was fired by Athletic Director Bo Schembechler.

The distraction did not seem to affect the Wolverines, however. They tore through the tournament averaging 92 points per game and the long-range bombing of Glen Rice helped them build a 51-39 second-half lead on Seton Hall, a surprising Final Four entry. But just when it looked as if it was going to be easy for Michigan, the Pirates fought back.

John Morton, who scored a game-high 35 points, sparked a rally that gave Seton Hall a 67-66 advantage with 2:13 to play and then hit a three-pointer that tied the score, 71-71, with 25 seconds left in regulation.

Seton Hall, with 11 seconds left in overtime, missed a short jumper and Robinson was fouled as he raced downcourt for the potential winning basket. Rice finished with 31 points and boosted his total to a record 184 for the tournament.

*Michigan's Rumeal Robinson pumps his fist after sinking the free throws that gave the Wolverines a one-point overtime victory over Seton Hall and their first NCAA championship.*

# Abdul-Jabbar honored

Los Angeles Lakers center Kareem Abdul-Jabbar concluded his 25-city National Basketball Association retirement tour, April 23, when he was honored by his home fans and teammates at the Forum in Inglewood, Calif., before the final regular-season game of his career.

Abdul-Jabbar sat on the court in an oversized rocking chair as fans, friends and teammates said their goodbyes in a variety of ways. He received a Rolls-Royce from the players, a tennis court from team Owner Jerry Buss and numerous ovations from a packed house during the 45-minute ceremony. Inglewood Mayor Ed Vincent even gave him his own street, announcing that the road bordering the Forum's east parking lot had been renamed Kareem Court.

Abdul-Jabbar, a six-time NBA Most Valuable Player, scored 10 points in 26 minutes during the Lakers' 121-117 victory over Seattle. That brought his career record totals to 56,446 minutes, 1,560 games and 38,387 points.

# Lemieux overtakes Gretzky as top gun

Pittsburgh's Mario Lemieux, a bigger, stronger version of Los Angeles scoring machine Wayne Gretzky, has been skating on hallowed ice the last two seasons and appears ready to replace The Great One as hockey's top performer.

Lemieux, a 6-foot-4, 200-pound center, finished the 1988-89 National Hockey League regular season with 85 goals and 114 assists for 199 points, the most ever for someone not named Gretzky. He missed five games because of injury, but still accounted for 57 percent of the Penguins' scoring.

The 23-year-old Lemieux, winner of last year's Hart Trophy, finished ahead of Gretzky in the scoring race for the second straight year. He recorded nine hat tricks, set an NHL record for short-handed goals with 13, had a hand in 109 of Pittsburgh's record 118 power-play goals and scored 26 points in his team's last eight games, helping the Penguins to 40 vic-

*Pittsburgh's Mario Lemieux, the NHL's new top gun.*

tories and a playoff berth.

En route to compiling the fourth-highest point total in history, Lemieux jumped off to a blistering start, scoring 41 points in his first 12 games.

# 1989

## MAY·AUGUST

# Pistons stun Lakers

Backup center James Edwards scored all 13 of his points in the fourth quarter, June 13, and Detroit's Bad Boys rallied for a 105-97 victory over Los Angeles and a convincing four-game sweep of the two-time defending champion in the NBA Finals at Inglewood, Calif.

The Pistons, who mauled and brawled their way through the regular season, were the epitome of efficiency as they rendered basketball's team of the 1980s helpless and rolled to the franchise's first championship. Throughout the series, they relied on guards Isiah Thomas and Joe Dumars and bench help from Dennis Rodman, John Salley, Vinnie Johnson and Edwards.

The Lakers entered the final quarter of Game 4 leading, 78-76. But with Edwards scoring almost at will, Detroit took control. With 19 seconds remaining, Lakers Coach Pat Riley removed Kareem Abdul-Jabbar from his final game to a thunderous ovation.

While Dumars and Thomas combined for almost 50 points per game, the Lakers played without injured guards Magic Johnson and Byron Scott.

# Another Strange win

*Curtis Strange, only the sixth golfer to win consecutive U.S. Opens, hugs his trophy after successfully defending his 1988 championship.*

Curtis Strange, content to play par golf while the other contenders fell by the wayside, shot a final-round 70 and successfully defended his U.S. Open championship, June 18, with a one-stroke victory on the East Course of the Oak Hill Country Club at Pittsford, N.Y.

The 34-year-old Strange became the sixth golfer to win consecutive Open titles and the first since Ben Hogan in 1950-51. He parred 16 holes, birdied one and bogeyed one to finish at 2-under-par 278.

Starting in third place behind Tom Kite and Scott Simpson, Strange maintained an even course while the two leaders faltered. A triple-bogey seven at the fifth hole ruined Kite and sent him reeling to a final-round 78. Simpson struggled to a 75.

Strange gained a share of the lead with Jumbo Ozaki on the 10th hole when Kite bogeyed, and he took the lead when Ozaki bogeyed 14. He never gave it up, finishing one stroke ahead of Chip Beck, Ian Woosnam and Mark McCumber.

# Chang conquers Paris

*Michael Chang, the 17-year-old American in Paris.*

Michael Chang, a 17-year-old American in Paris, came back from a two-set deficit and pulled off a stunning upset in the French Open, June 5, when he defeated top-seeded Ivan Lendl in a 4-6, 4-6, 6-3, 6-3, 6-3 thriller.

Adding to the drama of a tense fifth set were severe leg cramps that almost forced Chang to withdraw. He was in so much pain at one point that he served underhanded, a move that surprised Lendl and resulted in an unforced error. Lendl helped Chang with a number of final-set miscues, just when the youngster appeared on the verge of collapse.

Lendl jumped out quickly against the 15th-seeded American, but Chang fought back to win the third and fourth sets. Chang had won the first two games of the fifth set when the cramps started.

Turning to his soft game, Chang hit the ball hard only when he had a clear winner. Lendl, apparently unnerved by the change of pace, fought back against his feeble opponent to 2-2, but Chang somehow managed to break serve. Lendl broke back—and then died.

Surviving on guile, courage and Lendl mistakes, Chang won the next three games and became the youngest male ever to win a major championship.

# American captures playoff at Troon

Mark Calcavecchia birdied the final hole of regulation to tie and then dropped a six-foot birdie putt on the final green of the first four-hole playoff in Open history, July 23, to win the championship at the Royal Troon Golf Club in Scotland.

The 29-year-old Calcavecchia parlayed two pars and two birdies into an unlikely victory over Australians Greg Norman and Wayne Grady. Norman, who shot a course-record 64 to come from seven strokes back after three rounds of regulation, birdied the first two holes of the playoff, bogeyed the third and picked up on the last hole after a wild bunker shot put him out of contention. Grady, who led the tournament from the second round to the 17th hole of the final round, recorded three pars and a bogey in the playoff.

Calcavecchia started the day three strokes behind Grady and still trailed by two with five holes remaining. But Grady opened the door with bogeys at 14 and 17 and Calcavecchia birdied two of the final three holes to tie.

The major title was Calcavecchia's first and he became the first American to win a British Open since Tom Watson triumphed in 1983.

# LeMond rides to glory

Greg LeMond's sensational 26-minute, 57-second sprint from Versailles to Paris wiped out a 50-second deficit to Laurent Fignon and allowed the American to capture his second Tour de France in stunning fashion. LeMond's 8-second victory was the smallest ever in the world's most prestigious bicycle race.

Few believed the 28-year-old LeMond could wipe out the Frenchman's lead in the July 22 final stage of the 2,000-mile, three-week event—a 15-mile time trial. But LeMond flew across the course, finishing 33 seconds faster than Frenchman Thierry Marie and 58 seconds faster than Fignon.

The victory was especially gratifying for LeMond, whose career had plummeted after he was shot during a 1987 hunting accident—nine months after becoming the first American ever to win the race. He had not won a major event since and finished 39th in the Tour of Italy only a month ago.

LeMond and Fignon dominated this race, the American leading after eight stages and the Frenchman after nine.

*Greg LeMond during a victorious moment in the Tour de France.*

# Ryan fans No. 5,000

Texas righthander Nolan Ryan, the 42-year-old fireballer, threw a 96-mile-per-hour fastball past Oakland's Rickey Henderson to start the fifth inning, August 22, and became the first pitcher in history to record 5,000 career strikeouts.

Ryan entered the game at Texas' Arlington Stadium with 4,994 strikeouts. He struck out Jose Canseco in the first inning, Dave Henderson and Tony Phillips in the second and Rickey Henderson and Ron Hassey in the third. When he fanned Rickey Henderson again in the fifth, the crowd of 42,869 roared its approval and Ryan doffed his cap.

The Rangers went on to lose, 2-0, but Ryan allowed only five hits and finished the night with 5,007 strikeouts. He has a record of having fanned 1,066 different batters in his 23 seasons, including 17 Hall of Famers.

Ryan is working in uncharted territory. Lefthander Steve Carlton is second on the all-time list with 4,136 strikeouts.

*Oakland's Rickey Henderson swings and misses, becoming Texas righthander Nolan Ryan's 5,000th career strikeout victim.*

# 1989

## 2 baseball tragedies

Baseball Commissioner A. Bartlett Giamatti, former National League president, died of a heart attack at his summer cottage in Massachusetts, September 1, eight days after banning Pete Rose from baseball for life.

Giamatti had replaced former commissioner Peter Ueberroth, April 1, and spent much of the next five months directing an investigation into the gambling activities of Rose, baseball's all-time hit leader (4,256) and one of the game's top personalities for three decades.

That ordeal concluded, August 24, when Giamatti, saying he believed Rose had bet on baseball games, announced an agreement that banned Rose from baseball.

Rose, buried under a mountain of evidence that chronicled his gambling, ended months of legal maneuvering by signing a carefully-worded agreement in which he accepted punishment while neither admitting nor denying his guilt. Giamatti reaffirmed the authority of his office and granted Rose the ability to continue denying allegations publicly.

The document also stipulated that Rose could apply for reinstatement after a year, but did not issue any guarantee. Giamatti stated at the news conference that he believed Rose had bet on baseball games and the former Reds manager, at his own news conference in Cincinnati, denied it. Rose is the 15th major leaguer to receive a lifetime ban.

Giamatti is the second commissioner, the first since Kenesaw Mountain Landis, to die in office.

*Former baseball Commissioner A. Bartlett Giamatti.*

## The "Quake" Series

*Players, officials and fans at San Francisco's Candlestick Park shortly after the Bay Area earthquake.*

Rickey Henderson stroked three hits, including a home run to lead off the game, and Oakland closed out an unexciting Bay Area World Series sweep of the Giants, October 28, with a 9-6 victory at San Francisco's Candlestick Park.

Exciting, no! Memorable, yes! While the Series lacked the classic moments or drama of past fall classics (the A's never trailed in their four-game romp), it will go down in history as an unforgettable sports event. Mother Nature's intervention saw to that, at 5:04 p.m. on October 17, just moments before the start of Game 3 at Candlestick.

As the crowd of 60,000-plus awaited the introduction of lineups, the ballpark suddenly started shaking and electric power stopped. Fans, players and the media remained remarkably calm as reports circulated that the Bay Area had been hit by an earthquake measuring 7.1 on the Richter scale.

Baseball Commissioner Fay Vincent reacted quickly, postponing the game and clearing the park before darkness could set in. The mood turned somber as reports of death and destruction circulated.

That death and destruction eventually would total 67 lives and billions of dollars. As Californians dug through the rubble and counted their blessings in the ensuing days, winning and losing baseball games became low priority. Vincent postponed the Series indefinitely and repairs were made to the ballpark. Finally, amid some calls for cancellation, the Commissioner and San Francisco Mayor Art Agnos endorsed October 27 as the resumption date. The 10-day postponement and 12-day gap in games were the longest in Series history and marked the first interruption for anything other than weather.

For the record, the A's recorded 5-0, 5-1, 13-7 and 9-6 victories and Dave Stewart was a two-game winner. But everything the A's accomplished was dwarfed by the raw power of Mother Nature.

### "SPORTS TALK"

*"At the start, I realized what a privilege it was to be in the Series. Now, I realize what a privilege it is to be alive. When people think of the 1989 Series, they're not going to remember who won, but who survived. . . ."*
**BRETT BUTLER**
San Francisco center fielder

# Raiders' coach breaks color bar, sparks revival in fortunes

Art Shell, the first black coach in the National Football League since the circuit's formative days, received good reviews after guiding the Los Angeles Raiders to seven victories in 12 games and a final 8-8 record.

Shell made history, October 3, when he was selected by Raiders Managing General Partner Al Davis to replace Mike Shanahan. The team had struggled to a 1-3 start after going 7-9 in 1988 and the former offensive tackle was asked to light a spark. Under Shell's direction, the Raiders won seven of their next 10 games before losing their final two and falling out of the playoff picture.

The appointment capped a big year for Shell, the 15-year Raiders' star who was inducted into the Pro Football Hall of Fame in the summer.

Fritz Pollard, a black running back, was the NFL's first black field boss, serving as player-coach for the Hammond (Ind.) Pros from 1923-25. Since then, however, no black had advanced beyond the position of offensive or defensive coordinator. The National Basketball Association has had 18 blacks serve as head coach 25 times since 1966 and major league baseball has had four blacks serve six times as manager.

Los Angeles' Art Shell, the NFL's first black head coach since the league's formative days in the 1920s.

# Chicago wins in a fog

The Chicago Bears groped their way to a 20-12 divisional play-off victory over Philadelphia, December 31—literally. Much of the game was played in a dense fog that engulfed Chicago's Soldier Field and limited visibility to as little as 10 yards.

The officials considered calling the game at halftime, but decided to continue play as long as they could make out both goal posts. The 65,534 fans spent much of the game wondering what was happening and CBS-TV was limited to four ground-level cameras that delivered a murky, but distinguishable, picture.

The game turned into a conservative, run-only proposition. Only nine points were scored after the fog rolled in—six by Philadelphia on two Luis Zendejas field goals and three on a field goal by Chicago's Kevin Butler.

The only saving grace for the fans was that Chicago won the best game they never saw.

# 43-40: A Grey Cup record

*Saskatchewan's Harry Skipper (left) and Vince Goldsmith hoist the Grey Cup after the Roughriders' 43-40 victory over Hamilton.*

David Ridgway's 35-yard field goal, his fourth of the game, gave Saskatchewan a 43-40 victory over Hamilton, November 26, in a wild Canadian Football League championship game that set a Grey Cup record for total points.

Ridgway's game-winning kick culminated a desperation drive that started at Saskatchewan's 36-yard line with less than a minute remaining and gave the Roughriders their second CFL championship and first in 23 years. Hamilton had tied the game with 44 seconds left when quarterback Mike Kerrigan hit Tony Champion with a nine-yard TD pass.

The Roughriders trailed by 12 points three times in the first half and rallied behind the passing of quarterback Kent Austin, who connected on 26 of 41 throws for 474 yards and three touchdowns. Kerrigan, almost as effective, completed 23 of 35 for 303 yards and three scores.

The previous record for total points had been set in 1956, when Edmonton had the better of Montreal by 50-27.

# 1990

# Douglas floors Tyson in heavyweight shock

*Mike Tyson watches as the referee counts over Buster Douglas during the eighth round of a heavyweight title fight in Tokyo. Douglas got up and knocked out the champion two rounds later.*

James (Buster) Douglas, so heavy an underdog that Las Vegas oddsmakers refused to post a betting line, battered undefeated heavyweight champion Mike Tyson to the canvas in the 10th round of a February 11 bout at Tokyo and scored one of the greatest upsets in boxing history.

Douglas, who figured to be just another patsy for Iron Mike, softened up the champion with three left jabs and then landed five brutal punches

that sent him spinning. He was counted out 1:23 into the round.

A post-fight controversy developed over Tyson's eighth-round knockdown of Douglas. Tyson supporters claimed that Douglas was given a long count on a mistake by the referee and the fight should have been over at that point. The videotape appeared to support that claim and officials said they would review the matter.

The bout was much livelier than expected and the three judges had it rated even at the time of the knockout. Tyson, 37-0 with 33 knockouts going into the fight, appeared astonished and disoriented. He also had a difficult time seeing out of his swollen right eye, courtesy of a big Douglas right hook in the fourth round.

Douglas lifted his record to 29-4-1 while recording his 20th knockout.

## « SPORTS TALK »

*"It's hard to find heels that don't have Mickey Mouse on them."*

**BRANDY JOHNSON**
5-foot, 95-pound gymnast, who wears a size 1 dress and size 3 shoes

# Shoemaker's last ride

Bill Shoemaker dropped the curtain on his legendary career, February 3, but his last ride was not a heroic one into the sunset. The 58-year-old Hall of Fame jockey rode Patchy Groundfog to a fourth-place finish at Santa Anita in Arcadia, Calif.

Riding his final mount in the Legend's Last Ride Handicap, Shoemaker had his 3-5 favorite in the lead on the homestretch. But Patchy Groundfog wilted as 63,200 fans watched in disappointment.

Shoemaker finished with

8,833 wins from 40,350 mounts. He also recorded 6,136 second places and 4,987 thirds while winning more than $123 million in purses. He has ridden four winners in the Kentucky Derby, five in the Belmont Stakes and two in the Preakness. Shoemaker is 1,490 wins ahead of second-place Laffit Pincay.

The Santa Anita sendoff was the culmination of a farewell tour that began last June and included appearances in 20 countries and most of the major tracks across North America.

*Record-setting jockey Bill Shoemaker closes out his career with a fourth-place finish aboard Patchy Groundfog at Santa Anita race track.*

# 49ers bust Broncos

Joe Montana threw five touchdown passes, January 28, at the New Orleans Superdome, leading San Francisco to a 55-10 demolition of Denver in the biggest Super Bowl mismatch in the classic's 24-year history.

Montana continued his record assault as he led the 49ers to their second straight Super Bowl victory and fourth since 1982. He completed 22 of 29 passes for 297 yards against the Broncos, finishing an incredible postseason (three games) with 65 completions in

83 attempts for 800 yards and 11 touchdowns. None of those passes were intercepted and the 49ers won the three contests by 100 points. Montana now holds Super Bowl career passing marks for completions (83), yards (1,142), touchdowns (11) and completion percentage (.680).

The Broncos, who suffered their third embarrassing Super Bowl defeat in four years and fourth overall, were never in the game. With Jerry Rice catching a pair of TD passes, the 49ers led 27-3 at halftime.

# UNLV crushes Duke

The University of Nevada-Las Vegas' Runnin' Rebels, the oft-investigated and much maligned whipping boys of the NCAA, released their frustrations, April 2, and demolished the Duke Blue Devils, 103-73, in the most one-sided NCAA Tournament final in the event's history.

In this battle of Good vs. Evil, Coach Jerry Tarkanian's bad boys were flawless and overpowering. They controlled

Duke with a full-court chest-to-chest defense that produced a tournament-record 16 steals and 23 turnovers. They shot 61 percent from the field, making 18 of 29 three-point attempts and pushing the ball inside to big Larry Johnson. The Rebels, in lifting their final record to 35-5 and capturing the school's first national championship, became the first team ever to score 100 points in a title game.

With guard Anderson Hunt connecting from the outside (12 of 16 for 29 points) and Johnson (8 of 12 for 22 points) inside, UNLV owned a comfortable 57-47 advantage with 16:24 remaining. But the Rebels were just getting started. Applying intense full-court pressure, they ran off 18 straight points and turned the game into a rout.

*UNLV guard Anderson Hunt (12), a 29-point scorer in the NCAA Tournament final against Duke, leads the Runnin' Rebels' sideline cheer.*

## ★ SPORTS WATCH ★

**JAN:** Miami captured an undisputed national championship when it defeated Alabama, 33-25, in the Sugar Bowl while top-ranked Colorado was losing, 21-6, to Notre Dame in the Orange Bowl.

**MAR:** Houston center Akeem Olajuwon became the third player in NBA history to perform a quadruple-double when he finished a game against Milwaukee with 18 points, 16 rebounds, 10 assists and 11 blocked shots.

**MAR:** Baseball's players and owners reached agreement on a new collective bargaining agreement, ending a 32-day lockout of spring training camps.

**APR:** Stanford's women defeated Auburn, 88-81, and captured their first NCAA basketball championship.

# Gathers collapses in game

*Former Loyola Marymount star Hank Gathers.*

More than 5,000 friends, fans and family members said an emotional goodbye on March 6 to former Loyola Marymount basketball star Hank Gathers at a memorial service at Gersten Pavilion in Los Angeles, the same arena where he collapsed and died two days earlier during a game against Portland in the West Coast Conference postseason tournament.

Gathers, a 6-foot-7 scoring machine projected as a first-round National Basketball Association draft pick, went down near midcourt, seconds after slamming an alley-oop pass midway through the first half. He was later pronounced dead of cardiomyopathy, a heart-muscle disorder, at age 23.

Gathers had been placed on medication to regulate his heartbeat after the senior fainted during a December 9 game against California-Santa Barbara. He missed two games but grew stronger and asked doctors to cut back the dosage. The autopsy showed he had not taken the medication within eight hours of his death.

Last season, Gathers became only the second player in NCAA history to lead the nation in both scoring (32.7 points per game) and rebounding (13.7). He was averaging 28.8 points this season.

# Faldo Masters Floyd

Nick Faldo captured his second straight Masters tournament, April 9, coming from behind over the last few holes to beat Raymond Floyd on the same sudden-death playoff hole that he birdied last year to beat Scott Hoch.

Faldo, who shot a final-round 69 at Augusta National, made up four strokes over the last six holes to catch the 47-year-old Floyd. Faldo needed a bogey from Floyd at 17 to tie and then watched as his veteran opponent had to scramble for his par on the final hole to finish at 10-under-par 278 and force the playoff.

Floyd had a chance to win on the first extra hole, but missed a 15-foot birdie putt. Faldo won it with a par on 11, after Floyd had pulled his second shot into the water.

In winning his third major championship, Faldo joined the great Jack Nicklaus as the only players to win back-to-back Masters. Ironically, he played his final round with the 50-year-old Nicklaus, who shot a 74 for an unspectacular sixth-place finish.

# 1990

## MAY-AUGUST

# Hale to the champion

Hale Irwin dropped an eight-foot birdie putt on the first hole of sudden death following an 18-hole playoff, June 18, defeating Mike Donald and capturing his third U.S. Open.

At age 45, Irwin became the oldest golfer ever to win this prestigious event and the first to do it while playing under a special exemption. He had to travel an uphill road over the difficult Medinah (Ill.) course.

Irwin needed a sizzling five-under-par 31 on the back nine of Sunday's final round to tie and then found himself two strokes down with three holes to play in the playoff round. But he birdied Medinah's fearsome 16th hole with a splendid 2-iron shot and made a solid par on 18 as Donald bogeyed. That put both golfers at two-over 74 and forced sudden death.

The 34-year-old Donald, who struggled through a four-bogey playoff after making only six in the first four rounds, fell quickly

*Hale Irwin begins his U.S. Open celebration as his ball rolls toward the cup and a sudden-death victory birdie.*

in sudden death. Irwin became the fifth golfer to win three U.S. Opens when he attacked Medinah's par-4 first hole with a perfect drive, a near-perfect wedge shot and a center-of-the-hole birdie putt.

## ★ SPORTS WATCH ★

**MAY:** Arie Luyendyk drove his Chevrolet to victory in the fastest Indianapolis 500 ever, averaging 185.981 mph.

**JUN:** It took the Detroit Pistons only five games to dispatch Portland and win their second straight NBA championship.

**JUN:** Baltimore shortstop Cal Ripken played in his 1,308th straight game and moved into second place on the all-time consecutive-games list.

**JUL:** Nolan Ryan became baseball's 20th 300-game winner when he defeated Milwaukee, 11-3, in a complete-game effort.

**JUL:** Martina Navratilova beat Zina Garrison, 6-4, 6-1, and captured her ninth Wimbledon singles championship.

# Post-Gretzky Oilers capture Stanley Cup

*Stanley Cup celebrants (left to right) Kevin Lowe, Mark Messier and Jari Kurri of the Edmonton Oilers.*

The Edmonton Oilers, the team that let Wayne Gretzky get away, proved they were good enough to win the Stanley Cup without him, May 24, when they defeated the Boston Bruins, 4-1, in Game 5 of the finals at Boston Garden.

The Oilers, who won four National Hockey League championships in five years with The Great One leading the charge, made their fifth title something special. They won behind the goaltending of playoff MVP Bill Ranford, a fill-in for the injured

Grant Fuhr, a stingy defense and speedy forward lines that consistently beat the slower Bruins to the puck.

After scoring a dramatic 3-2 triple-overtime victory in Game 1, Edmonton reeled off a 7-2 win, lost 2-1 and won the fourth game 5-1. The Oilers allowed Boston, the team with the best overall regular-season record, only eight goals in the series.

The Oilers took control of Game 5 in the second period on goals by Glenn Anderson and Craig Simpson.

# Ryan's sixth no-hitter

Texas righthander Nolan Ryan, defying age like no pitcher before him, hurled the sixth no-hitter of his career, June 11, and added to his growing list of major league records.

Ryan, who had thrown his record fifth no-hitter in 1981 as a member of the Houston Astros, struck out 14 Oakland A's and walked two while pitching the Rangers to a 5-0 victory at Oakland. The 43-year-old became the oldest pitcher to

throw a no-hitter and the first to do it for three different teams. Baseball's all-time strikeout king pitched four no-hitters for California in the 1970s.

Ryan was making only his second start since coming off the disabled list with a bad back. He gave up five runs to Oakland last week, but the A's did not come close to getting a hit in this game. Only two balls were hit hard and Texas outfielders caught both without difficulty.

# King continues reign as Sheehan collapses

Defending champion Betsy King shot a double-round 70-71 and captured her second straight U.S. Women's Open, July 15, when Patty Sheehan self-destructed and surrendered a 10-stroke lead on the last day at the Riverside course of the Atlanta Athletic Club.

Sheehan entered the final day with a six-shot advantage over Jane Geddes. She had withstood six rain delays over the first three days to post rounds of 66 and 68 and she birdied two of the first three holes on the rain-forced double round to increase her lead to eight. At that point she was 10 strokes ahead of King.

But nothing went right for Sheehan the rest of the way. After the first 18, her lead was down to four over Mary Murphy and five over King. When Sheehan bogeyed the eighth and ninth, King took a one-stroke lead. Sheehan made a courageous attempt to rebound with two late birdies, but she left a 25-foot birdie putt three feet short on 18.

The 34-year-old King finished with a 284 in becoming only the fifth golfer to win two straight Opens.

Betsy King salutes the gallery after an 11th-hole birdie during the final round of the U.S. Women's Open.

# New York Yankees owner banned

Former New York Yankee boss George Steinbrenner during happier times.

Commissioner Fay Vincent banned controversial George Steinbrenner from further involvement with the management of the New York Yankees, July 30, because the team's principal owner had acted in a manner "not in the best interests of baseball."

Vincent took surprisingly severe action against Steinbrenner after determining that he had maintained a three-year association with Howard Spira, a "known gambler," and paid Spira $40,000 to uncover unfavorable information about Dave Winfield, the Yankee outfielder with whom he had engaged in a long-running feud. He said Steinbrenner could remain only as a limited partner.

Vincent said he was "able to evaluate a pattern of behavior that borders on the bizarre" after conducting a two-day interview with Steinbrenner. Many fans, players and associates had felt that way throughout Steinbrenner's stormy 17½-year reign as keeper of "the Bronx Zoo."

Under his leadership, the Yankees did win four American League pennants and two World Series, but the team was constantly in turmoil as Steinbrenner hired and fired managers on no more than a whim and conducted a hands-on policy that frustrated managers and players alike.

# Rose begins sentence at Illinois prison camp

Pete Rose, on top of the world five years ago when he broke baseball's all-time hit record, completed his abrupt downhill slide, August 8, when he reported to a Federal work camp at Marion, Ill., to begin serving a five-month sentence.

The 49-year-old Rose was sentenced, July 20, by U.S. District Judge S. Arthur Spiegel after pleading guilty to two counts of income-tax evasion. He failed to report more than $350,000 from autograph signing and baseball memorabilia sales. The sentence followed his lifetime ban from baseball last August because of his alleged gambling activities.

Rose turned himself into the Southern Illinois prison camp two days before his court-ordered deadline and is scheduled for release January 7. The start of his sentence was delayed to allow him to recover from knee surgery. Warden John Clark said Rose will not be accorded special privileges and he will be matched to one of 35 available prison jobs. The former Cincinnati manager said he will not grant interviews.

# 1990

## Reds get nasty, beat A's in World Series

*The Cincinnati Reds had reason to celebrate after their shocking four-game World Series sweep of the Oakland Athletics.*

Jose Rijo and Randy Myers combined on a two-hitter and Hal Morris drove in the winning run with an eighth-inning sacrifice fly as the Cincinnati Reds posted a 2-1 victory over Oakland, October 20, and completed their stunning four-game World Series sweep of the powerful Athletics.

The Reds had entered the fall classic as heavy underdogs to the team that had a lot of every-thing—power, speed, pitching and defense. The A's also had three straight American League pennants and were coming off a four-game sweep of San Francisco in the 1989 World Series.

But with Rijo, Rob Dibble and Myers combining on an opening-game shutout and Cincinnati hitters battering Oakland ace Dave Stewart in a 7-0 victory, the Reds set the tone. They followed with a 10-inning 5-4 win and rode Chris Sabo's two-homer third game to an 8-3 triumph.

With Oakland's aura of invincibility now shattered, Cincinnati delivered the final blow with a two-run eighth-inning Game 4 rally that required only one hit.

Dibble and Myers, Cincinnati's "Nasty Boys," combined for 7²/₃ scoreless innings in the Series while Billy Hatcher batted .750.

## Holyfield claims title

Evander Holyfield delivered a crushing right hand to the jaw of James (Buster) Douglas, October 25, and recorded a third-round knockout that gave him undisputed claim to the heavyweight championship during a bout in Las Vegas.

Holyfield dominated the first two rounds and delivered his haymaker one minute, 10 seconds into the third when Douglas missed connecting on a big uppercut. Holyfield stepped back and then crushed Douglas to the canvas with a long right. The champion landed on his side, rolled onto his back and remained down through the count.

The loss ended a short championship reign for Douglas, who had shocked the world in February with his 10th-round knockout of Mike Tyson. He entered his first title defense outweighing his 28-year-old opponent, 246-208, but Holyfield was superior in every way.

The victory was the 25th straight for Holyfield, a former cruiserweight who has recorded 21 knockouts. The 30-year-old Douglas dropped to 30-5-1.

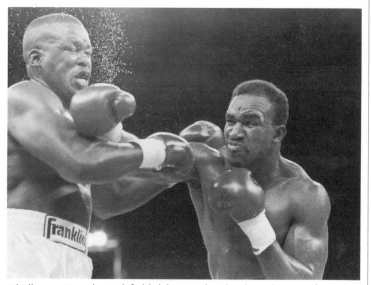

*Challenger Evander Holyfield delivers a hard right to the jaw of champion James (Buster) Douglas during their title fight.*

## A no-hitter—finally

Dave Stieb, Toronto's unlucky righthander who had lost four previous no-hit bids in the ninth inning, finally took his place in the record books, September 2, when he pitched the first no-hitter in Blue Jays history to beat the Indians, 3-0, at Cleveland.

The 33-year-old Stieb began his run of bad luck, September 24, 1988, when he took a no-hitter against Cleveland into the ninth and retired the first two batters. That was spoiled by a bad-hop grounder. Six days later, he lost a no-hit bid against Baltimore, also two out in the ninth, on a bloop single.

Stieb was one out away from a perfect game on August 4, 1989, when the Yankees' Roberto Kelly doubled. He lost another 1989 no-hit bid in the ninth and pitched another one-hitter, his fifth in less than a calendar year.

This time Stieb got the final three outs—and his 17th victory. He induced Chris James to fly out, made Candy Maldonado his ninth strikeout victim, walked Alex Cole and got Jerry Browne on a line drive to right.

The no-hitter was the ninth in the major leagues this season, a modern record.

*The triumphant U.S. Davis Cup team (left to right): Jim Pugh, Rick Leach, Michael Chang, Andre Agassi and captain Tom Gorman.*

# U.S. recaptures Cup

America's top-ranked doubles team of Rick Leach and Jim Pugh overwhelmed the Australian tandem of Pat Cash and John Fitzgerald in a fourth-set tiebreaker, December 1, and recorded a 6-4, 6-2, 3-6, 7-6 victory that clinched the United States' first Davis Cup triumph since 1982.

Leach and Pugh were the world's top-ranked pair last year but they were bypassed for the American squad. There was no such slight this year and they responded by winning all four matches they played as the U.S. marched to victory. It was evident from the beginning that Cash and Fitzgerald were over-matched in a must-win situation for Australia.

The key was the Americans' ability to bear down in break situations and win service. Fourteen times the Australians had break points and 13 times they failed. The Aussies did force the tiebreaker, but lost, 7-2.

The doubles victory on the clay courts of the Suncoast Dome at St. Petersburg, Fla., followed on the heels of Andre Agassi's five-set victory over Richard Fromberg and Michael Chang's three-set pounding of Darren Cahill. It gave the U.S. an insurmountable 3-0 lead in the best-of-five matchup and clinched its 29th Davis Cup.

# A quarterback duel

Houston quarterback David Klingler threw for 563 yards and seven touchdowns, November 3, to offset the NCAA-record 690-yard passing performance of Texas Christian University quarterback Matt Vogler and gave the Cougars a 56-35 victory at Houston.

The win lifted the Cougars to 8-0 and left them as the only undefeated, untied major college team in the country. Klingler, the nation's leader in total offense, completed 36 of 53 passes and surpassed the 400-yard barrier for a record seventh time this season.

Vogler, subbing for injured starter Leon Clay, picked apart Houston's defense, completing 44 of 79 passes and throwing for five touchdowns. His 690 passing yards surpassed the record of 631 set in 1988 by Utah's Scott Mitchell.

After falling behind 28-14 at the half, TCU pulled even in the third quarter. But it took Klingler only four plays to get Houston back into the lead and the Cougars steadily pulled away.

Both quarterbacks topped the Southwest Conference single-game record for passing yards (517) set by Houston's Andre Ware in 1989.

*Houston QB David Klingler.*

# Patriots punished by NFL

National Football League Commissioner Paul Tagliabue fined the New England Patriots and three players $72,500, November 27, for a locker-room incident that degraded a female reporter for the *Boston Herald*.

Football writer Lisa Olson was in the Patriots' locker room attempting to interview cornerback Maurice Hurst following a September 17 practice. That's when she was humiliated by the lewd comments and suggestive behavior of Zeke Mowatt, Michael Timpson and Robert Perryman.

Mowatt, the instigator, was fined $12,500 and the other two $5,000 apiece. The Patriots organization, owned by Victor Kiam, was fined $25,000 and charged an additional $25,000 to defray cost for instructional material for all league personnel on how to deal with the news media.

A 60-page report compiled by the commissioner's office was critical of Patriots' management for not taking any action before, during or immediately after the incident. There was no attempt immediately to discover the truth.

# 1991

## Bills miss a Super chance

Scott Norwood's 47-yard field goal attempt sailed wide with eight seconds remaining as the New York Giants survived Buffalo's late challenge for an exciting 20-19 Super Bowl victory, January 27, at Tampa Stadium.

The Giants used a relentless ball-control offense that consumed huge amounts of time and a defense designed to slow down Buffalo's high-powered passing attack. The strategy worked to perfection as New York kept possession of the ball for a Super Bowl-record 40 minutes, 33 seconds.

The 16-3 Giants dominated the clock behind 34-year-old Ottis Anderson, who rushed for 102 yards and a touchdown, and quarterback Jeff Hostetler, who outplayed Buffalo's Jim Kelly and completed 20 of 32 passes for 222 yards and a touchdown.

Buffalo jumped to a 12-3 lead, but Hostetler's 14-yard touchdown pass to Stephen Baker with 25 seconds left in the half cut the deficit. New York opened the second half with a 14-play 9:29 drive that ended with Anderson's one-yard run.

After 135-yard rusher Thurman Thomas had given the Bills a 19-17 lead in the fourth quarter with a 31-yard TD scamper, Matt Bahr provided the winning points on a 21-yard field goal with 7:20 remaining.

*New York defender Leonard Marshall (70) celebrates after sacking Buffalo quarterback Jim Kelly during second-quarter Super Bowl action.*

---

## Buffaloes win, lose

A funny thing happened to Colorado on its way to a first-ever national championship. The Buffaloes, ranked No. 1 by both the Associated Press and United Press International polls entering their January 1 Orange Bowl clash with Notre Dame, won the battle but unfortunately lost half the war.

Colorado defeated the Fighting Irish (fifth ranked by AP, sixth by UPI), 10-9, lifting its final record to 11-1-1. The Buffaloes scored the winning touchdown on Eric Bieniemy's one-yard run in the third quar-

ter and then breathed a deep sigh of relief when a scintillating 91-yard punt return for a touchdown by Raghib (Rocket) Ismail was called back on a clipping penalty with 43 seconds left in the game.

That near slip must have been enough to turn some voters in the UPI coaches' poll toward second-ranked Georgia Tech, a convincing 45-21 Citrus Bowl victory over Nebraska. The 11-0-1 Yellow Jackets outpointed the Buffaloes, 847-846, and stole half of Colorado's national championship.

## Terry Norris batters Sugar Ray Leonard

Terry Norris, a 23-year-old WBC junior middleweight champion, worked over Sugar Ray Leonard with numerous jabs, hooks and counter punches that produced a one-sided 12-round decision, February 9, and convinced the winner of five world championships that it was time to call it a career.

The 34-year-old Leonard, sporting cut lips and a nearly closed left eye, somberly announced his retirement after the bout—his first fight in more than a year. He goes out with a career record of 36-2-1.

Norris (27-3) sent Leonard to the canvas in the second and seventh rounds. He controlled his older opponent from start to finish and even won over the 7,495 fans at Madison Square

*Terry Norris connects with one of the many punches that brought a sad end to the outstanding career of Sugar Ray Leonard.*

Garden with his speed and accuracy. By the eighth round, many of the pre-fight Sugar Ray supporters were joining in the chant, "Terry! Terry!"

# A Battle of the Ages

*George Foreman fends off heavyweight champion Evander Holyfield with a long jab during action in their "Battle of the Ages" title fight.*

Youth triumphed in the "Battle of the Ages," April 19. Heavyweight champion Evander Holyfield scored a unanimous 12-round decision over 42-year-old George Foreman in a fight that many had predicted would end shortly after the bell for the opening round.

Holyfield, 14 years younger and 49 pounds lighter than Foreman, dominated as expected with his hand speed and footwork while showing respect for the former champ's punching power. The 257-pound Foreman, undefeated over the last four years after a 10-year retirement, connected with several solid rights but couldn't string his punches together.

The undefeated Holyfield was never in trouble and appeared to have Foreman on the ropes late in the ninth round. The champion delivered a strong six-punch barrage and Foreman stumbled to his corner at the bell, a painful look covering his face. He regained his composure, however, and finished the fight without incident.

## ★ SPORTS WATCH ★

**JAN:** Kevin Bradshaw of U.S. International set an NCAA scoring record against a Division I opponent when he totaled 72 points in a game against Loyola Marymount.

**APR:** Bill Shoemaker, horse racing's winningest jockey, suffered paralysis of his extremities when the car he was driving crashed at Covina, Calif.

**APR:** St. Louis winger Brett Hull finished the season with 86 goals and earned his first Hart Trophy as the player most valuable to his team.

**APR:** The Detroit Tigers spoiled Chicago's debut in new Comiskey Park by pounding out a 16-0 victory over the White Sox.

**APR:** Raghib Ismail, Notre Dame's Heisman Trophy runnerup, spurned the NFL and signed the richest contract in CFL history—a four-year deal with Toronto worth a guaranteed $18.2 million.

# Duke pulls shocker, defeats UNLV

Christian Laettner swished two free throws with 12 seconds remaining and Duke pulled off one of the biggest shockers in NCAA Tournament history, March 31, knocking off top-ranked and undefeated University of Nevada-Las Vegas, 79-77, in a semifinal contest at the Indianapolis Hoosier Dome.

Jerry Tarkanian's Runnin' Rebels entered the Final Four matchup with a 45-game winning streak, the fourth longest in NCAA history, and a chance to become college basketball's first repeat champion since 1973. UNLV had blown away opponents by an average margin of 27.6 points per game.

But the Duke players refused to give an inch. And with Laettner (28 points) playing an inspired game and the Rebels seemingly for once out of sync, it soon became apparent UNLV was in for a rare struggle.

With 2½ minutes remaining, the Blue Devils trailed, 76-71. But Bobby Hurley hit a three-pointer, Brian Davis hit a layup and free throw and, after UNLV had tied on Larry Johnson's free throw, Laettner stepped to the line for his game-winners. The Rebels rushed the ball downcourt, but Anderson Hunt's desperation shot was off target.

The Blue Devils went on to defeat Kansas, 72-65, in the April 1 final.

*The 1991 NCAA champion Duke Blue Devils and Coach Mike Krzyzewski.*

# Hip injury threatens Bo's baseball career

Bo Jackson, released 16 days earlier by Kansas City because of a football hip injury, agreed to a share-the-risk contract with the Chicago White Sox on April 3 and revived his sagging baseball career.

The 28-year-old Jackson, a worldwide celebrity because of his two-sport prowess, television commercials and endorsements, suffered the injury during the Los Angeles Raiders' January 13 playoff victory over Cincinnati. The Royals, based on a report by their orthopedist that Jackson would not be able to play this year and maybe never again, released him and paid a termination price of $391,484.

The remaining 25 teams could have picked him up on waivers, but they also would have had to pick up his bulky salary. The White Sox, believing Jackson's injury was not as bad as reported, decided Bo was worth a gamble.

The contract calls for a guaranteed salary of $700,000 this year, whether or not Jackson plays, and two option years. The $700,000 is the minimum Jackson could earn, but he could get as much as $1.5 million this year, $2.9 million next year and $3.75 million in 1993.

# 1991

## Raging Bulls charge past injured Lakers

Scottie Pippen scored 32 points and Michael Jordan added 29, lifting Chicago to a 108-101 victory over Los Angeles and carrying the Bulls to their first National Basketball Association championship.

The Bulls' June 12 victory at Los Angeles' Forum erased Chicago's reputation as a one-man team. Jordan, who has won five straight NBA scoring titles, averaged 29.8 points over the five-game final series, but Pippen and John Paxson (20 points) also played vital roles and the Bulls held the Lakers to 91.6 points per game.

The Lakers, without injured starters James Worthy and Byron Scott, managed to put up a good fight. They held a 93-90 advantage in the finale before the Bulls rallied on Paxson's outside shooting.

Chicago finished the playoffs with a 15-2 record. Lakers guard Magic Johnson closed with a triple-double: 16 points, 11 rebounds and 20 assists.

*Chicago's Michael Jordan pays an emotional tribute to the NBA championship trophy after the Bulls' five-game victory over the Los Angeles Lakers.*

## 2 baseball milestones

Rickey Henderson raced into the record books with his 939th career stolen base and 44-year-old Nolan Ryan continued his record assault by pitching his seventh career no-hitter in May 1 milestone performances.

Henderson broke former St. Louis star Lou Brock's all-time stolen base record at the Oakland Coliseum in the fourth inning of a 7-4 A's victory over New York. Henderson, caught stealing second in the first, swiped third base on a 1-0 pitch from Tim Leary to Harold Baines, beating Matt Nokes' one-hop throw. The game was stopped for a ceremony that included Brock and Henderson's mother.

Henderson set the record on his 1,154th attempt in 12 seasons. Brock needed 1,245 attempts over 19 years.

Ryan was masterful in shutting out Toronto, 3-0. He walked only two while striking out 16 in what he called the most dominating performance of his 25-year career. The Blue Jays, baseball's top hitting team, did not hit a ball hard and flailed helplessly at Ryan's assortment of 96-mph fastballs, curves and changeups.

## Penguins win 1st Cup title

Mario Lemieux's shorthanded goal broke open a tight game and Pittsburgh defeated the surprising Minnesota North Stars, 8-0, May 25, to capture the franchise's first Stanley Cup.

The Game 6 victory in Minnesota was no contest as Joe Mullen scored twice, Lemieux notched three assists and goaltender Tom Barrasso recorded 39 saves. Lemieux finished the playoffs with 44 points and earned the Conn Smythe Trophy as the postseason MVP.

It was a nice finish for the talented center, whose career had been put on hold late in 1989-90 and early this year by a serious back injury. He sat out Game 3 against Minnesota when he suffered spasms, and the North

*Pittsburgh captain and Stanley Cup victor Mario Lemieux.*

Stars took a two games to one advantage.

But it was all Pittsburgh the rest of the way. With goalie Jon Casey allowing 10 first-period goals in the last three games, the North Stars fell into a deep hole. The team that had finished with the 16th-best National Hockey League record before upsetting Chicago, St. Louis and Edmonton in the playoffs went down quietly in the end.

---

### "SPORTS TALK"

*"When I was little, I used to go to bed thinking about carrying the Stanley Cup over my head. Hey, it's heavier than I dreamed."*

**RON FRANCIS**
Pittsburgh center after the Penguins' first NHL championship

# Records tumble in Tokyo

Carl Lewis, a young 30-year-old, and Mike Powell, a man lost in Lewis' shadow for years, took center stage, August 25 and 30, at Tokyo with two of the most dazzling track and field performances in history.

Lewis grabbed the World Track and Field Championships spotlight first when he posted a world-record 9.86-second clocking in the 100-meter dash. Not only did Lewis beat the 9.90 record set by Leroy Burrell two months earlier, he did it against a field that included Burrell and four others who finished under 10 seconds. Burrell was clocked in 9.88.

Racing in front of 60,000 fans at National Stadium, Burrell jumped out fast and led at 90 meters. Lewis, second to last out of the blocks and fifth at the 50-meter mark, caught Burrell with five meters remaining. It was an amazing performance for a man who *should* be past his prime.

But Lewis turned from victor to victim five days later when Powell made an historic long jump that shattered one of the most cherished records ever posted. Powell took one mighty

Carl Lewis (second from left) raises his arms and smiles after breaking the 100-meter dash world record in competition at the World Track and Field Championships at Tokyo.

leap into the record books when he soared 29-4½ to surpass Bob Beamon's 1968 world record by two inches and snap Lewis' 10-year, 65-meet long jump winning streak.

The 27-year-old Powell posted the record on his fifth try, after Lewis had broken the 29-foot barrier for the first time in his outstanding career on his fourth leap. Lewis recorded a wind-aided 29-2¾ and then added jumps of 29-1¼ and 29-0. His final four jumps ranked among the best seven in history.

But they were not good enough to catch Powell, whose second-best effort was 28-0¼. He broke the long-standing record in muggy conditions at sea level, in contrast to Beamon's 1968 feat in the 7,375-foot altitude of Mexico City during the Olympic Games. Beamon's jump, which broke the previous mark by almost two feet, was considered the greatest accomplishment in track and field history.

Mike Powell soars to a world-record leap of 29-foot-4 ½, breaking Bob Beamon's 23-year-old mark by two inches.

# John Daly captures PGA title

John Daly, a rookie who hits moon-shot drives, shot a final-round 71 over the Crooked Stick Golf Club course in Carmel, Ind., August 11, and captured the PGA Championship by three strokes over Bruce Lietzke.

Daly's monster drives and poise under pressure amazed the rest of the field. The 25-year-old, a non-winner who got into the tournament as the last alternate, averaged 302 yards off the tee through the first three rounds.

The long course suited Daly's game. He played the four par-5s in 12 under par, which is precisely where he finished the tournament at 276. He entered the final round with a three-stroke lead and extended it to five by the sixth hole. A double-bogey five at 17 cut his lead, but he never was in danger of losing the tournament.

Daly, who receives a 10-year qualifying exemption on the tour and a lifetime exemption in the PGA Championship, is the first rookie to capture a major since Jerry Pate won the 1976 U.S. Open.

# basketball

## It was pure Magic

*The man who put the fun and personality back into basketball*

Earvin Johnson gingerly made his way toward the center jump circle at the Philadelphia Spectrum, measuring each step like an old man with sore feet. When he reached his destination, he fidgeted uncomfortably, shook hands with Caldwell Jones and grinned at the 7-foot-1 forward much like Davy Crockett must have grinned at that bear more than a century earlier.

The significance of this moment was not lost on players from both the Philadelphia 76ers and Los Angeles Lakers as they prepared to tip off Game 6 of the NBA Finals. The Lakers held a three games to two lead, but the 76ers were at home and Los Angeles was playing without dominating center Kareem Abdul-Jabbar, who was nursing an ankle

*Magic Johnson in 1979.*

injury. The Lakers' 6-foot-9 point guard jumping center? Were they conceding this game?

Johnson lost that center jump, but he found the formula to lead the Lakers to a most unlikely 123-107 victory and their first NBA championship in eight years. Without Kareem! Johnson played center, he played forward, he played guard . . . he did everything. In 47 minutes, he scored 42 points (14 of 23 from the field and 14 of 14 from the free throw line), grabbed 15 rebounds, handed out seven assists, made three steals and blocked a shot. One moment he was mixing it up in the paint with the big boys; another he was leading the Lakers' fast break. It was one of the greatest performances in NBA playoff history, and it was delivered by a 20-year-old kid three years out of high school.

"It was amazing, just amazing," said Philadelphia superstar Julius Erving.

It was pure *Magic*.

The Philadelphia victory completed an amazing run for the passing fancy with the effervescent smile and happy-go-lucky outlook on life. In just over a year, Magic (the nickname came from his high school playing days) led his hometown Michigan State University team to an NCAA Tournament championship and the Lakers to the top of the

NBA mountain. After the Spartans had downed Larry Bird's Indiana State team in the 1979 NCAA final, the talented sophomore who could thread a no-look pass through the eye of a needle entered the NBA draft in search of a new world to conquer.

He conquered professional basketball the first time he stepped onto the court in a

*The toast of Los Angeles after Lakers' 1980 NBA Finals victory.*

Laker uniform. The NBA of the late 1970s was a league badly in need of a facelift, an image booster . . . a smile. Its athletes were almost mechanical, their demeanor serious. Drugs had cast a pall over the league's reputation.

Magic and Bird, who had been drafted by the Boston Celtics, helped change all that. While Johnson brought fun and personality back into pro basketball, Bird was popular and marketable. It is interesting how the careers of these two NCAA Tournament adversaries were woven

together in the fibers of the NBA's 1980s popularity surge.

A nation separates their home arenas, but Magic and Bird have never been far apart in terms of celebrity status. They arrived in the NBA at the same time, they brought incredible passing skills and basketball savvy to their new teams, they helped turn two struggling franchises into

winners and they gave the league a long-awaited credibility transfusion. They became instant superstars and watching NBA basketball became a trendy thing to do.

For Magic's part, success can be measured in championships. He combined with such stars as Abdul-Jabbar, James Worthy, Michael Cooper, Keith Wilkes and Byron Scott to turn the Lakers of the 1980s into the most dominant NBA franchise since the Celtics of the late 1950s and '60s. Starting in 1980, Los Angeles captured five titles, lost in the finals three

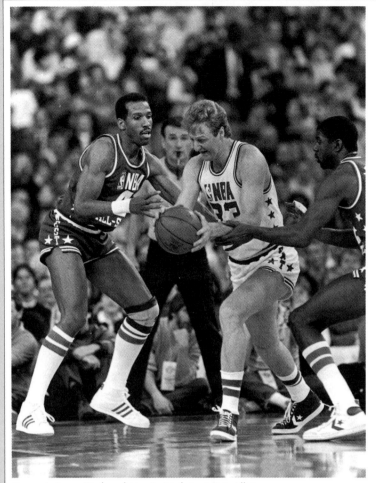

*Boston's Larry Bird and Magic (right) – NBA All-Stars.*

*A passing fancy.*

more times and became the league's first repeat champion in 19 years (1987 and '88).

The Celtics won three championships and lost in two finals—both defeats to the Lakers. Bird collected three consecutive Most Valuable Player awards starting in 1983-84; Magic was named MVP three times in four years, beginning in 1986-87. Magic was the NBA Finals MVP three times, Bird twice.

The Magic and Larry Bird shows were class acts that fans everywhere flocked to see. The tone for the 1980s was set when Johnson played his first regular-season game for the Lakers.

Los Angeles won that contest on a last-second shot and Magic joyfully raced around the court, hugging Abdul-Jabbar and everybody else he ran into. The big center told the rookie to calm down, there were many more games to be played over the long

season. But it was soon easy to detect a new enthusiasm among the Lakers—and especially Abdul-Jabbar.

## "More than anyone else, Kareem made me a better player."

**MAGIC JOHNSON**

"He penetrates with the ball so well and finds the open man so consistently that he has helped everybody's offense," said Abdul-Jabbar, on his way to becoming the NBA's all-time leading career scorer. "In regards to myself, he has been excellent in getting me the ball in spots where I like it best. He has really helped make a difference."

"More than anyone else, Kareem made me a better player," Johnson countered years later. "He wasn't just talented, he was smart. You

couldn't help but learn from him."

Johnson's emotion and excitement, worn like badges of honor on his expressive face, were contagious. It was full alert when Magic had the ball because his teammates knew they could be on the receiving end of a surprise bullet pass at any time or in any situation.

Johnson did have his basketball disappointments. After his big 1980 finish, Magic suffered through an injury-plagued 1980-81 campaign and played in only 37 games. The early 1981-82 season was difficult because of a feud with Paul Westhead that eventually led to the coach's dismissal and he was the goat in the 1984 NBA Finals, a 4-3 loss to Bird and the Celtics.

But the plusses far outnumbered the minuses as Johnson directed the Lakers' methodical march through the '80s and built his case as one of the game's all-time great players. The most satisfying victory came in 1988 when Pat Riley's team defeated Detroit, 4-3, and Johnson triumphed over close friend Isiah Thomas in the series that broke the long string of no-repeat champions.

But the real feathers in his cap came in 1990, when Magic was voted MVP for the third time, and in April 1991, when he became the NBA's all-time leader in assists. His career came to a sudden and sad end in November 1991 when he announced to the world that he had tested positive for HIV, the virus that causes AIDS.

A shocked nation reacted as if it had just lost its best friend. Emotional sentiments were expressed nationwide and tears were shed over the plight of one of the most popular athletes in American sports history. Magic stories dominated newspaper headlines as well as radio and television news programs for several days.

No longer able to compete, Johnson, the man who had

averaged 19.7 points, 7.3 rebounds and 11.4 assists over a 12-year career, embarked on a crusade to make the world aware of the AIDS disease and to urge people to avoid making the same mistake he had made.

Through it all, one thing never changed. Magic's ever-present smile was as big and sincere as ever.

*Magic's career came to a screeching halt in 1991 when he announced he had contracted HIV, the virus that causes AIDS.*

# 1991

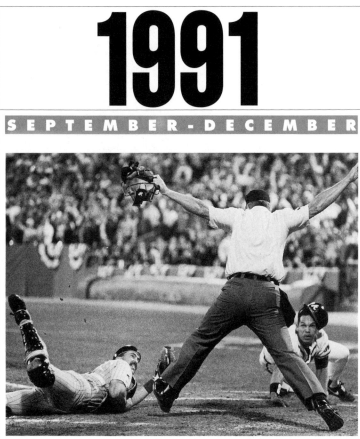

*Atlanta's David Justice scores the winning run in Game 3.*

## "SPORTS TALK"

*"It's like the Kennedy assassination. Everyone tells me where they were and what they were doing when Gibson hit that home run."*

**DENNIS ECKERSLEY**

Oakland closer who served up the game-winning homer to Dodger Kirk Gibson in the 1988 World Series

## ★ SPORTS WATCH ★

**SEP:** Brigham Young quarterback Ty Detmer became the NCAA's all-time career passing leader (11,606 yards) in a 27-23 loss to UCLA.

**SEP:** Miami's Don Shula picked up his 300th NFL career coaching victory in the Dolphins' 16-13 triumph over Green Bay.

**OCT:** The Toronto Blue Jays became the first big-league team to surpass 4 million in attendance.

**NOV:** Raghib (Rocket) Ismail returned a kickoff 87 yards for a touchdown and Toronto defeated Calgary, 36-21, to win the Grey Cup final at Winnipeg.

**NOV:** Pittsburgh Coach Bob Johnson died of brain cancer three months after directing the Pittsburgh Penguins to their first Stanley Cup title.

## Twins scalp Braves in outstanding Series

Pinch-hitter Gene Larkin drove a long single to left-center field with the bases loaded and one out in the 10th inning, October 27, giving the Minnesota Twins a stirring 1-0 victory over Atlanta and a seven-game triumph in one of the most exciting World Series ever played.

Larkin hit the first pitch he saw from Braves reliever Alejandro Pena and drove in Dan Gladden with the run that gave the Twins their second championship. Gladden, who had doubled to lead off the inning and was sacrificed to third, danced down the line when Larkin drove his game-winner over the drawn-in outfield.

The timely single delighted a loud Metrodome crowd of 55,118 and ended an outstanding pitching duel between veteran Jack Morris, who gutted out all 10 innings for the victory, and Atlanta youngster John Smoltz, who left the game after $7\frac{1}{3}$ innings of six-hit pitching. It also settled a World Series that duplicated the Twins' 1987 triumph over St. Louis: four victories at the cozy Metrodome, three losses on the road.

The Twins continued their Metrodome magic in Games 1 and 2, recording a 5-2 decision behind Morris in the opener and a 3-2 win the next night when light-hitting Scott Leius hit an eighth-inning home run.

But the Braves fought back, sweeping to 5-4 (12 innings), 3-2 and 14-5 victories at Atlanta. The Braves needed one more victory, but it would have to come at the Metrodome.

Twins center fielder Kirby Puckett made sure that didn't happen in Game 6, keying Minnesota's 4-3 victory with an RBI triple, a sacrifice fly, a leaping catch of a 400-foot drive by Ron Gant and a decisive 11th-inning home run.

Both teams had their scoring chances, but neither could break through. The Braves missed an opportunity to win in regulation when Lonnie Smith led off the eighth with a single and then failed to score on Terry Pendleton's drive off the left-center field wall. Smith, who lost the ball and hesitated at second, ended up at third on Pendleton's double but failed to score when Morris got an infield out before inducing Sid Bream to hit into a double play.

## Chip Beck shoots 59 in Las Vegas tourney

Chip Beck, a 13-year tour veteran, carved his name alongside Al Geiberger's in the record book, October 11, when he carded the second 59 in the history of PGA tournament play. Beck's 13-under-par effort was compiled on the 6,914-yard Sunrise Golf Club course in the third round of the Las Vegas Invitational.

The 35-year-old recorded 13 birdies and five pars while claiming a share of the third-round lead with Bruce Lietzke. His 59 came 14 years after Geiberger's in the 1977 Memphis Classic.

But Beck's record-tying performance was not good enough to lift him to victory. He finished two strokes behind Andrew Magee and D.A. Weibring, both of whom shot final-round 66s and tied for the lead after 90 regulation holes at a record-setting 31-under-par 329. Magee won the $270,000 first prize on the second hole of a sudden death playoff when he parred and Weibring struggled to a bogey.

# Jayhawk sets new rushing record

Diminutive Tony Sands finished his collegiate career in spectacular fashion, November 23, running for an NCAA single-game record 396 yards in Kansas' 53-29 victory over Missouri at Lawrence, Kan.

The 5-foot-6 Sands carried the ball a record 58 times and scored four touchdowns. He broke the record of 386 yards set earlier this year by San Diego State's Marshall Faulk against Pacific. It marked the fourth time this coveted football mark had been tied or broken in the last two years.

Sands rushed for 240 yards in the second half, breaking the record in the game's final minute. He averaged 6.8 yards per carry with a long-gainer of 38 yards. He finished the regular season with a school-record 1,442 yards and the Jayhawks

*Record-setting Kansas running back Tony Sands.*

recorded their first winning campaign (6-5) since 1981.

Washington State's Rueben Mayes broke the record with 357 yards in 1984 and that was tied, November 4, 1989, by Cal State Fullerton's Mike Pringle. Indiana's Anthony Thompson ran for 377 a week later and that stood until Faulk ran wild September 14.

# Disease forces Magic to retire

Earvin (Magic) Johnson, the effervescent quarterback of five Los Angeles Lakers National Basketball Association championships, announced his retirement from basketball, November 7, because he tested positive for HIV, the virus that causes AIDS.

Johnson, supported by his wife, Cookie, Lakers Owner Jerry Buss, General Manager Jerry West and NBA Commissioner David Stern as he made the difficult disclosure at the Los Angeles Forum, said the

discovery was made when he underwent tests for an insurance policy. He emphasized he does not have AIDS at this time and that his wife had tested negative for the disease.

The announcement created national shockwaves and evoked an emotional outpouring of concern and affection from friends and fans everywhere. It also prompted a massive upsurge in AIDS testing around the nation, a reaction Johnson was hoping to trigger. Johnson, who said that he was exposed through heterosexual sexual activity, will devote his life to informing the public about the virus.

Johnson captured three NBA Most Valuable Player awards during his 12-year career and finished as the league's all-time assist leader with 8,932.

# Frenchmen beat U.S. in Davis Cup shocker

Guy Forget banged out an emotional 7-6, 3-6, 6-3, 6-4 victory over American Pete Sampras, November 30, clinching France's first Davis Cup triumph in 59 years and touching off a patriotic country-wide celebration.

Forget's win, inspired by a chanting, flag-waving crowd in Lyon, France, gave his country an insurmountable 3-1 lead over the defending champions and climaxed one of the biggest upsets in Davis Cup history. When Forget hit a match-ending forehand, the French team celebrated by running vic-tory laps around the court carrying the French flag.

Forget, who had dropped his opening singles match to Andre Agassi, served 17 aces against Sampras. The American, who had lost to Henri Leconte in the second singles match, won only three fewer points than Forget, but the Frenchman won them when it counted.

The U.S. was down 2-1 after the doubles upset by Forget and Leconte over Ken Flach and Robert Seguso. The final singles match, Agassi versus Leconte, was not played.

*Frenchmen Guy Forget (left) and Henri Leconte run a patriotic victory lap after recording their unlikely Davis Cup win over the United States.*

# 1992

## Redskins bury Buffalo

Washington quarterback Mark Rypien passed for two touchdowns, Gerald Riggs ran for two more and Chip Lohmiller added three field goals as the Redskins powered their way to an easy 37-24 Super Bowl victory over Buffalo, January 26, at the Metrodome in Minneapolis.

The Redskins were in control all the way, even though they squandered several great first-quarter scoring opportunities. After Lohmiller's 34-yard field goal opened the scoring early in the second period, Rypien passed 10 yards to Earnest Byner for a touchdown and Riggs made it 17-0 with a one-yard run. At this point, the Redskins had outgained the Bills, 264 yards to 31.

A two-yard Riggs TD run early in the third quarter stretched the lead to 24-0 and virtually sealed the outcome. Buffalo, which lost in last year's Super Bowl to the New York Giants, fought back to make the final score respectable on Jim Kelly's passing. But the top running team in the NFL finished with only 43 rushing yards on 18 carries. Kelly threw a Super Bowl-record 58 passes, four of which were intercepted. Rypien, the game's Most Valuable Player, completed 18 of 33 passes for 292 yards.

The Super Bowl victory was the eighth straight for NFC teams. Joe Gibbs has coached the Washington Redskins to three Super Bowl championships in four tries.

*Washington coach Joe Gibbs gets a celebratory drenching from his players after guiding the Redskins to a Super Bowl win over Buffalo.*

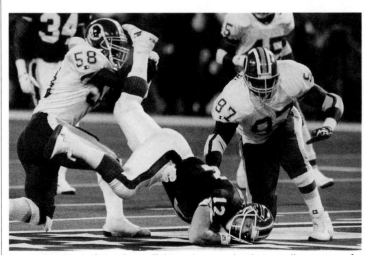

*It was that kind of day for Buffalo and quarterback Jim Kelly, victims of Washington's swarming Super Bowl defense.*

## Hurricanes, Huskies share championship

The Miami Hurricanes, well aware that Washington had completed its perfect season earlier in the day with a 34-14 victory over Michigan in the Rose Bowl, blasted Nebraska, 22-0, on New Year's night and matched the Huskies' 12-0 final record. The pollsters proclaimed both teams national champions the next day, the Associated Press' top honor going to Miami and the USA Today-CNN coaches' poll selecting Washington.

For the first time since 1973 two major universities completed perfect seasons, and it set up an interesting dilemma because Miami had entered its bowl game No. 1 in the AP poll and tied for the top spot in the coaches' poll. But Washington's victory came against the No. 4-ranked Wolverines while the Cornhuskers were No. 11.

Washington used a stingy defense and the strong play of quarterbacks Billy Joe Hobert and Mark Brunell to end Michigan's eight-game winning streak. Hobert ran two yards for Washington's first touchdown in the second quarter and passed for two touchdowns in the second half. Brunell, Hobert's backup, completed seven of eight passes for 89 yards and a fourth-quarter touchdown.

Michigan managed only 205 total yards, converted two of 15 third-down plays and was tackled for a loss 13 times. The Wolverines boasted one of college football's best offensive lines.

Miami's 18th consecutive victory was fashioned by a defense that handed Nebraska its first shutout since 1973 (covering 220 games). The Cornhuskers, the nation's leading rushing and scoring team, managed only 82 yards on the ground against Miami, the country's top defensive team (nine points per game).

The Hurricanes took control early, scoring 1:42 into the game on quarterback Gino Torretta's eight-yard pass to Kevin Williams. Carlos Huerta kicked 24-yard field goals on Miami's next two possessions and the rout was on.

---

### ★ SPORTS WATCH ★

**FEB:** A Superior Court jury found former heavyweight boxing champion Mike Tyson guilty of rape and two counts of criminal deviate sexual conduct.

**FEB:** Martina Navratilova passed Chris Evert on the all-time list when she rallied for a 7-6, 4-6, 7-5 win over Jana Novotna and her 158th career victory.

**FEB:** Davey Allison, driving a Ford Thunderbird, avoided a 14-car crash on lap 92 and went on to win his first Daytona 500, averaging 160.256 mph.

**MAR:** New York Yankee pitcher Pascual Perez tested positive for cocaine and was suspended for one year by baseball Commissioner Faye Vincent.

**MAR:** Tom Watson ended a five-year drought with a three-stroke victory over Ronan Rafferty in the Hong Kong Open.

# U.S. women win gold

The United States walked away from the Winter Olympic Games at Albertville, France, with 11 medals, well behind Germany, the Unified Team and several other European snow and ice powers. But the American showing was respectable, a tribute to a women's contingent that produced all five golds and seven of the overall medals.

Speed skater Bonnie Blair and figure skater Kristi Yamaguchi were the brightest of the U.S. stars. Blair, a 27-year-old from Champaign, Ill., earned gold medals in the 500-meter and 1,000-meter sprints and became the first American woman to win three golds in Winter Olympics competition. Blair also won the 500 event at Calgary four years ago.

Struggling on ice that turned mushy from unseasonably warm weather, Blair won the 500 meters on February 10, by 18 hundredths of a second over China's Ye Qiaobo. After failing in the 1,500 meters two days later, she came back, February 14, to beat Qiaobo in the 1,000, this time by a hair-raising 2 hundredths of a second.

Yamaguchi, the reigning U.S. champion, was the height of elegance and artistry as she became the first American woman since 1976 to win a figure skating title. She finished comfortably ahead of Japan's Midori Ito and fellow American Nancy Kerrigan in a competition filled with falls and flawed performances.

Yamaguchi, of Fremont, Calif., went down on a triple loop and cut a triple salchow to a double. But it didn't matter. All the other competitors also fell and Yamaguchi was clearly the deserving champion.

American Paul Wylie, a Harvard student with a reputation for succumbing to nerves in major competitions, was a surprising silver medalist in the men's competition.

The American hockey team appeared headed for a medal when it went undefeated (4-0-1) through the preliminary competition. But consecutive losses to the Unified Team and Czechoslovakia in the medal round resulted in a fourth-place finish.

*Bonnie Blair speeds to her second Winter Olympic gold medal in the 1,000-meter competition.*

*American Kristi Yamaguchi was the height of elegance as she soared to a figure skating gold.*

# Another Magic moment

Magic Johnson, voted by fans to a starting berth for the National Basketball Association All-Star Game despite his November 7 retirement, made a dazzling one-game return, February 9, and put on a show that fans and other NBA superstars will long remember.

Displaying no rustiness from his three-month layoff, Johnson outshined Michael Jordan and 23 of the NBA's other top stars. He sparked a 153-113 Western Conference victory with 25 points, nine assists and five rebounds in his 29 minutes of work. He connected on 9 of 12 field-goal attempts, 3 of 3 from three-point range and 4 of 4 from the free throw line. Not surprisingly, Magic won his second All-Star MVP award.

The day belonged to the man who led the Los Angeles Lakers to five NBA championships in his 12-year career before testing positive for the HIV virus and calling it quits. Johnson was the last of the 25 All-Stars introduced and received an emotional reception from players, coaches and fans.

When the game got underway, he scored eight points in the first five minutes, including a 10-foot "Junior Skyhook" from the baseline and a fake-pass layup. He also capped his big day spectacularly, hitting all of his three-point bombs in the final 2:42.